MAJOR EUROPEAN GOVERNMENTS

THE DORSEY SERIES IN POLITICAL SCIENCE

EDITOR **NORTON E. LONG** *Brandeis University*

MACRIDIS & BROWN *The De Gaulle Republic*

MACRIDIS & BROWN (eds.) *Comparative Politics: Notes and Readings*, rev. ed.

DRAGNICH *Major European Governments*, rev. ed.

ROBINSON *Congress and Foreign Policy-Making: A Study in Legislative Influence and Initiative*

JACOBINI *International Law: A Text*

MANGONE *The Elements of International Law: A Casebook*

GRIPP *Patterns of Soviet Politics*

MINAR *Ideas and Politics: The American Experience*

MEEHAN *The Theory and Method of Political Analysis*

EDELMANN *Latin American Government and Politics: The Dynamics of a Revolutionary Society*

JACOB & ATHERTON *The Dynamics of International Organization: The Making of World Order*

MAJOR EUROPEAN GOVERNMENTS

by Alex N. Dragnich, Ph.D.

PROFESSOR OF POLITICAL SCIENCE
VANDERBILT UNIVERSITY

1966

THE DORSEY PRESS
HOMEWOOD, ILLINOIS

© 1961 AND 1966 BY THE DORSEY PRESS

First Printing, January, 1966

Library of Congress Catalogue Card No. 66–11821

PRINTED IN THE UNITED STATES OF AMERICA

To Paul

PREFACE TO THE REVISED EDITION

THIS edition, in its basic approach, is much like the first. New materials have been inserted at many places, however, not only in an effort to bring the book up to date but, also, to provide more adequate treatment of certain topics. Some new sections have been included and others rewritten. Finally, a new concluding chapter on the study of comparative government has been added.

In the preparation of this edition, I was greatly aided by the extensive comments of Professor Carl J. Schneider of the University of Nebraska and Professor Andrew Gyorgy of Boston University. I am also indebted to Professor Fritz T. Epstein of Indiana University for his observations on the section on Germany. I am particularly indebted to Bette Benjamin Hunt for her meticulous efforts in preparing the index.

A. N. D.

Nashville, Tennessee
January, 1966

PREFACE TO FIRST EDITION

NORMALLY, a preface is where the author sets forth what he has attempted to do in the pages that follow. But only those pages can reveal how well he has succeeded, and the reader's standard of measurement will not always be the same as that of the author. Moreover, what appeals to one reader may not appeal to another. While realizing that the book will have to be judged on its own merits, I should nevertheless like to call attention to some of its features.

I have sought to produce a book of moderate size covering four major political systems of Europe. Because two of these systems (those of France and Germany) do not seem so strange after one has studied Great Britain, they can, in my opinion, be treated more briefly. Be that as it may, the length of the book is such as to make it possible for the instructor to utilize such other materials as he may choose. Secondly, I have frankly thought of this work as a textbook for students, and I have attempted to write it for them. Consequently, it will disappoint those readers who may be looking for something profound. To be sure, textbook writers and instructors do not always agree on the proper level of writing for college students, but here again the students themselves will have to pass judgment. Suffice it to say that I have always believed that political phenomena could be explained without indulging in involved and complicated prose. Thirdly, although the treatment follows the standard country-by-country approach, an effort is made, where it seemed appropriate, to relate the new with what the student already knows about his own government or that of another nation which he has studied. I am aware, however, that the most meaningful comparisons will be made by the students and their instructors as the opportunities arise and as the insights occur.

The bibliographical notes at the end of each chapter are not designed to provide an exhaustive list of source materials. Rather, they are merely suggestive of some of the principal works on the particular subject.

In the preparation of this volume, I owe many debts, to former teachers as well as to colleagues who have written in the field of political science. Several of my colleagues have read all or parts of the manuscript, and they have given me valuable suggestions, even though I may have ignored some of their major criticisms. Professors Norton E. Long of Northwestern University and Roy C. Macridis of Washington University read the whole manuscript. Professor Manfred C. Vernon of the University of Alabama read the sections on Great Britain and the Soviet Union. Professor Andrew Gyorgy of Boston University read the section on France. Professor Louis Nemzer of Ohio State University read the Soviet section and Professor David A. Booth of Michigan State University read the British section. Two of my graduate students, William H. Hunt and Bette Benjamin Hunt, read the French and British sections respectively. My thanks are also due to Cleo Wescoat Sandlin who bore the burden of typing the manuscript.

A. N. D.

Nashville, Tennessee
March, 1961

TABLE OF CONTENTS

PART ONE. GREAT BRITAIN

INTRODUCTION

MAN is a gregarious animal; he does not live in isolation. In the society which he has created there is considerable interdependence, and this interdependence has been greatly magnified since the Industrial Revolution. Because many of man's activities affect other people there is a need to regularize or systematize these relationships. Much of this is done through private organizations, or in what some observers call the realm of private governments. When it is done by publicly constituted authority which has the power to compel obedience, we have reference to the realm of public governments, or usually just government.

Historically, the organization of public authority has taken a number of different forms. Consequently, political scientists often speak of types or forms of government. The introductory pages that follow are designed to explore briefly some elemental concepts that may be useful in the study of the four political systems treated in this book. Some of the questions raised here, together with others that will come to the fore as these systems are examined, are treated within a more analytical framework in the concluding chapter.

CLASSIFICATION OF GOVERNMENTS

Since Aristotle, one of the most enduring classifications of government has been that based on the extent of popular participation, that is, the "government of the few" and the "government of the many." While this classification is useful even today, particularly as we look at contemporary democracies and dictatorships, it does not apply in many situations. For example, the evolving governmental forms in many societies which are now emerging from colonialism do not fit the mold. And while this book does not attempt to treat all forms of government, the reader should nevertheless be aware that the traditional classification of governments is overly simplified for today's world.

The governments we are to study in this book—Great Britain,

1

France, Germany, and the Soviet Union—can be classified in the traditional sense. The first three are democracies, although there are significant differences between them. The Soviet Union, on the other hand, is the world's most powerful dictatorship, which presents a challenge such as democracies have never before confronted. In a sense, this type of challenge is new, for most of man's political experience has been under authoritarian forms of government. Representative democratic institutions have played a significant role only in relatively recent times.

In some ways this makes the challenge of dictatorship all the more a matter of life and death, for there is a real question as to whether the world can survive half slave and half free. And the struggle is not confined to democracies and dictatorships already existing. Vast areas of the world hang in the balance, especially the new nations of Asia and Africa. Perhaps it is in these countries that the fate of democracy and dictatorship will be decided.

WHAT CHARACTERIZES DEMOCRACIES?

The word "democracy" has been so misused by its enemies and sometimes by its avowed friends that we sometimes have difficulty in defining it. Historically, however, the political aspect of the concept has the earliest roots in time. Democracy is government by the people. Although there are many implications in this simple definition, the ultimate test of democracy lies in whether or not those who govern us can be removed peacefully when they no longer represent the majority will. In studying democracy, therefore, the student must look for (1) some basic ideas and assumptions of the democratic faith, (2) some principles in the application of the democratic idea, and (3) the ways of institutionalizing democracy, that is, the ways in which democratic government is organized. In all democracies, there is general agreement on the basic ideas and principles, but considerable variation in the institutional arrangements through which democracy operates.

BASIC IDEAS AND ASSUMPTIONS

At the center of democratic theory is the concept that man is important, that government exists by virtue of his consent, and that the state is therefore the servant of the community. All men are created equal. And as they come from the hand of their maker, they are endowed with certain inalienable rights (for example, life and liberty) with which no earthly authority should interfere. Any system of political oganization which denies these rights is intolerable, in the view of most democratic theorists. By implication, this means that whatever government exists does so by virtue of the consent of the governed.

Closely related to the above is the assumption that man is capable of managing his own affairs, that is, that the people can manage their own affairs better than some one else could do it for them. This implies that intelligence, honesty, and even rationality will be brought to the task, but it does not assume an absence of mistakes and blunders. It does assume that people are good judges of wise or unwise policies, and that mistakes are preferable to unbridled authority, no matter how efficient the latter might be.

Nevertheless, there is in democratic theory a basic assumption that government is necessary to avoid the extremes of liberty and equality. Democracy seeks to foster an environment in which each man can develop to his fullest capacity, freely and in ways determined by himself. In doing so, however, he must not be permitted to infringe upon the freedom of others. In other words, government in a democracy should promote the "greatest good of the greatest number." In sum, the importance of the individual is tempered by the need for authority, an authority which man controls.

Equally important for its citizens is the idea that a democratic society is a flexible and not a permanent and fixed order, an open society where change can take place without destroying its basic character. This idea constitutes a state of mind, a belief that man is master of his fate, and that change therefore results from the conscious effort of the society's citizens. This idea suggests that government can be organized rationally and that trust can be placed in one's fellow man. There is thus the unspoken assumption that in such a society the continuing diversity of interests can find an acceptable compromise.

PRINCIPLES IN APPLICATION OF DEMOCRATIC IDEA

Some of the principles that are adhered to in the application of the democratic idea are commonplace, and yet they should be stated briefly. First among these is the rule that there should be a wide distribution of the right to vote. In other words, there should be no political, economic, religious, or racial qualifications for the right to vote. Moreover, elections must be free and honest, and should be held at relatively frequent intervals. The people must, in short, be given an opportunity periodically to pass judgment on their rulers, with assurance that their desires will prevail.

Secondly, there is the rule that popular differences concerning issues of public policy will be resolved by the principle of majority rule. In operation, this means that major desires for change must be possible through constitutional means. The minority, on the other hand, will acquiesce, but in doing so it does not abdicate its right to try to become the majority. The majority must realize that it is a majority only for the time being and must, therefore, respect the rights of the minority. It is in this process that the forces of compromise and accommodation play their roles. Without these modifications, the principle of majority rule could not long continue to operate.

Closely related to majority rule is the principle that there should be toleration of opposition. This suggests that groups and parties should be free to organize, to assemble, and to speak and write freely to the end that people may be persuaded to support their programs and policies. If there is to be effective competition for political leadership, there must be a large measure of tolerance for differences of opinion.

Fourthly, there is the principle that the rule of law shall prevail in democratic societies. This means that everyone shall be equally subject to the law. There must be no favoritism. It means, also, that there is a lack of arbitrariness, that is, that the rules are clear and known in advance. Every society faces the problem of law and right, which raises the issue of justice. In democratic societies, the rule of law assures adherence to well-defined norms and the protection of personal rights.

Finally, there is the usually unspoken principle of political consensus, which in a sense sums up the rules discussed above. Consensus means, essentially, an agreement on fundamentals, or the rules of the political game. In this sense, democracy is a method of arriving at political decisions. Its hallmark is a set of generally accepted rules which regulate the political process. Democracy does not signify that certain things will be done, but rather that it is a *certain* way of doing things politically. Without this basic political consensus, no society which considers itself democratic could long hope to survive as a democratic order.

INSTITUTIONALIZING DEMOCRACY

While adhering to the fundamental precepts of democracy, democratic nations vary in the institutional arrangements through which they are governed. These arrangements are set forth in what are called constitutions, usually in the nature of written documents, although not necessarily so. But every written constitution is augmented by certain political practices, generally known as usages or conventions, which are not mentioned in the constitution but which are nevertheless very much a part of the political process. Consequently, the nature of constitutions in democratic countries constitutes a focus for comparison.

To be sure, all democratic constitutions have something in common. In their different ways, democratic constitutions (1) set forth the powers of government, (2) define the rights of individuals, and (3) prescribe certain procedures for the exercise of governmental powers. In doing these things democratic constitutions vary a great deal, as any study of different democratic governments readily reveals. Some of them are more explicit than others in putting certain matters beyond the reach of government. Some are more precise in enumerating individual rights and in allocating governmental powers. And some are more detailed than others in setting forth the procedural limitations on the exercise of governmental authority.

Democratic constitutions therefore constitute an agreement among the nation's citizens concerning the machinery of government and the powers which the various components of that government will exercise. In this sense, constitutions order the relations between the citizen and his government as well as the relations among governmental institutions. When there is a serious breakdown concerning this compact or its meaning, civil war may result, or at least an effort to write a new constitution. Consequently, providing means for an orderly amendment of the constitution is of great importance. Yet, the amending process cannot in and of itself guarantee long life for a constitution. Some nations have had few constitutions and others many during comparable periods of time, the United States and France, respectively, being good examples.

Constitutions have been justified and defended on various grounds. With the growth of democracy in the West, the original justification emphasized natural law, i.e. the need to make explicit certain precepts of justice and right which were thought to be divinely-inspired and therefore eternal. Subsequently, the defense of constitutionalism became more pragmatic, i.e. the need to have an ordered political system in which stability, agreed-upon procedures, and specified individual rights would prevail, thus minimizing arbitrariness and the likelihood of revolutionary disruptions. Moreover, in republics particularly, constitutions serve as symbols of unity and majesty of nations. But even non-democratic nations seem to find constitutions necessary, however false their pretended "constitutionalism," for today any nation would feel naked without a constitution.

Generally speaking, when we look at the organization of political authority, we find significant variations among democratic states. Electoral procedure and practices, that is, the ways in which popular participation takes place, will vary. The relations between a central government and those of the nation's subdivisions will differ, particularly if one nation is organized on the federal principle, where authority is divided between a central government and governments of the nation's territorial units, and another nation is organized on the unitary principle, where all authority is vested in the central government.

Moreover, the functional allocation of power, whether there is a separation-of-powers scheme or not, produces many important variations. Parliamentary systems, as we shall see in this book, are not all alike despite their many similarities. Likewise, the United States system, usually depicted as an example of the presidential type of government, offers interesting examples of how the mechanics of democracy can vary. This becomes all the more obvious as we look at specific institutions, such as the executive, the legislature, and the courts.

Finally, democratic systems offer many similarities and differences in their political dynamics. At the heart of this question is the manner in which the struggle for power proceeds. The chief manifestations of this struggle are political parties, although in some democratic systems formally organized interest groups also play a decisive role. Of particular importance in the dynamics of any democratic political system is the nature of the leadership which the system produces. As a general rule, this leadership is intimately connected with the respective political parties. And since parties are the institutions through which the electorate is presented with alternatives, popular participation has an impact on the leadership of any democratic system, because it is to the leadership that the people look to translate their verdict into meaningful political programs.

DEMOCRACY AND THE ECONOMIC ORDER

The question of whether democracy is necessarily associated with any particular economic system has often been raised. Those who answer in the affirmative argue in favor of private enterprise. They point out that the greatest economic progress was achieved in an era when the free market regulated economic activity and the government pursued a laissez-faire attitude toward economic matters. They argue further that the freedom associated with democracy means also freedom from governmental interference in the functioning of the economic system. Those who argue in the negative readily admit that the development of modern democracy and the extraordinary growth of private economic enterprise took place side by side. But, they point out, the evolving capitalist system has changed creating problems which could be handled only by the government. They insist, moreover, that it is for the people of any democracy to decide what policies their government should follow concerning economic questions.

A historical note at this point may be instructive. In the first place, governments of modern democratic states never accepted a completely "hands off" policy with respect to economic matters. They imposed tariffs on imports, granted tax relief, and took other steps to create a favorable economic climate for infant industries. Moreover, as industries developed, a trend toward mergers (monopolies) threatened to destroy competition, which is the essence of a private enterprise economy. Thereupon democratic governments were called upon to pass anti-monopoly legislation so as to preserve competition. In addition, other types of regulation (e.g. transport, broadcasting, etc.) became necessary to avoid chaotic situations in an increasingly interdependent and complex industrial civilization.

Before long, however, democratic governments moved beyond regulation to more positive programs designed to promote economic welfare. This step was prompted by several factors. One of these was the determination of labor to use the strike and other weapons in order to improve the lot of the workers. Another factor was large-scale unemployment and its consequences. Still another factor was the imbalance between the incomes of industry and agriculture. These in turn called attention to poverty, to poor housing, and to unequal opportunities in education. The result was an aroused social conscience among a large part of the voters. Democratically elected governments responded with considerable legislation, calculated not only to redress the economic balance, but also to promote the general economic welfare.

More recently the trend toward economic and social welfare legislation has continued. Social security acts, civil rights acts to protect minorities, acts to improve housing and education, and government-sponsored projects to eliminate or minimize poverty have come into being. These have been accompanied by legislation concerning oil exploitation, regulation of the stock market, control of interest rates, and other economic activity to assure a type of balance and thereby avoid drastic economic fluctuations. Democratic governments have thus assumed considerable responsibilities in the economic realm, leading most qualified experts to describe the economic systems of most democratic states as mixed economies.

In some democratic nations, such as Sweden and Great Britain, the governments embarked upon considerable state ownership of economic enterprises. This raises the question of the limits, if any, to which democratic governments may go in the economic sphere. It also poses the question of government responsibility, particularly when big labor and big business sometimes appear to be following policies and programs at the expense of the consumer. There probably is no answer that is acceptable to all citizens. At the same time, there would seem to be little doubt that governments in democratic states must have ample power to deal with matters of public concern in today's immensely complex industrial society. Moreover, these governments must be concerned with safeguarding basic freedoms, without which democracy has no meaning. To achieve such a balance will be no easy task, a task to which all citizens in democratic nations would do well to devote more of their attention.

WHAT CHARACTERIZES DICTATORSHIPS?

As suggested above, man has for the most part lived under authoritarian forms of government. These have varied greatly in time and place. We shall be concerned, in this book, with one dictatorship— that of the Soviet Union. There are, however, many other types of dictatorship, and some reference to these would seem to be in order, particularly by way of comparison with the modern totalitarian type of which the Soviet model is a good example.

EARLIER TYPES OF DICTATORSHIP

Perhaps the earliest form of authoritarian rule was exemplified by the chief of a tribe or clan. Such rulers survived in tradition-bound societies and in relative isolation. Some are still to be found in places like the more remote regions of Africa. Subsequently, we find potentates ruling over greater numbers of people and assuming the title of king or emperor. Sometimes they took on an aura of holiness and became in fact god-kings, one of the best modern examples being the ruler of Tibet before he was forced to flee as a result of the conquest of his nation by Communist China.

Monarchy, as a form of authoritarian rule, is familiar to all. The history of Europe in the past 2,000 years is replete with examples of monarchical rule. For the most part, however, monarchy in Europe has either disappeared or has changed radically. Most modern European monarchies have become constitutional monarchies, with real political power being vested in popularly elected officials. Elsewhere, however, particularly in some of the countries in the Middle East, the monarch remains virtually unlimited.

The oldest formalized dictatorship was found in ancient Rome. It was far different, however, from modern dictatorships. A man was brought in and given dictatorial powers to deal with a certain crisis. He was elected and not self-appointed. He served for a limited period, never more than six months, and then returned to whatever he had been doing before. Perhaps the best known of such dictators was Cincinnatus (fifth century B.C.), a farmer who went back to his plow after having dealt with the situation that brought about the emergency grant of power. Modern democracies have on occasion granted the executive extraordinary powers to deal with crises, which has given rise to the term "constitutional dictatorship."

MODERN TOTALITARIAN DICTATORSHIPS

There are several types of dictatorship in the modern world. Some, including the quasi-military strong man type found in certain Latin American countries, may be described as "partial" dictatorships. This does not mean that their authority is limited, for it is not. Rather, it signifies that the aims of the dictatorship are limited. Generally speaking, in such regimes the dictator has complete control of the political and military establishments, including the direction of the nation's foreign relations. Threats to internal security are met by the use of the police, press censorship, and such other measures as are deemed necessary. The dictator, however, may have little or no interest in the operation of the economy or in other activities of the society. People may be left to pursue economic and social goals without hindrance, so long as these do not constitute a threat to the dictatorship. Such regimes often seek to freeze the status quo.

The most prominent of modern dictatorships, however, have been the totalitarian dictatorships of the Nazi-Fascist and Communist varieties. While there are significant differences between Fascist and Communist dictatorships, an attempt to discuss those differences here would lead us far afield. More important for this brief introduction is to note that they have a great deal in common. Consequently the discussion that follows is in large measure applicable to both types.

First of all, modern totalitarian dictatorships, whether Communist or Fascist, are characterized by an official ideology, that is, a set of ideas concerning society and how it should be run. These ideas are totally at variance with basic democratic beliefs. There is a total rejection of any and all ideas that stress man's ability to govern himself, although the dictatorship may allege that it speaks for the people. On the other hand, there is an elaborate justification of dictatorial authority. In addition, no other ideology is permitted to compete for public favor. In short, there is one official ideology, determined and altered by those who wield the dictatorship.

Secondly, modern totalitarian dictatorships have a great deal in common in the ways and means they employ in the establishment and perpetuation of the dictatorship. They are, first of all, more or less dedicated to a thorough remaking of society. In some ways, the Communist revolution is more complete, but the Fascist revolution, even though it may leave some things relatively untouched for a while, is nevertheless dedicated to the ultimate transformation of society as a whole. Totalitarianism, as the word suggests, means that the dictatorship concerns itself with everything in the society. Some dictatorships have confined themselves to the exercise of political or military power or a combination of the two, but literally nothing escapes the attention of a totalitarian dictatorship.

Thirdly, modern totalitarian dictatorships are characterized by mass movements, exemplified by the Communist party and the Nazi party. This is the basic instrument of rule, sometimes leading observers to use the term "party dictatorship." This is also the vehicle employed to capture power in the first place, by capitalizing on or whipping up mass discontent. Once in power, the party and the dictator become symbols of the regime and what it seeks to accomplish. As such, they are above criticism and take on an aura of infallibility.

Fourthly, the party spews forth a variety of auxiliary agencies as instruments of its rule. As in all other forms of authoritarian rule, there is a distrust of people. This distrust is total, and to the end that the people should be harnessed to do the bidding of the dictatorship there are created secret police establishments, youth movements, women's organizations, various newspapers, and other instruments for manipulating public opinion, together with a variety of instruments in the political, economic, and military fields. Nothing is left to chance.

Fifthly, modern totalitarian dictatorships have been characterized by unabashed efforts to demonstrate popular support for the dictatorship. Well-planned and minutely supervised massive demonstrations, parades, and plebiscites have been put on so as to impress foreigners, and perhaps citizens too, with the size and enthusiasm of their following. In this effort, the dictatorship often borrows such popular terms as democracy and seeks to employ them to its own ends.

Finally, totalitarian dictatorships have been engaged in the pursuit of aggressive foreign policies. These have a twofold purpose: they may help the dictatorship achieve certain foreign policy goals and at the same time serve to focus domestic dissatisfaction on the foreigner rather than on the dictator. Because they can so effectively control available information about foreign affairs, the wielders of the dictatorship can more easily shape popular thinking about foreign policy matters and their impact on the regime's difficulties and problems. In this way, they seek to explain many of their failures, domestic and foreign.

A slightly different approach to a definition of totalitarian dictatorships is offered by Carl J. Friedrich and Zbigniew K. Brzezinski. They conclude that such dictatorships are characterized by a "pattern of interrelated traits" consisting of

an official ideology . . . covering all vital aspects of man's existence . . . ; a single mass party led typically by one man . . . ; a system of terroristic police control . . . ; a technologically conditioned near-complete monopoly . . . of all means of effective mass communication . . . ; a similarly technologically conditioned near-complete monopoly . . . of all means of effective armed combat; a central control and direction of the entire economy . . . .[1]

In a later book, Brzezinski credits the above to Friedrich and proposes a concise definition which he says points to the essence of totalitarianism—"its institutionalized revolutionary zeal." Totalitarianism, he says,

is a system in which technologically advanced instruments of political power are wielded without restraint by centralized leadership of an elite movement, for the purpose of effecting a total social revolution, including the conditioning of man, on the basis of certain arbitrary ideological assumptions proclaimed by the leadership, in an atmosphere of coerced unanimity of the entire population.[2]

Certain elements or attributes of modern totalitarian regimes can be found in earlier authoritarian or despotic systems, but that does not

---

[1] C. J. Friedrich and Z. K. Brzezinski, *Totalitarian Dictatorship and Autocracy* (Cambridge, Mass., Harvard University Press, 1956), pp. 9–10.

[2] Z. K. Brzezinski, *Ideology and Power in Soviet Politics* (New York, Frederick A. Praeger, publisher, 1962), pp. 19–20.

mean that those systems were totalitarian. Unlike modern totalitarianisms, they did not seek to destroy all existing political, economic, and social relationships. They were not bent on undertaking large scale social engineering, with the aim of building a new unity around one ideology—that of the rulers. Totalitarianism is a phenomenon of our age.

*   *   *   *   *

As indicated earlier, democracy and totalitarian dictatorship are exemplified by the four political systems treated in this book. It is my hope that the reader will keep this broader framework in mind as he proceeds to study these systems, their organizational aspects, the procedures they typify, the problems that confront them, and the challenges they pose to one another. These are the more important features in any meaningful comparative analysis and not the details, although details are necessary to an understanding of each individual system.

BIBLIOGRAPHICAL NOTE

A convenient collection of the constitutions (or constitutional documents) of the political systems discussed in this book are to be found in William G. Andrews, *Constitutions and Constitutionalism* (Princeton, N.J.: D. Van Nostrand, 1961).

The literature dealing with democracy is vast. The following will provide the student with a good beginning: Robert A. Dahl, *A Preface To Democratic Theory* (Chicago: The University of Chicago Press, 1956); Charles Frankel, *The Democratic Prospect* (New York: Harper and Row, 1962); A. D. Lindsay, *The Modern Democratic State* (New York: Oxford University Press, 1943); Walter Lippmann, *Essays In The Public Philosophy* (Boston: Little, Brown and Co., 1955); Leslie Lipson, *The Democratic Civilization* (New York: Oxford University Press, 1964); Henry B. Mayo, *Introduction To Democratic Theory* (New York: Oxford University Press, 1960); J. Roland Pennock, *Liberal Democracy: Its Merits and Prospects* (New York: Rinehart, 1950); Clinton L. Rossiter, *Constitutional Dictatorship: Crisis Government In Modern Democracies* (Princeton, N.J.: Princeton University Press, 1948); Joseph A. Schumpeter, *Capitalism, Socialism and Democracy* (New York: Harper-Row, 1950); Thomas Landon Thorson, *The Logic of Democracy* (New York: Holt, Rinehart and Winston, 1962).

There is a growing literature on dictatorship. The following titles offer a good beginning: Hannah Arendt, *The Origins of Totalitarianism* (2nd ed., New York: Harcourt, Brace and World, 1958); Zevedei Barbu, *Democracy and Dictatorship: Their Psychology and Patterns of Life* (New York: Grove Press, 1956); Betty B. Burch, *Dictatorship and Totalitarianism: Selected Readings* (Princeton, N.J.: D. Van Nostrand, 1964); Alfred Cobban, *Dic-*

tatorship: Its History and Theory (New York: Scribners, 1939) ; Carl J. Friedrich and Zbigniew K. Brzezinski, *Totalitarian Dictatorship and Autocracy* (Cambridge, Mass.: Harvard University Press, 1956) ; Robert Jay Lifton, *Thought Reform and the Psychology of Totalism: A Study of "Brainwashing" in China* (New York: W. W. Norton & Co., 1961) ; Franz Neumann, *The Democratic and Authoritarian State* (Glencoe, Ill.: The Free Press, 1957).

PART ONE
GREAT BRITAIN

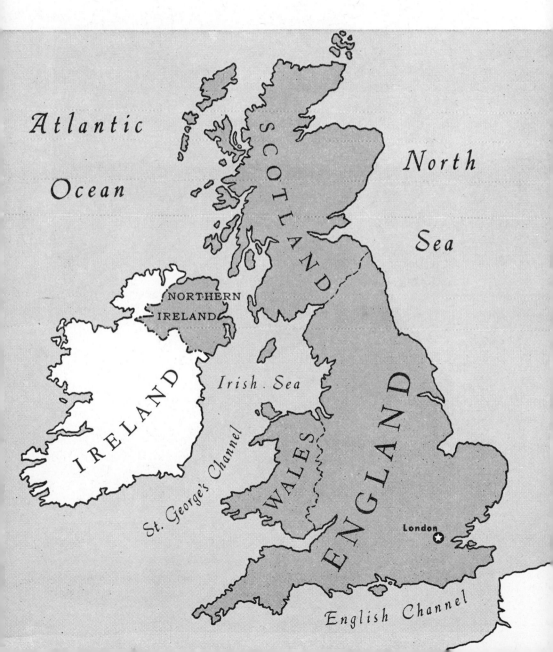

Atlantic

Ocean

North

Sea

SCOTLAND

NORTHERN
IRELAND

IRELAND

Irish Sea

St. George's Channel

WALES

ENGLAND

London

English Channel

CHAPTER 1

THE COUNTRY AND
ITS PEOPLE

THE political system which prevails in Great Britain[1] is deeply rooted in the past. A familiarity with that past would contribute greatly to an understanding of the nature and operation of contemporary British political institutions. Unfortunately, an adequate treatment of the past is beyond the scope of this book. Yet some basic information about the country and its people, however brief, will acquaint the reader with a number of factors which contributed to the origin and growth of these political institutions, and may, it is hoped, lead him to probe deeper into the historical and environmental conditions which favored the growth of the British political system.

THE GEOGRAPHIC SETTING

Great Britain is an archipelago (the British Isles), separated from the continent of Europe by the English Channel. The principal island, approximately 750 miles long and no more than 300 miles at its widest point, constitutes the bulk of the territory of England, Wales, and Scotland. Six counties at the northeastern tip of Ireland, which is a separate island, are known as Northern Ireland. The total area of the United Kingdom of Great Britain and Northern Ireland is relatively small—some 94,300 square miles, or about the size of the state of Oregon. With a population of over 53 million, Great Britain is one of the most densely settled countries in the world, exceeded only by Belgium and the Netherlands. The heaviest concentration of people is in England, where 44 million live. Scotland has 5⅓ million, Wales 2½ million, and Northern Ireland about 1½ million.

The climate of the British Isles is fairly even and moderate. The summers are cool and the winters mild, due in part to the warming effect of the Gulf Stream. The rainfall is generous (between 30 and

---

[1] The formal name of the country is the United Kingdom of Great Britain and Northern Ireland.

17

60 inches in the heart of the country), helping to produce a cloak of green the year around throughout most of the country.

The moderate climate, together with sizable acreages of good agricultural land, enabled the British to produce a large part of their foodstuffs prior to a hundred years ago. But as the country was becoming industrialized, its population grew and with it the importation of large quantities of food. With the advances in ocean transportation, and because much of the land was not suited to wheat farming in any case, the importation of many food products became more economical than to have them produced domestically. This became ever more evident as the income from British manufacturing grew by leaps and bounds, and as an increasing number of Britishers became engaged in commerce and manufacturing. In short, Britain became a highly industrialized nation. Today four out of five of her people are city dwellers.

Topography and other natural conditions favored the Industrial Revolution in Great Britain. Britain was blessed with the requisite natural resources. Coal was found in abundance and near it iron ore. Mining and manufacturing concentrations grew up, as did shipping and commercial centers. Good harbors became important grain-milling, leather-tanning, shoe-manufacturing and ship-building centers. They also became important as centers for the manufacture of cloth, paper, chemicals, drugs, and dyestuffs. Their docks, warehouses, and storage facilities, particularly those of London and Liverpool, added to the importance of shipping and commercial activities. Over the years the centers of British industry shifted. Initially, the position of the coal fields determined the location of mining and manufacturing centers. But as iron and steel industries became more dependent upon imported ores, and as more and more of the manufactured product was destined for export, the manufacturing centers moved steadily toward coastal cities, where they are, for the most part, to be found today. Difficulties there were, but British circumstances were, by and large, favorable to the Industrial Revolution.

CONSEQUENCES OF INSULAR POSITION

Britain's position played an influential role in the development of her political institutions. First of all, it helped to cement a feeling of nationalism a good deal earlier than was the case with the peoples of the European mainland. Invasions from the Continent, from the Roman Conquest, which began A.D. 43, to the Norman Conquest of 1066, helped to forge national unity. Interestingly enough, the latter was the last great invasion, and although each left its unique imprint, all of them served to augment a feeling of national unity.

Secondly, Britain's insular position provided a shield against involvement in the quarrels of Europe, especially after the development of the British Navy. The absence of land frontiers meant that the people had no need to turn to the state for the defense of their homes and farms. There was no standing army, which in many another country was the instrument of autocratic rule. Being relatively free of the threat of foreign tyranny, the people could devote more time to combatting tyranny at home. But the English Channel was more than a protective shield. It was also, especially in times of peace, a means of easy access to the Continent, to its ideas, and to its contributions to science, trade, and industry.

Thirdly, Britain's geographic position was in large measure responsible for her subsequent commercial and military position. The discovery of the New World and the establishment of new trade routes via the Atlantic made Britain the center of world commerce. Her industry, her cities, and her commerce grew apace. Trade and the need to control the waters around the British Isles for defense purposes went hand in hand. At the same time, Britain's dependence on sea power encouraged the growth of the empire. In short, the seas not only became commercial highways but also avenues which led to discovery, exploration, empire, and naval supremacy.

Finally, Britain's insular position, together with industrialization and its attendant consequences, resulted in her being the first nation to be compelled to develop public policies in an age of urbanized society. The transition from an agricultural to a primarily urban society created many new problems. Among these was the problem of providing such services as water, transport, fire protection, sewage disposal, and, later, electricity and gas. But frequently these problems also forced local authorities to find local solutions, and in the process assisted the development of local self-government. Hence, Britishers were ahead of other people in learning to grapple with many local political problems—an experience that influenced their thinking about national politics. This thinking was aided by the smallness of the British Isles, which facilitated a centralized government and a national point of view. This is in part evidenced by the fact that none of the great issues in British politics are sectional. A combination of circumstances, therefore, put Britain ahead of other nations in adjusting her political institutions to the problems of modern urbanized society.

THE PEOPLE

The racial origins of the people are to be found in two basic strains—Nordic (North European) and Mediterranean (South European). The Romans came first to mix with the native but numerically few Britons and Welshmen. The Roman withdrawal in the fifth century was followed by the arrival of Germanic peoples (Angles and Saxons), followed by Danes and Normans. Intermarriage over the centuries has resulted in a considerable mixture of the races, although the people have no common name. They think of themselves as Englishmen, Scots, Welshmen, or Ulstermen.

The common language is English, although no one is required to speak it. The Welsh have, in fact, retained their language, but its use is declining; 40 per cent of those who speak it are over 65 years of age. As in the matter of race, the common language is the product of mixing. English is supposed to be a Teutonic tongue, yet over half of the words in current ordinary use are of Latin origin.

In religion, as in race and language, there is a combination that has brought unity in diversity. Great Britain is overwhelmingly Protestant, although Roman Catholicism is the religion of approximately 8 per cent of the people. Of the Protestants, more than half are adherents of the Church of England (Anglican), of which the monarch is the head. The others are "Nonconformists" (Baptists, Methodists, Congregationalists, *et al.*). Scotland has its own national church (Presbyterian), while in Wales the Anglican Church is on the same footing as other churches.

The Church of England is not so important politically as it once was. Historically, it tended to be upper middle class, while the nonconformist churches were inclined to be lower middle class, and the Roman Catholic Church tended to be working class. In the period from 1680 to 1830, religion in large measure constituted the basis for political parties, the Tories being identified with Anglicanism and the Whigs with Nonconformity. While this was regretted by some, others have argued that it was good because it prevented the basing of parties on class. In any case, studies of recent British elections indicate that religious differences do not seem to affect the political choices of the voters.

Class differences have long been a part of British life, although in some significant respects these have varied from class divisions elsewhere. First of all, the British nobility always remained a relatively small group since only the oldest person in the family inherits the title, while the other members continue as commoners. Secondly, because the barrier between classes was not rigid, and because there were manifold differences within classes, it was possible for persons to move up the social ladder. Thirdly, class divisions were only partially based on economic differences, with education perhaps being an even more important consideration. Moreover, although titled personages occupied, until recent times, a large share of the privileged positions, no class or group has stood in any privileged *legal* relationship to the state since the first part of the sixteenth century. Also, many of the peerages created in the last century constituted rewards for achieving eminence in the arts, science, or government service (diplomacy, military service, and politics).

Today there is still a gradation of classes, from the comparatively rich to the comparatively poor, but a leveling process has been under way for some time. A large proportion of the people do not regard themselves as either relatively rich or relatively poor. The great bulk of them tend to think of themselves as lower middle class. But this is a new development, resulting from an upward movement of those in the labor ranks who have done well and the downward movement of many who had once identified themselves with the upper class, but who in recent decades have suffered economic decline. Sometimes, however, an economic overlap between groups makes class identification less meaningful. A skilled worker, for example, may think of himself as working class while a clerk or teacher may prefer the designation middle class, yet the best-paid skilled workers earn considerably more than the lowest-paid teachers and clerks. But it should be noted that manners, speech, social habits, and other class attributes do not change with anything like the speed that may bring about change in income levels.

Some evidence of leveling, however, is also to be found in the social and political realms. Although the upper middle class is still powerful and influential, it no longer occupies as dominant a position as it once did in the House of Commons, in the civil service, or in the field of education. And in education, where social inequalities persisted the longest, the evidence of leveling is dramatically portrayed by the fact that approximately three-fourths of all university students receive financial aid, most of it coming from national or local government. Moreover, during the past decade several new universities have been built with the aim of drawing students from all over Britain, thus providing an opportunity to lessen the educational and social monopoly of Oxford and Cambridge. Consequently, the narrowing of the gap between the classes has resulted in the lower layers of the middle class, as well as the working class, being better represented in British public life at all levels. This is not to suggest, however, that the lower classes are represented in anything like their relative numerical strength in the society at large.

It must also be noted that the British educational system has emphasized the training of an elite. Even the Labor party has not deviated too much from this principle; what it has wanted is an equal opportunity for the talented from the lower classes to rise along with those who had money. But there is a general belief that the privately financed schools constitute a surer avenue for university entrance, particularly to Oxford and Cambridge. Consequently, many lower class parents make a real sacrifice to provide their children with what they believe to be superior educational training.

The leveling which has been taking place over the last 50 years can be ascribed to a number of factors. The two world wars, with their legacies of large debts, high taxes, and the accompanying losses of India, Burma, Ceylon, and other dependent areas, have played the most important role. Simultaneously, popular education and the organization of labor for political action brought extensive social services, but at a cost to all. The nationalization program of the Labor party furthered the process. The result has been an economic and social revolution whose net effect has been to improve the living standard of the working classes and to lower it for the more well-to-do.

Class barriers still exist and still are felt, but they do not exert nearly the importance or influence which they did in the past. A lot of perfectly ordinary people are now earning tremendous salaries (compared to 1945), which has opened the world of clubs, hotels, resorts, restaurants, and theaters to an entirely new body of people. It is now a little more difficult to distinguish the miner from the civil servant and the shopkeeper from the barrister. Debutantes no longer exist in the old sense and are no longer presented to Court. The importance of the changes that have taken place is reflected in public opinion surveys which indicate a general agreement that opportunities for social advancement for the upcoming generation (in all groups) are better than they have been for the present one. Even an acrid critic like C. A. R. Crosland admits that "the distribution of opportunity stands today in closer relationship to that of ability . . . than ever before."[2]

[2] C. A. R. Crosland, *The Conservative Enemy: A Programme of Radical Reform for the 1960s* (New York: Schocten Books, Inc., 1963), p. 170.

He insists, however, that leadership is still disproportionately drawn from too narrow a base and although "the way to the top is being rebuilt," it is perhaps a narrow ladder rather than a broad highway.

At the same time, the changes that have occurred in Britain since 1945 are much more profound than the above paragraphs would seem to indicate. Not only has there been a social revolution, but in addition, the forces of science and technology have been altering the face of the nation. Changes in industry—diversification, development of new techniques of professional management, the new role of insurance companies (to mention a few)—and the impact of these on British society generally may not yet be appreciated or understood, to say nothing of the challenge to the political system to provide the needed accommodation.[3]

POLITICAL LIFE

Any attempt to explain a nation's political system or way of life solely in terms of national character raises difficulties, but one cannot deny that aggregate behavior patterns are revealing. National character may find its main expression in art, literature, architecture, or politics. In Britain, it is perhaps best expressed in her political institutions. Although Britain has made great contributions in other fields, notably literature, those in the areas of law and government are of major concern to the present discussion, and it may be that they will turn out to be the most enduring.

Perhaps the most characteristic feature of British political life is its history of long and, on the whole, peaceful development. Except for a brief experiment with a republican form of government in the middle of the seventeenth century, British political institutions have experienced a steady and cumulative growth over some thirteen or fourteen hundred years. In the process much was changed and much was preserved. The net result has been political unity, stemming in large part from the existence of a political consensus, that is, an agreement on the principles and basic rules that determine how society is to be governed.

First among these principles is *freedom*, exemplified both in the individual and the collective actions of Britishers. It has been said that a Britisher is not only free, he is truculently free. He has a determination "not to be put upon," a determination to resist all tyranny. He

---

[3] For a detailed recent study, see Anthony Sampson, *Anatomy of Britain* (London: Hodder & Stoughton, 1962).

is not accustomed to remaining silent when there is any effort to interfere with his rights as a free man. This principle is exemplified collectively in the long tradition of safeguarding freedom of speech and freedom of the press, as well as other freedoms, although Britain has no bill of rights in the American sense. It also finds expression in the fact that there is no un-British activities committee of Parliament. And it finds dramatic expression in a legal system and its rules of evidence which are designed to protect the innocent by safeguarding the rights of the accused.

Closely related to freedom is the principle of *toleration*, which forms the basis for workable political compromise. It was not always like this; some periods in British politics were marked by violence. Ultimately, however, moderation and balance were restored. If it can be said that national character changes, one of the most important changes in Britain is to be found in the latter half of the seventeenth century, when it was decided to try the way of toleration in the field of religion and the way of discussion and compromise in matters of politics. Perhaps one result of the temper of compromise is the tendency toward temporary solutions which the British "make do" for the time being. This habit of "muddling through," although sometimes accompanied by dire consequences, puts a premium on the value of experience, which has often demonstrated that many serious problems cease being problems with the passage of time. The result of such a philosophy in practice has been the "softening of sharp edges," which in other settings have produced disastrous social conflicts.

A final principle, basic to the British consensus, is a *practical approach* to the job of self-government. This has been exemplified by a sense of social obligation, a feeling of responsibility toward society as a whole. The tradition of Britishers doing things for themselves on a voluntary basis and in free association with others is well known. This is particularly true in the realm of local government, which is based on voluntary unpaid service. There is a salaried staff, to be sure, but it is the servant of an unpaid local council. The conviction that people should take part in government is based not only on the principle that politics is an honorable profession, but also on the practical consideration that if citizens do not bother to decide questions of public policy someone else will decide for them.

A corollary of the practical approach to self-government is that if citizens are to decide questions of public policy they should be well informed. To this end Britishers read avidly about political questions. They are aided in this by newspapers of differing opinions which have a national and a local circulation (most of them published in London), by weekly periodicals and books, and by a BBC news service that is listened to by half the population. Moreover, they read the political tracts put out periodically by the major political parties. All in all, there would seem to be little doubt that the people of Britain are better informed politically than the citizens of any other country.

A second corollary of the practical approach to self-government holds that differences of opinion about questions of public policy should be resolved by counting heads instead of breaking them. This means acceptance of the principle of majority rule. At the same time, British political practice reveals respect for rights of the minority. Major desires for social change can be realized without unreasonable delay, while at the same time there is no allegation that minority rights are violated.

In short, freedom, toleration, and a practical approach to self-government combine to constitute the essence of the British political consensus.

BIBLIOGRAPHICAL NOTE

Among the studies that have characterized the people of Great Britain and their approach to politics, useful insights may be gained from Sir Ernest Barker, *Britain and the British People* (London: Oxford University Press, 1955); *The Character of England*, edited by the same author (London: Oxford University Press, 1947); Denis W. Brogan, *The English People* (New York: Alfred A. Knopf, Inc., 1943); Drew Middleton, *These Are the British* (New York: Alfred A. Knopf, Inc., 1957); K. B. Smellie, *The British Way of Life* (New York: Frederick A. Praeger, Inc., 1955); and Michael Stewart, *The British Approach to Politics* (London: Allen and Unwin, 1954).

Stressing the impact of post World War II developments are: Robert Brady, *Crisis in Britain: Plans and Achievements of the Labour Government* (Berkeley: University of California Press, 1950); C. F. O. Clarke, *Britain Today: A Review of British Political and Social Trends* (Cambridge, Mass.: Harvard University Press, 1951); G. D. H. Cole, *The Post-War Condition of Britain* (New York: Frederick A. Praeger, Inc., 1957); Angus Maude, *The English Middle Classes* (New York: Alfred A. Knopf, Inc., 1950); Anthony Sampson, *Anatomy of Britain* (London: Hodder & Stoughton, 1962); and Francis Williams, *Socialist Britain: Its Background, Its Present, and An Estimate of Its Future* (New York: The Viking Press, Inc., 1949).

CHAPTER 2

THE DEVELOPMENT OF BRITISH POLITICAL INSTITUTIONS

GREAT BRITAIN is a democracy, being governed by representatives elected by and responsible to the people. But she did not become a democracy on any specific date. The transition from a more or less absolute monarchy to democracy required several centuries of slow but steady growth. Consequently, her constitution does not date from a specific time, as does ours. Nor is it to be found in one compact document. Rather, it consists of a number of charters, important statutes, judicial decisions, and certain political practices resulting from custom and usage. All of these are generally identified with important landmarks in the gradual growth of British political institutions, and will be discussed subsequently in this chapter.

THE BEGINNINGS OF REPRESENTATIVE GOVERNMENT

The first significant step toward democracy coincided with the establishment of the practice of representation. It is now generally agreed that representative government originated in England during the thirteenth century, growing out of the royal need for unusual sums of money for war and other enterprises. Because the sums of money forthcoming from the upper nobility (the monarch's immediate associates and counselors) proved insufficient, the king decided to tax the lower nobility. In order to do this, King John in 1213 asked the sheriff of each county to send four "discreet Knights" (presumably persons friendly to the crown and hence willing to tax their compatriots) to meet with his advisers in the Great Council. This practice of summoning an equal number of knights from each county was continued by other monarchs. By the turn of the century, the towns or boroughs were also sending a like number of "representatives."

From these feeble beginnings a collective body of representatives came into being and acquired the name Parliament, whose attributes for many years to come were, however, judicial and not legislative. It is generally agreed that this term came into use in the latter half of the thirteenth century, although there is some disagreement as to the

26

actual date. In any event, all members of Parliament met as one body for the first time in 1295. Afterward, they broke up into groups or "estates" consisting of nobles, clergy, and commons. A subsequent realignment resulted in only two groups, which have continued to this day—the House of Lords and the House of Commons.

In the beginning, however, Parliament had very little authority of its own. It was not popularly elected and it met only at the discretion of the king. Sometimes several years separated its meetings. Moreover, it was not a deliberative body, but a kind of high court of justice concerned with judicial and administrative matters. And even in these matters, the commoners from the counties and the boroughs did not sit with the king and his lords to take part in their decisions. In time, they developed into a gathering which could present grievances to the monarch. But not until the fourteenth century were the commoners told to elect a speaker (to speak for them), and not until the reign of Henry V (1413–22) did they begin putting their petitions in the form in which they wished them enacted.

THE ASCENDANCY OF PARLIAMENT

Initially, no one ever dreamed of making Parliament into an instrument for controlling the king's government. Gradually, however, this gathering of nonelected feudal representatives was converted by stages into a parliamentary assembly, which was first to control the monarch and later to be controlled itself by a popular electorate. But a great deal of time was to elapse before this double transition was completed.

The growing power of Parliament was made significantly evident as the House of Commons, by degrees, acquired the right of originating all bills for raising or disbursing revenue. As a result, the support of the Commons became essential to the Crown. However, the members of the Commons were more independent and less subject to royal influence than the peers, and therefore inclined to support government programs and bills only if they understood and approved them. Nevertheless, Parliament did not gain control over finance until the fifteenth century.

By and large, however, the period 1603 to 1688 represents the era in which parliamentary supremacy was vindicated. In actuality, English kings had few real difficulties with their parliaments, or at least few that they could not successfully resolve, until James VI of Scotland became James I of England. James became the symbol of the Divine Right of Kings, but neither he nor Charles I was a very skillful ruler, with the result that the Stuarts were driven from the throne. The bloodless revolution of 1688, which brought William and Mary to the throne, constituted a sharp break in constitutional development. By their acceptance of the throne, William and Mary acknowledged the supremacy of Parliament. At a time when continental European feudal kingdoms were turning into absolute monarchies, feudal limitations on the royal prerogative in England were developing into parliamentary restrictions on the exercise of crown powers. The crucial question was whether the king could make laws outside of Parliament. The Civil War confirmed that the king was not above the law and that the common law could be amended only in Parliament. Since 1689 no monarch has ever challenged the supremacy of Parliament.

This is not to suggest that after 1689 monarchs lacked influence in government. On the contrary, many of them exercised great influence, but they had to depend upon Parliament for funds and for the laws that they administered. Moreover, in the long, peaceful evolution of British political institutions since that time, the power and influence of the monarch has steadily declined. Individual monarchs, through their intimate knowledge of affairs and their persuasiveness, may and do exercise influence from time to time, but effective political power is exercised solely by Parliament.

There is some question, however, as to how effectively Parliament exercises its powers in practice, or indeed, if it has not abdicated them in favor of the ministers. These questions will be examined in subsequent chapters, particularly the ones on the Cabinet and Parliament.

THE TRIUMPH OF PARLIAMENTARY DEMOCRACY

Today the British system can be said to be monarchical in form and democratic in substance. With the rise of Parliament to a position of supremacy, it was inevitable that Parliament would settle the question of political leadership and determine its conditions. Moreover, as the basis of the suffrage was widened, the popularly elected house was bound to eclipse the House of Lords. And as political parties organized to present alternative programs to the electorate, it was inevitable that party government should become synonymous with democratic government. To understand this significant transition in British government, a brief discussion of the major developments is essential.

THE EVOLUTION OF RESPONSIBLE GOVERNMENT

As the influence of the monarchs declined, the "meetings of the King in Parliament" became increasingly more formal, while the real work of Parliament was being done in the two Houses sitting separately. Parliamentary supremacy, therefore, meant that the monarch would have to govern through ministers who were acceptable to Parliament. During his wars with France, for example, William III experienced difficulties with the House of Commons. Hitherto his ministers had been chosen from both political parties. Between 1693 and 1696, however, he dismissed the Tories and allotted all the great offices to the Whigs, who had a majority in the House of Commons. Heretofore turbulent, the House now became docile. For the monarch this was a matter of convenience, for political circumstances forced him to make use of ministers who could manage the House. By winning its confidence, they were able to control it.

Out of these circumstances grew the practice of selecting the chief ministers exclusively from the party or faction having effective control of the House of Commons. With the views and policies of the crown being determined by the party having a majority in the House of Commons, the ministers of necessity became in effect a committee of that party. By countersigning the king's acts, the ministers thereby assumed responsibility for them. Although they were the king's advisers, they were limited in the advice which they could give by the political complexion of the party they represented. It is true, of course, that until political parties became strong, the king could play off one group against another, but in the end he could not prevail against a united party commanding a majority in the House of Commons.

Under these circumstances, it is understandable that the king's advisers should begin meeting without his presence to decide what advice they were going to give him. This development was aided considerably by the fact that George I (1714–27) could speak no English, and therefore found it singularly unprofitable to attend meetings of his advisers, who were to become known collectively as the cabinet. What this was to mean in the end was that the cabinet would give the monarch only such advice as the political party of which it was a part was willing to have translated into public policy. Indeed, it could give no other advice, unless it wished to risk being removed from office by adverse votes in Parliament. In the end, the cabinet's policies could only be those which could command the support of its party, as represented in Parliament.

It is out of these developments that the now well-known practice of ministerial responsibility came into being. The cabinet must enjoy the confidence of the House of Commons or else resign, or, alternatively, dissolve the House and hold new elections, the latter to indicate if the electorate's wishes had been correctly represented by the existing House.

Within the cabinet, the monarch's main adviser was the First Lord of the Treasury, a post traditionally held by the modern prime minister. It is now commonly agreed that the first prime minister was Sir Robert Walpole, although he rejected the term. When he lost support of the majority in the House of Commons in 1742, he resigned. But it was not until the resignation of Lord North and his whole cabinet in 1782, as a result of hostility in the Commons, that the practice of collective responsibility began. From that time on, the cabinet became the symbol of united and responsible collective endeavor, both in policy and administration. A demonstrated lack of confidence in one of its members or in the way it governed, collectively or individually, signified a lack of confidence in the cabinet as a whole.[1]

Political leadership in the British system, therefore, evolves from Parliament or, more specifically, from the House of Commons, to which it is always responsible for its exercise of that leadership. More precisely, the posts of political authority are filled by leaders of that political party which has a majority in the House of Commons. These leaders are held accountable by the House of Commons not only for the political decisions they may make, but also for the way in which they perform the day-to-day tasks of governing the nation.

THE DEMOCRATIZATION OF THE COMMONS

In the struggle for political power, the monarch had lost out to Parliament, but Parliament was anything but a democratic body. Political leadership evolved from Parliament, and the practice that ministers could stay in office only so long as they were able to retain the confidence of the House of Commons became accepted long before the members of the Commons were elected on the basis of a broad suffrage. With the broadening of the suffrage, perhaps the most

---

[1] In large measure, the idea of collective responsibility developed as a protection against the king. If they were to be regarded as individual advisers, the ministers could be played off one against another. If they stuck together, the king had to accept their advice or find an alternative government. Collective responsibility thus became a device for maintaining the unity and strength of the party, for if the cabinet stuck together, the king would have to turn to the opposition for an alternative government.

important single development in nineteenth century British government, political leadership in effect became accountable to the people. Political power had passed from the king to Parliament, and from Parliament to the free electorate.

By the beginning of the nineteenth century, suffrage rules had become confused and lacking in uniformity. In some towns nearly every adult male could vote, whereas in others not 1 per cent could do so. In some towns property determined eligibility; in others, membership in the municipal corporation—membership which was acquired by birth, marriage, or purchase. Moreover, representation in the Commons was not according to population. Each county and each borough, irrespective of its size, was entitled to two members in the Commons.

From a democratic point of view, the injustices inherent in this situation are obvious. This is especially so inasmuch as the Industrial Revolution had brought many people to the newer factory towns such as Birmingham, Manchester, Leeds, and Sheffield. In turn, many previously thriving rural towns were virtually deserted and came to be known as "rotten boroughs," or in the American vernacular, "ghost towns." These rotten boroughs continued to send two members each to the House of Commons, often selected by no more than a handful of "freemen," usually nonresidents, who owned a few dilapidated buildings. Under such circumstances, membership in the House of Commons was frequently bought and sold, with the consequent ability of a few men to swing the balance of power.

Another way of depicting the suffrage situation on the eve of the Great Reform Act of 1832 would be to compare the number of eligible voters with what it would have been under the rules of universal suffrage. At that time the population of Great Britain and Ireland stood at approximately twenty-four million. If universal suffrage had prevailed, nearly ten million would have been entitled to vote, whereas the total actually eligible was considerably under one million.

The most significant step in the democratization of the suffrage was the Great Reform Act of 1832, the first successful result of a movement for reform which had begun some fifty years earlier. It did two things: it redistributed seats in the Commons and it broadened the suffrage. Representation in the Commons was still not in proportion to population, but the most glaring inequalities were cleared away, with the more populous towns gaining some 150 seats. By providing for uniformity of suffrage requirements in the towns and through the extension of the suffrage to certain classes of tenants in the counties, the

Act added more than a half million votes to the rolls, thereby nearly doubling the number of eligible voters.

The process begun by the Great Reform Act of 1832 was carried forward through a series of other acts, culminating in the establishment of universal suffrage in 1928. The Reform Act of 1867 provided for a further redistribution of seats and added almost a million new voters. The secret ballot and the requirement that voting take place on a single day in each constituency were made law by the Act of 1872. This was followed by acts dealing with the suppression of corrupt practices (1883), a further extension of the suffrage (1884), and a considerable redistribution of seats in the Commons (1885). The Representation of the People Act (1918) made all adult males eligible to vote, abolished the distinction between county and borough suffrage, provided for university representation (abolished by the Labor Government in 1948), and extended the suffrage to some women. The limited franchise extended to women was regarded by the militants among them as an insult, and their activities finally culminated in the Act of 1928, which gave women the same suffrage rights as those enjoyed by men.

The effect of the Great Reform Act of 1832, and the chain of events it set in motion, was to rest political power upon popular election, although this was not obvious until some time later. In the eighteenth and early nineteenth centuries, representation in the Commons was based essentially on property, which meant, in effect, that the landowners determined who was to sit in the Commons. The growth of industrial and commercial interests in the nineteenth century tended to modify this situation. Political parties, ceasing to be collections of great landowners and their associates, were becoming more and more dependent on the consent of the rapidly expanding middle-class electorate. Moreover, within the electorate after 1832, the power and authority of the House of Commons rapidly increased, while that of the Lords declined. Votes of confidence or the lack thereof in the House of Lords became irrelevant after 1850. The authority of the popularly elected Commons, on the other hand, was dramatically recognized by Prime Minister Disraeli when, in 1868, he resigned forthwith after his party was defeated at the polls, not waiting for an adverse vote in the newly elected House of Commons.

THE DECLINE OF THE HOUSE OF LORDS

The House of Lords is no longer an upper house in any meaningful sense of that term. As the Commons gained in power and prestige, through the changes recounted above, the House of Lords, which underwent no similar modification, was being relegated to an inferior status. Although the cabinet, as late as 1850, regarded an adverse vote in the Lords as requiring a confidence vote in the Commons, the power and influence of the upper house declined rapidly in the latter half of the nineteenth century. The significant test of power between the two houses came in 1909, and was resolved by the Parliament Act of 1911, in favor of the Commons.

The Parliament Act of 1911 followed in the wake of the defeat of the Government's[2] budget in the Lords in 1909, an unusual occurrence, for in the preceding fifty years the Lords had seemingly accepted the principle that the budget could neither be amended nor rejected in the House of Lords. Following an election in 1910, in which the power of the Lords was the issue, the Parliament Act of 1911 was passed in the next session of Parliament, with the House of Lords assenting. The prime minister and his associates had realized that the House of Lords would not desire to curb its own powers voluntarily. Consequently, he had asked for and received the king's assurance that he would assent to the creation of a sufficient number of peers to insure the passage of the Parliament Bill, should it be initially rejected by the Lords.[3] Once it became known that the threat "to pack" the Lords had the king's advance support, opposition to the bill dissipated and the Lords voted to pass it.

Under the provisions of the Parliament Act of 1911, money bills become law in thirty days whether passed by the House of Lords or not. For all other bills (except a bill to extend the duration of Parliament), the Lords could delay action for as much as two years. The Parliament Act of 1949, however, reduced the maximum delaying period to one year. While these two acts may seem to have destroyed the need for the continued existence of the "upper house," a good deal of useful work is still performed there, and perhaps better performed than in the Commons.[4]

THE GROWTH OF POLITICAL PARTIES

In the triumph of parliamentary democracy in Britain, one of the essential ingredients was the development of political parties. Today, democracy, or representative government, is everywhere party government—government by and through political parties. The active

---

[2] The British use the term "the Government" in somewhat the same way we use the term "the Administration."

[3] Sir Ivor Jennings, *Cabinet Government* (2d ed.; Cambridge: Cambridge University Press, 1951), p. 395ff.

[4] See Chapter 4.

functioning of more than one political party is one of the distinguishing features of democracy. Where parties peacefully compete for power a certain consensus exists—an agreement on the fundamentals or principles which constitute the foundation or basic framework of the society. The emergence of such a consensus in Britian made possible the organized mobilization of groups (parties), based on differences of a less fundamental nature, differences that do not constitute a life-and-death matter for any group.

Theoretically, there is no limit on the number of political parties in a democracy, but experience seems to teach that a two-party system facilitates the more effective functioning of democratic government. Or, conversely, democracies having a multiparty system, except perhaps some of the smaller countries of western and northern Europe, have experienced considerably greater troubles in the operation of their political systems than those nations having a two-party system. Great Britain, except for brief transition periods, has had a two-party system.

The Whigs and the Tories, although in some ways scarcely more than factions, can be said to be the earliest of English political parties. They developed more or less definite principles and the concept of a unified leadership, which was to characterize their successors. Not until the nineteenth century, however, did the two-party system, symbolized by the Conservatives and the Liberals, blossom into full flower. The beginning of this century saw the birth of the Labor party and its subsequent emergence as a major party, accompanied by the decline and virtual demise of the Liberal party.

The growth of political parties went hand in hand with the evolution of the cabinet system. That the two should be closely connected is understandable, for the existence of at least two parties means that there is always an alternative to the Government in power, a vital prerequisite to the cabinet system of government. This alternative is now officially recognized under the name of Her Majesty's Loyal Opposition. In a broader sense, parties periodically provide alternatives for the voters, while at the same time serving as links between the Government (or the opposition) and its supporters in the country.

THE BRITISH CONSTITUTION TODAY

THE NATURE OF MODERN DEMOCRATIC CONSTITUTIONS

The origin of modern constitutions is closely associated with the rise of democratic political systems. Constitutionalism in democratic countries has in effect become synonymous with effective restraints on political power. It has also come to mean that the powers conferred upon government will not be exercised arbitrarily but in conformity with certain rules or principles. Thus, democratic constitutions not only limit the powers of governments, but also obligate them to adhere to definite procedural safeguards in the performance of their functions, so as to guarantee the preservation of the fundamental principles that make up the democratic creed. Ultimately, democratic constitutions, like democracy itself, rest on acquiescence, for the source of the power to govern is popular consent.

More concretely, democratic constitutions can be viewed as instruments which impose limitations on what governmental authorities may do, defining the spheres of governmental activity and providing for the protection of the citizen's rights, procedural (for example, impartial and speedy trial) as well as substantive (for example, freedom of speech). They can also be viewed as instruments for allocating governmental powers territorially (for example, in federal systems, between a national government and the territorial subdivisions of the nation). Finally, they can be looked upon as instruments for allocating powers functionally among the specific institutions of government (legislative, executive, or judicial).

While the usual emphasis, at least in the United States, is on the written document called the Constitution, the constitutions of modern democratic states are more inclusive. To be sure, a written charter or a collection of written documents constitutes an important element of all constitutions. But there are other components that are as much a part of all living democratic constitutions as the written documents. Binding judicial interpretations, for example, constitute a part of the nation's constitutional framework. Likewise, certain statutes which regulate or determine some of the basic democratic processes fall in the same category. Finally, customs or precedents, which through long usage become an integral part of the country's political practice (such as political parties) must be looked upon as forming part of that nation's constitution. In Great Britain, as we shall see in the following section, there are ample illustrations of all of these, but they are also to be found in the United States and other democratic countries.

When modern democratic constitutions are viewed as more than written documents, it should be readily appreciated that they are altered or amended in several ways. Most constitutions provide for means of formal amendment, but none of them has escaped being amended in significant ways through judicial interpretation, legislative statutes, or customs and usage, or all of these. This suggests that one cannot judge the flexibility or rigidity of a constitution by merely examining the article or section which specifies how it may be amended.

ELEMENTS OF THE BRITISH CONSTITUTION

For a long time, the British Constitution was referred to as unwritten. Tom Paine, in a trans-Atlantic debate with Edmund Burke, insisted that the Constitution did not even exist and challenged Burke to produce it. Today, no one questions its existence and few people refer to it as unwritten. It is unwritten mainly in the sense that it is not to be found in one compact document, for a large part of it is written. The written part, sometimes referred to as the "Law of the Constitution" (as opposed to the unwritten "Conventions"), consists of the great charters or historic documents, statutes of constitutional importance, the common law, and judicial decisions. The unwritten elements are chiefly the Conventions of the Constitution.

LAW OF THE CONSTITUTION

Heading the list of the historic documents is Magna Carta (1215) or the Great Charter. It did not result from popular revolution and it contained little that was new. It was brought about by the action of a handful of barons who insisted upon a redress of grievances which flowed from the autocratic rule of King Richard and King John. And it was primarily intended as a statement of existing feudal law.[5] As a constitutional landmark, however, Magna Carta is important. It reinforced the notion that the king and the government were not above certain principles of law, and that in the event of a refusal to obey them, the nation has the right to force them to do so. Secondly, the Great Charter embodied provisions that were in the interest of persons other than the barons. Although the clauses which sought to protect baronial privilege have never been repealed, they fell into disuse. The clauses which breathed the spirit of benevolent reform, however, have survived. Finally, Magna Carta achieved importance as a touchstone or bulwark of the nation's liberties. Englishmen invoked its principles whenever they felt that the monarch was exceeding his authority.

. Among the other historic documents are the Petition of Right (1628), the Bill of Rights (1689), the Act of Settlement (1701), the Act of Union with Scotland (1707), the Great Reform Act (1832),

---

[5] Magna Carta was not signed as we now sign a document, for neither King John nor his opponents could sign their names. But the seal of the realm and the individual seals of the barons served to make the document legally valid.

the Parliament Act (1911), the Statute of Westminster (1931), and the India Independence Act of 1947.

The Bill of Rights and the Act of Settlement sought to make sure that the principle of parliamentary supremacy, which the Revolution of 1688 attempted to establish, would be preserved. The former, among other things, forbade a standing army in time of peace and denied to the King the right to make or suspend laws except by consent of Parliament. Moreover, Parliament had to be called at least once a year to vote funds. The latter act provided that the monarch may not be a Roman Catholic nor may he marry one. It also outlawed special courts and denied to the monarch the right to dismiss judges at will.

Statutes, like the Reform Act of 1867, are of a constitutional nature, but perhaps constitute less distinct landmarks in British constitutional development. Other laws which regulate the suffrage, election methods, rights of individuals, and the powers and duties of public officials, fall in a similar category. They cannot be classified among the great charters, and yet they are not in the same category as ordinary laws. Such legislative enactments are called organic acts or organic laws so as to distinguish them from ordinary legislation.

While enacted statutes did not, by and large, produce constitutional changes until after 1832, the body of legal rules known as the common law, which grew up apart from any action by Parliament, has helped to shape British political institutions over the centuries. The sources of the common law must be sought in the customs and mores of English communities and the application of these by the King's judges in cases which came before them. With the passage of time, a whole body of legal rules was thus developed. As these became fairly uniform throughout the country, common to the whole realm, they acquired the designation the *common law*. Most guarantees of civil rights under the British constitution, for example, are rooted in the common law.

In addition to the common law, the courts have contributed to constitutional growth through their interpretation of the great charters, the organic acts, and the common law itself. These judicial decisions, like the common law, although not set down in the precise form of a legislative act or a formal constitutional document, are nevertheless written and may be found in various legal and judicial collections or commentaries.

THE CONVENTIONS OF THE CONSTITUTION

As suggested earlier, customs, conventions or usages develop around most constitutions. While they are less precisely formulated than law, leaving some room for argument and misunderstanding, the distinction between them is not really of fundamental importance. Laws, like conventions, ultimately rest on public acquiescence, although they are not regarded with the same sanctity as laws, nor is a breach of one of them always so obvious. The source of conventions is precedent, but precedents do not create a rule unless it is generally recognized that they do create a rule. Moreover, some conventions are of greater importance than others, and some receive greater attention than others.

The core of the British constitutional system, the cabinet, and the most important person in the cabinet, the prime minister, were not established by legislation or recognized by the courts of law. They acquired legal recognition in the Ministers of the Crown Act of 1937, which provided a salary for the prime minister and higher salaries for those ministers who were in the Cabinet, making it necessary to define who are members. But the act says nothing about the place of the Cabinet in the British system or about the powers of its members. The practice of basing all important political acts on Cabinet advice is rooted in usage or convention.

The fact that the prime minister is the leader of the majority party is the result of convention. That he must come from the House of Commons is also based on a rule created by precedent, although a more recent one. The supremacy of the Commons over the House of Lords, moreover, stemmed from usage some time before being legally recognized in the Parliament Act of 1911.

The practice of convoking Parliament at least once a year, the fact that it is organized in two houses, and the principle that its acts must be assented to by the monarch are all based on convention. Similarly, through usage was evolved the basic attribute of the parliamentary system—that a ministry must collectively resign after it loses the confidence of the House of Commons or go to the country, that is, hold a new election. Moreover, should such an election indicate a defeat for the Government, convention dictates that the ministry must resign forthwith and not wait to meet the new House of Commons.

The conventions are obeyed and workable simply because they are conventions. If general acceptance of the practices outlined above had not prevailed they would not have become conventions. It is true, however, that it may not always be easy to tell when a certain practice has gained general acceptance over a sufficiently long enough period of time to have it designated as a convention. Constitutional authorities agree, however, that just because some political usage goes unchallenged for a time, this does not necessarily make it a convention.

SOME BASIC PRINCIPLES OF THE CONSTITUTION

As the fundamental law of a constitutional monarchy, the British constitution is in reality the constitution of a parliamentary democracy. The history of its development has been characterized by a tendency to let fundamental issues work themselves out. In its present form, certain basic principles seem to stand out, which may be summarized conveniently under six general headings.

The Neutrality of the Monarch. In matters of politics, except for the choice of the prime minister under certain circumstances, the queen acts only on the advice of her ministers. The saying that the queen can do no wrong means that crown decisions of a political or controversial character cannot be her personal decisions. Moreover, she does not show partiality toward any political group and remains free of the conflicts which take place in the political arena. She is not only neutral, but also believed to be neutral. Herbert Morrison, a onetime Labor party leader, suggests that respect for the monarchy and its popularity have grown in the present century chiefly because of a general acceptance of its political impartiality.[6] The glamor and color of the monarchy, he continues, "helps the wheels of democracy to move smoothly round."[7]

Parliamentary Democracy. Parliament is legally omnipotent; no British law can be unconstitutional in the American sense. There is no legal distinction between a constitutional rule and an ordinary statute. "Within the limits of physical possibility and the limits of public opinion, Parliament can decide anything."[8] But the significantly powerful part of Parliament, the House of Commons, is popularly elected and therefore periodically accountable to the people.

Ministerial Responsibility. There is no separation of powers in the American sense; rather there is fusion. The people elect the legislature—the House of Commons—and the leaders of the majority party in fact become the executive, but in doing so they do not give up their legislative seats. This fusion of executive and legislative powers, as will become evident in the next chapter, is at the core of the parliamentary form of government.

---

[6] Herbert Morrison, *Government and Parliament: A Survey from the Inside* (London: Oxford University Press, 1954), p. 85.

[7] *Ibid.*, p. 88.

[8] Sir Ivor Jennings, *Parliament* (Cambridge: Cambridge University Press, 1939), p. 9.

Independence of the Judiciary. While the political branches of the government are fused, the judiciary is independent. It applies and interprets the law with impartiality for high and low alike, for its basic task is to preserve the rule of law. The judges are selected because of their judicial competence and are appointed for life. In their decisions, they are free from political interference or pressure, partly because they do not possess the power to declare legislative acts null and void.

Unitary Government. The central government is not compelled to share governmental powers with the authorities of the geographical subdivisions of the country. There is no federal system. What powers local units of government may possess have been granted to them by the central authorities and may be taken away by them.

Protection of Civil Rights. Unlike the United States, Great Britain does not list specific rights which are to be secured, although they are, in essence, identical with those found in our Bill of Rights.

BIBLIOGRAPHICAL NOTE

Walter Bagehot, *The English Constitution* (London: World Classics Edition, 1928) ; Anthony H. Birch, *Representative and Responsible Government: An Essay on the British Constitution* (London: Allen & Unwin, 1964) ; Albert Dicey, *Introduction to the Study of the Law of the Constitution* (10th ed.; New York: The Macmillan Co., 1961) ; and Frederic W. Maitland, *The Constitutional History of England* (Cambridge: The Macmillan Co., 1908) are considered among the classics of British political literature. Equally perceptive contemporary works are Leopold Amery, *Thoughts on the Constitution* (London: Oxford University Press, 1953) and Harold Laski, *Reflections on the Constitution* (New York: The Viking Press, Inc., 1951).

Useful surveys of the development of British political institutions are George B. Adams, *Constitutional History of England* (rev. ed., New York: Henry Holt & Co. Inc., 1934) ; Winston Churchill, *The Birth of Britain* (New York: Dodd, Mead & Co., 1956) ; Cecil Emden, *The People and the Constitution, Being a History of the Development of the People's Influence in British Government* (2d ed.; London: Oxford University Press, 1956) ; H. R. G. Greaves, *The British Constitution* (3rd. ed.; London: Allen & Unwin, 1955) ; George L. Haskins, *The Growth of English Representative Government* (Philadelphia: University of Pennsylvania Press, 1948) ; Sir David C. Keir, *The Constitutional History of Modern Britain* (6th ed.; New York: Black, 1960) ; and Faith Thompson, *Magna Carta: Its Role in the Making of the English Constitution, 1300–1629* (Minneapolis: University of Minnesota Press, 1948).

Standard works, more limited in scope than those suggested above, include those of Lord Campion, *et al.*, *British Government Since 1918* (London: Allen and Unwin, 1950) ; Robert K. Gooch, *The Government of England* (New York: D. Van Nostrand Co., Inc., 1937) ; Wilfred Harrison, *The Government of*

Britain (London: Hutchinson, 1955); Sir Ivor Jennings, *The British Constitution* (Cambridge: Cambridge University Press, 1950) and *The Law and the Constitution* (London: University of London Press, 1952); A. Lawrence Lowell, *The Government of England* (New York: Macmillan, 1908); Andre Mathiot, *The British Political System* (Stanford: Stanford University Press, 1958); Frederick Austin Ogg, *English Government and Politics* (2d ed.; New York: The Macmillan Co., 1936); William A. Robson, *The British System of Government* (rev. ed.; New York: Longmans, Green & Co., Inc., 1953); D. C. Somervell, *British Politics Since 1900* (London: Andrew Dakers, Ltd., 1950); Diana Spearman, *Democracy in England* (New York: The Macmillan Co., 1957); Harold Stannard, *The Two Constitutions: A Comparative Study of British and American Constitutional Systems* (New York: D. Van Nostrand Co., Inc., 1949); Hiram Miller Stout, *British Government* (New York: Oxford University Press, 1953); and K. C. Wheare, *Government by Committee: An Essay on the British Constitution* (London: Oxford University Press, 1955).

CHAPTER 3

THE GOVERNMENT:
THE CABINET SYSTEM

WHEN political control slipped from the king's hands, as we noted in the last chapter, the cabinet fell heir to the crown powers. The concept of crown powers remained, and it became well-established that these powers were exercised by ministers and not by the king. Subsequently, the ministers were made answerable to Parliament for their acts. Early in this century, A. Lawrence Lowell was able to declare (in his book *The Government of England*) that "the cabinet is today the mainspring of the whole political system." It was several decades later, however, before political scientists began generally to use the term "cabinet government" as descriptive of the British form of government, thereby recognizing the predominant role which the cabinet plays in it. The aptness of this term will become evident as we look at the elements of the cabinet system, its operation, and its relationships to other political institutions. To understand the British system of government, therefore, is in large measure to appreciate the central role of the cabinet and how that role is played.

THE ELEMENTS OF CABINET GOVERNMENT

Put in the simplest terms, the elements of cabinet government are three. First of all, the people periodically elect members to the House of Commons. Secondly, the leaders of the party which has a majority in the Commons constitute themselves as the executive, collectively known as the cabinet. Thirdly, the cabinet is responsible for governing the country, that is, for making all the basic policy and administrative decisions, but it can continue to exercise this responsibility only so long as the House of Commons has confidence in the way it handles the public's business.

Essentially what this means is that in the British system there is a fusion of legislative and executive powers. The people decide only which party is to have a majority in the House of Commons. The principal leaders of that majority, while retaining their legislative seats, become the executive—the cabinet, usually numbering about 20 members.

Because these leaders are also responsible for the appointment of ministers who are not members of the cabinet, as well as of other high officials, the executive is sometimes referred to more broadly as "the Ministry" or as "the Government." In short, the cabinet, as a type of committee of the Commons—indeed its most important one—is the executive.

The job of the cabinet is to lead. It is responsible for the final determination of what programs and policies are to be submitted to Parliament. But it must also lay down the main principles, in accordance with policies prescribed by Parliament, that govern the administration of various government departments. And it must be ever ready to defend, before Parliament, its policies as well as the manner in which they are being implemented. Indeed, it must account to the House of Commons for everything that goes on in the day-to-day workings of a far-flung bureaucracy. In short, the cabinet possesses ample power to govern, but its members are collectively accountable for what they do or fail to do.

FORMATION OF THE GOVERNMENT

The British cabinet forms around the prime minister, who has sometimes been referred to as the "first among equals," but who in actuality occupies a more powerful position than that phrase suggests. Because his party selects him as its leader, it in effect chooses a potential prime minister. The people, by giving his party a majority in the House of Commons, make the actual choice. Formally, he is summoned by the monarch, who asks him to accept the post of prime minister, although the monarch has no real discretion if one party has an undisputed majority. There is no legal requirement that he be a member of the Commons, but practice since 1902 indicates that he must be, although prior to that time a number of prime ministers had come from the House of Lords.[1]

The choice of a prime minister presents more of a problem when no party commands a majority in the Commons or when the post is

[1] Complete agreement on this point is lacking, although the fact that in 1923 the king sent for Stanley Baldwin instead of Lord Curzon has led most observers to conclude that the king's action constituted a recognition of this principle. In 1963, the Earl of Home was made prime minister, but this was after the passage of the Peerage Act, 1963, which permits a peer to give up his title. Lord Home promptly gave up his title, became Sir Alexander Douglas-Home, and was elected to the House of Commons, where he had served for a number of years before he became a peer.

vacated through death or resignation. In the former instance the result may be a coalition or a minority government, discussed later in this chapter, in whose formation the monarch may play more than a passing role. In the latter instance, however, his discretion may be more limited. If the retiring or deceased prime minister has an accepted second-in-command who is ready to take over, the monarch has little real discretion. Since Winston Churchill's wartime Government, the position of deputy prime minister has been in existence (publicly announced although constitutionally unrecognized), but this does not mean that the queen would necessarily turn to him in case of the death or resignation of the prime minister. This was borne out by the appointment of Harold Macmillan instead of R. A. Butler following Anthony Eden's resignation at the time of the Suez crisis in 1956. The available evidence suggests, however, that the queen's advisers (top Conservative party leaders, including the outgoing prime minister) were in agreement that she should send for Mr. Macmillan. A similar situation occurred when in 1963 Macmillan resigned and advised the queen to send for Lord Home. Where a resignation is occasioned by dissensions inside the Government and where agreement on a successor is lacking, the monarch's discretion would be considerably enhanced.

The first task of a newly designated prime minister is that of appointing persons to fill some 100 offices which are at his disposal. Among these, the most important are the ministers who will head the various ministries, but most important of all is the decision as to which ministers will be in the cabinet. The prime minister decides who shall be in the cabinet, and appointment is simply in the form of a note from the prime minister asking the minister to attend.

In the making up of his cabinet, however, the prime minister is governed by certain considerations. First of all, the persons he appoints to the key administrative positions and to the other posts from which the cabinet members are drawn must be, by well-established custom, either peers or members of the House of Commons. Secondly, while certain ministries are always represented in the cabinet (for example, the Chancellor of the Exchequer and the Secretary of State for Foreign Affairs), not all ministers heading the important departments can be included in the cabinet without making it a large and unwieldy body. Finally, certain political considerations serve to influence the prime minister's choices. Uppermost among these is the fact that he is only one, albeit the most important one, of his party's leaders. Several of his colleagues, because of their experience and accomplishments, will in effect be chosen for him. As a rule they will have had parliamentary experience together as members of the "shadow cabinet," a term used to designate the leaders of the opposition party who would likely constitute the cabinet if their party achieved a victory at the polls, and frequently they will have had experience in office during a previous Government. In his choice of ministers, the prime minister can hardly avoid consulting some of these other party leaders. He needs a coherent cabinet, as free as possible of personal antagonisms. Yet it is desirable that the cabinet should command general respect among its supporters in Parliament and exercise authority among them. Often this means including leading and influential members of varying political temperaments, provided the chances are fairly good for their being able to work together. As a general rule, there will be, among his party colleagues in Parliament, two or three men who carry great weight and three or four times that number who carry some weight and who have the confidence of a particular segment of the party. No prime minister can ignore such men.

Moreover, other considerations guide the prime minister. In the cabinet it is desirable to have persons who head ministries, else the cabinet "would be deficient in that day-to-day administrative experience which makes a real contribution to collective decisions."[2] But it is also essential that, in order to have time for thought and deliberation in policy making, some of its members have light or no departmental duties. The number of ministers without portfolio is not large, but several other posts require little of the cabinet member's time. Among these are: Lord President of the Council (Privy Council, which meets infrequently), Lord Privy Seal (no duties except safekeeping of the Privy Seal), Chancellor of the Duchy of Lancaster (duties relate to certain crown estates requiring about 30 minutes of work per week). Moreover, certain other offices have some departmental duties which are basically not administrative.

The prime minister is further limited in his appointment of ministers by the Ministers of the Crown Act (1937), which requires that a minimum number be from the House of Lords. The act establishes two lists of ministers and provides the maximum number of House of Commons' members on each. In effect, this means that at least a small number of ministers will be members of the upper house. But this limitation is not really a serious one, for the prime minister would, in any event, want to have persons in the Lords who could act as spokesmen for the Government. When a minister is in the Lords, his

---

[2] Herbert Morrison, *Government and Parliament: A Survey from the Inside* (London: Oxford University Press, 1954), p. 34.

undersecretary or secretary must be in the Commons (although the reverse is not necessarily true), where the crucial defense of the Government's policies takes place.

Ministers who are in charge of departments but who are not in the cabinet have substantially "the same rights and responsibilities as cabinet ministers apart from the fact that they are outside the cabinet."[3] They may be appointed to serve on cabinet committees and they usually have an opportunity to appear before the cabinet when matters affecting their departments are being discussed.

Ministers usually serve as long as the prime minister wants them. Formally, they are appointed by the queen and hold office during Her Majesty's pleasure, but it is the prime minister who advises the queen and therefore ministers serve at his pleasure. When he desires a change, ministers submit resignations as a matter of courtesy, although this would not be necessary, since the crown can dismiss one of its servants at any time.

POSITION OF THE PRIME MINISTER

A prime minister owes much to his party, for by choosing him as its leader it in effect decides that he shall be prime minister if it comes to power. But once he accepts the office from the monarch he is endowed with the power and the prestige of the office which no party can give or take away, although he may have difficulties in certain crisis situations. He is the queen's first minister and as such he is more than just a first among equals. His power to appoint, dismiss, or reshuffle his colleagues makes his personal authority great. He must consult with his cabinet colleagues, and he cannot afford to alienate otherwise naturally deferential and loyal colleagues in the Commons, but once he and his cabinet are in agreement, there is little need to worry about Parliament. He may not have the constitutional power of our president, but because of the absence of such impediments as the separation of powers and a system of checks and balances, he has greater strength whenever he pursues policies that have been hammered out in cabinet meetings.

It has been suggested that his power depends "in part on his personality, in part on his personal prestige, and in part upon his party support."[4] As in the case of the American president, no prime

---

[3] Morrison, *op. cit.*, p. 58.

[4] Sir Ivor Jennings, *Cabinet Government* (Cambridge: Cambridge University Press, 1959), p. 187.

minister combines all of the desired qualities. Yet he is chosen by his party perhaps because he comes closer to possessing them than any other one of his party colleagues. As a general rule, conflicts in the cabinet are rare and disagreements, when they do occur, lead to resignation and not to dismissal. The prime minister can, within limits, commit the cabinet by publicly announcing policies prior to consultation with his cabinet, but this is rare. Individual ministers, on the other hand, may find themselves disowned by the cabinet when they make basic decisions without consulting the cabinet, particularly if such decisions meet with public hostility. In such eventualities the minister resigns, theoretically without impairing the cabinet's standing and prestige.

As a rule, however, the cabinet is collectively responsible to Parliament. Its members stand or fall together. Disowning a minister is an exception.

The prime minister's functions are varied. He is, first of all, chairman of the cabinet, a body which he must select and keep going as a team. In this role he gives advice and engages in preliminary consideration of plans long before these can be brought before the cabinet. Every prime minister has a sort of "inner cabinet," a few close associates with whom important and delicate questions are discussed informally before they are brought before the cabinet. In addition, he must keep an eye on what goes on in the various departments, for if he does not he risks possible embarrassment. Moreover, he is the leader of the Commons, although the day-to-day arrangements are made by a prominent cabinet colleague who is known as the leader of the House of Commons. The ultimate responsibility, however, is his. Furthermore, he advises in the appointment of bishops, superior judges, permanent secretaries, and others. Last, but not least, he must manage the party majority in Parliament and in the country. He must be concerned constantly not only with views within his own party but also with the moods of public opinion which affect the popularity of his Government and which will affect the political life of his party at the next election. Technically, at election time he stands for election to the House of Commons in a single constituency, but as prime minister he goes to the country as leader of his party.

THE WORKING OF THE CABINET SYSTEM

As suggested earlier, the broad basic decisions of any Government are hammered out in meetings of the cabinet. Questions or proposals may be initiated by the prime minister or any one of his colleagues.[5] A minister must decide what matters require the attention of the cabinet, knowing that the cabinet expects him to make all decisions which are not of fundamental political importance. He should not expect the cabinet to solve his difficulties, but neither should he seek to avoid collective discussion of significant political questions. "The minister who refers too much is weak; he who refers too little is dangerous."[6] Sometimes a matter is of such urgency that there is insufficient time to consult the cabinet. In such instances consultation with the prime minister must suffice. This is most likely to occur in the realm of foreign affairs, and for that reason the important Foreign Office telegrams and dispatches are circulated daily to members of the cabinet.

The cabinet meets for about two hours twice each week. These deliberations are in secret and the proceedings are confidential. Prior to 1916 there was no cabinet office and no secretary. The only record of cabinet decisions was a letter which was sent to the monarch by the prime minister, who retained a copy. Under pressure of war, a cabinet secretariat was instituted in 1916 and is now firmly developed. The secretariat circulates memoranda and other documents, makes up the agenda (under direction of the prime minister), issues summons to cabinet meetings and to meetings of cabinet committees, takes down and circulates cabinet conclusions, and prepares reports of its committees.

Two standing items of business are before the cabinet once each week (usually not the same day), even though papers about them may not have been circulated. These are: foreign affairs and, when Parliament is sitting, parliamentary business, matters requiring attention and matters to be brought up in the course of the week. During the latter discussion the chief whip is in attendance. In case of urgency, of course, the prime minister may permit alterations in the agenda.

As a general rule, many matters receive informal and formal consideration before they reach the cabinet, especially among departments which are directly concerned. This may take place in a minister's office in Parliament, at lunch, in the lobbies, at a club, or outside the cabinet room while waiting for the meeting to begin. Matters to be placed before the cabinet are first circulated in memo-

---

[5] The personnel of the cabinet, the conferment of honors, and the making of appointments are not as a rule discussed in sessions of the cabinet. Neither is the exercise of the prerogative of dissolving Parliament discussed in the cabinet.

[6] Jennings, *op. cit.*, p. 215.

randa form to interested departments at least "two clear days" before they can be put on the cabinet agenda.

In cabinet discussions all members are equal and they are expected to express their views with the utmost frankness. A minister must master the affairs of his department and be able to stand on his own two feet, for he can bring civil servants to cabinet meeting only if the prime minister or the chairman of a cabinet committee gives consent. Discussion continues until a consensus has been reached. The prime minister, when he thinks appropriate, will sum up the views of the members, a summary that may be at variance with the views that he has expressed. Silence signifies acceptance of the prevailing view, although not necessarily precise agreement. Voting in cabinet is rare, for an agreed conclusion is preferred, else the very existence of the government would be in danger if the minority could not support the majority decision.

Members of the cabinet, while they may differ in the secret confines of the cabinet room, are obligated to tell the same story in public. Any one of them who does not resign is responsible for everything that is done in the cabinet. Although the obligation is less strong for a minister outside the cabinet, he, too, must be prepared to defend cabinet decisions or else resign. He cannot at some later time reject criticism on the ground that he had not originally agreed with the decision.

Since there are no references to opinions of individuals by name, cabinet minutes, which are secret in any case, reveal little except the actual conclusions. Recording these is the most delicate task of the cabinet secretariat. After the prompt circulation of a preliminary draft, the conclusions may receive wide circulation. Each minister receives a copy, whether he is a member of the cabinet or not. If a matter is of exceptional secrecy the cabinet conclusions will not be circulated.[7] The cabinet secretariat is also charged with the duty of verifying that actions in accordance with the cabinet conclusions have been taken by the respective departments.

The load which the cabinet must carry has increased considerably in recent years because of the large number of matters with which government has become occupied. To help ease this load, a system of cabinet committees has been devised. Because of the need to preserve secrecy and because the cabinet has final responsibility, little is known about the actual work of these committees. We do know that some of

---

[7] Morrison, *op. cit.*, pp. 11–13.

them are temporary and others are standing committees; some are occupied with major problems while others deal with matters of lesser concern. For more important matters, their conclusions are in the nature of reports and recommendations, while for matters of lesser importance, although an appeal is always possible, their conclusions are usually in the nature of decisions. Little is known, however, as to who are the chairmen of what committees, or what committees deal with what questions and in what frames of reference. It is known that the prime minister acts as chairman of many of the really important committees, although many of the committees are frequently chaired by ministers who have few if any departmental responsibilities. And because of the importance of financial and foreign matters, it is safe to conclude that the Chancellor of the Exchequer and the Foreign Secretary must serve on more committees than other ministers.

Because so many problems are competing for the cabinet's time, and because so little of it is available for general issues of policy after routine business is dispensed with, some observers have suggested the creation of a type of supercabinet.[8] It would consist of some half dozen members entirely free of ordinary departmental duties. They would devote their efforts to policy planning and would endeavor to reconcile departmental conflicts and iron out contradictions and difficulties in administrative policies. While concerned mainly with broad policy problems, they would not be divorced completely from administration. This suggestion was at least partially put in practice by Sir Winston Churchill after his return to power in 1951. Sometimes referred to as directing ministers, they commonly acquired the name "overlords." It appears that the institution was of brief duration, for the practice has seemingly been discontinued. Herbert Morrison, a Labor leader, has expressed disagreement with the idea of a supercabinet, although he recognizes the need for coordination.[9] But coordination, he argues, must be voluntary and not imposed, for direction or supervision would be resented by the ministers being supervised. Moreover, he asks, since authority would be divided in such circumstances who would be responsible to the House of Commons—the minister or the overlord? While indicative of a problem which constantly faces the cabinet, the suggestion of a supercabinet seems to have raised more problems than it has solved.

Whatever the nature of the cabinet, it is collectively responsible for the political and the administrative acts of the Government. An attack

---

[8] L. S. Amery, *Thoughts on the Constitution* (London, 1947), p. 88ff.

[9] Morrison, *op. cit.*, p. 45ff.

upon a minister is an attack upon the Government and a defeat of a minister is a defeat of the Government. This does not mean, however, that a Government must accept responsibility for the personal mistakes of ministers. But if it is unwilling to stand by a minister, and thereby risk its political life, he must resign. Similarly, a Government may withdraw a proposal which meets opposition, and if the minister's credit has not been impaired in the process, he need not resign.

Ordinarily, however, the cabinet is in no danger of being overthrown. A Government with a clear majority can only be defeated in the Commons by virtue of a party split, and all members of the majority know that to vote against the Government is tantamount to inviting the opposition to take over. Under such circumstances, therefore, the cabinet has the upper hand in its relations with the Commons.

It does not follow, however, that the result is "cabinet dictatorship." The Government's authority is not the police or any other weapon of dictatorship; its authority is the majority, which expects to be treated with respect. Moreover, the majority rests upon popular support. If either the majority or the popular support disappears, the Government will also disappear in due course. And the Government is not obliged to wait until a general election to know where it stands, for public opinion is constantly expressed through the various instruments at the disposal of a free people. "It is the fear of defeat and the threat of dissolution that supply the most effective elements of the Government's power over its majority."[10]

There must be a balance, as one Labor party leader has indicated when he wrote: ". . . just as the Government has not, and ought not to have, absolute power, neither have nor ought the back-benchers to have absolute power. If back-benchers could freely do just as they like . . . we should have parliamentary chaos. . . ."[11] But neither must it be forgotten that a "Government and its supporters are not a collection of strangers brought together for a particular purpose but a group, most of whom have lived together in the House and their party for many years and who share the same broad aims."[12]

If, however, the Government meets defeat in the Commons, through an adverse vote on legislation on which it is insisting or if it fails to receive a vote of confidence for which it is asking, or if an opposition

[10] Jennings, *op. cit.*, p. 458.
[11] Morrison, *op. cit.*, p. 95
[12] *Ibid*, p. 99.

motion (expressing a lack of confidence in the cabinet or in an individual minister by whom the cabinet is willing to stand) passes, the cabinet has the choice of resigning or asking the monarch to dissolve the House so that new elections can be held. This choice is made by the prime minister, usually after consultation with his more intimate colleagues. Dissolution may also be requested when, because of an exceedingly small majority, the prime minister finds the going difficult or impossible. He may also decide on dissolution when he believes that his party stands a good chance of being returned with a safe majority. The likelihood of such a dissolution increases as the term of a Parliament approaches its statutory limit of five years. Similarly, the appointment of a new prime minister, in the event of death or resignation of the occupant of that office, is often followed by dissolution and new elections, particularly if a general election has not been held in the recent past.

COALITION AND MINORITY GOVERNMENTS

The cabinet system, in normal times, is controlled and operated by the leaders of the political party commanding a majority in the House of Commons. Two exceptions to this practice need to be noted. First, there have been times when cabinets were formed by the leaders of more than one party acting in concert. These have been referred to as coalition governments. Secondly, there have been occasions when no party commanded a majority in the Commons, but the leaders of one of them were nonetheless asked to form a government. These acquired the name of minority governments.

Since the growth of modern political parties, Great Britain has in the main been blessed with two major parties, with the result that the verdict at the polls usually gave one of them a majority. This is in sharp contrast with the situation prevailing in some other countries (for example, France under the third and fourth republics) where no party ever has a majority and consequently every government represents a coalition of parties. The very concept of coalition has been abhorrent to the British, and they have not employed it successfully except in time of war, notably the two world wars. The only other instance in this century when a coalition was attempted was in 1931, when the so-called "National Government" was formed in the hope of providing a united approach to the problems of the economic depression. Shortly after its formation, however, new elections resulted in an overwhelming victory for the Conservative party, although the coalition technically continued to exist until 1935.

The two wartime coalitions were prompted by the need for a maximum effort in the prosecution of World Wars I and II. The pattern of a small war cabinet, set by Lloyd George in World War I, was adopted in 1939, although the Labor party refused to enter the cabinet until Winston Churchill became prime minister in 1940. Their attitude was due, not to any lack of support for the war effort, but to their lack of confidence in Mr. Chamberlain because of his appeasement background. These wartime coalitions concentrated on a common end—victory—and were, in a sense, largely politico-administrative machines.

Coalition cabinets can unite on the issue, such as war, which brings them into being, but once that issue passes from the scene they are apt to pass with it. In World War II, for example, the coalition came to an end following Churchill's determination to hold new elections after Germany's surrender but prior to the defeat of Japan. Moreover, there is little likelihood that coalitions can successfully cooperate on problems over which they divide. The usual destiny for such matters is evasion, postponement, or weak compromise.

Unlike a coalition government, a minority government is organized by one political party, but a party which does not have a majority in the Commons. A minority government cannot continue to exist without the active or passive support of one or more parties in addition to its own. And it must recognize that it cannot hope to put through any measure for which it cannot obtain support beyond its own ranks. Not having a disciplined majority, a minority government is less stable than a majority government, for the threat of impending dissolution does not frighten the members of the non-Government parties. On the other hand, the lack of a majority party imposes an unwritten obligation of fair play (at least in British experience) on the non-Government parties; they must not seek to oust the cabinet just on any pretext.

The two British experiences with minority governments in this century came during the 1920s, a transition period in which the Labor party was replacing the Liberal party as one of the two major parties. The first minority government was formed in 1923 by Labor, which had the second largest number of seats in the Commons. The Conservatives had 67 more members than Labor, but they had gone to the country, as the majority party, in support of a protectionist program and were roundly defeated, losing 86 seats and the majority which they commanded before the election.[13] This Government lasted only nine months, with the Conservatives winning a majority in 1924. While Labor lost 40 seats, the Liberals lost 119, a blow from which they never recovered. The second minority government was formed in 1929, again by Labor. This time, however, they commanded a plurality[14] in the Commons, making for a more stable government, for it could only be defeated by a combination of the other two parties. The Government was in office two years, and it might have remained longer if it had not been for the economic crisis, which resulted in some division in Labor ranks as to the appropriate program the Government should undertake. In the elections since the 1930s, one party (Conservative or Labor) has always had a majority (although sometimes a very small one), with undisputed authority to constitute a government.

POSITION OF THE MONARCH

The monarchy has survived in Britain, and has indeed become a revered institution, because of its successful transition from a position of virtually absolute authority to that of political neutrality. The queen accepts and acts on the advice of her ministers who enjoy confidence of the House of Commons. She may seek to influence them in this advice by pointing out objections to the course they propose, by furnishing them relevant information, or by suggesting an alternative policy. She must be listened to with respect and consideration, and her proposals, even if the prime minister should think them stupid, must be answered respectfully. But in the end, the advice of her ministers prevails.

This political neutrality of the sovereign is but one phase in the evolution of the British system. In no small measure it stemmed from changes that followed the Reform Act of 1832, which made cabinets dependent upon the vote of the people and not upon the favor of the monarch. The institution of ministerial responsibility made it possible for the people's representatives in the Commons to hold the Government accountable for the way it governed. The throne was thus spared from the "gusts of political conflict and the storm of political passion."

---

[13] The election of 1923 returned the following to the House of Commons: Conservatives, 258; Laborites, 191; Liberals, 159.

[14] Labor, 289; Conservative, 264; Liberal, 58.

It can readily be appreciated that if the queen were to identify herself with a particular group of party politicians or a specific political program, she would become a politician, subject to criticism and attack like all other politicians. She could not appeal to the people against the cabinet without expecting the cabinet to appeal to the people against her. Moreover, she is not only impartial but, what is perhaps more important, she is believed by the public at large to be impartial. This position was not attained until relatively recent times. Queen Victoria, for example, was a political partisan during many years of her reign. In recent years the political neutrality of the queen has resulted in a more positive advantage: the people can serve the queen while damning her Government.

The extent to which the monarch can influence political policy is greatly circumscribed by the ability, the capacity for hard work, and the personality of the occupant of the throne, as well as the political climate of the times. As Jennings has written: "The crown adds dignity but not capacity."[15] Given the latter, the monarch can, over the years, accumulate much information and experience. Cabinet minutes and papers, Foreign Office telegrams, and other official papers are sent to the palace daily. Moreover, newspapers and other publications are made available. In addition, the queen may ask for information and she may talk with distinguished persons. If she is willing to read, to study, and to ponder questions of public policy, she can be a most learned person. But learning is perhaps less important than the capacity to understand the nature of a problem.

Outside opinions not clouded by political partisanship are often useful to the prime minister, especially when they come from one with long experience. At the end of his reign of 25 years, for example, King George V had had four prime ministers. Queen Elizabeth, by the time she was forty, had already known six prime ministers. When taken together with the generally accepted conclusion that in the last 100 years British monarchs were above average in their capacity for hard work and sound judgment, it may be that the opinions of recent British monarchs have been more important than has generally been realized.

Yet, it must be noted that it is possible to exaggerate the value of the queen's opinions. She leads a sheltered life and has little personal contact with the people. Moreover, irrespective of her wisdom, the policies of the Government cannot, in the main, diverge too much from

---

[15] Jennings, *op. cit.*, p. 345.

the political program of the party on whose support the Government depends. The queen can influence her ministers only to the extent that her views are considered sound, and provided that they do not go contrary to important party aims and programs.

An important political function of the queen is that of seeing to it that she has a Government. She names the prime minister. So long as one party has a majority in the House of Commons with a recognized leader, this choice has been made for her. She may be able to exercise some discretion in this matter in the event of the resignation or death of a prime minister, or in circumstances where no party has an indisputable majority in the Commons. If a Government is defeated and resigns without advising dissolution, however, the monarch is bound to send for the leader of the opposition. This is done without the advice of anyone, for the seeking or the receiving of advice could only be interpreted as an effort to keep the recognized leader of the opposition out of office.[16]

Theoretically, the monarch can refuse to accept advice that Parliament be dissolved, but such advice has not been refused for more than 100 years, and it is difficult to foresee the development of circumstances which might prompt such a refusal. Should such advice ever be refused, however, the issue of the monarch's personal role in politics would become uppermost in the public mind. Similarly, the queen can, in theory, dismiss her Government, but in practice there has been no dismissal for more than 150 years. In the unlikely event that some future Government should seek the enactment of controversial legislation that had not been discussed in the previous electoral campaign, especially if highly repugnant to a large majority, the queen might resort to dismissal. All in all, however, it would seem a rather remote possibility that the queen would either refuse dissolution or seek the dismissal of her Government.

The symbolic function of the monarchy would seem to be equally as important as the political. The monarchy personifies the state; it stands for the country and its cherished institutions, and provides a focus for patriotism. The queen speaks for the nation and for the members of all political parties. She is head of the Anglican Church.

---

[16] Under somewhat exceptional circumstances (the Government had not been defeated), Mr. Chamberlain, when his own resignation had been accepted in 1940, apparently did volunteer advice to the king to send for Mr. Churchill. See Winston S. Churchill, *The Second World War* (Boston: Houghton, Mifflin Co., 1948), Vol. I, p. 523. In similar circumstances, Mr. Eden's resignation in 1957 was apparently accompanied with advice that the queen send for Mr. Macmillan.

Her name is "the cement that binds the Constitution."[17] Moreover, the monarchy serves as a link between Great Britain and the Dominions across the seas. It is the institution which facilitated the conversion of an empire into the commonwealth of free and independent nations. As the head of the state, the queen devotes much time and energy to ceremonial functions—the formal appearance in Parliament, the dedication of public institutions and memorials, and the visits from foreign dignitaries and their diplomatic representatives, to mention a few.

Socially, the members of the royal family give of their time in the support of charitable organizations, art, literature, the theater, sports, science, and other activities and pursuits of merit that ordinary people engage in. Titles, honors, and other awards are usually conferred by the queen on advice of the prime minister, while military orders are made on advice of the appropriate minister. The one exception is the Royal Victorian Order, which is a private order and is bestowed by the queen alone.

The queen enjoys certain privileges. She cannot be arrested or hailed into court. Generous allowances are made from the public treasury for the maintenance of her civil list. She is accorded deference and respect. Aside from limitations that have been mentioned elsewhere, it should be noted that she cannot become a Roman Catholic without forfeiting the Crown. Similarly, a Catholic cannot become a monarch nor can a monarch marry a Catholic.

BIBLIOGRAPHICAL NOTE

The most comprehensive study of the British executive as a whole is Sir Ivor Jennings, *Cabinet Government* (3d ed.; Cambridge: Cambridge University Press, 1959). A somewhat different approach but also excellent is John P. Mackintosh, *The British Cabinet* (London: Stevens, 1962). Standard works on the cabinet system also include A. B. Keith, *The British Cabinet System* (rev. ed. London: Stevens, 1952) and Wangteh Yu, *The English Cabinet System* (London: King, 1939). Also useful are Walter Bagehot, *The English Constitution* (London, 1867), chaps. 1 and 6; Harold J. Laski, *Parliamentary Government in England, A Commentary* (New York: The Viking Press, Inc., 1938); Sir John Marriott, *English Political Institutions: An Introductory Study* (4th ed.; London: Oxford University Press, 1938); and Ramsay Muir, *How Britain Is Governed* (4th ed.; Boston and New York: Houghton Mifflin Co., 1940). Particularly informative are Herbert Morrison, *Government and Parliament: A Survey from the Inside* (3rd ed.; London: Oxford University

---

[17] Jennings, *The Queen's Government* (London: Penguin Books, 1954), p. 33.

Press, 1964) and Lewis Broad, *Anthony Eden: The Chronicle of a Career* (New York: Thomas Y. Crowell Co., 1955).

Specialized studies include those of Byrum E. Carter, *The Office of the Prime Minister* (Princeton: Princeton University Press, 1956) ; Hans Daalder, *Cabinet Reform in Britain, 1914–1963* (Stanford: Stanford University Press, 1963) ; Bernard Schwartz, *Law and the Executive in Britain: A Comparative Study* (New York: New York University Press, 1949) ; and K. C. Wheare, *Government by Committee: An Essay on the British Constitution* (London: Oxford University Press, 1955).

CHAPTER 4

PARLIAMENT:
THE HOUSE OF COMMONS

THE British Parliament consists of two chambers, the House of Commons and the House of Lords. Because the latter was relegated to a distinctly secondary position in this century, there is now a tendency to use the terms "Parliament" and "House of Commons" interchangeably, a practice adopted in this book. Although the House of Lords cannot be dismissed outright as an institution of British government, it is so far overshadowed by the Commons that, as a rule, one is justified in speaking of the House of Commons as the parliament of Great Britain. The role of the Lords, however is discussed in a subsequent section of this chapter.

THE HOUSE OF COMMONS AND ITS MEMBERS

The House of Commons currently consists of 630 members elected in single-member districts (constituencies) on the basis of universal suffrage.[1] Almost every British subject who is 21 years of age or over is legally qualified for a seat in the Commons. Among those specifically excluded are members of the peerage (except Irish nobility), clergymen, and persons holding offices of profit under the crown (ministers of the crown excepted). The party affiliations of the members elected in 1964 were as follows: Labor, 317; Conservative, 304; Liberal, 9.

Prior to 1911, members of the House of Commons received no compensation. At that time a salary of £400 annually was provided. This was raised to £600 in 1937 and to £1,000 in 1946, and is now £3,250 (a maximum of £750 is tax free). While members have a free railway pass, they do not have office space, nor are they provided with clerical and other essential assistance enjoyed by American congressmen and senators. They have lockers in the corridor in which to place their papers, and they must seek refuge in a crowded library when

---

[1] For a discussion of the electoral process, see Chapter 5.

59

preparing their speeches. Ministers and chairmen of important committees, however, have offices of their own. Because of the country's geographic compactness, members can visit their constituencies during week ends, enabling them to transact many matters at home which American legislators must do in Washington or by mail. In the past, a substantial portion of the Commons membership has had some outside income, but this is less true today.

The occupational background of the members is considerably different in the two parties. Among the Conservatives, the largest group (about a third) is made up of businessmen, with barristers (trial lawyers) a strong second. Farmers and military men come next in roughly equal numbers. Not far behind are men of journalistic background. Among the Laborites, teachers and miners constitute the largest number and in approximately equal proportions. Barristers and journalistis are not far behind and in about the same numbers. As is clearly evident, businessmen, farmers and soldiers are almost totally absent from Labor ranks. It is interesting that at a time when government is engaged in operating large businesses, there are few managers, engineers, scientists, or administrators represented in either party in the House of Commons.

In addition to individual immunities accorded to its members (unlimited freedom of speech in the House, immunity from arrest arising from a civil suit, exemption from jury duty), the House in its corporate capacity can protect its dignity against members and non-members. A member may be expelled or punished for contempt. Nonmembers may be summoned by the House, on recommendation of its Committee on Privileges, and, if found guilty of a breach of privilege, may be imprisoned (limited to the remainder of the parliamentary session), but the House is often satisfied if the offender appears at the bar of the chamber and apologizes. Parliament, however, is usually reluctant to take actions which might be regarded as efforts merely to silence or discourage criticism.

The physical chamber in which the House of Commons meets is a unique structure. Most Americans are inclined to think of a legislative chamber as being semicircular in arrangement, with the presiding officer facing the members. The House of Commons chamber (located inside the Palace of Westminster along with the House of Lords chamber and other rooms) is oblong, with a wide aisle lengthwise down the center, at one end of which is the speaker's chair. On opposite sides of the aisle, and facing it, are tiers of benches on which the members sit. The Government supporters, the majority, sit on the benches to the speaker's right, while the opposition benches are on his left. The front benches on each side are occupied by the respective party leaders, ministers, and would-be ministers. The remaining benches can, however, accommodate only about two thirds of the House membership.

Following its destruction by Nazi bombs in World War II, the chamber was rebuilt along its old lines, except for more modern lighting, air conditioning, leather-covered foam rubber on the benches, and less ornate design of interior decoration. Winston Churchill, supported by his colleagues (including the Labor leader, Clement Attlee), wanted the House rebuilt along the old lines for two reasons. First, he was convinced that an oblong chamber facilitated the preservation of a two-party system. Crossing the floor (that is, changing parties), which he had done twice, was, in his opinion, difficult and required serious consideration, whereas a semicircular arrangement permitted members to move easily from left to right, or vice versa, in varying shades of political opinion. Secondly, he believed that a chamber which could not seat all of its members, which was not too large, would be better suited to the conversational style of speaking which had prevailed in the House. If it were large enough to accommodate all its members, he argued, "nine tenths of its debates will be conducted in the depressing atmosphere of an almost-empty or half-empty chamber."[2]

The atmosphere inside the House is conditioned by the speaker, who is the number one man of the House. He presides over its proceedings and acts as its ceremonial head. He sits in the canopied chair in the traditional dress of knee breeches, wig, and long black gown. At the long table beneath him sit the clerks of the House, also in wig and gown, recording its proceedings. On this table rest two dispatch boxes and the mace, the latter the symbol of the queen's authority. The speaker has no gavel or bell, but merely rises and says, "Order, Order." He is accorded great respect, and his moral and psychological authority is far greater than any written rules would imply.

Unlike the speaker of the United States House of Representatives, the speaker of the House of Commons is impartial. He is selected by the prime minister and his colleagues and then formally elected by the

---

[2] Winston Churchill, *The Second World War: Closing the Ring* (Boston: Houghton, Mifflin Co., 1951), p. 169.

House, usually without opposition from the minority. As a rule, he is a back-bencher, or at least a man who has not been prominent in his party's affairs. In addition to such personal traits as tact, patience, and judicial temperament, he must be thoroughly versed in the rules and procedures of the House. He is paid a salary of £8,500 annually and is provided with an official residence in the Palace of Westminster. Once elected, he becomes politically inactive and refrains from any future association with his party. Customarily, he is not opposed for re-election in his constituency, nor does he advocate the claims of his constituents. Although they are in effect denied representation, they are at least partially compensated by the exalted office which "their" representative holds. From time to time, the chairman and deputy chairman of the Ways and Means Committee relieve him, the former presiding when the House meets as a committee of the whole. Although nominated by the Government, they, too, are expected to be impartial, but they change with a change in government.

The speaker has long-standing precedents to guide him in presiding. These precedents extend even to the way he should vote in case of a tie, usually an unlikely event. If the motion is to adjourn, for example, he always votes "no" in the event of a tie. And if a negative vote would defeat a proposal and a positive one mean more consideration, he votes "aye." Although the debate is often spirited and on occasion pungent, the atmosphere gives the speaker little reason for concern. "There is no banging of desks; there are no desks to bang; and they would not be banged if there were." All members are "honorable" or "right honorable," although the verbal thrusts across the aisle might sometimes lead an unsuspecting visitor to think otherwise. As in other parliamentary bodies, the speaker's rulings may be appealed.

PARLIAMENTARY PROCEDURE IN THE HOUSE OF COMMONS

Procedure in every legislative body, although subject to change, in time becomes regularized and the subject of one or more treatises.[3] We are here not concerned with the details of parliamentary procedure

---

[3] Generally regarded as the authoritative book on the subject is: *Sir Thomas Erskine May's Treatise on the Law, Privileges, Proceedings and Usage of Parliament*, edited by Sir Edward Fellowes, T. G. B. Cocks, and Lord Campion (16th ed.; London: Butterworth & Co., 1957). For a brief popular discussion, see Eric Taylor, *The House of Commons at Work* (Baltimore: Penguin Books, Inc., 1951).

but rather with some of its basic principles and with those rules which will throw light on the ways in which the cabinet and the House of Commons conduct their joint business.

THE DOMINANT ROLE OF THE GOVERNMENT

The first principle to note is that in parliamentary procedure the dominant role is played by the Government of the day, that is, by the cabinet. In general, it determines what matters are to be considered and how much time is to be allotted to each. It decides what legislative program will be presented to Parliament and how its time will be apportioned to this and other matters which demand parliamentary action. In collaboration with the leaders of Her Majesty's opposition, the Government decides how much time and what days the opposition may have to discuss what it wants to discuss. Moreover, the Goverment must find some time to allot to private members' motions.

The Government's legislative program is presented at the opening of Parliament through the "speech from the throne." It is usually delivered by the sovereign in person from the throne in the House of Lords, with members of the Commons and their speaker, who have been summoned to attend, packed in behind the bar. While the speech is addressed to the Lords, the queen turns to the Commons alone when she refers to financial requests which will be presented to them. For more than a hundred years the speech from the throne has been looked upon as a statement of ministerial policy. It is drafted by the cabinet, but the monarch has an opportunity to see it, to ask questions about certain parts of it, and to make suggestions for changes in wording The basis of its language, however, is significant, for the queen speaks of "my ministers" and of what they think and propose to do.

It is the cabinet, therefore, that must decide, prior to each legislative session, what legislative proposals, taken from the party platform, should be introduced and passed in the time available. The demands on the Parliament's time are such, however, that considerably less than half of the available days can be assigned to Government legislation. Usually, each ministry has bills it wants passed. Moreover, a number of matters require enactment each year and consume a great deal of time. In view of these and other demands upon the Parliament's time, many desirable bills each year cannot receive consideration. The cabinet must determine which proposals for new legislation can be considered in each session and which ones are to be postponed. But cabinet business always has priority.

How the House Uses Its Time

According to Herbert Morrison, some 80 to 85 sitting days of the House are likely to be devoted to "essential business," leaving between 60 and 70 days for Government legislation.[4] In the category of essential business, he includes the debate on the address in reply to the speech from the throne, provision for essential legislation and supply (budget and finance bills, army and air force annual bills, supply days, and the less important expiring laws), opposed private bill legislation, private members' time, days set aside for consideration of the works of public corporations, debates on delegated legislation, debates on adjournment, and contingencies (for example, a two-day debate on foreign affairs). Some six or eight of the "essential business days" are devoted to the debate on the address in reply to the speech from the throne, the principal time when general debate takes place. General debate also occurs three or four other times during each session when the consolidated fund bills are brought up for second and third readings.

Since more than 70 per cent of the yearly expenditure must be voted annually by the Commons and authorized by legislation, it is to be expected that financial matters would occupy much of the time of the House. Twenty days are allotted for the consideration of the estimates, which is done by the whole House sitting as the committee of supply. Similarly, taxation proposals are handled by the House sitting as the committee of ways and means. Because the House is really too large to conduct a significant and useful discussion of public expenditures, the debate tends to center on public policy rather than public expenditure. In practice, the opposition chooses the subjects it wants to discuss and criticize. The Government, in turn, must defend these items, which means that only the dominant subjects are discussed.

Unlike American practice, the raising and spending of money in England can be proposed only by ministers of the Crown. A bill which authorizes expenditure, although it does not appropriate the money, also requires a recommendation from the Crown at some point. Motions to increase expenditures are contrary to standing orders (rules of the House), thus preventing "pork barrel" legislation. Motions to reduce expenditures are in order but would no doubt be regarded as questions of confidence by the Government, whose responsibility it is to exercise initiative in the raising and spending of money. Since ministers of the Crown play such an important role in money

---

[4] Herbert Morrison, *Government and Parliament: A Survey from the Inside* (London: Oxford University Press, 1954), p. 233.

matters, it is obvious that the voice of the Treasury would be significant. All departmental requests for money must undergo scrutiny in the Treasury. In the end, however, the position of the Treasury is perhaps no stronger than the influence of the Chancellor of the Exchequer on his cabinet colleagues, for the cabinet is collectively responsible for all policy, including fiscal.

Four days each week some time is set aside to enable ministers to answer questions that have been submitted by House members. This practice, known as question time, is discussed more fully in a subsequent section of this chapter. In addition, other times are reserved for private members for the consideration of matters of their choice. For example, the first 20 Fridays after the debate on the address are private members' days.[5] Moreover, the last half hour of each day, as a rule, is set aside for private members to use as they wish. Generally speaking private members' bills stand a good chance of passage if the Government is inclined to help. They stand no chance if the Government is opposed.[6]

Since more than half of the average seven-month session of Parliament is devoted to "essential business," as discussed above, the amount of time available for *new* government-sponsored legislation is limited, therefore, to some 60 or 70 days in each session. In this time only a few pieces of major legislation can be considered. Although cabinet committees carry a heavy load in the shaping of a legislative program, a similarly heavy burden is borne by parliamentary counsel in the drafting of bills, a time-consuming process. Herbert Morrison reports that of five major Labor bills, the average number of drafts made before presenting them to Parliament was 17, with 12 being the fewest and 23 the maximum.[7] Considered in the light of this and other aspects of the legislative process, it can readily be appreciated that in each session there is time for no more than a few pieces of major legislation.

CONSIDERATION OF BILLS

All legislative acts begin as bills. Those introduced by a minister or his deputy are known as Government measures, while bills dealing

---

[5] Motions and bills are taken on alternate Fridays. The first six bill Fridays should be for second readings and the last four for the report stages and third readings.

[6] According to Jennings, private members' motions are for the most part of little value, except that "they enable ministers to put in half-a-day's work on administrative business." See *Parliament* (2d ed. New York: Cambridge University Press, 1957), pp. 347–48. Private members cannot avail themselves of the services of the Office of Parliamentary Counsel in the drafting of bills but must arrange for their drafting elsewhere.

[7] Morrison, *op. cit.*, p. 238.

with matters of public policy which are introduced by individual members are referred to as private members' bills. Measures of purely local concern are termed private bills. All bills must go through three readings, although in an emergency all three readings can take place during the same day. The first reading serves merely as a public notice that legislation on the subject is imminent, and a date is set for its second reading. At first reading the actual text of the bill is not available and no debate takes place, for there is no motion before the House.

The second reading is unquestionably the most crucial stage for any bill. There is no actual reading of the bill at this time, but a printed text becomes available prior to the date set for its second reading, and members have an opportunity to study it. The essence of this stage is the debate on the main principles of the bill. The outcome of this debate determines whether the bill is passed or defeated. The usual procedure is for the minister in charge of the bill to move "that the bill be now read a second time," and then to launch into his main speech in favor of the proposed measure. Since not the bill but merely the motion that it be read a second time is before the House, amendments to it cannot be proposed. If the opposition wishes to present an alternate motion, it usually moves an amendment "that the bill be read a second time upon this day six months," when, under previous conditions, the session would have finished, or "that this House declines to give a second reading," stating the objections. Should either of these amendments pass or should the motion "that the bill be now read a second time" fail, the bill is dead and cannot be revived prior to the next session of Parliament.

If the bill weathers the storm of second reading, its enactment is virtually assured. The speaker declares that the bill is read a second time, and it is then sent to committee. But unlike American committees, which do not have the benefit of ascertaining the will of their respective houses through the device of second reading, British committees have a more precise job, that of putting into final form a bill which has already, in effect, been passed. Moreover, they do not spend time on bills which may never see the light of day or which may even be defeated, as is often true of American committees. They have a right to feel that their work will not be in vain.

Controversial bills, as a rule, go to the committee of the whole, that is, the House sitting as a committee. There are distinct advantages in having bills considered by the committee of the whole. Rules of procedure arc informal. Many more members have an opportunity to participate than would otherwise be the case. Moreover, the Government can exercise firmer control and actually facilitate faster consideration if the matter is before the committee of the whole. Finally, the report stage does not open the way for new amendments as would be the case when the bill has been in one of the standing committees. Although committees are used, "the main emphasis," a one-time leader of the Commons has written, "still remains on work in the chamber rather than in the committee room."[8] The obvious disadvantage is that the committee of the whole can consider only one bill at a time, but the House has shown little inclination to have important measures considered by other committees.

In addition to the committee of the whole, there are four other types of committees—select committees, sessional committees, standing committees, and committees on private bills. Select committees are created for the purpose of looking into a particular subject and reporting to the House; their membership is determined either by the Committee of Selection or by the resolutions which bring them into being. Sessional committees are select committees which are chosen for the life of the particular parliamentary session. Party representation on all committees is roughly proportionate to the party complexion of the House.

There are five standing committees, simply designated as Committees A, B, C, D, and the Scottish Committee. Their membership, and also that of the committees on private bills, is determined by the Committee of Selection, an 11-member committee chosen at the beginning of each session, following informal consultations among the party leaders. In its work, the Committee of Selection is guided by the recommendations of the whips, although not bound by them. Each of the standing committees (except for the Scottish Committee) is composed of from 20 to 50 members. Since there is no functional specialization, except for the Scottish Committee, there is no competition for membership on any particular committee.

Committee procedure in Great Britain varies in several respects from that in this country. First of all, the seniority principle is not too important, and there is no competition for committee membership. Secondly, the chairman of the committee, like the speaker, is neutral and impartial. Bills do not carry his name, nor is the committee named after him. Thirdly, bills are guided by the appropriate minister or his deputy, one of whom is always present. Although commit-

---

[8] *Ibid.*, p. 147.

tee members representing the majority party are not bound by rigid party discipline as they are in the House (no whips are employed), the minister's parliamentary secretary helps keep them in line. Only those committee members who heard the debate on a particular phase of the pending legislation are allowed to vote. A defeat for the Government in committee, however, is not regarded as a vote of no confidence. Finally, the manner in which amendments are voted upon differs from American practice. When an amendment has been proposed and debated, the vote is first taken on the original language. This is advantageous to the supporters of the original motion, for they have assurance that their motion will be voted on. And, if the vote is favorable, further amendments to the particular words involved cannot be offered. Moreover, there would seem to be a general gain, for if the original wording meets with approval, time is not utilized in discussing various and sundry proposals to change it.

Committee consideration is followed by the report stage, at which time new clauses or major amendments may be proposed, debated, and voted upon, unless, of course, the bill has been in the committee of the whole. This is followed by the third reading, which is similar to the second reading in that no amendments can be offered to the text of the bill and in that the question is put in the same way. On occasion, there is lively debate on third reading, but in most instances the battle has been fought and victory won before the time for the third reading arrives.

MANAGING THE HOUSE

Subject to cabinet direction, the leader of the House of Commons is responsible for the business of the House and the Government's program.[9] His responsibilities, however, are not to the cabinet alone. He must also guard the legitimate rights of the opposition, as well as the rights of the House as a whole, including those of the backbenchers. Historically, of course, opposition was equated with disloyalty, if not treason. But the constitution was gradually changed, and the opposition is legally known as Her Majesty's Loyal Opposition.

Under the supervision of the leader, the Government chief whip manages things and makes the detailed day-to-day arrangements. This is done in consultation with the chief whip of the opposition, who receives advance notice of the matters which the Government intends

---

[9] According to a former leader of the House, this consumed from one fourth to one third of his 15- to 18-hour workday. See Morrison, *ibid.*, p. 116ff.

to submit to the House during the following week. The two chief whips are known as the "usual channels." They do not normally engage in debate, "for it is desirable that at all times some people representing Government and opposition should be on speaking terms . . ."[10]

The Government chief whip has the title of Parliamentary Secretary of the Treasury, although he is more often referred to as the patronage secretary, a title that was appropriate at times in the past when he exercised material influence on many government appointments. He is assisted by a deputy chief whip and by a varying number of junior whips. All of the whips are members of Parliament and most of the Government whips are ministers, and as such receive salaries. The chief whip has an office at 12 Downing Street (No. 10 is the prime minister's residence), where there are accommodations also for the junior whips. The main opposition party has the same number of whips, but they are unpaid, except for their salary as members of the House.

The Government whips are extremely busy men. They must be available to ministers, to other whips, and to party leaders of the opposition. They must attend various meetings and they must be on the floor of the House a good deal of the time. Moreover, they must find time for private members of the Commons who want to see them. More specifically, Government whips arrange, in consultation with the whips of other parties, the days on which various matters will come before the House. In general, they must see to it that Government business is not hindered by procedural failures. It is their duty to see that the members of the Government party attend House sittings and that they vote "right" when votes are taken. In dealing with their party colleagues, whips employ persuasion rather than bullying. Such tasks require men of tact, patience, restraint, and a willingness to be self-effacing.

Since whips cannot dictate, except in rare instances, they must convey to ministers the worries, the anxieties, and the complaints of the back-benchers. It is imperative that leaders know the mood of their followers in order to judge the impact of proposed or pending Government measures, or the lack thereof. For this purpose, there is a close and systematic contact between the whips and the party's rank and file in the House. This is usually the duty of the junior whips rather than the chief whip. The way it is done, however, is not in itself

---

[10] *Ibid.*, p. 103. The general personal cordiality which prevails in the Commons is in sharp contrast to its absence in the German Reichstag during the days of the kaiser, when different political parties even had separate dining rooms.

important. What is imperative is that communication between leaders and followers continues without interruption.

Formal communications to the respective party members are issued in the form of written messages, known as whips.[11] On Thursday of each week, the leader of the House announces the business that is to be brought before the Commons during the following week (beginning the following Tuesday and ending the Monday thereafter). On Friday, whips are mailed to all party members, although there are occasions when special whips are circulated. The whip informs party members of the various matters to come before the House each day of the following week, and it may indicate who the main speakers will be. The relative importance of each subject is indicated by underlining it once, twice, or three times. If underlined only once, the matter is not considered of great importance. Items twice underlined are fairly important, and may indicate a possible vote. A three-line whip suggests that a vote is almost certain, and every member is expected to be present, unless ill or unavoidably absent. A debate or a vote on a motion of censure is always three-line business.

Party members who violate party rules or in other ways impair their party's position may be disciplined by warning or, in extreme cases, by having the whip withdrawn. Withdrawing the whip is virtually tantamount to expulsion from the party, although there have been instances where the whip was restored at a later date. In the Conservative party, the power to withdraw the whip is vested in its leader. In the Labor party, however, it can be done only by a majority vote at a meeting of the Labor members of the Commons.

LIMITATIONS ON DEBATE AND VOTING

Every legislative body in a democracy is at one time or another confronted with putting a limit on debate if a vote is to be taken on the matter before it. Closure is the term most often used in Britain to describe a method of procedure designed to prevent obstruction. It may be applied to all types of motions. A proposal to limit or cut off debate requires a simple majority, provided that at least 100 members vote for it.[12] The speaker, however, may refuse to put the question if he believes that it would constitute an infringement of the rights of the minority. Since he is not a political partisan, the speaker is admirably suited to prevent the majority from riding roughshod over the minor-

---

[11] For a sample of Labor and Conservative whips, see Morrison, *ibid.*, pp. 110–13.

[12] Forty members constitutes a quorum in the House of Commons.

ity, while at the same time assuring the majority a vote on the issue after the minority has had ample time to state its case.

Moreover, the speaker, on his own initiative, may take steps to facilitate more prompt decisions by the House on measures that are before it. This is referred to as kangaroo closure or just kangaroo. It is the power of the speaker to ignore proposed amendments, that is, to select for consideration only those amendments which he thinks are representative of important sections of opinion. The speaker exercises this power during the report stage of a measure, but it is also exercised by the chairman of ways and means when the House is meeting as a committee of the whole, and it is also employed by the chairmen of the standing committees.

Another form of closure utilized in the Commons is the guillotine, or closure by compartments. Officially it is referred to as "allocation of time orders." It is most often employed when a bill is likely to arouse lengthy and fierce opposition.[13] The guillotine sets time limits for each stage (committee, report stage, and third reading) in the consideration of a bill. Moreover, it makes dilatory and adjournment motions out of order, and it removes other impediments (such as time regularly set aside for the consideration of certain subjects) to a speedy consideration of a legislative matter. Through the employment of the guillotine, the opposition's great weapon of delay is nullified before the debate begins. The kangaroo is particularly significant when a measure is being considered under allocation of time orders, for it enables the House to concentrate on the most important amendments in the time allotted.

Once a question is put by the speaker, he can usually determine the result and proceeds to announce it. On occasion, his estimate of the voting is disputed and he is forced to call for a division, a literal filing of members past tellers, who count them aloud. When a division is called, members go into one of two lobbies, known as "division lobbies." They are allowed six minutes for this purpose. Whips are on hand to make sure that party members go into the right lobby. They also supply the speaker with the names of tellers, whose names he announces. There are two from the "ayes" and two from the "noes," one of each going into the two lobbies. When the speaker puts the question a second time, members file out past desks, giving their names to the clerks, and then past the tellers, who count them aloud. Some pairing (agreement by members of opposite parties not to vote) takes place,

---

[13] For an example of "allocation of time orders," see Appendix B (pp. 338–47) in Morrison, *op. cit.*

but only when arranged through the whip's office. If the matter coming up is three-line business, the whips will be reluctant to arrange pairing. Sometimes the division is called off simply because the opposition is not resolved to go through with it.

Calling a division may, on first thought, seem like a cumbersome and time-consuming method of providing a recorded vote. Actually, a division takes about 10 minutes, compared with something like 45 minutes for a roll call vote in the U.S. House of Representatives. In fact, the only speedier method of taking a recorded vote involves the use of one of the systems of electrical recording utilized in some American state legislatures. Aside from other possible arguments against electrical recording systems, they would be largely inapplicable in a legislative chamber where members do not occupy fixed places.[14]

THE FUNCTION OF THE HOUSE OF COMMONS

The basic task of the House of Commons is to give or to deny assent to the proposals or actions of the Government, and thereby either to keep the Government in office or to force it out. In order to decide which it should do, the Commons functions as an arena for debate, criticism, and the ventilation of grievances. It is in the House that the Government is forced to defend and justify its actions and proposals. In short, the House forces it to have sound and sufficient reasons for the way it is governing as well as for the changes that it proposes to bring about.

Such is the theory.[15] In practice, however, certain circumstances stand in the way of anything like an ideal performance of this role by the Commons. An analysis of these factors and the problems involved therein is the subject of a subsequent section of this chapter.

OPPOSITION AND CRITICISM

One hundred years ago, John Stuart Mill, in discussing representative government, wrote:

Instead of the function of governing, for which it is radically unfit, the proper office of a representative assembly is to watch and control the government: to throw the light of publicity on its acts; to compel a full exposition and justification of all of them which any one considers questionable; to

---

[14] Electronic voting has been introduced in the French National Assembly, but its members have assigned seats.

[15] For a useful guide, see A. H. Hanson and H. V. Wiseman, *Parliament at Work* (London: Stevens, 1962).

censure them if found condemnable, and, if the men who compose the government abuse their trust, or fulfil it in a manner which conflicts with the deliberate sense of the nation, to expel them from office, and either expressly or virtually appoint their successors. This is surely ample power, and security enough for the liberty of the nation. . . .[16]

A few years later, Walter Bagehot asserted that among the functions of the House of Commons were these: "to express the mind of the English people . . . to teach the nation what it does not know," and to make us "hear what otherwise we should not."[17] More recently, another Englishman observed that "the main task of Parliament is still what it was when first summoned, not to legislate or govern, but to secure full discussion and ventilation of all matters, legislative or administrative, as the condition of giving its assent to bills, whether introduced by the Government or by private members, or its support to ministers."[18]

Since the members of the majority party are by and large obliged to support the Government, "the main responsibility for what was once the critical function of Parliament as a whole" rests on the opposition.[19] The role of the opposition was legally recognized by the Ministers of the Crown Act (1937), which provided a salary for the leader of the opposition. The largest party in opposition is designated as the "official" opposition and its leader is designated by the speaker as the leader of Her Majesty's loyal opposition.

It should not be assumed, however, that an individual supporter of the Government in the House must say the same thing as the minister. The important point is the manner in which disagreements are stated. If they are stated in a spirit of friendship and courtesy, there is no need to fear retaliation or disruption of party harmony. A former leader of the House has even said that occasional revolts (if not too frequent) against the Government among its own supporters are, although annoying, not to be wholly deplored.[20] While the Government should not, in his opinion, be careless in estimating parliamentary opinion, neither should it make too many concessions on the floor, else "it will get the reputation of a Government that does not know its

---

[16] John Stuart Mill, *Considerations on Representative Government* (London: Parker and Son, 1861), p. 104.

[17] Walter Bagehot, *The English Constitution* (London: World's Classics Edition, Oxford University Press, 1928; originally published in 1867), p. 116.

[18] L. S. Amery, *Thoughts on the Constitution* (London: Oxford University Press, 1947), p. 12.

[19] *Ibid.*, p. 31.

[20] Morrison, *op. cit.*, p. 160ff.

mind."[21] In practice, much will depend on the size of the Government's majority. If it is too large, there is a danger that it may be difficult to manage. If it is too small, the legitimate freedom of the M.P. is certain to be gravely limited.

THE PURPOSES AND AIMS OF OPPOSITION

Since the real function of the House is to question and to debate the policies and the actions of the Government, it seems pertinent to ask: to what purpose? Under normal circumstances, the opposition does not expect to defeat the Government in the Commons. Nor, indeed, does it hope to modify the Government's policy in any important respect. Therefore, its main aim is to utilize its position in the House to persuade enough people in the country to give it a majority at the next election. The opposition seeks to convert the electorate and not the Government's party. Nevertheless, Governments at times have modified or even withdrawn proposals which met with criticism in the House. For the most part this has happened on questions of minor importance only. Apart from results, however, opposition constitutes a valuable outlet for minority opinions, and for a ventilation of grievances. Certain things occasionally need to be said publicly and forcibly, and the House is the one place where they can be said most effectively. The attitude of the House is often a reflection of electoral dislikes, and this is what makes debate important.

By criticizing the Government, the opposition sets before the electorate the major conflicts of policy. In doing this, it must demonstrate a responsible attitude, for it is Her Majesty's alternative Government. The duty of Her Majesty's opposition is to oppose, but there is mutual forbearance, for the minority knows that the majority's duty is to govern. The opposition is aware, moreover, that it must be ready to accept office should it succeed in defeating the Government either in the House or in an election.

By and large, the Government may also be in a position to benefit from debate. The existence of the opposition keeps the Government on its toes. By being forced to explain and defend its actions, the majority contributes its share to the shaping of public opinion. The prime minister does not need a weekly press conference, for when the House is sitting, he has, in effect, a press conference four days a week through the question hour. Moreover, being currently attuned to the winds of popular belief, the Government is in a better position to cope with discontent before being engulfed by it at a future election. In

---

[21] *Ibid.*, p. 167.

addition, debate may also reveal a multitude of small complaints among the Government's supporters, and these will be listened to by astute managers of the majority, if they are to avoid more serious trouble later.

THE INSTRUMENTS OF OPPOSITION

One of the most effective instruments of the opposition is the question hour. Four times a week (no question hour on Friday) the first order of business (beginning at 2:45 P.M.) consists of ministers' replies to questions that have been submitted at least two days in advance by nonministerial members of the House. Up to two questions may be submitted by each member (no limit when written replies will suffice), and they are addressed to ministers in whose sphere of responsibility the matter inquired about falls. Questions may be designed to embarrass a minister, to call attention to minor injustices in the bureaucracy, or simply to extract information. This power is not only a potent weapon in the hands of the opposition, but it is also a significant way of informing the people about current problems and developments inside their government.

Ministers have experts in their departments to prepare answers to questions. Once an answer is made to a question, however, any member may ask a supplementary question, provided it is related (the speaker will not permit unrelated ones), and the supplementaries must be answered then and there. At this point the minister is on his own,[21a] although civil servants may be in the "box" (a row of seats at the end of the House to the right and behind the speaker). The "box" is separated from the House chamber by a low partition and technically is not a part of it. Because no messenger boys are used, conversation and notes pass over the partition if the minister needs help. The minister's private secretary, a member of the House, is also there to assist if necessary. If the minister is a member of the House of Lords, questions in the Commons relative to his department are handled by the parliamentary secretary of the department, who is a member of the Commons.

A minister may refuse to answer a question on the ground that to do so would be injurious to the national interest. This is particularly true with respect to questions in the realm of foreign affairs, when delicate negotiations may be in progress. The Government usually seeks to avoid such a course if possible, for the impression may quickly spread that the question has embarrassed it or that it has something to hide.

[21a] A recent rule of procedure permits ministers of state and parliamentary secretaries to act as departmental spokesmen.

The House expects candor and forthrightness from a minister. Even more, it demands respect. A former minister, in discussing the relationship between the House and the ministers, observed candidly: "But above all, if one is to be effective in the House of Commons one must love the place. . . . The House will forgive much in a minister if it likes him and if it knows he likes the House."[22]

On occasion the Government itself makes use of the question hour by getting friendly members to ask questions, so as to enable it to correct false or misleading information or to quell rumors. The Government may also benefit from questions of the opposition to the extent that these call attention to inefficient administration or bureaucratic blunders, which the Government is anxious to correct.

Normally, question hour lasts something less than a full hour and comes to a close by 3:30 P.M. Often it is impossible to answer all the questions that have been set down for a specific day. Those questions which have not been reached in time will automatically receive a written reply. If the member concerned still wants an oral reply, he can get it by having it postponed to a subsequent day.

In addition to the question hour, the last half hour of the first four days of the week is used by members to discuss anything they wish. Public business comes to an end at 10:00 P.M., followed by the so-called debate on adjournment. The House stands adjourned at 10:30 P.M. without question being put. The last half hour is used chiefly to ventilate grievances, but if a member expects an answer from a minister at this time, he must notify the minister so as to insure his presence. During certain times, the Government may move to suspend the 10 o'clock rule, and in such cases, when public business has occupied the House after 10 P.M., there is no debate on adjournment.

Debate on adjournment can take place earlier in the day under certain circumstances. After question hour, a member may move adjournment to consider "a definite matter of urgent public importance." If the speaker decides that the subject meets this definition, and if the motion is supported by 40 members, the time for such discussion is usually set for 7:30 P.M. that same evening.

THE WORK OF THE SELECT COMMITTEES

Significant (although uneven) control over the work of the Government is achieved through the select committees, which are set up as circumstances may require to look into specific matters. Some of these

---

[22] Morrison, *op. cit.*, p. 170.

are re-established regularly, the most important ones being those of the estimates (expenditures), public accounts, statutory instruments, and nationalized industries. These committees are relatively small, usually 15 members, although the one on the estimates has grown in size (now 43 members) and utilizes the technique of sub-committees. Through their power to send for persons, papers and records, they exercise significant control, although by and large they may not raise policy questions (the one on nationalized industries being an exception in this respect).

The debates that take place in the House on the reports of the select committees, however, constantly involve policy questions. This is to be expected in view of the fact that it is primarily the opposition that performs the function of criticism and control, a function which was once the province of the House as a whole. The Government realizes this, and therefore permits the opposition to decide in the main what is to be discussed. This is particularly evident when the report of the estimates committee is taken up. It is generally agreed that when the Government's proposed expenditure (estimates) for the following year are considered by the House acting as the committee of supply, it is the opposition that determines what items are to be debated. Although 26 whole days are devoted to this matter each year, only a relatively small number of selected items can be considered in that time. Consequently, most of the debating touches on policies of the Government in relation to the services rendered, with the result that at the end of this period many things are voted on which have not been debated. Technically, the committee of supply authorizes expenditures, then resolves itself into the committee of ways amd means which orders the actual issuance of money through the exchequer.

Once money is appropriated, financial control is exercised by the comptroller and auditor general, a quasi-judicial officer acting as an agent of the Commons, and by the Select Committee of Public Accounts, to which audit reports are submitted, and which in turn reports to the House. The comptroller and auditor general controls the issues of public money by seeing to it that large uninvested balances do not exist and that no more is spent than was authorized by Parliament. Moreover, with a staff of several hundred, he audits the accounts of all departments,[23] but he has discretion as to what accounts he should audit in detail, except that his powers do not extend to auditing "grants-in-aid." His reports are looked over by the Select Committee

---

[23] Each department also has its own audit staff.

of Public Accounts, whose chairman, by convention, is from the opposition and usually is the financial secretary of the treasury in the previous Government. From time to time, the Select Committee reports to the House. Departments seem to stand in awe of this committee, and its mere existence seems to contribute to honest financial administration.

The Select Committee on Statutory Instruments, which is relatively new, provides another way in which the House seeks to control the Government. This is, in effect, a committee on delegated legislation. Contrary to earlier British practice, much legislation in recent years has been drawn up in general terms, providing ministers with far-reaching powers to fill in the details by making rules and regulations. The nationalization legislation of the Labor Government accelerated this trend. Statutory instruments fall into four general categories: those that do not need to be laid before Parliament, those that do but which may not be debated by Parliament, those that must be laid before Parliament and which may be debated and annulled within a period of 40 sitting days after they have been laid, and those which require an affirmative resolution of the House before they can have the force of law. The greatest bulk of them are to be found in the third category. The Select Committee must scrutinize these for unexpected or unusual exercise of powers confirmed by the general act, as well as for vagueness and ambiguity, and to call the attention of the House to those of them that, in its opinion, require House consideration.

Finally, the youngest of the select committees is the one on the nationalized industries. Its main function is to secure such information as it may need to pass judgment on the reports and accounts of the nationalized industries. It may also criticize those aspects of the orgaization and operation of these industries for which the respective minister is responsible, i.e. those areas of activity in which he is authorized or required to make decisions.

The work of the select committee on nationalized industries, as well as the one on statutory instruments, will receive further attention in chapter six.

How Effective is Parliamentary Control?

Certain circumstances and developments have served to weaken the importance of Parliament, leading a number of observers to suggest that the function of control is poorly and inadequately performed. First of all, they point out, events such as the Suez fiasco, the Profumo affair, and the failure of the Cabinet's Common Market policy would have resulted in the fall of Governments in the nineteenth century, despite the fact that M.P.s did not have a great deal of influence in policy even then. But party discipline is such today that there is little need to fear an adverse vote. Secondly, parliamentary control is weakened by virtue of the fact that the leaders decide policy in advance of presenting it to the House. For example, the 1962 defense decision to switch from the Skybolt missile to Polaris submarines was simply announced to Parliament by the prime minister without any prior consultation. Thirdly, given the complexity and sheer size of governmental operations, the average M.P. cannot be effective even in asking questions. And administrator-ministers do very little by way of elucidating problems and situations so as to make his position less difficult.

These considerations suggest that the real debate on issues takes place in the Cabinet, in the party caucus, and in the party committees. Much of what happens on the House floor is shadow-boxing. Moreover, while M.P.s can confidently talk in generalities about social reform and foreign and colonial affairs, they are singularly unprepared to discuss industrial organization, scientific spending or Treasury control. It must not be forgotten, however, that in parliamentary and party committees, particularly the latter, the back bench member has a wide opportunity to raise issues and to voice opinions. But these go unreported, and the public is left no better informed than if the debate had not taken place.

A number of suggestions have been put forth to improve parliamentary procedure—streamlining finance bill procedure, the provision of offices and secretaries for M.P.s, along with better salaries and a research staff. Moreover, it is suggested, Parliament could be considerably revitalized if the Cabinet would stop treating every vote in the House as a vote of confidence. While the extent of public discussion concerning parliamentary reform would lead one to expect some steps toward reforms, perhaps in the near future, it remains a fact that no Cabinet is anxious to create difficulties for itself by making the House of Commons more powerful.

THE PLACE OF THE HOUSE OF LORDS

In popular language, the word Parliament is frequently used to refer to the House of Commons alone. In view of the shift of political power away from the Lords and to the Commons, this use of the word Parliament was perhaps inevitable. Yet Parliament is bicameral, at least in form. Therefore, it is necessary to discuss the House of Lords, however briefly, and to consider its place in British political life.

COMPOSITION AND CHARACTERISTICS

Some 900 persons are entitled to sit in the House of Lords. Of this number, some 675 are hereditary peers, over half of them created in this century. Their origin dates back to Parliament's formative stage, when the king summoned the more important barons and clergy to share in the councils of state. Once summoned, they considered themselves entitled to attend sessions of future Parliaments. Moreover, they insisted that this right could be passed on to their heirs; hence the establishment of the concept of hereditary peerage. Since the title passes to the oldest child (the others remaining commoners), hereditary peerage has not developed into a caste system.[24]

Scotland and Ireland, in the acts of union with England, were accorded the right of electing a number of representative peers. The 16 peers from Scotland were elected by the Scottish peers for the duration of Parliament. Since 1963, however, all Scottish peers may sit in the Lords. The peers from Ireland were elected for life, but as none has been elected since the establishment of the Irish Free State in 1921, the Irish representative peers have ceased to exist.

Other peers include the nine lords of appeal in ordinary (the law lords), as well as the lords spiritual—the Archbishops of Canterbury and York, plus 24 bishops of the Church of England. Moreover, new peers may be created at any time. Usually new peerages are announced in the honors list, published on the queen's birthday and at New Year's. The actual selection of new peers is made by the Government of the day, after consultation with the leader of the opposition, through recommendations to the monarch.

A majority of the peers are not active. Attendance at House of Lords' meetings rarely runs over 100, three being a quorum. Those who do attend are men of ability and extensive public experience. Many of them are former members of the House of Commons. Others include leading industrialists, ex-ambassadors, and many who have served the crown in important capacities, such as colonial governors, generals, and admirals. By virtue of their previously held positions, they receive pensions, which is desirable since members of the Lords do not receive a salary, although those who actually attend have their expenses paid.

---

[24] The ranks of the hereditary peerage, in descending order are: duke, marquess, earl, viscount, baron. There may be women peers, but they were not allowed to sit in the House of Lords until 1958. Moreover, the royal dukes take no part in its proceedings, although they may attend on ceremonial occasions.

The House of Lords is presided over by the Lord Chancellor, a minister who is also speaker. Unlike the speaker of the Commons, the Lord Chancellor takes part in debate freely. In general, procedure is much more relaxed than in the Commons. There are no standing committees, no closure, and only two standing orders. The first order provides that a peer cannot speak more than once on any motion, and the second states that debate must be relevant to the question before the Lords. Since the peers have no constituents to impress, there is no compulsion for a person to join in the debate unless he believes that he has something of importance to say.

The provision in 1958 for life peerages, that is, appointment of nonhereditary peers, and the acquisition by women of the right to sit in the upper chamber would seem to be indicative of a trend to "modernize" and "democratize" the House of Lords. These actions are but the partial culmination of a long process—of many studies and discussions, engaged in by all major political parties, on how and in what ways the House of Lords might be altered to enable it to play a more useful and constructive role in the British political system.

In 1963 Parliament passed a new peerage act which permits a person to disclaim a peerage for his lifetime. This disclaimer is irrevocable, but the peerage does not die. A successor may accept the peerage but not while the one who has disclaimed it is still alive. A person who has disclaimed the peerage cannot again receive a hereditary one. The act applies to inherited peerages; a person who accepts a newly created peerage cannot subsequently disclaim it.

LEGISLATIVE FUNCTIONS

As noted earlier, the House of Lords was shorn of much of its legislative power by the Parliament Act of 1911, which permits a money bill to become law within 30 days of its submission to the Lords irrespective of the latter's action. It should be noted in passing that the House of Commons cannot engage in the practice of the U.S. Congress of passing legislation by tacking it on as a rider to appropriation bills. In nonfinancial matters, the Parliament Act of 1911 specified that the Lords could delay legislation for as long as two years. By the Parliament Act of 1949, put through by the Labor Government, this was reduced to one year.[25]

While the limited power of delay may not be viewed as a significant

---

[25] At its annual conference in 1934, the Labor party decided that it would "take steps during its term of office to pass legislation abolishing the House of Lords as a legislative chamber." But 15 years later it apparently did not feel so strongly about the Lords.

legislative function, the more careful consideration which measures receive as a result of this power ought not to be underestimated. A leader who helped guide most of the Labor program through the Commons in the years 1945–50 has said that drafting imperfections would have been materially more numerous if it had not been for the House of Lords.[26] In addition, the House of Lords has more time to debate the lesser political issues, and it can approach some of the larger issues of principle, such as those involved in foreign and imperial affairs, with a less obvious partisan manner.

Moreover, the House of Lords can save the more harried House of Commons much valuable time through a careful working out of the less controversial bills. In many noncontroversial bills, too, the Lords can be of invaluable assistance. In the private bill field, for example, there is need for a great deal of committee work, which can often be done better in the Lords. The House of Commons has few persons who are expert in local legislation, which is not true of the Lords. The time and expertness available is particularly important at the committee stage, when the purpose is as much to find common ground for promoters and opponents of a measure as it is to safeguard the public interest.

With the increasing use of delegated legislation by ministries, the House of Lords is in a far better position than the House of Commons to look for probable abuses resulting from delegated legislation, provisional orders, and so on. The Lords have the time, they have men of experience, they have the legal talent, and some can usually be found who are interested in matters regarded as dull or unspectacular by others. But even if the politically unromantic local matters were more rewarding, the rules of the Commons so rigidly ration its time that a private member has little chance of doing much about statutory instruments even if he were disposed to do so.

As a Judicial Body

The House of Lords performs a judicial function as a court of appeal. With some exceptions, it is the final court of appeal in civil and criminal cases tried in the courts of Great Britain (civil cases only in the case of trials in Scotland). All peers are eligible to participate in the judicial activity of the House, but in practice, supported by custom for more than a century, its judicial functions are performed by the Lord Chancellor, the nine law lords, and those others of the

---

[26] Morrison, *op. cit.*, p. 195.

peers who have held high judicial office and who wish to participate. All of these men have had exceptional experience in the legal and judicial field. In their work they do not act as a committee, for their decisions are the decisions of the House of Lords.

BIBLIOGRAPHICAL NOTE

Sir Ivor Jennings, *Parliament* (2d ed. New York: Cambridge University Press, 1957) stands out as the most able analysis of the Parliament, while *Parliament: A Survey*, edited by Lord Campion (London: Allen and Unwin, 1955), also gives evidence of much insight. Other general works include those of A. H. Hanson and H. V. Wiseman, *Parliament at Work* (London: Stevens, 1962); Horace M. King, *Parliament and Freedom* (London: John Murray, 1953); Kenneth MacKenzie, *The English Parliament: A Study of Its Nature and Historic Development* (London: Pelican Books, 1950); Peter G. Richards, *Honourable Members: A Study of the British Backbencher* (New York: Praeger, 1959); Eric Taylor, *The House of Commons at Work* (London: Pelican Books, 1955); and Norman Wilding and Philip Laundy, *An Encyclopaedia of Parliament* (London: Cassell, 1958). Among the works written by members of Parliament, the following are of interest: W. J. Brown, *Everybody's Guide to Parliament* (2d ed. London: Allen and Unwin, 1946); Quintin M. Hogg, *The Purpose of Parliament* (London: Blandford Press, 1946); and Christopher Hollis, *Can Parliament Survive* (London: Hollis and Carter, 1949).

Sir Thomas Erskine May's Treatise on the Law, Privileges, Proceedings, and Usage of Parliament, 16th ed., edited by Sir Edward Fellowes, T.G.B. Cocks, and Lord Campion (London: Butterworth & Co., 1957), is regarded as the authoritative work on Parliamentary procedure. Other informative studies are Alfred C. Bossom, *Our House: An Introduction to Parliamentary Procedure* (London: James Barrie Publishers, Ltd., 1948); Lord Campion, *An Introduction to the Procedure of the House of Commons* (3d ed. New York: The Macmillan Co., 1950); and Lord Winterton, *Orders of the Day* (London: Cassell, 1954).

Two more specialized works deserve noting: D. N. Chester and N. Bowring, *Questions in Parliament* (London: Oxford University Press, 1962); S. E. Finer, et al., *Backbench Opinion in the House of Commons, 1955–1959* (New York: Pergamon Press, 1961).

Discussions of the position of the House of Lords may be found in *The Future of the House of Lords*, edited by Sydney Bailey (New York: Praeger, 1954), and P. A. Bromhead, *The House of Lords and Contemporary Politics* (London: Routledge and Kegan Paul, 1958).

CHAPTER 5

POLITICAL PARTIES

ALTHOUGH political parties are of relatively recent origin, it would be difficult, if not impossible, to visualize democratic government functioning without them. Where representatives are chosen by a broad electorate, the problem of ascertaining the will of the people and translating it into effective action requires organization. That organization is provided by political parties. They develop programs and select leaders to present to the electorate. They seek to persuade voters and to agitate them sufficiently so that they will go to the polls. Between elections, the party in power, by defending the policies and actions of its leaders, seeks to create and to maintain the impression that the country is being governed in a desirable way and that the opposition could not do so well. The party out of power, by criticizing the policies and actions (or lack thereof) of the Government, desires to promote the opposite impression: that it could certainly govern more effectively than the party in power. It is no exaggeration to assert, therefore, that today democratic government is everywhere party government.[1]

THE NATURE OF BRITISH PARTIES

Although the rudimentary origins of British political parties can be traced back several centuries, many writers prefer to date their origin about 1700, when the two major political groupings were called the Tories and the Whigs. In the modern sense, however, British parties can be said to begin in the early nineteenth century when the Tories began calling themselves Conservatives and the Whigs began calling themselves Liberals.

One of the major attributes of the British party system, like that of the American, is its two-party character. During the nineteenth century and the early years of the twentieth, the Conservatives and the Liberals continued to be the two major parties. With the formation of

---

[1] Edmund Burke defended parties in these words: "When bad men combine, the good must associate; else they will fall one by one, an unpitied sacrifice in a contemptible struggle." In a later era, Benjamin Disraeli defined party as "organized opinion."

the Labor party early in this century and its subsequent growth in the 1920s and 1930s and the corresponding decline of the Liberal party, the British party system underwent a transition. The transition was nearing completion in the 1930s and was certainly complete with the election of 1945, when Labor won a large majority while the Liberal party was meeting its demise. Subsequent elections merely confirmed what had already happened; the Labor party had replaced the Liberals as one of Britain's two major parties. Although the British party system has undergone changes, the tendency toward the two-party nature has remained reasonably constant in British politics.[2]

The reasons for the existence of a two-party system in England are not self-evident. Winston Churchill infers that the nature and shape of the House of Commons chamber discourages many parties and is, therefore, important to the preservation of a two-party system.[3] Other writers have suggested that British electoral arrangements are a partial explanation. Among these are the single-member district, the rule that plurality elects and the requirement of a monetary deposit by all candidates, which is forfeited unless the candidate obtains a certain percentage of the total vote cast. Sir Leopold Amery has maintained that the two-party system is in large part the consequence of the British system.[4] What he suggests is that the British have always had a strong government and that the cabinet has never been buffeted about by an irresponsible assembly. The purpose of British elections, he says, is not to ascertain the "national will" or "the majority will" but to confirm a Government with a working majority. The voters really have only two alternatives: to confirm the Government in office or to reject it in favor of an alternative team. As a general rule, a governing team which has a majority in the Commons can only be displaced by another team which is capable of securing an alternative majority. Perhaps all of the above-mentioned considerations have played some role in the existence of the two-party system in Britain. Be that as it may, Britishers seem to have preferred to vote for a party which had a reasonable chance of forming a Government; this has meant that independents and smaller parties tend to be pushed aside.

As in the United States, no mention of the party system is to be

---

[2] For a brief summary of changes in party affiliations and attempts to form third parties, see Chapter 4 in Ivor Bulmer-Thomas, *The Party System in Great Britain* (London, 1953). For a discussion of party factions in the 1930's and after, see his Chapter 8.

[3] Winston Churchill, *The Second World War: Closing the Ring* (Boston: Houghton, Mifflin Co.: 1951), p. 169.

[4] L. S. Amery, *Thoughts on the Constitution* (London: Oxford University Press, 1947), p. 15ff.

found in the British written constitution, yet it is central to the operation of the two countries' respective political processes. The British carry this further in that they avoid party labels more than we do. At election time, for example, the ballot does not indicate the party affiliations of the candidates, although party affiliations are made amply clear in the electoral campaign, and the voters are never in doubt. And although party considerations, in practice, enter into almost every act and decision of the House of Commons, party labels are studiously avoided in parliamentary deliberations and in official publications. In party literature, however, party designations are used as a matter of form.

WHAT THE PARTIES HAVE STOOD FOR

Throughout most of the eighteenth century Parliament was dominated by the landed interests. But by 1832 the merchants and manufacturers of the towns had gained considerable political influence. Moreover, the Reform Act of 1832 enfranchised the middle class of the towns, which served to produce a political balance between town and countryside and reflected the balance of economic power.

The Conservative party tended to be identified with wealth. Yet, in the nineteenth century it gained a considerable volume of working-class support, especially after the Conservatives, in an astute move, passed the Reform Act of 1867, which enfranchised the householders of the urban working class. While continuing to be identified with wealth and the general conservative tradition, the party has managed to attract a substantial middle-class vote, and at the same time to retain a significant working-class following.

The combination of Whigs and Peelites, which succeeded in repealing the Corn Laws, led to the establishment of the Liberal party. Based largely on manufacturing interests and "the Nonconformist Conscience," the Liberal party came to be known as the party of free trade and of the British middle class. It was the party of traditional liberalism, that is, maximum freedom and a minimum of governmental interference. Unlike the Conservatives, who emphasized the positive values of tradition and preferred normal growth to deliberate creation, the Liberals looked upon change with favor as long as it promoted and strengthened free institutions.

The Liberals were in office from 1868 to 1874 and again from 1880 to 1885. From 1886 to 1905, except for one brief interval, they were eclipsed by the Conservatives. Their majorities in 1906 and in several subsequent elections were deceptive because they were made possible largely by the developing trade-union influence, which was lost to the

Liberals after the establishment of the Labor party. By 1918, the Liberals were further weakened by an intraparty split over the party's participation in the Coalition Government of 1916. In the 1920s and 1930s, the decline of the Liberal party was precipitous, although it staved off its political demise until the 1945 elections.

The Labor party was founded in 1900. It is known as the party of socialism, but it was not until 1918 that socialism was adopted as the party program in the following words:

. . . to secure for the producers by hand or by brain the full fruits of their industry and the most equitable distribution thereof that may be possible, upon a basis of common ownership of the means of production and the best obtainable system of popular administration and to control each industry and service.

In practice, however, the Labor party is based on trade-union support much more than on any ideological doctrine.[5] Although it has accepted much of the Marxian analysis, the Labor party has not emphasized doctrine. Its program is founded more on a simple demand for distributive justice, that is, a more equitable sharing between rich and poor. Moreover, even its trade union base would not be sufficient to win a national election. For this, a much broader appeal is necessary.

In and out of power, the Labor party has behaved like other democratic parties and quite unlike Communist parties. After its victory in 1945, it engaged in a limited amount of nationalization, but always with respect toward due process and the rights of the minority. Unlike Communist confiscations, provision was made by the Government for compensation to the owners of the nationalized properties. At no time while Labor was in office was there fear that democratic political processes would be suspended or that the Labor party would attempt to hold on to political power beyond the period for which its members were elected. Perhaps no one was surprised when the Labor party began increasingly to resemble the other great parliamentary parties as it came to rival them in size and strength.[6]

While various issues have tended to divide British political parties,[7] there is reason to believe that while important differences remain, "British parties today are in closer agreement on 'fundamentals' than

---

[5] It is interesting to note that none of the so-called ideological founders of British socialism, the seven authors of the *Fabian Essays in Socialism* (1889), displayed any interest in the trade unions.

[6] R. T. McKenzie, *British Political Parties: The Distribution of Power Within the Conservative and Labour Parties* (London: St. Martins, 1955), p. 584.

[7] For different issues with which successive Governments since 1900 have had to deal, and the dominant political personalities involved, see D. C. Somerwell, *British Politics Since 1900* (London: Oxford University Press, 1950).

they have been for many years."[8] The Conservatives, with one or two notable exceptions, have accepted the nationalization legislation of the Labor Government and have embraced the idea of the welfare state. This does not represent a drastic change by the Conservative party, for it has a long history of social reform. The Labor party, on the other hand, has in the practices of the welfare state accepted much from the Conservatives. Although it once advocated nationalization of the land, the Labor party has in recent years actively sought the support of the farmers. The Conservatives, for their part, continue their appeals to the working class and gain considerable support from it. Both the Labor and the Conservative parties recognize that the growing strength of the so-called middle class (clerks, mechanics, insurance agents, shop assistants, and white-collar workers generally) has given it a balance of power. Consequently, both parties appeal to this group, especially in marginal constituencies. Neither party has at any point "threatened to disrupt the parliamentary system in order either to impose its own policies or to prevent its opponents from implementing theirs."[9]

The Labor party's awareness of its broader responsibility was well stated by one of its leaders, Herbert Morrison, when he said: "A Government is entitled to take into account what is politically advantageous to its party, but it must never forget that it is responsible to the community as a whole for the well-being of the country as a whole. In the framing of the legislative program, as in other matters, it is morally wrong and in the end politically suicidal to forget that the public interest comes first."[10]

What Divides the Parties Today?

There are matters, of course, over which the two parties divide, and although generalizations are subject to error, an attempt will be made to summarize the party positions on the major issues.[11] It is necessary, however, to keep in mind that a considerable division of opinion exists within each party; that it is more pronounced in the Labor party; that

---

[8] Samuel H. Beer, "Pressure Groups and Parties in Britain," *The American Political Science Review*, Vol. 50, pp. 1–23 (March, 1956). Also, see McKenzie, *op. cit.*, p. 581.

[9] McKenzie, *ibid.*

[10] Herbert Morrison, *Government and Parliament* (London, Oxford University Press, 1954), p. 224.

[11] This section owes much to the excellent study by S. E. Finer, H. B. Berrington, and D. J. Bartholomew, *Backbench Opinion in the House of Commons 1955–59* (New York, Pergamon Press, 1961). Declarations by the parties and their principal leaders have also been utilized.

it does not always take easily ascertainable or classifiable forms. In the Conservative party differences of opinion are perhaps more over priorities and emphases, while in the Labor party they are apt to involves matters of substance. The Conservative party is in some ways like a collection of pressure groups, while the Labor party resembles a coalition of parties.

Some one has suggested that what characterizes the Labor party is a set of attitudes instead of a body of doctrine. Hugh Gaitskell, the then leader of the party, reflected this in a speech to the party conference in 1959. In it he summarized what he called the party's "first principles." They are: (1) a broad human movement "on behalf of all those who are oppressed, or in need or hardship"; (2) a belief in social justice, in a distribution of wealth on the basis, not of the accident of birth, but on "how much effort, skill, and creative energy we contribute to the common good"; (3) a classless society, "a society without the snobbery, privilege, or restrictive social barriers which are still too prevalent in Britain today"; (4) a belief in "the fundamental equality of all races and all nations"; (5) a belief "that the pursuit of material satisfaction by itself is empty and barren, and that the good society is one in which the human personality is developed to the full"; (6) a belief that while the pursuit of private gain is desirable it "should not take precedence over the public good"; (7) a belief that the above goals "must be achieved through freedom and democratic self-government."

Gaitskell was really replying to factions in the party which were concerned with the practical application of one or more of these activities. A number of party spokesmen had warned against the danger of the party's becoming an impotent appendage of the welfare state. They had argued that Labor had succeeded so well in reforming capitalism that it had not only civilized it but, in addition, made it practically indestructible. Gaitskell was aware, however, that if the party emphasized nationalization, controls, policies in housing, education, etc.—at the expense of "first principles"—there would be little chance of success at the polls. He noted that general prosperity (as evidenced by television sets, refrigerators, washing machines, automobiles, and new housing developments) had contributed to a diminished loyalty to Labor. Technical changes produced more white collar jobs and fewer manual labor jobs. Workers were moving out to semi-detached homes. These and similar developments spelled somewhat altered attitudes, attitudes that are less favorable toward unionization and toward the Labor party.

While keeping in mind that serious divisions exist within the Labor party, the position of the vast majority of its members on a number of foreign and domestic issues can be stated at least in tendencies. In foreign affairs, for example, the party has a tendency towards pacifism. It has a revulsion against the employment of force (or threat thereof) in international relations. A strong and vocal group, although seemingly a minority, has advocated the unilateral abandonment of the H-bomb, the withdrawal of the American Polaris base, and even the withdrawal from NATO. There is a considerable distrust of the capitalist, materialist U.S.A., and a hope for cooperation with the Soviet Union on the international level despite hostility toward its form of government. During the 1950's and early 1960's, however, the leaders have managed to have the party committed to collective security including the retention of nuclear weapons. The party is fairly united in its hostility toward colonialism. It is equally united in its support of the United Nations. The party's leaders have expressed opposition to Britain's joining the European Common Market on the terms that the Conservatives were willing to accept.

On the domestic front the party exhibits a tendency toward humanitarianism in social policy (e.g. penal reforms) and a tendency toward improved material standards for workers in the economic field. The party is concerned about the cost of living, wants to increase social security payments, and desires to direct the economy in the interest of the common good. During the past decade and a half its leaders have managed to follow moderate and reformist policies in domestic affairs, but they have continually been challenged by a vocal group of their supporters demanding a more aggressive economic program. In the educational realm, the party seeks reforms that will increase still further the number of university students and that will somehow reduce or minimize the divisions existing in secondary education.

Generally speaking, the Conservative party is less dissatisfied with the way things are than is the Labor party. In the realm of foreign affair there is no serious opposition in Conservative ranks to Britain's role in the cold war on her membership in the western alliance. On the other hand, Conservatives have been far from united with respect to Britain's relationship to Europe and to the Commonwealth and the Empire. The majority, particularly the younger generation of Conservatives, has tended to lean toward a closer association with Europe. The party's policy of seeking membership in the Common Market (which Labor opposes) is an indication of this tendency. Many

Conservatives have insisted, however, that closer unity with Europe should not be at the expense of the Commonwealth and the Empire. The party is reconciled with the realization of self-government by its one-time colonies and has pursued policies toward that end. The Suez crisis of 1956 did provoke a serious crisis within the party, but this has been healed without permanent scars. There are significant fears in the party about national sovereignty, leading it to be less enthusiastic about the UN than is Labor.

In domestic affairs the Conservative party is not opposed to change, but it is not in a hurry. Although there was a good deal of support for the abolition of capital punishment, the party is by and large opposed to the relaxation of penalties for crime. In the area of social services the Conservatives are responsive to working class claims, but they must reconcile these with the claims of other classes. Due to the expansion of production in the late 1950's they were able to increase social services in some areas while at the same time providing some relaxation (e.g. private building and tax relief) to the middle class. By and large Conservatives are less enthusiastic than the Laborites about the welfare state. They are opposed to further nationalization and they believe that government should be more discriminating in the distribution of social service benefits.

THE BEGINNINGS OF PARTY ORGANIZATION

The modern British party system is the product of the gradual expansion of the electorate since 1832. Prior to that year there was in Great Britain "nothing that could seriously be called a party system either inside or outside Parliament."[12] Before that date parties were groups of men in Parliament who on great issues thought, talked, and for the most part voted alike. But even inside Parliament there was no party organization in the modern sense.

Prior to 1832 there was little or no need for party organization. The franchise was so limited and parliamentary seats controlled by so few people that there was no need for an organized effort to persuade the public and seek its votes. With the Great Reform Act of 1832, however, the electorate was enlarged, necessitating the compilation of lists of qualified electors. Consequently, it was important to each party to see that all of its qualified supporters were registered and the names of all unqualified opponents were removed from the voting lists. For

---

[12] McKenzie, *op. cit.*, p. 3.

this purpose, "registration societies" were formed; these groups constituted the beginning of party organization at the constituency, or district, level.

It was not until 1867, however, that a grouping of constituency associations was begun. In that year the Second Reform Act was enacted, further extending the suffrage and, in effect, making the national organization of parties a necessity. In that year was formed the first of the great party organizations, the National Union of Conservative and Constitutional Unions, now known as the National Union. Thus, more than a third of a century elapsed between the initial founding of the registration societies and the effective mobilization of party organizations in support of party candidates. Ten years later, in 1877, the Liberal party founded the National Liberal Federation, which resembled the National Union of the Conservatives. The existence and functioning of these national party organizations furnished a pattern for other parties which were to come into being at a later date.

THE PARTIES IN ACTION: CONSERVATIVE

Party organization in Great Britain may be understood best through a consideration of the principal component parts. These are the leader, the party organization inside Parliament, and the party organization (national and local) in the country. In terms of power, prestige, and influence in decision making, they generally rank in the order named and will be discussed in that order.

THE CONSERVATIVE LEADER

The leader of the party is the one person to whom party adherents, both in and out of Parliament, look for day-to-day leadership. He is either an actual or a potential prime minister. By virtue of this fact he has enormous authority over his followers, who have only two real alternatives—they must "back him or sack him." As long as he remains his party's leader, he is the authoritative voice of the party and the symbol of what it stands for.

Although the Conservatives in 1965 altered the method of selecting the leader, the unique way in which they did it in the past merits brief discussion. In the history of the party no actual contests for the leadership, that is contests in which a formal vote was taken, seem to have occurred. The party elected a leader "only after he had been called to the office of prime minister."[13] This election, at a meeting composed of the Conservative members of Parliament, the party's prospective parliamentary candidates, and the executive committee of the National Union, constituted a formal ratification of a choice made by a few party stalwarts after whatever consultation they had chosen to make among their colleagues. Normally, there was always a leader, because once made prime minister, and then designated leader, he remained in the post of party leadership until he died or retired. If the post became vacant when the party was out of power, it formally remained vacant; the Conservatives in the Commons elected a leader and those in the Lords did likewise. In the normal course of events, through the cabinet and the shadow cabinet, the leader groomed a successor, but rivals sometime arose to supersede a potential successor, but this usually took place long before the party got together to select a new leader. When the post became vacant while the party was in power, the outgoing leader was usually able to name his successor, as Harold Macmillan did in 1963 when Sir Alexander Douglas-Home was made prime minister. There was some disagreement among Conservative leaders at the time, but once Macmillan had indicated his choice, no one was predisposed to question it openly. When the party leader stepped out at a time when there was an internal party crisis, as at the time of Suez when Anthony Eden resigned, the voice of other Conservative leaders was seemingly more important. After consultations among these top leaders, they decided that the Queen should be advised to send for Mr. Macmillan. This is not to suggest that Eden disagreed with them, but that under the circumstances their judgment as to who should be designated prime minister would have been decisive irrespective of what Eden might have thought. It is not known to what extent rank and file Conservative M.P.s were consulted, but some complained that they were not asked their views. It seems clear, however, that those who held strong views had indicated a preference for Macmillan over the other leading contender, R. A. Butler, and that they made this preference known privately to the party's Chief Whip.

Partly because of the dissatisfaction which arose following the selection of Sir Alexander Douglas-Home in 1963, the Conservatives decided in 1965 that the leader should be elected by the party's members of the House of Commons. He is then presented to a larger party gathering, consisting of the Conservative members of the Com-

---

[13] *Ibid.*, p. 33.

mons and prospective candidates, the active Conservative peers from the Lords, and the members of the executive committee of the National Union. Ratification of the election by this larger group will doubtless be perfunctory.

There have been brief periods when the Conservative prime minister was not the leader of the party, but for the most part the leader of the party in Parliament is also its leader in the country. Normally, once designated the prime minister, he automatically becomes leader of the party. One exception was Winston Churchill in 1940, but somewhat unusual circumstances were involved. Both Churchill and the outgoing prime minister, Neville Chamberlain, agreed that it was desirable and in the interests of unity not to have Churchill take over as party leader. Within a few months, however, Chamberlain resigned the post and Churchill became leader of the party. Churchill suggests that this would have been necessary in any case.[14]

As mentioned above, the position of the leader in the Conservative party is a strong one. He does not attain that position except after many years of close association with his party colleagues. In the past 80 years the party has had ten leaders; they averaged more than 20 years in Parliament prior to election to the leadership. But despite their position of strength, Conservative leaders have generally discovered that their authority in opposition is less than when their party is in office. Moreover, the position of the leader is demonstrably weak when there is much sentiment against him among his party colleagues. This was true of Balfour,[15] for example, when he was indecisive on the question of tariff reform, and also when he in effect urged capitulation in the House of Lords to Liberal party proposals to reduce the power of the Lords. His position was no doubt weakened by the fact that he did not present his views to his followers in person but instead presented them through a letter to The Times. Austen Chamberlain, on the other hand, was forceful enough, but his views in 1922, in favor of continuing the coalition with the Liberals, were unacceptable to his party colleagues in Parliament, who forced him to resign as leader. The simple fact is that he "tried to lead a party in a direction in which the great majority of its members both inside and outside Parliament did not want to go."[16]

---

[14] Winston Churchill, The Second World War: Their Finest Hour (Boston: Houghton Mifflin Co., 1949), p. 496.

[15] For a detailed discussion of the relationship of some Conservative leaders and their followers, see McKenzie, op. cit., p. 68ff, p. 83ff, p. 110ff.

[16] Ibid., p. 109.

A leader, despite weaknesses, may survive if he does not have a strong rival or an obvious successor. This seems to have been true of Stanley Baldwin, who was a Conservative leader for 14 years. At times he seems not to have consulted his colleagues on important matters of policy, such as calling an election in 1923 and his espousal of the protective tariff. On other issues he seems to have been lethargic and indecisive. In 1926 he had to be goaded into action on trade-union legislation by the party conference. The years 1927–29 have often been labeled "the years of decay" in describing the Conservative Government because they culminated in the party's defeat at the polls in 1929. Although this defeat further weakened Baldwin and challenged his leadership, there does not seem to have been an obvious successor. The economic and political crisis of 1931 gave him a reprieve by ending internal party struggles for the time being. Thereafter his position was never challenged. He retired in 1937.

A recitation of some of the difficulties which have beset some Conservative leaders ought not, however, to lead one to minimize the authority they traditionally wield. The leader may receive aid from the party's Advisory Committee on Policy and from other party bodies, but the ultimate responsibility for the formulation of policy and the party's program is his. He has control over the party's central office (discussed below). He appoints the chairman of the national party organization, the two vice-chairmen, the treasurers of the party, and the chairman and deputy chairman of the Advisory Committee on Policy. These appointees are responsible to him alone. To be sure, he holds these vast powers with the consent of his followers in Parliament and in the popular organization of the party outside, although the latter is less important than the former. While his position is normally strong, it is also potentially precarious.

CONSERVATIVE PARTY ORGANIZATION IN PARLIAMENT

Prior to 1922 the Conservative party in Parliament was almost completely devoid of formal organization. The leaders and the whips in effect were the organization. The downfall of Austen Chamberlain as party leader in 1922 convinced many Conservatives of the need for a more formal party organization in the House of Commons. As a consequence, the Conservative Members Committee, popularly called the "1922 Committee," was established. When the party is in power, all Conservative private members are eligible for membership, which for all practical purposes means that it is an organization of the entire back-bench membership of the party. The leader does not attend meetings of the committee except when it has been arranged for him to speak. Neither do ministers or junior ministers attend. The whips attend but do not have a vote. When the party is out of power, however, all are private members and eligible. Although the leader still attends only on special occasions, members of his shadow cabinet and the party whips attend but are considered ineligible for organizational office and have no voting rights.

The 1922 Committee, usually meeting once a week for an hour or two, is normally chaired by a prominent back-bencher who has direct access to the leader and to whom he conveys the views of the back-benchers. Since votes are not normally taken in the committee, it becomes the duty of the chairman to interpret the "sense of the meeting." In addition, the leader also gets regular reports on the moods of the committee from the whips, whom he appoints. Although the 1922 Committee is not authorized to formulate policy for the party, rank and file M.P.s speak their minds freely and name representatives to policy-advisory bodies of the party. Moreover, their more detailed discussion of problems and policies takes place in one of the functional committees.

The party's functional committees, not to be confused with the committees of the Commons, correspond to the several ministries or groups of ministries. It is in the functional committees, chaired by back-benchers when the party is in power (by members of the shadow cabinet when out of power), that the great issues are debated and the party's attitude with respect to them crystallized. The sessions of functional committees, while sometimes troublesome, constitute an excellent training ground for future ministers. Here, also, differences are hammered out in private, helping to insure a united front before the public. The views of the functional committees are brought to the leader by a Business Committee, which consists of the main officers of the principal functional committees.

Although the views of the back-benchers are kept constantly in mind by the leader, his most intimate advisers are apt to be his cabinet colleagues. When out of power, they are technically known as the Consultative Committee, or more popularly, the shadow cabinet. Unlike their Labor colleagues, Conservative members of Commons play no role in selecting the shadow cabinet. The leader has the same authority in choosing shadow cabinet members as he has in appointing the cabinet.

CONSERVATIVE PARTY ORGANIZATION OUTSIDE PARLIAMENT

Mass party organizations developed in the late nineteenth century. They were in large part made necessary by an expanding electorate, which was becoming more and more independent as a result of the secret ballot, restrictions on campaign expenditures, and other safeguards against control of the vote by a limited number of party workers. The rise of the need for many voluntary party workers coincided with the advancement of education and the spread of literacy, making possible a greater utilization of printed party literature.

The official name of the Conservative party organization is The National Union of Conservative and Unionist Associations, hereafter referred to as the National Union. While cognizant of the need for a national party organization, Conservative leaders from the beginning conceived of it as a servant of the party inside Parliament. They did not want the National Union to usurp any of the functions of leadership. Their fears, however, seem to have been unfounded, for the National Union has continued to operate as little more than "an electoral machine and a channel of communication between the parliamentary leaders and their followers in the country."[17] From time to time, ways of keeping the leader more intimately in touch with the rank and file of the party have been explored, but the leader and his colleagues have persistently fought every suggestion that the National Union should be accorded effective control over the party in Parliament or over the party's central office, which is under the control of the leader. In addition to serving as a two-way channel of communication between the leaders in Parliament and the rank and file party members in the country, the National Union is an educative political force and a vehicle for winning elections. In addition, it provides the party's politically active supporters with an opportunity to play some limited part in the selection of party leaders and in the formulation of party policies.[18]

The party organization outside Parliament, although having no national party constitution, is arranged on a fairly precise basis. It can best be viewed as a dual hierarchy, one part voluntary, the other professional. At the base of the voluntary organization are the constituency associations and at the top is the annual Conference. The real

---

[17] *Ibid.*, p. 180.
[18] *Ibid.*, p. 185ff.

governing bodies in the voluntary structure, however, are the Central Council and executive committee of the National Union. On the professional side, the most important institution is the central office, which is directly responsible to the leader. In addition, there are area offices, which are really branches of the central office. At the base of the professional pyramid are the agents and organizers. The constituency agent, although under considerable influence from the central office, is the one person in the party's professional staff who is responsible to the voluntary side of the organization. The voluntary and professional sides of the National Union will now be examined in more detail.

The Conference is a yearly meeting which lasts about two and a half days. Each constituency association irrespective of its size has the right to send seven members (exclusive of M.P. or prospective M.P., certified agent, and certified organizer) to the Conference. More than 5,000 persons have the right to attend, but since 1945 attendance has averaged between 3,000 and 4,000. Although the first Conference was held in 1867, nearly 20 years passed before current political questions were debated and resolutions regarding them adopted. It must be reiterated, however, that even today the Conference does not formulate party policies. In the main, it has tended to serve as a demonstration of party unity and support for its leaders. The leader does not participate in the formal sessions of the Conference but he does address the members in a mass meeting immediately after the Conference adjourns. The extent to which the debates and resolutions of the Conference have influenced the Conservative party in Parliament on policy matters is uncertain, for specific examples are few. There are, on the other hand, a number of examples of Conference resolutions that have been ignored by the party leadership. Demands for the reform of the House of Lords were made with monotonous regularity for many years, but without any effect. While leaders cannot be bound by conference decisions, they can be embarrassed by them.

The Conference, besides being unable to formulate policy, lacks the power to act as the party's governing body. This authority is vested in the Central Council, which normally meets once a year and is, in effect, a briefer and smaller version of the annual Conference. It consists of the party leader, all Conservative members of Parliament (including peers), prospective Conservative candidates, members of the executive committee of the National Union, representatives of the National Advisory Committee of the National Union and four representatives of each constituency organization. Meetings of the Central

Council afford constituency representatives an opportunity to express their opinions on any matter that especially concerns them and to get firsthand reports from the leader and his associates.

The executive committee of the National Union, with a membership approximating 150, normally meets every other month. It consists of the leader and other principal officers of the party, together with representatives of the areas, each of which encompasses several constituencies. It concerns itself, in the intervals between the meetings of the Central Council, with matters under the jurisdiction of the Council. Much of the detailed work is performed by the General Purposes Subcommittee, created in 1933 and consisting of 56 members; the subcommittee also prepares the agenda for the annual Conference as well as for the Central Council. It is in this subcommittee that a great deal of sifting and sorting takes place of matters that various party bodies want discussed at the Conference or by the Central Council.

Last, but not least, in the framework of the voluntary party structure are the constituency associations, which constitute the basic units in the party organization. In theory they have complete autonomy in the management of their affairs, but the central office does provide them with model rules for guidance. The usual governing body of an association is an executive council, which, among other things, has the authority to expel members for political heresy and intraparty disputes. As a rule, it meets quarterly and annually appoints a number of committees. The chairman, who is the effective head of the association, presides at these sessions, and the salaried constituency agent serves as secretary to the executive council. The model rules recommend that the constituency agent "should be recognized as the chief official of the party in the constituency." He is supposed to help the association and serve his party's M.P. (or the party's prospective candidate) as an executive assistant and as his eyes and ears in the constituency. The association as a whole meets once a year to hear and discuss reports from its executive council and its committees. Their member in the Commons (or their prospective candidate) customarily addresses the annual gathering.

Membership in a constituency association "is open to all men and women resident in 'or connected with' the constituency who declare their support of the objects of the association and subscribe annually to its funds,"[19] normally in nominal annual dues. Although the size of

---

[19] *Ibid.*, p. 244.

constituency associations varies greatly, the average membership is approximately 5,000. The number of members, however, does not seem to bear any particular relationship to the party's electoral strength in the constituency, for some of the strongest constituencies are weak in formal party membership. It is in the marginal constituencies that formal memberships are often large, for here organization and hard work often make the difference between victory and defeat.

Although the primary function of the constituency association is to conduct publicity and raise money with the view to securing the election of Conservative candidates, the association's role in the selection of parliamentary candidates is also important. For this purpose the executive council appoints a selection committee. The committee may invite seven or eight would-be candidates for interviews but ultimately recommends two or three who are invited to a special meeting of the council where they make brief speeches and answer questions. Afterward, the council chooses the constituency's candidate, usually requiring a series of ballots since a majority vote is required. This choice may be vetoed by the central office but only in instances where the prospective candidate would be regarded as clearly detrimental to party interests.[20]

Earlier in the selection process, the chairman of the association sends a request to the central office for a list of persons considered suitable as candidates. He may personally visit the central office vice-chairman responsible for candidatures and discuss prospective candidates with him, and he may also talk with the area agent of the party. In any case, the selection committee is informed of the views of the central office. At times, much informal pressure may be brought to bear on behalf of a person desired by the central office, particularly a prominent party man who had been defeated in another constituency.

To remove the temptation from selective committees and executive councils to nominate only candidates who are wealthy enough to pay their own campaign expenses, party rules permit a candidate to pay only the "personal expenses" of the campaign, which cannot exceed £100. If elected, he may contribute up to £50 a year to the constit-

---

[20] There seems to be general agreement that irrespective of who the candidate might be, the party's vote in the constituency would be altered by a few hundred votes at most. This is as true of the Labor party as it is of the Conservative. See *Ibid.*, p. 5; Bulmer-Thomas, *op. cit.*, p. 260; David Butler, *The British General Election of 1951* (London, 1952), pp. 273–75.

uency association, but only up to £25 if he is a prospective candidate.

Certain ancillary organizations, although not a part of the formal party structure, seek to promote party aims and policies. Among these are the Carlton Club, the Association of Conservative Clubs, the working men's clubs, the women's clubs, and youth groups. The Carlton Club is considered the most influential, but observers have encountered considerable difficulty in attempting to appraise the influence of the Conservative and working men's clubs, where members meet friends, play billiards, or have a drink, with politics perhaps low on the list of conversation topics.

While constituency associations and other organizations may in various ways exert influence on party programs and policies, they, like the Conference, do not make policy or control the affairs of the Conservative party. The leader and his parliamentary colleagues, however, "must win at least the acquiescence and, if at all possible, the willing support of the constituency associations."[21] When these associations are in revolt, as they were in 1922, they may contribute significantly to a leader's downfall.

The professional, as opposed to the voluntary, side of the Conservative party organization outside Parliament has already been referred to. The role of area and constituency agents has been described. The central office, which appoints and pays them, is the heart and soul of the party's professional structure. It is officially described as the headquarters of the party organization, and sometimes referred to as the "civil service" of the party.

The central office is in a way the personal instrument of the leader, for he appoints a member of Parliament, known as chairman, to run it. He also appoints the vice-chairman and the other principal officers, who, along with the salaried staff, do not change from year to year. The total staff of the central office is about 200.

The chairman supervises the work of the central office, but the detailed management is left to the general director and his staff. Most of the chairman's influence is exerted behind the scenes. He must try to keep the National Union from embarrassing the party in Parliament. If need be, he will defend parliamentary leaders at the party Conference and elsewhere. He may defend the central office and he may pledge to convey to the leader the feelings of party organizations.

The role of the central office, according to a National Union

[21] McKenzie, *op. cit.*, p. 243.

committee report, "is to guide, inspire, and coordinate the work of the party throughout the country, to advise and assist constituency associations and area councils and to provide such services as can best be organized centrally."[22] Party literature seeks to refute suggestions that the affairs of the party are directed or managed by the central office by emphasizing that its purpose is to provide advice and assistance, rather than directions, to the constituency associations.

It remains a fact, however, that the really vital functions of the party (policy, finance, candidatures) are controlled by the leader or by the chairman, or another one of the leader's appointees. *"It would be difficult to envisage a more tight-knit system of oligarchical control of the affairs of a political party."*[23] But it should never be forgotten that a leader and his associates recognize that there are limits beyond which the party rank and file will not go. And what may be even more important, the leader and his colleagues are keenly aware that the limits beyond which a majority of the electorate will not go may be reached before those of the party's rank and file members.

Finally, some mention should be made of the more important committees of the National Union. Although the National Union, through its various official bodies, selects a number of the members of these committees, the committees themselves are responsible to the leader and not to the National Union; the committees have the effect, however, of tending to link the leader and the National Union. The Advisory Committee on Policy, the Consultative Committee on Party Finance, the Central Board of Finance, and the Standing Committee on Parliamentary Candidates are all more or less run by personal appointees of the leader. They could not, of course, be run for long in a manner which clearly offended the sensibilities of the party's rank and file.

THE PARTIES IN ACTION: LABOR

The Labor party functions not too differently from the Conservative party, but some facts about its origin and brief history are unique. Its founding dates from about 1900, when the Trades Union Congress instructed its parliamentary committee to call a meeting to consider labor representation in Parliament. Its founders did not, however, think of themselves as establishing another political party. A labor

---

[22] *Interim and Final Reports of the Committee on Party Organization, 1948 and 1949* (London, 1949), p. 31. This is popularly known as the Maxwell Fyfe Report, after the committee's chairman.

[23] McKenzie, *op. cit.*, p. 291. Italics are his.

movement designed to improve the lot of the workers had existed for some years, but prior to 1900 the general rule was to work through existing parties. The decision of the Labor Representation Committee in 1900 that members of Parliament whom it helped elect should take a position completely independent of the Conservative and Liberal parties set in motion the tide that led to formal adoption of the name Labor party in 1906 and in a few short decades swept the Liberal party into political oblivion. Within 23 years after its founding, the Labor party had a prime minister at No. 10 Downing Street, although 20 additional years were to elapse before it commanded a majority in the House of Commons.

Moreover, the Labor party is unique in that most of its membership is made up of members of affiliated organizations, principally the trade unions. There was no individual membership in the party prior to 1918, and even today individual membership constitutes only a small part of the total. The reason is mainly historical. Workers' associations, such as the Miners' Federation, which helped elect persons to the House of Commons began affiliating with the Labor party once it became active. Trade unions which affiliate pay a political levy to the party on those members who have not "contracted out," that is, signed a statement of refusal to pay.

It was not until 1918, however, that the Labor party was converted to socialism, that is, to work for "the common ownership of the means of production." In its analysis of capitalist society and in its belief in the common ownership of the means of production, the party can be said to have something in common with Marxism. At that point, however, any similarity between it and modern-day Communist parties ceases. The Labor party is dedicated to the preservation of the democratic political order, to the principle of peaceful change, and to the principle of compensation for nationalized property. Moreover, it never espoused complete socialization of all economic activities, and more recently its leaders have tended to limit or modify previous nationalization goals. At the international socialist conference in 1950, Labor party secretary Morgan Phillips declared that British socialism was "Methodist, not Marxist."

THE LABOR LEADER

The leader of the Labor party is elected annually at the beginning of each session of Parliament by the Labor members of the House of Commons. Once elected, leaders usually are assured of re-election. Since 1922 only one leader has had to face a contest for re-election.

The one exception was Hugh Gaitskell in 1960, and he won easily. The term "leader" was formally adopted in 1922 only when it became clear that the leader, who previously was known as chairman, would become the leader of His Majesty's Loyal Opposition.[24] In the latter capacity he became a potential prime minister, a capacity which is the main source of his influence and authority. As a potential prime minister he has been able "to acquire a degree of authority that is nowhere acknowledged in the constitution of the party,"[25] and to acquire a role as party leader that is not much different from that of the leaders of other British parties.

When it has been necessary to choose a new leader, actual contests have developed, instead of the leader evolving in the Conservative party tradition. In 1935 the contest was between Clement Attlee, Herbert Morrison, and Arthur Greenwood. In 1955, the contenders were Hugh Gaitskell, Herbert Morrison, and Aneurin Bevan. With the death of Gaitskell in 1963, the contest was between Harold Wilson, George Brown and James Callaghan.

Once named prime minister, a Labor leader acts much as his Conservative counterpart. The first Labor prime minister, Ramsay MacDonald, went about choosing his cabinet without sharing any formal responsibility in the task with Labor organizations inside or outside Parliament. Despite subsequent party conference resolutions that sought to limit the prime minister's cabinet-making powers,[26] the party has now come to recognize that the final responsibility for choosing ministers must rest with him. Clement Attlee, who was Labor prime minister for some seven years following World War II, has put it this way:

> In my view, the responsibility of choosing the members of the Government must rest solely with the Prime Minister though, in practice, he will consult with his colleagues. If he cannot be trusted to exercise this power in the best interests of the nation and the Party without fear, favour or affection, he is not fit to be Prime Minister.[27]

---

[24] During each Labor Government, a back-bencher was elected chairman of the party in Parliament. In opposition, however, the leader assumed the role of chairman.

[25] McKenzie, *op. cit.*, p. 299.

[26] These were primarily the consequence of Ramsay MacDonalds' decision (without consulting his colleagues) in 1931 to lead the so-called National Government (with all major parties participating), in an effort to deal with the economic emergency.

[27] Clement Attlee, *As It Happened* (London: William Heinemann; 1954), p. 156. Attlee was the first Labor party leader whose origins were upper middle class. His successor, Hugh Gaitskell, also had a middle-class background. For a discussion of the factors contributing to Attlee's rise as leader, see McKenzie, *British Political Parties*, pp. 357–61. Harold Wilson, like Gaitskell, is an intellectual.

After Attlee became prime minister, his relationships with his party in and out of Parliament were almost the same as those of a Conservative prime minister. Not unlike his Conservative counterpart, he always had to keep two considerations in mind. He must not outrage his followers in the House of Commons, lest his Government fall. And he must not outrage his followers outside Parliament, lest he find himself without an electoral machine. In practice, therefore, the principle of leadership in the Labor party is much the same as it is in the Conservative party.

In some ways, however, the Labor leader differs from the leader of the Conservative party. When out of power, the Labor leader did not, prior to 1955, choose his "shadow cabinet" (the parliamentary committee); it was chosen for him by the Labor members of the Commons. Since 1955, however, Attlee, Gaitskell, and Wilson have appointed full shadow governments, including many members who had not been elected to the parliamentary committee, thus attaining a degree of control over their party colleagues comparable to that when in office. In other respects, the Labor leader seems weaker than his Conservative counterpart. He is obligated more than the Conservative leader to attempt to implement the party's program, which is determined jointly by the Labor members of the Commons and the mass party organization. In addition, the whips are not the leader's personal appointees. The chief whip is elected annually by the party organization in Parliament, and he in turn appoints the junior whips. Finally, the Labor leader does not exercise personal control over the party's head office. Yet some of the most careful studies of British politics suggest that even these differences may be more apparent than real.[28]

LABOR PARTY ORGANIZATION IN PARLIAMENT

There are similarities and differences between the Conservative and Labor party organizations in Parliament. Both organizations are autonomous in the sense that they do not permit the party organizations outside Parliament to direct or control them. They have their own rules, choose their own leaders, and acknowledge responsibility only to the electorate. It was some time before the Parliamentary Labor Party (official name of the party organization in Parliament) acquired a clearly autonomous position, for the early Labor members were but agents of an extra-parliamentary body. But the efforts of the

---

[28] For example, see McKenzie, *op. cit.*, p. 297ff. For a different view, however, see Saul Rose, "Policy Decisions in Opposition," *Political Studies*, IV (June, 1956), pp. 128–38.

early years to impose a political program on the PLP from the outside were successfully resisted. Following the decision of the leader to head a coalition with the Conservatives in the early 1930s, there were other efforts to limit the leader, but there was no serious challenge to PLP's leadership after Attlee became the party's leader.

The organizational machinery of the Labor party is well defined, while that of the Conservative party is loose and informal. The Conservative party organization in Parliament is for the most part a meeting of back-benchers, which the leaders do not attend. The Parliamentary Labor Party, however, expects its leader to attend its meetings, at which he usually presides. He would want to attend in any case, for unlike the Conservative back-benchers' organization, the Parliamentary Labor Party may make binding policy decisions. This is much more important when the party is out of power, because when it is in power the cabinet makes policy decisions. Also, when the party is out of power the PLP is more subject to extra-parliamentary influence than when it is in power.

Conservative publicists have occasionally asserted that the Parliamentary Labor Party is subject to control by an insidious body outside Parliament. Laborites have retaliated by labeling the Conservatives undemocratic because of their unwillingness to hold themselves responsible to their mass organization outside Parliament. Both of these contentions are not accurate, for in practice the Laborites are not dictated to from the outside and the Conservative organization, especially in Parliament, has more democracy than meets the eye. Exaggeration aside, it must be said that the Labor party does make more elaborate efforts to give the rank and file a greater sense of participation than do the Conservatives.

Discipline among Labor members of the Commons is more strict in theory than in practice. This is especially true in the committee rooms. At one time, however, Labor members had virtually no liberty of action, but this has been relaxed. According to the standing orders of the PLP, as revised in 1952, the party "recognizes the right of individual members [of the Commons] to abstain from voting on matters of deeply held personal conscientious conviction." Moreover, in cases involving alleged violations of discipline, the member or members concerned "shall have the right to be heard at the Party Meeting before the Whip is withdrawn." But, "for the purpose of securing concerted action in the House, Members shall consult the Officers of the Parliamentary Party before tabling any motion, amendment or prayer, or other proposal which may involve Party policies or decisions."

There are differences of opinion in all political parties, particularly democratic ones, but some parties, such as the Conservative, manage to keep these closely guarded secrets. Differences in Labor party ranks have tended to "leak" or to result in public argument. As one of its leaders has said, ". . . Parliamentary Labor Party meetings were and still are, notoriously liable to leaks; both accurate and inaccurate information about the proceedings finds its way into the press."[29]

Meetings of the PLP take place once a fortnight when the party is in office but about three times during the same period when the party is out of power. Special meetings may also be held. Labor members from the House of Lords may attend PLP meetings, but they have no vote when the leader is chosen.

The PLP has "subject groups" that are similar to the functional committees of the Conservative 1922 Committee. There are some 20 of these, all chaired by back-benchers, with functions similar to their Conservative counterparts. They appear to have had little influence on the formulation of Government policy, and there is no evidence that they have played any significant role.[30]

LABOR PARTY ORGANIZATION OUTSIDE PARLIAMENT

Because of its trade union origins, the Labor party had "what a new party usually lacks, an organization in depth through the trade union system."[31] Most of the party membership is still attained through trade union affiliation. But not all trade-union members are members of the party—only those on whom the union pays a political levy to the party. In 1964, the party had a total membership exceeding 6,000,000, including 1,000,000 individual members, organized into about 600 local constituency parties. A few thousand members are members by virtue of their membership in cooperative and socialist societies which affiliate with the party.

The main functions of the party organization outside Parliament are not too different from those of its Conservative counterpart. They are: (1) to act as a vote-getting agency, and (2) to serve as a "two-way channel of communication between the party in Parliament and its more active supporters in the country."[32] In so far as the organization has an ultimate sanction (refusing to perform the first of the above-mentioned tasks), it possesses some limited power in the selec-

---

[29] Morrison, *op. cit.*, p. 136.
[30] McKenzie, *op. cit.*, p. 447.
[31] Sir Ivor Jennings, *The Queen's Government* (Baltimore: Penguin Books, 1954), p. 64.
[32] McKenzie, *op. cit.*, p. 455.

tion of party leaders and in influencing party policies. But these are minor and subordinate functions, and are no more characteristic of the Labor party than of the Conservative.

Outside Parliament, the highest party authority is the Conference, which meets once a year, although more frequent meetings are possible. Members of the Labor Conference number around 1,200, or less than one third the size of a Conservative Conference. The delegates are selected by constituency party organizations and by the affiliated trade unions. Each constituency party may send one delegate for every 5,000 members or fraction thereof, and each trade union may send one delegate for every 5,000 members on whom affiliation fees have been paid. Members of the Parliamentary Labor Party and prospective parliamentary candidates, as well as members of the National Executive Committee (discussed below), are ex officio members, but they have a vote only if they come as duly chosen delegates.

It is of interest to note that the final speaker in any resolution debate is either a member of the National Executive Committee or a minister, or someone else designated by the NEC. He advises a course of action, and in a very real sense speaks for the leadership. Voting at the Conference is by card, or bloc system; this is customary and not required by the written rules. Each delegation is given a card on which appears the number of votes to which the delegation is entitled. The larger unions have several hundred votes (for example, transport workers have 835), which dwarf the hundreds of cards with one, two or three votes each.

Labor partisans have sought to depict their Conference as a deliberative body which determines party policy, while characterizing the Conservative Conference as a party demonstration. In practice, however, the differences are minor and the similarities remarkable. First of all, the Labor leaders have been in a position either to control the vote of the Conference or to ignore it and act on their own responsibility.[33] Secondly, no proposals can be included in the party program unless adopted by at least a two-thirds majority of the Conference. Thirdly, the Conference declares itself on broad issues, but it is left to the National Executive Committee and to the Parliamentary Labor party to decide what items to include in the election manifesto.

---

[33] This is not to suggest that the leaders of any democratic party can easily ignore the annual assembly of its most militant supporters. It is interesting, however, that for years Labor Conferences passed resolutions supporting the setting up of a Jewish state in Palestine, but when the Labor Government took office in 1945 it tried to ignore these resolutions and sought to promote a unitary state there including both Arabs and Jews.

Perhaps even more important is the bond of mutual confidence which seems to exist between the parliamentary and trade union leadership of the Labor movement. Although there is some dissatisfaction with the bloc system of voting, the union leaders maintain that the present system reflects trade union solidarity. Parliamentary leaders, who are usually the dominant figures at the Conference, are also not anxious to change the existing system. The chief advantage it holds for them is that it is much easier to attempt to satisfy the trade union leaders than to attempt to satisfy the whole membership. The majority of the big unions are traditionally represented by moderate men, whereas the "fanatics, cranks and extremists" seem to be dominant among the delegates from the constituency parties.

It may be, however, that the great trade unions are ceasing to be a moderating influence. At the party conference in 1960, for example, the trade unions succeeded in passing resolutions opposing Britain's continued association with the North Atlantic Treaty Organization (NATO) and her production of nuclear weapons, resolutions which had been opposed by the party leader, Hugh Gaitskell. After the vote had been taken, Gaitskell announced that he would seek to have these resolutions reversed, and was successful in doing so at the 1961 Conference, thereby emerging an even more powerful leader than he had been. But the 1961 Conference adopted a resolution demanding the withdrawal of the American Polaris submarine base from Britain. Again Gaitskell and the PLP refused to be bound by this resolution. And it is significant that upon his election as leader in 1963, Harold Wilson declared that he could not be bound by this resolution because it had not been adopted as Labor policy by the PLP.

Although, in practice, the Labor Conference has held its leaders in just as much awe and pride as has the Conservative Conference, especially when Labor has been in power, two differences need to be noted. First, the Labor leader reports to the Conference on the work of the party in Parliament, instead of simply addressing the delegates after they adjourn, as is characteristic of the Conservative Conference. Secondly, the professional organization of the Labor party is responsible, through the National Executive Committee, to the Conference, while the "civil service" of the Conservative party is responsible to the leader alone.

The Labor party organization at the constituency level is more complicated than its Conservative counterpart. This is due to the existence of two types of membership—individual and affiliated organizations. Fairly definite rules, laid down by the national office, govern the functioning of the local organizations, which are subject to more central control than is true of Conservative constituency parties.

Individual members of the party do not meet as a group at the constituency level. They do meet at the ward level about once a month, but the proportion of the membership that is continually active falls below five per cent. Some surveys indicate that these are persons of extreme views on public policy, while other studies indicate that ward parties are more social than political, especially in districts where the party is assured a majority.

At the constituency level, delegates from ward committees and from the affiliated organizations (mostly trade unions) constitute the General Management Committee and are in control of party organization affairs. There is a proviso, however, that members of affiliated organizations may not take an active part in the affairs of the constituency organization unless they are also individual members of the party organization at the ward level. As this suggests, members of affiliated organizations are eligible for individual membership in the party at the ward level but this, of course, entails the payment of additional dues. Although such membership is not obligatory, the reverse is true of an individual member, who is required, if eligible, to belong to a trade union affiliated with the Trades Union Congress, but many local parties do not enforce this rule. Constituency parties are supposed to apply annually for a renewal of their affiliation with the national party, but this proviso is likewise not enforced.

The General Management Committee meets annually. It selects persons to serve on its various committees, the most important of which is the executive committee, which usually meets once a month. Persons named to the executive committee must be members of the General Management Committee. If the General Management Committee is small, it may act as the executive committee. If the constituency employs a party agent, he normally becomes the secretary. Often he is the most important official in the constituency, for he is encouraged to think of himself as "the managing director of the party," although reminded that he is not a dictator. Ideally, he is supposed to be a disinterested servant of the party in its various activities. The recruitment and training of constituency agents has been emphasized by both parties in recent years.

One of the functions of the constituency organization, as in the Conservative party, is the selection of parliamentary candidates, although national organs of the Labor party perhaps play a more prominent role than the Conservative national offices in this process. The National Executive Committee may take the initiative in proposing candidates, although the constituency executive committee, a ward committee, or an affiliated organization also may do so. Unlike Conservative practice, individuals who aspire to become Labor candidates cannot, except privately, suggest their own names. Before the executive committee submits names to the General Management Committee (usually convened in special session), it may have interviewed the different prospective candidates and it will have consulted with the NEC "to determine the validity of the nominations received." Although interference from the national office is limited, and in most cases resented, party rules do require that the selection of a prospective parliamentary candidate "shall not be regarded as completed until the name of the member selected has been placed before a meeting of the National Executive Committee, and his or her selection has been duly endorsed." Until that endorsement is received, the constituency party is not permitted to introduce the candidate to the public. Once a person is selected as a candidate he need not test his strength against other potential candidates when the next election rolls around, for readoption is virtually automatic.

Labor rules permit larger personal financial contributions to the constituency party by members of the Commons or prospective candidates than is the case in the Conservative party. The maximum permitted is £250 in the boroughs and £300 in the counties. Trade union nominees often have an advantage in being selected as candidates because the union will pay a large part of the election expenses. Of the total expenditure in the constituency which the law permits, unions may contribute up to 80 per cent.

The National Executive Committee, subject to guidance from the annual Conference, is responsible for the work of the party outside Parliament. It not only supervises party work at all levels but also has the responsibility of enforcing the party's constitution, rules, and standing orders. It has the power to expel a Labor M.P. from the party and, should the constituency organization stand by him, it has the power to disaffiliate it from the national party. The NEC reports on its work to the Conference and submits to it such resolutions and declarations as it believes are called for by political circumstances. In almost every case of disciplinary action, the NEC has been upheld by the subsequent party Conference.

The 28 members of the NEC are selected by the Conference. Actually, 12 members are nominated by the trade unions and elected by their delegations to the Conference. Socialist and cooperative organizations affiliated with the party select one member. Seven members are nominated and elected by the constituency and other local subdivisions of the party. Five women members are elected by the whole Conference from among those nominated by affiliated organizations; the trade unions are in a position to choose all five of these. The same is true of the treasurer of the party, who is nominated by affiliated organizations and elected by the whole Conference. The leader and deputy leader of the party are ex officio members.

The trade unions are therefore in a position to select 18 of the 28 members on the National Executive Committee. In practice, especially in recent years, the tendency has been for the Parliamentary Labor Party to have a majority on the NEC. The preponderance of members and ex-members of Parliament on the NEC and its committees for a time seemed to guarantee that the views of the NEC would not be at variance with those of the majority of the Parliamentary Labor Party. Moreover, the latter's leaders were usually able to rely on trade union member support in the NEC, especially against disaffected minorities. This was true in part because the more powerful union leaders have preferred to serve on the General Council of the Trades Union Congress rather than on the NEC, making it easier for the party's Parliamentary leaders to influence the less powerful trade union representatives on the NEC.

As result of the struggles over party policies in the 1950s, however, "the presence of a majority of M.P.s on the NEC no longer in itself operated as a factor tending to insure that the NEC's views conformed to those of the Parliamentary leaders."[34] And although the Parliamentary leaders have remained in effective control, "the *public* struggle to retain that control has sometimes given the impression that the party was about to lapse into anarchy."[35]

Through the NEC, the leaders of the party in Parliament have for the most part been able to advise the Conference as to what it should advise them to do, although the Conference has often been reminded that its resolutions and declarations are advisory. There is a provision in party rules for periodic consultations between the PLP and the NEC, but in practice the latter has no authority over the actions in Parliament of the party's ministers or its other members.

The party's professional staff operates under the NEC and its

---

[34] See McKenzie's revised edition of his *British Political Parties* (New York: Frederick A. Praeger, Publisher, 1963), p. 595ff.

[35] *Ibid.*, p. 605. Italics are his.

subcommittees. Its activities are not unlike those of the Conservative professional organization. The Labor head office, popularly known as Transport House, is located in London. Unlike the Conservative central office, Transport House is not the personal machine of the party leader. It is the servant of the Conference and of the NEC. Since the parliamentary leaders of the party have generally played a dominant role in the NEC, and consequently in the Conference, this distinction has not been too meaningful. In practice, for the most part, the head office and its regional offices have served the purposes of the leader and his colleagues in Parliament.

PARLIAMENTARY ELECTIONS

British elections are in some ways similar to and in other ways strikingly different from our own elections. The basic similarity is to be found in that they are democratic. There is freedom of speech and press; candidates campaign freely and openly. There is a two-party system. Virtually everyone can vote, and voting is secret. Candidates must meet certain qualifications, and there are laws forbidding corrupt practices. The dissimilarities are to be found mainly in the nominating process and in the differences that characterize electoral practices and campaigns.

It has been argued that British elections, more than any other, embody the notion of a "mandate," that is, that the victorious party is expected to carry out the program it had put before the voters and that it should not depart from it in any important respect. While the concept may appear vague at times, there is a general belief that the policies and approaches of a new cabinet may be predicted on the basis of the election results and the program that had been presented to the electorate. It is obvious, however, that circumstances may change and with them the relative importance of issues. Consequently, a cabinet may feel less bound by the mandate and may in certain circumstances even depart from it. Hence, while the doctrine of the mandate is important, it is neither a blueprint nor a straitjacket under all circumstances.

PARTY CONTROL OF NOMINATIONS

The nominating of party candidates for seats in the House of Commons is, as indicated earlier in this chapter, largely in the hands of party organizations at the constituency level. There are no national or state nominating conventions. And there are no primary elections.

Only the person selected by the respective party organization has the right to call himself a candidate of that party. An individual may become a candidate as an independent but his chances of election are virtually nil. Occasionally a member of the Commons leaves his party and crosses the floor to join a party on the other side or to remain an independent member, but in doing so, he must be aware that his political future is dark indeed. Historical proof of this is to be found in the fact that since 1945 no member of the Commons who crossed over to the opposition benches has been re-elected.

While nominations are party affairs, there are laws which impose legal limits on what parties can do. First of all, certain classes of persons are not eligible for nomination. Among these are judges of the High Court and the Court of Appeal, ordained priests or deacons of the Church of England, ministers of the Church of Scotland and priests of the Roman Catholic Church, persons holding an office of profit under or from the crown, persons convicted of treason or felony, and those found guilty of corrupt or illegal practices in connection with elections.[36] There is no requirement, however, that a candidate be a resident of the constituency. Secondly, certain formalities need to be complied with. These include a nomination paper signed by at least ten persons, consent of the candidate, and a deposit of £150 (about $420), which is returned if the candidate polls at least one eighth of the total vote cast. The requirements of a monetary deposit effectively discourages nonserious candidates and helps to preserve a two-party system.[37]

SOME ELECTORAL PRACTICES

Aside from the established rules mentioned above, some other electoral practices deserve attention. One of these is the time of election which, contrary to American practice, does not occur on some fixed day of a certain month in a pre-determined year. Aside from the fact that an election must take place at least once every five years, although even this may be altered by Parliament in times of great crises (such as war), a British election may come at any time. The time is by and large determined by the party in power, whose leader "advises" dissolution of Parliament. The election of a new Parliament takes place within a month after the dissolution of the old one.

---

[36] The disability in connection with the last category extends for five years, and the holding of an office of profit under the crown no longer applies to members of the armed forces. Minors, lunatics, and aliens are, of course, also excluded.

[37] In 1964, deposits were forfeited by 187 candidates. Fifty-three of them were Liberals, while only five Conservatives and eight Laborites lost theirs.

Also at variance with United States usage is the practice of government officials in Britian assuming the responsibility of getting voters registered. This is done once a year, usually in a house-to-house canvass. This list of registered voters is posted on bulletin boards in public buildings or other public places. Any person who is not on the list, and believes he should be, may protest to the registration officer and, if the decision is not to his satisfaction, may appeal to the county court. Similarly, any person may protest the inclusion of persons he considers ineligible. The British approach to registration serves to produce a larger percentage of qualified voters than is to be found in the United States, but it alone does not explain the fact that in recent British elections more than 80 per cent of the qualified voters went to the polls.

Voting in British national elections is simple and easy—no long ballots, no multiple offices to be filled, and no propositions to vote on. The voter's task is to choose a candidate to represent the constituency in the House of Commons. The ballot is hardly larger than an ordinary envelope. It contains only the names of the candidates (in alphabetical order), their addresses, and their vocations. No party designations are used on the ballot, but the voters are aware of the party affiliations of the candidates.

The counting of the ballots is different from the procedure employed in the United States. All the ballot boxes in each constituency are brought to a central place. After the seals have been examined, the total number of ballots in each box is ascertained. Then the ballots from all the boxes in the constituency are dumped together and subsequently sorted into piles according to the candidates for whom they are marked. Consequently, no candidate knows how he did at any particular polling place. Moreover, no public announcement of the count is made until the counting has been completed, hence there is no custom of conceding elections. The person receiving the highest number of votes is elected. Should there be a tie, the winner is determined by lot.

CAMPAIGNS

In contrast with American campaigns, which go on for months, British campaigns are brief, lasting no longer than three weeks. It should be pointed out, however, that important parliamentary debates are nearly always in the nature of a campaign. This is particularly true as the Parliament's legal limit of five years is approached and new elections are near at hand. Sometimes, when the cabinet is beset with difficulties, such as too small a majority or factional struggles, an early election becomes a safe forecast. In such circumstances, virtually every occurrence in Parliament is part and parcel of the forthcoming political struggle.

British campaigns are more limited than American ones in other ways besides length. The principal limitation which Americans would notice concerns radio and television. The government-owned British Broadcasting Corporation (TV and Radio), as well as the Independent Television Authority, seek to make a fair division in the time available among the parties which have put a certain number of candidates (50 in 1964) in the field. In the 1964 campaign this resulted in the Conservative and Labor parties getting four TV broadcasts each (two of 15-minute, one of 20-minute, and one of 25-

RESULTS OF THE LAST SIX GENERAL ELECTIONS IN GREAT BRITAIN
IN HOUSE OF COMMON SEATS ACCORDING TO POLITICAL PARTY

	1945	1950	1951	1955	1959	1964
Conservative	213	297	321	345	365	304
Labor	393	315	295	277	258	317
Liberal	12	9	6	6	6	9
Other	22	4	3	2	1	0

RESULTS IN PERCENTAGE OF THE POPULAR VOTE

	1945	1950	1951	1955	1959	1964
Conservative	39.9	41.7	48	49.8	49.4	43.4
Labor	48	46.4	48.8	46.4	43.9	44.1
Liberal	9	9.1	2.5	2.7	5.8	11.2
Other	3.1	2.8	.7	1.1	.9	1.3

minute duration). In addition, they were allotted four ten-minute and three five-minute radio broadcasts. The Liberal party was allotted one TV broadcast of twenty-five minutes and two radio broadcasts (ten and five minutes). In addition, the major parties are allotted a certain amount of broadcast time each year. To the extent that they do not utilize this time, they may employ it during the formal campaign and thus have additional broadcasts. Only in the last two national campaigns have the broadcast services reported on the activities and utterances of candidates.

Newspapers, however, report fully on campaign activities, although political advertising in them is not common. If a voter wants to see a candidate and to hear him in person, he must attend one or more of the large number of small local meeings or the few large rallies. Although usually not seen or heard via radio or TV, the candidate for the House of Commons is seen and heard in person by large numbers of his constituents.

Aside from the time made available to the parties on radio and television, each candidate is permitted to use the mails free of charge to send to each registered voter a copy of his "election address." This is in the form of a letter which sets forth his stand on issues that are before the voters.

CAMPAIGN EXPENDITURES AND CORRUPT PRACTICES

Each candidate must appoint an election agent (campaign manager) who is required by law to handle and account for *all* election campaign expenses, except the personal expenses of the candidate himself.[38] No one except the candidate, the election agent, or persons authorized by the latter in writing can spend money in an effort to get a candidate elected or another one defeated. The courts have ruled that general political propaganda does not come under this limitation. But any unauthorized expenditure on behalf of a particular candidate (or against his opponent) for a particular constituency is prohibited. Expenditures between elections are not covered by the corrupt practices acts.

In addition to this restriction, there is an upper limit on the amount of money which may be spent. Each candidate may spend up to £450 (about $1,260), plus 1¾ cents for each elector on the register in urban areas and 2⅓ cents for each elector in rural constituencies. In addition, each candidate is allowed to spend $280 for his personal expenses, including travel and hotels, of which he must give an accounting. There is no limit, however, on the amount of money spent by the national party organizations in publicizing party policies and pleading for party victory. But individual candidates may not be backed in the process. Consequently, even the name of the party leader can not be mentioned in such publicity.[39]

Moreover, many campaign methods which Americans regard as more or less innocent are prohibited in England. Treating, for example, is forbidden. A candidate cannot (for the duration of the campaign) buy a round of drinks at the local pub, nor can he treat a friend to a lunch. Candidates who live in a hotel during a campaign usually refrain from tipping, lest this be interpreted as an attempt to

---

[38] Should a candidate knowingly and personally appoint as his election agent a person guilty of corrupt practices, the election of such a candidate would be invalid.

[39] Following the general election in October 1959, however, there were charges of legal and illegal evasion of the limits on election expenses by both of the major parties. These charges were accompanied by pleas for revising the limits upward so as to meet the increased costs of conducting campaigns. In the general election of 1964 there were virtually no cases of charges concerning election expenses.

buy a vote. Candidates may not dress their supporters in uniform, nor may they hire bands to attract a crowd for a street corner meeting. The number of motor vehicles used to transport voters to the polls is limited to one for every 1,500 registered voters in a county constituency and one for every 2,500 in an urban district. All such conveyances must be registered with the appropriate election official. A voter may use his automobile to take himself and members of his household to the polls, but he cannot take a friend, unless his is one of the registered vehicles.

A violation of one or more of the legal limitations on electoral campaigns is sufficient to invalidate the election of the candidate involved. Despite the various limitations, however, British political campaigns are vigorous affairs.

The two major parties finance their campaigns in somewhat different ways. In the Labor party, the chief source of campaign funds is the accumulation of affiliation fees which trade unions pay annually on their members.[40] In an election year the trade unions provide additional funds in the form of special contributions. In the Conservative party, by their own admission, the bulk of their campaign funds (until recently) came from a few hundred people. More recently, however, they have sought to broaden the base from which party funds are solicited.

INTEREST GROUPS

In the United States we are accustomed to witnessing various special interests plead their cases before congressional committees and before individual congressmen. Although they have received little attention, British pressure groups "are numerous, massive, well organized, and highly effective."[41] The objects of their attention, as well as the tactics they employ, differ somewhat from those we are accustomed to observing in the United States.

First of all, British pressure groups would find their efforts unrewarding if they were to center their activities around committees or individual members of the Commons. As indicated earlier in this chapter, Commons committees do not possess powers comparable to

---

[40] Trade unions are not obligated to contribute for their members who have "contracted out," that is, signed a slip of paper refusing to pay.

[41] This is the conclusion of a recent and highly useful study by Professor Samuel H. Beer, "Pressure Groups and Parties in Britain," *op. cit.* Also see his "The Representation of Interests in British Government: Historical Background," *The American Political Science Review*, Vol. 51 (September, 1957), pp. 613–50.

those exercised by our congressional committees. Moreover, due to the party discipline which the cabinet can enforce, the individual member of the Commons is not apt to have his vote changed as a result of pressure group activity. If they are to be effective, therefore, British pressure groups must seek to exert their influence on those having the power of making decisions.

Since only the Government has a majority, special interests seek to persuade it that what is desired is not contrary to the national interest. Their approach is twofold. If new legislation is the object, they will attempt to convince the minister of the appropriate department. If money is involved, it is imperative that the Chancellor of the Exchequer also be convinced, for proposals to spend money require recommendations from the Crown. The Chancellor keeps the "pork barrel" locked and those who would dip in it must prove that the expenditure of public funds for their benefit would also be for the benefit of the nation. If, on the other hand, the object is not new legislation but a more favorable interpretation of administrative regulations, efforts will be made to convince the appropriate agency or department that it is in the national interest to amend them. If the proposed change would result in decreased revenue, the Chancellor of the Exchequer will expect to be consulted.

Although pressure groups do not attempt to win over individual members of the Commons, they do seek to exert their influence in the selection (nomination) of candidates by the respective parties. In other words, they strive to get their interests represented in Parliament and then hope that that person (or persons) will be a persuasive spokesman for them in the counsels of the Government. Of course, the cabinet must decide how important are the pleas of its individual supporters for a particular legislative or administrative policy, and the cabinet must think first of the national interest of the country and of the party, and only secondarily of the interest of individual groups.

The Government, for its part, generally makes it a practice of consulting with group interests. Before major bills are introduced, for example, the interests concerned are given an opportunity to state their case. Similarly, when administrative authorities must draw up new regulations, these are usually submitted in draft form to the special interests concerned for their comments and criticism. Local authorities are likewise consulted on local government legislation. From time to time, royal commissions or departmental committees are set up to study a problem and to submit recommendations. Outside interests are usually well represented on such bodies. Moreover, some departments have permanent advisory committees, where special interests are similarly represented on a continuing basis.

The increasingly close association between the Government and interest groups has been augmented by the general acceptance in Britain of the welfare state and a controlled economy. Because of this acceptance, governmental authorities are making decisions having a wide impact upon various sectors of the economy, and pressure groups are more and more concerned with these decisions at the administrative level, for the battle on the legislative plain has been fought and decided. Some opportunities for discretion in the making of rules and regulations still exist at the administrative level. Pressure groups continue to exert influence and to share in this administrative decision making. "The main substance of this system is continued, day-to-day contacts between public bureaucrats in the government departments and private bureaucrats in the offices of the great pressure groups. . . ."[42]

BIBLIOGRAPHICAL NOTE

Perhaps the outstanding work on the British party system is R. T. Mc-Kenzie, *British Political Parties: The Distribution of Power Within the Conservative and Labour Parties* (2nd ed., New York: Praeger, 1964). Also quite useful are *Political Parties and the Party System in Great Britain*, edited by Sidney Bailey (New York: Frederick A. Praeger, Inc., 1952); Ivor Bulmer-Thomas, *The Party System in Great Britain* (New York: The Macmillan Co., 1953); and Edgar R. Pike, *Political Parties and Policies* (3d ed.; London: Pitman, 1950). More historical, but excellent is Sir Ivor Jennings, *Party Politics*, 3 vols. (Cambridge: Cambridge University Press, 1960, 1961 & 1962).

Two specialized recent studies deserve mention: Samuel H. Beer, *British Politics in the Collectivist Age* (New York: Random House, 1965); W. L. Guttsman, *The British Political Elite* (London: MacGibbon & Kee, 1963).

Insight into the organization and practices of the Conservative Party may be found in Nigel Birch, *The Conservative Party* (London: Collins, 1949); Anthony Eden, *Days for Decision* (London: Houghton Mifflin, 1950); and Timothy Raison, *Why Conservative?* (Baltimore: Penguin Books, 1964).

In the voluminous literature of the Labor Party, some of the more informative works are Clement R. Attlee, *The Labour Party in Perspective—And Twelve Years Later* (London: Longmans, Green, 1949); G. D. H. Cole, *A History of the Labour Party from 1914* (London: Routledge and Kegan Paul, 1948); Jim Northcott, *Why Labour?* (Baltimore: Penguin Books, 1964); Henry Pelling, *The Origins of the Labour Party* (New York: St. Martin's

---

[42] Samuel H. Beer, "Pressure Groups and Parties in Britain," *ibid.*, p. 7.

Press, 1954) ; Philip P. Poirier, *The Advent of the British Labour Party* (New York: Columbia University Press, 1958) ; and F. H. Stewart Reid, *The Origins of the Labour Party* (Minneapolis: University of Minnesota Press, 1955).

Also useful is the special number of the *Political Quarterly* (London, 1960), devoted to the Labor party.

The rapidly increasing number of studies of British elections includes those of Joseph Baker, *The Law and Practice of Parliamentary Elections* (London: Just, 1940) ; John Bonham, *The British General Election of 1955* (New York: The Macmillan Co., 1956) ; David E. Butler, *The British General Election of 1955* (London: The Macmillan Co., 1955) ; ——, *The British General Election of 1959* (London: Macmillan, 1959) ; and R. B. McCallum, and Alison Readman, *The British General Election of 1945* (London: Oxford University Press, 1947).

Among the numerous studies of pressure politics in Great Britain, especially informative are S. E. Finer, *Anonymous Empire: A Study of the Lobby in Great Britain* (London: The Pall Mall Press, Ltd., 1958) ; Allen Potter, *Organized Groups in British National Politics* (London: Faber & Faber, 1962) ; and J. D. Stewart, *British Pressure Groups: Their Role in Relation to the House of Commons* (Oxford: Clarendon Press, 1958). Other studies of a specialized nature include P. A. Bromhead, *Private Members' Bills in the British Parliament* (London: Routledge and Kegan Paul, 1956) and William B. Gwyn, *Democracy and the Cost of Politics in Britain* (London: Athlone Press, 1962).

CHAPTER 6

NATIONAL ADMINISTRATION

IT IS axiomatic that legislative enactments require the services of countless persons in order that their intent be accomplished. To the work of this collective body of persons, political scientists have applied the term "public administration," although the terms "civil service" and "bureaucracy" are frequently used as synonyms. A knowledge of the nature of administration and its place in the political process is therefore a prerequisite to an understanding of the government of any particular country. This requires, among other things, a familiarity with the organization of the bureaucracy, the powers it wields, and the functions it performs, as well as its relationship to the public and to the policy-making branch or branches of government. An appreciation of the role of public administration should be of more than passing interest to the average citizen, for it is here that he experiences his most intimate contact with government.

With the expansion of governmental activities in recent decades, especially in the economic and social fields, the impact of the bureaucracy on everyday life has increasingly been felt. The programs which provide old-age assistance, help to farmers, unemployment benefits to workers, credit to businessmen, etc.—all call for a larger, increasingly complex, and a more expensive public service. The net result very often is to make more difficult the application of the yardsticks of good administration—efficiency and responsibility. For the British, the situation has been further complicated by the nationalization and subsequent government operation of several industries.

In this chapter our discussion will, in the main, center on the organization and operation of the administrative apparatus at the national level. Because the management of the nationalized industries is through public corporations, operating under the direction of specific ministries, they will be accorded separate treatment. But it must not be forgotten that the ultimate responsibility for the way a nationalized industry functions rests with the minister under whose department it falls.

ORGANIZATION OF THE ADMINISTRATION

The principal activities of the British government are carried out through some 30 ministries, whose heads are responsible to the House of Commons. These ministries developed gradually as the need for the performance of certain functions became publicly recognized, in much the same way as the departments in our government came into being. The organization of British ministries is fairly uniform,[1] although terminology is sometimes different. The arrangement of ministries is hierarchical, with various divisions and subdivisons fanning out from the top. Each ministry is staffed from top to bottom by permanent civil servants, with the permanent secretary at the top. Superimposed over these, and giving direction to the department, are the political appointees—the minister and two or three associates. The minister (in some ministries the title is secretary of state) serves at the pleasure of the prime minister, which is also true of his associates, who are selected by the prime minister in consultation with the minister. The Treasury now has two ministers of cabinet rank (the Chancellor of the Exchequer and the Chief Secretary of the Treasury and Paymaster General).

POLITICAL HEADS OF DEPARTMENTS AND THEIR ASSOCIATES

Policy and administration fuse at the ministerial level in Britain. The minister, as a member of Parliament and as a member of the prime minister's executive family, is at once a policy maker and an administrator. In other words, he is only a part-time administrator, but responsible nevertheless. Much of his time must be spent in the House, where he listens to and makes speeches. Moreover, he must keep in touch with the voters, attend party conferences, and take part in party propaganda. He must take part in various functions and be accessible to the politically important. If he heads one of the ministries that is normally represented in the cabinet, he spends some time in its meetings.[2]

---

[1] For an excellent treatment of British administration, see W. J. M. Mackenzie and J. W. Grove, *Central Administration in Britain* (London: Longmans, Green, 1957). Also see Sir Ivor Jennings, *Cabinet Government* (2d ed.; Cambridge: Cambridge University Press, 1951), chaps. iv, v and Appendix III.

[2] Herbert Morrison reports that his work day ranged between 15 and 18 hours. He got to bed between 1 and 2 A.M. as minister of supply and about 3 A.M. when he headed the Foreign Office, in each case arising about 8 A.M. *Government and Parliament* (London: Oxford University Press, 1954), pp. 62–63, 117.

The minister has a parliamentary secretary to assist him, and in some of the larger departments there is also a minister of state (in some cases more than one), to whom some phase of administrative activity is delegated by the minister. In practice, the minister of state occupies a position somewhat higher than the parliamentary secretary, since he is vested with discretionary powers beyond those considered appropriate for the parliamentary secretary. In the case of a department whose head is referred to as secretary of state, instead of minister, the "parliamentary secretary" is known as the "parliamentary undersecretary of state."

Like their chiefs, parliamentary secretaries are members of the majority party and members of either the Commons or Lords. In those instances where the minister is in the Lords, it is imperative that the parliamentary secretary be in the Commons, for it is there that the crucial defense of departmental policies must take place. By relieving the minister of his less important duties and by learning the business of government departments, parliamentary secretaries qualify themselves for future ministerial positions. It should be remembered, however, that parliamentary secretaries do not determine policy without reference to their chiefs.[3] They cannot, for example, override the opinions of permanent civil servants, but must refer such cases to their ministers.

The minister is also assisted by his parliamentary private secretary. He is a member of the Commons who performs a variety of duties for the minister, although he gets no additional pay. He is expected to know the temper of the House. He conveys the minister's views to the party's back-bench supporters and their grievances to the minister.

The minister alone is responsible to the House of Commons for what happens in his department; he takes the credit as well as the blame. The British operate on the principle of protecting the civil servant, for if he should be subject to questioning by committees of the Commons or other bodies, the minister could not expect faithful services and absolute loyalty from him. The names of the top civil servants are not even known except to an exceedingly small group of people. The British do not believe that the civil servant should be dragged into the political arena, nor do they believe that his prestige and influence should be subjected to the hazards of popular prejudice. These are the occupational risks of the politician and not of the expert administrative official.

---

[3] Parliamentary secretaries are not ministers of the crown and there is some question as to whether ministers of state are. See *ibid.*, p. 57ff.

Inside the department, the minister "will no doubt criticize whoever is responsible" for mistakes "but publicly he must accept responsibility as if the act were his own." It would be in order, however, for him to explain to Parliament that something went wrong in the department, that he apologizes for it, and that he has taken steps to prevent the recurrence of such a mistake in the future.[4]

Rarely is responsibility for bad administration pinned on particular officials. The best known recent case is the Crichel Down affair of 1954, where serious complaints were lodged against civil servants who had not given proper attention to the claims of a landowner for the return of land taken earlier under emergency powers. The minister of agriculture, who was not personally to blame, ordered a public inquiry, during which departmental files were made available, bad administration was demonstrated and responsibility fixed on specific officials. Yet no civil servant lost his job (although some rearrangement of duties resulted), but the minister resigned. And while the public revelations may have had a salutory effect on the civil service, the case seemed to prove that misconduct on the part of a civil servant was more likely to lead to the minister's downfall than his own.

What has been said above suggests that a minister ought to possess a combination of qualifications. He must be honest and incorruptible, and must appear to possess these qualities. Since he makes all major decisions of principle or refers them to the cabinet, he must be competent. He is responsible for the administration of his department both to the cabinet and to Parliament. This signifies that he ought to have had parliamentary experience which is clearly essential in the case of the more important ministries. As a general rule, a person who becomes a minister has already had departmental experience, which would be unusual in the case of members of the president's cabinet in the United States. If a minister is to reach the top, however, all of his qualifications will not get him there if his party colleagues in the Commons do not believe that he is the man for the job.

PERMANENT SECRETARIES

The permanent secretary of a ministry is in actuality the administrative chief of the department. In departments whose heads are known as secretaries of state, the "permanent secretary" is known as

---

[4] Morrison, *ibid.*, pp. 320–24. Morrison reports how three years went by, when he was home secretary, before it was discovered that certain regulations had not been laid before Parliament. Morrison forgot, the department forgot, neither house had noticed the failure, and the press had not spotted it. This was embarrassing to Morrison, but he was completely frank with Parliament.

the "permanent undersecretary of state." He is responsible for the general organization and efficiency of the ministry, and for the advice which he gives to the minister on behalf of the permanent civil service of the department. In recent times, the permanent secretary has also become the department's accounting officer. The Treasury now has two permanent secretaries, one being concerned with general administration and the other with economic and financial matters.

On many matters the minister deals directly with the undersecretaries or assistant secretaries of the department. For the most part, however, he works with his principal private secretary (usually a promising young man on his way up in the department) and with the permanent secretary. The former is a delicate and important office, calling for discretion in the shielding of the minister from unnecessary engagements and needless paper work. Simultaneously, he should be close to the permanent secretary and see to it that a continuous link is maintained between the minister and the permanent secretary.

Although the permanent secretary is not a politician, he should know enough about politics to avoid blunders as well as to help his chief from committing them.[5] In those rare instances where the minister and the permanent secretary cannot get along personally, the latter is usually moved to a corresponding position in another ministry. That this happens so rarely is a real tribute to the British system.

MINISTER AND THE CIVIL SERVICE

The number of civil servants with whom the minister is in actual contact is few. These normally include the permanent secretary, the deputy secretaries, one or more under secretaries, the minister's private secretary, and the legal adviser. The legal adviser, whose post is of first-rate importance, is in a position to know more about the day-to-day activities of the department than anyone, except possibly the permanent secretary. Civil servants below the grade of those named above carry out instructions given by others, although many of them, through their chiefs, have a hand in shaping those instructions. But only the top officials are in a position to exercise a real and direct influence on important policy matters.

These top advisers are from the departments. They are trusted and

---

[5] Morrison, *ibid.*, pp. 312–13. Sir William Harcourt has said that the "value of the political heads of departments is to tell the permanent officials what the public will not stand." (*Life of Sir William Harcourt*, II, p. 587.)

loyal servants of each succeeding minister. This is in sharp contrast to American and French practice; in the former there is a large turnover in top posts, while in the latter the minister brings in a personal cabinet of trusted advisers to protect him from the civil servants.

When the Labor party came to power in 1945, many of its adherents were fearful lest an unsympathetic civil service sabotage the party's nationalization program. These fears were ill founded, and disappeared with experience. One of the Labor ministers of that day has said that his general experience led him to conclude that if the minister "knows what he wants and is intelligent in going about it, he can command the understanding cooperation and support of his civil servants."[6] Moreover, "in my experience our civil service generally prefers a minister with a mind of his own to a mere rubber stamp."[7]

The dedication and loyalty of British civil servants to their respective ministers is best illustrated by the following apocryphal question of a civil servant to his minister: "Well, sir, if you are bound to do a deuced silly thing, must you do it in a deuced silly way?" And he then proceeded to advise the minister how best to carry out a policy of which he strongly disapproved. A good civil servant will study the minister's habits of work if he is to be of maximum help to him. Some ministers like to read and to study matters for themselves, while others prefer digests and interpretation. Some will concentrate better on essentials, while others will be masters of detail.

THE PERMANENT CIVIL SERVICE

THE CIVIL SERVICE AND ITS RECRUITMENT

The British civil service today combines most of the characteristics (for example, ability, integrity, selection on the basis of merit, efficiency) associated with a good bureaucracy. Scarcely more than 100 years ago it could properly be described as a spoils system. Patronage as a qualification for holding appointive office began to disappear in the 19th century largely as the result of the administrative reforms of some of the great prime ministers, Pitt, Peel and Gladstone.[8] The British Civil Service Commission was established in

---

[6] Morrison, *op. cit.*, p. 311. Also, see ex-Prime Minister Attlee's chapter in William A. Robson, *The Civil Service in Britain and France* (New York: The Macmillan Co., 1956).

[7] Morrison, *op. cit.*, p. 317. Similar views are voiced by Attlee, *op. cit.*

[8] It has been suggested that the American spoils system has been more difficult to eradicate, in part because it grew up side by side with popular participation in government. In Britain, on the other hand, the wide extension of the suffrage came *after* the merit system was well on its way.

1855. From 1870 to the present, most vacancies in the public service have been filled on the basis of merit—through competitive examinations.

The civil service is conveniently divided into five classes. At the top is the Administrative Class, a relatively small group of some 3,500 persons who staff the most important positions in the various departments. About 100 new appointments are made to this class annually, although in recent years the number of acceptable candidates has not always been sufficient to meet the demand. Next is the Executive Class of some 60,000 officials who occupy positions of considerable responsibility but not of the same order as those in the Administrative Class. Third in the administrative hierarchy is the Clerical Class, which is large and important, and which is divided into two grades—clerical officer and higher clerical officer. A fourth class, the Clerical Assistants, is reserved to women, as is the fifth class, the Typist Class. The foreign service falls in a separate category.

Recruitment for each class is by competitive examination, the most severe of which is the one for those who aspire to the Administrative Class. There are age and educational requirements which must be met before one is permitted to take an examination. In the case of the Administrative Class, the age span is between 20½ and 24. Moreover, appointments to this class provide for a two-year probationary period, after which candidates must pass a central board conducted by the civil service commissioners. The age groups from which recruitment to the next three classes takes place are 17½–18½, 16½–17½, and 15–16, respectively. Considerable variation from these age requirements is permitted to ex-service personnel. In the case of the Typist Class the entrance ages range from 18 to 33.

As the above suggests, the British recruit for the civil service on the basis of ability and not on the basis of preparation and training for a specific job. With minor exceptions, recruitment to the federal civil service in the United States is based on the latter—that is, training and experience for the specific job to be filled. The British believe that it is more important to channel the best minds into the Administrative Class at the outset. There they can be taught the specific requirements of the position and allowed to advance as rapidly as their industry and talents permit. Similarly, they emphasize ability, as opposed to training for a specific job, in recruitment for all but the Typist Class.

The examinations are mostly written, although interviews have become more important in recent years, especially for the Administrative Class. The written examination tests a candidate's general knowledge, his proficiency in English, and his knowledge of two or three academic subjects which he chooses from a large number of alternatives. The written part of the examination is the most important, although the importance of the interview increases as one goes up the administrative pyramid.

A slightly modified method for recruitment to the Administrative Class was inaugurated on an experimental basis after World War II. This method requires a "full course of study for an honors degree at a recognized university," with the candidate obtaining at least second-class honors. Such candidates are given written examinations, which require the writing of papers designed to test knowledge of English, general information, reasoning power, capacity to distinguish the important from the less important, and the quality of being able to perceive implications. A general intelligence test is also given. Following this, the Civil Service Selection Board provides an opportunity for observation and informal testing of the candidate over a period of two or three days. At the outset of the experiment candidates were assembled to live together in a house in the country for a few days. This came to be known as the "country house" or "week-end" test. This is now done in London, and in some instances is replaced by an interview.

TREASURY CONTROL

The civil service is controlled by the Treasury, under the direction of the prime minister, who is its First Lord. The prime minister's consent is necessary "for the appointment of permanent heads of departments, their deputies, principal financial officers, and principal establishment officers."[9] This means, in a sense, that the Treasury has two important outposts in every large department.[10] The one is financial, which is responsible for regularity in accounting and in scrutinizing proposals for new expenditures. The other, the principal establishment officer, is responsible for office organization and for matters affecting the staff which may develop anywhere in the ministry.[11] Both the principal financial officer and the principal establishment officer work closely with their opposite numbers in the Treasury.

---

[9] Royal Commission on the Civil Service (1929), *Minutes of Evidence*, p. 1269.

[10] A former permanent secretary of the Board of Trade argues, however, that each department is more a master in its own house than my statement implies. See William A. Robson (ed.), *The Civil Service in Britain and France* (New York: The Macmillan Co., 1956), p. 109ff.

[11] A minister must have Treasury approval for appointments and dismissals in the two top grades of the civil service.

The Treasury exercises powers similar to those exercised in the United States by the Civil Service Commission and the Bureau of the Budget. It reviews budget estimates, issues general regulations with respect to the civil service as a whole, supervises the work of the Civil Service Commission, and gives day-to-day advice to departmental establishments officers with respect to the problems confronting them.

The Treasury also exercises an accounting control. It designates an "accounting officer" in each department, usually the chief financial officer or the permanent secretary. He is responsible, through the minister, to Parliament for departmental expenditures. Moreover, he is personally and pecuniarily liable to the Treasury for unauthorized or irregular expenditures unless he has protested to the minister in writing and has received authority from the minister to incur such expenditures.

From the foregoing it is evident that most other departments stand in a somewhat inferior position to that of the Treasury. While the control over finance is the most effective power exercised by the Treasury over other departments,[12] its predominance is also psychological. The very fact that other departments must seek Treasury approval in money matters and personnel constitutes a psychological barrier. Moreover, it is generally agreed that the Treasury gets the best brains, and since their job is to scrutinize proposals that require the expenditure of money, they tend to develop their critical faculties to a high point. Finally, departments which are overruled by the Treasury, by being obligated to defend Treasury decisions, cannot avoid a certain sense of inferiority in arguing contrary to the way they argued before being overruled.

Major decisions of the Treasury are, of course, subject to cabinet approval, but the Chancellor of the Exchequer is a powerful force in most, if not all, cabinets. On the other hand, if the Treasury were to interfere indiscriminately in the affairs of other departments, it certainly would be overruled some of the time. Departments do not object to Treasury interference per se quite so much as they object to the manner and spirit in which it is done.[13]

THE FUNCTIONS OF THE HIGHER CIVIL SERVICE

In the words of the Royal Commission on the Civil Service (1929), "determination of policy is the function of ministers," while the

---

[12] See Jennings, *op. cit.*, p. 137ff.

[13] Robson, *op. cit.*

"business of the civil servant [is] to strive to carry out that policy with precisely the same good will whether he agrees with it or not."[14] But some 75 per cent of the business of every Government is conducted pretty much as it would have been by its predecessors in similar circumstances.

"The most important function of the great permanent official," therefore, "is not to carry out decisions already taken by ministers, but to advise them what decisions they should take. . . ."[15] Crises come frequently. Questions can not always be settled on their merits. The higher civil servant must ask not only what is the right thing to do, but also what are the difficulties of doing the right thing. What is practicable? What means are available? What will be the opposition and how can it be overcome? Although there are the necessary memoranda to prepare, the conversations to record, committee decisions to set down, etc., it seems agreed that the higher a man advances in a department, "the less he writes and the more he talks and listens."

The higher civil servants are in a position to exercise real and direct influence on policy matters, but understandably on questions within their respective areas of competence. Most of them have a more than usual interest in prospective decisions. On the average, they will be around 10 or 15 years, and hence will, in all likelihood, have to cope with the long-term consequences of today's decisions. Therefore, it makes more sense to face difficulties immediately than to wait for future complications. Under such circumstances, the higher civil servant often advises that the best decision is to take no action, and nine times out of ten they are perhaps right.

The functions of the British civil service, generally, have been aptly summarized by Sir Ivor Jennings in the following words:[16] "The civil servant's function is thus to advise, to warn, to draft memoranda and speeches in which the Government's policy is expressed and explained, to take the consequential decisions which flow from a decision on policy, to draw attention to difficulties which are arising or are likely to arise through the execution of policy, and generally to see that the process of government is carried on in conformity with the policy laid down."

---

[14] Royal Commission on the Civil Service, *op. cit.*, p. 1268.

[15] H. E. Dale, *The Higher Civil Service of Great Britain* (London: Oxford University Press, 1941), p. 46. This work gives a particularly good account of the operations of the top few hundred people in the British civil service.

[16] Jennings, *op. cit.*, p. 116.

Honesty and integrity are notable characteristics of the British civil service. Nowhere is this more noticeable than in the higher civil service, where acceptance of bribes, direct or indirect, is completely unknown. Even attempts to obtain special favors or to bring improper influence to bear are apt to lead to trouble. The British attitude in these matters was well expressed in a report of a board of inquiry, which stated, among other things that ". . . the State is entitled to demand that its servants shall not only be honest in fact, but beyond the reach of suspicion and dishonesty." Not only must the civil servant not make use of his official position to further his private interests, "but neither is he so to order his private affairs as to allow the suspicion to arise that a trust has been abused or a confidence betrayed."

THE CIVIL SERVICE AND PARLIAMENT

Charges have been made in and out of Parliament that the people's ancient liberties were being snuffed out by a powerful bureaucracy hiding behind weak and overworked ministers.[17] Such allegations have not been given wide credence. Criticisms continue to be made, but few people view the civil service as an autonomous and powerful force which threatens to extinguish their liberties.

Nowhere are civil servants more respected than in Parliament. It is true that members of Parliament look upon civil servants with perhaps a tinge of condescension (politicians are wielders of authority), but they also view them with friendliness, confidence and respect.[18] For their part, civil servants view the House of Commons with "a mixture of distaste and respect; distaste for its general intellectual level, respect for its decency of feeling, sound judgment of men, and good sense in large affairs."[19] This mutual respect between politician and civil servant is unknown in France and in the United States.

SOME RECENT TRENDS IN ADMINISTRATION

The vast increase in governmental activity in economic and social fields has tended, in some respects, to alter the role of the civil service. The older regulatory functions have in the main given way to service functions (for example, national health service). Regulatory functions remain, but they are of a different type, and really incidental to the implementation of specific policy and developmental plans (for

---

[17] For example, see Lord Hewart, *The New Despotism* (New York: Cosmopolitan Book Corp., 1929).

[18] Dale, *op. cit.*, p. 152.

[19] *Ibid.*, p. 153.

example, town and country planning). There is a greater association with international organizations than in the past. A much larger place in the governmental sphere is being allotted to science. Moreover, relations between business and the civil service are considerably closer than before World War II. Shifts in Britain's position in the world and her altered relationships with various areas have made necessary adjustments in her civil service abroad and at home. Finally, increased governmental activities have in our time meant that the average citizen continuously feels the impact of government. Hence the need for "a high degree of communication between the governors and the governed."[20]

Although proud of their civil service, many British citizens have continued to suggest that it could be improved. Some Labor party spokesmen have asserted that the service is not open sufficiently to men and women from the lower classes. In order to remedy this alleged imbalance, they want to broaden the opportunities for entrance into the service by significant changes in the educational system. Others, while acknowledging the desirability of excellence irrespective of class background, have warned of the dangers of a "meritocracy," i.e. the development of a bureaucratic class that might set itself apart from, and lose respect for, the democratic masses that it is supposed to serve. Moreover, there are numerous recommendations for administrative reorganizations to promote efficiency and to insure responsibility. All of the above-mentioned observations merely suggest that the demands on the civil service are never-ending, and that as long as this condition continues, there will be a need for changes and adjustments in the bureaucratic machine.

THE OPERATION OF NATIONALIZED INDUSTRIES

As the state has become more active in economic matters, the coordination of economic policy and the development of appropriate administrative machinery has been a growing problem. In addition to the older ministries, there are now also ministries for housing and local government, education, health, labor, agriculture, etc. And now there is the widespread use of the public corporation to manage and operate the nationalized industries.

These developments did not come about overnight, nor were they the consequent product of the Labor victory in 1945. In the nineteenth

---

[20] The foregoing is based primarily on Robson, *op cit.*, Chapter 5.

century the view was widely held that the government should have as little as possible to do with economic affairs. It was thought that free competition would result in the production of more and cheaper goods, which would be of benefit to the consumer. But almost simultaneously the idea was taking root that the government should take the responsibility for freeing women and children from unsuitable work and from excessive hours of labor. Legislation in this field was to be followed by legislation for health and unemployment insurance, old age pensions, etc. To be sure, all of this did not mean that the government should accept the responsibility of seeing that industry functioned so as to provide full employment and a more equitable distribution of the economic earnings of society. But few will argue against the proposition that once the government accepted the responsibility of mitigating some of the unfavorable consequences of industrialization, it made more plausible and more persuasive the arguments of those who urged increased responsibility of the state in the realm of economic and social affairs.

Although nationalized industries represent a large segment of the economy in Britain, they employ no more than ten per cent of the total labor force, and hence operate largely in the context of a predominantly private enterprise economy. Some of the nationalized industries, however, conduct large operations. The coal industry, for example, is the largest single employer in the country, while the biggest investment requirement of any industry is in the production and distribution of electricity.

THE PUBLIC CORPORATION

Parliament, on recommendation of the cabinet, chose the public corporation (for example: British Overseas Airways Corporation, National Coal Board), as the instrument through which nationalized industries would be managed. In doing this, two objectives were held uppermost. First, efficient management seemed to require a certain degree of autonomy, that is, freedom from constant interference on the part of the bureaucracy of a ministry. Secondly, the principle of responsibility to Parliament had to be preserved. To achieve these ends, public corporations were put under ministers who would ultimately be responsible for their work to Parliament. But the corporations were given considerable latitude in making many decisions without reference to ministers. Hence, ministers are not responsible for all decisions.

The board of a public corporation is appointed by the appropriate minister, who has power to remove members and who is responsible to Parliament for his appointments. He also determines the salaries and conditions of service of the board members. While the minister is given certain powers of control and direction, the board has the duty of operating and managing the industry in the public interest. It is provided with the necessary powers to do so. The minister is required, however, to approve the borrowing and the capital investments which the board wishes to undertake. Also, he has to approve programs of research and development. In addition, the minister has control over the consumer councils (discussed below). Finally, he is required to lay before Parliament the annual report and statement of accounts of the board.

Since the Labor Government was well aware that governing boards of government corporations would be more subject to attack, in Parliament and in the press, than private undertakings, there was a deliberate effort to minimize such attacks. To this end, consumer councils were established.[21] They constituted the machinery for systematically bringing to the boards and to the minister the views of the consumers. It was the Government's conviction that while public relations men have the duty of interpreting the policies of the board to the public, they have as much of a duty to convey public criticisms and complaints to the board.[22]

The consumer councils are appointed by the minister. As a general rule, he is obligated to consult representative consumer groups, often specified by statute, before making the appointments. In practice, he asks for a panel of nominees from which most of the members are chosen, although some (for example, civic leaders) are his personal appointees. Most councils have representatives from the board or corporation governing the industry. The size of the councils varies from three to thirty. Some councils exist on the national level only, while some are regional and local only. None exists on all three levels. On the average they meet about six to eight times a year, with the national councils meeting less often than regional or local ones.

The duties of the councils are to consider and to make recommendations in matters of consumer interest which are raised by actual or potential consumers, initiated by the councils, or referred to them by the minister. The implementation of recommendations depends in large part upon the minister. There is reason to believe, however, that

---

[21] For a discussion of consumer councils, see Eldon L. Johnson, "Consumer 'Control' in British Nationalized Industries," *Journal of Politics*, Vol. 15 (Feb., 1953), pp. 88–113.

[22] Morrison, *op. cit.*, pp. 265–67.

councils in many instances do not even have the opportunity of making recommendations. "Many council meetings hear of the majority of complaints only through the secretary's report on how satisfactory disposition has been achieved."[23] On the other hand, councils are sometimes informed of general plans, and can make representations on the basis of these, which comes closest to sharing in policy formulation by consumer councils. Some councils are closely enough tied to industry, through direct representation, to have a voice in policy, while others have no direct relation to their industries.

The most obvious defect in the consumer councils is that they are too little known and too little used. One reason is consumer indifference. Another is to be found in the fact that there are no effective organizations which represent general consumer interests. Moreover, there are competing channels: advisory committees in government departments and the continued practice of ministers to meet directly with representatives of the great interest groups. Often the councils find themselves in a dilemma. They must depend on the agency for information and remedial action, but at the same time they must be independent of the agency to assure the consumer a vigorous voice. They must, at one and the same time, have the confidence of both the minister and the consumers.

THE PROBLEM OF ACCOUNTABILITY TO PARLIAMENT

In creating the public corporation and in vesting it with what seemed to be the necessary authority, the British were aware that situations would probably arise which would make it impossible to assess responsibility. The older concept that the minister was responsible for every administrative act in his department was forced to give way to significant modification. While some questions remain to be resolved, the present rule would seem to be that a minister cannot be held accountable for actions of autonomous authorities unless the law requires his consent for such actions (for example, borrowing, capital investments, etc.).

This is not to suggest that in areas where the minister's explicit consent is not required, the boards are under no control. On the contrary, the minister may have frequent informal discussions with the board chairman. He has the right to question the chairman about those aspects of policy or management which have given him cause for apprehension, and he has the authority to urge suitable action. The Treasury,

---

[23] Johnson, *op. cit.*, p. 96.

too, may exercise a good deal of control through its inquiries concerning income and expenditures. The Parliament and its Public Accounts Committee, together with the more recently established Select Committee on Nationalized Industries, scrutinize and debate the annual reports and statements of accounts which the boards are required to make, and which the minister is required to lay before them. Morrison reports that the Labor Government usually allotted three days of Government time for a debate of the reports of socialized industries.[24] Moreover, letters from individual members of Parliament to chairmen of boards constitute another way of getting information and ventilating grievances. Finally, at the end of the day (as discussed in a previous chapter) any subject may be discussed on the adjournment motion.

There is some debate as to the effectiveness of the Select Committee on Nationalized Industries. Its primary purpose is to scrutinize the reports and accounts of the nationalized industries, with the aim of informing Parliament about the aims, activities, and problems of the corporations operating these industries. Some critics insist that the Committee does not probe deep enough. Other observers contend that if it probed deeper it would interfere with the day-to-day operation of the industry involved, and hence contribute to lowered efficiency. Still other observers maintain that the Committee does an excellent job, but no one really reads its reports. There would appear to be some truth in each one of these contentions. The Select Committee is an imperfect instrument of parliamentary control. Most students of the problem are agreed that it could be improved, but this will require, first of all, a willingness on the part of members of Parliament to devote more time and effort in this direction. They could be assisted considerably if Parliament were to provide its members with a research staff and an adequate secretarial service.

Labor party leaders seem to have been aware of and on guard against a particular danger often associated with government-operated enterprises—a large and cumbersome bureaucracy. Morrison has referred to it as the "danger of elaborating machinery for its own sake," the danger "of large-scale duplication in the ministries of the supervisory, technical, and administrative staffs of the public corporations."[25] What the parent ministry needs, he said, is "a quite small, brainy, constructive branch which studies the work of the boards, examines their statistics, takes note of parliamentary, press,

---

[24] Morrison, *op. cit.*, p. 262.
[25] *Ibid.*, pp. 298, 273.

and public criticisms, and so on."[26] Efficiency of government-operated enterprises requires, he observed, "suitable organization and the more streamlined the better. *But what is still more necessary are able men with clear minds and the right policy—doing things, and doing them well.*"[27]

DELEGATED LEGISLATION AND ADMINISTRATIVE TRIBUNALS

The expansion of governmental activities in the economic and social realms brought about a realization that Parliament could not draft statutes in such a way as to take care of all eventualities. Hence, the trend to draft laws in more or less skeleton fashion, vesting in ministeries the authority to fill in the details. Two major problems have tended to arise as a result. First, the problem of providing adequate safeguards so that the rule-making authority will be exercised in conformity with the basic statute. And secondly, the problem of the possible violation of citizen's rights by administrative boards or tribunals, many of whose decisions are judicial in nature, without recourse to appeal in the courts. It is to these problems, together with a survey of the growth of delegated legislation, that we now turn.

The Growth of Delegated Legislation

The power of government departments to make rules having the effect of law grew out of nineteenth century regulatory legislation (for example, on railroads and other public utilities). It was given added impetus by the social legislation which was soon to follow. The social and economic legislation of the twentieth century, particularly the nationalization program of the Labor Government following World War II, augmented the practice of administrative rule-making manyfold.

The extent of the rule-making authority is sometimes breathtaking. In recent years the British Parliament has passed many laws which declared that where a minister is satisfied that certain facts exist, or where it seems to him that something has happened or is necessary, he can then exercise the powers specified in the law. The National Coal Board (1946), for example, is authorized to perform all such activities "as it may appear to the Board to be requisite, advantageous or convenient for them to carry on for or in connection with the discharge

---

[26] *Ibid.*, p. 273.

[27] *Ibid.*, p. 298. Italics are mine.

of their duties. . . ." Not all government corporations are given such broad powers, but that some are suggests the twin problems mentioned above.

The reasons for delegation of rule-making authority are, however, compelling. For fairly obvious reasons, Parliament cannot set out in an act all of the details of administration. The pressure upon parliamentary time does not permit adequate consideration. In addition, the subject matter of much modern legislation is often of a technical nature, and technical matters cannot easily be included, for they cannot be effectively debated. Moreover, in large and complex schemes of reform it is impossible to foresee all contingencies which may arise; it cannot be known whether conditions will change, requiring modifications in detailed statutory provisions. Flexibility is essential, for it permits experimentation and makes possible adaptations in accordance with actual practice. Finally, statutory rules can be prepared in greater leisure and with more care, minimizing the possibility of serious errors.

SAFEGUARDS IN DELEGATED LEGISLATION

The fear that administrative rule-making might go beyond the intent of the original legislative enactment is enhanced by the absence in Britain of constitutional limitations on the legislature. Moreover, the role of the courts is far more modest than in the United States. British courts cannot ask if Parliament had the right to legislate, and consequently to bestow rule-making power. They can merely ask: Is the rule-making body acting in accordance with the procedural framework prescribed by law? They do not inquire into the reasonableness of any action; that is for the executive to decide.

In view of these and other considerations, the British have tended to establish certain safeguards in the exercise of rule-making authority. First of all, Ministers are empowered to make rules and regulations having the effect of law only if authorized to do so by statute. Secondly, the rules must be confirmed by the ministers. Thirdly, an increasing number of statutes are requiring consultation with advisory committees prior to the making of regulations. All departments in the economic and social sphere use advisory committees. The effectiveness of consultation, however, depends upon how the minister conceives his duty to consult and the extent to which advisory bodies are representative of the interests affected.

Moreover, Parliament may, by adverse resolution, nullify regulations laid before it. As a rule, this must be done within forty days, but in practice neither house exercises much control via such resolutions. As a general rule, Parliament has neither the time nor the knowledge to supervise the minister or to call him to account for administrative decisions. The House of Commons Select Committee on Statutory Instruments, on the other hand, which is empowered to call to the attention of Parliament certain rules which are unusual or where there is an unexpected use of powers or where there is delay, serves a useful purpose. Although the committee cannot criticize the rules themselves, it can amplify certain features so as to enable the House to make a more competent decision. Administrative agencies know this, and consequently they are on the alert for abuses, errors, or procrastination, factors which, in all likelihood, would lead to parliamentary criticism.

Within the limits set for it, the Select Committee on Statutory Instruments seems to have done a good job. It cannot amend any statutory instrument, but it can and does call to the attention of the House any mis-use or abuse of authority, any unjustifiable delays, and any poorly formulated rules. As a result, the Committee has had an important influence in the field of procedure, partly because it is often in direct touch with civil servants. Perhaps the best indication of its success is to be found in the fact that the number of cases about which it has complained has steadily diminished.

ADMINISTRATIVE TRIBUNALS

Until fairly recent decades, the view has prevailed in Britain that there was no such thing as administrative law in the British system.[28] Yet, administrative decisions were being made by public authorities other than Parliament or the courts of law, resulting in a body of administrative rules. As disputes arose between persons whose rights were allegedly invaded and a public authority bent on enforcing a policy, administrative tribunals were set up by ministries to resolve such disputes.[29]

The work of administrative tribunals has come in for a great deal of criticism. One of the fundamental rules of Anglo-Saxon justice has been that no person should have his rights impaired without being heard in his defense. Yet, administrative bodies often hand down decisions without a hearing and without any statements as to the

---

[28] This was due in large part to the influence of A. V. Dicey's, *The Law of the Constitution* (London: Macmillan, 1885). Subsequent editions published through 1939.

[29] The tendency has been to set up three-man tribunals. See Lord Campion, *et al.*, *British Government Since 1918* (New York: Macmillan Co., 1950), p. 127.

findings of fact or the reasons for the decision taken. Decisions are merely announced. The exercise of such authority has sometimes resulted in injustice to individual persons who have had no recourse to judicial appeal from the administrative decisions. Moreover, the work of administrative bodies is usually attended by a lack of publicity, in sharp contrast with the courts of law, which must function openly.

Anglo-Saxon judicial tradition is further violated by administrative tribunals where the person does not know what is the case against him. Often, the issues have not been formulated sufficiently, and there is no opportunity for cross-examination. Moreover, in many tribunals there is a rule against legal representation by the citizen.

Another Anglo-Saxon judicial principle is that a person may not be a judge in his own case. Yet, administrative tribunals have to decide cases in which the department is a party to the case. And the head of the department appoints the members of the administrative tribunal. On the other hand, it would be difficult to conceive of these tribunals performing their vital functions if they were not a part of the administrative machine.

Administrative tribunals, therefore, often find themselves in a kind of no man's land, between the aggrieved citizen and the need for effective administration. Individual citizens argue that the law court judges, who are chosen for ability to assess and weigh evidence, occasionally fall into error. But the citizen has a right to appeal, however limited. Administrative tribunals, on the other hand, are likely to make more errors than the law courts, yet their actions are not sufficiently subject to review. This argument seems to be reinforced by the tendency to draft administrative powers in such a way as to give absolute rather than qualified descretion. Proponents of effective administration point out, however, that in many areas, some of them vital to national security, government would come to a standstill if every administrative decision were to become the subject of controversy, debate, and review in Parliament or in the courts.

In order to meet some of the criticism of administrative tribunals, Parliament passed the Tribunals and Inquiries Act, 1958. The purpose of this legislation was to establish a statutory provision for judicial appeal. The act provides for certain procedural reforms and it establishes the principle of judicial scrutiny on points of law. Moreover, it sets up a council to review and to make reports on the workings of some thirty designated administrative tribunals. Insufficient time has elapsed for a general judgment to be made at this time concerning the contribution of this legislation in meeting some of the problems to which the above-mentioned criticisms addressed themselves.

Many observers recognize the advantages which administrative tribunals possess in resolving disputes between individuals and public authority. They are at once cheaper and more speedy than the regular courts. In addition, they are manned by experts, individuals who possess special experience or training in a particular field. Moreover, there is room for considerable flexibility in the operation of administrative tribunals, and this is of much help to the department or ministry which from time to time may find it necessary to engage in adaptation.

By contrast, administrative tribunals in the United States have been more circumscribed than in Britain. Their actions are defined by the Administrative Procedure Act of 1946. The purpose of this act was said to be to prescribe a code of fair administrative procedure for all cases where the decision is preceded by a hearing. Hence, interested parties can learn the nature of the case against them, submit evidence, subpoena witnesses and documents, and engage in cross-examination. And they have the right of counsel. Under this law, an agency inspector hears the evidence and the arguments, but the agency head makes the decision. The hearing officer prepares an intermediate report that summarizes the evidence and arguments, and often recommends a decision. This report is available to the parties, who can raise objections to it. Moreover, the agency decision must be accompanied by findings and the reasons upon which it is based. Finally, the regular courts are given considerable scope to review agency decisions.[30]

BIBLIOGRAPHICAL NOTE

Although no single book discusses the entire subject of public administration in Great Britain, S. E. Finer, *A Primer of Public Administration* (London: Mullers, 1957), and W. J. M. MacKenzie and J. W. Grove, *Central Administration in Britain* (London: Longmans, Green, 1957) may serve as a useful initial presentation. Sir William Henry Beveridge, *Full Employment in a Free Society* (New York: Norton, 1945) suggests the problems arising from the government's expanded social and economic responsibilities, but it is necessary to consult several specialized books in order to gain a general view of contemporary public administration. Among these,

---

[30] For a discussion of state liability for wrongful acts of government officials in Britain, France, and the United States, see the next chapter. The French Council of State will receive fuller treatment in the next section of this book.

some of the more informative are Samuel H. Beer, *Treasury Control* (London: Oxford University Press, 1957) ; *The Organization of British Central Government, 1914–1956,* A Survey by a Study Group of the Royal Institute of Public Administration, edited by D. N. Chester (London: Allen and Unwin, 1957) ; and Sir Oliver Franks, *Central Planning and Control in War and Peace* (Cambridge, Mass.: Harvard University Press, 1947). In addition, chapters of Jennings, *Cabinet Government* and *Parliament* are particularly relevant.

Studies of national planning include those of John Jewkes, *Ordeal by Planning* (New York: Macmillan, 1948) ; Ben W. Lewis, *British Planning and Nationalization* (New York: Twentieth Century Fund, 1952) ; and W. Arthur Lewis, *The Principles of Economic Planning* (London: Allen and Unwin, 1949).

Among the general studies of nationalization are D. N. Chester, *The Nationalised Industries: An Analysis of the Statutory Provisions* (2d ed.; London: Allen and Unwin, 1951) ; A. H. Hanson, *Parliament and Public Ownership* (London: Cassell, 1961) ; William A. Robson, *Nationalised Industry and Public Ownership* (London: Allen & Unwin, 1960) ; and *The Public Corporation: A Comparative Symposium,* edited by Wolfgang Friedmann (Toronto: Carswell, 1954).

There are numerous studies of the British public service, among which the more useful include Philip W. Buck, *Amateurs and Professionals in British Politics, 1918–59* (Chicago: University of Chicago Press, 1963) ; Frank T. A. Ashton-Gwatkin, *The British Foreign Service* (Syracuse: Syracuse University Press, 1950) ; G. A. Campbell, *The Civil Service in Britain* (London: Pelican Books, 1955) ; H. E. Dale, *The Higher Civil Service of Great Britain* (London: Oxford University Press, 1941) ; Frank Dunnil, *The Civil Service: Some Human Aspects* (London: Allen and Unwin, 1956) ; Herman Finer, *The British Civil Service* (London: Allen and Unwin, 1947) ; Edgar N. Gladden, *The Civil Service or Bureaucracy* (London: Staples, 1956) ; Roger Keith Kelsall, *Higher Civil Servants in Britain, From 1870 to the Present Day* (London: Routledge and Paul, 1955) ; and Bosworth Monck, *How the Civil Service Works* (London: Phoenix, 1952).

CHAPTER 7

LAW AND THE JUDICIARY

THE relationship between the law and the judiciary, on the one hand, and the prevailing political system, on the other, varies in time and place. Dictators have, as a rule, either created new legal systems as protectors of their political order, or they have "harnessed" the existing legal systems to do their bidding. In democratic states, legal systems have shaped and influenced the political order, and have themselves been altered and influenced by it. In those democratic countries (for example, the United States) where judicial review of legislative acts exists, the law and the judiciary in no small degree influence the future evolution of their respective political systems. In Britain, where political and constitutional principles often stemmed from usage and judicial decisions, the law and the judiciary helped shape the evolution of the political system itself. Hence, the British legal order may be considerably less the product of a political system than is usually the case.

LAW AND THE JUDICIARY IN THE MODERN STATE

The sum total of the rules of human conduct which the courts will enforce is known as law. The test of law, therefore, is judicial recognition. These rules can be placed into two categories: those that set up standards governing the relationship between individuals and public authority (government), and those which regulate the relationships between individuals and other individuals. The former is usually called public law and the latter private law. Public law embraces three types of law: constitutional, administrative, and criminal. Court actions under crimininal law are referred to as criminal cases, whereas most other legal actions, notably those between individuals, are designated as civil cases.

The criminal law embraces offenses against the state and those offenses against individuals which are judged sufficiently grave (such as murder, arson, etc.) to be offenses against society as a whole. Aside from this distinction, perhaps the vital difference between criminal and civil law is to be found in the sanctions. The sanction of criminal law is punitive. The object of prosecution under it is punishment of the guilty party. The object of a civil action, on the other hand, may be to compensate the injured party, to force compliance with the law, or to restrain a person (or persons) from embarking on actions which would be injurious to others.

Law, public as well as private, has its origin in several sources. It may emanate from custom or usage when recognized by the courts. It may originate in legislative enactments. Or it may stem from judicial interpretation.

In primitive societies the enforcement of law was in the hands of private individuals or agencies. Even in the early history of British courts there were, in addition to the king's courts, several other types, including private feudal courts. Over the long run, however, the king's courts superseded the others simply because they provided better justice. Royal justice became the most popular justice. "One of the chief attractions of royal justice was its readiness to proceed against great offenders and the certainty that its decisions would be enforced."[1] By the end of the fourteenth century, the central courts sat at Westminster and were staffed by professional judges appointed by the king from among the practicing barristers. These courts were known as the *common law* courts, as a way of distinguishing them from the ecclesiastical courts and other special tribunals.

Today we generally assume that the administration of justice constitutes a significant function of government. We look to the courts to investigate and to determine the pertinent facts, to apply the law to these facts, to determine and to construe the law, and to prevent infractions of law and violations of individual rights. And we expect the courts to mete out the appropriate punishment.

ORIGIN AND MEANING OF THE COMMON LAW

COMMON LAW AND OTHER SYSTEMS OF LAW

The common law is one of the two or three great systems of law existing in the world. It and the Roman law system are the best known, partly because they have been copied extensively. Although less well-known and not extensively copied, the Mohammedan system of law needs to be recognized as a significantly important law system. It is to be found chiefly in north and central Africa, western and southern Asia and in the East Indies. The common law system has spread to

---

[1] E. M. Sait, *Political Institutions: A Preface* (New York: Appleton-Century-Crofts, 1938), p. 208.

most areas which came under British influence,[2] including the United States, while the Roman law prevails in Japan, China, Turkey and on the European continent. Interestingly enough, Scotland retains a separate system of law in the Roman tradition and, of course, a separate system of courts.

The common law has its origin in judicial decisions, which were initially based on the customs or usages of various English communities where the traveling justices held court. One decision tended to set the pattern for deciding future cases, hence the occasional use of the term "case law" to describe common law. In time, the king's judges applied the same body of legal rules to the entire nation. Hence the term "common," that is, common to the whole realm of England.[3] Traditionally, therefore, the common law left many areas of human activity untouched until specific cases arose to make it necessary.

The Roman law, on the other hand, is code law. It seeks to have a specific code for every conceivable type of case which may arise.[4] Carefully drawn statutes enable the Roman law justice to turn to "the law" for every case, instead of seeking "to find" it, as is often the case in common law.

The trade mark of the common law is *stare decisis,* the principle that previous cases decide present ones. Precedent is all important and binding. The Roman law systems have in recent decades made considerable use of precedent, especially in France, but there is no rule that it is binding on future cases. This is not to suggest that the English did not borrow from Rome, for they did, "but what they borrowed chiefly was logic, method, and spirit, rather than matter."[5]

The Roman law and the common law also differ with respect to legal concepts in certain types of cases. For example: Suppose your neighbor's roof is blown off by a tornado while he is on vacation and you get it repaired after unsuccessfully trying to get in touch with him. When he gets back he refuses to pay you. Roman law recognizes an

---

[2] Some exceptions might be noted: the Roman-Dutch law prevails in the Union of South Africa and the Roman (French) law prevails in the French-populated regions of Canada.

[3] Sometimes "common" was used in contrast with special or particular surviving local custom or canon law. See R. M. Jackson, *The Machinery of Justice in England* (4th ed.; Cambridge: Cambridge University Press, 1964), p. 10ff.

[4] It has been argued that this is an over-simplified distinction, that Roman law has much in common with common law in that the need for Roman law emerged from past litigation. See Sait, *op. cit.,* p. 189. His chapters on Roman and common law are particularly recommended.

[5] Sait, *op. cit.,* pp. 250–51.

obligation on his part to indemnify you for having incurred an expense to protect his interests in his absence. In the common law, however, there is generally no such obligation.

Another difference in the two systems concerns the personnel of the judiciary. In the Roman law tradition, a lawyer must choose at an early age whether he is going into the judiciary or whether he is going to practice before the courts. In the Roman system, the judiciary is a part of the administrative hierarchy and is a separate profession from that of the practicing lawyer. The justices are trained for the courts through the ministries of justice. In common law systems, on the other hand, judges are drawn from the legal profession.

THE DEVELOPMENT OF COMMON LAW

The common law was aided in its development by the medieval notion that law existed (divinely ordained), and that the problem was to find it, for it was not conceived that the state could alter the law. Moreover, in administering the "law and custom of the realm," the courts had in large measure to rely on custom simply because there was little formal law to administer.

Initially, reported cases served as precedents, first simply as evidence of the law or some principle, and later as a rule that became binding upon future cases and lower courts. After a time, noted jurists, such as Glanville, Coke, and Blackstone, made an attempt to bring together (1) decisions which had been made with respect to certain subjects (for example, marriage, inheritance, etc.) and (2) decisions made at various places but essentially based on the same or a similar set of facts. These collections or commentaries served in effect to "codify" much of the common law.

In the process of bringing the rules of common law together, certain defects became obvious. Certain types of cases required finer distinctions, and hence new rules had to be formulated and applied. Other cases pointed to the need for statutory enactment. But even before the great commentaries came into existence, it had been discovered that in some instances the common law rules would not promote justice or prevent injustice. Hence the need for modification in some form.

MODIFICATION OF COMMON LAW: EQUITY

A whole system of legal rules known as equity (or chancery) grew out of the decisions of the Lord Chancellor in cases where persons had appealed to the king for relief from common law decisions that constituted injustices. All legal systems, at one time or another, are confronted by the question of how, while preserving rigidity of law, to prevent that rigidity from causing real suffering in individual cases. In England the Lord Chancellor, in effect, acted as the king's conscience. After a time a whole series of equity cases established well-defined principles, which by the early part of the nineteenth century had become "a set of rules which could be invoked to supplement the deficiencies of common law or to ease the clumsy working of common law actions and remedies."[6]

Under the common law, certain types of disputes were not covered or covered only imperfectly. In some cases real injustices resulted. Under the common law, for example, contracts made under threat of life or limb were invalid, but contracts facilitated by the more subtle influences, such as alcoholic drinks, were valid. Under equity, of course, the latter type of contract would be considered fraudulent, and hence illegal. In another type of case (tort as well as contract), the only remedy known to the common law was damages. In many instances the remedy was akin to bolting the barn door after the horse had been stolen. Money damages, for example, could not replace a large shade tree which had been cut down or irreparably damaged. Therefore, the equity court, in the case of a threatened injury or a nuisance, established the practice of issuing an injunction. Equity, it should be noted, has to do with civil controversies and not with criminal cases.

At the beginning, equity was not a legal system. The early Chancellors were not lawyers but ecclesiastics. As "keepers of the king's conscience," they exercised that reserve of justice which was inherent in the king as the fountain of all justice. Their spasmodic decrees, issued in individual cases over the years, tended to create precedents, which by the eighteenth century began more and more to resemble the common law in their rigidity.

Until late in the nineteenth century, the equity courts were separate from the regular law courts. The Judicature Acts of 1873–75, however, ended the separation of law and equity, and provision was made that *all* courts should apply and use both sets of rules. In case of conflict between them, equity was to prevail. Where statutes are applicable, however, they supersede both the common law and equity.

---

[6] Jackson, *op. cit.*, p. 7.

MODIFICATION OF COMMON LAW: STATUTES

Prior to 1832, the role of parliamentary statutes in court cases was not really significant. Since that time, however, it has often been found that Parliament has deemed it necessary to legislate in some area previously governed by the common law or equity. Yet, this has been brought on more by the expansion of governmental activity in new spheres than by any desire to change the common law. There have been statutory modifications in both criminal and civil law, but judge-made law is still basic in most areas of British jurisprudence. There are *habeas corpus* acts, but much of the liberty of the subject is guaranteed by case decisions. And almost the whole law of torts is still judge-made law.

In the matter of civil rights, for example, the British operate on the common law principle that one may lawfully do anything which is not forbidden by law. This does not mean that there are few limitations; indeed there are many, especially with respect to printed utterance. For example, English law imposes severe limits on the reporting of criminal cases in the press, and the British law of libel affords greater protection to individual persons than its American counterpart. On the other hand, the British have resisted efforts to limit the basic freedoms of antidemocratic movements. The inhabitants of Great Britain, although not possessing a formal bill of rights, are perhaps more passionately dedicated to the preservation of civil liberties than any other people in the world.

It should be noted, however, that the term "common law" is sometimes also used to include statutes, particularly when one is thinking of "the whole body of law administered by the common law courts, or of the principles and rules that rest entirely upon precedent."[7] Similarly, when it is sometimes contrasted with other systems of law, it may be thought of as broadly embracing the legal system, as well as the habits of legal thought which the British have evolved.

THE COURT SYSTEM

Like so many other institutions of British government, the court system was shaped and altered by usage over a period of years. As nearly as one can tell, one-time itinerant royal commissioners, who

---

[7] *Ibid.*, p. 14.

were mainly concerned with looking after the king's financial affairs, were after a time to become itinerant judges. As royal commissioners, they had little judicial authority; as itinerant judges their main function became judicial. These itinerant judges visited each county three or four times per year to hear and determine the validity of the allegations of serious crime, the lesser offenses being dealt with by the sheriff and later by justices of the peace.

Consequently, the practice of hearing virtually all criminal cases in the county where the crime was committed became well established. In civil cases of any importance, however, the proceedings were held at Westminster, which meant that participants, witnesses, and others with an interest in the case had to travel to Westminster for the trial. Because of the difficulties which arose as a result of civil proceedings being heard at Westminster, a change was introduced—a compromise was made between centralization and decentralization. Justices of the Assize Courts, who were the best available justices, were sent to the counties to hear cases. The points of law, however, were argued mainly at Westminster and the formal judgment was rendered there.

Perhaps the greatest strides in the systematization of the British judicial system were made during the reign of Henry II. At that time the system of royal writs, which are the root of common law procedure, was inaugurated. These writs required that disputes be brought before royal authorities for settlement. Moreover, Henry II adopted and perfected the system of itinerant judges. In addition, he established the principle of the "king's peace," that is, that a crime should no longer be considered a wrong against the individual but rather a wrong against the state. Finally, he asserted the exclusive jurisdiction of the Curia Regis in the case of all serious crimes, and he hastened the demise of the older methods of trial (such as ordeal, battle, etc.), which led to the development of trial by jury.

The Courts of Justice

Unlike courts in the United States, British courts do not as a rule exercise both criminal and civil jurisdiction. Consequently, there are two judicial hierarchies in Britain, which need to be considered separately.

Minor criminal cases are dealt with by justices of the peace (unpaid) or by magistrates. There are no juries in such cases. Summary offenses (those not requiring an indictment) are also tried here, as well as indictable offenses which are triable summarily when the accused consents and the court thinks this expedient. Appeals from such decisions may be taken to Quarter Sessions (which is usually a county court), the court of first instance where a jury is employed, and one in which the more serious cases are tried. The magistrates' courts also make preliminary inquiry into indictable offenses. In case of the most serious crimes, such as murder, the prisoner is held for trial in the Assize, which is the designation for the court periodically held in each county by one or more judges of the High Court of Justice who go around on circuit. An example of such courts is the Central Criminal Court in London, popularly known as Old Bailey.

The most serious crimes, therefore, are tried by the Assizes, made up of judges assigned to it from the High Court of Justice (queen's bench division),[8] while the less serious crimes are tried in Quarter Sessions. Appeals from both may be taken to the Court of Criminal Appeal. If the attorney general consents (which is rare), appeals in criminal cases may be taken to the House of Lords, the highest court of appeal in the land.

Civil cases of no great importance usually originate in county courts,[9] which sit at frequent intervals. Appeals may be taken from them to the appropriate division of the High Court of Justice, discussed below. More important cases, such as those relating to civil liberties or cases which are or are likely to become test cases, are first brought to the appropriate division of the high court. Similarly, cases involving large sums of money also come to the high court in the first instance.

The High Court of Justice, referred to above, is divided into three divisions: (1) queen's bench, (2) chancery (equity), and (3) probate, divorce, and admiralty. The queen's bench division assigns justices to both civil and criminal courts, but "circuit work and the Court of Criminal Appeal has first claim on judicial time."[10] These three divisions of the high court, along with the Court of Appeal, are sometimes referred to as the Supreme Court of Judicature, as if it were one court. The civil side of Assizes is sometimes considered as a separate division, although in reality it is primarily a perambulating sitting of the queen's bench division.

Decisions of the lower civil courts may be appealed to the Court of Appeal, and a few cases may eventually reach the House of Lords if

---

[8] The queen's bench assigns judges to both civil and criminal courts.

[9] Despite the name, their jurisdiction does not coincide with the boundaries of the counties.

[10] Jackson, *op. cit.*, p. 44.

permission to appeal is granted by the Court of Appeal or the House of Lords itself.

All courts of appeal sit in London. The Court of Appeal and the Court of Criminal Appeal, which have already been mentioned, do most of the appeals work. Two other appeals courts, however, need to be mentioned. They are the Judicial Committee of the Privy Council and the House of Lords. The former has traditionally been the highest court of appeal in cases arising in the British controlled areas overseas. Since the self-governing members of the Commonwealth (see next chapter) now prefer to keep appeals within their own

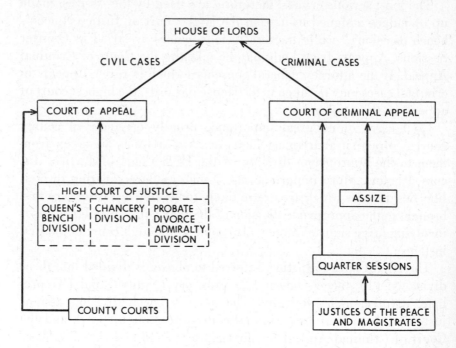

judicial systems, it is now the ultimate court of appeal for cases arising in the Channel Islands, the Isle of Man, the colonies, protectorates, and trust territories. It is also the final court of appeal from the ecclesiastical courts. The House of Lords, on the other hand, is the highest court of appeal domestically, but not as a matter of right, for its permission, or that of the Court of Appeals, is necessary before it will hear cases. Actually, it is not the House as a whole that hears cases, but the law lords (the normal number is seven but the law permits nine), although they act in the name of the House. Since the House is technically the highest court of appeal, the law lords can not sit as a court when the House of Lords is in session. Therefore, in order not to interrupt their work, the device of an appellate committee was inaugurated in 1948.

BRITISH JUDGES

Most British judges are appointed upon the advice of the Lord Chancellor, who is head of the judicial hierarchy. A few of the top judicial appointments are made by the prime minister, usually after consultation with the Lord Chancellor. Appointments are made from the legal profession, or more precisely, from those of its members, known as barristers, who are principally engaged in court work (see next section). Before he is eligible for appointment, a person must have been a barrister for at least seven years. Once appointed, judges serve, not "at the pleasure of the Crown," but "during good behavior," which means permanence of tenure.

One of the outstanding characteristics of British judges is their independence. In the words of Jennings, "No allegation of partiality or corruption or political influence is ever made against British judges."[11] The explanation, in large measure, is to be found in the fact that it is not easy to become a barrister. Before a person can practice, he must be "called to the Bar" by one of the four Inns of Court, incorporated associations but not subject to government control, which will admit him only if he possesses those high qualities of education and discipline that will help to perpetuate the long tradition of professional independence which the Inns have built up. And his Inn of Court would condemn any judge who bowed to political pressure or the pressure of public opinion. But it should also be added that British judges, because they do not have the power of judicial review, that is, the power to declare laws null and void, are not subject to the type of pressure with which American judges are often confronted.

JUDICIAL PROCEDURE

Because British courts operate on legal foundations which are very much like our own, it is not surprising that procedure in them should also be similar. Perhaps the most significant similarity is that the rules of evidence are designed to protect the accused and to place the burden of proof on the prosecution. Here we find such things as habeas corpus, indictments, trial by jury, protection against self-incrimination, and the presumption of innocence until proof of guilt has been presented. Another similarity concerns publicity; the courts

---

[11] Sir Ivor Jennings, *The Queen's Government* (Baltimore: Penguin Books, 1954), p. 147.

are open to the public. But there are some differences, and these should also be noted.

One significant difference involves the legal profession. In Britain, it is divided into solicitors and barristers. The former do not try cases in court, while the latter do virtually nothing else. The solicitors advise clients, engage barristers to try cases, and prepare such cases for trial. A man cannot be both at the same time. Nor can a barrister and a solicitor enter into a partnership. The standard of professional honor is high among both, maintained in large part by the Law Society (for solicitors) and the Inns of Court (for barristers). One interesting and significant result of this division is that the total number of barristers is relatively small, which enables the judges to get to know them, and thus be in a better position to dispense justice.

Another significant difference concerns the British approach to criminal prosecutions. There is no system of public prosecutors comparable to our district or prosecuting attorneys, although there is a well-established principle that all reasonable prosecution costs are to be paid out of public funds. Generally speaking, prosecution is by private individuals, by the police, and by the office of the public prosecutor. In certain lesser crimes a private person employs a solicitor, who is given full cooperation by the police. In the great bulk of criminal cases, especially those involving professional criminals, prosecution is by the police. In all cases where the offense is punishable by death, as well as in certain other categories of offenses, prosecution is by the office of the public prosecutor.

Other differences include the fact that British judges play a more active role in the course of the trial. They may, for example, comment on the evidence presented as well as on the failure of the defendant to testify. Moreover, the press may not report on cases until a verdict has been rendered. Finally, the use of grand juries for making indictments has been abolished. Indictments are now drawn up by a judicial clerk, with the aid of the prosecuting solicitor. Even trial by jury is on the decline, particularly in civil cases, where litigants must pay the jury fees. But it is also on the decline in the lesser criminal cases where the defendant has a choice of being tried before a jury or a judge. A desire for a speedy trial seems to be one of the main reasons, together with the belief that the results would not be materially different.

At one time, a major criticism of British justice was that it favored the rich, a reproach with a great deal of truth in it. Shortly after World War II, however, a system of legal aid and advice was established.

This enables those who are unable to meet the costs of litigation to obtain legal aid and advice free, or to pay for it according to a scale adapted to their means. The government provides the necessary subsidy, but the program is administered with complete independence by the legal profession. Consequently, the old charge about "equal justice for the rich" no longer has any validity in Britain.

STATE LIABILITY FOR WRONGFUL ACTS

The adage, "The king can do no wrong," has traditionally applied to all of the king's servants. In Common Law, this meant that an employee of the government who exceeded his authority was personally liable. As a rule, the injured party had no other recourse but to sue the person as an individual, for the state could not be sued. This situation was modified somewhat by the Crown Proceedings Act of 1947, which, in substance, makes the state responsible for the actions of its servants.[12]

Under this act, the immunity of the crown in tort is abolished, as is the cumbersome procedure of "petition of right." The injured party may now sue as a matter of right. Government departments are made responsible to their employees for any breach of statutory duties and also for duties which at common law an employer owes his servants or agents. With some exceptions, civil proceedings against the crown can be instituted in county courts. While this act is regarded as a great step forward, it, like its American counterpart, leaves much to be desired. Many ambiguities and exceptions remain.[13]

BIBLIOGRAPHICAL NOTE

William M. Geldart, *Elements of English Law* (5th ed.; New York: Holt, 1954) may serve as a useful introduction to the complexities of English law. Also quite informative are Carleton K. Allen, *Law in the Making* (4th ed.; Oxford: Oxford University Press, 1946) and Sir Alfred Denning, *The Changing Law* (London: Stevens, 1953). Additional supplementary studies include F. T. Giles, *The Criminal Law* (London: Penguin, 1955); Harold Potter, *An Historical Introduction to English Law and Its Institutions* (3d ed.; London: Sweet and Maxwell, 1948); *Rule of Law: A Study by the Inns of Court* (London: Conservative and Unionist Central Office, 1955); Harry Street, *Governmental Liability: A Comparative Study* (Cambridge: Cambridge Uni-

[12] Interestingly enough, a similar action was taken in the U.S. with the passage of the federal Tort Claims Act in 1946, although it contains many exceptions as well as ambiguities.

[13] For an excellent brief survey, see H. Street, *Governmental Liability: A Comparative Study* (Cambridge: Cambridge University Press, 1953).

versity Press, 1953) ; and E. C. S. Wade and G. Godfrey Phillips, *Constitutional Law* (4th ed.; London: Longmans, Green, 1955).

The British court system is discussed in Jfan Kyrle Flecher, *The British Courts: Its Traditions and Ceremonial* (London: Cassell, 1953) ; Harold G. Hanbury, *English Courts of Law* (2d ed.; London: Oxford University Press, 1953) ; R. M. Jackson, *The Machinery of Justice in England* (4th ed.; Cambridge: Cambridge University Press, 1964) ; and Caleb P. Patterson, *The Administration of Justice in Great Britain* (Austin: University of Texas Press, 1936).

Contrasting views of administrative law are presented in Carleton K. Allen, *Law and Orders, An Inquiry into the Nature and Scope of Delegated Legislation and Executive Powers in England* (London: Stevens, 1945) and Sir Cecil Thomas Carr, *Concerning English Administrative Law* (New York: Columbia University Press, 1941). General studies include *Administrative Tribunals at Work, A Symposium,* edited by R. S. W. Pollard (London: Stevens, 1950) and William A. Robson, *Justice and Administrative Law: A Study of the English Constitution* (3d ed. London: Stevens, 1951).

CHAPTER 8

GOVERNMENT IN
THE COMMONWEALTH

UNLIKE other empire builders, the British have produced a unique phenomenon—a novel way for subject peoples of the empire to achieve independence and self-government, while at the same time retaining and preserving a bond of unity. The resulting free association of independent nations is known as the Commonwealth, or sometimes as the Commonwealth of Nations. In 1965, the Commonwealth had twenty-one member-nations. They were: Great Britain, Canada, Australia, New Zealand, India, Pakistan, Ceylon, Ghana, Malaysia, Nigeria, Sierra Leone, Tanzania, Trinidad and Tobago, Jamaica, Gambia, Malta, Zambia, Cyprus, Kenya, Uganda, and Malawi. Each may freely leave the association; Burma did so in 1947, Ireland in 1948, and the Union of South Africa in 1961.

The Commonwealth was once described by the late prime minister of India, Mr. Nehru, as "that strange and odd collection of nations which seems to prosper most in adversity." In another context, he referred to it as "an international organization that works." Queen Elizabeth, in her 1956 Christmas message, spoke of the Commonwealth as "one of the most hopeful and imaginative experiments in international affairs that the world has ever seen." More recently, the *Times* of London said that it "is shapeless, unorganized, unstructured, anomalous, illogical. Equally, it is flexible, adaptable, pragmatic, useful."

The Commonwealth does not, however, have any common government. Every member nation has complete control over its own affairs. It determines its domestic and foreign policies, defines its citizenship and immigration regulations, negotiates and signs treaties with other nations, and maintains its own diplomatic service and its own defense establishment.

OLD AND NEW COMMONWEALTH

As in the case of many other aspects of British politics, the Commonwealth is not the result of deliberate creation. Nor has it

157

remained static. It has grown and developed, and its nature has changed. Some things have, however, remained fairly constant. The Commonwealth has continued to be a free association. Its members have maintained a free and frank exchange of views on matters of common interest. In addition, they have sought to develop and to retain democratic forms of government, although there have been some recent setbacks in this respect.

EVOLUTION OF SELF-GOVERNMENT

The development of the concept of self-government for parts of the British empire cannot be identified with any specific date. In general, however, it can be said that the loss of the thirteen American colonies gave considerable impetus to the realization of self-government. Canada was perhaps the first to benefit, with Australia, New Zealand, and other colonies following closely behind. It was during the nineteenth century, for the most part, that these and other areas became self-governing, although progress did not proceed at the same tempo in each.

Several imperial conferences in the twentieth century led to a more precise definition of the status and rights of these self-governing colonies, then including Canada, Australia, New Zealand, Ireland, and Union of South Africa. At the conference of 1907, the representatives of these colonies were successful in their request that the term "self-governing Dominions" be used with reference to their countries. The first formal attempt to describe the status and mutal relationship of the member nations came at the Imperial Conference of 1926. It described them as "autonomous communities within the British Empire, equal in status, in no way subordinate one to another in any aspect of their domestic or external affairs, though united by a common allegiance to the crown, and freely associated as members of the British Commonwealth of Nations."

The imperial conferences of 1929 and 1930 revealed that the Dominions were of the opinion that certain inequalities continued to exist. Consequently, appropriate resolutions, which had the approval of Dominion governments, were adopted. These and previous statements in the same vein were, in effect, enacted into law in 1931, with the passage of the Statute of Westminster.

THE STATUTE OF WESTMINSTER, 1931

In a sense the Statute of Westminster represented the culmination of a process. In large part, it recognized or reaffirmed already existing rights and practices, except perhaps in the case of South Africa, where self-government had not advanced to the same degree as in the other Dominions. Yet, the Statute is a significant constitutioned landmark. Although its terms did not cover the whole of the subject, the Statute marks a great step forward in the process of readjustment, redefinition, and classification of Dominion status.

The principal provisions of the act may be summarized as follows: First, it provides that laws of Dominion parliaments cannot be disallowed on the ground that they are repugnant to the laws of Great Britain or to a future act of the British Parliament. Secondly, it says that future laws of the British Parliament shall not extend to a Dominion unless the Dominion parliament had requested and consented to its enactment. Thirdly, the act provides that any change in the law dealing with the succession to throne will require assent from the Dominions. Finally, the act assures the Dominions of autonomy in their internal and external affairs.

The Statute is quite precise in dealing with Dominion autonomy. It asserts that the formal executive, the governor general, shall be appointed on the advice of the Dominion. Secondly, each Dominion is free to legislate concerning its own affairs. Moreover, judicial appeals from Dominion courts to the Judicial Committee of the Privy Council in London could be cut off by any Dominion that wanted to do so, thereby making Dominion courts the final courts of appeal. Finally, each Dominion is sovereign in the realm of foreign affairs. Each can send and receive ministers (ambassadors), participate in or abstain from wars engaged in by Great Britain, acquire membership in the League of Nations, and make treaties with other countries. In the case of treaties, however, the act provided for notification of other members of the Commonwealth.

EXPANDING COMMONWEALTH

Although the Statute of Westminster applied originally only to the older self-governing Dominions, its provisions have been extended in recent years to new members of the Commonwealth. In the independence acts of India, Pakistan, Ceylon, Ghana, and Malaya sections of the act were repeated either verbatim or in a slightly modified form. Some adaptation, however, was necessary, because India, and subsequently Pakistan and the Federation of Malaya, wished to avoid even the appearance of British control. These three countries did not want a governor-general, and yet they wanted to stay within the Commonwealth, but not the "British" Commonwealth. With British ingenuity, they were accommodated by being able to decide on their own head of state (elected or hereditary), by dropping the term "British" from the formal title of the Commonwealth, and by agreeing that in relation to them, the queen was simply the "Head of the Commonwealth." Subsequently, a number of other members have indicated their intention of following India by becoming republics.

Nevertheless, the general nature of the Commonwealth has changed considerably with the inclusion of Asian and African nations. Australia, Canada, New Zealand, and, to a considerable extent, also South Africa, all had a tradition of association and cooperation with Great Britain. The racial and cultural traditions of their peoples are similar. On the other hand, the cultural patterns of most of the Asian and African members differ greatly from those which are predominant in the other Commonwealth countries. And today more than four fifths of the people in the Commonwealth are Asians or Africans. Moreover, there are areas of conflict among the new members, two of which might be mentioned in passing. India and Pakistan are at odds with respect to the status of Kashmir, while Ceylon and Malaysia are at odds with India concerning the status of persons of Indian origin within their borders, to say nothing of explosive situations in Africa. The fact that no machinery exists for the settlement of disputes between members constitutes a weakness in the Commonwealth. The importance of this shortcoming is likely to become increasingly noticeable. In short, the unifying factors seem to be decreasing and becoming weaker, whereas the divisive ones seem to be getting stronger and more numerous.

This is not to say that conflicts and the cultural heterogeneity of the member states will destroy the Commonwealth. Although some of the factors that once bound the members together are now gone or diluted, the Commonwealth still has considerable value as a symbol. Perhaps its chief asset is good will, which is a rare commodity in international relations today. But there is also a wide range of interests that overlap—economic, cultural, and military. Trade and sterling continue to help bind most members together. Great Britain is still the best customer for all Commonwealth countries except Canada. True, the Commonwealth is in a stage of transition, but the leaders of the respective member states continue to believe that their countries have something in common and that membership in the association is valuable. Moreover, the Commonwealth may provide a type of moral laboratory where the explosive chemistry of race can be studied and, hopefully, controlled.

RELATIONS AMONG COMMONWEALTH MEMBERS

Members of the Commonwealth, prior to 1964, dealt with one another through high commissioners whom they sent to each other's capitals, and who ranked as ambassadors. They were accredited to the respective foreign offices, except in London, where they dealt with the Commonwealth Relations Office, which was responsible at that end for the interchange of information on subjects of mutual interest among the Commonwealth members. Where foreign policy is concerned, the Commonwealth Relations Office works in close cooperation with the Foreign Office. In 1964, at a meeting of prime ministers in London, it was decided to establish a Commonwealth Secretariat, which is to be largely a clearing house of information. Much of the Commonwealth relations staff will be merged with the British Foreign Office, although a small coordinating staff will remain. A number of Commonwealth organizations and standing committees will remain. Among these, are the Commonwealth Parliamentary Association, the Commonwealth Air Transport Council, the Commonwealth Shipping Committee, the Commonwealth Telecommunications Board, and the British Commonwealth Scientific Offices.

Of considerable importance in recent years have been the conferences of ministers of Commonwealth countries. These have included prime ministers, foreign ministers, defense ministers, finance ministers and supply ministers. The prime ministers have met in London, while many of the other conferences have been held in other Commonwealth countries. These meetings are held in private, where a frank and uninhibited exchange of views and information can take place. In addition to the conferences, ministries in one country may deal directly with their opposite numbers in other member nations. Moreover, all sorts of informal meetings take place on a more or less regular basis; the get together of the ambassadors of the Commonwealth countries in Washington is but one example.

GOVERNMENT IN THE COMMONWEALTH COUNTRIES

Despite many dissimilarities, most Commonwealth countries chose the parliamentary form of government. Subsequently, this form has been substantially modified in some of these countries. In others there has been a departure from democracy itself, notably in Ghana (which is an outright dictatorship) and Pakistan (which purports to be building democracy, but is probably a long way from it). Ceylon, along with some of the newer African members, may be drifting in the direction of dictatorship. Obviously, it would be impossible, in a chapter such as this, to discuss the government and politics of all of the Commonwealth countries. Consequently, only a few of these countries have been selected, somewhat arbitrarily, for discussion here.

POLITICAL HERITAGE: CANADA, AUSTRALIA, NEW ZEALAND

Despite the existence in Canada of French elements in the population, the political heritage of these three countries is derived from Great Britain. They not only inherited British political forms but, in addition, passed through similar stages of development. Moreover, the environments to which these forms were transplanted were remarkably similar. The territory of each, especially of Canada and Australia, was extensive and sparsely populated. To an extent, therefore, the political life of each country was influenced by a frontier spirit similar to that in the United States. These countries became the homes of immigrant pioneer peoples to whom social and other class distinctions were distinctly secondary, making for an environment favorable to democratic ideas and institutions. These countries have evolved into tolerant, pluralistic societies firmly based upon common liberal-democratic principles.

The constitutions of these nations consist of the respective acts of the British Parliament granting self-government, together with such amendments as have been made locally and at Westminster, as well as judicial interpretation and those constitutional practices which have stemmed from custom and convention.

Politically, Canada and Australia are organized along federal lines, while New Zealand is a unitary state. The Canadian and Australian federations are composed of ten and six political subdivisions, respectively, known in Canada as provinces and in Australia as states. The founders of the Canadian federation were determined to have a strong central government, hence stipulating that powers not granted to the provinces are reserved to the central government. A number of judicial decisions, however, tended to strengthen the provinces at the expense of the central government. In Australia, on the other hand, residual powers are vested in the states. By and large, however, problems stemming from war and economic depression have tended to enlarge the scope of activities undertaken by the central governments of both countries.

POLITICAL HERITAGE: INDIA, CEYLON, PAKISTAN, NIGERIA, MALAYSIA

In each of these countries there was a large indigenous population when the British arrived. In each there is mass illiteracy and in each only a small western-educated and politically active minority. In varying degrees each country is characterized by tribal or family clan systems, and in India, and Ceylon caste divisions are a continuing problem. Moreover, within each nation, linguistic, ethnic, and religious conflicts persist. In Ceylon, for example, the largest single group is the indigenous Sinhalese, whose religion is Buddhism, but the Tamils are a sizable group, and most of them are Hindus, Moslems, or Christians. Similarly, in Malaysia there are three distinct ethnic groups: Indian, Chinese, and Malay, who differ from each other also in religion and language. In Nigeria, too, there are different religious as well as tribal groupings.

The most complex situation, however, is that of the Indian subcontinent. In the case of Pakistan, for example, its two widely separated areas are different cultural entities, with Islam being the only major feature shared in common by people whose political union is largely artificial. In India, there are 14 major linguistic groups and 6 religious communities. And it is in India that the caste problem has assumed its greatest proportions.

It is not unfair to say that each of these new countries is characterized by a degree of cultural heterogeneity which has complicated considerably the establishment and operation of secular democratic governments. Suspicion and intolerance among the various groups, as well as the general low level of literacy, education, and economic development, often inhibit their working together in voluntary associations. This, in turn, increases the burden which governments must bear, particularly in the areas of social and economic improvement.

For many years no effort was made to introduce British political institutions in these countries. With the exception of Malaysia and Nigeria, demands for self-government along British lines began in the nineteenth century. Gradually, institutions of colonial government were democratized, and aspects of the British system of government took root. Progress was slow, however, with the result that the achievement of independence, except in the case of Ceylon (and perhaps Nigeria), was of a quasi-revolutionary character.

As in the four original Dominions, the new commonwealth countries have specific constitutional documents. The constitutions of Pakistan,[1] India, and Nigeria are the products of constituent assemblies of the respective countries. That of Malaysia is based upon a draft

---

[1] The original constitution of Pakistan was abrogated by presidential proclamation in 1958, but a new one, drafted by a committee appointed by the president, was promulgated in 1962.

constitution submitted by a commission directed by Lord Reid. That
of Ceylon is based upon proposals made by Ceylonese ministers, and
promulgated through a series of Orders in Council in London. That of
Nigeria came about in similar fashion. In the case of all of these
countries the constitutions were ratified by representative assemblies,
except for the 1962 Pakistani one.

India, Pakistan, Nigeria, and Malaysia arc organized as federations, although there are significant differences. The least complicated
situation is found in Pakistan where division into two provinces was
dictated by a geographic separation of nearly 1,000 miles. Originally,
the Indian constitution provided for 27 states, but since the boundaries were not conterminous with ethnic and linguistic lines, there was
considerable agitation for change. In 1956, a reorganization that
satisfied the demands of the more vocal groups reduced the number to
14. Nigeria is composed of four states, although the federal capital
(Lagos) enjoys a separate status. In 1963, the Malay federation was
enlarged and its name changed to Federation of Malaysia. To Malaya
were added three other constituent states: Singapore, North Borneo
(Sabah), and, Sarawak. The original Malay federation was composed
of 11 states, 9 of them corresponding to the traditional states which
were ruled by the Sultans, plus the two crown colonies of Penang and
Malacca which the British ceded to the federation. In 1965, Singapore
was forced to leave the federation. Ceylon is a unitary state.

The constitutions of India and Malaysia specify the exclusive and
concurrent powers of the national and state governments. In India
residual powers belong to the central government. Under certain
circumstances, the national parliament may legislate on subjects
normally falling under state jurisdiction. By comparison, Malaysia is
quite decentralized. Not only are residual powers vested in the states,
but, in addition, the states alone may legislate upon matters which
have been assigned to them. There is no indication as of this date to
what extent, if any, custom and judicial interpretation will
significantly reduce the powers of the Malay states. In the case of
India, however, the events of the past decade indicate that the states,
which were designed to be weak, are almost powerless to oppose the
central government.

HEADS OF STATE

As in Great Britain, the executive power in Commonwealth countries is formally vested in a head of state. In Canada, Australia, New
Zealand, and Ceylon, the head of state is the governor-general,

presumably representing the British monarch but actually the nominee of the respective governments. The trend seems to favor the appointment of persons who are citizens of their respective countries. By and large, the governor-general exercises powers similar to those of the British monarch. As in Britain, the major opportunity for discretionary action comes when no party has a majority in the legislature or when the incumbent prime minister resigns or dies. In New Zealand, the governor-general is authorized, for specific cause, to reject the cabinet's advice.

India and Pakistan (joined in 1963 by Nigeria) chose to be republics, with elected presidents playing the role which governors-general play in the other member states. When another member of the Commonwealth would use the words "queen" or "crown," India employs "union" and "state." Pakistani practice in this respect is similar to India's. Malaysia, on the other hand, has a monarch of her own who is the head of state. He is elected at a conference of the rulers of the Malay states, serves for five years, and is not eligible for re-election. In practice, however, the rulers are placed on a list, in order of seniority, and are chosen in this order. Presumably, the majority could find a senior ruler unsuitable and consequently turn to someone else.

THE REAL EXECUTIVE

Except for Pakistan, which under the 1962 constitution established a presidential system, executive power is effectively exercised by a group of ministers, collectively referred to as the cabinet. As in Great Britain, the cabinet is presided over by the prime minister, who, by virtue of his being the leader of the majority party in the legislature, is appointed to this office by the head of state. In Ceylon, the largest group in parliament is a coalition party, with the prime ministership going to the man with a strong personal following in the largest faction of the coalition.

As in Great Britain, other members of the cabinet are chosen by the prime minister. Some of the factors which limit his choice are not too different from those that operate in Great Britain. Personalities, regional diversities, and rural-urban conflicts play their part in the choice of cabinet colleagues. In Canada and Australia it is necessary to include representatives from as many provinces and states as possible. In countries like India, the numerous racial and cultural cleavages complicate the problem of appropriate representation in the cabinet. In Australia and New Zealand, under labor governments, the prime minister's choice of colleagues is limited by the party's parliamentary caucus. In Australia, it is customary to nominate a panel from which the prime minister makes his selection. In New Zealand, the prime minister's nominations are subject to approval by the caucus.

Commonwealth cabinets, by and large, are collectively responsible to the lower houses of their respective parliaments. In the older member countries British practices were, in essence, taken over without much fanfare. In the newer countries, however, there has been a tendency to write into law (in their constitutions) many of the practices and conventions which in the older members of the Commonwealth govern the relations between the cabinet and other institutions of government.

Although written into the constitutions of some of the new Commonwealth countries, the collective responsibility of the cabinet has been weakened to some extent. Perhaps because of a lack of experience, ministers have sometimes disagreed vigorously and publicly with government policy, and yet did not resign from the cabinet. Secondly, oftentimes there is no effective opposition in parliament, and the large party that supports the cabinet is unlikely to attempt to call it to account. Moreover, even when some opposition is manifest, the attitude of the dominant party toward criticism has been negative. But it is still too soon to pass judgment on the workings of cabinet government in these nations.

LEGISLATURES

Except for New Zealand, whose upper house was abolished in 1956, the Commonwealth countries we have been considering have bicameral parliaments. In each of these countries (except for Pakistan), it is in the lower house that the significant debates on finance and other legislation take place. It is here that criticisms are voiced, grievances ventilated, and, in the final analysis, governments upheld or voted out.

Lower houses in the Commonwealth countries generally are smaller than the British House of Commons. India's House of the People is the largest, with a membership of 505. The size of the others is as follows: Canada's House of Commons, 263; New Zealand's House of Representatives, 80; Australia's House of Representatives, 123; Ceylon's House of Representatives, 151; Malaysia's House of Representatives, 159; Nigeria's House of Representatives, 312.

Members of the lower houses usually are elected on the basis of a broad suffrage and single-member districts with approximately the same number of inhabitants for each district in the respective countries. Some variations exist, however, because of a failure to redistrict or because of a desire to insure some representation to religious and national minorities or castes. In some instances this results in multimember districts, while in others there is provision for a few appointive members. Among the federations, Canada is unique in that it assures each province a minimum number of representatives irrespective of population.

The internal organization of the lower chambers does not differ significantly from the patterns established in London. In the older member nations, there are two variations that deserve being noted. First, although the speaker is impartial in his rulings, he serves only as long as his party commands a majority, and in general elections he is actively opposed in his consituency. This is also true of Ceylon and India. Secondly, parliamentary scrutiny of accounts is far less rigorous than in Great Britain. In the lower chambers of the newer member countries, the main variation is in the extent and nature of the opposition. The central fact is that at the time of their independence, these nations had one political party whose main reason for existence was to fight for independence. There was no need for a second party. After independence was achieved, however, an effective opposition, if it developed at all, required several years to reach an effective stage.

The absence of an effective second party determined the nature of the opposition that developed. First of all, so long as the opposition was numerically weak and thus had no hope of forming an alternate government, its criticism tended to be irresponsible. Moreover, such criticism tended to be unconstructive, with the most constructive criticism coming from groups or individuals in the government party. Finally, the opposition parties that developed tended to represent either extreme right or extreme left political opinion, making it almost impossible for them to unite. This not only limits their effectiveness, but, in addition, makes it difficult to determine who is the leader of the opposition.

In the countries that have them, the upper chambers are called senates, except for India, whose upper house is known as the Council of States. Their respective sizes are as follows: India, 232; Ceylon, 30; Malaysia, 50; Nigeria, 40; Australia, 60; Canada, 101. All of them have one thing in common: a singular lack of power. They may neither originate nor amend financial legislation, although they do have power of limited delay. Nonfinancial bills may be delayed for a longer period, but this does not constitute a significant hurdle.

The establishment of upper chambers was motivated by diverse considerations, with the result that the selection of their members varies. The Canadian Senate was intended to approximate the House of Lords, that is, to represent wealth and property. Hence the senators are appointed by the governor-general, on the advice of the Cabinet. Interestingly enough, the Canadian Senate is not viewed primarily as an aspect of Canadian federalism, for although seats are apportioned among the provinces, Quebec and Ontario have 24 members each. By contrast, the Australian Senate is designed as a federal and democratic institution, with 10 senators from each state. Because one party frequently captured all seats in one state, a system of proportional representation was introduced in 1948 to insure minority representation.

In Ceylon, 15 senators are elected by the House of Representatives and 15 are appointed by the governor-general, on the advice of the prime minister. In Malaysia, 28 senators are elected by the 14 state legislatures (two each), while 22 are appointed by the monarch. Members of the second group are supposedly selected for their distinguished service in the professions, in public affairs, and in industry. In India, 220 members of the Council of States are apportioned among the states and selected indirectly by the elected members of the state legislative assemblies. The remaining 12 seats are filled by appointment by the president, whose constitutional instructions require him to select persons having special knowledge or practical experience in literature, science, art, and social service.

POLITICAL PARTIES: CANADA, AUSTRALIA, NEW ZEALAND

Each of these countries has basically a two-party system, although third parties have from time to time exerted significant influence. The major parties are based upon nationwide support and thus represent a composite of regional, economic, ethnic, and religious interests. In Australia and New Zealand, however, labor parties have achieved the status of major parties, which has served to emphasize class as the basis of party strength, although in both countries their appeal has been broadened so as to include many small farmers and portions of the urban middle class. New Zealand's other major party is the National, while in Australia it is the Liberal, although the Country party refuses to pass from the scene and is, in effect, in permanent coalition with the Liberals. Canada's major parties are the Progressive-Conservative and the Liberal.

As in Great Britain, the party leader is the dominant personality in the political process, although less so in the labor parties. The non-labor parties choose their leaders by parliamentary caucuses, except in Canada where they are selected by party conventions. The labor parties of New Zealand and Australia also employ the parliamentary caucus in choosing their leaders, who are subject to removal by the caucus if they do not live up to its expectations. Moreover, labor caucuses are influential in determining party policies and, when in power, legislative programs. In essence, therefore, non-labor party leaders, as in Britain, are more powerful within their party organizations than are the labor party leaders, but both are less powerful than their counterparts in London. Correspondingly, the parliamentary caucus is more powerful, both in policy matters and in influencing Cabinet membership.

Party organization outside parliament is similar to that in Great Britain, although it is not so well developed. Prior to World War II, for example, constituency organizations were more the exception than the rule. Even now, many local organizations tend to lie dormant between elections, which seems to accord them greater autonomy than in Great Britain. There are party staffs and professional workers, but they appear to devote most of their time to educational activities rather than seeking to enhance national control over local units of the party.

To a large degree, these generalizations do not apply to the labor parties of New Zealand and Australia. In those Dominions, workers have been well organized for several decades, with the labor parties being an outgrowth of trade unionism. From the outset, local units of these parties have been more active than corresponding units of the non-labor parties, especially in the intervals between elections. Moreover, the national offices of these two labor parties have maintained a closer and tighter organizational control over their regional and local units.

POLITICAL PARTIES: INDIA, CEYLON, MALAYSIA, NIGERIA

Political parties in these newer members of the Commonwealth are less fully developed than in Great Britain or the other member states. Except for the Congress party in India, which began in 1883 under somewhat unusual circumstances, political parties in the newer states of the Commonwealth are the products of this century.

Moreover, there has been a tendency toward one-party dominance. The parties which since independence have exercised effective control of the government are, except in Ceylon, the parties which led the fight for independence. The identification of these parties with the independence movements has apparently enhanced their prestige among the people and raised their leaders to the position of national heroes. Conversely, these same factors have made it difficult for opposition parties to develop and to acquire respectability.

The importance of the leaders of the dominant parties can scarcely be overemphasized, Prime Ministers Nehru of India, Nkrumah of Ghana, and Abdul Rahman of Malaysia led parties primarily because of their roles in the independence movements. Not only have these men exercised effective control over the organization of their respective parties, but, in addition, their personal influence has been important with the educated elites of their countries. Moreover, the tasks which these men have faced have tended to enhance their positions as leaders. And they have endeavored to present themselves as representatives of their respective nations rather than of any particular group or subculture.

The relationship of party leaders to the party organization, in and out of parliament, may change in the future. At the moment, however, their position is seldom challenged. As new leaders arise, and as opposition parties gain in respectability, lesser leaders and the rank and file will no doubt demand a greater voice.

The organization of parties is still in the process of development, with greater strides being made in some countries than in others. In view of the recent rise of political parties in these nations, however, it is surprising that political organization has proceeded to the extent that it has. The dominant parties have developed their organizations on the national, regional, and local level by utilizing professional workers. Where universal suffrage is a novelty, party workers have faced a monumental task in spreading information and educating the voters.

The question has been raised as to how democratic are countries where one-party systems are dominant. Perhaps some time must elapse before a definitive answer can be provided. Certainly, the danger of a drift from one-party rule to authoritarian dictatorship is very real. But it seems worth noting that these parties and their leaders in power have been elected by universal suffrage. Moreover, parties, elections and parliaments—all these institutions of democratic government—have been established under conditions of poverty, ill health, illiteracy, in some cases civil strife, and in all cases cultural heterogeneity. In the light of these and other factors, one cannot but marvel at the degree of tolerance which has prevailed, and tolerance is one of the basic prerequisites for democracy.

BIBLIOGRAPHICAL NOTE

There are numerous books on the Commonwealth as a whole as well as on particular aspects of the political, economic, and social relationships. Among the more informative are the following:

BAILEY, SIDNEY D. *Parliamentary Government in Southern Asia.* New York: Institute of Pacific Relations, 1953.

BAUER, PETER T. *Economic Analysis and Policy in Underdeveloped Countries.* Durham, N.C.: Duke University Press, 1957.

BELL, PHILIP W. *The Sterling Area in the Postwar World, Internal Mechanism and Cohesion, 1946–1952.* Oxford: Clarendon Press, 1956.

BRADY, ALEXANDER. *Democracy in the Dominions.* 3rd. ed., Toronto: University of Toronto Press, 1958.

CROCKER, W. R. *Self-Government for the Colonies.* London: Allen and Unwin, 1949.

EMERSON, RUPERT. *Representative Government in Southeast Asia.* Cambridge, Mass.: Harvard University Press, 1955.

HARVEY, HEATHER J. *Consultation and Co-operation in the Commonwealth: A Handbook on Methods and Practice.* London: Royal Institute of International Affairs, 1951.

HUSSEY, W. D. *The British Empire and Commonwealth, 1500–1961.* Cambridge: Cambridge University Press, 1963.

JENNINGS, SIR IVOR. *Constitutional Laws of the Commonwealth.* Oxford: Clarendon Press, 1957.

———. *Problems of the New Commonwealth.* Durham, N.C.: Duke University Press, 1958.

———. *The Approach to Self-Government.* Cambridge: Cambridge University Press, 1956.

———. *The British Commonwealth of Nations.* London: Hutchinson's University Library, 1954.

———. *The Commonwealth in Asia.* Oxford: Clarendon Press, 1951.

KAHIN, GEORGE, McT. *Major Governments of Asia.* Ithaca, N.Y.: Cornell University Press, 1958.

KING, JOHN KERRY. *Southeast Asia in Perspective.* New York: Macmillan, 1956.

MANSERGH, NICHOLAS. *The Commonwealth and the Nations.* London: Royal Institute of International Affairs, 1948.

NICHOLSON, MAJORIE. *Self-Government and the Communal Problem: A Study of Colonial Constitutional Problems Arising in Plural Societies.* London: Gollancz, 1948.

SIMMONS, JACK (ED.). *From Empire to Commonwealth: Principles of British Imperial Government.* London: Odhams, 1949.

UNDERHILL, FRANK H. *The British Commonwealth.* Durham, N.C.: Duke University Press, 1956.

WHEARE, K. C. *The Statute of Westminster and Dominion Status.* 5th ed. Oxford: Oxford University Press, 1953.

Books on individual countries, especially on the postwar members of the Commonwealth, are less numerous. In addition to the studies suggested below, current periodicals and the learned journals are excellent sources of information.

AUSTRALIA

CRISP, L. F. *The Parliamentary Government of the Commonwealth of Australia.* 2d ed. New York: Longmans, Green, 1954.

DABIS, S. R., ET AL. *The Australian Political Party System.* Sydney: Angus & Robertson, 1954.

DAVIES, A. F. *Australian Democracy: An Introduction to the Political System.* Melbourne: Longmans, Green & Co., 1958.

ENCEL, S. *Cabinet Government in Australia.* Melbourne: Melbourne University Press, 1962.

GREENWOOD, GORDAN (ED.). *Australia: A Social and Political History: 1788–1950.* New York: Praeger, 1956.

————. *The Future of Australian Federalism: Commentary on the Working of the Constitution.* Melbourne: Melbourne University Press, 1946.

HORSFALL, J. C. *Australia.* New York: Praeger, 1956.

MILLER, J. D. B. *Australian Government and Politics,* 2d ed. London: Blackwell's, 1959.

NADEL, G. H. *Australia's Colonial Culture.* Cambridge, Mass.: Harvard University Press, 1957.

OVERACKER, LOUISE. *The Australian Party System.* New Haven, Conn.: Yale University Press, 1953.

SCARROW, HOWARD A. *The Higher Public Service of the Commonwealth of Australia.* Durham, N.C.: Duke University Press, 1957.

CANADA

CLOKIE, H. M. *Canadian Government and Politics.* 2d ed. New York, London: Longmans, Green, 1950.

COLE, TAYLOR. *The Canadian Bureaucracy: A Study of Canadian Civil Servants and Other Public Employees, 1939–1947.* Durham, N.C.: Duke University Press, 1949.

DAWSON, ROBERT MACGREGOR. *The Government of Canada.* 4th ed. Toronto: University of Toronto, 1963.

LAUGHARNE, GRACE. *Canada Looks Ahead.* London: The Royal Institute of International Affairs, 1956.

LOWER, A. R. M.; SCOTT, F. R., ET AL. *Evolving Canadian Federalism.* Durham, N.C.: Duke University Press, 1958.

CEYLON

BAILEY, SIDNEY D. *Ceylon.* New York: Longmans, Green, 1952.

JENNINGS, SIR IVOR, AND TAMBIAH, H. W. *The Dominion of Ceylon: The Development of Its Laws and Constitution.* London: Stevens, 1952.

OLIVER, HENRY M. *Economic Opinion and Policy in Ceylon.* Durham, N.C.: Duke University Press, 1957.

TRESIDDER, ARGUS JOHN. *Ceylon: An Introduction to the "Resplendent Land."* New York: Van Nostrand, 1960.

WRIGGINS, W. HOWARD. *Ceylon: Dilemmas of a New Nation.* Princeton, N.J.: Princeton University Press, 1960.

INDIA

BERKES, ROSS N., AND BEDI, MOHINDER S. *The Diplomacy of India.* Stanford, Calif.: Stanford University Press, 1958.
BROWN, W. NORMAN. *India, Pakistan, Ceylon.* Ithaca, N.Y.: Cornell University Press, 1951.
GLEDHILL, ALAN. *The Republic of India.* London: Stevens, 1951.
HARRISON, SELIG S. *India: The Most Dangerous Decades* (Princeton, N.J.: Princeton University Press, 1960.
MENON, VAPAL PANGUNNI. *The Transfer of Power in India.* Princeton, N.J.: Princeton University Press, 1957.
MORAES, FRANK. *Jawaharlal Nehru.* New York: Macmillan, 1956.
MORRIS-JONES, W. H. *Parliament in India.* New York, London: Longmans, Green, 1957.
MURTI, B. S. N. *India in the Commonwealth.* New Delhi: Beacon Information and Publications, 1953.
PARK, RICHARD L., AND TINKER, IRENCE (EDS.). *Leadership and Political Institutions in India.* Princeton, N.J.: Princeton University Press, 1959.
WEINER, MYRON. *Party Politics in India.* Princeton, N.J.: Princeton University Press, 1957.

MALAYSIA

CARRINGTON, C. E., ET AL. *Malaya and Singapore.* London: Royal Institute of International Affairs, 1956.
GINSBURG, NORTON, AND ROBERTS, CHESTER F. *Malaya.* Seattle: University of Washington Press, 1958.
GULLICK, J. M. *Malaya.* New York: Praeger, 1963.
MILLS, LENNOX ALGERNON. *Malaya: A Political and Economic Appraisal.* Minneapolis: University of Minnesota Press, 1958.
PYE, LUCIAN W. *Guerilla Communism in Malaya.* Princeton, N.J.: Princeton University Press, 1956.

NEW ZEALAND

BEAGLEHOLE, J. D. (ED). *New Zealand and the Statute of Westminster.* Wellington: Victoria University College, 1944.
LIPSON, LESLIE. *The Politics of Equality: New Zealand's Adventures in Democracy.* Chicago: University of Chicago Press, 1948.
MILLER, HAROLD. *New Zealand.* New York: Longmans, Green, 1950.
MILNE, R. S., ED. *Bureaucracy in New Zealand.* London: Blackwell's, 1957.
REED, A. H. *The Story of New Zealand.* New York: Roy, 1955.
ROBSON, J. L. (ED.). *New Zealand.* London: Stevens, 1954.
SIMPSON, FRANK A. *Parliament in New Zealand.* Wellington: Reed, 1947.
WEBB, LEICESTER. *Government in New Zealand.* Wellington: Department of Internal Affairs, 1940.

NIGERIA

BRETTON, HENRY L. *Political Power and Stability in Nigeria.* New York: Praeger, 1962.

EZERA, K. *Constitutional Developments in Nigeria.* New York: Gregory Lounz, 1960.

MITCHISON, LOIS. *Nigeria: Newest Nation.* New York: Praeger, 1960.

SKLAR, RICHARD. *Nigerian Political Parties: Power in an Emergent African Nation.* Princeton: Princeton University Press, 1963.

SMYTHE, HUGH H. AND MABEL M. *The New Nigerian Elite.* Stanford: Stanford University Press, 1960.

PAKISTAN

AHMAD, MUSHTAG. *Government and Politics in Pakistan.* Karachi: Pakistan Publishing House, 1959.

BOLITHO, HECTOR. *Jinnah: Creator of Pakistan.* London: Murray, 1954.

CALLARD, KEITH B. *Political Forces in Pakistan, 1947–1959.* New York: Institute of Pacific Relations, 1959.

KHAN, LIAQUAT ALI. *Pakistan, the Heart of Asia.* Cambridge, Mass.: Harvard University Press, 1950.

QURESHI, I. H. *The Pakistani Way of Life.* New York: Praeger, 1956.

STEPHENS, IAN M. *Pakistan.* New York: Praeger, 1963.

SYMONDS, RICHARD. *The Making of Pakistan.* London: Faber & Faber, 1950.

PART TWO
FRANCE

CHAPTER 9

FRANCE AND THE FRENCH

THOSE of us who are a part of Western Civilization see in France certain attributes common to the West—an emphasis on the importance of man as an individual, a belief in political democracy, and a dedication to fundamental civil rights. We find, however, that there is less agreement among the French people in the acceptance of these concepts, and more conflicting interpretations of them, than in England or the United States. Since the last quarter of the nineteenth century, France has been functioning as a parliamentary democracy, with significant variations (to be noted later) from the British model. These differences are to a large extent rooted in the past, in France's experience as a nation, and in the character of her people.

GEOGRAPHY AND ECONOMICS

The geophysical configuration of France has facilitated the development of a closely knit society, while enabling the country to maintain diversified contacts with the outside world. The area is compact, and there are no formidable mountain barriers inside the country. Navigable rivers, an extensive network of canals, and a railway system provided the country with a superb system of internal communication long before the coming of the airplane. On the north, west, and south France is surrounded by water, while the Alps and the Pyrenees offer partial protection to her southeast and southwest. The Rhine river and the open country of the northeast constitute the one break in the natural protection pattern. France's geographical location enables her to look in three main directions. In the west, her orientation is Occidental, looking toward Britain and the Americas. In the east, her orientation is continental; she is typically European. In the south, she looks to the Mediterranean, North Africa, Italy, and Greece, a window looking back on the past 2,000 years of Western civilization.

The city of Paris has played a unique role in the history of modern France, sometimes identified with France herself, while on other occasions considered something other than an integral part of the nation. Irrespective of how one looks upon the city, it cannot be denied that

Paris has influenced the destiny of France. The phenomenal population growth of the city (one Parisian for every 50 Frenchmen less than 200 years ago as compared with one for every 8 today) enabled it to monopolize many facets of French life—national administration, banking, industry, and intellectual and artistic life. More than one third of all industrial and commercial profits are earned in the Parisian area, while more than half of the turnover of French businesses takes place in the same area. While a moderate trend toward dispersal seems to be in progress, Paris still employs the vast majority of French workers in several important industrial and commercial sectors of the economy. This would seem to suggest that Paris is more than a frivolous, brilliant, and superficial place, an impression that some visitors may acquire. Yet there are differences between the hectic, hurried life of Paris and the more deliberate, less hustled and philosophical attitude of the provinces. On the other hand, there are some indications that Paris no longer impresses the provincial, that there is a movement away from Paris toward the provinces, with a corresponding increase in provincial pride—pride in cathedrals, legends, landscapes, and local products.

Because of the variety in her climate, soils, and natural resources, France for a long time was looked upon as economically the best balanced nation in Europe. The abundance of fertile soil in differing climates and the blessing of adequate rainfall combined to make for a productive and diversified agriculture. A base for industry was provided by the abundance of iron ore, bauxite, and potash. Deficiencies in coal, oil, and textile raw materials were in large part made up from resources in the French empire. Partly because she resisted the Industrial Revolution, or could not accommodate to it, France for a long time remained a nation of small farmers, artisans, and shopkeepers, with the urban and rural populations relatively balanced. Even today this balance is maintained better than in any other modern industrial nation.

The evolution toward industrialization has been slow, mainly because of (1) the Frenchman's attachment to the soil, (2) his artisan conception of manufacturing, and (3) the achievement in France of a balanced and prosperous economic order prior to the Industrial Revolution.

The Frenchman's attachment to the soil is not easy for an American to understand, for we sell one farm, buy another, and perhaps repeat the process. In the case of the average French peasant, however, his particular piece of land has been in the family for generations. It is more than just a piece of land, and he wants it to remain that way. Unfortunately, he has done little to improve the productivity of his land, for he has not wanted to invest in chemical fertilizer, in tractors or other elements of modern agriculture, with the result that output per acre has dropped.

The Frenchman has been slow to adopt power-driven machinery in many industries. Traditionally, his conception of work has been that of the artisan and artist with pride in work well done. He has a passion for conceiving and creating fine products, but he abhors the notion of mass producing them with machines. He likes to emphasize quality instead of quantity, moderation and not bigness, craftsmanship and not impressive production figures.

Having achieved a prosperous and balanced economy, the French saw little reason for change. During the seventeenth and eighteenth centuries, agriculture, commerce, and handicraft production were the dominant features of economic life in France. Her soil, climate, and industrious peasants made France relatively self-sufficient. Manufacturing was limited to a few people and tended to emphasize luxury goods. But this balance was to be upset in the nineteenth century, which became the century of coal, iron, and applied science, with an emphasis on mass-produced consumer goods. Large-scale enterprises left the craftsmen behind. The France "that functioned so well in the age of wood, wind, and water was falling behind in an age of steam and iron."[1] The French economy resisted change at the time technical advances were enabling foreign agriculture and foreign industry to compete successfully with its own counterparts.

France entered the twentieth century a comparatively rich nation, largely self-sufficient, and still maintaining a nice balance between agriculture and industry. Her answer to competition, at home and abroad, consisted principally of cartels, tariffs, and subsidies, and not improved production. Although the French still pay lip service to individualism and the profit motive, the essential feature of their economy is a kind of collectivism. Certainly, there is little room for free enterprise. Cartels protect industrialists from domestic competition, while high tariffs and restrictive quotas shield them from foreign competition. The peasants demand subsidies so they can buy the expensive French-produced goods, while workers seek wage supplements and other benefits. Prior to the formation of the De Gaulle republic, which has been reducing subsidies, approximately one third of

---

[1] John B. Wolf, in E. M. Earle, *Modern France: Problems of the Third and Fourth Republics* (Princeton, N.J.: Princeton University Press, 1951), p. 27.

the French national budget went for direct or indirect subsidies.

Most observers of modern France agree that the country has been suffering from economic stagnation. She has sought to maintain herself as a nation of villagers in a world of cities. She has been unable or unwilling to submit unproductive ideas and institutions to external competition, from which they have long been protected. Modern industry, as well as industrial workers, have been regarded as foreign intruders. Some students of contemporary France have argued that the unwillingness of the French to abandon traditional ideas and structures—as shown by the absence of economic expansion—may well be the cause of protectionism rather than the effect. However that may be, there seems little doubt that France has been trying to remain aloof from the real world of the twentieth century.

Developments in the late 1950s and early 1960s, however, seemed to constitute a reversal of the earlier trend. The rate of economic growth has shot up phenomenally, and a general economic expansion is taking place, due in large part to the government's reform in tax and investment policies. New resources have been uncovered and developed, particularly oil, atomic energy, and electricity. Industrial enterprises are becoming more and more efficient, with less and less reluctance to employ the laborsaving devices of modern technology. In agriculture, too, more advanced methods and techniques are being introduced. And although the small man still dominates in industry and commerce (about 65 per cent of the French firms employ one to five persons), some uneconomic enterprises are falling by the wayside. In short, the Industrial Revolution is being accepted.

A number of legislative enactments in the 1960s helped to promote modernization in industry and agriculture. Some of these dealt with tax and budgetary policies, others promoted scientific research and technical education, while still others improved rural public utilities and trade and distribution channels. All of these developments have helped Frenchmen to meet increased international competition which was brought on by France's entry into the European Common Market.

* * * * *

France has in some circles been depicted as a nation of tax evaders. Although there is evasion, Frenchmen pay more taxes than we or the British do. Her tax burden (national and local) amounts to more than 40 per cent of her national income, while ours is around 30 per cent. And it should be remembered that the average income of a Frenchman is scarcely more than one fourth that of an American.

French tax laws are, however, inequitable and uneconomical. More than half of the tax revenue derives from consumers' (sales) taxes, which one finds at all stages of production and distribution. All goods sold and delivered (milk and bread are exempt) and all services rendered are subject to sales taxes. At each stage, the taxes are passed on to the consumer, and are thereby borne primarily by those who can least afford them. An unknown degree of evasion occurs at some points along the way.

Income taxes, on the other hand, account for less than 30 per cent of the government's revenue. And it is interesting to note that workers pay a disproportionate share of that, while the peasants and corporations pay a small part of it. The disproportionate privileges which the tax system establishes and protects are more serious, in the opinion of French treasury officials, than the evasions.

In the 1960s, however, the government granted tax relief and enacted measures to equalize the tax burden. Industrial and business taxes were simplified and depreciation on diminishing values was introduced. The income tax was simplified and adjustments made in it so as to institute greater tax equality. Inheritance taxes were reduced, but taxes were placed on the appreciation of property values (and hence on real estate speculation). Moreover, these measures were accompanied by a drive to eliminate tax evasion.

THE PEOPLE

The population of France is approximately 48 million. A decade ago France was being referred to as a country of old people; the birth rate had been going down since the early part of this century, and many of her young men had been lost in World War I and II. In the past ten years, however, the birth rate has been sharply on the increase, with the result that today people are talking about a new France, a young France. Because of wartime losses, women still predominate (over 52 per cent), but the increasingly dominant theme tends to emphasize youthfulness and growth.

Although the inhabitants of France refer to themselves as Frenchmen, they are the least race-minded of any people in Europe. As a matter of fact, there is "no such thing as a French race."[2] The unity which the nation possesses is not based on racial elements, for in the north they are German, in the south they are Mediterranean or Latin,

---

[2] Andre Siegfried, in E. M. Earle, *op. cit.*, pp. 4–5.

and in the west they are Celtic. Ethnically, the primary form is perhaps Celtic, but the Romans determined the essential cultural patterns, including language, religion, and concepts of law and government. And after the fall of the Roman Empire, the various invaders contributed to the admixture that resulted. As a consequence, Frenchmen have little sympathy for racial prejudices or racial theories.

The basis of French unity is to be found more in a way of life. A noted Frenchman has said that it would be more appropriate to refer to his countrymen as "a culture group, delimited by the diffusion of its language."[3] A Frenchman's loyalty is to the nation, and his concept of the nation is that of "a glorious personification of a civilized cultural entity," and not that conveyed by the contemporary political system or the government of the moment, both of which he may detest.

In their attitude toward other cultures and nations, however, the French may appear intolerant. They have believed in the superiority of French culture and have been convinced that they had a civilizing mission to perform in the world. To this end, they exerted efforts which were in the nature of real sacrifices, national and personal. The motivation, although not always so interpreted by others, was not the aggrandizement of France but rather the improvement of the whole world community.

In religion, France is nominally Catholic. Of some 48 million inhabitants, about 37 million have been baptized, and these are overwhelmingly Catholic. The Protestants and Jews constitute no more than a million, with the latter numbering less than 200,000. The great mass of Catholics are not practicing Catholics in the American sense, because they are in the main Catholics only at four moments of their lives—birth, first communion, marriage, and death.

Although most Frenchmen are sincerely religious, they are also sincerely anticlerical. The *ancien régime* was founded on a double absolutism, king and church, while the republic has been characterized by a double revolt. Throughout the nineteenth century, the church was opposed to republican institutions, which in large measure led to a formal separation of church and state in 1904.

Whether faithful to the church or not, the Frenchman bears an imprint of Catholicism. "French Catholicism—like all Catholicism— is a religion of authority, encasing France in an armor of ecclesiastical

---

[3] A. L. Guerard, *France: A Short History* (New York: W. W. Norton, Inc., 1946), p. 44.

discipline."[4] As a consequence, religion in France fosters neither a tradition of individual moral responsibility nor a feeling for political liberty. Yet while they are conformists from the outside, most Frenchmen, having made a pact with the church, feel free and are determined not to sacrifice their freedom of mind.

As in the case of other peoples, Frenchmen are said to exemplify certain characteristics. They are practical and matter of fact; they are quiet, orderly, thrifty, suspicious, and serious. Their material interests are highly developed; they value property for the independence it will give them. Insofar as "bourgeois" is defined as a man with some resources to fall back upon, all Frenchmen are bourgeois, or want to be. Since money is difficult to earn, one should keep it. As Siegfried has often said, "a Frenchman will give his life for his country, but he does not want to give his money."

Moreover, a Frenchman is proud of his individualism and his independence of mind. He does not want ready-made opinions; his is the critical approach. He wants to discuss, to think, to analyze, and to reach conclusions on his own. He seeks to inject intelligence and reasoning into everything. He resists advertising and inquiries into his personal life and beliefs. The Frenchman's individuality has no doubt made for high cultural achievements, but it has also led to frustrations. For example, the analytical approach made it difficult to determine the final resting place of France's Unknown Soldier. If placed in a location associated with the Revolution, this would be offensive to those who never accepted it. A similar difficulty was encountered when a chapel was suggested, because there was no proof that the Unknown Soldier was even a Christian, let alone a Catholic, hence the risk of blasphemy. By contrast, no one in England considered the theological implication of the decision to bury the country's Unknown Soldier in Westminster Abbey.

Paradoxically, the Frenchman's practical bent is no handicap when he engages in a discussion of abstract ideas and high principles. He becomes an idealist, a universalist, an internationalist, and a humanist. While accepting tolerance as an intellectual necessity, he is skeptical about men and about compromise. He has a vigorous interest in the ideas which underlie politics, but he is cynical towards those who practice politics.[5] This attitude, coupled with the Frenchman's

---

[4] Siegfried, *op. cit.*, p. 10.

[5] Patrick Edward Charvet, *France* (New York: Frederick A. Praeger, 1955), p. 246.

reluctance to forget injury, even if by doing so the common interest would be served, has made for anything but efficiency in government.

THE CHARACTER OF POLITICAL LIFE

In France, as in other countries, the nature of political life is in part shaped by the past. The dominant echo from the past portrays a theme of national greatness. In the seventeenth and eighteenth centuries, and during most of the nineteenth, France was undisputedly the leading nation on the Continent politically, economically, culturally, and intellectually. Many Frenchmen still remember an era of grandeur when French alliances controlled Europe and the French Empire extended over six continents. This cannot but be a factor in the nation's political subconscious, in the concept that the French have of themselves and their role among the nations.

Yet French political institutions in the age of greatness were absolutist—monarchical and clerical. They had bestowed upon France a certain unity, an organic conception of the state. The French Revolution swept away these political institutions, although it took another 100 years for republican institutions to gain a relatively firm, if not always decisive, foothold. For some, the absolutist institutions continued to be the ideal, although supported by a decreasing number of people. Yet, the impact of the Revolution was unsettling; the greater part of French political history since then has been characterized as a period in which Frenchmen have been searching for a new political consensus.

In these years of search, certain views have been dominant in French political life. One is that the state is something to be feared. The state possesses power and is therefore forever and always a potential tyranny. Consequently, one needs to be constantly on guard lest freedom be lost. It follows, therefore, that grants of authority must be limited and surrounded with safeguards. It is in this psychology—pessimism about human nature and the distrust of men—that the French belief in written law is rooted.

An outgrowth of this attitude is the view that the state is something apart from and above the individual, and not necessarily benevolent. In contrast to the Anglo-American idea that the state exists to protect and serve the people, the French view the state as a would-be master, an intruder, unrelated to the individual and a threat to him. The Frenchman suspects that if he joins an association (state or other), he will have to give more than he will receive. This concept gives rise to the tendency on the part of citizens to get as much as possible from the state, while at the same time contributing as little as possible. It is this attitude that has caused many observers of the French political scene to conclude that there is an absence of civic spirit in France.

The fear and distrust of the state has made it difficult for Frenchmen to organize a workable political authority. They have not wanted a system of government that vests significant authority in anyone, least of all in a strong executive. They have tried different forms of government, but none has been completely satisfactory. For the vast majority, the least unsatisfactory has been the republican form, provided it did not attempt to grapple with problems over which Frenchmen are seriously divided.

Moreover, French political life has been characterized by an emphasis on ideology and principle. This has meant that the various political factions could not be counted upon to embrace compromise as a workable system on a continuing basis. Certain factions might compromise on certain issues, and therefore constitute a majority in the resolution of those issues, but on other issues they might be determined to force the government out of office, rejecting all compromise proposals no matter how reasonable. In other words, the government of the day was forced, as a price of staying in office, to seek a new majority combination on each basic problem that it was compelled to tackle.

The inability to resolve the political problem effectively has made it more difficult for French governments to cope with the social revolutionary trends of this century. Industrialization and large-scale trade unionism brought in their wake social and economic problems whose solution could hardly wait until the French had reached agreement on basic political questions. The consequences have not always been decisive. While the moderate political groups managed to retain control (often precarious), many Frenchmen were expressing their exasperation by voting for extremist political parties of the left or right. The Communists, for example, have managed to poll over twenty per cent of the popular vote in most elections since World War II. While polling a considerably smaller percentage of the vote, groups on the far right have served to augment the size of antidemocratic blocs in the legislature and in a number of municipal councils. Fortunately for France, the extremist groups have been in a minority, but that minority has been large enough to constitute an ever-present danger to French democracy.

In brief, France has lacked the type of *practical* political consensus that exists in Britain. Whatever consensus has existed has been of a somewhat abstract nature, typified by the rallying cry of the Revolution—liberty, equality, fraternity. But many of the issues raised by that very Revolution have made practical political agreements difficult. More recently, the unsettling experience of defeat and occupation in World War II, including the experience of a collaborationist regime (Vichy) under Nazi auspices, has led to a more profound search for the source of France's difficulties. Or perhaps it was more of a search for a scapegoat, a search that did not leave the system of government and its leaders unscathed. Moreover, the costly, desperate, and largely unsuccessful battle to save the empire after World War II also contributed to France's difficulty in seeking to find a unifying political consensus.

BIBLIOGRAPHICAL NOTE

Among the general discussions of the people of France are D. W. Brogan, *The French Nation: From Napoleon to Petain 1814–1940* (New York: Harper, 1958); Stanley Hoffman, *et al.*, *In Search of France* (Cambridge: Harvard University Press, 1962); Hans Kohn, *Making of the Modern French Mind* (New York: Van Nostrand, 1955); Pierre Maillaud, *France* (London and New York: Oxford University Press, 1945); Charles Moraze, *The French and the Republic* (Ithaca, N.Y.: Cornell University Press, 1958); Charles Seignobos, *The Evolution of the French People* (New York: Knopf, 1932); and Andre Siegfried, *France: A Study in Nationality* (New Haven: Yale University Press, 1930); Edward R. Tannenbaum, *The New France* (Chicago: University of Chicago Press, 1961).

The cultural setting is discussed in Julian Park (Ed.), *The Culture of France in Our Time* (Ithaca, N.Y.: Cornell University Press, 1954) and Frederick C. Roe, *Modern France: An Introduction to French Civilization* (London: Longmans, Green, 1956). A. Maurois, *The Miracle of France* (New York: Harper, 1948) presents a general history of French civilization.

CHAPTER **10**

THE DEVELOPMENT OF FRENCH POLITICAL INSTITUTIONS

FRANCE was one of the first countries in Europe to develop a sense of national unity, symbolized by the monarchy. Unlike Great Britain, however, France did not make steady strides toward political democracy. And the strides she did make came considerably later than in Britain and were characterized by a number of interruptions and reversals. Moreover, the transitions, notably the Revolution of 1789, were more violent and more disruptive of political unity than those experienced by the British. In brief, a sense of national unity was not accompanied by an evolving agreement concerning the nature of the nation's political institutions.

THE ANCIEN REGIME AND THE REVOLUTION

France of the *Ancien Regime* was governed by the King, who wielded his powers through secretaries of state personally selected and directed by him. They, in turn, exercised their authority through a centralized bureaucratic machine, which was several centuries in the making and which was perfected under King Louis XIV by Cardinals Richelieu and Mazarin. After Louis XIV, however, the political structure lacked cohesion, being characterized by weakness and division. In the last fifty years of the Old Regime personal rule was symbolized by the nonexistence of a prime minister (although one was appointed in 1787), the King insisting on being his own prime minister.

A type of representative assembly, called the Estates General, had come into being in France in the fourteenth century. It was to represent the three estates (classes), the first being the clergy, the second the nobility, and the third the townsmen. The first two were by far the most important, although they represented only about five per cent of the population. The third type was a catch-all in which the middle class (bourgeoisie) was the most important. The feeble attempts of the Estates General to limit the monarchy were singularly unsuccessful. The fact that it was not convened between 1614 and 1789 is perhaps the best commentary on its role in the *Ancien Regime.*

What the Estates General did not do in the way of limiting royal authority, was attempted, to a degree, by the *parlements,* of which France had a number, the most important being the *Parlement* of Paris. Parlements were primarily law courts which had exercised some advisory powers in the medieval period. Because the promulgation of royal decrees was achieved by registering them with parlement, the latter attained the right of criticizing and even refusing to register them. Because kings could legally overrule such refusals, parlements were at worst a nuisance under strong monarchs. Under weaker governments, however, they became centers of opposition and were viewed by many Frenchmen as guardians of their liberties. Ironically enough, the opposition of parlements often prevented much needed reforms, thereby making it difficult for monarchs to take steps that would meet with popular acclaim.

The king's decision in 1788 to suspend parlements and to call a meeting of the Estates General for May 1789 was a confession of defeat, signifying the end of absolute monarchy. But the privileged classes, which had sided with the parlements, had not counted on the possibility of the Third Estate taking over the revolt and turning it to its own ends. Similarly, the Third Estate served to set in motion certain forces which it could not control. Within a brief span of time the constitutional struggle turned to civil war and a profound social revolution.

A CENTURY OF POLITICAL TURMOIL

The French Revolution had a tremendous impact, especially in Europe, raising the hopes of peoples in the struggle against monarchical regimes. On the other hand, it disappointed many of its supporters, not only because of the excesses (terror, etc.) but also because it seemed unable to produce a stable political order. For France it ushered in a century of political turmoil, which culminated in the establishment in 1875 of the Third Republic, an uneasy experiment which few expected to last, but which was to provide France with a political system that endured longer than any other that France has tried since the Revolution.

In the first years of the Revolution an unsuccessful effort was made to establish a constitutional monarchy. Following this failure, a republic was formed in 1792, which gradually assumed reactionary forms and was finally merged in the Empire of Napoleon. After Napoleon's downfall, the Bourbon monarchy was restored. This in turn gave way to a new monarchy in 1830, which recognized the theoretical sovereignty of the people as well as the tricolor flag of the Revolution. In 1848, monarchy was again replaced with a republic, only to be soon overthrown by its own president, Louis Napoleon, who became emperor, a position that he retained until the military disaster in the Franco-Prussian war ended in his capture in 1870 by the enemy at Sedan.

Following the armistice of 1871, and under its terms, a national assembly was elected to resolve the question of peace or war. It made peace with Germany, but it also governed France for the next five years, even though this was going beyond the stated purpose for which it was convened. And before it dissolved it formulated the constitutional instruments that were to govern France for the next sixty-five years.

Thus a century of political turmoil came to an uneasy and perhaps uncertain end. Unlike the English Revolution of 1688, which established the supremacy of Parliament (and without bloodshed), the French Revolution succeeded only in asserting the democratic ideal of popular sovereignty. It produced no lasting agreement, at least prior to 1875, on how this ideal was to be embodied in governmental institutions. The question of where responsibility for political acts was to rest was not adequately answered (or at best, answered provisionally) by any of the attempts at political organization from 1789 to 1875.

The Third Republic, which dates from the fall of the Empire in 1871 to the collapse of France in World War II in 1940, provided the longest period of stability since the Revolution. Its story, according to David Thomson,[1] can be divided into two equal parts. The first 35 years were spent in liquidating the past, "in thrashing out the old conflicts between Church and State, clerical and anti-clerical, Monarchy and Republic, militarism and parliamentarism" with the triumph of the anticlerical, Republican parliamentary forces. The next 35 years were spent "in seeking working compromise within the now established parliamentary Republic between new social forces—the new industrial working class . . . and the new indus-

---

[1] *Democracy in France: the Third and Fourth Republics* (2d ed., London: Oxford University Press, 1952), p. 72.

trial and financial oligarchy." Social and economic issues had in large measure replaced dynastic and ecclesiastical questions, even though some basic political questions remained.

THE CONSTITUTIONS OF THE THIRD AND FOURTH REPUBLICS

Between the Revolution and the establishment of the Third Republic the French experimented with a dozen constitutions. Although the average lifespan of each was brief, these constitutions were elaborate, long, and detailed documents. But, as history has demonstrated, the care and precision with which a constitution is drawn has no relation to its survival. Nor does practice in drafting constitutions guarantee their workability.

The most workable of French constitutions was that of the Third Republic. It consisted of three laws drawn up in 1875 as a temporary expedient by a monarchist assembly which could not decide which of two royal families should rule France. This was a compromise which neither faction wanted and which neither side believed would endure. The three laws do not resemble a constitutional document; there is no division into titles or chapters and no exact order. The Law on the Organization of the Public Powers vests legislative power in a Chamber of Deputies and a Senate, provides for a formal executive (president), prescribes that ministers are responsible to both houses of the legislature, and provides for a method of amending these arrangements. The Law on the Organization of the Senate prescribes in more detail the organization and powers of that body. The Law on the Relations of the Public Powers, passed several months after the other two, seeks to regulate more precisely governmental procedures involving the legislature and the executive.

The essential point to remember is that these three laws provided a mere structural framework, with the actual operation of the system to be worked out in practice. These laws did not place any limitations on the powers of government, except that the republican form of government would not be subject to amendment. The two houses, acting together, could presumably legislate about anything when and as they wished. And since there was no judicial review in the American sense, they had no fear of being overruled. Hence there was no real need to amend the constitution in a formal sense.

At the end of World War II, the people decided, by popular referendum, to write a new constitution. After turning down the product of the first constituent assembly, the people accepted that of the second. In the French tradition, the constitution of the Fourth Republic was detailed and logical, but, in the main, it ratified the political practices that had evolved under the Third. To be sure, some efforts were made to remedy the shortcomings that had evoked the most concern, primarily the relatively rapid turnover of cabinets. This was done by making impossible spur-of-the-moment votes of confidence, which had brought down so many governments in the prewar period. A cooling-off period of 24 hours was required, with the additional proviso that the only one who could ask for such a vote of confidence was the prime minister (premier), and not any minister. Moreover, the constitution provided that no cabinet could be defeated on a confidence vote or a censure motion unless an absolute majority voted against it. In practice, however, governments resigned when defeated, irrespective of the nature of the majority.

In addition, the constitution attempted further to protect the cabinet by making it responsible only to the lower house. Moreover, it sought to provide the cabinet with the power of dissolution, the important weapon of the British prime minister that had been nonexistent in the Third Republic. This effort was of little consequence, for the authority was so hemmed in with limitations and restrictions as to be meaningless.

FRENCH PARLIAMENTARISM UNDER THE THIRD AND FOURTH REPUBLICS

The French political system, under the Third and Fourth Republics, was essentially parliamentary. France was governed by ministers who were responsible to an elected legislature. There was a politically neutral head of state, and there was no judicial review in the American sense. But there were many significant dissimilarities from the British model, and these need to be pointed out, both as an aid to understanding the government of the Third and Fourth Republics and as a background for judging the governmental arrangements of the Fifth Republic.

France has always had a unitary form of government. Although Great Britain also has a unitary arrangement, its local units of government have more power than corresponding units in France. The latter country is much more centralized in the direction of affairs from Paris. What the British call local government, although it is limited, is for the French really a matter of administration.

Instead of a monarch, France had a president, elected for seven years by the two houses of Parliament meeting as one body. As in Great Britain, he was the ceremonial head of state. His political acts were the acts of ministers who were politically responsible to the legislature. But because no political party had a majority in Parliament, he had more discretion and influence in the choice of the man who would head and form the cabinet.

It was in the nature of the cabinet, however, that the main differences from British practice appeared. As indicated above, no political party ever had a majority, or anything approaching one, during the existence of the Third and Fourth Republics. Instead of two major parties, there were several major ones and a number of smaller ones, all electing some members to the legislature. In order to have a cabinet which could have the support of a majority in Parliament, it was necessary to include members from a number of political parties. Every cabinet, therefore, was a coalition government, reflecting the views of the respective parties represented therein.

This meant that every cabinet would be an uneasy combination, held together on the basis of what its members could agree upon. The basis of agreement was usually the lowest common denominator. Since they could not agree on most of the really crucial issues, the ones they could agree upon were in the main the more minor ones. Consequently, French cabinets could not seek to implement major and decisive party pledges as in Britain. Any attempt to do so, on the part of the prime minister or others, would bring an end to the coalition and the cabinet.

The average life of a cabinet was a little over six months, which suggests considerable instability. As a matter of fact, it was not so bad as it seemed, because a number of members of an outgoing cabinet would always be found in the succeeding one. Certain men served in cabinet after cabinet, in the same or different posts, which meant that there was a great deal more continuity and experience in cabinets than surface impressions indicated. This does not detract, however, from the fact that most major problems could not be dealt with in a forthright manner.

The cabinet was weak, partly because the prime minister could not be the strong unifying party leader that he is in Britain. His task was more that of a broker or compromiser seeking to get divergent groups to work together. Often one or more of these groups saw more advantage in voting against the cabinet than in supporting it. They could vote against the government, not only because they did not have to fear a new election but also because they had reason to believe that they might be more influential in the next cabinet.

They did not have to fear new elections because the prime minister did not have the power to dissolve parliament. In theory he possessed the power to dissolve the lower house, acting in the name of the president, but the consent of the Senate was required. Mainly because this power was employed in the early years of the republic by President MacMahon, acting without the consent of the prime minister and therefore contrary to the basic principle of parliamentary government, it fell into disuse. MacMahon had dissolved the Chamber of Deputies (with the consent of the Senate) at a time when the prime minister and the cabinet enjoyed the confidence of the Chamber of Deputies. This evoked such a storm of protest that dissolution came to be looked upon as an attempted *coup de 'Etat.* Thereafter it was never employed. The constitution of the Fourth Republic sought to institutionalize the power of dissolution, but it never became an actual political reality.

The cabinet was also weak because of certain political practices that had evolved in French parliamentary procedure. The cabinet could not, as in England, determine the way in which the time of Parliament would be spent. More than that, it could not even insist that cabinet measures have priority. And it did not have control of finance measures. Parliament could increase expenditures without any obligation to raise new revenue, an impossibility in Great Britain. Without control over finance and without priority for cabinet measures, the government of the day is in a weak position indeed.

Moreover, the practice of proxy voting in Parliament, that is, the possibility of one man casting all of the votes of his party group, made it difficult for a cabinet to keep a majority around. This would assure a sizable bloc of votes against the government on any issue. The groups supporting the coalition cabinet were not so united, for they would never give united, unqualified support, in advance, to the government on all questions. This situation forced the cabinet to look continually to its own defenses, canvassing its supporters and making sure that there were sufficient votes on hand at all times. In a sense, the prime minister was forced to worry more about the collective and individual dissensions of his majority than about the opposition. In brief, the nature of the coalition made for a lack of political cohesion.

Finally, the cabinet was at the mercy of parliamentary committees. Instead of being able to guide and shape the work of committees, as in Britain, cabinet members were often treated with hostility. Cabinet measures were often buried or so rewritten as to constitute but a faint resemblance of the original. It was not unusual for committees to report measures that could at best be described as undesirable by the government.

During the Third Republic, the cabinet had to please both houses of Parliament, although adverse votes in the Senate came to mean less and less in terms of the cabinet's political survival. The lower house increased its power and influence. During the Fourth Republic, France had essentially a one-house legislature, called the National Assembly, although an upper house, the Council of the Republic, was retained. The latter could at best merely delay measures for a brief time.

Because of the weakness of the cabinet, particularly in its relationship to Parliament, French parliamentarism came to be generally known as assembly government, signifying the predominant power of the legislature. This is in contrast to the employment of the term cabinet government, which is so often used in connection with British parliamentarism, signifying the predominant power of the cabinet.

COLLAPSE OF THE FOURTH REPUBLIC

In May 1958, the Fourth Republic collapsed. The country's political system had returned to a state of chronic instability, something most Frenchmen after World War II had hoped to avoid, with the consequence that many pressing problems could not be solved, or even relieved. Even so, the system would probably have survived if it had not been for the government's inability to maintain the French colonial empire. Economic conditions at home had improved greatly in 1953–57. Paradoxically, the increasing prosperity seemed to magnify the reverses in the foreign field, which were pulling France's international prestige downhill, and which had consumed much of her material and human resources.

The immediate circumstances leading to the downfall of the Fourth Republic can be summed up in one word—Algeria. The French settlers there, numbering at least 1,500,000, were determined to resort to violence, if need be, against what appeared to be the helplessness of the government in Paris to cope with the Moslem nationalist movement in Algeria. In this attitude they were supported by professional army officers, partly because of the humiliating defeat in Indochina and a no less humiliating withdrawal from Suez in 1956. Moreover, it was apparent that certain army units in Algeria and in France meant business. The threat of a military revolution was real.

The attitude of the populace in France was not reassuring to the established authorities. There was considerable sympathy for the nationalist attitude of the Algerian settlers and of the army. Many Frenchmen, particularly among the younger generation, were disinterested and apathetic about Algeria, but they did not come to the defense of the established order either.

In view of these circumstances, the government in Paris came to the conclusion that the only acceptable way of avoiding an almost certain military dictatorship was to call upon their World War II hero, General Charles de Gaulle, to form a government. On June 1, 1958, he was made prime minister, the last one under the Fourth Republic, with his stipulation that he would have power to revise the constitution drastically and that he could rule by decree for six months. The Parliament readily granted these powers and the Fourth Republic came to an end.

THE CONSTITUTION OF THE FIFTH REPUBLIC

The present French constitution was not drafted by a constituent assembly but by a handful of De Gaulle's men. After discussions by several groups, including a constitutional consultative committee, the draft was approved by the cabinet and submitted to the electorate for ratification in September 1958. It was approved by nearly 80 per cent of those who cast votes. The percentage in the overseas territories, except for the West African territory of Guinea, was even higher. In Guinea it was rejected in favor of independence.

The main aim of the drafters was to get away from a system in which Parliament predominated and which had failed to provide effective leadership. Their answer was to strengthen the executive in his relations with the legislature. This was done in two ways: first, by giving substantive powers, especially in times of crisis, to the formerly powerless chief of state, the president, and, secondly, by conferring greater powers on the prime minister by limiting the Parliament's policy-making powers and its powers to vote governments out of office.

On paper, the new constitution establishes the essential features of a traditional parliamentary government, but modifies it to give the executive (president and prime minister) the real power in policy making. Correspondingly, the powers of Parliament have been reduced or circumscribed. This in itself would appear to be a move in the direction of British practice. In actuality, however, the French Parliament has been shorn of its power to hold the executive politically accountable. To be sure, the cabinet is said to be responsible to the popularly elected lower house, the National Assembly, but the latter is severely hampered in the methods it can employ in seeking to hold the cabinet responsible. And the president is responsible to no one.

In a sense, this is leadership without accountability to popularly elected representatives. The constitution establishes a system which provides for leadership, but this leadership appears to be in large measure shielded from expressions of popular desires and aspirations. It is conceivable, however, that as the constitution is applied and the system evolves, a better balance will result, with a more successful combination of leadership and democracy.

In order to hold French overseas territories together, the constitution established the Community,[2] consisting of France and the "member states." Initially, common governmental institutions (president, executive council, senate, and court of arbitration) were created to handle common affairs. Before these could really be set in motion, however, a constitutional amendment in 1960 transformed the Community into an association of equal and independent states not unlike the Commonwealth that emerged from the British Empire. All members of the Community chose independence, and most of them elected to remain in the Community. They are now members of the United Nations. The president of France is recognized as "ex officio" president of the Community, but the senate, the executive council, and the court of arbitration have been abolished. The relations of Community members are now defined by special accords among the contracting parties. These provide for cooperation in matters of defense, education, telecommunications, finance, and foreign affairs. From time to time there are also meetings of the heads of the member states to discuss matters of common concern. France has extended considerable economic assistance to her former colonies, and has brought most of them into an associate membership in the Common Market.

An innovation for France is an independent body, called the Constitutional Council, composed of former presidents of the Republic and nine other members (three each chosen by the presidents of the two houses of Parliament and by the president of the Republic), the latter serving nine-year terms, and not eligible for reappointment.[3]

---

[2] The constitution of the Fourth Republic had sought to cope with this problem by establishing something called The French Union.

[3] Initial appointments were for three-, six- and nine-year terms, so that one third of them are replaced every three years.

The principal function of the Council, it seems, is to keep Parliament within the bounds set for it. The president, the prime minister, or the president of either house may ask that it strike down legislation when any one of them considers that Parliament is going beyond its powers. Moreover, the Council must approve all laws of a constitutional nature ("organic laws," that is, laws expanding on constitutional provisions), as well as the rules of procedure in Parliament. In addition, the Council is supposed to check on the regularity of elections to the presidency, to decide contested elections to Parliament, and to insure the proper conduct of referendums.

It may be futile to speculate about the future of the Constitutional Council or its impact on the future evolution of the Fifth Republic. Suffice it to say that for the present it is, and in the future could remain, a stumbling block to a significant expansion of the powers of the legislature. On the other hand, it could become the instrument of a looser interpretation of the constitution, thereby allowing for a great balance between executive and legislative authority. In 1962 it held itself incompetent to decide on an appeal charging that President De Gaulle was violating the constitution by seeking to amend it without reference to parliament.

The constitution provides that amendments to it may be proposed by the president, by the prime minister, or by members of parliament. In each case a proposed amendment must obtain a majority in each house of parliament. After passage by the two houses, the proposed amendment, if initiated by members of parliament, must be submitted for ratification by the people in a popular referendum. If the proposed amendment is initiated by the president or the prime minister, however, ratification (after passage by the two houses) may, at the discretion of the president, be achieved *either* by popular referendum, *or* by a three-fifths majority vote in a specially called joint meeting of the two houses of parliament.[4]

THE ARMY AND THE FIFTH REPUBLIC

The army, as suggested earlier, played a decisive role in the overthrow of the Fourth Republic. This was contrary to the well-established principle that in a democracy the civil power must be supreme, a principle that had been respected by French democracy no less than elsewhere. Because the events leading up to the overthrow of

---

[4] De Gaulle's circumventing of the amendment process is discussed in the following chapter in connection with his general use of the referendum.

the Fourth Republic pose a serious question for the future, the army's position should be stated, particularly since it conceivably could be used to justify the overthrow of the Fifth Republic.

The army reasoned that since a modernized fighting force could not cope with guerrilla actions, the only way out was to destroy the rebel organization and to put in its place a new political organization. But since the nation's political leaders seemingly did not understand this, the army was anxious to get the point across. At first, they only wanted to be heard. Subsequently, army and civilian authorities disagreed as to the need of certain administrative actions in Algeria. This conflict was resolved by having the civilian authorities retreat. Soon the army developed the doctrine that in a subversive war, only the army could be the final judge, although conceding that the civil and military authorities might work together.

Soon the army went even further. Certain army officers declared that civil administration was affected by partisan political considerations, a fact which could only give the rebels hope that France would capitulate. Hence the army, which was allegedly motivated by the national interest alone, was duty bound to bring an end to any encouragement of capitulation. In brief, the army was seeking to play a political role.

After De Gaulle came to power, the army's ideas for the reformation of the state were not adopted. Nevertheless, it sought to exercise a decisive influence in the new government's policies, particularly as they affected Algeria. Following De Gaulle's putting forth of the doctrine of self-determination for Algeria in 1959, a number of French army officers (some active and some retired) and their sympathizers made several desperate bids to prevent Algerian independence. These involved forthright efforts to defeat referendums, open rebellion in Algeria (and the seizure of power there in some areas for a brief period of time), as well as the creation of the Secret Army Organization (OAS) whose aim was to overthrow De Gaulle. These actions, as well as the attempt to assassinate President De Gaulle, ended in failure.[5]

In the light of these circumstances, it is not surprising that De Gaulle was forced to assume emergency powers, and to take extreme

---

[5] For a detailed discussion of the impact of Algeria on French politics, as well as of De Gaulle's various maneuvers to keep the army in line, see Roy C. Macridis and Bernard E. Brown, *The De Gaulle Republic: Quest for Unity* (Homewood: Illinois; Dorsey Press, 1960), as well as their *Supplement to the De Gaulle Republic* (1963). Also see William G. Andrews, *French Politics and Algeria: The Process of Policy Formation,* 1954–1962 (New York; Appleton, Century & Crofts, 1962).

measures to keep the army out of politics and to assure its loyalty to the politically constituted authority. The Algerian war, which dominated the evolution of the Fifth Republic in its first four years, came to an end with the grant of independence to Algeria in 1962. Now that the Algerian problem is past history, it remains to be seen if antirepublican elements in the army will make further efforts, particularly when De Gaulle passes from the scene, to determine the political structure of the state. It also remains to be seen how and in what ways the Fifth Republic will evolve now that the Algerian war is not there to dominate the political scene.

BIBLIOGRAPHICAL NOTE

Useful surveys of French political history are Dennis W. Brogan, *France Under the Republic: The Development of Modern France 1870–1939* (New York: Harper, 1940) ; ――, *The French Nation: From Napoleon to Petain* (London: Hamilton, 1953) ; J. P. T. Bury, *France 1814–1940* (Philadelphia: University of Pennsylvania Press, 1949) ; Alfred Cobban, *A History of Modern France* (2 vols., Baltimore: Penguin Books, 1961) ; and Albert Gueraud, *France: A Short History* (New York: Norton, 1946). Alexander Werth has written several accounts of modern French history, of which *The Twilight of France, 1933–1940* (New York: Harper, 1942) and *France, 1940–1955* (London: Holt, 1956) are particularly helpful.

Constitutional questions and political institutions under the Third and Fourth Republics are discussed in Patrick Edward Charvet, *France* (New York: Praeger, 1955) ; G. Lowes Dickinson, *Revolution and Reaction in Modern France* (London: G. Allen, 1892) ; Edward Mead Earle (ed.), *Modern France: Problems of the Third and Fourth Republics* (Princeton, N.J.: Princeton University Press, 1951) ; Jacques Fauvet, *La France Dechiree* (Paris: A. Fayard, 1957) ; Francois Goguel, *France Under the Fourth Republic* (Ithaca, N.Y.: Cornell University Press, 1952) ; R. K. Gooch, *Parliamentary Government in France: Revolutionary Origins, 1789–1791* (Ithaca, N.Y.: Cornell University Press, 1960) ; Herbert Luethy, *France Against Herself* (New York: Praeger, 1955) ; Ronald Matthews, *The Death of the Fourth Republic* (New York: Praeger, 1954) ; Saul Padover, et al., *French Institutions: Values and Politics* (Hoover Institute Studies, Stanford University Press, 1954) ; Dorothy Pickles, *French Politics: The First Years of the Fourth Republic* (London and New York: Royal Institute of International Affairs, 1953) ; O. R. Taylor, *The Fourth Republic of France: Constitution and Political Parties* (London: Royal Institute of International Affairs, 1951) ; David Thomson, *Democracy in France: The Third and Fourth Republics* (4th ed.; London: Oxford University Press, 1964) ; and Gordon Wright, *The Reshaping of French Democracy* (New York: Reynal and Hitchcock, 1948) ; ――, *France in Modern Times: 1760 to the Present* (Chicago: Rand McNally, 1960) ; ――, *Rural Revolution in France: The Peasantry in the Twentieth Century* (Stanford: Stanford University Press, 1964).

It is interesting also to consult two works which appeared shortly before the events of May 13th, Maurice Duverger, *The French Political System* (Chicago: University of Chicago Press, 1958); and David Schoenbrun, *As France Goes* (New York: Harper, 1957).

A useful recent commentary is Raymond Aron, *France, Steadfast and Changing: The Fourth and Fifth Republics* (Cambridge: Harvard University Press, 1960).

On the military and its relation to politics see: William G. Andrews, *French Politics and Algeria* (New York: Appleton, Century & Crofts, 1962); Edgar S. Furniss, Jr., *De Gaulle and the French Army* (New York: Twentieth Century Fund, 1964); J. H. Meisel, *The Fall of the Republic: Military Revolt in France* (Ann Arbor: University of Michigan Press, 1962).

CHAPTER 11

THE EXECUTIVE

THE CONSTITUTION of the Fifth Republic introduces a dual executive—a president and a cabinet—not too much unlike that existing in the Fourth Republic. The constitution does strengthen the position of the president, but political policy-making is clearly vested in the cabinet, which is responsible to the popularly elected National Assembly. In practice, however, De Gaulle has so interpreted the constitution—an interpretation acquiesced in at a time of crisis by the cabinet, Parliament, and the country generally—as to make the president's role predominant in the determination of national policy. When De Gaulle passes from the scene, if not before, questions as to the workability of this system, particularly in the matter of the relationship between the president and the cabinet and of these two to Parliament, will no doubt arise. The ability to find answers to such questions will in large part determine whether the Fifth Republic will survive when its first president is no longer at the helm.

THE PRESIDENT: NOMINATION AND ELECTION

The president of the Republic is elected for a seven-year term, with no limit on the number of terms he may serve. As originally provided for in the constitution, he was to be elected by an electoral college which included members of Parliament, members of general councils, and members of municipal councils in proportion to the population of each commune, as well as representatives of municipal councils from overseas territories. In all, there were approximately 80,000 electors, the great majority of whom represented communes with a population of no more than 2,000 inhabitants.

In 1962, however, on De Gaulle's insistence the constitution was amended by popular referendum—contrary to the amendment procedure established by the constitution—to provide for the direct popular election of the president. Nominations are made by petitions signed by at least 100 members of Parliament, members of the Economic and Social Council, general councilors, or elected mayors, provided that such signatures include citizens from at least ten of ninety departments into which the country is divided. Election is by a majority of the votes cast; if no candidate obtains a majority there is a run-off election on the second Sunday following. The run-off is between the two candidates who had obtained the highest number of votes in the first election.[1] As long as De Gaulle wants to stay in the office, however, another candidate is not likely to unseat him.

THE PRESIDENT: POWERS

The president's powers are impressive. Some of them, such as the power to pardon, the appointment of ambassadors, and nominations to civil, army, and judicial posts, require the signature of the prime minister (and possibly another minister), in true parliamentary form. But a number of substantive powers are exercised on his own, without any reference to advice from those who can be held politically accountable in Parliament. The following are the most important:

The president appoints the prime minister, although he cannot dismiss him. Nevertheless, he exercises a type of veto in policy making, for the constitution says that he shall see to it that the constitution is respected; that he shall ensure, by his arbitration, the regular functioning of the governmental authorities, as well as the continuity of the state; that he shall be the guarantor of national independence, of the integrity of the territory, of respect for Community agreements, and for treaties. Since he is president of the Community, his is the dominant voice in France's relations with the overseas territories.

Moreover, the president may send messages to Parliament, but they cannot be the subject of debate. He may dissolve the National Assembly, although he cannot do this more than once a year. He need only consult the prime minister and the presidents of the two assemblies. And he may ask the Constitutional Council (three of whose members he appoints and whose president he designates) to rule on the constitutionality of parliamentary bills and laws.

The president's emergency powers are in some ways the most impressive, particularly since he decides when an emergency exists. "When the institutions of the Republic, the independence of the nation, the integrity of its territory, or the fulfillment of its international commitments are threatened in a grave and immediate

---

[1] In the event that the office becomes vacant or the president is incapacitated, the President of the Senate acts as president. In case of a vacancy or permanent incapacity, there is to be a new election within fifty days.

manner," says the constitution, "and the regular functioning of the constitutional governmental authorities is interrupted, the President of the Republic shall take the measures required by these circumstances." He need only consult the prime minister, the presidents of the assemblies and the Constitutional Council, and he must inform the nation of the measures he is taking. While so ruling, however, he may not dissolve or adjourn Parliament. The constitution stipulates that the measures he takes "must be prompted by the desire to ensure to the constitutional governmental authorities, in the shortest possible time, the means of fulfilling their assigned functions."

THE PRESIDENCY UNDER DE GAULLE

De Gaulle, although often seeking to convey the impression that he stands above the partisan battles of the political arena, has been the prime mover in the politics of the Fifth Republic. In exercising personal leadership he has often violated both the spirit and letter of the constitution. But since he arrogated to himself the power to interpret its meaning whenever he believed it important or necessary to do so, no serious challenge to his personal rule has arisen. His actions have, however, evoked criticism and thereby made him the subject of political controversy.

De Gaulle has exercised his personal leadership in several ways. First of all, through visits to foreign heads of states and their visits to him, and through declarations in the realm of foreign and domestic policy, he has become the spokesman for the nation. His insistence on pomp and ceremony has caused the limelight to focus on him. Secondly, through his employment of the referendum, he has sought to buttress his authority by demonstrations of popular approval. It should be noted in this connection that the constitution does not give him the right to initiate referendums, only to refuse to call for them when asked to do so by the cabinet or by Parliament. Yet it is evident that those which were held came as a result of his initiative. The one which amended the constitution to provide for popular election of the president was opposed by the National Assembly, but this was to no avail. Even the Constitutional Council was powerless to stand in the way.

It was most disturbing to many Frenchmen to be told by the president that the referendum had become a normal feature of government, a way, in effect, of circumventing Parliament. On the other hand, it could not be denied that De Gaulle had used the referendum effectively, demonstrating that a vocal opposition often constituted but a minority. It is likely that another president, should he find himself in conflict with Parliament or the cabinet, would not overlook the potential of the referendum.

Thirdly, De Gaulle has actively sought to determine cabinet policy in fields he considered vital, and he was instrumental in the dismissal of certain ministers and the appointment of their successors. At times he has made policy and simply communicated it to the cabinet without the benefit of discussion or deliberation in the cabinet. Often, by consulting technical committees or his personal advisers, he by-passed the ministers. Sometimes he contradicted previous statements of his prime minister, who was forced to "change his mind" publicly.

Finally, in the exercise of the president's emergency powers, De Gaulle insisted that he was the sole judge of the propriety of all governmental actions for the duration of the emergency. He thus refused to permit the convocation of a special session of the National Assembly during such a period, even though a majority of the deputies demanded one in accordance with constitutional provisions. The manner in which the president conducted himself during the five months of emergency rule in 1961 at the time of the military insurrection in Algeria was in many ways reassuring. But there was some question as to whether the situation in Algeria met the constitutional requirements for emergency rule. And there was considerable doubt as to whether he could rightfully prevent a special session of Parliament, particularly since the constitution explicitly states that during a period of emergency rule the president may not exercise his right to dissolve Parliament.

The general consensus among experts on French politics seems to be that the presidency under De Gaulle is unique. Thus Dorothy Pickles has asserted that "Parliament would have made short work of Presidential constitutional interpretations, if the President had been anyone else, holding offiice at any other time."[2] And a French writer declared: "We are living in a strange and contradictory regime—a liberal dictatorship, in which one man carries the whole burden of the State, yet cannot act as a dictator and impose his will by force, because he is a liberal and a Christian."[3] Other writers have been less

[2] Dorothy Pickles, *The Fifth French Republic: Intitutions and Politics* (2nd ed., New York: Frederick A. Praeger, Publisher, 1962), p. 155. See also Macridis and Brown, *Supplement to the De Gaulle Republic* (Homewood, Ill.: The Dorsey Press, 1963) chap. II.

[3] As quoted in Pickles, *op. cit.*, p. 227.

charitable, but in the main they have not denied the uniqueness of the presidency under General De Gaulle.

THE CABINET

During the Third and Fourth Republics, the prime minister and his colleagues were usually referred to as the cabinet, although their official name was the Council of Ministers. The bulk of their deliberations were held in an informal atmosphere under the chairmanship of the prime minister. In such a capacity they were known as the cabinet council. In order for their acts to be valid, however, they had to meet as the Council of Ministers, over which the president of the Republic presided. The latter were brief meetings to give legal form to what had been hammered out at length in the cabinet. Under the Fifth Republic, on the other hand, meetings of the cabinet have been infrequent. All major discussions have taken place in meetings of the Council of Ministers, with the president presiding.

The cabinet is composed of the prime minister, appointed by the president, and an indefinite number of ministers (currently 27) whom he nominates. During the Third and Fourth Republics, ministers were usually members of Parliament, although practice did not dictate that they must be as in Great Britain. The present constitution makes this impossible. Article 23 states that "the office of members of the Government shall be incompatible with the exercise of any parliamentary mandate, with the holding of any office at the national level, in business, professional or labor organizations, and with any public employment or professional activity." Members of Parliament can, and have, become ministers, but when doing so they resign from the house to which they had been elected.[4] They retain access to both houses, however, and have a right to be heard. In practice, they sit in Parliament and engage freely in the debates, but they do not have a vote.

The prime minister and his colleagues in the cabinet, according to the constitution, "determine and direct" the policies of the nation. Moreover, the prime minister directs the operation of the Government and is responsible for national defense. In practice, however, these powers have in the main been exercised by the president and his close advisers. The cabinet ministers have not protested this transfer of

---

[4] The electoral law provides for the election of alternates at the regular election who can easily step in when a vacancy occurs for whatever reason.

authority; indeed they seem to have willingly acquiesced, being content with implementing the president's policies. Under other circumstances and with a change in personalities, practice might very well be significantly different.

The broad constitutional grant of authority to the cabinet (aside from corresponding limitations on the legislature which will be discussed below) is augmented by Article 38 of the constitution, which says: "The Government may, in order to carry out its program, ask Parliament to authorize it, for a limited period, to take through ordinances measures that are normally within the domain of law." In February 1960, the prime minister, pursuant to this article, demanded and received a broad delegation of authority to govern by decree for a period of 14 months. This grant of power was ostensibly made "for the maintenance of law and order, the safeguarding of the State and the Constitution, and the pacification and administration of Algeria." The sole limitation on this grant of authority was the express proviso that Parliament could not be dissolved during this period. Article 41, however, prevents Parliament from seeking to legislate in areas where it has delegated decree powers to the cabinet.

In two areas where French cabinets were notoriously weak in the past, areas where British Governments are strong, the constitution is unequivocal in making them strong. These are the areas of fiscal control and priority for cabinet measures. Article 40 states that "Bills and amendments introduced by members of Parliament shall not be considered when their adoption would have as a consequence either a diminution of public financial resources, or the creation or increase of public expenditures." And Article 48 states that "the discussion of bills filed or agreed upon by the Government shall have priority on the agenda of the Assemblies in the order set by the Government." Other articles give the Government sufficient power to speed the passage of finance bills, and in the event Parliament fails to act within a specified time (70 days), the budget bill can be put into effect by decree (a power that the Government has thus far not needed to use). Moreover, the cabinet may force a vote on a bill and the amendments it approves, rejecting all other attempts to amend.

For a cabinet to exercise this type of power in a parliamentary system is not unusual, provided, of course, that it is responsible to a popularly elected legislature for the way it exercises its authority. Reference has already been made to the exercise of substantive powers by the president, who is accountable to no one, which constitutes a serious modification of the parliamentary system. The constitution does provide, nevertheless, that for the powers exercised by the cabinet, the latter is responsible to Parliament. More precisely, the cabinet is responsible to the National Assembly.

The methods for exacting ministerial responsibility are not always precise. Article 49 states: "The Prime Minister, after deliberation in the Council of Ministers, may pledge the responsibility of his Government to the National Assembly with regard to the program of the Government, or with regard to a declaration of general policy, as the case may be." This has been interpreted to mean that when a cabinet is formed, the prime minister will make a general statement of policy to the National Assembly, which may reject the cabinet by a simple majority, and thus force its resignation. In the case of future general statements of policy, however, the cabinet cannot be ousted by a simple negative majority, although it might choose to resign on its own volition.

Secondly, a cabinet can be defeated by a censure motion, if adopted by an absolute majority (that is, a majority of the total membership) of the National Assembly. Such a motion may be voted upon only if it has obtained the signatures of at least one tenth of the members of the Assembly, and only after 48 hours have elapsed after its filing. If the motion is defeated, the signers cannot sign another censure motion for the remainder of the session.

In a three year period (1959–1962) there were nine censure motions; all but one were defeated. The one which received the necessary votes (October, 1962) censured the Government for proposing to amend the constitution by referendum. This was followed by a dissolution of the National Assembly and the holding of new elections, as well as a vote on the referendum in question, with the outcome in both cases being a victory for General De Gaulle.

Thirdly, the Government can be defeated on a censure motion which follows some issue the Government makes a matter of confidence. The prime minister, after deliberation in the Council of Ministers, may stake the life of his Government on a general issue of policy or a specific legislative text. The cabinet is presumed to have the confidence of the National Assembly unless a censure motion is filed in the following 24 hours. If such a motion receives an absolute majority, as outlined in the above paragraph, the cabinet is forced to resign. But if the motion fails to pass, the policy or legislative text concerned is considered approved. It is possible in this way to have a bill become a law with a majority of *those voting* expressing their disapproval. The general effect of this procedure is that the cabinet can go on with its program unless the Assembly is willing to turn it out.

As indicated above, the limit on the signing of censure motions does not apply when the cabinet poses the question of confidence. The same persons may sign censure motions as often as the Government stakes its political life. The limit on the frequency with which members could sign censure motions was designed not so much to save governments from possible defeat but rather to make it impossible for a small number of members to employ the censure motion as a propaganda or obstructionist device. Present indications point to the use of censure motions as means of forcing the prime minister to debate important policies.

The cabinet is held to account in other ways, such as the debates in committee and in the assemblies. Moreover, one day each week is set aside for members of Parliament to question cabinet members orally. Initially, questions were of two types—with or without debate. The former were followed by a vote, and sometimes resolutions. The Government opposed debate, votes, and resolutions. In its opinion, this would be a type of vote of confidence each week. Upon the Government's urging the Constitutional Council ruled that votes and resolutions on oral questions were beyond the power of the National Assembly or the Senate, even though the latter cannot hold the cabinet to account. The Senate, by being denied the right to express its criticism in terms of a vote, is virtually reduced to the status of a mere consultative body. And now neither the Assembly nor the Senate can express political views by a vote other than a vote of censure. The cabinet is thus shielded from receiving unpalatable popular views through public expressions in Parliament.

Although the cabinet can be overthrown only by the National Assembly, it is authorized to seek approval of a general policy statement in the Senate, and thus apply at least moral pressure on the Assembly if the Senate concurs. Also, the cabinet can convoke a joint conference committee if there is disagreement between the two houses. Moreover, the cabinet can seek Senate action on the budget if the Assembly does not act within 40 days, which is also a type of pressure.

Aside from the censure mentioned above, the cabinet has experienced no serious difficulty with Parliament, partly because it has abdicated real power to the president. There have been a relatively large number of changes in cabinet posts, however, suggesting that individual ministerial instability remained high. Yet by comparison with the Third and Fourth Republics, the cabinet has been markedly stable.

PRESIDENTIAL OR CABINET GOVERNMENT?

French cabinets in the Third and Fourth Republics were characterized by weakness, resulting in general governmental instability. What is the Fifth Republic's answer to "Assembly government"? Is it the establishment of a strong cabinet along British lines, or is it the forsaking of parliamentary traditions and the inauguration of presidential government along American lines? The aim of the framers of the new constitution was to strengthen the executive and to produce greater stability, but, as the preceding discussion has indicated, the new government of France is neither presidential nor cabinet, as these terms are generally understood in Great Britain and in the United States. It is largely personal rule.

The governmental system of the Fifth Republic has been so dominated by the president that some writers have simply asked: "What kind of presidential government?"[5] Other writers who initially viewed the Fifth Republic as a temporary phenomenon are no longer so sure.[6] Important, and in many cases irreversible, changes have been made. Ideological quarrels seem less important, while the pragmatic approach to government and its functions seems to be gaining ground. The built-in possibilities for conflict, not only between the executive and the legislature, but also between the president and the prime minister, are still there. But De Gaulle's rule seems to have considerably weakened the traditional French hostility to a strong executive, offering hope for the development at some future time of a real French consensus around a more workable party and cabinet system.

On the other hand, De Gaulle has been disinclined to associate Parliament and the parties in the tasks of governing. Men hold positions of responsibility in the government because they enjoy his confidence and not because they represent powerful groups in Parliament. Often it has been difficult for Parliament or the people to know

---

[5] Macridis and Brown, *op. cit.*, p. 48.

[6] Compare for example, the views of Dorothy Pickles, *The Fifth French Republic* (New York: Frederick A. Praeger, Publisher, 1960) with Pickles (second edition), *op. cit.*, as well as those of Macridis and Brown, *The De Gaulle Republic* (Homewood, Ill.: Dorsey Press, 1960) and *Supplement, op. cit.*

what he thinks or what policies he intended to pursue. He has had little or no interest in political machinery, and he has refused to become a party leader. Often he gave the impression that he was concerned only with lofty principles, expecting the administrative apparatus to devise the means of achieving them. This attitude was aided and abetted by the public, which seemed anxious that he shoulder the burdens and devise miraculous solutions for near-insoluble problems. The opposition parties for the most part failed to come forth with concrete alternatives to the president's policies. In such circumstances it is difficult for workable parliamentary machinery to develop.

The result is that the basic problem remains. Assuming that France is to be governed democratically, it is necessary that suitable and workable political machinery evolve. If it is to be a presidential system, the people must have an opportunity to elect a president at more frequent intervals than the present seven-year period. Moreover, the president must also be made more responsible by making it possible for Parliament to override his opposition in some way. If it is to be a cabinet system, two conditions are necessary: (1) the coming into being of a governing majority in Parliament, and (2) ways of regulating relations between the cabinet and parliament so as to facilitate a strong but responsible government.

In the Third and Fourth Republics no single party had a majority. Furthermore, no combination of parties, even those with similar policies, could command a majority. Hence there was no group or party which could be said to represent the majority of the public. Correspondingly, while governments often met with defeat in the legislature, there was never an alternative government, that is, there was no party or group with coherent policies to take over. It was easy for combinations to develop for the purpose of ousting a government, but it was much more difficult to constitute governments dedicated to the pursuit of definite and important legislative objectives. The legislature was so divided that formulation of policies was made almost impossible.

The Fifth Republic does give some evidence, however tenuous, of remedying this situation. Although the coming into existence in 1958 of a new political party, the Union for the New Republic, did not produce a majority in the first election, in the elections of 1962 the UNR came within a few votes of capturing a majority of the seats in the National Assembly. When the seats of other pro-UNR deputies were added, there were 274 Gaullists out of a total of 482, a clear majority for one political group for the first time in the history of Republican France. Because of the uniqueness of De Gaulle, and because it is far from clear how stable a political formation the UNR is, it would be hazardous to speculate on the likelihood of coherent majorities in Parliament after De Gaulle leaves the scene.

Another factor needs also to be noted. The Fourth Republic, and to a large degree the Third also, was criticized because of the popular apathy it engendered. People did not seem too cognizant of political crises and, what is worse, they did not seem to care. The Fifth Republic does not seem to have remedied this situation either. More than that, there are indications that reliance on De Gaulle has given people less and less of a sense of participation and involvement in the political process. And since political parties are denied the great political prizes, there is no particular incentive for them or their leaders to seek the establishment of larger and more effective political organizations. In any case, political apathy, so much criticized by the opponents of the Fourth Republic, does not seem to have diminished.

Yet there is dissatisfaction. Political groups other than the Gaullists dislike the constitution. There are arguments over its interpretation. Many Frenchmen feel that the constitution is being treated with contempt and have said so. The parties have been free to criticize the cabinet as well as the president, and those in opposition have done so. Most Frenchmen realize that the making of important political decisions, while Parliament looks on, is foreign to the French Republican tradition. Parliamentary groups, even the Gaullists, have come to realize that idleness does not encourage a sense of responsibility. Macridis and Brown have asserted that one of the crucial failings of Gaullism has been its inability "to establish any institutions through which political conflicts in the future may be resolved."[7] While this indictment may be overly harsh, there is certainly an element of justification in it. Processes for resolving conflicts in a democratic political order do not just happen, they have to be painstakingly created and shaped.

BIBLIOGRAPHICAL NOTE

There are no works that deal exclusively with the executive under the Fifth Republic. The following recent works, however, provide specific and useful treatment of the executive: Raymond Aron, *France: The New Republic* (New York: Oceana, 1960); Peter Campbell, *Constitution of the Fifth Republic* (Oxford: Blackwell, 1958); E. Drexel Godfrey, Jr., *The Government of France* (2nd ed., New York: Crowell, 1963); Roy C. Macridis and Bernard

[7] Macridis and Brown, *Supplement, op. cit.*, p. 97.

E. Brown, *The De Gaulle Republic: Quest for Unity* (Homewood, Ill.: Dorsey Press, 1960) and, *Supplement to the De Gaulle Republic* (1963); Dorothy Pickles, *The Fifth French Republic: Institutions and Politics* (Rev. ed., New York: F. A. Praeger, 1962); Nicholas Wahl, *The Fifth Republic: France's New Political System* (2nd ed., New York: Random House, 1962); and Philip Williams and Martin Harrison, *De Gaulle's Republic* (New York: Longmans, 1960).

Also useful, although pertaining to the Fourth Republic, is Edgar S. Furniss, Jr., *The Office of the Premier in French Foreign Policy-Making: An Application of Decision-Making Analysis* (Princeton, N.J.: Princeton University Press, 1954).

CHAPTER **12**

PARLIAMENT

FRANCE has returned to a bicameral legislature not unlike that of the Third Republic. The popularly elected National Assembly consists of 482 members—465 from France proper, 10 from overseas departments, and 7 from overseas territories. They are elected for five years by direct, equal, and universal suffrage. The Senate has 274 members, elected indirectly by electoral colleges consisting in the main of local councillors. Their term of office is nine years, with one third of the members elected every three years.

ELECTORAL PROCEDURES

The French have changed their electoral system a number of times since 1875, with no particular scheme ascendant. They have not been addicted to proportional representation, as is sometimes assumed. And even at times when they have employed proportional representation, it has been in combination with majority voting. In any case, studies of French voting indicate no necessary relationship between the electoral system employed and cabinet stability.

The present electoral system was established by decree in October 1958, but Parliament has authority to change it. Under this system, France is divided into single-member districts, with one deputy elected for every 93,000 inhabitants. There is a proviso, however, that no department (of which there are 90 in France) may have fewer than two deputies. There are, in effect, two elections, or ballots, held one week apart on Sundays. Candidates receiving a majority, provided that at least one half of the registered voters cast a ballot, in the first election are elected. In the districts where no one receives a majority, there is a runoff, or second ballot, in which the winner is determined by a mere plurality. In the interval between the two ballots, candidates may drop out (those who receive less than 5 per cent of the vote must do so), and several parties may seek to combine their support in favor of a single candidate. No new candidate may appear, however, on the second ballot.

Except for minor differences, such as the injunction against new candidates on the second ballot, this system was employed in 13 out of 22 elections between 1875 and 1958, inclusive, and is by far the most simple of those that have been used.

To be a candidate for the National Assembly, one must be a French citizen who has attained his 23rd birthday. Moreover, he must deposit 1,000 francs (approximately $200), which he forfeits if he does not receive 5 per cent of the votes cast. Candidates who poll at least 5 per cent are also reimbursed for a certain part of their campaign costs, such as those for posters, printing, and mailing. In theory, these are the only costs, but unofficial posters and private letters are not illegal. Since there is no maximum on campaign costs, a candidate may even put out a newspaper which will support his candidacy. Political parties which can show that they are running candidates in at least 75 districts are provided a certain amount of free radio and television time.

An innovation in the electoral system, alluded to in the previous chapter, is the requirement that each candidate must have a substitute whose name appears on the ballot and who replaces the deputy if his office becomes vacant. There are two limitations: (1), if the substitute replaces a deputy, he may not run against him at the next election, and (2), deputies may not be substitutes for senators or *vice versa*. The latter limitation is to preclude the possibility of a deputy or a senator who becomes a minister from retaining a post in the other chamber.

Political campaigns are brief (about three weeks), as in Britain. The electoral lists are revised annually, at present having about 27 million registered voters; about 21 million voters cast ballots in the election of November 1958, and 19 million did so in the election of October 1962. Women have been enfranchised only since World War II.

PARTY REPRESENTATION IN PARLIAMENT

In past French elections the two-ballot system helped the moderate parties, primarily because the extremist parties could not or would not combine on the second ballot. This was especially true in 1958. This, together with the crisis atmosphere in which so many voters were anxious to express confidence in De Gaulle by voting for candidates identified with him, produced a most unrepresentative Assembly. For example, some 7 million votes, cast for Socialist and Communist candidates, were represented by 50 Deputies, while one half that number, cast for Union for the New Republic candidates, were represented by over 200 Deputies. In 1962, however, the Socialists and Communists observed a form of electoral alliance by withdrawing in each other's favor where their combined vote on the first ballot had indicated sufficient strength to prevent the election of the Gaullist candidate. In this way, with a somewhat smaller total vote than they had in 1958, they elected 66 and 41 Deputies, respectively. UNR voters, on the other hand, were nearly twice as numerous in 1962 as in 1958 yet elected only 233 Deputies.

The party representation (including affiliates) in the National Assembly after the 1962 election was as follows:

Union for the New Republic (UNR)	233
Socialists	66
Democratic Center (MRP and Independents)	55
Communists	41
Democratic Rally (Radicals and Independents)	39
Independent Republicans (Gaullist)	36
Unidentified or nonaligned	12

In the Senate elections, held in March 1959, the UNR did not repeat its Assembly triumph. The result was a virtual return to the Fourth Republic. In France proper, of 255 senators elected, only 85 were new. Among the latter, nearly half had been members of the National Assembly, and many incumbents did not seek re-election. Hence, the new Senate was almost a duplicate of the old Council of the Republic. This was reflected in the election of a Radical as president of the Senate, the same man who had held the position since 1947. The renewal of one third of the Senate in 1962 did not materially change its political complexion.

LEGISLATIVE POWERS OF PARLIAMENT

Unlike the basic law of the Third and Fourth Republics, the constitution of the Fifth seeks to spell out the powers of Parliament, and, by stating that in other areas the Government can legislate by decree, seeks to limit them. One of the first limitations is on the length of legislative sessions, of which there are two annually; each session is limited in duration to three months. Special sessions, not to exceed 12 days in length and to deal with a specific agenda, can be called at the request of the prime minister or a majority of the Assembly, although the president refused to permit the latter during a period of emergency rule in 1960. Moreover, the cabinet has control over how the time of Parliament is to be used, for Government matters have priority.

It should be noted that matters in the following categories are to be regulated by legislation: civil rights and obligations; nationality, contracts, gifts, and inheritance; crimes and criminal procedures; taxation and currency; electoral systems; public institutions; economic plans, including nationalization and denationalization of enterprises; general organization of national defense; education; property rights; employment, unions, and social security; administration of local government units. Moreover, Parliament authorizes the declaration of war, ratifies treaties, votes the budget, and can initiate amendment of the constitution. Finally, it can delegate any of the above powers to the cabinet.

The constitution says that in all other areas the Government may legislate by decree. Since the enumerated powers seem quite broad, this would not seem to be as serious a limitation as the cabinet's control of parliamentary time and its control of the budget, mentioned above. The practice of enumerating, in a limitative manner, the functions of Parliament does, however, represent a reversal of past practice in France, and in this sense represents a serious limitation upon Parliament.

The constitution gives the Senate equal power in lawmaking, although some matters, such as finance bills, must be submitted to the Assembly first. Presumably if the cabinet and Senate were of like mind, and the Assembly hostile, the Senate could be employed to exercise a veto power in legislation. On the other hand, it can be overruled only if the cabinet and the Assembly are in agreement. The Senate lacks the power to initiate censure motions as a means of ousting the cabinet, but the latter presumably may raise the question of confidence in the Senate, with all the consequences such a move entails.

In case of disagreement between the Assembly and the Senate, the cabinet can force the convening of a conference committee in case of failure to pass identical bills after two readings or after a single reading if the Government has declared the matter urgent. If the conference committee fails to adopt a common text, the cabinet can, after a new reading in each chamber, ask the National Assembly "to rule definitively."

Parliament, partly because the Parliamentary Standing Orders (over which the Constitutional Council has final authority) prevent it from expressing its collective sentiment (except in the Assembly via the cumbersome censure motion route), has played a subservient role. The cabinet has not been willing to debate policy any more than it had to. The Constitutional Council early upheld the cabinet in its contention that no votes could be taken or resolutions voted upon in connection with questions addressed to ministers. The above observations apply to the Senate as well as to the National Assembly, even though the cabinet is not responsible to the former. The result has been that relations between the cabinet and Parliament have worsened. And the Senate, which was initially thought of as a device to thwart hostile majorities in the National Assembly, has in the main served to delay measures and thereby irritate the cabinet.

LEGISLATIVE PROCEDURE

The present constitution deals with legislative procedure in greater detail than past ones. Reference has already been made to the fact that the constitution now gives the cabinet such control over parliamentary time and over finance that the interminable debates that used to take place on the budget and other bills, often designed to embarrass and defeat the Government, are no more. Moreover, the constitution stipulates that parliamentary standing orders cannot go into effect until they have been examined by the Constitutional Council so as to make sure that they are in conformity with the constitution.

Each chamber is presided over by a president. Unlike the speaker of the House of Commons, however, French presiding officers remain members of their respective political parties, and do not have his unchallenged authority. In the past, they were elected to their posts annually, but the constitution now provides that the president of the Assembly is elected for its duration, while the president of the Senate is elected every three years, that is, after each partial renewal of its membership. Moreover, the standing orders now give the presiding officer more authority in controlling debate and calling members to order than his predecessors had. Each of the two presiding officers holds a position of great prestige, the president of the Senate replacing the president of the Republic if the latter is incapacitated.

The physical arrangement of each house is much more like that of the United States Congress than of the British Parliament. Members sit in a semicircular scheme, but because of the many parties it is difficult to have a clear-cut dividing line between Government and opposition. Deputies are grouped according to political coloration, from the far "left" (presiding officer's left) to the extreme "right." As the accompanying illustration indicates, the Union for the New Republic occupies the left-center position, with the Communists on the far left. Certain traditionally left-of-center parties (MRP and Radicals) could hardly be moved left or right, and since they are not affiliated with the UNR, they occupy a "position within a position."

In order to be represented on committees, according to standing orders, a parliamentary group must have at least 30 members. It is partially because of this requirement that certain party representatives in the Assembly have affiliated. At present there are six parliamentary groups entitled to committee assignments, with each group receiving committee appointments in proportion to its strength.

The number of committees has been reduced from 19 in the Fourth Republic to 6. The number was decreased for two reasons: to reduce

SEATING ARRANGEMENT IN THE NATIONAL ASSEMBLY

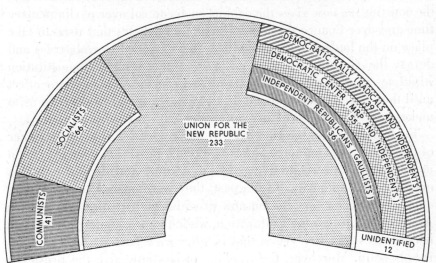

the authority of committees and to avoid the time-wasting practice of submitting identical matters to several committees. Each of the six committees is supposed to number from 60 to 120 deputies. As originally constituted, two had 60 each, two had 90 each and two had 120 each. A suggestion that each committee create subcommittees was rejected as being contrary to the constitution. Subsequently, special committees were authorized to which bills may be sent. However, such committees may not have more than thirty members and no more than fifteen of these may come from the same permanent committee. There are also committees of inquiry, comparable to the select committees of the House of Commons.

The six permanent committees are: Foreign Affairs; National

Defense and Armed Forces; Finance, General Economy and Planning; Constitutional Laws, Legislation, and General Administration of the Republic; Production and Trade; Cultural, Family, and Social Affairs.

Since the Assembly meets in the afternoon, committees meet in the morning.[1] Unlike the situation during the Third and Fourth Republics, when a minister was virtually helpless, he now pilots his own measure through a committee. He may refuse to consider amendments not previously submitted to the committee, and he may insist on a single vote on the whole bill (or a part thereof), including only those amendments which are acceptable to the Government. Moreover, he can bring about a vote once he believes that the differing points of view have been stated.

Another innovation in legislative procedure concerns proxy voting. In the past, French legislators quite frequently gave to one of their colleagues, usually the leader of their party bloc in Parliament, the right to cast their votes when they were away. This practice of proxy voting grew up rather than the practice of pairing, with the result that often one man could cast a sizable number of votes. The new constitution, in theory, abolishes this practice. Proxy voting is still possible, but only in case of a specific reason (for example, illness, being away on government business, etc.), and no member may cast more than one proxy vote.

In practice, however, proxy voting continues to a considerable degree. This is made possible because of the installation of electronic voting in the National Assembly. A member who plans to be away simply gives his key to the voting instrument on his desk to one of his colleagues, who votes for him. One reason for this practice may be the requirement that deputies vote regularly or else they may lose some of their salary, and they may lose their places on committees for unexcused absences. Each house decides on the penalties for parliamentary absenteeism of its members.

THE FUTURE OF PARLIAMENT

The Fifth Republic makes a deliberate effort to break with the past, so characterized by Assembly dominance. In the two previous republics, deputies ousted cabinets with impunity and with no fear of dissolution which might jeopardize their seats in the Assembly. The resulting instability was further complicated following World War II

[1] The Assembly decided that its committees could also meet when Parliament is not in session.

by the presence in the Assembly of a large antidemocratic bloc—the Communists on the far left and the ultraconservatives on the far right. Both the Government and the democratic opposition had to contend with this political fact of life. This is one reason why each cabinet was in large measure a reshuffle of the previous one.

To avoid Assembly pressure and harassment, the cabinet is now provided with certain procedural safeguards, discussed in the preceding chapter. In turn, the Assembly's powers have correspondingly been reduced. The net result, based on the practice of the first six years of the Fifth Republic, seems to be that whereas in the past Parliament tried to do too much, today it does not have enough to do. As indicated earlier, it does not even have the traditional right of determining its own procedure and hence is unable to exercise pressure on the Government. Its alternatives are limited: either turn out the Government or let it go on with its work. As pointed out in the previous chapter, it is possible for a bill to become a law, by having the Government pose and win a vote of confidence, without the Deputies voting on the actual bill. It is not likely that the Assembly will be content indefinitely with such procedure and with its severely limited role.

There is some uncertainty about the powers which the prime minister and the cabinet will in the future exercise vis-à-vis the president of the Republic. Under General de Gaulle, real executive power is largely wielded by him, while the prime minister and the cabinet have been reduced to little more than his agents. If a future president returns to, or moves in the direction of, the position of a nonpolitical head of state, the prime minister and his colleagues will exercise real executive power. When and if they do that, they will be accountable to the National Assembly, something the president is not. In such circumstances, the Parliament will be able to evolve into its proper role, that of criticism and control.

There is general agreement that the first years of the Fifth Republic have witnessed a worsening of relations between the cabinet and Parliament. This is due in part to the fact that the cabinet has abdicated its powers in favor of the president. Parliament believes that it could more readily "get at" the ministers if they were playing the role which the constitution confers on them. Moreover, the Fifth Republic's first two prime ministers, Michael Debré and Georges Pompidou, were more inclined to lecture the Deputies, even their own supporters, rather than attempt to work with them. Finally, the constitutional prohibition against ministers simultaneously being members of Parliament has resulted in many ministers being recruited from the civil service, with the consequence that ministers are often isolated from public opinion. In brief, the alleged quest for a separation of powers has resulted in a greater gulf between ministers and the political arena. In a democratic parliamentary system this is at best a tragedy, and in the long run may be incompatible with it. Unless something can be done to devise ways for Parliament to do more in the realm of criticism and control, the outlook for its future may not be bright.

Finally, the prime requisite for the successful operation of parliamentary government is still a homogeneous or coherent majority. Parliament will be able to exercise its proper function only when there is a majority which will view its main role as that of seeking to keep the Government in office. It may criticize the ministers, and in other ways show its displeasure, but, except for gross breaches of trust, it will vote to keep the cabinet in power. Correspondingly, the minority will have to develop into something beyond merely being negative. It will need to develop a program with which to attract the electorate. And it will need to be prepared to act as a majority if it succeeds in getting the confidence of a majority of the voters. The development of coherent majorities and minorities in French politics may seem a long way off, as it does at this writing, but this must remain a yardstick by which the future of Parliament will have to be measured.

BIBLIOGRAPHICAL NOTE

A particularly useful study of Parliament under the Fourth Republic is D. W. S. Lidderdale, *The Parliament of France* (London: Hansard, 1951). Also of interest are Peter Campbell, *French Electoral Systems and Elections 1789–1957* (London: Faber and Faber, 1958) ; and Nathan Leites, *The Game of Politics in France* (Stanford, Cal.: Stanford University Press, 1959). The recent books on the Fifth Republic, listed at the end of the previous chapter, should be consulted for their references to Parliament.

CHAPTER 13

POLITICAL PARTIES

POLITICAL parties usually are the bones and sinews of politics, but in some political settings they can be quite dissimilar. This is best illustrated by France, whose party system is different from what an American or a Britisher is accustomed to. An understanding of these differences is essential to a fundamental grasp of French political processes, as well as to a sound approach to the study of comparative politics.

HISTORIC NOTE ON FRENCH PARTIES

French political parties have been characterized by their multiplicity. In past general elections national parties have sometimes numbered between 10 and 20, in addition to a number of purely local or regional ones. The usual fluctuation has been between 12 and 15 national parties. Moreover, until 1962 no one party ever approached getting a majority of the vote. Consequently, there has been nothing in France that even remotely approached the two-party system which is prevalent in the United States and Great Britain.

The multiplicity of French parties is matched by their diversity in organization and politics. Politically, they range from parties that emphasize principle and rigid adherence to it, such as the Communist party, to parties that espouse no principle and are the personal followers of one man. Organizationally, they vary from the tight discipline that the Communists and Socialists have imposed to the largely unorganized groups on the far right. The parties of the center, which have governed France in the past eight decades, are also largely unorganized in that they do not have an organization outside Parliament of the nature operated by the major parties in Great Britain. The only major exception is the Radical Socialist party, which has held party conferences where issues were debated and where leaders made reports. To a lesser extent the Socialists and the Popular Republican Movement (MRP) also are exceptions. French parties do emphasize personal, card-carrying, dues-paying membership. In this sense, however, all French political parties are small, with the Communists being the only possible exception, and their paid membership probably does not exceed 450,000.

Another characteristic of French parties is their fluidity. Parties appear and disappear. This does not symbolize significant shifts in political opinions and tendencies. Studies of French voting behavior indicate a fairly steady and consistent pattern. To be sure, Gaullism is new, but even it possesses characteristics that are an inheritance from the past. What changes, in the main, are the party labels. There has always been a large protest vote, for example, but from election to election it may be recorded under differing party labels. A large portion of the vote cast in 1958 for the party that supported De Gaulle was a protest vote.

There is no simple explanation for the multiplicity of French political parties and the diversity of their approaches to the problem of politics. In part the reason can be traced to an absence of consensus or a common understanding concerning the basis and form of government. There is a basic idealism that is dissatisfied with compromise and halfway measures, hence the striving for one pure party. On the other hand, there is a fundamental distrust of one's fellow man, and hence a fear of efficient organization. Moreover, French governmental practices encouraged many parties. "Assembly government" helped to perpetuate divisions. There was no real need for discipline, because a deputy could do what he wanted and still be secure in his seat for the duration of any one Parliament. The method of election, whether combined with proportional representation or not, encouraged many parties and candidates, at least on the first ballot. Finally, the sharp divisions among Frenchmen as to the type of economic system which France should have merely added fuel to the fire of already existing differences.

A comparative note suggests another reason for the multiplicity of political parties in France. At the time when political parties were forming in the United States and in Great Britain, the nature of the form of government in those two countries was not really in question. The differences that divided men into parties were primarily over policies which government should follow. In France, on the other hand, the formation of political parties preceded agreement on the nature of the system of government. Differences over the question of how the state should be organized could not help but creep into party positions. Moreover, by the time that the Third Republic was organized and a certain consensus achieved (1875–1885), parties organized along class lines had appeared (first the Socialists and in this century the Communists). In other words, just when Republicanism had become respectable, a new source of division had arisen to perpetuate the multi-party system. With France now apparently moving toward a more widely shared prosperity, accompanied by a decline in ideology, perhaps the conditions are ripe for fewer parties. But we must always remember that political habits and political practices do not change rapidly.

THE CONSTITUTION AND PARTIES

The French constitution says that "political parties and groups may compete for votes. They may form and carry on their activities freely. They must respect the principles of national sovereignty and of democracy." It is obvious that the last sentence lays the foundation for possible action against antidemocratic parties of the right or left. The largest and most powerful of these is the Communist party. It is rather common knowledge that it, like other Communist parties, owes its primary allegiance to Moscow. Moreover, it respects the principles of democracy only when its own interests would be served thereby. No action has yet been taken, however, against the party or its principal publications. But in 1959, the government did dissolve the small Nationalist party, an extreme rightist group formed with the avowed aim of fighting against French democracy. Subsequently, the cabinet has banned certain protest meetings scheduled by Communists or their sympathizers, as well as similar meetings by rightist groups. Moreover, the government has banned about 150 newspapers at both ends of the political spectrum. It is obvious that this proviso of the constitution on respect for the principles of national sovereignty and democracy gives to the government of the day a considerable latitude in actions it may take against extremist political groups.

There are six major political parties in France. Four of these—the Radicals, the Socialists, the Communists, and the Independents—have a relatively long history. The Popular Republican Movement (MRP) and the Union for the New Republic (UNR) are post World War II creations. Operating alongside these six major groupings, and often in cooperation with them (particularly in Parliament), are a number of small parties. After the Fifth Republic was launched, for example, a number of pro-UNR followers, who believed that the UNR did not have a sufficiently positive labor program, and who feared that the conservative forces were getting too strong in the party, created the Democratic Workers Union (UDT). For all practical purposes, however, the UDT is part of the UNR. Similarly, there are small groups (or parties) allied with the MRP, with the Radicals, and with the Independents.

UNION FOR THE NEW REPUBLIC (UNR)

The Union for the New Republic, the largest of French political parties, was created in unusual circumstances. Its history goes back to 1947, when De Gaulle and his followers founded the Rally of the French People (RPF). The RPF was said to be not a party but a movement or rally that advocated a reform of the constitution. De Gaulle had withdrawn from the political arena. Initially, the RPF had considerable success, but after 1954 its strength diminished. By refusing to accept the responsibility of governing, although it had the largest number of deputies at one time, it constituted an essentially antidemocratic bloc in the National Assembly. Following the return of De Gaulle to power in 1958, however, his followers founded the Union for the New Republic. Although De Gaulle refused to have his name associated with it in any way, this did not stop the organizers of the UNR from proclaiming their loyalty to him.

In the elections of November 1958, the UNR was quite successful. On the first ballot it polled some 18 per cent of the vote, about what the Communists polled, but on the second ballot their percentage was increased to 28. As a result, they won 189 seats in the National Assembly. This number was increased to 211 through affiliations of small right-wing groups. This number, together with the 66 deputies from Algeria, constituted a slender majority. While one could not say that the UNR had become a majority party, it could be looked upon as the first French party to approach that position since the beginnings of the Third Republic.

In the elections of 1962, the UNR nearly doubled its 1958 vote, polling 32 per cent on the first ballot and 40.5 per cent on the second. It elected 233 members out of a total of 482, but when 41 other pro-Gaullist deputies were added the total was 274, a clear majority. Some observers were prone to look upon the election as a second referendum in which the voters had reasserted their support of General De Gaulle—a victory for him rather than the party.[1] But a majority for one political group for the first time in the history of Republican France cannot be minimized.

---

[1] R. C. Macridis and B. E. Brown, *Supplement to the De Gaulle Republic* (Homewood, Ill.: Dorsey Press, 1963), p. 84.

Both in 1958 and 1962, UNR strength was general throughout the country. In 1958, the heavy losers seemed to be the Communists, Socialists, and Radicals. In 1962, UNR gains were made largely at the expense of the Independents, the MRP, and the extreme Right. In 1958, as well as in 1962, about half of the UNR deputies were without previous parliamentary experience. They come from a variety of occupations—business, engineering, liberal professions, and the white-collar group—although they are mostly from urban areas. Workers and peasants are not strongly represented among the UNR deputies.

Aside from the Gaullist followers, many of whom are extreme rightists, the UNR appealed to all those who were opposed to the Fourth Republic because of its Algeria policy or because of other considerations. Moreover, the UNR registered considerable appeal among the younger generation of industrialists, engineers, and professional men. It also received support from the lower middle class, such as the salaried elements in plants and industrial firms. Finally, the UNR received some working class support, and is working through the Democratic Workers Union to get more. Almost from the beginning of the Fifth Republic, a number of UNR deputies were cognizant of the importance of the worker to the party's future, and sought labor support through autonomous workers' syndicates and through worker representatives on the central committee of the party.

The UNR does not have a well-articulated program or an elaborate organization. The primary reason is that its leaders have not been able to take a definite stand on either. Although not formally associated with the UNR, De Gaulle has preferred that it limit its activities to providing support for him. His most devout followers, however, have been divided. One group has favored a great organization drive to enlist members on at least as large a scale as the Communists, while another faction has preferred avoiding all the responsibilities which such a move would entail. One such responsibility would be the party's program. In the early years of the Fifth Republic, the party preferred to tackle problems pragmatically—to aid in the settlement of the Algerian question, to promote economic expansion, to improve relations between industry and labor, to carry out fiscal and administrative reforms—and by and large it has experienced considerable success.

Some UNR followers fell by the wayside because of what they regarded as a "sell-out" in Algeria, and some even sought to overthrow the regime by unconstitutional means. But the settlement of the Algerian question has made the party more homogeneous, and perhaps more inclined to develop long-range programs for the problems which France faces. Nevertheless, the party continues to exhibit some uncertainties, and no doubt will continue to do so in the future, particularly in those areas where it is unsure of General De Gaulle's position. On the other hand, many UNR deputies have not been satisfied with their "do nothing" role, and have been calling for "the rehabilitation of the function of Parliament."

There is evidence that the UNR has become a durable political force in France. The results of the local elections in early 1965, for example, seemed to demonstrate that the party was establishing solid roots in the French countryside and in a number of the medium-sized provincial towns.

THE COMMUNIST PARTY

The Communist party of France is a Marxian party, loyal to Moscow. Like its Soviet counterpart, it is ruled from above by a handful of men who are not responsible to the rank and file, and, of course, were not elected by the rank and file. Nevertheless, aside from a small number of defections, they have been successful in imposing an iron discipline on the membership.

After being founded in 1920, the party gradually gained strength, emerging after World War II as the strongest single party in France. But in 1958 it managed to poll only 18 per cent of the vote on the first ballot, a decline of some 30 per cent from its postwar high. On the second ballot, chiefly because no one would affiliate with them, the Communists lost many seats. From a high of 144 deputies in 1956, the party dropped to 10 in 1958. Consequently, the Communists' influence in Parliament was nil. Because they were so few, they were deprived of committee assignments and of the right to introduce motions of censure.

In the 1962 elections, however, the Communists made a modest recovery, polling 21.8 per cent of the vote on the first ballot. More important perhaps, the party succeeded in electing 41 deputies, partly because of an arrangement with the Socialists that the candidates of their two parties withdraw in each others favor in those districts where their joint vote might prevent the election of the UNR candidate. Communist deputies are now numerous enough to get committee assignments and, with only a handful of deputies from outside their ranks, have the strength to present at least one censure motion per session.

There are a number of factors which explain Communist strength in France. There is a tradition of voting for the revolutionary left in France, partly because the left was the historical defender of republican institutions, and partly because it was the antirepublican forces that brutally suppressed the workers' uprisings in 1848 and 1871. The Communist party, more or less fortuitously, inherited the leftist position, and thereby became the beneficiary of the leftist voting tradition. In addition, the Communist party devotes a great deal of time and effort to its organizational and propaganda drives. It sponsors youth groups, discussion and protest meetings, and it puts out numerous publications. Moreover, it has managed to gain control of a large part of the trade union movement. It has convinced many workers that the Communist party is the working class party. These workers are not really interested in the Soviet Union; they are disturbed by the real or fancied injustices of French society. Once in control of the largest trade unions, the Communist party has been able to exercise its tyranny through them. Workers are mobilized to vote, to contribute to the party treasury, and to participate in Communist-organized demonstrations.

Aside from the workers, the Communist party has found some support among lower class peasants. To them the party does not talk of collectivization. Rather, the party has systematically attempted to place one man in each village who knows the peasants and their problems. His main job is to help the peasants in their problems with the local bureaucracy. And the peasants have demonstrated their gratitude with votes for the party.

Finally, the Communist party has in large measure been the recipient of support from the discontented in various social and economic groups. Included here are some intellectuals, particularly elementary school teachers and some civil servants, and persons with no party allegiance who are anxious to cast a protest vote. They are not necessarily convinced that the Communists would straighten out "the mess"; they are just voting against conditions as they are.

Although the party continues to poll a sizable vote, there are indications that all is not well inside and outside the party. In spite of its labored dynamism, it gives the appearance of being old and tired, with the same party bureaucracy and the unchanging slogans. It is in financial trouble. Its best source of funds, the salaries of parliamentary deputies, has been severely cut by virtue of the sharp drop in the number of Communist deputies. In 1958, many of its one-time supporters deserted the party because De Gaulle represented the only sensible solution to France's most pressing problems of the moment. Many of these probably resumed their former voting habits in 1962, because they were convinced that De Gaulle's one-man rule constituted a victory for the traditional forces of conservatism. Destalinization and the Soviet suppression of the Hungarian revolution (1956) hurt the party some. Party membership has declined, as the official figures indicate. As important as anything else, however, in reducing the effectiveness of Communist appeals is the growing prosperity and the steadily rising standard of living for more and more Frenchmen. One indicator of this was that in 1962 the Communists won only 13 out of 103 straight fights with the UNR.

THE SOCIALIST PARTY

The Socialist party is the party of democratic socialism. Although formally still Marxian in outlook, believing in the collective ownership of the means of production, it abhors the authoritarian structure of the Communist party, as well as its intellectual and political subordination to Moscow. In practice, the Socialist party seems to have modified its belief in collective ownership, and seems more interested in reforming French capitalism so as to achieve a more equitable distribution of income for all groups, but especially for the workers. In spite of its emphasis on socialism, the party draws its membership in large measure from middle-class intellectuals, teachers, civil servants, and the more conservative workers.

In the postwar period, the Socialist party has alternated between being third and fourth in votes polled. In 1958, the Socialists maintained their voting strength on the first ballot (15 per cent), but lost heavily when it came to Assembly seats. In the 1962 elections, they lost ground in the popular vote (13 per cent), but gained several Assembly seats, for a total of 66, enabling them to stay alive politically.

The Socialists participated in several postwar governments, including the interim De Gaulle Government (1958). Following the inauguration of the Fifth Republic, however, the Socialists have formed a "constructive opposition" to De Gaulle. They have supported his foreign policies, including his efforts to bring peace to Algeria. But they have opposed some of his domestic policies, including aid to

Catholic schools and those social and fiscal policies whose costs they believe will be borne disproportionately by the working class. And they are critical of what they regard as a lack of respect for the constitution by both the president and the cabinet.

There have been some rumblings of dissatisfaction among the rank and file with the policy of "constructive opposition." In the debates, however, the leaders have won out. Moreover, an effort in 1959 to form an Autonomous Socialist party was largely unsuccessful, although the prospects for more splinter parties on the left seem excellent.

There is reason to believe, however, that the causes of dissatisfaction go deeper than the disagreement over qualified support for De Gaulle. There seems to be a gap between leadership and many of its supporters. There is a feeling in some Socialist circles that the party's doctrinal foundations are in serious need of re-examination. The old slogans and oft-repeated remedies do not seem to make sense in the light of the new problems of an increasingly industrialized society. Yet, the leadership has refused to examine its doctrinal foundations critically, although other Socialist parties, notably the British Laborites and the German Social Democrats, have done so.

Moreover, Socialist party rules tend to discourage young people. A person must be a party member for five years before he can be a delegate to the party congress, a member of the executive committee, an editor of a party paper, or a candidate for Parliament. It is no accident that the average age of Socialist deputies in the Assembly, as well as their delegates at party conferences, is higher than that of any other party.

While still seeking working class support, the Socialists have lost ground among the workers. This was almost inevitable, for the Socialists, when in power, were forced to be reasonable and hence compromised on trade union claims. Yet, in doing so, they were forfeiting some worker support to the Communists. Similarly, in seeking long overdue reforms, the Socialists were frustrated by peasant and petty bourgeois opposition, which could only result in a net gain for the Communists.

POPULAR REPUBLICAN MOVEMENT (MRP)

The Popular Republican Movement is a new party that grew out of the World War II resistance movement against the Nazis. It is essentially a party of Christian socialism. It is anti-Marxist and anticlass war, but it is also critical of free enterprise. Aside from supporting liberal social and economic policies, however, the MRP has been in favor of basically conservative policies. It is strongly influenced by Catholicism and has supported aid to Catholic schools. Because of the latter, it parted company with the Socialists, with whom it otherwise had a good deal in common. For the same reason, as well as because of other conservative tendencies, the MRP became respectable as a party for ultraconservative voters.

In 1946, the MRP polled more votes than any other party, but dropped to third or fourth place in subsequent elections, polling slightly below 11% in 1956. Experiencing some resurgence because of the influence of vigorous liberal Catholics and the actions of the Christian Trade Union Confederation, the MRP improved its strength slightly in 1958, but it managed to elect only 56 deputies. In the Senate, however, it increased its strength from 21 to 29, the largest net gain recorded by any party. In the 1962 elections, however, it again lost ground, polling 9 per cent of the vote and electing only 38 deputies. These, together with their allies, make up the Democratic Center in the National Assembly.

The MRP for several years cautiously supported De Gaulle and a number of its leaders held cabinet posts. Although anxious to assist De Gaulle in finding a solution to the Algerian question, the party was from the outset uneasy about several developments in the Fifth Republic. It was opposed to some of the economic policies of the Government, as well as the latter's inclination to rely too much on technocrats. And it was anxious about the role of the army in the new regime. Nevertheless, its ministers stayed in the cabinet until May 1962.

The departure from the Government of the MRP ministers was precipitated by De Gaulle's ridiculing (at a press conference) the idea of European political integration. The party had for some time prior to May 1962 been unhappy with De Gaulle's nationalistic defense policies. And, as the party that had in the postwar period been the strongest proponent of European unity and European integration, it could not tolerate De Gaulle's attack upon its cherished program. The party's departure from the cabinet was also aided by virtue of the fact that its leaders did not like the trend toward a presidential system in France.

The best known of MRP's postwar leaders, Georges Bidault, seemingly became too nationalistic for the party, and in the early years of the Fifth Republic formed a small and unsuccessful splinter party.

Subsequently, he became involved in the unconstitutional efforts to overthrow General De Gaulle, and fled France to avoid arrest.

Although determined to be a party of the left, as shown by its backing of progressive economic and social policies, the MRP found its most effective support coming from traditionally conservative areas, areas in which the church had always been strongest. Thus the enthusiasm of the party militants for social reform was not shared by the vast bulk of the party's electoral supporters, the principal exception being its supporters among the workers.

THE RADICALS AND ALLIES

The Radical Socialist party, the oldest of French political parties, was the largest and most powerful of the prewar parties. Championing political democracy, separation of church and state, civil rights, and fundamental reforms, it was generally conservative in the economic realm. Characteristic of its philosophy and program was the not infrequent reference to its being neither radical nor socialist. Although the Radical Socialist was still the largest party in the late 1930s, it declined from that time because of the growing strength of the Socialist party.

In the elections following World War II, the Radical Socialists were all but wiped out. Nevertheless, they made a gradual comeback, polling about 10 per cent of the vote in 1955. Always a party of personalities, it provided many ministers and several prime ministers during the Fourth Republic. Partly because of internal splits after 1955, it lost heavily in the election of 1958. Its popular vote dropped to 8 per cent, but along with its allies managed to elect 41 deputies. One of its best-known postwar leaders, Pierre Mendès-France, was defeated in a constituency that had elected him continually since 1932. In the Senate elections of 1959, however, the party improved its position, with 51 senators out of a total of 306.

The divisions that occurred within the party, now known simply as Radical, stemmed mostly from the determination of several of its leaders to lead it in particular directions. Some of the differences were more personal than political. Mendès-France, now no longer in the party, created a considerable stir when he sought to alter the party's organizational structure and its economic policies. He wanted to modernize the party organization so as to build more of a mass party on the national level. Moreover, he urged government intervention to modernize the economy, particularly to bring about the reconversion of its backward sectors. His personal defeat in 1958, however, seems more attributable to the fact that he was bucking a nationalist tide on the question of Algeria.

By 1962 the Radicals had achieved a partial reunification within their ranks. In the elections, however, they dropped slightly below their 1958 vote, but managed (along with their allies) to elect 39 deputies. In the Assembly they are known as the Democratic Rally.

In the early years of the Fifth Republic, the Radicals supported General De Gaulle, but were increasingly suspicious of the new political institutions. They were particularly unhappy about the failure of the system to provide effective parliamentary control of the cabinet. Even as they developed a dislike for the regime, and signed censure motions, they for the most part avoided attacking it directly. They opposed De Gaulle's efforts to develop an independent atomic striking force, and they have been critical of his position with respect to NATO. In a sense, their general attitude very much resembled the "constructive opposition" of the Socialists.

INDEPENDENT REPUBLICANS

A loose organization of conservative parties, using some variation of the name Independent, has been a significant force in French politics. In the postwar years these groups were known collectively as the Independents and Peasants party. They represented the conservative elements of rural France, as well as the conservative sectors of the business community. They opposed economic and social reform, and they rejected state interference in economic affairs, except for subsidies for farmers and protective tariffs for business. In conformity with conservative opinion generally, they favored state aid to Catholic schools.

As the above suggests, the Independents and Peasants party has received support primarily from conservative elements, among them people who never reconciled themselves to the republic, who deplored the Revolution, and who would like to have reversed it. Such antirepublican elements, prior to World War II, did not succeed in organizing for effective parliamentary action. Rather, they found themselves in open antiparliamentary organizations. After World War II, however, a small number of right wing deputies, mainly from poor, strongly Catholic areas, came together to form a parliamentary group, which was to become the nucleus of the future Independents and Peasants party. Since 1949, other small conservative parties joined and thus augmented the size of this political formation.

In the 1958 elections, the Independents and Peasants party polled

20 per cent of the vote on the first ballot, the largest vote cast for any party. In fact, it was the only party closely associated with the previous regime to make such gains. This is all the more remarkable because the conservative tide behind the UNR could have been expected to decrease their strength. The only explanation seems to be that the Independents made their gains at the expense of the Radicals and the MRP. With 120 seats they were the second largest group in the National Assembly and the largest party in the Senate.

Between the 1958 and 1962 elections a number of divisions, referred to below, tended to shatter this alliance of conservative parties. The nucleus that remained took on the name, Independent Republicans. In 1962, they polled less than half the 1958 vote that was cast for the Independents and Peasants party. In the National Assembly they have 36 seats. They are known as Gaullists, supporting the UNR.

Although the Independents and Peasants had some doubts about De Gaulle, they supported him in the early years of the Fifth Republic. In fact they joined the cabinet and did not decide to abandon it until mid-1962, and even then the Independent ministers decided to stay in their posts on an individual basis. What divided the party more than anything else was De Gaulle's Algerian policy, and his granting of independence to France's former African colonies. Some of their parliamentary leaders remained cautious and non-committal, but many of them became increasingly hostile, with some demonstrating sympathy for the Secret Army Organization (OAS) that was seeking to overthrow De Gaulle by force. Moreover, in the domestic field, the party was never happy about De Gaulle's desires for modernization of the economy, national planning, and increased taxes.

It would be hazardous to predict the future of the traditional alliance of conservative forces. The elections of 1962 indicated considerable disarray in their camp. And what remains of this bloc, under the name Independent Republicans, seems to be going along with De Gaulle and the Union for the New Republic.

INTEREST GROUPS IN FRANCE

The very idea of interest or pressure groups, at least in theory, is repugnant to the French. Influenced by Rousseau's concept of the general will, they like to maintain that no one should stand between the citizen and his government. In practice, however, pressure groups have been important and active in France. The traditional attitude seemed to be that if pressure groups are to win favors, they should do so unseen via the back door. To some extent this attitude has changed in recent times.[2] The constitution of the Fourth Republic officially recognized pressure groups when it set up an economic council whose members were chosen by trade unions, business associations, and agricultural organizations. A similar institution, the Economic and Social Council, is provided for by the constitution of the Fifth Republic. In both instances, however, the powers of the council were said to be advisory.

Among the multitude of organizations that lobby for favors, the most effective have been the agricultural associations (especially the alcohol lobby), the veterans, and those championing the interests of small (usually inefficient) business. Organized labor is split into several federations, often hostile to each other, and has been weakened thereby. Moreover, the large Communist-controlled trade unions have been more concerned with activities designed to overthrow the system rather than to extract concessions from it.

The methods which pressure groups have employed have varied, although they have sought usually to keep in close touch with political parties and their representatives in Parliament, particularly the committees. In political campaigns, they have given financial support to their favorite candidates in unknown amounts, which is perfectly legal, since there is no maximum sum which a candidate may spend. In some ways, the existence of many political parties meant that a number of them resembled interest groups or at least acted as spokesman for the principal ones.

In the Fifth Republic, because of the shift of power from parliament to the executive, interest groups altered their focus of action. They have been paying less attention to Parliament than in the past. At the same time, they have been more active in the executive branch of government. Their task has not been made easy, however, by General De Gaulle's known hostility to pressure groups.

BIBLIOGRAPHICAL NOTE

A basic work on French politics which is particularly valuable for its discussion of political parties is Philip Williams, *Politics in Post-War France: Parties and the Constitution in the Fourth Republic* (2d ed.; London and New York: Longmans, Green, 1958). Additional general works on parties include

---

[2] See the excellent studies by Bernard E. Brown, "Pressure Politics in France," *The Journal of Politics*, 18 (November, 1956), pp. 702–19; "Alcohol and Politics in France," *American Political Science Review*, LI (December, 1957), pp. 976–94; "Pressure Politics in the Fifth Republic," *Journal of Politics*, 25 (November, 1963), pp. 509–25.

those of Richard William Barron, *Parties and Politics in Modern France* (Washington, D.C.: Public Affairs Press, 1959) ; Maurice Duverger, *Political Parties* (New York: Wiley, 1954) ; Jacques Fauvet, *Les Forces Politiques en France, de Thorez a de Gaulle; Etude et Geographie des Divers Partis* (Paris: Le Monde, 1951) ; Jean A. Laponce, *The Government of the Fifth Republic: French Political Parties and the Constitution* (Berkeley: University of California Press, 1961) ; and G. E. Lavau, *Partis Politiques et Realites Sociales: Contribution a une Etude Realiste des Partis Politiques* (Paris: Armand Colin, 1953).

More limited in scope, but equally useful, are Mario Einaudi and François Goguel, *Christian Democracy in Italy and France* (South Bend, Ind.: University of Notre Dame Press, 1952) ; E. Drexel Godfrey, Jr., *The Fate of the French Non-Communist Left* (New York: Doubleday, 1955) ; Charles A. Micaud, *Communism and the French Left* (New York: Praeger, 1963) ; Aaron Nolan, *The Founding of the French Socialist Party, 1893–1905* (Cambridge: Harvard University Press, 1956) ; Francis de Tarr, *The French Radical Party from Herriot to Mendès-France* (New York: Oxford University Press, 1961) ; and Angelo Rossi, *A Communist Party in Action: An Account of the Organization and Operations in France* (New Haven: Yale University Press, 1949).

Two interesting critiques, written by former members of their respective parties, are Jean Baby, *Critique de Base: Le Parti Communiste Francais Entre le Passe et l'Avenir* (Paris: Cahiers Libres, 1960) ; and Andre Philippe, *Le Socialisme Trahi* (Paris: Tribune Libre, 1957).

For a discussion of interest groups, see Henry W. Ehrmann (ed.), *Interest Groups on Four Continents* (Pittsburgh: Pittsburgh University Press, 1958) ; ———, *French Labor from Popular Front to Liberation* (New York: Oxford University Press, 1947) ; ———, *Organized Business in France* (Princeton, N.J.: Princeton University Press, 1957) ; V. Lorwin, *The French Labor Movement* (Cambridge, Mass.: Harvard University Press, 1954) ; J. Meynaud, *Les Groupes de pression en France* (Paris: Armand Colin, 1958).

CHAPTER 14

ADMINISTRATION

THE OUTSTANDING characteristic of French public administration is its centralization. Like Great Britain, France is a unitary state, yet French administration, which retains a great deal of the absolutist tradition, is more centralized. What the British call local government is more appropriately referred to in France as administration. The centralized bureaucracy of Napoleon's time has survived and has played an important role in French public life largely because of the weakness and instability of the political executive. Stability in administration in the midst of political instability was no doubt recognized and appreciated by Frenchmen. There have been efforts on the part of political parties, however, to combat the autocratic aspects of the bureaucracy. But since the average tenure of a minister was approximately six months (Third and Fourth Republics), little could be done to carry through with reform measures. Under the Fifth Republic important reforms have been made, some of which are discussed below.

Next to centralization, the most important characteristic of French public administration is the system of administrative law which has been developed, and which will be discussed later. This system, operating through an independent system of courts, provides for an efficient, easy, and inexpensive method of testing the validity of governmental actions, as well as providing for adequate restitution to injured parties.

A more recent attribute of French administration concerns its deep involvement in the national economy. Economic planning, national and regional, designed to eliminate glaring contrasts between "private wealth and public poverty," has required both new authority to administrative subdivisions and machinery for coordinating the efforts of the private and public sectors of the economy.

ORGANIZATION OF THE ADMINISTRATION

As in Great Britain, the administrative system is directed by the ministers. The organizational structure of the ministries is similar. As a rule there is a secretary and/or an undersecretary who is supposed to assist the minister. Below them are the directors, who are the equivalent of assistant secretaries and who head *directions,* or divisions. Their immediate subordinates are the bureau chiefs. Only a few departments have a general secretary, who corresponds to the permanent head of a department in Britain. All of these people, together with the rank and file civil servants, are permanent appointees and usually not subject to removal by the minister.

In the past all ministers designated to head departments came to their posts distrusting the bureaucracy of their respective departments. Their distrust was usually well-founded, not so much because they could not remove the permanent officials, but mainly because the brief tenure of ministers created an attitude among the civil servants that any radical departures or innovations desired by an incoming minister should not be taken too seriously, because his place would soon be taken by another man. This was less true of some departments, notably foreign affairs, and particularly when the same man held the same ministerial post in several succeeding cabinets.

Because of his distrust of the permanent officials, a French minister appoints a small group of men who enjoy his absolute confidence and who share his ideas. These men, who advise and assist the minister and who act as intermediaries between him and the permanent staff, are known collectively as the cabinet. Sometimes they are referred to as "ministerial cabinets." Each such cabinet has a chief, an assistant chief, a secretary, and several attachés. The minister is in no way limited by civil service regulations in the choice of these men. The more important ones are usually mature and experienced, but the attachés are bright young men who have just completed their education in law or politics. The attachés work without a salary. They are anxious to make government a career, and are glad to get the experience. Moreover, their positions carry prestige. Before leaving office, the minister usually finds places for his cabinet in the permanent service.

Recruitment to the civil service, however, is usually free of political influence or partisan considerations. Basically, there is equality of opportunity. Moreover, the principle that there ought to be a significant relationship between the public service and schools and universities is generally accepted. Prior to 1945, however, there was nothing comparable to a civil service commission, individual departments having a relatively free hand in selecting persons for the public service. Recruitment was unified by law after World War II, with general conditions established to govern promotion and discipline. But some areas remain outside the civil service code (for example, nationalized enterprises and technical branches such as mining and engineering).

Another aim of the post–World War II reforms was to provide for the recruitment and training of persons for the higher civil service. For this purpose, the National School of Administration was established. Admission to the school is through keen competition from two groups: (1) persons not over 26 years of age who hold degrees or diplomas from universities or technical schools, and (2) bureaucrats between the ages of 26 and 30, and with at least five years of service. From those admitted are recruited the "superior" functionaries and civil administrators. One impact of this school on the civil service is that attendance considerably improves one's chances for promotion to the higher rungs of the bureaucratic ladder. Moreover, the school has helped promote the practice of in-service-training.

The school course lasts for two years, with a third year possible. In the first year, the "student" serves as an intern with some high functionary, but away from Paris. At the end of the year, he is required to submit an original study (at least 50 pages) on some phase of administration. The second year is spent in Paris interning in one of the central ministries, where he acquires experience in general administration, economic and fiscal administration, social administration, and the foreign service. At the end of the year, he takes an examination in each of these areas and, on the basis of his rank in each, he makes a choice of career among the positions available. For those who are selected to participate in the third year, there are specialized studies and other internships.

For a long time the pay of French civil servants was regarded as very low, but the situation has improved. In the lower and middle grades, the civil servant is better off than his counterpart in private business. At higher levels, however, the position of the civil servant is relatively poorer, particularly in such technical areas as scientific research.

Paradoxically, although there is a widespread public distrust of the bureaucracy, there is prestige in being part of it. There is no dearth of applicants for civil service positions, and morale is high, particularly among those in the upper ranks. Personal ties are particularly close between influential public servants. There is ability, honesty, and mutual respect. Members of powerful control bodies, such as the Council of State and the Court of Accounts, wield considerable power and influence in the bureaucracy as well as among political leaders. Because of the historical brief tenure of ministers, civil servants have been more influential in policy making than their British counterparts. And under De Gaulle many of them have become ministers or other important advisers.

On the other hand, as indicated earlier, the civil service in France has been less accountable and less responsive to the political leadership than is true in Great Britain. Moreover, much of the bureaucratic structure is cumbersome and inefficient, mainly at local levels. In recent years, however, much has been done to simplify administrative procedures and to streamline administrative practices generally.

*   *   *   *   *

Below the national level, for purposes of administration, France is divided into some 90 principal areas, called departments. Although each department is subdivided into about 35 cantons and although in each canton there are a number of communes, the really important administrative unit is the department. Each department has a general council, which is a type of departmental assembly, although general councils do not possess powers usually associated with local government. Members of general councils are popularly elected for six-year terms, and although they receive no pay, the quality of the men who serve is high. Many of them are members of the National Assembly or the Senate. General councilors are members of the electoral colleges which elect members of the Senate. In general, it may be said that departments serve the interests of national administration rather than those of local autonomy.

The executive officer of the department is the prefect, who is the appointed representative of the central government. As such, his is a dual role: chief administrator of local affairs and agent of the Ministry of Interior.

THE PROCESSES OF ADMINISTRATION: MINISTER OF INTERIOR AND PREFECT

Characteristic of the centralization of French public administration is the fact that one ministry, the Ministry of Interior, supervises the carrying out of all national laws throughout France. This is done through the prefect, who is appointed by the minister of interior and may be removed by him at will. Thus there is direct and centralized control of the administration of public affairs. Unless one can visualize the central control of everything from the police to the supervision of elections, he cannot appreciate the far-ranging powers of the minister of interior.

As the foregoing suggests, the prefect exercises vast powers, but as an agent of the minister of interior he is usually bound by detailed instructions. In the exercise of some powers, however, he has a free hand. Aside from transmitting information and giving effect to ministerial instructions, the prefect directs all the state services within his department. He exercises control over subprefects and mayors. He appoints many officials, such as school teachers, letter carriers, and tax collectors. Moreover, he may also be asked to perform political tasks for the ministers he serves. To perform his many tasks, the prefect has a considerable staff to assist him.

Like other effective administrators, the prefect relies more on persuasion than on dictation. He must anticipate conflicts and seek to compromise differences. While serving his political chief, he must seek to be impartial in local matters, show discretion, and be cheerful, prudent, and accessible. He is constantly beset by various claims, demands, and ambitions. He usually comes to his job after having extensive experience as a subprefect.

Associated with the prefect in administering the affairs of the department is the general council. By comparison with his powers, those of the council are meager. It may not make representations of a political nature to the central government, and it may take up only such things as are brought before it by the prefect. In some matters, its decision is final, but in many others it requires the approval of the central government, and in still others its decisions may be revoked within three months. Similarly, in case of municipal councils, there is a long list of subjects on which they cannot make a final decision without the prefect's prior approval. In his dealings with departmental authorities, therefore, the prefect is really master rather than servant.

Because administration is so centralized, political party activity tends to be greatest at focal points in the administrative hierarchy, which means principally in Paris and at the department prefectures. It is interesting to note that while the newer parties, notably the UNR, have gained ascendancy in Paris, the older parties continue to dominate in the departmental administration.

* * * * *

From what has been said in the preceding pages, it can be seen that coordination and control of administration is in the hands of the minister of interior and the prefects, as well as in the hands of such control bodies as the Court of Accounts and the administrative courts (discussed below). Parliament does have committees of inquiry, but these are less effective than the select committees in Great Britain.

FIFTH REPUBLIC REFORMS

In the early years of the new regime several steps were taken, aside from some that have already been mentioned, to improve the administrative system. On the national level, in order to facilitate cooperation among the 90 geographic departments, and in particular to promote the central government's plans for economic growth, the departments were grouped into 21 economic regions. For the most part these groupings conform to the historic regional areas (e.g. Normandy, Burgundy, Brittany). The Government designates "superprefects" to act as coordinators, mainly with respect to the regional economic programs. Moreover, the prefects have been given increased responsibility for management, arbitration, and coordination of economic activities in their respective departments.

In addition, the Government undertook a number of reforms designed to improve local administration. One of these was the creation of the Paris Area Authority, which seeks to deal more effectively with the enormous problems of this vast concentration of people, comprising one fifth of the population of France and affecting several units of administration. The Central Markets (*Les Halles*), which were inefficient, unhygienic, and monopolistic, constituted one of the most serious problems of the Paris area. The Paris Area Authority has now decentralized and reorganized many of the Central Market's operations. Similarly, the acute problem of the operational deficits of the public transportation system, due in part to conflicting jurisdictions and in part to the refusal of the communities to invest in necessary modifications, has now been faced and solutions worked out. Other problems of the Paris area are also being realistically attacked.

Another effort to improve local administration was a series of measures designed to give local areas more freedom by lessening state supervision, rendering local taxation more flexible and broadening the scope of local administration. As a means of lessening central control, departmental budgets no longer need state approval as long as they are balanced and as long as the interest due on loans does not exceed 10 per cent of the departmental tax revenues. Similarly, financial supervision of communes with populations exceeding 9,000 has been reduced, and other activities, affecting even those with fewer than 9,000, are subject to less state supervision.

Moreover, the local tax structure has been reformed. A number of taxes which have yielded mediocre returns have been abolished and replaced by taxes which are more flexible and better adapted to present economic conditions. At the same time, a complete revision of land assessments has been undertaken and the local system of business turnover taxes modified. Moreover, the maintenance of highways within communes is now the responsibility of the communes rather than the departments.

In order to facilitate cooperation between communes and between departments, the old regulation prohibiting lateral communication—intercommunal or interdepartmental—has been modified. The prohibition was initially motivated by the desire to avoid any danger of concerted action or opposition to the central government. It has now been made easier for two or more communes to associate for the purpose of setting up joint services or for planning and implementing joint public works programs. In large population areas, urban districts that involve several communities may be created to perform necessary services that the localities may not be able to perform individually. This may be done by local initiative or by "request" of the central government. Also, the consolidation of small communes has been made easier.

While some of these efforts to improve local administration are couched in terms of greater local autonomy, and in some areas more local independence will no doubt result, the basic aim is to improve a highly centralized administration and not to decentralize it. In all fairness, however, it should be noted that some observers believe that there is a genuine effort to decentralize, especially in nationally owned industries.

ADMINISTRATIVE LAW AND ADMINISTRATIVE COURTS

Unlike British or American practice, the French have a separate body of law, called administrative law, which determines the rights and liabilities of the servants of the state as well as the rights and liabilities of citizens in their relations with these agents of the state. The basic philosophy embodied in such a system is contrary to the notion that the "king can do no wrong." In the French view, the state is a responsible person and its administrators are agents or instruments, and hence cannot be held personally liable for wrongful acts. Consequently, special courts, called administrative courts, have been established to hear administrative law cases.

This system seems to have originated in the French Revolution and the events that preceded it. Even the *ancien régime* had been subjected to intolerable restraints by the law courts. With the coming of the Revolution, all parties were agreed that the courts would be a stumbling block to the new order, and all were determined to change things. A revolutionary law of 1790 declared that judicial functions must remain distinct from the administrative ones, while the constitution of 1791 forbade the courts from engaging in actions that would infringe upon the administrative field.

These actions were in line with Montesquieu's interpretation of the separation of powers as understood by Frenchmen, that is, that the courts must not interfere with the freedom of administrative action. Theoretically, under this philosophy, the government can do anything it pleases without any fear from the ordinary courts. But over the decades, safeguards evolved in the form of administrative courts with definite procedures and a coherent body of law to guide them. The result is a system which makes government responsible for its acts and which protects the individual citizen from administrative excesses. Under this system, the Frenchman is perhaps better protected from official oppression than is an Englishman or an American.

There are a number of other, and perhaps more important, advantages of the administrative law system. First, the costs are negligible. Secondly, the citizen knows that his claim will be decided promptly, and he knows that if he wins his adversary has enough money to pay the judgment.

This does not mean that the administrative courts have unlimited powers. In a country that has not had judicial review one would hardly expect this. As a matter of fact, only administrative acts, and not other governmental actions, are subject to control by administrative courts. Actions by administrative agencies may be nullified if the agency or person in question was not empowered to do what he did or sought to do, if there was nonobservance of prescribed forms or procedures, if there was an abuse of power (that is, legal acts performed for purposes not contemplated by the law), or if there was an error in the law. In short, an administrative court may not challenge the right of a law to exist, but only the way it is being administered. In recent years, however, there has been a tendency to expand the scope of review, as well as to emphasize merit instead of technicalities in reaching decisions.

At the top of the administrative hierarchy is the Council of State. Its membership is approximately 150, but it is divided into five bodies or sections. Only one of the five sections is concerned with judicial business; the other four acts in a consultative capacity to the Government on administrative questions. The advice rendered does not, however, bind the judicial section in litigation that may come before it. The public prestige which the Council enjoys stems from its judicial section. In all of its work, despite the fact that its members are appointed and may be removed by the cabinet (upon recommendation of the minister of justice), the Council seems relatively free from subservience to the executive, and some observers believe that if it has a bias it is in favor of the citizen. As a way of protecting its interests, each ministry designates an official of high rank who participates in all meetings of the Council of State when matters of concern to the ministry are being considered.

If the administrative exercise of discretionary power is challenged, the Council of State will require the department concerned to set out its reasons. In judging the sufficiency of these reasons, the Council has the power to call for documents and files. In exercising the authority to rule that a department may be attempting to go beyond the discretionary powers vested in it, the Council seeks at one and the same time to require that administrative acts be reasonable, while preserving the administrator's freedom of action which properly belongs to him. In large part it succeeds in securing such a balance, for it seems to have the confidence of the executive as much as of the citizen. The fact that the public knows of the existence of an institution empowered to redress grievances tends to make the administrator act more responsibly.

Prior to 1954, the Council of State heard the majority of claims in administrative matters, although claims in minor matters were heard in prefectural councils. In that year, a radical change in the hearing of cases was introduced. The prefectural councils of the Seine (Paris) and Alsace and Lorraine (Strasbourg), together with 21 interdepartmental prefectural councils, were transformed into 23 administrative tribunals. The majority of claims are now channeled to these administrative tribunals, but the Council of State still retains control, mostly through appeals, which it must hear. Also, the Council may exercise original jurisdiction in matters that affect several administrative tribunals. Similarly, the Council still acts as the court of first instance in disputes that concern the rights of civil servants.

In its advisory capacity, the Council of State gives opinions to the cabinet on all matters on which the latter seeks advice. In some areas the cabinet is obligated to ask for advice, for example, on cabinet measures submitted to Parliament, on its decree laws, and on all its nonlegislative decrees. Since 1945, the Council has been empowered to take the initiative in directing the cabinet's attention to areas where it believes legislative or administrative reforms are needed. As suggested above, advisory opinions of the Council are not binding upon the cabinet or the Council's judicial section.

Because the government has in recent years gone into areas where the ordinary law already applied (such as nationalization and the protection of property rights), the line of demarcation between private law and administrative law has become less clear. If the government does violence to the right of property or public freedom, it may find itself subject to the jurisdiction of the ordinary courts. In cases of disagreement as to jurisdiction, the Court of Conflicts decides.

BIBLIOGRAPHICAL NOTE

Two works by Brian Chapman, *Introduction to French Local Government* (London: Allen and Unwin, 1953) and *The Prefects and Provincial France* (London: Allen and Unwin, 1955) are penetrating studies of local government and administration in France. See also his *The Profession of Government: The Public Service in Europe* (New York: Macmillan, 1959).

Still useful is Walter R. Sharp, *The French Civil Service: Bureaucracy in Transition* (New York: Macmillan, 1931). An interesting analytical study from the point of view of organizational theory is Michel Crozier, *The Bureaucratic Phenomenon* (Chicago: University of Chicago Press, 1964). A comparable study of the bureaucracy under the Fourth Republic does not exist, but some insight into the administration in postwar years may be found in Mario Einaudi, et al., *Nationalization in France and Italy* (Ithaca, N.Y.: Cornell University Press, 1955). Also of interest is William A. Robson (ed.), *The Civil Service in Britain and France* (New York and London: Macmillan, 1956).

CHAPTER 15

LAW AND THE JUDICIARY

THE FRENCH judicial system is based on Roman law. Because of its systematic codification under Napoleon, French law is often referred to as the Napoleonic Code. In our treatment of Britain, we noted that common law is largely case law as modified by legislative enactments. Roman law, on the other hand, is code law. Carefully drawn statutes enable the Roman law justice to turn to "the law" for every case, instead of seeking "to find" it, as is often the case in common law. The trade-mark of the common law is *stare decisis* (adherence to decided cases); in other words, previous cases decide present ones. Roman law systems have in recent decades made some use of precedent, especially in France, but there is no acceptance of the principle that precedent is binding in future cases.[1]

ORGANIZATION OF THE COURTS

The constitution of the Third Republic made no reference to the judiciary or a judicial system. In practice, as already indicated in the preceding chapter, a dual system of courts developed: ordinary courts and administrative courts. In the discussion of the latter, it was also pointed out that any conflict of jurisdiction between the two court systems is resolved by the Court of Conflicts. This judicial system, as it evolved, received general acceptance and was virtually untouched by the constitution of the Fourth Republic. In the early years of the Fifth Republic, however, a number of changes were made. These sought (1) to reform the court structure which was devised when 75 per cent of the population was rural, (2) to improve rules of procedure and to clarify jurisdictions, (3) to improve the training of judges, and (4) to establish the Constitutional Council, mainly as a check on Parliament.

At the bottom of the court hierarchy are the minor (local) courts of first instance (*Tribunaux d'Instance*), which replace the justices of the peace. Each of these courts may have several judges, who are required

---

[1] For a discussion of some differences between common law and Roman law, see Chapter 7 under Great Britain.

to reside in the place where the court is situated. Each case, however, is heard by a single judge, who has more power than did the justice of the peace. These courts are intended to be the most important units in the judicial system, courts that will ensure prompt and inexpensive settlement of the most common types of civil cases.

Above these courts are the major courts of first instance (*Tribunaux de Grande Instance*). These courts have jurisdiction throughout a department, although the larger departments may have two or more of them. These courts try the more important civil cases and hear some appeals, such as those from the special technical labor and commercial courts. Each case is heard by an uneven number of judges who render a verdict by majority vote.

Criminal cases are heard by police courts or correctional courts, depending upon the seriousness of the offense. Criminal cases of the utmost seriousness, such as murder, are tried in the assize courts. These usually convene quarterly in each department. They are composed of three judges and nine jurors (the only jurors used in any French court), who make up a jury of twelve. Eight votes are necessary for conviction.

There are 27 courts of appeal, one for each of the existing judicial districts. They were untouched by the recent reforms except that their jurisdiction has been extended, particularly to cases arising from the field of social legislation. The decisions of the children's courts, commercial courts, farm lease courts, labor conciliation boards, and social security commissions may now be appealed to the courts of appeal.

At the top of the judicial hierarchy is the Court of Cassation. It has three sections: the criminal chamber, the civil chamber, and the chamber of requests. Each section has a president and 15 judges. Criminal appeals go directly to the criminal chamber, but civil appeals are funneled through the chamber of requests, which forwards only those appeals that it believes contain substantial grounds for reversal. Unlike the American or British highest courts, the Court of Cassation does not pronounce guilt or innocence. A reversal of a lower court decision, that is, a successful appeal, merely means that the case is sent back for retrial by another court of the same standing.

Finally, there is provision for the establishment of a high court of justice to try the president or other members of the government for high crimes and misdemeanors. Before they can be tried, however, the National Assembly and the Senate must vote indictments, which require a majority of the membership of each body.

In 1963, the Government succeeded in getting Parliament to establish a special Court for the Security of the State as a means of combating subversion. This action stemmed mainly from the various terrorist acts of civil and military elements who sought to impede De Gaulle's efforts to settle the Algerian problem. The new court is composed of civilian magistrates and high military officers. There is no jury, and appeals may be made to the Court of Cassation.

FRENCH JUDGES

The independence of the judiciary is well recognized in France. Judges hold office during good behavior and are not subject to removal by the executive. Instead of recruiting judges from the legal profession, as is done in the United States and Great Britain, the French view the judiciary as part of the administrative hierarchy and a separate profession from the practice of law. Hence, French legal graduates must choose at an early age whether they are going into the judiciary or whether they are going to practice before the courts. In France, the bench is a career.

Judges are recruited from law graduates under 27 years of age who have passed a competitive examination and then spend four years in the newly established National Center of Judicial Studies. The center is designed to do for the judiciary what the National School of Administration is supposed to do for the civil service, namely, produce a judiciary of competence and high standing. In the past, would-be magistrates were recruited in a similar way, but after their successful admission they usually learned the practical aspects of judicial business by spending a year or two in subordinate positions while awaiting appointment to judicial posts. Presumably, the Center of Judicial Studies will now prepare a man for appointment to a judicial post without his serving what in the past amounted to a type of apprenticeship.

Other changes in recent years have simplified judicial procedures and have altered the rules governing the classification and promotion of judges. There is now only one corps of judges for all courts, except for the Court of Cassation, which is considered "outside" the hierarchy. Moreover, there are only two main ranks: judges of lower courts and judges of the courts of appeal. Promotions are based on seniority and merit. Unlike in the past, judges can now be promoted without having to move to a new court.

The general supervision of the judiciary is in the hands of the High

Council of the Judiciary. It is presided over by the president of the Republic and the minister of justice. There are nine members appointed by the president for four-year terms. The Council presents names for appointments to the Court of Cassation and for first presidents of the courts of appeal. Actual appointment is by the president. Moreover, the Council gives its advice concerning the appointment of other judges whose names are proposed by the minister of justice. The Council also acts as a disciplinary council for judges. Finally, the president must consult the Council before he can pardon persons under conviction for capital punishment, and he may consult it in cases of petition for reprieve of sentence.

FRENCH JUDICIAL PROCEDURE

French judicial procedure is sometimes said to be characterized by the *inquisitorial* system, as opposed to the *accusatorial* system, which characterizes British and American judicial practice. The principal difference is that the former emphasizes the rights of society and seeks a prompt repression of crime, while the latter places emphasis on the rights of the accused and attempts to safeguard him from possible injustice. The basic aim may be the same, but the manner in which it is to be reached may differ.

After an arrest has been made, it is up to the examining magistrate (*juge d'instruction*) to decide if there is a prima facie case against him. He examines witnesses, including the arrested man (but in the presence of his lawyer), and studies other pertinent information. Neither the accused nor his counsel is present at the examination of witnesses, although a confrontation in court subsequently is a fairly regular practice. However, the defense counsel has access at all times to the dossier which the examining magistrate is compiling. The record compiled mixes facts and rumors, which may tend to incriminate the accused, and may include a survey of the accused's past. If the examining magistrate decides that there is a case, the man is committed for trial, otherwise he goes free.

Under this system, despite the declaration of the Rights of Man, which asserts that a man is "considered innocent until he had been found guilty," the accused is not presumed to be innocent. If the examining magistrate decides that the accused is to be tried, he is, in effect, saying: "After a careful examination of witnesses, including yourself, and anyone else who knows anything about the case, we believe you are guilty. But if you can explain your conduct to the satisfaction of the majority of the jury, they have the power to free you if they wish." Frenchmen are apt to observe, however, that this is not far different from what happens in Britain or the United States, except that the French are less hypocritical about it. It may be significant, however, that in the Anglo-American system the accused does not have to take the witness stand, something he cannot escape doing in France.

At the trial, the presiding judge does not act as an umpire of a duel between two opposing sets of lawyers. Rather he conducts the trial from beginning to end. He has the complete dossier before him, with which he is fully familiar. He interrogates the witnesses, beginning with the accused. His sole aim is to discover the truth. During the trial, witnesses are able to talk at length and there is no rule of evidence which excludes irrelevant eloquence on their part. Lawyers do not cross-examine witnesses directly; they only suggest questions to the judge, who propounds them. There is no summing up of a case in the British-American manner.

It is of interest that in addition to the criminal action, the injured party may seek damages. This action may be taken separately or the injured party may join the criminal action of the prosecution, being represented by counsel. Strangely enough, it is possible for a man to be ordered to pay damages for the murder of someone whom, according to the jury, he did not kill.

On the whole, French courts are free from technicalities, they are trusted to do substantial justice, and the law is less likely to be tortured out of its obvious meaning than is true in the United States or Great Britain. Justice in France is also more accessible and cheaper. Just as France considers crime an offense against society, and therefore engages actively in the prosecution of the accused, it also provides legal aid to those who cannot afford it.

THE CONSTITUTIONAL COUNCIL

Traditionally, France, like most other European countries, has not had the American equivalent of judicial review. Courts could not question the right of the legislature to legislate on anything it wished. This was due in part, perhaps, to the fact that French constitutions have been unlike the American. They did not impose specific limits on what the legislature could do; there were no prohibitions, and no powers reserved to subordinate units such as the states. The very concept of judicial review did not arouse much enthusiasm or support.

The constitution of the Fourth Republic established a Constitutional Committee, whose purpose was to determine whether the laws passed by the National Assembly imply amendment of the constitution. The committee could not nullify acts of the legislature, yet the constitution gave it power to send measures back to the legislature for reconsideration if in its opinion they implied amendment of the constitution. Should Parliament persist, says the constitution, the law cannot be promulgated until the constitution was amended in ways prescribed by the constitution itself. Since the constitution could be amended by the legislature, no one regarded the Constitutional Committee as a judicial hurdle to the aims and desires of the legislature.

The present constitution, as indicated in an earlier chapter, sets up the Constitutional Council. While this may be regarded as a far cry from establishing the power of judicial review, there would seem to be much more substance to it because of the limitations the constitution places on the legislature. Moreover, the powers granted to the council are far more extensive than those conferred upon the Constitutional Committee under the Fourth Republic, powers that are designed to protect the executive in its large domain of power. In the first years of its existence, the Constitutional Council seemed to be on the side of the executive in the latter's disagreements with the legislature.

BIBLIOGRAPHICAL NOTE

A general description of the French court system is provided in Robert C. K. Ensor, *Courts and Judges in France, Germany and England* (London: Oxford University Press, 1933). Discussions of French law and legal philosophy may be found in Rene David and Henry DeVries, *The French Legal System: An Introduction to Civil Law Systems* (New York: Oceana, 1958) ; A. Fouilee, et al., *Modern French Legal Philosophy* (New York: Macmillan, 1921) ; and Sir Maurice S. Amos and F. P. Walton, *Introduction to French Law* (Oxford: Clarendon Press, 1935).

More recent material is available on the subject of administrative law. One may consult profitably both C. J. Hamson, *Executive Discretion and Judicial Control: An Aspect of the French Conseil D'Etat* (London: Stevens, 1954) ; and Charles E. Freedman, *The Conseil D'Etat in Modern France* (New York: Columbia University Press, 1961). Also useful is the comparative study by Bernard Schwartz, *French Administrative Law and the Common-Law World* (New York: New York University Press, 1954).

PART THREE
GERMANY

CHAPTER 16

GERMANY AND THE GERMANS

GERMANY'S history as a nation-state is relatively brief, especially if compared to that of France or Great Britain. Yet much has been crowded into that brief span of less than 100 years, including two world wars and several different political systems. From late unification, Germany rose quickly to the position of a great power. Twice in the twentieth century she directed the forces of the losing coalition in world conflict. As a result of World War II and its aftermath, she remains a divided nation. The part occupied by Soviet troops became a Soviet satellite state (known as the German Democratic Republic), while the areas once occupied by the Western powers have been united to form the Federal Republic of Germany. It is the latter Germany that we are primarily concerned with in this book.

LATE UNIFICATION

During the period when Great Britain and France were strong nations, the area of Germany was occupied by a group of weak and divided states. To be sure, there had once been the Holy Roman Empire (German), but from the thirteenth century to the Napoleonic era there was no Germany in a political sense. The Reformation and the religious wars of the sixteenth century had split the Protestant north and the Catholic south. The Thirty Years' War of the Seventeenth century left much devastation and a greatly reduced population. As a consequence, after the Peace of Westphalia (1648) separate states grew apace. In 1800 there were 314 different states, some large, but most of them small.

Napoleon, more than any other one man, was responsible for smashing this conglomeration of small states, which was to lead to their ultimate unification. The struggle as to who should unify Germany was, in the end, between Austria and Prussia. The latter had been rising in power. Her rulers built up her strength by a combination of ruthless military power and the modernization of her economy. Frederick the Great (1740–86) raised Prussia from a weak principality to one of the strongest military states of Europe. But the real regeneration

255

of Prussia came after her disastrous defeat by Napoleon in 1806. Military conscription was introduced, certain feudal institutions were swept away, and the bureaucracy was modernized.

Under the impact of revolutionary France and the consequent developments in the Germanies themselves, the number of German states was sharply reduced. After Napoleon's fall from power, consolidation of the German states continued. At the Congress of Vienna (1815), the German Confederation, a loose combination of 38 states, was established. The most influential of the German states were Austria and Prussia, with the former predominating. In the end, however, it was Prussia that was to unify Germany.

The man who capped the unification efforts, and who, in a real sense, was the unifier of Germany, was Otto von Bismarck (1815–98). At the age of 47, he was made minister-president of Prussia, and was to guide the nation's destinies, and to a large extent Europe's destiny as well, for three decades. From the outset, he made it clear that he was no democrat. His method would be force: "blood and iron." In two quick wars, against Denmark in 1864 and against Austria in 1866, he established Prussia's dominance, following which he set up the North German Confederation (1867), a union of 22 states and principalities. The unification was made complete following the rapid defeat of France in 1870 and the subsequent ceding to Germany of Alsace and a part of Lorraine. In January, 1871, the North German Confederation was abolished and a German empire, consisting of Prussia and the North and South German states, was proclaimed. By "blood and iron" Germany had been unified.

But Bismarck did more than unify the nation. For the next twenty years (1871–1890) he manipulated and guided the social forces in the Empire, and made Imperial Germany a power among the nations of Europe.[1] His influence and his contributions deserve much more attention than this book can provide. A brief summary of his work in shaping the political life of the Empire, however, is presented in a subsequent section of this chapter.

GEOGRAPHY AND ECONOMICS

Germany's geographic position places her astride the center of the European continent. The Federal Republic lies to the east and north of

---

[1] See Arthur Rosenberg, *Imperial Germany: The Birth of the German Republic, 1871–1918* (Boston: Beacon Press, 1964), especially chapter one. This book was originally published in German in 1928.

France and stretches from the northern boundary of Switzerland to the North Sea and the southern boundary of Denmark. About half the size of prewar Germany, the area of the Federal Republic is comparable to that of Great Britain, or about half the area of France.

Germany does not have well-defined geographic frontiers except perhaps for the seacoast in the north, which is interrupted, however, by the Jutland peninsula. All the main rivers, except for the Weser and the Ems, either rise on foreign soil or leave Germany for other countries. Her greatest river is the Rhine, which originates in Switzerland and flows into the sea in Holland. Germany's North Sea boundary made possible the emergence of great ports, such as Bremen and Hamburg, and the development of sea trade.

There are considerable variations in climate and topography. In the north are the lowlands and river valleys, while much of the center is uplands, with moderate mountain ranges rising to the west and east. In the south the river valleys are low, while the mountains rise to greater heights, especially as one approaches the Alps. Rainfall is usually ample, particularly in the north, and the soil fertile.

Germany is a rich nation, particularly in those things that are necessary to a modern industrialized society. She has been particularly well endowed in coal and iron, as well as in many industrial chemicals. Her traditional agricultural areas, however, were in the eastern part of the nation, which are now within the boundaries of Poland or the so-called German Democratic Republic.

As already implied above, one of the really important keys to the growth of Germany as a power was its rapid transformation in the latter half of the nineteenth century from a primarily agrarian country to a modern industrial nation. Economic growth was particularly phenomenal after unification. German coal production jumped from about 30 million metric tons in 1871 to more than 190 million tons in 1914. Similarly, from a low of a few hundred thousand tons in 1850, Germany forged ahead in iron extraction to more than 8 million tons in 1900, equaling that of Great Britain, and more than doubling the output of the latter before World War I. By 1913, Germany had also become Great Britain's rival in merchant shipping. Considerable progress was made in organic chemistry and the consequent development of synthetic drugs, dyes, etc. Moreover, Germany developed a sizable electric power industry.

Germany's rapid industrial and commercial expansion was facilitated by a banking system which was purposely designed to promote economic growth. This enabled her to build an economic empire that extended far beyond her borders. Large enterprises evolved into cartels (monopolies) which were successful in fixing prices, regulating markets, and avoiding competition at home and abroad. The name I. G. Farben came to symbolize this economic giant, which was to become a tool of the state in two world wars.

World War I did not damage Germany physically since the fighting did not take place on German soil. World War II, however, inflicted heavy damage and destruction. Paradoxically, however, she has made a more rapid and a substantially sounder recovery than after World War I. To some extent this has been accelerated by American aid, but the Germans deserve the primary credit. Some have argued, also, that German recovery could not have been nearly so rapid if it had not been for the giant stream of refugees and expellees from the east, who represented almost insuperable problems in the immediate postwar years but whose manpower contributed greatly to the extent and speed of economic reconstruction.

In any event, the recovery was phenomenal. By 1953, Germany had achieved an industrial output that was 59 per cent larger than in 1936. By 1956, her gold and dollar reserves were larger than Britain's. Her exports quadrupled between 1952 and 1961, in part because of the heavy investment in the production of goods for export. In many areas, Germany's share of the export market exceeded that of Great Britain or the United States. Twenty per cent of the world's manufactured exports come from German shops and factories. By 1965, Germany was producing every 12th ton of steel and every 14th ton of coal of the world's output. She is today the third industrial power in the world, and her workers are among the best paid in Europe. Moreover, her farm output has also increased at a steady, although somewhat slower, rate. And she leads the world in new dwellings built in proportion to population.

THE PEOPLE

There are more than 57 million people living in the Federal Republic, an area in which less than 40 million lived before the war. This increase is accounted for largely by the 10 million refugees and expellees who have come from the Soviet zone and areas taken over by other Communist-controlled governments. The population density in the Federal Republic is almost as great as Britain's. Although of approximately the same size as the Federal Republic, the regions under Soviet and Polish control have only approximately 17 million inhabitants.

The refugees and expellees have, for the most part, been integrated and most of them regard the Federal Republic as their home (they do not even use the term "new home"). This integration was facilitated by a number of government measures, only some of which were of an economic nature. One of the latter was the law on the "equalization of the burden," passed in 1952, and designed to help others in addition to the refugees. Under this law, every able person was to contribute half of what he possessed for redistribution and equalization. Certain public organizations, such as the central banks and religious and charitable institutions, were exempt. The tax base of the lean year 1948–49 was used to determine a person's worth, and individuals and companies were given the opportunity of spreading their payments over thirty years. Out of the fund thus created, the refugees, as well as other Germans who had suffered war damages or who were wiped out by the currency reform, were assisted (according to a complex formula) through grants or loans for housing, furniture, and pension payments.

Because the nation is made up of the most varied ethnic components, some writers maintain that there is no such thing as a German "race." The main ethnic groups are the Swabians, the Bavarians, the Lower Saxons, the Franks, and several other less numerous ones. According to one German writer, "Germany has always been a sort of melting pot. North and south have developed independently: on the one hand we have the north with its coast line and Slav, Danish, and English influences; and on the other the mountainous districts of the south. A structure formed from a thousand warring elements is what we are finally left with."[2]

Some Germans have insisted, however, that there is a German race. Other Germans, notably Hitler and his followers, went further in their espousal of the doctrine of German racial purity. In view of the considerable intermarriage which took place among racial groups that moved about the European continent, any claim of racial purity would seem to be devoid of a scientific basis. Nevertheless, Germans are Germans. Many of them see in themselves certain racial characteristics that are "different." This, together with language, culture, and some measure of a common history, enables Germans to think in terms of an ethnic unity.

Because of the failure of democratic institutions to take root in Germany, and particularly in view of the fact that autocratic rulers took her to war twice in the first half of this century, many observers

[2] Eugen Diesel, *Germany and the Germans* (New York: The Macmillan Co., 1931), p. 8.

have sought the answer in traits of national character. Although an intriguing subject, a discussion of national character is beyond the scope of this book. Nevertheless, a few general observations may be in order, simply as a way of focusing interest on the subject.

Essentially, what we should note is the complexity of the subject. It certainly is a fact that liberal institutions, which emphasized the dignity of the individual and popular control of government, simply did not take hold in Germany. Perhaps the speed with which she became a powerful industrial nation simply precluded that. Industrialization was slower in Britain and in other Western European countries, and it was largely the work of private entrepreneurs. In Germany, on the other hand, liberal institutions not only did not have the time to take root but they also had to struggle against an industrialization tide that was spurred by government action.

Moreover, it should also be noted that when industrialization came, feudalism had not yet been swept aside. The aristocracy was still a power in the nineteenth century. The *bourgeoisie* had gained little headway and was excluded from public life. All this began to change, but the middle class was becoming influential long before it had learned to shoulder any political or social responsibilities. This is far too complex a subject to be explained away by the phrase "national character."

Some writers have pointed to the divergent behavior of Germans as individuals and as a group. One of the best known of their writers, Goethe, once remarked: "The Germans—so worthy as individuals, and so miserable in the mass!" The Germans are well known for their hard work. They have demonstrated their ability in science and technology. They have produced great masterpieces in music, art, and literature. And yet, collectively, they seem to have shown little resistance to authority and dictatorship. On the contrary, they have seemed willing to worship and to glorify naked force, and to lend willing support to military ventures of all types.

While it would be erroneous to contend that today's Germany is a totally different Germany, it would be equally erroneous to assert that Germany has not changed significantly. Change in any society is rarely rapid, yet great strides are evident in Germany. Most Germans are aware of the evils of their past, notably the Nazi era (discussed in the next chapter), but they do not like to talk about them. They have not fully come to terms with their recent past, yet the opinion that "all was not bad" under Hitler is seldom heard, by comparison with ten years ago. There has been a reluctance to root out and to punish former Nazis—the Germans would prefer to forget the past—but on the other hand, there is evidence that many of the judges have been fair and courageous. The radical right exists, but it is small, lacks money, and has no support from any significant quarter. The number of militant democrats may not be large, which is true of most democratic societies, but the Germans have come to realize what is and what is not a democratic order. And there are signs that the citizens have become more vigilant with respect to those who would subvert the democratic system. Yet no one is sure what would happen in the event of a severe economic or political crisis.[3]

The German Federal Republic is divided almost equally along religious lines, with the Protestants having a slight majority over the Roman Catholics. Germany's prewar population was roughly two thirds Protestant and one third Catholic. The difference is to be accounted for largely by the fact that the areas now under Russian and Polish control were overwhelmingly Protestant. The influx of refugees has resulted in the establishment of large Protestant communities in former Catholic areas, such as Bavaria.

CHARACTER OF POLITICAL LIFE

German political life until the end of World War I was characterized by autocracy. The lack of progress in the adoption of democratic institutions was in sharp contrast with the rapid strides Germany was making in the material realm (rapid industrialization, etc.). It was also in sharp contrast with the liberal political developments that were taking place in other Western European countries. It was not that the liberal ideas of the French Revolution were unattractive to the Germans, for they were. But they lacked the revolutionary drive to succeed, or they underestimated the strength of the established order and hence the need for revolutionary action, or both.

In 1848, the revolutionary tide swept across Europe, leaving many monarchs shaking in their boots. This was also true in Germany, where the revolution died aborning. At the Frankfurt Assembly, a great popular gathering, there was talk of basic rights and self-

---

[3] Several authors have been concerned with the new outlook of the Germans. Some of these include: Klaus Bölling, *Republic in Suspense: Politics, Parties, and Personalities in Postwar Germany* (New York: Frederick A. Praeger, 1964), especially chapter 9; Alfred Grosser, *The Federal Republic of Germany: A Concise History* (New York: Frederick A. Praeger, 1964); Hans Kohn (ed.), *German History: Some New German Views* (Boston: Beacon Press, 1954); Walter Stahl (ed.), *The Politics of Postwar Germany* (New York: Frederick A. Praeger, 1963).

government. A turning point in German history was at hand, but German history failed to turn. Characterized by a lack of determination, the Assembly was after a time dispersed.

As one historian has observed, "1848 was, indeed, a tragic year in German history. On the surface, it seemed that the streams of rationalism—liberalism, democracy, social contract, egalitarianism, tolerance, constitutionalism—were converging in a common stream at last in the Germanies . . . German intellectuals suddenly found themselves the spokesmen for their people at a critical moment in their history . . . [they] sought unity through persuasion, progress through moderation, and a better world through the practice of tolerance and goodwill. They failed."[4] Although a tragic year for Germany, 1848 was also an important year; it provided a taste of political freedom and democracy and thereby ushered in a new phase of German political history.

In the years after 1848, German political developments continued along the authoritarian path, especially after Bismarck came to office in 1862. Some gains for popular democracy were registered, however, in that Bismarck, avowedly no democrat, was forced to accept some of its trappings, such as a moderately free press, political parties, elections, and a legislature. Although Bismarck openly denounced parliamentarism, and although the legislature was in the main powerless, the German people were learning some of the rudiments of the democratic process. But the struggle against liberalism in all its forms continued, with no prospect for the realization of a responsible form of government.

THE BISMARCK LEGACY

Bismarck wanted a strong and united Germany. He believed that this could best be achieved by a certain balance of social forces, notably through a compromise between the middle class, too weak to achieve power on its own, and the military aristocracy of Prussia.[5] The king of Prussia and the military aristocracy were all-powerful politically, and Bismarck did not really change this. In the light of the existing international situation, he did not believe that he could take steps to weaken the military. And he did not think that the weak middle class could manage the domestic political disagreements in a

---

[4] Louis L. Snyder, *Basic History of Modern Germany* (New York: D. Van Nostrand Co., 1957), p. 38.

[5] This analysis is based in large part on Rosenberg, *op. cit.*, pp. 1–27.

defenseless Germany. At the same time, it would have been difficult, perhaps impossible, to extract concessions from the military or to expect the king to renounce important powers.

Bismarck did get certain concessions for the middle class, such as the appointment of liberals to important administrative posts and to certain posts in the Prussian cabinet. At the same time, he tried to show to the members of the Prussian aristocracy that they must learn to live with liberal ministers and to reconcile themselves with the growing wealth and power of the cities. Similarly, he attempted to induce the middle class to accept the modest concessions simply because the international situation did not permit a significant weakening of the military or of the Emperor. The result was a type of unstable equilibrium which was to collapse after the departure of Bismarck in 1890.

Politically, the one notable result of Bismarck's arrangement was the solidification of the power of Prussia, which in effect ruled the Empire. A real Imperial cabinet never even came into existence. The Federal Council (*Bundesrat*) was really a council of ambassadors of the state governments, while Bismarck, the Imperial Chancellor and simultaneously president of the Prussian Council of Ministers, formulated German policy.

In domestic policy, Bismarck is best known for his actions, first against the Catholic Church and then against the Social Democrats. The former, known as the *Kulturkampf* (fight for civilization), was not so much an antireligious campaign as it was an effort to undermine the moral and intellectual authority of the Church. Bismarck's memory of his conflicts with Catholic France and Catholic Austria were still fresh, and he suspected the political loyalties of German Catholics in a possible war of revenge. His actions against priests, nuns, and monks, and his expulsion of the Jesuits, together with the confiscation of Catholic Church property, no doubt contributed significantly to the formation of the Catholic Center party. But when this party became reconciled to the German Empire in its existing form, and when its political demands turned out to be exceedingly moderate, Bismarck readily repealed the anti-Catholic laws. More than that, he sought to enlist the Catholics in what he had come to regard as a more important struggle, his campaign against the Social Democrats.

Bismarck apparently had genuine fears that the Paris Commune of 1871 could be repeated in Germany. He seemingly did not seek or desire the cooperation of the workers. His laws against the Socialist press and Socialist associations also hurt the liberals. But the Social

Democrats continued to take part in electoral campaigns and to increase their strength, suggesting that the anti-Socialist laws were merely a propaganda move or ineffective, or both. Whether Bismarck would have pursued more repressive measures is a matter for conjecture, for he was dismissed by the new monarch (William II) in 1890, the year that the Social Democratic vote jumped from ¾ of a million to 1½ million.

Since Bismarck opposed the establishment of parliamentary government, the net effect of his policies was to strengthen the forces of Prussian conservatism. At the same time, these policies were to result in an intensification of the internal political struggle. Under Bismarck the *Reichstag* (parliament) was, on the whole, powerless. It could refuse to pass the budget, but such actions could be and were circumvented. The *Reichstag* could debate, but it had no influence on military or foreign policy. In short, the authority of the Emperor was not limited during Bismarck's long tenure as Chancellor.

In the remaining years of the Empire (after 1890), real power was in the hands of William II. Prior to Germany's entrance in World War I, he had several chancellors, and neither he nor they sought to make meaningful concessions to the middle class or to come to terms with the working class. The latter, it might be added, parenthetically, increased its voting strength during his reign from 1½ to 4¼ million ballots cast for the Social Democratic party. There was no real move to establish parliamentary government. On occasion, certain political groups were consulted before the introduction of measures in the *Reichstag,* but the latter was never taken into confidence on really important matters, and it did not seem to dare challenge the authority of the Emperor. It is true that the *Reichstag* did condemn the Government in the handling of certain affairs, but the outbreak of the war prevented any meaningful developments therefrom. Even the failure of the *Reichstag* to support Chancellor Bülow on a measure in 1909, and his consequent resignation, was interpreted by William II as an indication that the *Reichstag* was siding with him, and hence resumed his autocratic ways of governing.

TOWARDS A NEW POLITICAL CONSENSUS

Germany, as we have seen, entered the second decade of the Twentieth Century with a political legacy that did not auger well for the orderly establishment of a democratic form of government. The war destroyed the autocratic system and ushered in Germany's first real experiment in democracy, which turned out to be short-lived. Within a little more than a decade Germany reverted to an even more thoroughly authoritarian pattern under Hitler, which was brought to an end with World War II.

Out of this tortured political past a new political consensus seems to be emerging. A new democratic system is taking shape. Given the past, however, most observers are tempering their optimism with caution. Yet there is evidence that democracy is putting down solid roots. First of all, while differences of opinion exist about many matters, no political party of any importance questions the present democratic constitutional structure. The ideological quarrels that dogged Germany's first experiment in democracy seem to be totally absent. Secondly, political or civic education seems to be accepted as a fact of life. The press is interested in political questions and comments freely on them. Ordinary citizens write letters to the newspapers on burning issues of the day. Political lectures and discussions draw good audiences. Television programs dealing with topics of current interest seem to be popular. Thirdly, there is a growing awareness of the power of public opinion. There seems to be general agreement, for example, that the minister of defense was forced out of office as the result of public pressure, and that even Chancellor Adenauer's retirement was hastened as a result of public opinion. Finally, there are indications that young people are forming their own views. They do not seem to want much guidance from a generation that has been identified with the horrors of the past or with a narrow nationalism. This is not to suggest that most of the young people are militant democrats, but they are under no illusions about Germany's past. In general, therefore, it can be said that a democratic political consensus is well on the way to being established in Germany.

This democratic revival was one of the objectives of Allied occupation policies, but it is by no means clear how much they contributed. These policies were in the main associated with the words "denazification" and "demilitarization." The former, as originally conceived, turned out to be impossible, and the latter had to be revised once the conclusion was reached that Germany was needed to buttress the Western defense against the growing Communist threat.

The denazification program had two related objectives: (1) to acquaint the Germans with the horrors of the Nazi era, thereby also inculcating the moral values of a free way of life; and (2) the removal from positions in public and semipublic office, as well as from positions of responsibility in important private undertakings, of all persons who had been more than nominal participants in Nazi party activities. The latter objective could be attained only partially. The examination of millions of dossiers was not an easy task. Moreover, the conclusion was soon reached that most cases demanded individual consideration. Most important, perhaps, too many Germans who had Nazi connections were simply indispensable to the running of the country, with the frequent consequence that punishment was meted out to lesser offenders while some who had been more closely associated with Nazism were rewarded with jobs. In the initial period, however, denazification did remove a number of persons with Nazi connections from the judiciary, the communications media, teaching, and the civil service. In addition, many of the pre-Hitler trade union leaders were reinstated in their jobs.

The first objective, however, seems to have been achieved in considerable measure. Allied effort contributed significantly in assisting the Germans to revamp their educational system, and thereby to present to future German citizens a more objective view of their history and the world about them.

BIBLIOGRAPHICAL NOTE

Studies useful as introductions to Germany are: J. H. Clapham, *The Economic Development of France and Germany, 1815–1914* (Cambridge: Cambridge University Press, 1936); Robert E. Dickinson, *Germany, A General and Regional Geography* (New York: E. P. Dutton, 1953); Eugen Diesel, *Germany and the Germans* (New York: Macmillan, 1931); Raymond Ebsworth, *Restoring Democracy in Germany* (New York: Frederick A. Praeger, 1961); Klemens von Klemperer, *Germany's New Conservatism: Its History and Dilemma in the Twentieth Century* (Princeton, N.J.: Princeton University Press, 1957); Hans Kohn (ed.), *German History: Some New German Views* (Boston: Beacon Press, 1954); ———, *The Mind of Germany: The Education of a Nation* (New York: Charles Scribners Sons, 1960); Edgar McInnis, *et al.*, *Shaping of Postwar Germany* (New York: Frederick A. Praeger, 1960); Koppel S. Pinson, *Modern Germany* (New York: Macmillan, 1954); Kurt Reinhardt, *Germany: 2000 Years* (Rev. ed., New York: Unger, 1961); Arthur Rosenberg, *Imperial Germany: The Birth of the German Republic* (Boston: Beacon, 1964); Louis L. Snyder, *Basic History of Germany* (New York: D. Van Nostrand, 1957); Walter Stahl, ed., *Education For Democracy in West Germany* (New York: Frederick A. Praeger, 1961); and Henry C. Wallich, *Mainsprings of the German Revival* (New Haven: Yale University Press, 1955).

CHAPTER 17

THE DEVELOPMENT OF GERMAN
POLITICAL INSTITUTIONS

IN THE less than 100 years that have passed since unification, Germany has experienced several abrupt shifts in her political structure. From 1871 to 1918, she was known as an empire. After World War I and until 1933, she was a republic, usually referred to as the Weimar Republic, after the city in which the constitution was drawn up. With the rise of Hitler, Germany was officially referred to as the Third Reich (Empire). The present political organization, following the allied occupation of Western Germany, is now being called the Second Republic, although officially it is the Federal Republic of Germany.

THE EMPIRE, 1871–1918

The Empire was organized on the federal principle and consisted of 25 states. One of these, Prussia, held a predominant position in the federation, being able to veto any amendment of the constitution. Moreover, although powers not delegated to the central government were in theory retained by the states, more and more powers were transferred to the central authorities. State authorities were also made less meaningful by the fact that the central government made almost exclusive use of local administration for the implementation of imperial legislation, although different writers are not in agreement on this point. The principal civil servants of the nation were in and around the capital, Berlin.

The executive power was wielded by the emperor and by the chancellor (prime minister). The monarch occupied a dual position as king of Prussia and German emperor. Although he could not veto laws passed by the legislature (*Reichstag*), they were rarely passed except on the initiative of the chancellor, whom the emperor could appoint and dismiss. Moreover, as king of Prussia, he controlled the chancellor's vote in the Federal Council (*Bundesrat*). More important was the fact that Bismarck, the kingpin of the whole system, never really formed an Imperial Cabinet, but governed Germany from his position as prime minister of Prussia. The *Bundesrat* was to act as the Imperial Cabinet, but it was mostly a legal fiction, a collection of delegates from the separate states that never sought to play the part of a cabinet. Prussia, or more appropriately, the emperor and his chancellor ruled Germany.

The position of the chancellor vis-à-vis the legislature was strong, for the Parliament (*Reichstag*) could not compel him to resign. Moreover, as we have seen in the previous chapter, the *Reichstag* had no influence over military or foreign policy. Other ministers, chosen from members of the higher bureaucracy rather than from parliamentarians or party leaders, were only assistants to the chancellor and personally responsible to him. Because the *Reichstag* was more openly critical of certain governmental policies in the post-Bismarck period, and because it insisted on more budgetary powers, Bismarck's successors thought it desirable to make political bargains to get their budgets adopted, while at the same time not acknowledging responsibility to the *Reichstag*.

The *Reichstag* was elected on the basis of universal, direct, and secret franchise, but since its powers were insignificant it was unable to develop into a genuine instrument of the popular will and served mainly as a debating society. The center of political gravity was the *Bundesrat*, whose members were controlled by the separate states. It had the power to pass legislation, to consent to a declaration of war, to approve the ratification of treaties, and to confirm officials of the central government. Since Prussia had 17 votes out of a total of 48 (no other state had more than 6), it needs to be re-emphasized that the king of Prussia exercised firm, if indirect, control. The power of Prussia was further enhanced by virtue of the fact that the prime minister of Prussia was also the German chancellor.

Although the chancellor was responsible only to the monarch, the question of ministerial responsibility was raised. In the period of Bismarck's dominance (1871–1890), his leadership was unquestioned. In the second period (1890–1914), chancellors had more difficulties with Parliament. Although rejecting ministerial responsibility, they sought better relations with the *Reichstag*. In fact, they found it useless to try to remain in power unless they were able to create a parliamentary majority. In 1910, the *Reichstag* adopted a resolution favoring ministerial responsibility, but this principle did not receive recognition until the last days of World War I, a time when few noticed or even cared.

It seems ironic, in view of the past failures to achieve parliamentary government in Germany, that it was handed to the *Reichstag* by General Ludendorff, without a struggle, in October 1918, when he admitted that the war was lost. With the appointment of Prince Max of Baden as chancellor, parliamentary government was established in Germany. The Imperial constitution was quickly revised to provide that the Imperial Chancellor must possess the confidence of the *Reichstag* in order to remain in office, and that he was responsible for all political acts of the emperor. By the end of October, Germany was a constitutional monarchy, but this escaped general notice.

One of the factors in the growth in importance of the *Reichstag* was the development of German political parties. There were a number of them, ranging from the Conservative party on the right, which was mainly interested in protecting Prussia's privileged position and the welfare of the great landowners, to the Social Democratic party on the left, which espoused a radical reconstruction of the economic system and the establishment of political democracy. In between were the Center party, which was really a conservative Catholic party, often cooperating with the Conservatives; the National Liberals, a party of industrial leaders with a sizable middle class following and a program of political reform that would alter Prussia's favored position; and the Progressives, a free trade party which emphasized the desirability of inaugurating a genuine parliamentary system.

Two things need to be said about this party structure. First, the parties could talk but did not have real control over policy. And even in the case of a veritable political vacuum in 1916, they were unable to grasp power. Second, by 1912 the Social Democrats were the largest party in the *Reichstag*, yet they seemed ill-suited to govern. They refused to enter any cabinet unless the whole political system were changed. Because of this stance, they were regarded in some circles as unpatriotic.

In 1914, however, the Social Democratic deputies in the *Reichstag* voted to support war credits and entered into an agreement not to oppose the government. This was not easy, because for several decades they, like other socialists, had campaigned against war. Their action in 1914 was not so much a matter of demonstrating their patriotism as it was following the reasoning of the Marxist leader, Friedrich Engels, who in the 1890's had foreseen the possibility of a Franco-Russian war against Germany. Because he believed Germany to be the home of the strongest and best organized socialist movement, he was convinced that German socialists should fight not only against Russia but also against anyone allied with her, "for, if we are defeated, the Social Democratic movement in Europe is smashed for twenty years."[1]

By the end of 1915, the Social Democrats faced another dilemma. By that time it was evident that Germany was engaged in a war of conquest, and some Social Democratic deputies refused to support further war credits, thus splitting the party. The majority, however, believed themselves bound by the 1914 commitments. They argued, further, that if a reversal of their earlier position served to disunite the nation and Germany were to lose the war, the Social Democrats would be blamed for the defeat. This was not an enviable position for the strongest party in the *Reichstag* to find itself in, particularly a party that was dedicated to democracy and opposed to the whole Imperial system.

THE WEIMAR REPUBLIC

In January 1919, the Germans elected a constituent assembly which met the following month in the city of Weimar. It immediately set about drafting a new constitution for the nation. The delegates approached their work systematically; among them were some of the best constitutional experts in Germany. They knew that they wanted to provide for a democratic form of government. Consequently, they gave serious thought to the parliamentary system, the Swiss type, and the American presidential form (the last mainly because of the influence of Max Weber). Ultimately, they decided on the parliamentary system. The resulting constitution, a long but carefully drawn document, was mainly the work of Hugo Preuss, who can rightly be called the father of the Weimar Constitution.

Germany was organized on a federal basis, with seventeen states (*Länder*). Remembering Prussia's dominance of the previous federation, the framers made sure that her position would be weak in the new organization. The central government, however, was vested with strong authority, considerably stronger than that of our national government at the time. Moreover, its powers could be augmented by simple amendment, which could be brought into force by a two-thirds vote in each of the two houses of Parliament. In this way, even the boundaries of the member states could be altered, even against their wishes. In addition, Article 48, providing for the grant of extraor-

---

[1] As quoted in Bertram Wolfe, *Three Who Made a Revolution* (Boston: Beacon Press, 1955), p. 595. Also see Arthur Rosenberg, *Imperial Germany: The Birth of the German Republic* (Boston: Beacon Press, 1964), pp. 73–77 and 117–123.

dinary powers to the executive, became a path leading to increasing centralization. It was on the basis of this article that Adolf Hitler received his first grant of unusual authority, which was to lead to the downfall of the republic.

The legislature was made up of two houses, the *Reichstag*, which was elected by universal, equal, direct, and secret suffrage, and the *Reichsrat*, whose members were appointed by the governments of the member states. While the *Reichsrat* possessed legislative powers, it had in fact only a suspensive veto, for its actions could be nullified by a two-thirds vote in the lower house. The real legislature was therefore the *Reichstag*, which however, delegated considerable authority to the executive in the postwar crisis years (1919–23) and during the years of economic depression (1930–33). Partly because of the employment of proportional representation, many political parties were represented in the *Reichstag*, none having a majority.

The executive power was organized along traditional parliamentary lines. There was a president as head of state and a chancellor as head of government. The president possessed more power than the British monarch or the president of France under the Third Republic. Among other things, he could dissolve the *Reichstag* and he could dismiss the cabinet. It was the abuse of the latter power that contributed significantly to the destruction of the parliamentary system. The position of the chancellor was never too strong, due to the fact that, as in France, there was no majority party. All cabinets were coalitions representing varying political views. This circumstance also afforded the president greater flexibility in the choice of a chancellor. Perhaps the best known political personality of the Weimar period was Gustav Stresemann who, although a chancellor for a very brief time, was Germany's minister of foreign affairs from 1923 until the time of his death in 1929.

The political party configuration in the *Reichstag* was never propitious for the success of German democracy. As already indicated, no party could command a majority. Secondly, the antidemocratic parties represented a stumbling block. On the far right were the German National People's party and the Nazi party (National Socialist German Workers party or NSDAP). Although the former was more important in the early years as a focus of reaction and opposition to Weimar, the latter was to become the effective enemy of the republic. On the far left was the Communist party, patterned after the Russian model and exhibiting a consistently negative attitude toward the republic.

The center of political power during Weimar was to be found largely in the Catholic Center party and the German Democratic party, with the aid of the Social Democratic party. The Center party was the most influential and the most stable, its membership cutting across all social strata. As a real party of the center, it could lean either way, and did at various times, participating in all cabinets. The Democratic party, a continuation of the former Progressives, gave strong support to the republic but, as did many other liberal parties in Europe, it declined progressively. The Social Democrats fought against the extreme right as well as the extreme left (Communists), and helped to shape the Weimar constitution, although in the end few of their principles were adopted. Although Marxist in theory, it was much more like the British Labor party in practice. Its membership in the *Reichstag* rose steadily, and although it never gained majority support, its leaders headed coalition cabinets for approximately three years and participated in several cabinets headed by leaders of other parties.

In the end, however, the Weimar Republic fell. A combination of circumstances brought it about. The economic collapse in 1929 and the inability of the government to cope with it made many people ready to accept new leadership. Additional dissatisfaction with the general state of affairs stemmed from a rising tide of nationalism which fed on the real and imagined sins of the victorious powers and the Treaty of Versailles. The president of the republic, Paul von Hindenburg, contributed his share in making parliamentary government unworkable through his failure to respect the wishes of the *Reichstag*. In 1932, for example, he dismissed Chancellor Heinrich Brüning even though he had the confidence of the *Reichstag*. This was the beginning of several "presidential" governments, cabinets having the confidence of the president but not that of the Parliament. The *Reichstag* contributed to the confusion by "amending" the constitution without formal amendment. This was done by passing laws, sometimes conflicting, by a two-thirds majority (the majority required to amend the constitution) whenever the issue arose as to whether the *Reichstag* had authority to legislate in that specific manner or area.

There were other considerations, too. The courts were lenient with "rightist" enemies of the republic. The army was built up and remained a state within a state. The people and their government failed to understand the totalitarian techniques of Hitler and the Nazis. Strong democratic leaders simply were not on the scene. And finally, as some observers have noted, the republic committed suicide, as evidenced by the fact that in 1932 three fourths of the people cast their ballots for antidemocratic parties of the right and left.

In general, the Weimar republic never succeeded in creating a political consensus. The country was torn ideologically between the far right and far left, which represented sizable elements of the population that did not believe in a democratic order. The country was also torn economically and politically; to many Weimar became synonymous with poverty, national humiliation, and fruitless debate in the *Reichstag*. The climate of fear and frustration which Hitler sought to dramatize and exacerbate was in the end to help him get to power. But before the existing discontents could be shaped into a political force it was necessary to have a leader and an efficient organization. These Hitler and the Nazis provided.

THE NAZI PERIOD

From a small faction, the National Socialist German Workers party (Nazi) became the second largest political party in the *Reichstag* in 1930. Originally attracting demobilized soldiers who could not adjust to civilian life, it soon gathered a motley crew of social misfits, cranks, political adventurers, criminals, and some idealists. By 1930, it drew strong support from the lower middle classes, from the youth, and from the militarists. It also received the support of significant financial and business circles. With the economic depression at its height, the party's leader, Adolf Hitler, made a bid for the presidency of the republic in 1932 but was badly defeated. A few months later, however, his party became the strongest party in the *Reichstag* (230 seats out of 608), and he made a bid for the chancellorship.

Organized along military lines, the Nazi party stirred up delirious demonstrations and carried violence into the streets and into the gatherings of the other parties. In the midst of the chaos, President Hindenburg asked Hitler to form a cabinet of "national concentration" in which the Nazis and the Nationalists were to share power. Although initially keeping only three cabinet posts for themselves, the Nazis made sure that they were the key ones, which gave them control from the beginning. Moreover, they were immediately granted their request for a dissolution of the *Reichstag* and new elections.

The new elections were scheduled for early March 1933. On February 26, the *Reichstag* was set on fire, apparently by a half-crazed Dutchman. The Nazis blamed the Communists, but disinterested observers generally were in agreement that the Nazis themselves were responsible. More recent evidence, however, seems to absolve them of the blame. Two days after the burning of the *Reichstag*, the president issued an emergency ordinance, in accordance with Article 48 of the constitution. Allegedly designed to protect the people and the state, the ordinance suspended the basic freedoms, in effect authorizing the government to exercise unlimited power. Thus armed, the Nazis proceeded to curb their opponents' use of the radio, press, and assembly, while Nazi mobs proceeded to loot and destroy the offices and organizations of the other political parties. In the ensuing election, the Nazis won 288 seats and the Nationalists 52. The remaining parties won 307 seats.

On March 24, 1933, in an atmosphere of indescribable frenzy, coercion, and terror, an enabling act was passed which became the "constitution" of Nazi totalitarianism. The consolidation of the dictatorship was rapid. A secret police organization rooted out opponents, real or imagined. Other political parties were abolished and suspect newspapers shut down. Concentration camps were established and new recruits brought in continually. Controls on business and labor were soon invoked to preserve the totalitarian pattern. When President Hindenburg died in 1934, Hitler conveniently merged the two offices, making himself the unquestioned ruler of Germany.

The domestic record of the dictatorship, from the harnessing of German industrial might to the military machine and the development of an aggressive foreign policy to the horrors of the gas chambers and mass exterminations, is a matter of historical record. The ruthlessness of the Nazi leaders, the techniques of Nazi party control of the masses, the launching of World War II, and, finally, the end of the dictatorship are also a matter of record, but not really within the scope of this book.

Nazism was more than just exaggerated nationalism or antisemitism or a reaction to defeat and to Weimar. These were a part of the picture, to be sure, but only a part of it. Some of the ideas on which the Nazi movement was built go back at least a hundred years. They depicted a past golden age when the German people (the mystical *volk*) lived in harmony and happiness, partly because they were superior to other people and partly because they were close to the soil. The industrial revolution and its consequences—big cities, modern ways, and those who had brought this about (Jews)—uprooted the *volk* and corrupted many of them. The doctrines associated with this point of view were formulated and propagated by several generations of teachers and students.

Because these ideas were often set forth in philosophical and quasi-scientific language, they gained a certain amount of acceptance in respectable academic circles and were embraced by right-wing political groups. But it seems significant to note that these ideas did not become a serious political force until they were wedded with the genius of Adolf Hitler and the disciplined organization of the Nazi party. Even then they might not have become a powerful political force if it had not been for the combination of other circumstances (the economic crisis, the legacy of defeat, the ex-army officers unable to adjust to civilian life, the debt-ridden peasants, and the alleged Communist threat) which Hitler could and did exploit to the fullest.[2]

THE CONSTITUTION OF THE SECOND REPUBLIC

Following her defeat in World War II, Germany was, by prearrangement, divided into four occupation zones, one each for the major allied powers which had fought against her. Berlin, located inside the Soviet zone, was similarly divided into four sectors. Although designed as temporary transition measures, the occupation zones took on an air of permanence once it became clear that the Soviet Union was interested in the reconstruction and unification of the country only on its own terms. Thereupon, the three Western powers decided to permit the unification of their three zones, in order that the Germans could begin governing themselves. To this end, the Germans drafted a constitution (technically the "Basic Law") with the advice and assistance of Allied experts. On May 23, 1949, it went into effect and the Germans began their second experiment in self-government. Although the Basic law provides that it will cease to exist as soon as Germany is reunited and a new constitution drafted, it appears, as of this writing, to have achieved a type of permanence.

The constitution sets forth the organization of the Federal Republic along federal lines. It also provides for a basically parliamentary system, and a specific delineation of executive, legislative, and judicial functions. Moreover, there is a clearly defined bill of rights. An interesting innovation is the provision that empowers the Federal Republic, through legislation, to "transfer sovereign powers to international institutions," and to "join a general, comprehensive

---

[2] An excellent exploration of the roots of Nazism is George L. Mosse, *The Crisis of German Ideology: Intellectual Origins of the Third Reich* (New York: Grosset & Dunlap, 1964). Also valuable is Peter G. J. Pulzer, *The Rise of Political Anti-Semitism in Germany and Austria* (New York: John Wiley and Sons, 1964).

system of international arbitration" as a way of settling international disputes. The constitution also establishes the general rules of international law as a part of the nation's law and gives them precedence.

As in other parliamentary states, there is a formal head of state, the president, and the head of government, the chancellor. Real political power is vested in the latter who, however, is responsible to the popularly elected lower house, now called the *Bundestag*. Aware of the weaknesses of parliamentary government under Weimar, the drafters of the Basic Law sought to make the position of the chancellor more secure, with the result that he now occupies a strong position vis-à-vis the legislature.

The central government is given the exclusive right to legislate in such fields as foreign affairs, citizenship, currency and coinage, railways, posts and telecommunications, and copyrights. It is supposed to have concurrent powers (with the *Länder*) in civil and criminal law, laws relating to the economy, labor, agriculture, public welfare, ocean and coastal shipping, and in "the prevention of the abuse of economic power" (anti-trust actions). In other areas, notably education and cultural affairs, the *Länder* are supposed to exercise primary responsibility. In case of conflict between laws of the central government and those of the states, the former are said to prevail. And the central government is vested with sufficient authority to force states to fulfill their duties as prescribed by the Basic Law.

The division of the tax revenues between the states and the central government is through a somewhat complex arrangement. The central government keeps all revenues that result from taxes on business turnover, on imports, and on the consumer. The states retain all tax revenue on capital, on inheritances, and on automobiles. But the states must turn over to the central government 39 per cent (increased from original 35) of the taxes they collect on income and on corporations. One basic consideration in this arrangement is to give real meaning to federalism, i.e., to provide definite sources of finance to both levels of government.

The Basic Law may be amended by a two-thirds vote of the members of each house of Parliament. Some provisions, however, are said to be unamendable. These include those portions of the basic Law which affect the organization of the republic into *Länder*, as well as those sections which provide the basic form of democratic organization, including the protection of fundamental civil liberties.

Under American influence, the Basic Law sets up a Federal Constitutional Court, with powers to annul acts of the legislature or the administration if they violate the Basic Law. The court is also authorized to forbid unconstitutional parties if such action is recommended by the cabinet. On the basis of such requests, it banned a neo-Nazi party in 1952 and the Communist party in 1956.

BIBLIOGRAPHICAL NOTE

Recent works which are good sources for the study of German political history are G. Barraclough, *The Origins of Modern Germany* (2d ed., Oxford: Blackwell, 1949); E. Brandenburg, *From Bismarck to the World War* (London: Oxford University Press, 1927); Erich Eyck, *Bismarck and the German Empire* (London: Allen and Unwin, 1950); James K. Pollock and Homer Thomas, *Germany in Power and Eclipse* (New York: D. Van Nostrand, 1952); Carl Schorske, *German Social Democracy* (Cambridge, Mass.: Harvard University Press, 1955); A. J. P. Taylor, *The Course of German History* (New York: Coward-McCann, 1946).

For the Weimar period, the following are excellent: Arnold Brecht, *Prelude to Silence: The End of the German Republic* (London: Oxford University Press, 1946); Andreas Dorpalen, *Hindenburg and the Weimar Republic* (Princeton: Princeton University Press, 1964); Erich Eych, *A History of the Weimar Republic* (2 vols., Cambridge: Harvard University Press, 1962–1963). Also of interest are Arnold Brecht, *Federalism and Regionalism in Germany* (Ithaca, N.Y.: Cornell University Press, 1945); William S. Halperin, *Germany Tried Democracy* (New York: Crowell, 1946); and Godfrey Scheele, *The Weimar Republic* (London: Faber & Faber, 1946).

The most authoritative study of the Nazi period is Franz L. Neumann, *Behemoth, The Structure and Practice of National Socialism 1933–1944* (2d ed.; New York: Oxford University Press, 1944). Nazi theory is expounded in Adolf Hitler, *Mein Kampf* (New York: Reynal & Hitchcock, 1941). Other standard works are Alan Bullock, *Hitler: A Study in Tyranny* (London: Odhams, 1952); Rohan Butler, *The Roots of National Socialism* (New York: Dutton, 1942); Gordon A. Craig, *The Politics of the Prussian Army, 1640–1945* (Oxford: Clarendon Press, 1955); M. S. Mayer, *They Thought They Were Free* (Chicago: University of Chicago Press, 1955); Friedrich Meinecke, *The German Catastrophe* (Cambridge, Mass.: Harvard University Press, 1950); George L. Mosse, *The Crisis of German Ideology: Intellectual Origins of the Third Reich* (New York: Grosset & Dunlap, 1964); Stephen H. Roberts, *The House That Hitler Built* (New York: Harper, 1938); Telford Taylor, *Sword and Swastika, Generals and Nazis in the Third Reich* (New York: Simon and Schuster, 1952); and H. R. Trevor-Roper, *The Last Days of Hitler* (New York: Macmillan, 1947).

The best source for the postwar period include: Gabriel Almond, et al., *The Struggle for Democracy in Germany* (Chapel Hill, N.C.: University of North Carolina Press, 1949); Klaus Bölling, *Republic in Suspense: West Germany Today* (New York: Praeger, 1964); Ludwig Erhard, *Prosperity Through Competition* (New York: Praeger, 1958); Fritz Erler, *Democracy in Germany* (Cambridge: Harvard University Press, 1965); J. F. Golay, *Founding of the Federal Republic of Germany* (Chicago: University of Chicago Press, 1958); Alfred Grosser, *The Federal Republic of Germany* (New York: Praeger, 1964); Richard Hiscocks, *Democracy in Western Germany* (London: Oxford University Press, 1957); Edward H. Litchfield, ed., *Governing Postwar Germany* (Ithaca, N.Y.: Cornell University Press, 1953); Drew Middleton, *The Struggle for Germany* (Indianapolis: Bobbs-Merrill, 1949); Hans J. Morgenthau, *Germany and the Future of Europe* (Chicago: University of Chicago Press, 1951); James K. Pollock (ed.), *German Democracy at Work* (Ann Arbor: University of Michigan Press, 1955); Herbert J. Spiro, *The Politics of German Codetermination* (Cambridge, Mass.: Harvard University Press, 1958); Walter Stahl, ed., *The Politics of Postwar Germany* (New York: Praeger, 1963).

CHAPTER 18

THE EXECUTIVE

GERMANY follows the traditional parliamentary pattern in that there is a dual executive, that is, a head of state and a head of government. The former, whose position is largely ceremonial, is known as the president. The latter, who is the equivalent of a prime minister, is called the chancellor. The method of selecting the president and the chancellor and the powers which they are to exercise are clearly set forth in the Basic Law, but it must not be forgotten that actual practice in the operation of political institutions tends to modify legalistic provisions. In this respect Germany is no exception, but we must bear in mind that Germany's second experiment with democracy is in its initial stages and that during most of this brief period the all-important post of chancellor has been held by one man, Konrad Adenauer. Consequently, observations concerning possible trends must be viewed with this in mind.

THE PRESIDENT

Contrary to practice under Weimar, the president is not popularly elected. He is chosen by a body known as the Federal Assembly, which is made up of the members of the lower house (*Bundestag*) and a like number of persons chosen by the legislatures of the states (*Länder*). A majority is required for election on the first and second ballots, while a plurality suffices on the third. The president serves for five years and may be re-elected only once. He must, upon election, resign from other public offices and from offices in profit-making organizations. He may not be a member of Parliament or of the legislature of one of the *Länder*, and he may not practice a profession while in office. The first president, Theodor Heuss, even resigned his membership in his political party after his election.

The president's functions are largely ceremonial. Unlike his counterpart under Weimar, he does not have the power to dismiss the chancellor or the cabinet, and he cannot exercise any emergency powers. All of his political acts, save that of designating the chancellor, must be countersigned by the chancellor or an appropriate minister. In designating the chancellor, his choice is limited by the political party complexion of the *Bundestag*. If one party had a majority, he would have no alternative but to choose the leader of that party. If no parliamentary combination had a majority, or if the party situation was otherwise confused, he would have some discretion in the choice of chancellor.

Under Theodor Heuss, who was president the first two terms, the office acquired considerable prestige. Heuss proved to be human and accessible, combining dignity and an unassuming manner. He was ready and willing to participate in all activities which in his opinion served to advance the intellectual and political interests of his country. Under him the presidency became a symbol of national unity. His successor, Heinrich Lübke, re-elected in 1964 with the support of both major parties, has continued in the same high tradition.

There is no vice-president. If the presidency becomes vacant, the president of the upper house (*Bundesrat*) serves the remainder of the term.

As in the case of the British monarch, the influence which the president wields is dependent upon the qualifications he possesses, his inclinations to act, and the circumstances in which he must function. Heuss has said that the president "may not . . . take part in the practical decisions of day-to-day politics, but he is permitted to help in improving the atmosphere and in facilitating the putting into effect of certain quite simple, reasonable, and generally accepted points of view." But the chancellor, no more than the British prime minister, is not obliged to accept the advice of his head of state. Yet at certain times the president may exercise considerable influence.

THE CHANCELLOR AND THE CABINET

The chancellor is nominated by the president, but this nomination must be ratified by a majority vote of the entire membership of the *Bundestag*. Should the *Bundestag* reject him, it then has the power to elect someone else by the same type of majority, and the president is then bound to make the appointment formal. If the *Bundestag* is unable to agree on a choice within two weeks, it may then choose a chancellor by a majority of those voting. The president is not, however, obliged to accept such a choice, and may instead dissolve the *Bundestag* and call for new elections, provided he does this within seven days.

Thus far in the experience of the Second Republic, no difficulty has been encountered in the choice of a chancellor. In each case, the *Bundestag* has accepted the man designated by the president, although in the first instance it was by a majority of only one vote. In the elections of 1953 and 1957, the chancellor's party (Christian Democrats) won substantial majorities and no difficulty was encountered. In the 1961 elections, however, the chancellor's party failed to win a majority, and had to make considerable concessions to the Free Democratic party, with which it had been in coalition, in order to stay in power. It is obvious therefore that the president must, as in other parliamentary states, have due regard for the political complexion of the legislature when designating the head of the government. In 1961, he waited until an agreement had been reached between the strongest party and its coalition partner, thus ratifying the informal choice that the leaders of the majority in the *Bundestag* had already made.

Once his appointment has been confirmed, the chancellor appoints his cabinet colleagues, whose formal appointments are signed by the president. The president may advise on appointments, but, as the first chancellor indicated, such advice can easily be ignored. Because the Basic Law makes the chancellor, and not the cabinet, responsible to the *Bundestag*, his colleagues are decidedly his political inferiors. The first chancellor (Adenauer) treated them in much the same way that an American president treats his cabinet. On occasion he publicly criticized some of them for positions they had taken in some of their public speeches, but he was reluctant to dismiss even inefficient ministers who were loyal to him.

The members of the cabinet may be and usually are members of the *Bundestag*. The size of the Cabinet has varied from 15 to 20 members.

Under the Basic Law, the chancellor determines policies and is responsible for them. The extent to which he consults his cabinet is largely left to his discretion. There is no such thing as collective responsibility, as in Britain, and the chancellor alone can be held to account. The constitution does say that all ministers are subject to the call of the *Bundestag* and its committees, and are presumably obligated to appear and to answer questions. This requirement has been ignored on occasion, but the *Bundestag's* only recourse is to express a lack of confidence in the chancellor, which is not easy to do, as we shall see.

Article 67 of the constitution says: "The *Bundestag* may express its lack of confidence in the Federal Chancellor only by electing, by the majority of its members, a successor and by submitting a request to the Federal President for the dismissal of the Federal Chancellor. The Federal President must comply with the request and appoint the person elected." In other words, the *Bundestag* must agree upon a successor before it can oust the chancellor, who is presumed to have the confidence of the legislature until it is explicitly withdrawn. This is in sharp contrast with practice under Weimar, with parliament freely voting governments out of office without any responsibility for finding an alternative cabinet. This requirement of the new constitution has been referred to as the "constructive vote of no confidence."

The chancellor may of his own volition seek a vote of confidence. If he fails to receive the support of a majority of the *Bundestag*, he may request the president to dissolve the *Bundestag*. This must be granted within 21 days unless in that interval the *Bundestag* elects a new chancellor, in which case the right to request a dissolution lapses. Whether the confidence motion is initiated by the chancellor or by someone else, a vote cannot be taken until 48 hours have elapsed after the motion is made.

In Germany's experience since the constitution went into effect, no chancellor has been defeated in the *Bundestag*. The "constructive vote of no confidence" seems to insure stability, something Weimar sadly lacked. The chancellor's position also has been strengthened by the trend toward a two-party system, thus ensuring majority support most of the time. Most observers agree that the forceful personality and political astuteness of the first chancellor (Adenauer), who was in office continuously for 14 years, also contributed to the strength and stability of the office.

It seems safe to conclude, therefore, that stability of the real executive in Germany is no longer a problem. The matter of whether responsible government is weakened in the process, however, is very much of a problem. Some German political observers have said that the "constructive vote of no confidence" is such a high price to pay for opposing the chancellor that the effect has been to paralyze parliamentarism. This, coupled with Adenauer's determined leadership, led some of these same observers to characterize the German system as "chancellor democracy."[1]

There are other methods of enforcing responsibility than the "constructive vote of no confidence," although they are less dramatic. One of these is the debate that takes place in the *Bundestag* and its committees. But such debates have not as yet acquired real

---

[1] An effort to evaluate Adenauer's role is made in a subsequent section of this chapter.

significance, due in part to a disinclination in Germany for public participation in the legislative process. There is no such thing as public hearings on bills, for example, although some voices have been heard demanding the inauguration of such hearings. Moreover, committee meetings are not public and their reports are not easily accessible. Finally, the attitude of Chancellor Adenauer, in specifically ordering certain ministers not to appear when summoned by committees, has weakened the enforcement of responsibility through debates in the *Bundestag* and its committees.

Another method of exacting responsibility is provided by the interpellation and question procedures. Thirty members may initiate an interpellation. If their motion is supported by 50 members of the *Bundestag*, a debate may follow after a representative of the cabinet has replied to the interpellation. Should the government choose not to reply, the debate may proceed in any case. In either event, a motion based on the interpellation or the cabinet's reply may be voted upon if it has the support of at least 30 members. Such a motion may censure a cabinet member, as some have, but Adenauer retained ministers so censured, thus reducing the significance of interpellations and questions as means of exacting responsibility. Questions rather than interpellations are usually addressed to matters of lesser import. These may be brought up by as few as ten members of the *Bundestag*, but no debate follows the government's reply.

The right of individual deputies to address verbal questions to ministers is recognized. Originally, only one hour per month was set aside for this purpose, and written notice was required well in advance. Since 1960, however, there has been more of an approach to British practice. Now questions are brought up at the beginning of each meeting of the *Bundestag*, with only three-day's (in exceptional circumstances only one) advance notice required. In addition, supplementary questions may be asked from the floor. Moreover, if the normal question hour proves inadequate, there is a provision for scheduling other question sessions on certain specified days in the week.

The *Bundestag* may, upon the motion of one fourth of its members, set up "an investigating committee which shall take necessary evidence in public proceedings," from which "the public may be excluded." This authorization under Article 44 of the Basic Law has been used infrequently and with varying results.

Public opinion, which in most democratic countries serves to control the government to a significant degree, played only a minor role in the early years of the Second Republic. Initially, the public did not seem to recognize that the policies and plans of the cabinet should be affected by public opinion. The chancellor and his associates, aside from realizing that their actions might have an impact on the next election, did not particularly encourage public comment and criticism. More recently, however, public opinion has played an increasing role as a check upon the government's policies and programs. Adenauer was forced to dismiss at least two ministers as a result of political pressures in Parliament. Adenauer's successor as chancellor, Ludwig Erhard, publicly recognized the role which public opinion must play in a free society.

The Basic Law further strengthens the executive by providing that the *Bundestag* may not increase expenditures or taxes over what the cabinet wants. This is comparable to the control over finance long exercised by the British cabinet and more recently by the French.

Emergency powers are provided for but these are carefully limited. The framers wanted to prevent the abuse of such powers, as had occurred under Weimar. Hence, there is no general emergency grant of power but only provision for the passage of a specific piece of legislation which the *Bundestag* is unable or unwilling to enact, and which the cabinet has declared to be urgent. Provided the upper house (*Bundesrat*) agrees, the cabinet's request for a legislative emergency *may* be granted by the president. If a legislative emergency has been declared, the *Bundestag* must pass a bill acceptable to the cabinet within four weeks or the bill will be deemed enacted, provided the *Bundesrat* approves. In the ensuing six months other bills may be passed in the same way. Thereafter no declaration of emergency is available to the same chancellor in his term of office. Moreover, this procedure may not be used to amend or suspend the constitution wholly or in part.

The constitution also provides that decrees having the force of law may be issued by the central government or its ministers or by governments of the *Länder*. The extent and purpose of such powers must, however, be outlined in laws, which the decrees must cite. Moreover, the decree power may not be employed by the national government to get around the constitutional requirement of *Bundesrat* consent for certain types of legislation. In these areas, decrees by the national government or its ministers require the consent of the *Bundesrat*.

A number of efforts have been made to amend the constitution so as to define more precisely various types of emergencies and how and by whom emergency powers are to be exercised. But because the two major parties were unable to agree on their wording, no such amendments were adopted as of late 1965. Several so-called "simple" emergency laws, for which a two-thirds majority was not required, were enacted. They relate to civil defense matters and to the safeguarding of supplies and transport. Further efforts to adopt the so-called "emergency constitution" will no doubt be made following the September 1965 election.

THE FEDERAL CHANCELLERY

The Basic Law provides for a deputy chancellor, but in Chancellor Adenauer's fourteen years of office his deputy remained largely a figurehead. Far more important is the Federal Chancellery, provided for by the standing orders of the cabinet.[2] This office, headed by a person with the title of Under Secretary, is the personal appointee of the chancellor and in a sense his second in command. The under secretary, who is more powerful than any one of the chancellor's cabinet colleagues, and the administrative staff which he heads, perform primarily two types of functions. First, they issue relevant instructions, in the name of the chancellor, to all ministries, and thus decide many questions before they can reach the chancellor. Second, they act as coordinators by settling many disputes between ministries. Only those disputes that cannot be resolved by them come before the cabinet for settlement.

The chancellor's position in relation to his cabinet is also strengthened by his appointment of informal committees on special subjects. They report to him personally and thus he has the weight of expert opinion on his side when he goes to the cabinet with his proposals. Although he uses some of his ministers in these efforts, the net result is that the knowledge of affairs gained in this fashion puts him in a relatively stronger position than the ministers, and thereby reduces the latter's authority.

ADENAUER AS CHANCELLOR

In October 1963, Adenauer resigned at the age of 87, after serving as chancellor for 14 years. His role in the evolution of German

---

[2] For a translation of the text of the standing orders, see John C. Lane and James K. Pollock, *Source Materials on the Government and Politics of Germany* (Ann Arbor, Michigan, 1964), pp. 42–45.

democracy has been criticized and applauded. Generally speaking, his positive contributions stand out, particularly when viewed in the light of the times and problems that confronted him. He commanded the respect of even those who did not like him. His image was tarnished to a degree, however, because he stayed on too long. There was a general consensus, even in his own party, that he should have retired at least two or three years earlier. In those years he antagonized many people, including his closest associates, and he became somewhat of a burden and a liability. After 1960, his power and prestige declined, and his retirement in 1963 was part of the price exacted by the Free Democratic party for joining him in coalition after the 1961 elections.

By providing a stable and effective government, Adenauer demonstrated that democracy and authority are not mutually exclusive. In this way he contributed significantly to the German acceptance of democracy, a considerable accomplishment in a nation lacking a democratic tradition. He was given considerable credit for the rapid economic recovery and general prosperity, which stood in sharp contrast to the ruinous inflation of the early Weimar period and to the subsequent economic collapse. In short, Adenauer's strong leadership and clear-cut policies, together with the attendant prosperity, gave the Germans reason to believe that democracy can be a success.

Adenauer's prestige was enhanced considerably by his handling of foreign affairs, especially in the early years of the new regime when he was its sole spokesman. Even his opponents admit that in those years he won much ground for his country by knowing when to be patient and when to display firmness and tenacity. In brief, he was imaginative, flexible, and statesmanlike in the pursuit of Germany's national interest.

Adenauer dominated the government to such an extent that many observers described his rule as a chancellor-democracy. Charges that he ignored his parliamentary majority are only partially true. There is no doubt that he was clever in the exercise of his power and that he carefully built up his personal prestige. In this he was exploiting to the limit the opportunities that the constitution provided, but he was rarely charged with violating it. It is also true that he often treated many of his colleagues coolly and perhaps even unfairly, and demanded unanimous approval from them. And he discouraged the introduction of democratic practices in his party. But blame for much of his autocratic behavior must rest on the party, which simply capitulated to him.

Moreover, chancellor-democracy had its pragmatic attributes, which were not necessarily negative. Adenauer was faced with holding together in the Christian Democratic Union (CDU) a number of diverse elements. He did this very well. He mediated among all groups, and in doing so he was criticized for not wishing to offend any major one of them. But in doing this he was not playing a merely passive role, as has been sometimes suggested, because he also prevented any one group from dominating the CDU.[3]

Perhaps the most telling criticism of Adenauer as chancellor was his dislike of criticism, most of which he took personally. He often cast suspicion on the opposition Social Democrats, who in his view were not too different from Communists. He did not seem to understand that despite differences of opinion, the government and the opposition could cooperate in many matters. His attitude toward the opposition gave the impression that he was treating the *Bundestag* in a condescending manner, and its reputation suffered thereby. He did not seem to appreciate the fact that a successful parliamentary democracy requires the collective wisdom of the cabinet, subject to the collective judgment of the parliament.

A member of the opposition has described Adenauer in these words: "The term 'patriarch' is probably most descriptive of Adenauer. Yet he is a patriarch of broad vision—and of myopic provincialism as well. His towering political gifts were not confined to tactical maneuvers and stratagems. He donned the statesman's robe, and it fit . . . a man of undeniably great stature, despite all his faults, mistakes, and omissions."[4] History is not likely to revise that verdict, not much anyway.

ADENAUER'S SUCCESSOR: LUDWIG ERHARD

Ludwig Erhard became chancellor in October 1963, a remarkably brief time on which to base any meaningful evaluation. Nevertheless, a few observations may be helpful. A social scientist turned politician, he was Adenauer's minister of economics from the beginning, and no doubt deserves the major credit for Germany's phenomenal recovery and prosperity. Because of his contributions, the party owes more to him than he to it. As might be expected, however, he does not yet have either Adenauer's one-time prestige or power.

---

[3] See Klaus Bölling, *Republic in Suspense* (New York: Frederick A. Praeger, 1964), especially chapters 4 and 7.

[4] Bölling, *op. cit.*, pp. 160 and 169.

In many respects, Erhard is different from his predecessor. He has not demonstrated Adenauer's understanding of political tactics nor has he been inclined to engage in political machinations. He wants to be chancellor of all the people and not just of his party. He seems more open to most people. He is optimistic and direct, and these qualities have endeared him even to many who are not fond of his dedication to free enterprise. He seems to value the views of his party colleagues, although he will, no doubt, remain firmly in command.

Moreover, his relations with the opposition Social Democrats have been good, and he has exhibited good will toward the *Bundestag* generally, which was not among his predecessor's strong points. In his first official statement as chancellor, he said: "I regard the opposition as a necessary element of full standing in a parliamentary democracy and hope that our discussions and disputes, which are bound to arise, may be conducted in this spirit." In addition, Erhard has stressed the importance of popular participation, and the force of public opinion, in a democratic society.

BIBLIOGRAPHICAL NOTE

There are no books in English dealing exclusively with the German executive. Klaus Bölling, *Republic in Suspense: Politics, Parties and Personalities in Postwar Germany* (New York: Praeger, 1964) contains much valuable commentary on executive leadership. Two books on the CDU leaders are useful: Arnold J. Heidenheimer, *Adenauer and the CDU: The Rise of the Leader and the Integration of the Party* (The Hague: Martinus Nijhoff, 1960), and Jess M. Lukomski, *Erhard of Germany* (New York: Praeger, 1965). The following may also be consulted with profit: Richard Hiscocks, *Democracy in Western Germany* (New York: Oxford University Press, 1957); John Ford Golay, *The Founding of the Federal Republic of Germany* (Chicago: University of Chicago Press, 1958); Herman Finer, *The Major Governments of Modern Europe* (Evanston, Ill.: Row, Peterson & Co., 1960); and Karl Deutsch and Lewis Edinger, *Germany Rejoins the Powers* (Stanford, Cal.: Stanford University Press, 1959); Arnold J. Heidenheimer, *The Government of Germany* (New York: Crowell, 1961); Elmer Plischke, *Contemporary Government of Germany* (Boston: Houghton Mifflin, 1961).

The following German works are particularly pertinent: Ludwig Bersträsser, *Die Problematik des deutschen Parlamentarismus* (Munich: Isar Verlag, 1951); Rupert Breitling, *Die Verbände in der Bundesrepublik* (Meisenheim am Glan: Anton Hain, 1955); Hans Ehard, *Freiheit und Föderalismus* (Munich: Richard Pflaum, 1948); Theodor Heuss, *Verfassungsrecht und Verfassungspolitik: Vom monarchischen Konstitutionalismus zum demokratischen Parlamentarismus* (Krefeld: Scherpe-Verlag, 1950); Dolf Sternberger, *Lebende Verfassung, Studien über Koalition und Opposition* (Meisenheim am Glan: Anton Hain, 1956).

CHAPTER 19

THE PARLIAMENT

GERMANY has a bicameral legislature. The popularly elected *Bundestag* consists of 496 members, with an addtional 22 non-voting members from West Berlin. The *Bundestag* members are chosen for four-year terms in "universal, direct, free, equal, and secret elections." The upper house, the *Bundesrat*, consists of 41 members who are appointed by and may be recalled by the ten *Länder* governments. This is in keeping with past German practice of having the members of the upper chamber represent component federal units. *Bundesrat* members are usually ministers in their respective states and hence play a dual role. The *Bundesrat* has no specific legislative term and is not affected by national elections. The Basic Law provides that no state will have fewer than three members, with five being the maximum for the most populous *Länder*. West Berlin sends four "observers."

ELECTORAL PROCEDURES

The drafters of the constitution were aware that one of the difficulties of Weimar was that it was beset with a multiplicity of political parties. One of their principal aims, therefore, was to draft an electoral law which would eliminate or discourage the small parties. In this, as we shall see later, they were in the main successful. Many of the drafters of the electoral law believed that the multiplicity of parties stemmed from, or at least was aided by, the system of proportional representation. Consequently, when the electoral law was drafted in 1949, it provided that 60 per cent of the deputies be elected by direct vote from single-member districts and 40 per cent through a system of proportional representation. In 1953 the electoral law was changed so that now 50 per cent are elected by direct vote and the other 50 by proportional representation.[1]

Under this system, the nation is divided into 248 electoral districts. The candidate receiving the highest number of votes in each of these

---

[1] For a copy of the electoral law see Lane and Pollock, *Source Materials on the Government and Politics of Germany*, pp. 51–55.

districts wins. The remaining 248 deputies are chosen on the basis of proportional representation, i.e. each party getting seats in proportion to the vote it polls. Each voter marks his ballot in two places, in one place he votes for an individual candidate and in the other for the party list of his choice.

The system is complicated by virtue of the fact that each of the states is supposed to have as many deputies as the size of its population entitles it, yet the single-member districts are drawn in such a way that one-half of the deputies will not necessarily be chosen by the one method and the other half by the other. North Rhine-Westphalia, for example, elects 155 deputies, but only 66 of them by direct vote because there are only that many electoral districts in it. Schleswig-Holstein, on the other hand, elects 20 deputies, 14 of them by direct vote for the same reason.

The general rule is that each political party in each one of the states is entitled to a number of seats directly proportional to the votes received by that party's list. In Schleswig-Holstein in the 1961 election, for example, this would have meant 9 for the Christian Democrats, 8 for the Social Democrats, and 3 for the Free Democrats. From each one of these, according to the electoral law, are subtracted the seats won by direct vote in the single-member districts. Thus, if each of the three parties had elected candidates in two districts, the remaining deputies would come from the party lists as follows: 7 CDU, 6 SPD, and 1 FDP. But in 1961 the CDU elected deputies in all but one of the 14 districts in Schleswig-Holstein, hence *four* more than it was entitled under the proportional representation formula. In such a case the rule is to avoid penalizing any party insofar as possible. Hence, the SPD and the FDP were given their 8 and 3 seats, respectively, and the CDU the 13 they had won, giving Schleswig-Holstein a total of 24 seats rather than the 20 to which it was entitled. Because of this rule the size of the *Bundestag* may vary by a few seats from the pre-determined total.

Minor parties are penalized under this system in that the electoral law does not permit the allocation of seats to a party, under the proportional representation formula, unless its lists receive at least 5 per cent of the total popular vote in the nation as a whole or unless it has elected at least three candidates to the *Bundestag* by direct vote.

The party lists are drawn up by the respective party leaders, and the seats which each party receives as a result of the proportional distribution are given to persons on the list in the order in which their names appear. If a candidate on the list has already been elected in the direct election, the seat goes to the next person on the list.

Nominations are controlled by the parties at the state level. In the case of nominations for the single-member districts the nominating group is a small party caucus or a party convention. Nomination of list candidates is by party conventions at the state level, with national, regional, and local organizations exerting some influence. As in Great Britain and France, there are no nominations by primary. Candidates must be at least 25 years of age, and the parties that nominate them must prove that their executive bodies are democratically elected and that they have democratic constitutions and a political program. Moreover, the signatures of 200 eligible voters are required for a valid nomination in an electoral district. Party lists, however, require up to 2000 signatures, depending upon the number of eligible voters in the particular state.

As might be expected, the popularly elected executive body of the party in each state, together with the party's top career officials, play an important role in the nominating process. The delegates are far from united, with many favorites being put forward. In the resulting intraparty contest, the party's top leaders at the *Länder* level facilitate compromise and accommodation. This is perhaps as it should be, for the leaders are in the best position to judge which of the prospective candidates can best serve the party in the *Bundestag*.

Different occupations are well represented in the *Bundestag*. As a result of the 1961 election, the largest single group listed farming in the occupation category. Civil servants, who are permitted to take leave if they are chosen for elective office, constituted the second largest group. Because most school and university teachers have civil service status, they are included in this group. The legal profession was well-represented and so was industry and business. Business and middle-class organizations are better represented among the Christian Democrats and the Free Democrats, while representatives of the workers are more in evidence among the Social Democrats. Some of the members have had previous legislative experience, having served in *Länder* parliaments. In 1961, one of every twelve members of the *Bundestag* was a woman.

Voter participation in postwar German elections has been relatively high, averaging more than 80 per cent. This may have been facilitated by keeping the list of voters current, as is done in Great Britain. Lists of eligible voters (age 21 and over) are posted well in advance of an election, affording ample opportunity for complaints. High participation can also be attributed to the fact that, like the French, the

Germans vote on Sunday. Moreover, there are voting facilities at railway stations and at hospitals and sanatoria, enabling persons to vote who otherwise might find it difficult to get to the polls.

Salaries of *Bundestag* deputies are reasonably generous. They are set in relation to a certain percentage which the ministers receive. In addition, they receive monthly expense allowances and per diem allowances, and they have free use of all governmentally controlled communications. Those who own cars receive a mileage allowance, plus payment for a chauffeur. Those who fail to attend sessions of the *Bundestag* lose a proportionate share of their per diem pay.

CAMPAIGN EXPENDITURES

The electoral law does not impose limitations on campaign spending,[2] which has increased with each election. In the 1957 electoral campaign, for example, it was estimated that the three major parties spent upwards of 12 million dollars, or four to five times the total spent by the three political parties in the previous general election in Great Britain.[3] In the 1961 electoral campaign, the amount spent increased by at least one-third. Partly as a result of these rising expenditures, the three major parties reached an agreement in January 1965, not only limiting the amounts of money to be spent in that year's campaign, but also imposing other rules governing the nature of the election battle.

Under this agreement, the CDU and its Bavarian affiliate (CSU) were limited to slightly over 4 million dollars, while the Social Democrats and the Free Democrats were limited to 3.75 million dollars each. Moreover, the parties agreed to have their books audited by a certified accountant, who was to make a public finding by mid-1966. Alleged violations of the agreement were to be brought before a special court. Non-financial aspects of the agreement included: a prohibition on campaign posters prior to thirty days preceding the election, and their posting only in designated areas; a ban on newspaper or magazine advertising until eight weeks before the election; a prohibition against skywriting; and a limitation on the number (two) of leaflets that may be sent to German households.

The parties are provided with free radio and television time, roughly in proportion to the votes they received in the preceding elec-

---

[2] See the following chapter for a discussion of the sources of party income.

[3] Uwe Kitzinger, *German Electoral Politics: A Study of the 1957 Campaign* (London: Oxford University Press, 1960), p. 202.

tion. The government also provides a sizable annual monetary subsidy, initially designated for "political education," to each party on the basis of its strength in the *Bundestag*. In addition, the governments of each of the states make similar contributions to the parties in their respective areas.

PARTY REPRESENTATION IN THE BUNDESTAG

The election of 1949, following the adoption of the Basic Law, resulted in eight political parties obtaining ten or more seats. The two largest parties were the Christian Democratic Union and the Social Democrats, obtaining 139 and 131 seats respectively. The Free Democrats were third with 52 seats. In the election of 1953, however, the Christian Democrats won 244 seats, while the Social Democrats had 150. The Free Democrats were again third with 48 seats. The number of parties electing candidates dropped to six.

The distribution of seats in the *Bundestag* as a result of the last three elections was as follows:

	1957	1961	1965
Christian Democratic Union (includes Bavarian affiliate, Christian Social Union)	270	242	245
Social Democratic party	169	190	202
Free Democratic party	41	67	49
German party	17	—	—

If it is possible to talk about a trend on the basis of the elections (five) since the founding of the Federal Republic, it would appear to be in the direction of a two-party system. In the first three elections, the Christian Democrats were evolving into a majority party. At the same time, the second largest party, the Social Democrats, was also increasing its strength. In 1957, the percentage of the votes cast for the two largest parties was 82 per cent. In 1961, it was 81.6 per cent, rising to 87 per cent in 1965. In sum, the smaller parties have not done well, while the two major parties increased and solidified their strength.

The party complexion of the *Bundesrat* depends upon the political party control in each of the *Länder*, because the *Länder* governments determine who shall be sent to the *Bundesrat* to represent them. The deputies from each state vote as a bloc, and they vote on instruction from their state governments. To the extent that the *Bundesrat* is important in national politics, therefore, it is incumbent upon the national parties to seek control of *Länder* governments. In actual practice, state election campaigns have been dominated by national questions rather than state issues.

LEGISLATIVE POWERS OF PARLIAMENT

Legislative powers are divided between the central government and the governments of the *Länder*. The constitution specifies that in some areas the central government has exclusive jurisdiction, while in others there is concurrent authority. The central government has exclusive legislative power (Article 73) in such matters as foreign affairs, citizenship, freedom of movement (passports, immigration, etc.), fiscal regulations (currency, money, coinage, etc.), customs and tariffs, posts and telecommunications, national railroads and air traffic, the legal status of persons in the service of the central government, industrial property rights (patents, etc.), cooperation of the national government and the *Länder* in the field of criminal police, and in matters concerning the protection of the constitution. In the areas of exclusive national power, the *Länder* have the power to legislate only if, and insofar as, they are expressly so empowered by law of the central government.

The constitution sets forth a long list (Article 74) of matters that fall in the realm of concurrent powers, matters over which the *Länder* are empowered to legislate as long as, and insofar as, the central government makes no use of its legislative power. The constitution stipulates, however, that the national government is empowered to legislate in these fields only insofar as there is a need for regulation by national law because certain matters cannot be effectively regulated by the *Länder* or because action by one or more of the states will prejudice the interests of other states or the community as a whole. Article 75 lists several matters concerning which the central government may issue general directions, with the *Länder* doing the more detailed regulating.

Other articles of the constitution specify the legislative and administrative powers that rest with the *Länder*. Education and cultural affairs are left completely to the *Länder*. Moreover, administration, even of national government laws, is left largely to state officials.

The primary law-making body of the national government is the *Bundestag*. It is limited in two ways. First, there has been a tendency for legislative initiative to shift toward the executive. This has been partly due to the strong lead which the chancellor has given and partly to the influence of the expert bureaucrat who has the relevant informa-

tion; bills are drafted in executive departments by experienced jurists, whose services are not directly available to the *Bundestag*.
Secondly, the *Bundestag* is limited by the constitutional requirement
that gives the *Bundesrat* a share in law making.

The *Bundesrat* exercises legislative functions in three categories:
ordinary laws which do not require its assent, laws which require its
approval, and amendments to the constitution. In the first category
the *Bundestag* can override the upper chamber, but it must do so by a
comparable margin. If the *Bundesrat* rejects a bill by a majority vote,
it can be passed over its veto by an ordinary majority in the *Bundestag*. If the *Bundesrat* rejects a measure by a two-thirds vote, then a two-
thirds vote will be necessary in the *Bundestag* to override. This has
sometimes been referred to as a suspensory veto. In the second
category are laws that affect the interests of the *Länder*. An example is
financial legislation which distributes financial resources between the
national government and the states. In such matters the consent of the
Länder is necessary. In the matter of amending the constitution, too,
the consent of two thirds of the *Bundesrat* is required.

The *Bundesrat* has authority to initiate legislation (cabinet measures must go to it first), but it has made less and less use of this right.
Moreover, it has been reluctant to invoke either its suspensive or
absolute veto. This may have been due in part because the majority of
the *Bundesrat* deputies were *Länder* ministers who belonged to the
majority party controlling the *Bundestag*. In addition, the national
government seems to attract the more energetic political personalities
because they want to be where the major decisions are being made. On
the whole, however, the *Bundesrat* has made a valuable contribution
toward the improvement of legislation. Because the *Bundesrat* members are involved in the administration of national legislation at the
Länder level, their knowledge of local conditions equips them to tell
the national ministers, as well as *Bundestag* members generally, what
will and what will not work, and how legislation should be drafted so
as to achieve the best results.

In case of disagreement between the *Bundestag* and the *Bundesrat*,
the Conference Committee[4] seeks to promote a workable compromise.
Unlike conference committees in the U.S. Congress, which are established for particular bills as the need arises, this one has permanent
status. It is composed of eleven members from each body, with a like
number of deputies. Aside from ministers of the national government

---

[4] For the standing orders of the Conference Committee see Lane and Pollock, *op. cit.*,
pp. 73–74.

no others are permitted to attend its meetings except by express decision of the committee. In order to provide continuity, the standing orders permit no more than four changes of membership, including deputies, during the existence of a single *Bundestag*. Unlike in the *Bundesrat* itself, *Bundesrat* members of the Conference Committee are not bound to vote as their respective state governments should like them to. The record of the Conference Committee, judged by the agreements which it was successful in promoting, has been impressive. During the first three legislatures (1949–1961), 181 bills were submitted to it, and of these 177 were passed by the two houses in the form recommended by the committee.[5]

The constitution provides that the national government must keep the *Bundesrat* informed of the conduct of affairs. In order to do this, the Ministry of *Bundesrat* and *Länder* Affairs was created, although informing the *Bundesrat* is not its only task. Approximately once a week, the minister meets the permanent representatives from the *Länder* and tells them about cabinet policies. Since he usually attends *Bundesrat* meetings and remains in close touch with its members, he is in a position to convey back to his cabinet colleagues the views of the *Länder* representatives.

Reference was made in the previous chapter to the power of the *Bundestag* to elect and to dismiss the chancellor and to its other techniques for enforcing control over the executive. Most observers believe that the *Bundestag* has not been energetic in this role. Its debates have often lacked interest and importance, or they have degenerated into disorder. And its members have too readily acquiesced in the arrogance of the cabinet in ignoring some findings of the *Bundestag*. One observer, while admitting the insufficiency of parliamentary control over the executive, had this to say: ". . . in the first years of a young democracy a great deal depends on the efforts of individuals, and . . . it would be wholly unreasonable to expect many members of the *Bundestag*, with little or no parliamentary experience behind them, to master quickly the difficult art of combining party discipline and loyalty with a strong sense of personal responsibility."[6] Nearly a decade has passed since that judgment was rendered, and improvements have been noted, but they have been slow.

The *Bundestag* still lacks an imaginative and aggressive group of

---

[5] Alfred Grosser, *The Federal Republic of Germany* (New York: Frederick A. Praeger, 1964), p. 45.

[6] Richard Hiscocks, *Democracy in Western Germany* (London: Oxford University Press, 1957), p. 139.

well-educated and politically trained men who realize that their chief task is to depict and explain things as they are, and in the process to win the people's support for future policies. Many energetic deputies have spent a great deal of time on committee work and in trying to compete with the bureaucrats in mastering details. And while this is not to be deplored, it has often been done at the expense of debating the main issues of policy. The deputies seem to be groping to develop a style suited to their system, but the dislike for debate in the Adenauer era did not advance that development.

LEGISLATIVE ORGANIZATION

As do other legislative bodies, the *Bundestag* and the *Bundesrat* have standing orders of procedure. They have their organizational rules, their presiding officers, their committees, and their established modes of doing business. Because of the basic differences between the two bodies, notably the absence of a significant role for political parties in the *Bundesrat*, the organization of the two bodies is somewhat dissimilar.[7]

The basic unit of organization in the *Bundestag* is the party group, or "fraction." As a rule, "fraction" is synonymous with political party group in the *Bundestag*. For example, the Christian Democratic Union deputies constitute a "fraction." But standing orders stipulate that any group with fewer than 15 members does not qualify as a "fraction." The significance of this rule is that individual deputies or deputies representing a small party will not have much influence unless at least 15 of them can combine to form a party group. Unless a party group is qualified as a "fraction," it is not entitled to any committee assignments. And it is the "fraction" which assigns the persons from its ranks to committee posts to which it is entitled. Moreover, only "fractions" may introduce legislation. Hence, despite Article 38 of the Basic Law, which states that deputies are "not bound by orders and instructions, and subject only to their conscience," deputies can exert influence only if they are members of party groups.

The presiding officer of the *Bundestag*, known as the president, is elected by that body from among its own members by secret ballot, and serves until a new *Bundestag* is elected. Thus far, he has been a member of the ruling coalition or majority party. His authority extends to such things as the rights, prerogatives, and internal order of the *Bundestag*. He is vested with vague police powers, which have

---

[7] For the standing orders of the *Bundestag* and the *Bundesrat*, respectively, see Lane and Pollock, *op. cit.*, pp. 60–67 and 70–72.

been interpreted as authorizing him to exclude unruly deputies from sessions of the *Bundestag* up to 30 days at a time. Unlike the Speaker in the House of Commons, the president of the *Bundestag* is an active party leader.

Assisting the president are two vice-presidents and a number of recording secretaries, also elected by the *Bundestag* from among its members. In addition, there is the Council of Elders, which acts as a type of steering committee. It is a permanent committee of 15 members, with each party group ("fraction") designating members in proportion to its strength in the *Bundestag*, and selecting them on the basis of age rather than years of service. Among other things, the Council of Elders distributes committee chairmanships and seeks agreements among the party groups to facilitate the work of the *Bundestag*.

The physical arrangement of the *Bundestag* has been the subject of debate. For the first several years it was housed in a lecture-hall type of chamber, with the members of the cabinet sitting on a raised platform at the front. Deputies wishing to speak could not do so from their seats but had to proceed to the front of the chamber. Under the urgings of its president, the *Bundestag* in 1961 decided to have the chamber redone so as to resemble the British House of Commons (to a degree) by arranging to have the majority party and opposition parties face each other, thus enabling the deputies to speak from their seats. The cabinet would have a special area on the majority side. Partly because of the narrowness of the vote, and partly because of plans to build a huge new parliament building, the nature of the future chamber seems in doubt. There are some indications, however, that it will take the form of a horseshoe, as in the old *Reichstag* in Berlin.

The presiding officer of the *Bundesrat* is also known as president. He is elected annually, and there is a tendency to elect a new one each year, rotating the office so that over a period of years each of the *Länder* will have been represented in the presiding officer's chair.

LEGISLATIVE PROCEDURE

As with other parliamentary bodies, the really important work of the *Bundestag* is done in committees. Currently there are 26 functional committees, usually one for each ministry, with membership ranging from 17 to 31 on each. Each party group is represented in proportion to its strength in the body. An interesting departure from

American practice is the assignment of a fair number of committee chairmanships to the opposition. All committees have the services of a full- or part-time assistant from the *Bundestag* staff. His work consists of assisting the chairman in the organization of the committee's work, including the calling of witnesses, assembling the necessary material, and providing liaison with other committees.

The various party groups seek to assign members to committees in accordance with the special competence of their deputies, but the standard of performance varies a good deal from committee to committee. One reason for this is that at times a bill may be referred to as many as three committees, with all the consequences that divided responsibility may bring. On the whole, however, parties seem to work better in committees than they do in the *Bundestag*. Antagonism between cabinet and the opposition is far less in evidence in committees, perhaps due to the fact that committee work is not open to the glare of publicity. Also, as mentioned above, the opposition holds a number of chairmanships and deputy chairmanships, which may make for a greater sense of responsibility. In the opinion of one observer, "nothing would have a healthier effect than the extension of the spirit prevailing in the best committees to the *Bundestag* as a whole and to political life in general. Democracy is seen at its best in Germany in the work of the *Bundestag* committees."[8]

Committees are empowered to call in expert witnesses and, on important occasions, their sessions are attended by appropriate ministers and their assistants. In this way, committees have the benefit of the cabinet's point of view when it is needed most. Representatives from West Berlin who are assigned committee posts participate on the basis of full equality, including the right to vote.

The constitution empowers the *Bundestag* to set up a standing committee (a type of watchdog committee) whose task is to "safeguard the rights of the *Bundestag*" in relation to the national government "in the interval between two legislative terms." Moreover, this standing committee "has also the powers of an investigating committee." But this committee has no legislative or impeachment powers, and there is little evidence of its engaging in any noteworthy activity.

An interesting innovation was the creation by the *Bundestag*, at the time of the establishment of the new German army, of the post of Defense Commissioner. He is the agent of the *Bundestag*, elected by it and charged with investigating all complaints as to violations of the

---

[8] Hiscocks, *op. cit.*, p. 136.

basic rights of soldiers or of the principles of internal leadership in the military forces. He has the power to obtain access to the pertinent papers and such other information as he deems necessary. He may refer complaints to appropriate sources for settlement, but his main task is to act as a "watchdog" for the *Bundestag,* which wants to avoid the formation of an army on the old model. It wants politically aware soldiers and not the automatons of the Hitler era. While the work of the Defense Commissioner cannot be evaluated without greater perspective, it may be important to note that he has reported the occurrence of several of the practices that the *Bundestag* wanted rooted out.[9] Perhaps he will continue to perform an all-important function.

The *Bundesrat* also does the bulk of its work in committees. However, it has only 13 committees, with equal representation on each from the 10 *Länder.* West Berlin is represented in each committee by an observer who, however, does not vote.

Legislative initiative may stem from members of the two houses or from the cabinet. Government bills must first begin in the *Bundesrat,* which sends them to the *Bundestag* via the cabinet. In this way, the *Bundestag* may have the views of the *Bundesrat* as well as the cabinet's reaction to those views. The cabinet may, however, shortcircuit this process by getting a party group in the *Bundestag* to introduce bills as their own. As mentioned earlier, individual members of the *Bundestag* cannot introduce bills unless they do so on behalf of a party group ("fraction"). Bills which originate in the *Bundesrat* are submitted to the *Bundestag* via the cabinet, just as if the cabinet had originated them, and they must be accompanied by a statement setting forth the cabinet's views.

Legislative proposals, as well as treaties, are considered by the *Bundestag* in three readings. On first reading the basic principles are discussed, and a vote is taken. If favorable, the bill goes to committee, after which it receives a second reading, a time when the detailed provisions of the bill are debated and amendments considered. Discussion on third reading is largely confined to a general debate of the main features of the bill, although amendments are also in order if supported by at least fifteen deputies. On third reading, each deputy may speak a maximum of one hour unless the majority, by resolution, accords him more time. In urgent circumstances, all three readings of

---

[9] Klaus Bölling, *Republic In Suspense: West Germany Today* (New York: Frederick A. Praeger, 1964), pp. 184–85. Also see Lane and Pollock, *op. cit.,* pp. 127–28, and Walter Stahl, *Politics of Postwar Germany* (New York: Frederick A. Praeger, 1963), p. 260ff.

a bill can take place in a single day provided there is unanimous agreement. After passage in the *Bundestag,* all bills are transmitted to the *Bundesrat,* which, as indicated earlier, has a suspensive veto in some matters and an absolute one in others. Experience thus far indicates that most differences are ironed out by the Conference Committee.

Proposed legislation before the *Bundesrat* usually goes automatically to a committee. Thereafter it is considered by the *Bundesrat* in a single reading, where all voting is by roll call of the *Länder.* And, as indicated earlier, each state casts its vote as a unit.

Voting in the *Bundestag* is by a show of hands or by standing. In case of doubt, there is a division, similar to the one employed in Great Britain, where deputies file through doors past counting clerks. If as many as 50 members request it in advance, a roll call vote is taken. There is no excessive delay in reaching a vote, since there is no evidence of filibustering, and hence there is no need for devices to limit debate. The Council of Elders manages to expedite business and to control the parliamentary timetable.

* * * * *

Legislative leadership is largely in the hands of the cabinet, if one is to judge by the measures introduced and enacted. Approximately three-fourths of all bills were initiated by the cabinet. Initially, many bills were introduced by ordinary members of the *Bundestag,* but this number has declined sharply. Extremely few bills have been introduced by ordinary members of the *Bundesrat* and still fewer passed. Party discipline in parliamentary voting is high, which is further evidence of executive leadership in the legislative halls.

BIBLIOGRAPHICAL NOTE

One of the few studies of the German national legislature is R. K. Ullmann and Stephen King-Hall, *German Parliaments: A Study of the Development of Representative Institutions in Germany* (London: The Hansard Society, 1954). Also of interest are certain chapters in Karl Deutsch and Lewis Edinger, *Germany Rejoins the Powers* (Stanford, Cal.: Stanford University Press, 1959). The books by Bölling, Heidenheimer, and Plischke, listed at the end of the previous chapter, have much useful material pertinent to the legislature in Germany.

A very valuable treatment of the electoral system is U. W. Kitzinger, *German Electoral Politics, the 1957 Campaign* (Oxford: Oxford University Press, 1960).

The following German works are especially pertinent: Wilhelm Keil, *Das*

Parlament (Stuttgart: Verlag der Turmhaus-Druckerei, 1952) ; Albert Pfitzer, *Der Bundesrat* (Bonn: Bundeszentrale fur Heimatdienst, 1956) ; Hans Schä-fer, *Der Bundesrat* (Cologne-Berlin: Carl Heymanns, 1955) ; and Hans Tross-mann, *Der zweite Deutsche Bundestag* (Bonn: Bonner Universitäts-Buch-druckerei, 1954), and *Aufgaben und Arbeitsweise des Deutschen Bundestages* (Munich: Isar Verlag, 1953).

CHAPTER 20

POLITICAL PARTIES

THE PRIMARY task confronting German political leaders when self-government again became possible was the problem of resuming the democratic experiment. This task could be assumed, initially at least, only by political party leaders who were still alive and who had had some experience in democratic politics under Weimar. But their experience, and that of their parties, did not adequately equip them for what was ahead. The Nazi era, together with defeat, destruction, and a divided nation, had changed German society a great deal. New forces were at work, and yet it is understandable that older party leaders were living too much in the past. The German people, too, had to face a different world; the one with which they were familiar had been shattered. Hence, it was inevitable that a period of readjustment and re-evaluation was in the offing, the consequences of which are still in the making.

SOME FACTORS SHAPING GERMAN POLITICAL PARTIES

In their desire to promote democratic government in postwar Germany, the Western occupation authorities began authorizing political party activities on the local level as early as August 1945, which by 1946 was extended to the states. At the same time, parties suspected of having Nazi leanings were not permitted to operate. It was not until 1948 that the United States relinquished all control over the regulation of German political parties in its zone of occupation. The British and the French finally relinquished control in their zones in early 1950.

The German constitution which went into effect in 1949 refers briefly to political parties. Among other things, parties are said to "participate in the forming of the political will of the people," something that is taken for granted in most democratic countries. This may reveal a tendency to want to legalize the role of parties. Political scientists know, however, that legalistic provisions cannot completely channel the political process, which is an evolving and growing thing. Parties are free to organize, but those which, "according to their aims and the conduct of their members, seek to impair or abolish the libertarian democratic basic order or to jeopardize the existence of the Federal Republic of Germany are unconstitutional." The Constitutional Court, upon petition of the cabinet or of either house of the legislature, is empowered to pass on this question. Pursuant to this power, it banned a neo-Nazi party and the Communist party.

Despite the constitutional stipulation that parties participate in the formation of the political will of the people, the Germans have been aloof where parties are concerned. In spite of a party membership tradition, less than 1.5 million were party members in 1953, when 32 million of them were casting a ballot. No doubt, the Nazi experience (with denazification, etc.) has made people cautious about joining parties. But distrust of parties also stems from the German respect for authority and their distrust of government based on debate and controversy. Moreover, the exclusive and at times autocratic attitude of party officials has discouraged potential recruits. Even those who are party members seem to defer to the leadership. Although there is always the possibility of a rank and file revolt against the leaders, there is no evidence that such a development is likely to occur. In the case of the Christian Democratic Union (CDU, *Christlich-Demokratische Union*), a type of divided loyalty tended to develop between the party and the intimate and powerful circle that had grown up about Chancellor Adenauer, reflecting the latter's desire to run the party without consulting lesser leaders, or at least without having to worry about their views. What has been said above is less true of the Social Democratic party, which continues to emphasize party membership.

Popular aloofness from parties may signify that German parties are becoming electoral machines, like ours, and consequently less ideological. In the past, they have followed the general European tradition of being highly ideological, viewing compromise as betrayal rather than an important ingredient in a working democratic system. The declining emphasis on ideological content would seem not only to promote acceptance of compromise but also to reduce the number of parties. Emphasis on ideological purity has always tended to increase the number of parties in a freely functioning democratic society.

Foreign policy has had a significant impact on German political parties. Adenauer, as chancellor of a divided nation, emphasized foreign affairs and thereby brought into sharp focus the question of national unity, on which all German loyalties could converge. There is in Germany today an essentially bipartisan approach to foreign policy. The attitudes of the two major parties are strikingly similar concerning all major foreign policy issues, although there are differences in tone and concept of application. Both parties are realistically pro-American, both support NATO, both want friendship with France, both champion the Common Market, and both desire a united Germany. The Free Democrats do not really disagree with the stand of the two major parties, although in their view neither one of them is aggressive enough in the pursuit of certain foreign policy objectives.

CHRISTIAN DEMOCRATIC UNION (CDU)

The Christian Democratic Union is founded on a double compromise. Its hard core and that of its Bavarian counterpart, the Christian Social Union, are the Catholic voters in West and South Germany. But Catholics have always been a minority in Germany and both Protestants and Catholics suffered under the Nazis. This common experience and the determination of Adenauer, a Catholic who is opposed to clericalism, to weld a united party of Protestants and Catholics brought into existence the CDU, hence the Catholic-Protestant compromise. Adenauer's successor, Ludwig Erhard, is a Protestant, which has helped the party in its desire to have a nondenominational image. The CDU militants, however, tend to be Catholics in most regions. In the first *Bundestag*, 40 per cent of CDU members were Protestants.

Particularly in the beginning, the Christian aspect of the CDU had a particular appeal. The one organization in Germany whose leadership had not been discredited by association with the Nazis was the church. Moreover, Christian precepts afforded a rallying symbol for many who had been guilty of blindness toward the Hitler regime.

The second compromise is economic, a compromise between trade unionist followers and the more conservative economists. The party offers a political home to the Christian trade unionists as well as to big industry and finance. In the immediate postwar years, it advocated the nationalization of basic industries, but as German recovery progressed this part of its program was dropped. It now believes in a free enterprise tempered by social conscience, sometimes referring to its desired goal as a "socially minded market economy." The party has attracted the support of farmers and the urban middle classes. In large part, its political line is determined and influenced by the views of the middle classes. This merging of diverse economic interests has brought into being different interpretations of what the party stands for economically.

The CDU was successful in the early and mid-1960's in getting laws enacted which were designed to promote widespread ownership of stocks and securities, particularly among lower and middle income groups. Tax and other inducements were offered to both employers and employees as a means of encouraging more and more people to invest in the economy. It is still too early to appraise the impact of these laws.

The CDU party organization is governed by a charter or statute,[1] which designates the organizational levels (national, state, district, and local) and provides for party governing bodies. Among the latter is the annual party convention, which elects a party chairman (2 year term) and allegedly passes on the basic outlines of policy. The Federal Committee, selected in a complicated manner, concerns itself with political and organizational matters; chooses the Election Commission, which participates with the CDU *Länder* associations in the nomination of candidates to the *Bundestag;* and elects a treasurer and 15 members of the Federal Executive Committee, whose job it is to carry out the decisions of the party organs above it. Since the Federal Executive Committee meets only every three months, it elects the Managing Executive Committee to deal with the more current matters.

From the above, it would seem that the CDU is a hierarchical and centralized organization. This impression was enhanced by Adenauer's long tenure as leader and his patriarchal attitude toward his party associates. In actual practice, however, there is a good deal of decentralization. The party organizations in the *Länder* have a fair amount of freedom in the conduct of party affairs. There are paid party workers, but they are mostly at the *Länder* level. The CDU encourages dues-paying members, but has never succeeded in boosting this membership much beyond 300,000.

SOCIAL DEMOCRATIC PARTY (SPD)

By contrast with the CDU the Social Democratic party (SPD, *Sozialdemokratische Partei Deutschlands*), is not a postwar product; its roots go back into the 19th century. In 1912 and 1919 it was the largest party in the country, polling more than 45 per cent of the total vote. Revived in 1945, after being suppressed by the Nazis, the SPD polled 29 per cent of the total vote in 1953, 32 per cent in 1957,

---

[1] For a copy of the Statute of the CDU see Lane and Pollock, *Source Materials on the Government and Politics of Germany,* pp. 187–91.

36 per cent in 1961, and 39 per cent in 1965. Although the CDU was becoming a majority party in these years, it is significant that the SPD also made gains. It is also necessary to point out that the party has had much more success on the *Länder* level than it has nationally, participating in many *Länder* coalition governments.

The SPD continues to emphasize dues-paying membership, which now totals over 700,000. It is the only party which manages to meet most of its expenses from membership dues, and it is the only party which regularly publishes a financial statement. Traditionally, the SPD has been a workers party, although in the postwar years it has gained followers from the middle classes and from intellectual circles. More recently, it has revised its doctrines, to which more detailed reference is made below, so as to make its appeal general.

Featuring a strong hierarchy, so typical of German parties, the SPD is highly organized.[2] It holds a party conference every two years, although extraordinary conferences may also be convened. The real power in directing party affairs, however, is the Executive which the conference elects, although there is a larger body, the Party Council, which must be consulted *before* the announcement of resolutions dealing with policy matters, fundamental questions of organization, and election strategy. The party rules say that the executive is responsible for "the control of the party," for "conducting the party's business" and for guiding "the fundamental attitude of the party organs." Since the Executive meets only once a month, the day-to-day business of the party is conducted by the Managing Committee, which is made up of the two chairmen and the four or five paid officials of the Party Executive. Because of its role, the Managing Committee also exercises considerable influence on questions of party policy. At the local level, party affairs are handled mostly by volunteer workers, while paid secretaries are employed at higher levels.

The SPD organization outside Parliament exercises control over the party (fraction) in Parliament, much as the British Labor party did prior to its assumption of power. Speeches by its leaders in the middle 1960's indicated, however, that once in power, the SPD's parliamentary leadership would assume the responsibility of governing, just as happened in Great Britain.

Although resolutely anti-Communist, the SPD, as an old socialist party, had its doctrinal roots in Marxism. In the postwar years many of its Marxist tenets were gradually dropped by the wayside. At its .

---

[2] For organization statute of SPD see Lane and Pollock, *op. cit.*, 192–96.

1958 conference, the SPD approved a proposal for a systematic re-examination of the party's program and doctrines. In a special conference held in November 1959, the party revised its program, abandoning most of its Marxian baggage. Aside from continuing to reject Communism as antidemocratic, and as a betrayal of the social-ist idea, leaders declared that the SPD must become a national party, thus discarding class warfare. There was still talk of nationalization for the solution of certain economic problems, but the vague concept of public ownership was dropped The basic emphasis was on free-dom. ". . . the consumer's freedom of choice and the worker's freedom to choose his job are fundamentals of a socialist economic policy, while free enterprise and free competition are important features of it." The party's slogan in the middle 1960s was: "As much competition as possible—as much planning as necessary." In addi-tion, the party dropped its hostility toward religion and the church, declaring that it does not claim to be an ideological party or a substitute for any church.

Moreover, the party has come out openly for national defense, no longer opposing conscription, and has endorsed the NATO alliance that it once opposed. The party's one-time opposition to European union has given way to an enthusiastic support for the Common Market. It is still hostile to Moscow, but it believes that international realities dictate negotiations with the Soviet Union and the nations of Eastern Europe.

The Social Democratic party, by the thorough revision of its program and doctrine, became more like the British Labor party. Its selection of Willy Brandt, the youthful and colorful mayor of Berlin, as the party's candidate for chancellor should it win an electoral victory in 1961, was further evidence of the party's changed image. Although he did not win either in 1961 or 1965, the party gained strength. In 1964, upon the death of the party's chairman, Brandt was officially elevated to this post. In connection with the party's changed image, it is interesting to note that at least one-third of the Germans view the SPD as bourgeois.

THE FREE DEMOCRATIC PARTY (FDP)

The Free Democratic party (FDP, *Freie Demokratische Partei*), heir of old German liberal parties, began its political life champion-ing political, economic, and religious freedom. Gradually, the party has moved to the right, so that sincere champions of democracy and political freedom were heard less and less in party councils. This shift toward more conservative positions was due in part to the party's decision to admit many ex-Nazis, with the consequent departure of the more liberal elements.

When the constitution was being drafted, FDP delegates expressed a preference for a unitary form of organization, although stressing the desirability of decentralization. Moreover, they favored a presidential rather than a parliamentary form of government. The party favors a national ministry of education, and is more opposed to the demands of the trade unions than are the two major parties. It is a more vigorous opponent of the Social Democrats than of the Christian Democrats, with whom it has been in coalition from the beginning.

The FDP is really a loose federation of *Länder* parties, although the standing orders adopted in 1960 seek to impose more control from the center.[3] Despite its support of the unitary principle of governmental organization, its own organization is federal. The chairman of the party has less authority over its members than is true of the two major parties. Moreover, the party has prided itself on the lack of strict party discipline. Its members in the *Bundestag* and in the *Länder* legislatures exhibit a great deal more independence than do the deputies of other parties. Paradoxically, its leaders have not seemed too sensitive to rank and file opinions. As in the case of the other parties, the FDP holds an annual conference.

In general, the electoral fortunes of the Free Democrats have not been particularly good. In 1949 it polled just under 12 per cent of the vote. In 1953 and 1957 it experienced a decline, polling 9.5 and 7.7 per cent of the popular vote, respectively. In 1961 it experienced a slight upsurge, polling 12.8 per cent. Most observers attributed this recovery to the alleged defection of some CDU voters as a form of protest against the refusal of Adenauer to retire. In 1965, its fortunes again declined, polling only 9.5 per cent of the total vote. At the *Länder* level, however, the FDP has done better, and has participated in coalitions in several state governments, in some instances with the CDU and in others with the Social Democrats.

THE DECLINE OF MINOR PARTIES

Eleven parties elected deputies to the *Bundestag* in the election of 1949, no one approaching a majority. The two largest parties, the CDU and the SPD, together polled 60 per cent of the vote, with the

---

[3] For Standing Orders of the FDP see Lane and Pollock, *op. cit.*, pp. 197–99.

CDU having an edge of less than two percentage points. Four years later, the CDU achieved the position of a majority party, and the number of parties represented in the *Bundestag* was reduced by approximately one-half. At the 1957 election, the CDU improved its majority status, and the number of parties with *Bundestag* representatives was reduced to four. The four became three before the following election because most of the German party deputies had joined the CDU. While the CDU was achieving its majority standing, the SPD also gained steadily. In the 1961 elections, the Free Democrats (the third party) gained a few seats, although the two major parties together polled approximately the same percentage (81.6) of the popular vote which they had won in the 1957 election. In the election of 1965, the CDU and the SPD polled nearly 87 per cent of the popular vote between them, while the Free Democrats fell to 9.5 per cent.

A new right-wing party, mainly a coalition of three small parties, was formed in late 1964 to contest the election of September 1965. Calling itself the National Democratic party, the group succeeded in polling only 2 per cent of the popular vote and failed to elect any deputies to the *Bundestag*.

The trend toward a two-party system has been unmistakable, but the reasons for it are less evident. The electoral system does not account for it, although it has served to discourage small splinter parties. Some observers have suggested that Adenauer's domineering roll in his long tenure as chancellor encouraged his opponents to support the only significant opposition party, the SPD. His success, at the same time, brought additional supporters to the CDU. Other analysts have pointed out that the old causes of faction—class lines and a dominant Prussia—were no longer a fact of political life in Germany. And a potential new source of faction—the refugees and expellees—quickly disappeared with the successful integration of these elements in German society. It has also been suggested that the actions of political leaders and interest groups tended to stress the importance of the two major political formations in postwar Germany. While it is difficult to assign specific weight to these various factors, in combination they were a force behind the trend toward a two-party system.

The question of how well integrated are the two major parties is another matter. There are divisive forces in both. The CDU represents a type of coalition—conservatives and liberals, businessmen, farmers, and workers—which was held together by the force of Adenauer's astute leadership. Erhard, able political leader that he is, must nevertheless face the problems of keeping this coalition together. The problems facing the Social Democrats are similar. Their abandonment of the Marxian ideology, which for long was the distinctive feature of the party, has made some adherents unhappy. Moreover, the party's appeal to all electors signifies that it has taken on the attributes of a coalition, with all that this implies. At present, however, differences of opinion within the two parties are not such as to suggest the likelihood of splits leading to the formation of a new party or parties.

EXTREMIST PARTIES

At both ends of the political spectrum, the "lunatic fringe" of German politics has dwindled. Remnants of political extremism remain but these are small. Attempts to revive a Nazi-type party were doomed to failure almost from the beginning. One party, the Socialist Reich party, received a fair measure of support in northern Germany in 1950–52, but was banned by the national Constitutional Court in October 1952. Since that time no one has succeeded in rallying the dispersed latecomers to rightist extremism. Several small groups exist, but their membership has declined and they have fallen to quarreling among themselves.

The story of the Communists is similar. After World War I they had been a sizable party, but after World War II their fortunes were completely different. In 1949 they polled 5.7 per cent of the vote, but dropped to 2.2 per cent at the 1953 elections. Their lack of success can be attributed to several factors. Many German soldiers had an opportunity to see the Communist system in Russia at first hand. Adding to their experience were those who escaped from the Eastern zone. The rapid economic recovery in West Germany and the brutal Soviet blockade of Berlin in 1948 also added to the distaste for Communism among Germans. In 1956 the Constitutional Court ruled favorably on the cabinet's petition that the party be banned, in accordance with the constitutional injunction against antidemocratic parties. Many Germans doubted the political wisdom of this action, although legally sound, because it gave the Communists an opportunity to say that the government feared the victory of its ideas.

So long as German democracy continues to function with a fair degree of success, the climate for the growth of antidemocratic movements is bound to be unfavorable. Should an emergency occur, a great deal will depend on the popular determination to defend democracy. In the long run, democracy will survive only if it becomes an accepted way of life. At the moment the present order does not seem in dispute.

FINANCING THE PARTIES

The Basic Law says that political parties must give an accounting of the sources of their income, but this requirement was not implemented by appropriate legislation. The Social Democrats have voluntarily followed the practice of publishing figures on income and expenditure, but the CDU and the FDP have not. The SPD has therefore pushed for the enactment of legislation that would force a public accounting, but this move was successfully resisted by the other two parties.

The major sources of party funds are three: membership dues; contributions from individuals and groups; and allocations from public funds. The SPD is the only party that receives substantial income from dues, which are graduated according to the income of members. In addition, SPD asks its *Bundestag* deputies to contribute 20 per cent of their salaries. The CDU also expects its *Bundestag* and *Landtag* deputies to make yearly contributions, although these are considerably smaller than in the case of the SPD.

The most important source of funds for the CDU and the FDP are the so-called sponsor's associations, which are really intermediaries between these parties and business firms. The firms were induced to contribute because in this way they could fight "the socialists," and also because a *Bundestag* law permitted certain tax exemptions to firms making such contributions. The sponsor's associations have received support from a majority of all employers (more in the case of large corporations). The contributors could indicate to which party they wanted the funds to go, but actual distribution was roughly in proportion to the relative strength of the two parties. Some small parties have also received help, but this has been relatively insignificant.

The SPD, through the state government of Hessen acting as the petitioner, challenged the constitutionality of the tax exemption granted to a sponsor group that was formed to collect money from a restricted number of large firms in industry, banking, trade, and insurance. In 1958 the Constitutional Court ruled in favor of the petitioner, nullifying the law on which the exemption was granted. It held that a law which accords financially well-to-do citizens a privileged status violates "the basic right of citizens to equality."[4] Since this decision was handed down, the contributions to sponsor's associations have declined to a degree, and the CDU and FDP have turned more to trade associations for direct support.

Even before the decision, however, there was dissatisfaction among those administering the political funds as to the way the system was working. Nearly half of the business community was uncooperative. Moreover, once a party received support from a sponsor association, its partners in the coalition also demanded funds. Finally, many business men were doubtful about the results, because they found *Bundestag* members more interested in their party's popularity than in the contributors of funds. Yet the desire to keep the Social Democrats out kept the checks coming in.

The SPD could not expect contributions from large corporations, but it has managed to sell expensive advertising space in its publications to certain businesses, notably breweries and department stores. Moreover, "public relations" contributions come from the party's own business firms, primarily newspapers and newsprint importers.

Government subsidies provide parties with another source of funds. In addition to the free TV and radio time that the parties are allotted, as mentioned in the previous chapter, the national government in 1959 appropriated more than a million dollars annually as subsidies to political parties for "political education." Three years later this sum went up to 5 million dollars. In addition, many of the *Länder* governments have also voted subsidies to political parties. The subsidies from the national government are apportioned to the parties on the basis of their strength in the *Bundestag*.

INTEREST GROUPS

As in other democracies, interest groups are very much a part of the political process in Germany. Initially there was a general public distrust of them. This seems to have been in part anticipated by the constitutional provision that deputies are "representatives of the whole people, not bound by orders and instructions, and subject only to their conscience." Nevertheless, interest groups developed rapidly and sought to exert their influence on political parties both in and out of government.

The principal categories of interest groups are: religious, business,

---

[4] For text of decision see Lane and Pollock, *op. cit.*, pp. 231–33.

and labor.[5] The church groups were particularly important at the outset because in the chaos of 1945 they appeared to be the only solid institutions left. Allied occupation authorities often asked church leaders to take jobs in local government. Subsequently, many of them became influential in party circles, especially in the CDU. The activities of Roman Catholic groups and organizations are usually to be found on the side of the CDU. From their point of view, the SPD is suspect, because in its origins it was Marxist, materialist, and godless. The FDP, because of its secular attitude, was not much better. Some CDU supporters have been unhappy about Catholic activity on behalf of the CDU, fearing that the CDU would become solely a Catholic party. Moreover, many liberals in the CDU pointed out that the SPD had changed its outlook considerably and that Christians should be able to find a home in the SPD.

Among the Protestant churches there is less evidence of political partisanship. Many Protestants were attracted by the efforts of the CDU to unite Catholics and Protestants in a common political effort. On the other hand, many Protestants were attracted by the SPD because it seemed to promise the realization of the Christian social gospel.

There is no established church in Germany, but there has never been any formal separation of church and state either. Consequently, the state collects taxes and pays clergymen and church educators. In theory, each baptized German belongs to some church, and unless he makes an official declaration that he has left it, he is taxed for its support.

Labor is active primarily through the German Federation of Trade Unions, which has a membership of approximately 6.5 million. About one-third of the German workers are organized, as opposed to one-half in Great Britain. Most trade union officials (certainly a large majority), are card-carrying Social Democrats. In the immediate postwar years, labor union sympathy for the SPD was open. Since 1957, however, a formal neutrality in politics is the rule. While the preponderant majority of labor votes is cast for the SPD, labor demands generally are made in nonpolitical terms. German trade unions are owners or part owners of a number of businesses, including banks,

---

[5] For a brief discussion of interest groups in Germany see Klaus Bölling, *Republic in Suspense* (New York: Frederick A. Praeger, 1964), pp. 126–53; Alfred Grosser, *The Federal Republic of Germany* (New York: Frederick A. Praeger, 1964), pp. 88–104; Uwe Kitzinger, *German Electoral Politics* (London: Oxford University Press, 1960), pp. 222–48; and Walter Stahl, *Politics of Postwar Germany* (New York: Frederick A. Praeger, 1964), pp. 24–32.

cooperatives, breweries, hotels, insurance companies, and publishing houses.

The Federation of German Industry is the most powerful organization in the business field.[6] Nearly 90 per cent of all industrial and commercial firms belong to it. In politics it has been openly pro-CDU. It has been the driving force behind the sponsor's associations, discussed above. It has also engaged in the promotion of certain business leaders for elective office. It has no difficulty in presenting its views to CDU and FDP leaders.

The German Farmers' Association has been the principal spokesman for the farmers. It has generally been favorable to the CDU, but it has often provided a forum for members of other parties to present their views. Because the CDU has polled large majorities in the rural areas, and because the organization has on occasion indicated that it might not go on supporting CDU candidates, the Farmers' Association is listened to by CDU leaders and its demands are carefully considered.

All the major interest groups have been successful in getting men elected to the *Bundestag* who are favorable to them. In the *Bundestag* elected in 1961, for example, the number of CDU deputies known to be favorable to various interests were: farmers, 47; industry and commerce, 32; labor, 29; retail merchants and tradesmen, 20; leading business employees, 9. Among the SPD deputies 47 represented labor, while 9 were friends of business, 5 were leading business employees, 8 represented retail merchants and tradesmen, and only 3 the farmers. In the FDP, industry and commerce elected 18, the farmers elected 12, while leading business employees and retail merchants and tradesmen had 3 and 4 respectively. The workers could count only 2 supporters among the FDP deputies.[7] There were many more deputies in each of the categories, particularly in the CDU and SPD, who leaned toward a particular interest group, although not necessarily openly identified with it.

The techniques and methods which interest groups utilize are varied. First of all, they seem to have attempted to institutionalize their "rights." There has been a strong tradition in Germany of institutions where labor and employers are equally represented, for example, labor courts and employment and social security agencies.

---

[6] For detailed study see Gerard Braunthal, *The Federation of German Industry in Politics* (Ithaca, N.Y.: Cornell University Press, 1965).

[7] The foregoing figures are taken from Stahl, *op. cit.*, p. 29.

After World War II, a concerted effort was made to extend this to policy-making groups and management in industry generally. This program acquired the name "codetermination." Ostensibly, the motive behind the program of having labor share in management, first authorized by legislation in the iron, steel, and coal industries, was to improve labor-employer relations as well as to provide labor with a check on industrialists who might be tempted to finance extremist political groups, as some had done in the case of the Nazis. In 1952, a milder form of codetermination was adopted for the remainder of the economy. Under this law, labor holds one third of the seats on supervisory boards of directors, not to be confused with actual management, while in the case of coal and steel boards labor has one half of the membership. Most observers view codetermination as an important innovation, but they are by no means agreed as to how well labor has done its part or the extent to which the working man has benefited as a result of being represented on boards of directors.

Secondly, since ministerial officials draft legislation, interest groups have tended to go to them more often than to *Bundestag* members or to the ministers. In this respect, their work has been facilitated by the fact that advisory bodies of experts have been set up in a number of ministries. In these advisory bodies are to be found representatives of interest groups, providing a natural point of contact with officials of the ministries. Moreover, at times ministers have been unsure about proposed legislation, and hence have not wanted to take the responsibility of advocating it without knowing what the public reaction would be. Consequently, they have authorized their associates to try out the proposed legislation on the interest groups concerned. In this way, interest groups have often been able to act as a more effective check on the government than the members of parliament.

Thirdly, German interest groups have concentrated on *Bundestag* committees, where the tendency has been to assign members because of their special competence. More often than not, the expert is one who has, or has had, some association with an interest group. Moreover, interest groups have sought to increase the number of *Bundestag* committees, so as to emphasize specialization and in this way assure representation on them by their friends.

Finally, interest groups have sought the paid services of civil servants for periods of time. German law permits civil servants to take leave and return to their posts at a later time. Consequently, interest groups have been able to prevail upon civil servants to take leave of their jobs and to join them in a full-time paid capacity. One does not need much imagination to visualize the value of a qualified civil servant who knows the inside of the regulatory process which happens to affect some interest group.

The political parties, of course, seek to harmonize group interests with party principles. Where this can be done, no serious problem arises. Where this cannot be done, parties seek to play off one interest against another. Sometimes, however, the result is division in party ranks. The most important struggle, however, takes place not when votes are taken in the *Bundestag*, but rather when new proposals are being debated in the ministries and existing measures are being implemented, as well as when legislation is being hammered out in committees.

BIBLIOGRAPHICAL NOTE

Although a comprehensive study of German political parties has not yet appeared in English, Arnold J. Heidenheimer's *Adenauer and the CDU: The Rise of the Leader and the Integration of the Party* (The Hague: Martinus Nijhoff, 1960) constitutes an excellent first step. Two useful works on the SPD are: Douglas A. Chalmers, *The Social Democratic Party of Germany* (New Haven: Yale University Press, 1964), and Richard N. Hunt, *German Social Democracy, 1918–1933* (New Haven: Yale, 1964). Also useful is Klaus Bölling, *Republic in Suspense* (New York: Praeger, 1964). The following books also have useful information on German parties: Herman Finer, *The Major Governments of Modern Europe* (Evanston, Ill.: Row, Peterson & Co., 1960); Edward H. Litchfield (ed.), *Governing Postwar Germany* (Ithaca, N.Y.: Cornell University Press, 1953); Sigmund Neumann (ed.), *Modern Political Parties* (Chicago: University of Chicago Press, 1956); James K. Pollock (ed.), *German Democracy at Work* (Ann Arbor: University of Michigan Press, 1955).

The following works in German are pertinent: Ludwig Bergsträsser, *Geschichte der politischen Parteien in Deutschland* (Munich: Isar Verlag, 1952); Ossip K. Flechtheim, *Die deutschen Parteien seit 1945: Quellen und Auszüge* (Berlin: Carl Heymanns Verlag, 1955); F. A. von der Heydte and Karl Sacherl, *Soziologie der deutschen Parteien* (Munich: Isar Verlag, 1955); Max Gustav Lange, G. Schulz, K. Schulz, et al., *Parteien in der Bundesrepublik: Studien zur Entwicklung der deutschen Parteien bis zur Bundestagswahl 1953* (Stuttgart and Duesseldorf: Ring-Verlag, 1955); Wilhelm Mommsen, *Deutsche Parteiprogramme* (Munich: Isar Verlag, 1960); Rudolf Wildenmann, *Partei und Fraktion* (Meisenheim: Anton Hain, 1955).

For studies of interest groups, see the following: Gerard Braunthal, *The Federation of German Industry in Politics* (Ithaca, N.Y.: Cornell University

Press, 1965); Rupert Breitling, *Die Verbände in der Bundespolitik: Ihre Arten und ihre Wirkungsweise* (Meisenheim: Anton Hain, 1955); Karl Deutsch and Lewis Edinger, *Germany Rejoins the Powers: Mass Opinion, Interest Groups and Elites in Contemporary German Foreign Policy* (Stanford, Cal.: Stanford University Press, 1959); Theodor Eschenburg, *Herrschaft der Verbände?* (Stuttgart: Curt E. Schwab, 1956); and J. H. Kaiser, *Die Representation organisierter Interessen* (Berlin: Duncker und Humblot, 1956).

CHAPTER 21

NATIONAL ADMINISTRATION AND LOCAL GOVERNMENT

AS IN Britain and France, administration in Germany plays a more important role than in the past. By virtue of increasing government activity in the economic and social fields, the administration becomes more vast and complicated. The German constitution even refers to the nation as a "social-welfare state." But administration has always played a significant role in Germany. Prussia perhaps led other nations in the establishment of a systematically organized professional civil service as we know it today. It was one of the twin pillars on which the state rested. The other was the army. On the other hand, administration in Germany is somewhat different from that of Britain and France by virtue of the fact that Germany is organized on the federal principle, with some significant governmental powers being vested in the *Länder*.

MINISTERS AND ADMINISTRATION

As in Britain and France, administration in Germany has as its basic task the carrying out of legislative and ministerial decisions. But there are at least three important differences. The first of these is the dominant position of the chancellor. Other ministers are responsible to him alone; they are not responsible to the *Bundestag*. In other words, ministers need to be concerned much more about how they stand with the party leadership than how they are regarded by the deputies in the *Bundestag*. Because ministers are shielded from political contacts in Parliament, they tend to surround themselves more with bureaucrats than is true of ministers in England or even in France, although the Germans do not have "ministerial cabinets" as do the French ministers.

Secondly, because they are not responsible to Parliament, German ministers have tended to shift certain tasks to civil servants which in Britain and France would be their normal responsibility. Ministers sometime send bureaucrats to address the *Bundestag* in their place, and they often ask them to participate in committee deliberations. Moreover, ministers sometimes send ministerial officials to the *Bundestag* during question time. And at other times they have them sign unpopular orders. This deliberately fostered confusion tends to create a situation where there is no clear distinction between the responsibility of ministers and civil servants. Consequently, the average German does not have a clear picture of the minister being responsible. Because of the minister's failure to consider himself accountable, the public has at times centered its fire on the civil servants. At the same time, this confused situation makes it more difficult to assess the true power of the bureaucracy in German politics.

Thirdly, German ministries have little administrative machinery of their own. For the most part, the actual execution of the laws is performed by the *Länder* governments. The constitution states that the *Länder* "execute the federal laws as matters of their own concern insofar as this Basic Law does not otherwise provide or permit." Even where state and national government ministries exist side by side, the national ones are chiefly concerned with drafting uniform legislation and in seeing that the administration by the *Länder* is in conformity with the statutes and the constitution. National ministry offices are usually small and compact, with most ministries having supervisory offices in all the major cities. The bulk of detailed administrative activity takes place in the counties and municipalities, under the direction of the governments of the *Länder*.

It is of interest to emphasize, in this connection, that *Bundesrat* members serve in both a legislative and an executive capacity. They participate in the passage of legislation, but as officials in their respective *Länder*, they are engaged in the administration of legislation passed by the national government. And they are intimately connected with the administration of legislation passed by the parliaments of the *Länder*, chiefly in overseeing its implementation at the local level.

German ministries are staffed entirely by permanent civil servants. Ministers are, of course, political appointees, and each minister usually appoints one undersecretary, known as state secretary, although some departments have two.[1] The state secretary is the equivalent of the British permanent head of the department. Although he is usually promoted from the ranks of the higher civil service, the law permits the chancellor to appoint a few without any restrictions.

---

[1] The German term *Staatssekretär* (state secretary) is also used to denote the highest rank in the civil service.

THE CIVIL SERVICE

As indicated earlier, the Germans were the first modern nation to set up a civil service as we know it, even though it was subservient to the monarchy. It early earned the reputation of being competent, incorruptible, and objective. Since recruitment was based on expert training and knowledge, and since higher education remained largely a class affair, selection to the higher civil service was restricted to the sons of the upper classes. Moreover, an expression of democratic or liberal convictions on the part of civil servants was sufficient to endanger their positions. Consequently, the civil service tended to develop into a caste system.

During Weimar an attempt was made to liberalize recruitment to the civil service, with some decline in quality as a result. In the Nazi period, civil servants whose loyalty to the new order was in question were removed. Recruitment was also carefully controlled. The net result of the Nazi period was also a decline in quality. At the end of World War II, there was an attempt to denazify the service and to rebuild it. After the somewhat uncertain period of the first postwar years, the general quality and competence of the service has steadily improved.

The present status of the civil service is regulated by the Federal Civil Service Act (1961).[2] This law sets up three classes in the civil service. These are: the *higher* service, the *intermediate* service, and the *ordinary* service. In order to qualify for the higher service, a person must have a university education and have passed the initial examination, which is followed by three years' experience in the service and the passing of a second examination. The intermediate service requires a secondary education (or its equivalent), plus three years' in the service and the passing of the intermediate service examination. The ordinary service requires elementary school or its equivalent and an apprenticeship period.

Aside from defense, railways, and the post office, the national government employs some 100,000 persons. Of these more than 8,000 are in the higher civil service. They occupy the top positions in each department and include the chief secretaries, bureau chiefs (equivalent of), and their immediate staffs. The higher service is

---

[2] For partial text see Lane and Pollock, *Source Materials on the Government and Politics of Germany*, pp. 114–16.

roughly comparable to the administrative class in Great Britain.

As suggested earlier, the administration of most national legislation is by the *Länder*. Defense, the post office, the national railroads, and the frontier and customs authorities are the only real exceptions. It is no surprise, therefore, to find that *Länder* civil servants are at least five times as numerous as national ones. The national government has ample power to supervise and to direct the *Länder* governments in the carrying out of its laws, but in the light of the cooperativeness of *Länder* administrators, difficulties are rare indeed.

The constitution specifically states that every German "shall have equal access to any public office in accordance with his suitability, ability, and professional achievements." One result is that the social composition of the service has changed. It is now more representative of the population as a whole. Allied efforts to get the Germans to deemphasize legal background as a requisite for the civil service, however, were only partially successful. Ultimately, economics and political science were added to law as approved areas of study, but not without a struggle.

Moreover, the Germans have a national school of administration for the specialized training of civil servants, in addition to at least one local school (Hamburg). The school was initially set up by the French at Speyer in what was their occupation zone. The school now serves the whole of the Federal Republic and its costs are borne by the national government and the governments of the *Länder*. Young candidates for the civil service spend three or four months there, usually between their initial and second examinations. They spend their time studying history, political science, economics, and the principles of public administration. In addition, they have an opportunity to visit governmental institutions at work and to associate with colleagues from all parts of the country.

In order to regulate conditions of service and appointment, there is the Federal Personnel Committee, whose members are chosen from different branches of administration as well as from nominees from the trade unions, including the civil servants union. Working closely with the Personnel Committee are the personnel committees of the *Länder*. Grievances are handled by councils set up for such purposes. Civil servants may belong to trade unions, but there is no right to strike.

The civil service law requires bureaucrats to be the servants of the people and not of any political party, and that they carry out their tasks impartially. They are subject to the law and must support the democratic order. Their conduct is supposed to be exemplary; they are expected to so order their lives as to bring respect and trust to their profession. By and large, they live up to these demands. Graft, bribery, or other types of improper conduct are rare, both in the national bureaucracy and in local administration.

The nonpolitical tradition of the past has not, however, been preserved. A civil servant may enter national politics freely without resigning his office. If successful, he simply retires on a pension while serving in the *Bundestag*. When he ceases being a member, he may apply for reinstatement in the service. Moreover, there is nothing to prevent a civil servant from actively participating in politics on the *Länder* or on the local level. In most cases, however, if he is elected to a state assembly, he is given leave of absence or retired, but with the right of reinstatement. Because of this right, and hence the very real possibility of going back, civil servants tend to continue their official associations.

Germany was the first among modern nations to accept responsibility for the wrongful acts of her officials while performing their official duties. Part of the reason may have been due to the fact that state ownership of various enterprises was embarked upon early by Prussia. In any case, the present constitution acknowledges their responsibility, and special administrative courts, similar to those in France, exist to take care of cases arising under these circumstances.

A number of observers have criticized the German civil service for being unimaginative, authoritarian, and slavish to routine. Speaking of the higher civil service, Professor Finer has written that they are "more useful in a static than a dynamic state; excellent interpreters of the past but not inventors of the ways and means of the future; apter to explain than evaluate; and inflexible in the power to make exceptions. . . . Forms predominated over purpose; command over the substance of commands; discipline over free creation; routine over local and personal invention."[3] Although passed in 1932, this judgment, in the opinion of Professor Finer, is still valid.[4] He admits, however, that while the civil service is still rather authoritarian, its education has been slightly liberalized, and that the mass of civil servants "is willing to serve faithfully the political chiefs of whatever party . . ."[5]

[3] Herman Finer, *Theory and Practice of Modern Government* (London, 1932), vol. II, p. 1270.

[4] Herman Finer, *The Major Governments of Modern Europe* (Evanston, Ill.: Harper, 1960), pp. 523–24.

[5] *Ibid.*, pp. 527–28.

STATE AND LOCAL GOVERNMENT

As suggested earlier, the *Länder* and the national government exercise certain concurrent powers. Residuary powers rest with the former. Of the powers left entirely to the *Länder*, education is the most important, although cultural affairs are not unimportant. Also, the *Länder* have a significant voice in drawing up their budgets and levying the taxes from which their revenue comes. At the local level, in the cities and counties, the situation is similar to that in the United States, where local governments are creatures of the state, having such authority as the states vest in them. One difference is that the German constitution recognizes certain areas of local authority which it would be difficult for the *Länder* to deny them.

Government in the *Länder* is patterned after that on the national level. There are responsible parliamentary governments, each with a minister-president, who is comparable to the chancellor, presiding over a cabinet of ministers. But there are differences, most of them in terminology. Except for Bavaria, each of the states has a unicameral assembly called the *Landtag*. The counterpart of the cabinet is called the senate. In Bremen and Hamburg, however, the terms for both the assembly and the minister-president are different.

The cabinets in the *Länder* operate in much the same way as the one on the national level. They are smaller, however, and often the same person holds more than one portfolio. Moreover, in two thirds of the *Länder*, the "constructive vote of no-confidence" has been introduced,[6] and in the remaining ones a similar practice makes for executive stability. Similarly, in most of the *Länder* the minister-president appoints and dismisses the ministers, subject to the subsequent approval of the *Landtag*.[7] As in the case of the national government, legislative activities are in the main carried out through committees.

Most observers concede that the state governments have made an enviable record. They handled the difficult problems of administration in the postwar reconstruction period before there was any national government. Moreover, there has been much more interparty cooperation at the state level, with less bitterness and a greater inclination toward compromise, than at the national level. There has been more of a sense of common purpose at the state level, and activities in state assemblies have been more lively and less formal

---

[6] Richard Hiscocks, *Democracy in Western Germany* (New York: Oxford University Press, 1957), p. 155.

[7] *Ibid.*, p. 156.

than those at Bonn. There is little doubt that the *Länder* have provided excellent training for self-government in Germany; a number of *Bundestag* members served in a *Landtag* before coming to Bonn.

One astute observer has given three main reasons for the general success of governments in the *Länder*. First of all, the political leaders in the *Länder* gained their experience at a time of great emergency, when only men of ability, courage and character could succeed and could rise above petty political considerations. Secondly, the major issues of policy that divide people sharply (foreign policy, rearmament, etc.) are not the concern of leaders at the state level, hence they do not impede cooperation. Finally, the caliber of leaders at the state level has been every bit as high as that of the men in national politics, and higher if they are to be judged in terms of the type of problem they have been forced to deal with.[8]

One unfortunate development has been the tendency of national leaders (government and opposition) to intervene actively in *Länder* elections. Because the *Bundesrat* plays a role in the determination of national policy, and because its deputies are officials of the *Länder*, national party leaders have sought to influence local elections as a way of getting friendly supporters in the *Bundesrat*. This has meant that often local elections have been fought out on questions of concern to the national government, with questions of local interest getting very little attention. Moreover, the Adenauer government sought to foster coalitions in the governments of the *Länder*, often in an attempt to prevent the largest party, the Social Democrats, from being a part of the governing coalition. Given the structure of the national government, perhaps this interference is unavoidable. And perhaps it is not all bad, for it has tended to increase the importance of the *Länder* in the federal system and it has made local people more aware of national issues.

BIBLIOGRAPHICAL NOTE

The following are useful on various aspects of German administration: Gordon Craig, *From Bismarck to Adenauer: Aspects of German Statecraft* (Baltimore: Johns Hopkins Press, 1958); Herbert Jacob, *German Administration Since Bismarck* (New Haven: Yale University Press, 1963); Edward L. Pinney, *Federalism, Bureaucracy, and Party Politics in Western Germany* (Chapel Hill: University of North Carolina Press, 1963); Roger H. Wells, *The States in West German Federalism: A Study in Federal-State Relations,*

---

[8] Hiscocks, *ibid.*, p. 161.

1949–1960 (New York: Bookman Associates, 1961). Also useful is Richard Hiscocks, *Democracy in Western Germany* (New York: Oxford University Press, 1957).

The following two German works by Theodor Eschenburg are good contributions to the study of administration: *Der Beamte in Partei und Parlament* (Frankfurt am Main: Alfred Metzner, 1952); and *Bemerkungen zur deutschen Burokratie* (Mannheim, 1955).

CHAPTER 22

LAW AND THE COURTS

THE German judicial system, as are those in other continental countries, is similar to the French pattern. The law is code law instead of case law, although precedent has become increasingly important in Germany. Moreover, the judiciary is identified with the state more than in Great Britain or the United States. This is largely a matter of emphasis, for courts everywhere are in a sense instruments of the state. In Great Britain and the United States, however, they are viewed as protectors of the individual, both from private and governmental actions. In Germany and in other continental countries, on the other hand, they are viewed as dispensers of justice, seeing to it that justice is done from the point of view of society at large, with less concern for the individual person. Finally, court procedure under the Roman law system, as already discussed under France, differs from the Anglo-American pattern.

THE COURT SYSTEM

Although Germany did not become a democratic state until after World War I, the German courts gained considerable independence as early as the first quarter of the 19th century. The Prussian constitution of 1850 had even proclaimed the rule of law principle, including the idea that courts were free of executive influence. As in the case of the higher civil service, judicial positions were open only to university graduates (law), a qualification that only the sons of the wealthy could hope to meet. This meant that judges were drawn from the conservative strata of society. It is therefore not surprising that most German judges developed a conservative political orientation, which became particularly evident in the Weimar and Nazi periods, when they did not seem to grasp the nature of the Nazi movement.

Despite its federal structure, Germany has a single integrated system of regular courts. There are state and local courts and there is a federal appeals court, but all are regulated by national codes, both as to procedure and the bulk of the substantive law which they apply. Moreover, all legal judgments and instruments are valid throughout the nation. In short, the law does not vary from state to state, as is so often the case in the United States. There are district courts, of course, and these will be treated in a subsequent section.

At the bottom of the court hierarchy are the local courts (*Amtsgerichte*), presided over by a single judge. In the smaller places he hears all types of small civil suits and minor criminal actions. In larger towns, the court may have several sections, or categories of cases, each presided over by a single judge. In both instances, the judge is joined by two lay assessors, and in the case of certain criminal cases, a second judge is added. The assessors are chosen by lot from lists of local inhabitants. An American-type jury is not used.

Standing above the district courts are the county courts (*Landgerichte*), serving both as courts of original jurisdiction and as courts of appeal. They are divided into sections, or chambers, some concerned with appeals and others with original jurisdiction. On the civil side there is usually a section that hears appeals cases and another section which hears original cases over which district courts have no competence. On the criminal side there are two appeals sections (little chamber and big chamber) and two original jurisdiction sections. One of the latter is also called the big chamber and the other the assize court, which tries the more grave criminal cases, such as murder.

All sections of the county court have three judges, except the little chamber which has one judge and two lay assessors. The judges in the big chambers are also assisted by two lay assessors. The assize court, however, has six jurymen who vote *jointly* with the three judges. A majority is always decisive, but there is reason to believe that the learned judges exercise preponderant influence.

The superior courts (*Oberlandesgerichte*) have two sections, civil and criminal. The civil section, staffed by three judges, reviews judgments of county courts and may alter them. The criminal section has a little and a big chamber, the former having three judges and the latter five. These decide points of law; they do not try cases but may order retrial in a lower court.

Decisions of the superior courts may be appealed to the federal appeals court (*Bundesgerichtshof*), which has approximately 80 judges. It is divided into sections of five judges each, some dealing with civil matters and others with criminal. The federal appeals court must review all cases submitted to it. Consequently, most of its work is concerned with appeals, and hence its major function is to ensure uniformity of legal interpretation among the courts of the *Länder*. Because some crimes are exclusively national, however, there is a criminal section which has original jurisdiction over them.

As in France, the German judiciary is under the supervision of the Ministry of Justice. Judges are recruited from law school graduates who seek a judicial career. They must first spend some three to four years in probationary and preparatory service, following which they must satisfactorily pass a final examination. Appointments are made by the minister of justice, who is assisted by nominating committees at both the national and state level. The nominating committees are selected by the respective legislatures. Promotion is through seniority and merit, handled by the minister of justice and a committee of judges.

Judges are independent, but they must not violate the principles of the constitution. They hold their positions during good behavior, and may only be removed by their fellow judges through procedures regulated by law.

Judicial procedure in Germany is much like that in France, with the judge dominating the proceedings. It is his job to ascertain the truth, and to this end he admits or excludes evidence. As in France, the rules of evidence are relatively flexible. And again as in France, there are pretrial investigations, with the accused seldom released on bail, although pretrial detention is reviewed periodically. In case of acquittal, however, the defendant may seek indemnification for his detention prior to the trial. It is interesting to note that the Germans have abolished the death penalty as a form of punishment.

Not unlike France, justice is relatively cheap in Germany. Lawyers' fees are usually fixed and appeals costs are often geared to the minimum money value of the case. Those who cannot afford trial costs are provided court-appointed legal talent which is paid for by the state. In general, justice in Germany is not only inexpensive but also accessible, fair, and not too cumbersome.

SPECIAL COURTS

There are several special courts in Germany, the most important of which are the administrative courts. Other special courts deal with labor relations, commercial disputes, tax disputes, and social security cases. Moreover, there are special disciplinary courts for actions entered against officials of the *Länder,* and the legal framework exists for the establishment of national disciplinary courts to hear proceedings against officials of the national government.

As in France, the government accepts liability for the wrongful acts of its officials while performing their official duties. Unlike in France, however, claims against individual officials, as well as salary and other pecuniary claims of civil servants, go to the ordinary courts. But, judgments are handed down against the state and not against the offending officials. The bulk of claims against public authorities, as well as conflicts between them, are, however, heard in separate administrative tribunals which have been set up for this purpose. There are administrative courts in the *Länder* and there is a supreme administrative court at the national level.

Where the jurisdiction of the Constitutional Court is involved, decisions of administrative courts may be appealed to it.

THE CONSTITUTIONAL COURT

Although Germany did not have a history of judicial review, American insistence upon it was readily accepted and a Federal Constitutional Court was established. Experience over the past fifteen years indicates that the Germans have taken to it quite readily. There is general acceptance of the Federal Constitutional Court. Moreover, the Germans established constitutional courts within the *Länder*, where review of state legislation is extensive.

The Federal Constitutional Court consists of two panels of eight judges each. One half of the members are elected by the *Bundesrat* and the other half by the *Bundestag*. Their choice is limited by several considerations. The judges must be 40 years of age and they must be qualified for judicial office in that they must have law degrees. Moreover, each panel must have three judges who are selected from the higher federal courts, and they serve for life. All other judges serve for eight years, but may be re-elected. Aside from these limitations, the *Bundestag* is required to choose its share indirectly through a special 12-member committee, which it elects by a proportional representation method. Selection of a judge requires eight votes in the committee. The *Bundesrat* elects its share of judges by a two-thirds vote of its membership.[1]

The jurisdiction of the Constitutional Court extends to several areas. First, it is its job to interpret the constitution "in the event of

---

[1] For a text of the Federal Constitutional Court Act see Lane and Pollock, *op. cit.*, pp. 94–110.

disputes concerning the extent of the rights and duties of a supreme federal organ or of other parties concerned who have been endowed with independent rights." Secondly, it decides in cases of differences of opinion as to "the rights and duties of the Federation and the *Länder*, particularly in the execution of federal law by the *Länder* and in the exercise of federal supervision." Thirdly, it resolves disputes of public law between the Federation and the *Länder* and between different *Länder*, or within a state, unless recourse to another court exists. Finally, and most importantly, the court is empowered to pass on differences of opinion or doubts on the formal and material compatibility of federal law or state law with the constitution, or on the compatibility of state law with other federal law.

In order for the court to exercise the last indicated jurisdiction, however, there must be a formal motion filed by the national government, a state government or one third of the members of the *Bundestag*, or by a court before which a law has been challenged as being in conflict with the constitution. Allegations that state legislation violates the state constitution are settled by state constitutional courts.

Moreover, as we have seen in a previous chapter, the Constitutional Court is empowered to pass on petitions by the cabinet or the *Bundestag* that a political party be banned because it seeks to overthrow the established democratic order.

The Constitutional Court has made a number of interesting decisions. As indicated earlier, it banned a neo-Nazi party and the Communist party, and it ruled unconstitutional a law that permitted certain tax exemptions to businesses contributing money to the sponsor's associations that were aiding the Christian Democratic Union and the Free Democratic party. In addition, it declared null and void a provision of the income tax law which would have forced married couples to file a joint return and thereby would have given a tax advantage to persons living together out of wedlock. Moreover, the court held that a person cannot be punished for membership in, and service to, a banned political party at a time when that party was not prohibited. In 1965, the court declared unconstitutional a law which authorized professional organizations to assess fines and to take away or suspend the professional rights of members, because of violations of ethics or standards. It did not say that professional courts could not sit in judgment of members, but it did rule that their actions must be under the supervision and ultimate authority of the public system of justice, including review of their decisions by the regular courts. There is general acceptance of the principle that all must abide by the judgments of the Constitutional Court.

CIVIL RIGHTS

Cognizant of what happened to their basic rights under Weimar, the Germans were anxious to provide all possible legal safeguards so as to avoid such dangers in the future. The first chapter of the constitution, consisting of 19 articles, deals with the people's rights in detailed fashion. At the outset, the constitution declares that the "dignity of man is inviolable" and that it is "the duty of all state authority" to "respect and protect it." The enumerated basic rights are said to be "binding on the legislature, on the administration, and on the judiciary."

Aware of how the rights of free speech, free press, and free assembly, guaranteed by Weimar, were abused by both the Nazis and the Communists to the end that these rights were destroyed, the framers sought to provide a shield against such abuses in the future. Article 9 prohibits associations whose aims and activities are in conflict with criminal laws or are directed against the constitutional order. Article 18 asserts that "whoever abuses freedom of expression of opinion, in particular freedom of the press, freedom of teaching, freedom of assembly, freedom of association, the secrecy of mail, posts and telecommunications, the right of property, or the right of asylum, in order to attack the free democratic basic order, forfeits these basic rights."

Moreover, the constitution (Article 79) asserts that the "basic principles laid down" in the first 20 articles cannot be the subject of constitutional amendment.

Elsewhere, the constitution forbids extraordinary courts, double jeopardy, and retroactive laws. The right of habeas corpus is also preserved. The police may not hold a person longer than until the end of the day following his arrest unless he is charged with a crime. The judge's decision in a habeas corpus proceeding is subject to appeal to higher courts. Also, provision is made against mental and physical ill-treatment of detained persons. And due process and the equal protection of the laws are declared to be part of the constitutional order.

BIBLIOGRAPHICAL NOTE

Published information on the law and the judiciary in present-day Germany is meager and scattered. Some information is to be found in several of the general books on Germany, listed in the bibliographical notes following Chapters 18, 19, and 20. Other information is to be found in the more recent periodical articles.

PART FOUR
THE SOVIET UNION

CHAPTER 23

THE COUNTRY AND ITS PEOPLE

THE USSR (Union of Soviet Socialist Republics), no less than other nations, is conditioned by the past, by her geography, by her people, and by her political and social heritage. While a detailed examination of that past is beyond the scope of this book, the author believes that even a cursory survey of the past will contribute to an understanding of the country and its political system. In this chapter we shall be concerned with presenting a few basic facts about the land and the people, and in the second we shall undertake a discussion of the historical development of Russia's political institutions. In this way, the Communist effort to impose a revolutionary system on the country can be viewed in the appropriate context, and the modifications in that system can be seen, in part at least, as the result of a need to compromise with social forces which have their roots in the past.

THE LAND

AREA

The present territories of the Soviet Union constitute about one sixth of the inhabited land surface of the world, or about 8.5 million square miles. This represents an area as large as the United States, Canada, and Mexico combined. It stretches from the Baltic Sea to the Pacific Ocean and from the Arctic to the frontiers of Iran, Afghanistan, and China. Much of the area was acquired in a rapid expansion to the Pacific. The Russians' march eastward across Siberia was as rapid as America's westward march to the other side of the Pacific.

The country is divided into 15 republics. By far the largest is the Russian Soviet Federated Socialist Republic (RSFSR), accounting for approximately three fourths of the nation's total area and over one half of its population. It stretches from the Baltic to the Bering Sea. The Ukraine, while territorially small, accounts for about one fifth of the country's total population. Among the remaining republics, Belorussia has over 8 million people, Uzbekistan and Kazakhistan

335

have over 10 million each, and Georgia and Azerbaijan have over 4 million each.

GEOGRAPHIC POSITION AND CLIMATE

Nearly all of the area of the Soviet Union is north of the 50th parallel (that is, north of the United States), although the most southerly parts reach below the 40th. For all its continental nature, it is largely landlocked, except for the Arctic. It has the longest and perhaps the most useless coastline. All seas and rivers are frozen part of the year. The great rivers flow to "locked seas." The only ice-free port, prior to the acquisition of Königsberg, Memel, and Liepāja (Lepaya), was Murmansk. Vladivostok is kept open year round with icebreakers.

For the most part, the Soviet Union has a cold climate, which is to be attributed more to its continental position, away from the moderating effect of oceans, than to its northerly latitude. There are extremes, nevertheless, ranging from the frigid Arctic to the intense heat found in the deserts of Central Asia, with some areas having moderate to semitropical climates. Generally speaking, however, large areas of the country are unsuited for agriculture, and the amount of new land that can be opened up is limited. Summers are brief: frosts occur late in the spring and early in the autumn. Conditions for the planting of winter wheat or rye are not favorable, due to the intense cold and the poor snow cover. Moreover, the quality of many of the soils is poor, and irrigation possibilities are limited. Because of variations and unreliability in rainfall, even the more favored regions experience great difficulties.

PHYSICAL GEOGRAPHY

One of the most striking geographical facts about the USSR is the immense Russian Plain. Across this plain flow a number of great rivers which have been, and to this day remain, important avenues of transport, commerce, and conquest. The low watersheds and short portages between the rivers have made it possible to connect them with canals. There are more than 180,000 miles of navigable rivers, although winter freezing prevents year-round use. The Volga is the most important single river, carrying half the country's total river freight. It drops less than 1,000 feet in some 2,300 miles. The great rivers of Siberia are of considerably less value, since they flow north into the frozen Arctic. Mountains in the Soviet Union are for the most part to be found along the periphery. The Urals, a low, eroded chain, are the one exception.

The importance of the rivers as arteries of commerce ought not, however, to be overemphasized, for the railroads still carry the bulk of the freight traffic (80 per cent in 1960). Moreover, it should be pointed out that Russia's continental vastness means that there are many empty spaces in the Soviet Union, which, in turn, suggest that much fuel is consumed in the transportation of goods.

From the Arctic southward, there are five zones, each with a characteristic soil and vegetation. The tundra of the far north, with the subsoil perpetually frozen, does not provide much vegetation or opportunities for its development. Gradually, it merges into the forest zone, covering nearly half of the total area of the Soviet Union. It is the largest forested area in the world and contains a mixture of trees. South of the forest zone is the famous steppe region of Russia, extending from the western boundaries all the way to the Altai Mountains in the east, an area that is on the whole rich but often lacking ample rainfall. The semidesert and desert zone lies partly in southeast European Russia and in areas of central Asia. The smallest, as well as the most southern, of the five main zones is the subtropical. It covers some 190,000 square miles along the Black Sea coast, the Caspian Sea coast, the Crimea, southern Transcaucasia, and the mountains of central Asia. Vegetation in the seacoast areas is extremely thick because of the humus soil and heavy rainfall. Central Asia, with its mild winters and hot summers, has sometimes been referred to as the "Imperial Valley" of the USSR.

NATURAL RESOURCES

In natural resources, the Soviet Union is perhaps the richest nation in the world. She has all of the raw materials necessary to contemporary civilization, although there is reason to believe she does not have all that she needs of each. These resources are scattered widely, although some areas seem particularly well endowed. The Ural Mountain range has a variety of minerals; the Ukraine has coal and iron ore; the mountains of central Asia and the Far East have many of the rare metals, including uranium; the Caucasus have an abundance of oil. The supplies of timber are large, although for the most part considerably removed from the principal population centers. Similarly, there is a great hydroelectric potential, which is only partially developed. Ironically, European Russia has been deficient in ordinary rock, making the construction of hard surfaced roads a difficult problem. Because so much remains unexplored, it is possible that the Soviet endowment in natural resources may prove richer than present estimates indicate.

THE PEOPLE

The population of the Soviet Union, according to 1965 estimates, is 225,000,000, with most of it concentrated in European Russia, and almost equally divided between rural and urban areas. More than 100 distinct and different ethnic groups are represented in this total, although the number of major groups is considerably smaller. More significant, however, is the fact that over three fourths of the popula-tion is Slavic, making for a greater ethnic unity than is sometimes sup-posed, although this does not mean that political unity necessarily follows.

Numerically, the women predominate in the Soviet Union, making up 55 per cent of the population. This disproportion stems in part from large losses in World War II, but it is perhaps even more attributable to the purges conducted over several decades by the Soviet regime.

THE SLAVS AND OTHER ETHNIC GROUPS

The Russian Slavs[1] are subdivided into three main groups. The most numerous are the Great Russians, who account for more than one half of the total population. The Ukrainians, sometimes called Little Russians, number over 37 million. The White Russians (Belorus-sians), not to be confused with the political "White Russians" (as opposed to the Red), number over 8 million. In addition, there are Slav minorities, chiefly Poles, Czechs, and Bulgarians. Traditionally, most Russian Slavs have been Orthodox Christians, although the Uniate Church, which had a connection with Rome and which for the most part was to be found in the Ukraine, was not insignificant. Protestant sects, however, made little headway in Russia.

The second largest ethnic group in the USSR is the Turkic or Turko-Tartar people, who number around 21 million. Predominantly Moslem, they are in the main the descendants of the Asiatic warriors who were led westward by Genghis Khan and Tamerlane in the

---

[1] The first mention of Slavs seems to have been made in the sixth century A.D. There is no agreement on the root meaning of the word "Slav." In certain West European languages it is synonymous with "Slave." In the languages of the Slavic peoples, however, the word means "praiseworthy" or "choicest."

thirteenth and fourteenth centuries. In this group are to be found the Uzbeks and the Kazaks of central Asia, the Kazan and Crimean Tartars, the Azerbaijanis of the Transcaucasus, the Kirgiz peoples who live in central Asia along the Chinese frontier, and the Yakuts in eastern Siberia.

In the third largest ethnic group are the Transcaucasian peoples, who number some 7 million. Prominent among these are the Georgians and the Armenians, together with smaller but closely related groups. They are of mixed religious affiliation, although preponderantly Christian at the time of the Revolution in 1917.

A fourth and final major ethnic group, the Finno-Ugrian, is linguistically and ethnically related to the Hungarians, the Turks, and the Finns. They number about 5,000,000. These peoples are mostly Estonians, Udmurts, Chuvash, Finns, and Karelians.

In addition to the main divisions already listed, there are about 5 million Jews living in the USSR. Most of these are scattered, although some are concentrated in the special Jewish autonomous region known as Birobidjan. One of the larger national minorities were the Germans; about 1.5 million of them lived on the Volga but were relocated to Siberia during World War II.[2]

PEOPLE AND NATIONAL CHARACTER

It has been popular in some circles to explain the behavior of the Soviet regime, as well as its very existence, in terms of traits to be found in the Russian character.[3] There is no doubt that certain characteristics or traits tend to stand out more in some people than in others. Efforts to relate the collective behavior of peoples who are today gathered together in nations to traits of national character ought not to be minimized. At present, however, the state of knowledge in this area is insufficient to justify firm conclusions.

The Russians have on occasion been depicted as loving, or at least easily accepting, authority.[4] It is true that they have often appeared to put up with a lot. On the other hand, they have at times demonstrated an independence of mind, a boldness of spirit, and outright resistance.

---

[2] Soviet policies toward religion and national minorities will be treated in subsequent chapters.

[3] For example, see Edward Crankshaw, "Russia in Europe: The Conflict of Values," *International Affairs*, Vol. XXII (October, 1946), pp. 501–10; and Dinko Tomasic, *The Impact of Russian Culture on Soviet Communism* (Glencoe, Ill.: The Free Press, 1953). Also see Joseph K. Folsom and Nikander Strelsky, "Russian Values and Character—A Preliminary Exploration," *American Sociological Review*, Vol. IX (June, 1944), pp. 296–307.

[4] See Geoffrey Gorer and John Rickman, *The People of Great Russia: A Psychological Study* (New York: W. W. Norton & Co., 1962).

The more one looks into the matter, the more he becomes convinced of the inevitable complexity and indecisiveness of national character. While certain traits may offer clues to a people's collective behavior, it is impossible to assign such traits any specific or precise weight.

Traits do not originate in something called the national make-up of a people but in the historical experience of those people. Human actions frequently are reactions to conditions of life which reach back into the past. The legacy of history, economic and social dislocations, the flow of new ideas and cataclysmic events such as wars—all play their part in shaping a nation's future, as well as the attitudes of the people toward that future and toward their ultimate destiny.

ISOLATION AND ITS CONSEQUENCES

It has often been pointed out that Russia's geographic vastness, coupled with the building of the Russian state largely in isolation from the West, resulted in a physical and a psychological separation from the influences that in Western Europe served to do away with or at least to modify political autocracy. The influences of the Renaissance, the Reformation, and the Counter-Reformation simply did not penetrate Russia. And Western liberal-democratic ideas of the 17th and 18th centuries did not make any significant inroads until the 19th century, and then in limited and often perverted form. It is noteworthy, as the next chapter will demonstrate, that throughout Russia's long political past no institutions that could limit or channel autocratic power took root. Isolation from the West, however, may have been only one factor, because institutions that might have shared power were created (e.g., Zemsky Sobor, Senate, State Council), but they did not succeed in assuming a role comparable to that of similar institutions in the countries of Western Europe.

BIBLIOGRAPHICAL NOTE

Among the studies which discuss the characteristics of the Russian people, some of the more informative are Raymond A. Bauer, *Nine Soviet Portraits* (New York: Wiley, 1955); Clyde M. Kluckhohn, Raymond A. Bauer, and Alex Inkeles, *The Soviet System: Cultural, Psychological and Social Themes* (Cambridge, Mass.: Harvard University Press, 1956); Sir John Maynard, *Russia in Flux*, edited and abridged by S. Haden Guest, from *Russia in Flux* and *The Russian Peasant and Other Studies* (New York: Macmillan, 1948); Klaus Mehnert, *Soviet Man and His World* (New York: Praeger, 1962); Wright Miller, *Russians as People* (New York: Dutton, 1961); Gerhart Niemeyer, *An Inquiry Into Soviet Mentality* (New York: Praeger, 1956);

and Albert Rhys Williams, *The Russians: The Land, The People, and Why They Fight* (New York: Harcourt, Brace & Co., 1943).

Frederick C. Barghoorn, *Soviet Russian Nationalism* (New York: Oxford University Press, 1956) is a scholarly treatment of nationalism, while *The Nationalities Problem and Soviet Administration*, edited by Rudolf Schlesinger (London: Routledge, 1956) and Nicholas P. Vakar, *Belorussia: The Making of a Nation, A Case Study* (Cambridge, Mass.: Harvard University Press, 1956) deal with particular aspects of the same topic. In *Soviet Opposition to Stalin* (Cambridge, Mass.: Harvard University Press, 1952) George Fischer discusses the problem of national loyalty, especially during the Second World War.

Useful studies of geography and natural resources and their relation to economic development include those of S. S. Balzak, V. G. Vasiutin, and Ia. G. Feigin (eds.), *Economic Geography of the U.S.S.R.* (American edition edited by Chauncey D. Harris, New York: Macmillan, 1949); Abram Bergson (ed.), *Soviet Economic Growth, Conditions and Perspectives* (Evanston, Ill.: Row, Peterson and Company, 1953); and Demitri B. Shimkin, *Minerals: A Key to Soviet Power* (Cambridge, Mass.: Harvard University Press, 1953).

CHAPTER 24

THE DEVELOPMENT
OF POLITICAL
INSTITUTIONS
IN RUSSIA

LONG HISTORY OF POLITICAL AUTOCRACY

RUSSIA as a nation has a long history. From its early beginnings to the Communist Revolution in 1917 is a considerable span of time. But it is not our purpose to review that history. Rather it is to call attention to a few of the more significant stages in Russia's development so as to provide some insight into her political past, and thus facilitate a better understanding of what happened in 1917 and after.

GROWTH OF IMPERIAL RUSSIA

Russia's long pre-Soviet history may, for the sake of convenience, be divided into four periods. The first is the pre-Mongolian period or the time of Kievan Russia, dating from the 9th century to about 1240. The second phase is the era of Tartar rule or the Mongolian period, which lasted nearly 250 years. The third period represents the resurrection of the Russian state, the rule of Ivan IV (the Terrible or the Dreaded) and the "Time of Troubles," an era covering some 130 years. The fourth period represents the rule of the Romanov dynasty (1613 to 1917). This somewhat arbitrary division of Russian history provides a mere chronological framework, although a convenient one, within which Russia's development and expansion can be viewed.

One of the outstanding features of Russia's long history is her growth and expansion into a great empire. This was far from a steady and firm development, for there were many setbacks. Although Russia of the Kiev period was strong enough to maintain and preserve the nation for some 400 years, she was considerably smaller and weaker than the Russia of later epochs. The ruling princes of that period were powerful, but a great deal less so than the later tsars.

The epoch of Tartar rule, and particularly its disruption, was accompanied by the growing predominance of Moscow. With the division of Russia into many principalities during the Mongol period, the princes of the Moscow area gained in power, mainly by obeying the Tartars and through their friendship with church leaders, which resulted in Moscow becoming the spiritual capital of Russia.[1] Gradually, Moscow gained a powerful economic hold over the smaller rival principalities. In 1340, the Khan singled out the Moscow prince as the Great Prince, making other princes subordinate to him. The succession of princes of Moscow, whose power and domain grew in comparison to the other principalities, provided a unifying force once the Tartar yoke was loosened. By the sixteenth century Moscow had become the political capital of Russia.

The unification of Russia in the post-Mongolian period was in no small part the work of Ivan IV, whose official rule dates from 1533 to 1584, although in effect others ruled for him in the early years, since he came to power as a child when Russia was in considerable turmoil due to quarrels among the princes for supreme control. By his determination and utter ruthlessness he became a powerful ruler and succeeded in unifying his country. With his death in 1584, however, Russia entered the "Time of Troubles," a period of strife, palace intrigue, and civil war—a period which also witnessed the attempt of the king of Poland to make himself tsar of Russia. This era came to an end with the election of the first Romanov as tsar in 1613.

The rule of the Romanovs, spanning some 300 years, was the period of Russia's greatest expansion and the era of her rise to a position of power among the nations. But most of Russia's achievements as a nation in this period were associated with a few of her rulers. Clearly predominant is Peter the First (the Great), although the works of Catherine the Second (the Great), and Alexander the Second also stand out. Peter, who ruled between 1682 and 1721, set out to Europeanize Russia within his lifetime. Russia was to be westernized deliberately and expeditiously in order that she might become a powerful nation. He brought Russia to Europe by building a new capital on the swamps where the Neva River flows into the Baltic, which he called St. Petersburg, later to be called Petrograd and now Leningrad. He traveled to France, Holland, Denmark, England, and Austria, and everywhere he went he gathered information and recruited artisans to build industry in Russia.[2] All of Russia's re-

---

[1] Russia had accepted Christianity in the tenth century.

[2] It may be argued that this was an inauspicious beginning, for it set the pattern of state intervention in the development of the economy, which at a later date tended to prevent the development of an energetic and imaginative system of free enterprise.

sources were harnessed to the building of a powerful westernized nation. Even the church, with the creation of the Holy Synod, was brought under state control.

Some 40 years elapsed after Peter's death, characterized by uncertainty, intrigue, and palace revolutions, before Catherine II came to the throne. She is regarded as a follower of Peter in that she sought to carry out his westernization policies. During her reign (1762–96), the Russian empire was enlarged and solidified. The non-Russian nationalities, however, constituted an internal weakness which was to plague Russia's rulers and which the Communists were to exploit at a much later date.

Although the Russian empire continued to grow, it was not until Russia's involvement in the Napoleonic Wars that she acquired the status of a first-rate power. From that time on she was to play a significant role in European affairs.

POLITICAL AUTOCRACY

"The heart and core of the old Russian state was the autocracy, born under the Mongols, cradled in the Muscovite period, and reaching maturity in modern times."[3] This is a succinct and apt depiction of Russia's political past under the tsars, although subsequent sections of this chapter will refer to some challenges to the autocracy and to attempts to modify it.

A few cursory observations about the development of autocracy in Russia may suggest the futility of seeking an easy explanation for its existence. One need but mention such things as the vast and interminable Russian Plain, which at one and the same time presented no barriers to foreign invaders and was conducive to free movement of people away from the center. In such circumstances, it was virtually impossible to maintain a compact homogeneous nation without autocratic authority. Moreover, these factors, together with Russia's geographic vastness, combined to produce a country in large part isolated from the rest of the world. This was especially true during the period of Tartar rule, when "the new Russia of the backwoods (the Moscow area) . . . was thus politically cut off from Europe.[4] And isolation certainly played a part, at a later date, in keeping out moderating influences and liberal ideas which flourished in Europe and which tended to modify the more objectionable aspects of European autocracy.

A noted historian has suggested that "it was not because of any

---

[3] S. R. Tompkins, *Russia Through The Ages* (New York: Prentice-Hall, 1940), p. 1.

[4] Bernard Pares, *A History of Russia* (New York: Knopf, 1926), p. 73.

alleged innate sympathy of the Russian soul to autocracy that the Tsardom of Moscow came into being but out of the stern necessity of organizing a military force sufficient to overthrow the Mongol yoke and then of securing control of a territory vast enough for strategic defense . . . Political freedom was sacrificed for national survival."[5] Another historian has asserted that tsarist autocracy was accepted as a necessary evil, in preference to the autocracy of the Polish nobles or other foreign rulers.[6]

There is some disagreement as to which of the Moscow princes was the first to assume the title of tsar (Caesar), but it is most often associated with Ivan IV (the Terrible or the Dreaded).[7] The beginning of autocratic rule in Russia is often associated with him. It was during his reign that the *Oprichnina*, a forerunner of the modern secret police, was established. It was also during his rule that slavery was introduced and a new nobility created. Ironically enough, it was during his reign that the *Zemsky Sobor* was established, an assembly which during the "Time of Troubles" (1584–1613) gained in power and which in 1598 elected Boris Godunov tsar and in 1613 elected the first Romanov, whose descendants were the ruling family until 1917.[8]

Other tsars who have stood out in Russian history for the most part continued in the traditions of Ivan IV, although their autocratic rule was not always accompanied by the degree of ruthlessness and brutality that is associated with Ivan and Peter I. Moreover, those who are known for their liberalization policies, such as Alexander II, did not accept limitations on their absolute power. Even the weaker tsars did not willingly accept limitations on their autocratic authority.

INFLUENCE OF THE CHURCH

The Russian Orthodox Church, over the years, became the most vocal defender in Russia of tsarist absolutism. Christianity was accepted in the tenth century by the Russian ruler, Vladimir. Since the parent body was the Eastern church, the Russian Church was from the beginning under the nominal control of the Patriarch at Constantinople. In time, the Moscow princes gained influence in the selection

[5] George Vernadsky, *A History of Russia: Kievan Russia* (New Haven: Yale University Press, 1948), Vol. II, p. 17.

[6] Edward Crankshaw, *Russia and the Russians* (New York: Macmillan, 1949), p. 52.

[7] D. S. Mirsky in C. J. Seligman, *Russia: A Social History* (London, 1931), p. 137, and M. T. Florinsky, *Toward An Understanding of The U.S.S.R.* (New York: Macmillan, 1939), p. 7. However, Pares, *op. cit.*, p. 89, and Tompkins, *op. cit.*, p. 110, assert that Ivan III was the first official tsar.

[8] No Sobors were held between 1654 and 1682, and after 1698 no Sobors were ever summoned.

of the Russian Metropolitan, the head of the Russian Church. With the fall of Constantinople to the Turks in 1453, or about the time that the Mongol domination ended in Russia, the Russian Church was completely severed from its Byzantine ties. Thereafter, the church fought for the unity and independence of the Russian Metropolitanate.[9]

With the establishment of the Holy Synod during the reign of Peter I, the church came under state control. The new princes of the church, especially the Ukrainian prelates, not only became subservient but also labored long to produce learned vindications of the new secular authority. "Thus, with the approval of the higher clergy, the Russian theocratic monarchy was transformed into a secular absolutism of the western type."[10]

The fact that most European countries had accepted Christianity from the Western church (Rome) made the West appear hostile to the Russians. This helped to make the Orthodox Church an ally of Russian nationalism. Hostile actions of western countries came to be viewed by the Russian Church as attacks upon "Holy Russia," the true interpreter and defender of Christ.

It was not until the late nineteenth century, however, that a full-blown exposition of the Russian version of the divine right of kings doctrine was produced. Its author was Pobiedonostsev, the former tutor of Alexander III and Procurator-General of the Holy Synod. He defended tsarist autocracy not only in terms of divine origin of his authority, but in addition he argued that Russia could be saved from the corrupting influence of foreign ideas only by a complete autocracy of state and church.

SERFDOM

During the long history of Russian autocracy the most persistent issue was serfdom. Popular concern with political, legal, and other reforms was important, especially in the 19th century, but clearly secondary. The main preoccupation seemed to center on the injustices of serfdom and the crying need for a solution.

It was during the reign of the Romanovs that serfdom became a firm and fixed institution. Land grants which had been made to the service gentry in payment for military service included the peasants

---

[9] Vladimir had from the beginning "made use of the higher clergy as counselors," and "the priests, as the only literate persons, were invaluable for civil purposes; for the keeping of records . . . for embassies and for other public services." See, Pares, *op. cit.*, p. 30. The priests also brought a system of law to Russia.

[10] Mirsky, *op. cit.*, p. 184.

who lived on the land. Many of these, however, made successful escapes to the more remote regions of Russia. In 1646 all squires who owned land were required to register it, together with the names of each of their peasants. These and their future descendants became legally attached to the land. Serfdom became hereditary. A code in 1649 confirmed serfdom as a state institution. By 1675, the sale of serfs apart from the land, although illegal, had become so widespread that it received legal sanction. Moreover, punishment for escape and for aiding fugitives became increasingly harsh.

But serfdom was more than an economic and social problem, with its legacy of economic backwardness, poverty, illiteracy, and human indignity. It was also a political problem in that it engendered attitudes of suspicion and distrust toward political authority and the agents of that authority. Serfdom was but the most notable symbol of Russia's peasant heritage, a heritage with which even the Soviet leaders have had to contend.

Despite a growing awareness of the acute nature of the problem of serfdom, and despite studies ordered by various rulers, no really significant step was taken to deal with it until the reign of Alexander II. What was done from time to time, even under Alexander II, left much more undone. It is a simple unadulterated fact that no tsarist regime found an acceptable solution to the most acute problem of Russian society.

PROTEST AGAINST AUTOCRACY AND SERFDOM

Russian autocracy, along with serfdom, did not go unchallenged indefinitely. Protests took several forms. In the earlier years they consisted chiefly of limited peasant revolts, along with two revolts of major proportions which were led by nonpeasants and which attracted considerable support. In the 19th century the protests were mainly political and literary, although limited peasant uprisings continued to take place.

The first of the major rebellions was led by a type of freebooter, a Don Cossack by the name of Stenka Razin. The rebellion continued for four years (1667–1671), but in the end it was suppressed and Razin was executed. A hundred years later (1773–74) another major rebellion broke out, which for a time gained considerable headway, even threatening St. Petersburg. It, too, was brutally put down and its leader, Emilian Pugachev, executed. For the most part, these were unorganized, spontaneous reactions against the oppressions of serfdom and the government's tax and other policies. Besides drawing support from the peasants, these revolts attracted outlaws and other elements which sought to profit from participating in them.

The first major political protest against tsarist autocracy is most frequently referred to as the Decembrist Revolt.[11] During the Napoleonic wars Russian soldiers had seen something of Europe and absorbed some disturbing ideas. The result of these new ideas was a liberal movement which contributed to the uprising that occurred in December 1825, following the death of Alexander I. It was led by officers of the guard regiments, some of whom had been in France following the defeat of Napoleon, who formed outside the Council of State shouting for "Constantine and Constitution." Constantine was a brother of Alexander's and in line for the throne, except that he had abdicated his right years earlier, although this fact was kept secret. Upon Alexander's death, Constantine proclaimed his younger brother Nicholas as Tsar. Certain regiments refused to take the oath to Nicholas, who thereupon opened his regime with a ruthless suppression of the Decembrists. The Decembrist uprising was not a peasant revolt. It was led by the nobles and a few liberals, loosely organized in secret societies. Although they lacked a coherent political program, they did talk of republicanism and of free speech. And they all agreed that serfdom was a crying injustice.

The intellectual atmosphere which helped make the Decembrist uprising possible was but the beginning of a literary protest against the evils of tsarism, which was to gain momentum during the 19th century, a century which produced Russia's greatest writers. Among these are Pushkin, Lermontov, Gogol, Herzen, Turgenev, Chekhov, Dostoyevsky, and Tolstoy. Most of these became absorbed with contemporary political and philosophical problems, much to the dislike of the ruling group. Censorship and imprisonment awaited those who advocated change. Gradually, however, they acquired boldness and experience, managing to circumvent the censors and to increase their popular following.

Nicholas I had inadvertently contributed to the rise of a generation of revolutionary writers. During his reign, the reorganization of the universities revealed the lack of competent instructors. Promising young intellectuals were encouraged to travel and to study abroad. Many of these went to Germany and upon their return were brimming over with ideas they had acquired from Hegel, Fichte, Schelling, and other philosophers and writers.

---

[11] See A. G. Mazour, *The First Russian Revolution, 1825* (Berkeley, Cal.: University of California Press, 1937).

One result of the nineteenth century Russian intellectual activity was the development of a cleavage between those who saw Russia's future in western ideas and ways of doing things and those who believed in indigenous solutions to Russia's problems. These schools of thought came to be known as Westernizers and the Slavophiles.[12] Following the reforms of Alexander II, this controversy tended to die down. As Alexander's regime moved on, however, a period of reaction set in, in part motivated by the Polish revolt and the various attempts on the tsar's life. The disillusionment with some of his reforms and the recall of Russian students from abroad contributed to the renewed spread of revolutionary doctrines.

The intellectual protest against tsarism and the evils of serfdom was but the forerunner of political activity in its various forms. New ideas and new political doctrines took root and were disseminated. Political organizations were being established, and political programs formulated. These and related questions will be discussed in subsequent pages. Suffice it to say at this point that these developments are but another indication that autocracy was being challenged, and as we now know, the end of its long history was approaching, only to be replaced, after a brief interval, by a far more systematic and ruthless totalitarian tyranny.

STEPS TOWARD REFORM

From what has been said above it should not be assumed that tsarist Russia took no steps toward reform. Although the various reforms in the end proved insufficient, many of them gave considerable promise at the time of their adoption. In a way, many of them can be looked upon as truly great advances, particularly those taken by Alexander II. Unfortunately, however, many of the promising reforms were either nullified by succeeding rulers, or they were not carried forward. Others, although significant, fell short of what Russian conditions demanded.

RUSSIA AT THE OPENING OF THE NINETEENTH CENTURY

Russia at the beginning of the nineteenth century was a country of contrasts, a phenomenon which prevails today. She had attained the position of a first-rate power on the continent and yet she was one of the most backward countries in the world. As the century wore on,

---

[12] Among the former were Alexander Herzen, who was forced into exile, and Michael Bakunin, the first of the Russian anarchists.

however, the weaknesses became predominant. This was to become glaringly evident at the time of the Crimean War and later during the Russo-Japanese War at the outset of the twentieth century.

Economically and socially, Russia was a picture of backwardness at the beginning of the nineteenth century. Although the small gentry class lived relatively well, the serfs were living in poverty and their number was increasing. Moreover, the serfs were virtual outcasts. There was mass illiteracy. Non-Russian nationalities, especially the Jews, were oppressed. Nowhere in the social or economic picture could one point to progress.

Politically, Russia entered the nineteenth century no less backward. There was no semblance of self-government or even a widespread discussion of it. The church and state were united behind the tsar-autocrat. The tradition of absolutism and authority characterized the Russian political scene.

REFORMS UNDER ALEXANDER I AND NICHOLAS I

The first two tsars of the nineteenth century were brothers who ruled for 54 years, which were divided almost equally between them. Steps toward reform during their reign were so few and so lacking in their approach to Russia's basic problems that there is a danger of overemphasizing them.

Alexander I (1801–1825) was primarily interested in foreign affairs, which occupied most of his attention. He seems to have favored the establishment of a constitutional monarchy, but only one of several projected constitutional reforms ever came into effect, and it was only partially realized. A State Council was established in 1810, which possessed only advisory powers. Its existence, therefore, constituted no effective limitation on autocracy.

Nicholas I (1825–1855) is regarded by many historians as the most reactionary among the tsars. He came close to establishing a police state. His Russification program among the non-Russian nationalities was symbolized by the concept of "one flag, one government, one church, one people." He ordered the opening of new schools to prove that the people did not want to go to school. When he was proved wrong, severe limitations were imposed on what was to be taught. Chairs of history and philosophy were considered dangerous. Many writers were placed under house arrest. Moreover, censorship generally became more stringent. His reign could appropriately be described as one long rear guard reaction against new ideas.

Some reforms, however, were inaugurated during the rule of

Nicholas I. The most notable among these was the codification of the laws under the direction of Count Speransky, who had been responsible for the 1810 reforms establishing the State Council. Speransky completed his monumental task of codification of the laws in 1833.

REFORMS OF ALEXANDER II

The most promising steps toward reform were those that were taken by Alexander II. These included the emancipation of the serfs (1861), reorganization of the institution of local government, the *Zemstvo* (1864), the reform of the judiciary (1864), the budget reforms (1862), the reorganization of municipal government (1870), and the introduction of conscription on a nonclass basis (1874). Moreover, at the time of his assassination, he had approved the project of Count M. T. Loris-Melikov for the creation of an advisory council to work with the State Council.

The emancipation of the serfs was hailed as a great and courageous act, which earned for Alexander the title of "Tsar-Liberator." The emancipation, however, was only partial and it was qualified. The state undertook to buy only one half of the land from the squires, which was to be given to the peasants, who would be given 49 years in which to pay for the land. The village assembly, the *Mir*, was given the responsibility of collecting the payments. Until all the payments were made, the peasant could not consider himself an owner of any part of the land. As time progressed, the peasants found the redemption payments an almost unbearable burden. At the same time, it was becoming increasingly evident that the lands originally purchased were proving insufficient for the number of peasants needing land. The liberation had been a great step forward, but other steps had to be taken if the peasant problem was to be dealt with successfully.

The reform of the *Zemstvo* was at least in part the consequence of the emancipation of the peasants. Earlier, the landlords had governed the local community, but now the newly liberated peasants wanted some voice in local affairs. The reorganization of the *Zemstvo* provided that the local government assembly be elected on a nonclass basis. Similarly, prior to the liberation, the land owners had dispensed justice. Under the changed circumstances, this could hardly be continued. Among the reforms in the judiciary was the introduction of juries and lawyers.

Among the other reforms, the requirement that the nobility serve in the army also seemed to recognize the greater equality acquired by the peasant. Some reforms, like the granting of a considerable amount of

self-government to the universities (1863), and making the budget
public for the first time in Russian history, were of a more general
nature.

None of these reforms, be it noted, limited the autocratic powers of
the tsar. They did, however, teach the people something of local self-
government, and they gave them some real hopes for the complete
extinction of serfdom.

It should be noted that Alexander, as well as others who sought
reform, labored under severe handicaps. The nobility was determined
to defend its economic interests. And the peasantry, in whose innate
political virtues the intelligentsia reposed such unjustified confidence,
was something less than capable of assuming its newly-acquired
responsibilities. Moreover, Alexander had to rely on an unenlightened
and often inept bureaucracy to carry out his policies. As a consequence some of his messages "never arrived," and others were "not
understood." In the light of such circumstances, it is perhaps surprising that considerable progress was achieved.

THE REACTION

The assassination of Alexander II doomed the prospects of further
reform, and ushered in a period of reaction. Even the Loris-Melikov
proposal, prepared during his reign as a modest concession to public
opinion, was never promulgated. The new tsar, Alexander III, agreed
with his antireform advisers. Among the most influential of these was
his former tutor, Pobiedonostsev, who was now Procurator-General of
the Holy Synod. Although the official terror was fairly general, it was
most felt in education and the press. The university autonomy, gained
under Alexander II, was revoked. Student clubs were banned. A
number of measures further restricted newspapers and their editors.
A program of intensified Russification was begun. A new set of
officials, called Rural Chiefs, was introduced to direct the work of the
locally elected institutions of government. Extraordinary measures,
ostensibly designed to deal with revolutionary organizations and their
activities, enabled the political police, the *Okhrana*, to exercise far-
reaching oppressive powers.

Economically, however, Russia experienced considerable growth
during the latter half of the nineteenth century. Industrialization
moved along at an increasing rate. Cities and towns grew apace, as did
the number of their inhabitants. The most notable achievement in the
transportation field was the building of the trans-Siberian railway.

BEGINNINGS OF CONSTITUTIONALISM

In 1900, Russia was a stronghold of absolutism. By contrast, in the United States, England, and a number of Western European countries the democratic system was widely accepted. Democratic ideas were spreading elsewhere. Even in Germany and Austria democratic institutions were making some inroads. Autocracy in Russia, too, was soon to experience setbacks.

POLITICAL FERMENT IN THE MAKING

Although political activities among Russian citizens were limited in 1900, a political ferment was in the making. The political movements which could function openly, and which therefore were not regarded as a threat to the government, were few. The most important of these were the *Narodniki* (populists), an intelligentsia-led revolutionary group that sought to enlist the support of the peasantry by "going to the people." Their movement had begun in the early 1870s. Much to their dismay, "the youthful agitators discovered that they could not arouse the people's 'pent-up revolutionary energy'. . . . [some] were stoned out of the villages and turned over to the tsarist police by the indignant peasants. The first waves of the go-to-the-people movement had broken against the wall of popular indifference and police repression. . . ."[13]

These failures tended to turn many of the youthful revolutionaries toward more and more direct action. The result was a split, out of which two rival organizations emerged, the terroristic *Narodnaya Volya* (the people's will) and the anti-terrorist *Chernyi Peredel* (the black partition), a defender of the *Narodniki* tradition. One of the great movers in the latter was George Plekhanov, who was to become one of the leading Russian Marxist theoreticians. By 1900 the *Chernyi Peredel* was a "respectable" organization.

A number of other political organizations were formed in secret and continued to function underground. Among these were the agrarian Social Revolutionaries, whose ideas were a combination of Marxism and the teachings of the Utopian Socialists; the *Kadets* (constitutional democrats), made up primarily of the liberal and moderate intelligentsia which desired the gradual and peaceful displacement of

---

[13] Leopold H. Haimson, *The Russian Marxists and the Origins of Bolshevism* (Cambridge, Mass.: Harvard University Press, 1955), pp. 13–14.

autocracy by a constitutional form of government; and the Social Democrats, who were the Russian exponents of Marxism.[14]

The Russian Marxists emerged from the underground revolutionary ferment in the 1880s. Many of those who had been identified with *Narodnaya Volya* and *Chernyi Peredel* were converted to Marxism. Despite police repression, the Marxian movement continued to grow and to remain active, although underground. The Russian Social Democrats were far from united, as exemplified by their split in 1903 into the Bolshevik and Menshevik wings.

The political ferment which flourished in the years around the turn of the century was given a considerable impetus by the evils stemming from industrialization, which came to Russia at a considerably later date than it did to the Western European nations. When it did come, industrialization came in a rush and brought about evils that have accompanied industrialization elsewhere, except that it produced them more precipitously. Neither society nor the industrial owners were in a position to cope with them, nor did they seem to feel any particular responsibility for doing so, although there was some progress toward efficient and enlightened management prior to the revolution. The growth of industrial enterprises, the rapid increase in the number of industrial workers, the great increase in the population of the cities and towns, together with the evils that are associated with industrialization everywhere—all occurred in Russia at a time when fresh Marxian ideas were attracting a large audience in European countries.

THE REVOLUTION OF 1905

The Revolution of 1905 was triggered by the disastrous consequences of the Russo-Japanese War (1904–05). Previously the protest against autocracy was in the main by individuals and small groups. In 1905, however, the Russian masses were moved to action on a large scale. To the impact of an unsuccessful foreign war were added the consequences of domestic hard times and the constant urgings of revolutionary parties, working in part through the *Zemstvos*.

The *Zemstvos*, the local government assemblies whose work the government had in many ways sought to impede, had gained considerable respect and popularity among the people. Among other things, they had done much in the field of public health and education, and they had organized relief during the famines in 1901–03. In

---

[14] Marxian ideas are discussed in detail in the following chapter.

November, 1904, the first all-Russian Congress of *Zemstvos* met in St. Petersburg. It put forward a number of demands, including the recognition and guaranteeing of civil liberties, the elimination of class and racial discriminations and the establishment of a representative assembly with real legislative powers.

The situation was made more acute by the massacre of several hundreds of peaceful petitioners, led by Father Gapon, who on Sunday, September 22, 1905, moved toward the Winter Palace, carrying portraits of the tsar and singing religious and patriotic songs, to present the grievances of the workers and to ask for the tsar's intervention and help. The immediate result was an increase in tensions, which found expression most frequently in strikes. Disturbances continued throughout the summer, aggravated by the returning soldiers after the formal conclusion of the war at the end of August.

The tsar's promise in June to a joint deputation of the *Zemstvos* and municipal councils that he would call together a national assembly, "as soon as possible," to set up a new regime, in which the public was invited to participate, had not quelled the disorders. When it was announced in August that the projected legislature—the *Duma*— would be elected on the basis of a narrow franchise and that it would have only consultative powers, the growing unrest spread to the Baltic provinces and the Caucasus. The situation continued to deteriorate, culminating in a general strike in October.

CONSTITUTIONAL MONARCHY

In the face of these conditions, Nicholas gave in. Although martial law was the tsar's reply to the revolution, he simultaneously proclaimed a moderate constitution, providing for a national legislature, the *Duma*, which was to be elected on the basis of universal manhood suffrage. It was to have legislative initiative and the right to pass on projects submitted by the tsar.[15] A bill of rights guaranteed the freedoms of speech, assembly, and conscience. A cabinet of ministers was made responsible to the *Duma*. The proclamation embodying these concessions by Nicholas came to be known as the "October Manifesto." Count Witte, who had a considerable hand in convincing the tsar to grant the constitution, was made the first responsible prime minister. Russia, at least in theory, became a constitutional monarchy.

In this new-found freedom, the pre-1905 secret societies blossomed

---

[15] See Serge L. Levitsky, "Legislative Initiative in the Russian Duma," *American Slavic and East European Review*, Vol. XV (October, 1956), pp. 313–24.

forth into political parties. The most active of these were the Social Revolutionaries, the Kadets (Constitutional Democrats), and the Russian Social Democrats, who about this time had split into the Bolshevik and Menshevik wings. All of these parties sponsored an exceptionally active discussion of current political, social, and economic problems. They held meetings, published newspapers and political tracts, and in other ways sought to propagate their programs and points of view.

THE DUMA PERIOD, 1906–1917

Russia's political experience under the constitutional monarchy is not easy to evaluate. The legislative beginnings were not auspicious, partly because of a lack of experience on the part of the participants. More important, however, is the fact that a number of the tsar's acts were clearly in violation of the constitution. In the midst of the uncertainties came World War I, which was to loom so large in the destiny of tsarism and Russia's future.

The first *Duma* convened in 1906, but was dismissed after a brief period of less than three months, most of which time had been spent in conflict with the government. It was dominated by the Kadets, "who devoted their full energy to expounding the indignation and disappointment experienced by the country at large at the inadequate reform and demanding a constitution on the English and the American pattern."[16] It thus earned the name "the *Duma* of the National Indignation." Count Witte was dismissed as prime minister and replaced by Peter Stolypin, who until his assassination in September 1911, ruled the country with an iron hand.

The second, and newly elected, *Duma* was convened in March, 1907. It met a similar fate after an existence of less than four months. Unlike its predecessor, it contained a strong group of Social Democrats, who had boycotted the first elections and who accounted, in part, for its hostile and revolutionary attitude. It achieved nothing in a parliamentary or legislative sense. When the *Duma* refused to consent to the arrest and trial of 16 Social Democratic members, who were charged with conspiracy and sedition, it was dissolved.

A third *Duma* was elected in the same year, but only after the electoral law had been changed, without even consulting the *Duma*, as the constitution provided. The revised electoral law did away with universal manhood suffrage. Some of the non-Russian nationalities

---

[16] Edmund A. Walsh, *The Fall of the Russian Empire* (Boston: Little, Brown, 1928), p. 85.

were disfranchised and severe limitations put on the electoral rights of the peasantry. The whole electoral procedure was involved and complex. Thus by a clever manipulation of the electoral regulations, the Government was able "to manage" the election of a conservative *Duma*, dominated by the propertied classes and the large landholders. It served its full term.

During the period of the third *Duma*, the Government introduced two significant reforms. One was the law calling for a gradual introduction of compulsory education for all children in the primary grades, a clear departure from past policies. The second important law introduced the Stolypin land reforms (1906–10), the completion of which was prevented by the outbreak of the war. Stolypin's aim was to free many peasants from their bondage to the *Mir* and to make of them free farmers. While this policy was attacked as discriminating in the favor of the relatively well-to-do peasants, it was, in fact, designed to create a group of free peasants who would feel that they had a vested interest in the established order so that they would defend it.

The fourth and last *Duma* convened in 1912. Like the third, it was conservative and docile. For a brief period during the war it rose to a position of leadership, simply because its members were appalled by the decay in the government and because they sensed the approaching doom of tsarism.

The period of the *Duma* (1906–17), while representing a significant step toward democratic government, left much to be desired. The tsar, as noted above, was far from being a constitutional monarch, that is, above politics. Not only did he from time to time exercise real political power, but in addition, violated the constitutional rights of the *Duma*. Also, he elevated the State Council, an administrative body, to the position of an upper house. Moreover, administrative officials were often found abusing the emergency powers still on the statute books. More important perhaps is the fact that the *Duma* really never acquired many of the essential powers associated with a true parliamentary legislature. For example, it never gained a really effective control of finance, and its power to call ministers to account, and to vote them out of office if need be, was not recognized in practice.

WORLD WAR I AND THE DISINTEGRATION OF THE OLD ORDER

A noted historian has said that Russia by 1914 was making such progress in the economic, social, and political realms that in another ten years "the possibility of a revolution in Russia would have been very slight."[17] Russian industry, in all its branches, experienced a remarkable and a sustained upsurge in the final decade of the past century and in the pre-1914 years of this one. During the same period no other nation approached Russia's economic growth rate. While workers were limited in what they could do to improve their lot, their economic position was nevertheless improving. Westernization and modernization reached also into the countryside. In brief, social and economic change, although creating problems in its wake, was proceeding at a rapid rate. But the promise of this period was cut short as the nation plunged into war in 1914. This is not to suggest, however, that Russia could have stayed out of the war once it came, for vital national interests were at stake.

War and Its Impact

The initial reaction of the people to the declaration of war was favorable and even enthusiastic. The German declaration of war aroused the people to a high sense of unity and dedication in the carrying out of their duties. This lasted for a long time. Moreover, the Russian soldiers, despite tremendous losses and lack of equipment, fought well. It is now generally agreed that the efforts of the Russians saved France from collapse in the west. When news of reverses at the front became known at home, however, particularly news of shortages of military supplies, news of bungling and inefficiency, together with a seemingly general ineptitude, the mood of the people seemed to change.

The attitude of the people was influenced in part by conditions on the home front. There was a feeling that much of the bungling was due to inept administrative personnel, together with the ministers in charge. The influence of Rasputin, a self-appointed "man of God," on the domestic scene is not to be underestimated. His influence was in large part due to the tsarina's belief that Rasputin could cure her son, the heir to the throne, who was suffering from hemophilia. Because he seemingly had certain magic healing powers, the tsarina looked upon him as a man sent by God, and abided by his advice in the political and military realms. Constantly, she urged Nicholas to follow the advice which he was getting from Rasputin. Many Russians noted that the result was the removal of able men who had been appointed in the summer of 1915 by the tsar. After several plots on his life, Rasputin was finally killed in December, 1916.

[17] George Vernadsky, *A History of Russia* (New York 1944), New Home Library Edition, p. 214.

The regime's answer to popular dissatisfaction with the way things were going in the military as well as in the domestic field was to send Nicholas to the front to take personal command of the army. Aside from the fact that Nicholas had no military training, his departure for the front resulted in his being politically isolated. The Bolsheviks, for their part, were spreading defeatist propaganda and making the most of a revolutionary situation.

It was at this time that the *Duma* requested the appointment of a responsible cabinet and the inauguration of much needed reforms. Army commanders, *Zemstvos*, and the general public joined in the *Duma's* request for the appointment of a responsible cabinet. But the tsarist regime seems to have been oblivious to any danger.

COLLAPSE OF TSARISM

The beginning of the collapse of Tsarism came in the form of food riots in the capital in March, 1917. Actually, food was not in short supply, but the distribution was bad and people had to wait long hours in queues to get their rations. Troops of the Petrograd garrison were asked to put down the disorders, but they refused to do so, and in a day or two went over to the side of the rioters. Thus, the Revolution and the collapse of Tsarism came without much bloodshed.

The *Duma* leaders, who were witnessing the collapse of tsarism, finally asked for the tsar's abdication. When asked to do so, he abdicated in favor of his brother, who refused to become tsar unless this position were offered by a constituent assembly. In these circumstances, the *Duma* leaders (liberals and moderate socialists) created a provisional government, and thereby made the Revolution complete.

The *Duma* leaders realized that they did not possess the authority to create a new government, but nevertheless proceeded to do so because they were convinced that the leaders of the Petrograd Soviet of Workers' Deputies, which had come into existence even before the tsar's abdication was announced, would do so. Indeed, the Soviet, whose name was soon changed so as to include soldiers' as well as workers' deputies, lost no time in challenging the provisional government, and in a few months was to become the vehicle for the Bolshevik seizure of power.

THE PROVISIONAL GOVERNMENT

Once established, the provisional government faced two basic decisions. The first had to do with the question of the war, whether to continue it or to make a separate peace with Germany. The second was the question of domestic reform, whether it should be initiated or postponed. The government decided to carry on with the war and to put off reform until a later date. These decisions were to contribute to its downfall. In themselves, they would not have been disastrous if the government had possessed real authority. From the beginning, however, it was to be harassed by the soviets of workers' and soldiers' deputies which were springing up throughout the country.

It was on the home front that things began to deteriorate first. The first decree of the provisional government had, among other things, proclaimed a general amnesty; established freedom of speech and press, the right to strike, the right of universal suffrage; and declared for a summoning of a constituent assembly. These freedoms permitted the socialist parties to begin agitating anew. Many of their leaders who had been imprisoned on various charges in 1915, were released by the provisional government. Since the land problem was not yet solved and since the army was composed mainly of peasants, the demoralizing effect of this socialist propaganda was disastrous. But it must not be forgotten, however, that the offensives of 1917 on the Austrian and Rumanian fronts, although successful in their initial stages, were a serious drain on the resources of the provisional government, and hence contributed to its weakening.

On the same day that the provisional government had issued its first decree, under pressure of the Petrograd Soviet, the latter issued its famous "Order Number 1," which "was the principal agency in the destruction of the Russian army."[18] Under this order, soldiers' committees were to be set up in each military detachment and all weapons were to be under their control and not that of the officers. Moreover, each detachment was to obey the political decisions of the Soviet and only those orders of the military commission of the state *Duma* which did not contradict the orders of the Soviet.[19] Since the collapse of the Russian army came *after* the Revolution, not before, it could be said that the collapse was the result of the Revolution, but that would be an oversimplification, for the Revolution was in part made possible by reverses at the front and the impact of these reverses on the domestic scene.[20]

THE STRUGGLE FOR POWER IN 1917

It is obvious, therefore, that from the first days of the Revolution there were two governments in Petrograd—the provisional government and the Soviet of Workers' and Soldiers' Deputies. The struggle

---

[18] Vernadsky, *op. cit.*, p. 236.

[19] *Ibid.*, pp. 236–37.

[20] See John Shelton Curtiss, *The Russian Revolutions of 1917* (New York: D. Van Nostrand Co., 1957), p. 29ff.

for power between them was to continue from the spring of 1917 until the Bolshevik seizure of power in the fall of 1917. Initially, the Bolsheviks were skeptical of the Soviet. In any case, they were a minority in the soviets of Petrograd and Moscow, as well as elsewhere. Moreover, the Petrograd Soviet was, in their opinion, too friendly toward the provisional government. When it was clear, however, that the soviets were following a course which was increasingly independent of the provisional government, and with Lenin's agitation in favor of a seizure of power, the Bolsheviks began working inside the soviets in pursuit of their aims. After a time, they succeeded in winning a majority of the delegates, first in the Petrograd Soviet and then in the Moscow Soviet. Subsequently, upon Lenin's urgings, the Bolsheviks were instrumental in having the Petrograd and Moscow soviets establish "military revolutionary committees," which were to be instruments for the seizure of power.

In the meanwhile, the First Congress of Soviets was held in June, 1917. At this congress the Bolsheviks and their allies had but a scant fraction of the total number of delegates.[21] The Social Revolutionaries had by far the largest number of delegates, with the Mensheviks next. Despite their lack of strength, the Bolsheviks proposed that the soviets should seize power. This proposal was defeated, mainly by being ignored. Shortly after the congress had adjourned, the Bolsheviks became the leaders of the abortive July insurrection, which resulted in the arrest of many of their prominent leaders. Lenin, however, succeeded in escaping to Finland, from where he attempted to direct the second layer of leaders in their agitation and their work of organizing the workers and soldiers.

Simultaneously, the provisional government resumed the war effort with the launching of the July offensive. Initially a success, the offensive ended in failure. This failure and the growing inflation, plus the Soviet-inspired demands for reform and withdrawal from the war, resulted in increasing difficulties on the home front. More and more workers were becoming Bolshevik followers. The peasants, too, were becoming increasingly restive. At the same time, some of the national minorities were getting restless, partly because of the provisional government's failure to enunciate a nationality policy.

A radical effort to deal with the situation on the home front took place in September. This was the famous Kornilov affair. General Kornilov, the commander-in-chief of the army, was persuaded by his

---

[21] Curtiss, *ibid.*, p. 41, says that the Bolsheviks and their allies had 137 out of 1,090 delegates.

advisers, and by emissaries of Alexander Kerensky, the head of the provisional government, to bring a detachment of troops to Petrograd, in order to put an end to the inimical activities of the Soviet. His mission, however, was subsequently viewed by Kerensky as an attempt to seize power. Thereupon, Kerensky appointed himself as Supreme Commander and sought to dismiss Kornilov, who refused to be dismissed and marched on Petrograd. Kerensky appealed to the Soviet for help. Spurred on by the Bolsheviks, who otherwise detested the provisional government, the Soviet responded to Kerensky's call to fight a common battle against Kornilov. The net result was Kornilov's defeat and arrest, as well as a strengthening of the Soviet in its struggle with the provisional government.

THE BOLSHEVIK SEIZURE OF POWER

After the Kornilov affair, the growing strength of the soviets throughout the country was accompanied by an increase of Bolshevik power and influence inside the most important soviets, those of Petrograd and Moscow. The Bolshevik party had at the beginning of 1917 some 30,000 members. By October, the number had jumped to 200,000. Their strength was also reflected in their gaining control of factory committees and of some trade unions. But most importantly, they gained majorities in the Moscow and Petrograd soviets, and were soon to gain control over others.

In spite of their growing strength, the majority of Bolshevik leaders were not optimistic. Lenin was the exception. From nearby Finland, he urged preparation for an immediate uprising. Bolshevik leaders in Petrograd did not believe that power could be held even if they were successful in seizing it in the capital. As if in desperation, Lenin returned to Petrograd in disguise (in late October) to personally urge acceptance of his position. Within a few days, he succeeded in winning over to his position all except two of the important Bolshevik leaders.

Employing the military revolutionary committees of the Petrograd and Moscow soviets, Lenin and his collaborators prepared to seize power on the eve of the meeting of the Second Congress of Soviets. In the night (November 6–7), they seized the important buildings (palace, railway stations, and telephone and telegraph centers) in Petrograd and in Moscow and arrested the members of the provisional government who had not succeeded in fleeing. The next day (November 8), they appeared before the Second Congress of Soviets with the request that their actions be endorsed. This the congress did, vesting power in a Council of People's Commissars, headed by Lenin.

Although in power, the Bolsheviks and their allies permitted the elections for the Constituent Assembly to be held. These had been scheduled by the provisional government, after considerable prodding by the Bolsheviks and their allies in the soviets. In one sense, the results were disastrous for the Bolsheviks, for they received a relatively small portion of the delegates. In view of the party's small membership, however, polling one fourth of the total vote could be interpreted as a moderate success. The Social Revolutionaries won a majority. Nevertheless, the Bolsheviks permitted the Constituent Assembly to convene in January 1918. When they were convinced that the Assembly would not do their bidding, the Bolsheviks disbanded it with force after its first day in session. The Assembly was never to be heard from again.

THE BOLSHEVIKS CONSOLIDATE POWER

Once in power, the Bolsheviks were forced to deal with several problems if they were to consolidate their authority. In the foreign realm, they had to liquidate the war with Germany and the Allied intervention which was to follow. Domestically, they had to liquidate the tsarist system and to build one of their own. Moreover, they had to embark upon the building of a new society.

WAR AND ALLIED INTERVENTION

The Bolsheviks, who had clamored for an end to the war, had little choice but to make peace at almost any price. At Brest-Litovsk in March, 1918, they signed such a peace, with great losses of territory.[22] The signing of a separate peace by Russia was viewed by the Allies as little short of treasonous. The first thought in Allied circles, even before they could know the nature of the new Russian government, was how to prevent Allied munitions and other materiel which had been sent to Russia from falling into the hands of the Germans.

The Allied landing of marines at Murmansk in the early part of 1918 was the beginning of an Allied effort to deal with the consequences of the Russian withdrawal from the war. Later this was to acquire the label "Allied Intervention," and the Bolsheviks, as well as many non-Bolsheviks, were to ascribe to it a purely political motive. Although there was no political motive initially, within a brief period

---

[22] See John W. Wheeler-Bennett, *The Forgotten Peace: Brest-Litovsk, March 1918* (New York: St. Martin's Press, 1939). See also George F. Kennan, *Soviet-American Relations, 1917–1920: Russia Leaves the War* (Princeton, N.J.: Princeton University Press, 1956).

after its inception, the intervention did acquire a political motive.

As opposition to the Bolshevik regime developed into a civil war, with many troops and officers of the old Russian army forming units to fight the hastily organized Red Army, some Allied assistance to the anti-Bolsheviks was forthcoming. Additional Allied troops, although the total was never great, were landed in European Russia and in Siberia. In the latter case, some Allied forces were much more concerned with watching the Japanese than with any attempt to overthrow the new Bolshevik regime. A comprehensive recent study, however, concludes that the intervention in Siberia was directed at neither the Japanese nor the Bolsheviks, but against the Germans.[23] It was believed in the West that a large number of German (Austrian) prisoners in Siberia were given arms by the Bolsheviks (at Germany's bidding) and that they were about to take large parts of Siberia.[24]

Although one ought not to underestimate the psychological impact on the Bolsheviks of the intervention, particularly when one remembers that Allied troops were landed in Russia as late as January, 1919, one cannot overlook the fact that the Allied victory in November, 1918, really knocked the heart out of the intervention. Allied troops, aware of the original intent of the intervention, soon became restive and had to be withdrawn. If one looks at the intervention with a balanced view, it is difficult to escape the conclusion that while it was a political fiasco, it was, at least partially, a military success because it "played its part in stopping the flow of German troops from east to west."[25]

One needs also to remember the so-called American intervention in the years 1921–23, which was primarily a mission of mercy and good will. It took the form of the American Relief Administration, a private organization which responded to the urgent appeal of the Russians. Later, the U.S. Congress joined in by appropriating millions of dollars. This "intervention" saved millions of Soviet citizens from starvation.

REPLACING THE TSARIST POLITICAL ORDER

Closely related to the intervention was the civil war which was precipitated by the Bolshevik revolution. Although Bolshevik intentions and aims had been well advertised, their strength had been

---

[23] Christopher Lasch, "American Intervention in Siberia: A Reinterpretation," *Political Science Quarterly*, LXXVII (June, 1962), pp. 205–223.

[24] *Ibid.*

[25] Sir Edmund Ironside, *Archangel, 1918–19* (London: Constable, 1953), p. 220.

consistently underestimated by the provisional government. Having awakened to the rude realities of the situation, the opponents of the Bolsheviks rallied around certain tsarist army generals who organized fighting forces to challenge the new regime. In the end, although they fought for approximately three years, they could not reverse the tide.

In the meantime, the newly formed regime was occupied with the task of liquidating the tsarist political order and building one of its own. Smashing the old order was easier than building a new one, for Marxian theory had provided virtually no guideposts for the latter. Lenin had said that it had to be a dictatorship of the toiling masses but he had not worked out any detailed plan. There was much improvising to meet the demands of the moment. The Red Army had been hastily organized to meet the threat to the regime posed by the civil war and the intervention. Equally hastily, the new regime organized a security police, first known as the Cheka, the so-called extraordinary commission for combating counterrevolution, sabotage, and dereliction of duty.

The Red Army and the secret police were basically negative in that they were to guard against the revival of the old order, although, as time was to prove, the new regime came more and more to be based on force and terror. While the one-party state was not immediately instituted, the Bolsheviks lost no time in beginning the liquidation of other political parties, even those that had initially collaborated with them. Moreover, the problem of organizing a competent and loyal bureaucracy did not prove so easy as Lenin had predicted.

BUILDING THE NEW SOCIETY

The overriding consideration in all of the new regime's efforts was the vast and complex problem of building the new society. One economic and social system had to be displaced by another.[26] The initial period of the attempted rapid transformation has come to be known as "war communism" (1918–1921). The efforts, in this period, of the workers to run the factories and of the government to force the peasants to deliver their produce to government-owned enterprises were soon recognized as failures.

This initial period was followed by a compromise with capitalism or, as described by some Soviet spokesmen, a strategic retreat. This was the period of the so-called New Economic Policy, which was to

---

[26] For a perceptive discussion of the major problems that the Bolshevik leaders had to face in this regard, see Barrington Moore, Jr., *Soviet Politics—The Dilemma of Power* (Cambridge, Mass.: Harvard University Press, 1950), p. 85ff.

terminate about 1928, with the launching of the new "socialist offensive" in agriculture and the beginning of the era of successive five-year plans. This was also the period of Lenin's death and the first gigantic struggle for power.[27]

BIBLIOGRAPHICAL NOTE

Among the general histories which may serve as an introduction to understanding the Soviet System are J. D. Clarkson, *A History of Russia* (New York: Random House, 1961); Bernard Pares, *A History of Russia* (New York: Knopf, 1953); Georg von Rauch, *A History of Soviet Russia* (New York: Praeger, 1957); N. V. Riasanovsky, *A History of Russia* (London: Oxford University Press, 1963); George Vernadsky, *Political and Diplomatic History of Russia* (Boston: Little, Brown & Co., 1936); and Warren Bartlett Walsh, *Russia and the Soviet Union, A Modern History* (Ann Arbor: University of Michigan Press, 1958). Additional background material may be gained from George Fischer, *Russian Liberalism: From Gentry to Intelligentsia* (Cambridge, Mass.: Harvard University Press, 1958); Leopold Haimson, *The Russian Marxists and the Origins of Bolshevism* (Cambridge, Mass.: Harvard University Press, 1955).

Bertram D. Wolfe, *Three Who Made a Revolution* (rev. ed.; Boston: Beacon, 1955) is a valuable discussion of the events leading up to the Revolution, while Edward Halett Carr, *A History of Soviet Russia* (New York: Macmillan, Vol. I, 1951; Vol. II, 1952; Vol. III, 1953; Vol. IV, 1954) is a scholarly treatment of post-Revolutionary events.

Studies which deal, in various ways, with developments during the period of the Revolution include those of Lord Edmund Ironside, *Archangel, 1918–19* (London: Constable, 1953); George F. Kennan, *Soviet-American Relations, 1917–1920:* Vol. I, *Russia Leaves the War;* Vol. II, *The Decision to Intervene* (Princeton: Princeton University Press, Vol. I, 1956; Vol. II, 1958); Alan Moorehead, *The Russian Revolution* (New York: Harper, 1958); Richard Pipes, *The Formation of the Soviet Union* (Cambridge, Mass.: Harvard University Press, 1954); John Reed, *Ten Days That Shook the World* (New York: Modern Library, 1935); Leonard Schapiro, *The Origin of the Communist Autocracy: Political Opposition in the Soviet State, First Phase, 1917–22* (Cambridge, Mass.: Harvard University Press, 1955); I. N. Steinberg, *In the Workshop of the Revolution* (New York: Rinehart, 1953); N. N. Sukhanov, *The Russian Revolution, 1917* (New York: Oxford University Press, 1955); John Wheeler-Bennett, *The Forgotten Peace, Brest-Litovsk, March 1918* (New York: W. Morrow & Co., 1939); and Lionel Kochan, *Russia and the Weimar Republic* (New York: Praeger, 1955).

C. E. Black (ed.), *Rewriting Russian History* (New York: Praeger, 1956) discusses Russian interpretations of the history of the country.

---

[27] See Chapter 26.

CHAPTER **25**

IDEOLOGICAL BASE:
MARXISM

THE IDEOLOGICAL foundations of the Soviet political system are
to be found in the writings of Karl Marx, Friedrich Engels, V. I.
Lenin, and other Marxists. As the word "Marxist" suggests, the common body of doctrine is known as Marxism or, in the Russian version,
Marxism-Leninism. It is necessary to have a working knowledge of
this body of doctrine if one is to understand the Soviet system. What
follows is designed, understandably, to provide a summary only of
the most essential elements of that doctrine.

HISTORICAL DEVELOPMENT OF SOCIALIST IDEAS

All socialists agree in the desirability of securing a fairer and more
satisfactory apportionment of wealth and economic opportunity,
through some substantial limitation on the private ownership of
property. This idea is not new; its historical roots can be found in
the Old Testament. In different epochs, however, the arguments in its
behalf have varied and the emphases and motivations of its proponents have not been the same.

EARLIER SOCIALIST IDEAS

Early socialism was motivated by religious and moralistic considerations. Each person was viewed as equal in the sight of God,
and therefore entitled to share relatively equally in the fruits of this
earth. In the early modern period (about 1500), socialism became
a combination of social revolt and religious zeal. Even as an increasing importance was being attributed to economic life, through the
development of trade, etc., socialistic ideas were for the most part still
utopian, idealistic, and visionary. The primary motivation among
the pioneers of socialism was an urgent desire to get men to realize
the good, rather than the bad, that is in them.

MARXISM AS SCIENTIFIC SOCIALISM

Although all beginnings are more or less relative, especially in the field of social history, the year 1848 may be viewed as the birth year of modern socialism. The Industrial Revolution had by the nineteenth century considerably altered the economic order in the West. Large-scale industry had developed, and with it a large class of propertyless wage earners, the proletariat. These developments were accompanied by evils (inadequate housing, poor sanitation, poor working conditions, long hours of work, absence of safety measures, etc.) which came in the wake of the industrialization of modern society. In 1848, Karl Marx and Friedrich Engels published the *Communist Manifesto,* which not only sought to explain these evils but, in addition, put forth a program of why and how they were going to pass from the scene.

Marxism is often described as "scientific socialism." It is in part the result of two converging developments—modern science, and the Industrial Revolution and its attendant consequences. While there is no effort here to pass judgment on modern science, its development enabled Marx to say, in effect: let us not be led down the mythical paths of the past if we are to explain social phenonema. Let us put society under the microscope in order that we might get a scientific answer to the question of what makes it tick. Modern science had pointed the way to a mundane and realistic approach to the study of society.

Society itself had provided many of the tangible and visible factors which would enter into the analysis. There was the development of steam and machinery, with the replacement of manpower by steam power. There was discovery, exploration, and commerce. There was the trading merchant class, the *bourgeoisie,* which rose to a position of dominance. There was the proletariat. There were the glaring evils accompanying this economic and social revolution.

Since these evils had their gravest impact upon the proletariat, it is perhaps not unusual that socialism, since about the time of the publication of the *Communist Manifesto,* should have concerned itself primarily with the interest of hand laborers in industrial society. This will become even more apparent as we comprehend the nature of the Marxian analysis concerning the rise and development of capitalism, as well as its projection of the impending future evolution of capitalist society.

THE TERMS "SOCIALISM" AND "COMMUNISM"

Before setting forth the basic ideas of Marx, however, it is well to be clear about the meaning of the terms "socialism" and "communism," for when they are used in different contexts they have considerably varied meanings. Historically, over the past hundred years or so, they have come to be associated with different means of approaching a similar goal. The word "communism" came into use in 1840. From 1840 to 1872, it came to imply revolutionary action aimed at the violent overthrow of capitalistic society. Socialism, on the other hand, was employed to designate constitutional activities aimed at the reform of the economic system through national control of the means of production. Between 1872 and 1917, however, the two terms became more or less synonymous, or more precisely, the term communism was dropped. Within 25 years of the writing of the *Communist Manifesto,* its authors were referring to themselves as socialists or social democrats. With the seizure of power in Russia by the Bolsheviks, the old distinctions were revived and even accentuated. In more recent years, the degree to which the economy should come under collective ownership or direction has also tended to distinguish communists and socialists.

As employed by the Russians and their allies, the term "socialism" is frequently used to designate a stage in the transition from capitalism to the new society. It is the period in which the government has taken over the economy but one in which the ultimate stage of development has not been reached, the ultimate stage being communism—a classless and stateless society.

The term "communism" has been used to designate the Marxian doctrine, particularly as it has been modified and applied by the Russians. This has perhaps been done more frequently by non-Russians, although the Russians have also used the term quite extensively to signify the same thing. The Russians seem to prefer to use "socialism" or "Marxism-Leninism" when referring to the doctrinal ideology on which their system is based. Non-Russian socialists, even when they accept the Marxian analysis, prefer not to call the Russian system socialist, whereas Russian leaders do not recognize any system but their own as truly socialist. The Russians, however, use the term "communist" freely when talking of their party and party leaders.

As employed in the pages that follow, unless otherwise indicated explicitly or in context, the term "socialism" will refer to the ideology or doctrine as expounded by Marx and other Marxists. When speaking of the political and economic system built up by the Russians, it will be more appropriate to speak of communism or Bolshevism. The important thing to note, however, is that the reader should be aware of the different ways in which the terms socialism and communism are used. The person using the terms, on the other hand, ought to make it quite clear how he is using them.

MARXISM AS AN INTERPRETATION OF CAPITALISM

By far the greatest part of Marxian writings can be said to consist of an interpretation of capitalism. To be sure, Marx and his disciples concerned themselves about the establishment and the nature of the future society. But the bulk of their literary output deals with the "laws" of social evolution, and particularly with the factors governing the rise of the *bourgeoisie*, the modern capitalist class, and its "inevitable" demise. Therefore, Marxism is, first of all, an interpretation of capitalist society.

DIALECTICAL MATERIALISM

Different men have sought an answer to the question of what is the moving force in history. Some have found it to be the will of God; others became convinced that the culture cycle was the law of history. Marx, on the other hand, concluded that on the basis of his researches societies rise and develop along a well-established path, the path of dialectical materialism.

The word "dialectics" was employed originally in ancient Greece to refer to a method of argument or disputation. A logical presentation of a point of view, or thesis, would provoke an opposition, or an antithesis. As a result of such a clash of views the opinions of the disputing parties underwent a change, with the result that something new, higher, or more profound developed, a synthesis. There was a negation of the old and the creation of the new. Marx contended that the dialectic was at work in the social order, that each social order provoked or created an inner opposition. The result was a new and better society, which itself would become the new thesis, and in turn create a new opposition, etc., etc.

What is the moving force in the dialectic process? Earlier, the German philosopher Hegel had argued in favor of the dialectic process, but he believed ideas to be the moving force in that process. Marx, on the other hand concluded that the material factors in life were primary and all-important. They were the original force, while ideas, art, religion, philosophy, forms of political organization, etc., were but derivative forces. They were not even autonomous forces, but dependent upon the material conditions of any given society.

MATERIALISTIC CONCEPTION OF HISTORY

According to the materialistic conception of history,[1] man makes history by trying to satisfy his needs, which are originally imposed by nature but later modified by man's artificial environment. These needs (food, clothing, shelter) are satisfied by man's productivity, which consists of extracting things from nature, in working them up, and in adapting them to his needs.

The productive forces (scientific and technical know-how) which man has at his disposal to satisfy his needs will determine all of his social relations. "The organization of any given society is determined by the state of its productive forces." (Plekhanov) In other words, "occupational activities determine the fundamental modes of social behavior and in this behavior are formed ideas, attitudes, and habits which express themselves in other fields of culture." (Marx and Engels) It follows, therefore, that as the nature of the productive forces changes, the organization of society will also change. For example, the change in the state of the productive forces under capitalism resulted in the building of urban communities, with the consequent need for urban services (garbage collection, fire protection, etc.). This in turn required a change in the organization of society so as to bring about these services. Urban local government with which we are familiar would have been unthinkable 2,000 years ago, for the state of the productive forces then available to man created no need for it.

Moreover, the Marxists argue, the prevalent mode of economic production in any society gives rise to definite interests, which are essentially antagonistic, thus dividing society into classes. These interests become expressed in law. "All positive law is a defense of some definite interest." (Plekhanov) For example, at a time when horses were domesticated and economically useful (for hunting or transport), the owners of horses needed a law against horse stealing. But all interests cannot be protected equally, for they are in fundamental conflict. The net result of the conflict of interests between antagonis-

---

[1] One of the clearest expositions of the materialistic conception of history is to be found in a brief essay by one of the earliest Russian Marxists, George Plekhanov, entitled "The Materialist Conception of History," originally published in 1897.

tic classes is a state organization (government, law, etc.) whose function is to protect the interests of the dominant group or class. The state is therefore an organization of class domination, an organ of oppression of one class by another.[2]

When new productive forces evolve, the existing social institutions —government among them—do not permit their proper utilization. In the end, the class struggle becomes more and more acute and can only logically be resolved by revolution. Thus, revolution is the inevitable result of the contradiction between the new scientific and technical know-how and the inability of social institutions to bring about the creative potentialities that the new forces of production offer.

To substantiate their theory, Marx and his followers cited historical examples, the most notable being the feudal system, which was overthrown when it stood in the way of the proper utilization of the new productive forces (the Industrial Revolution) of bourgeois capitalism. Capitalist society, therefore, was not only a necessary step in social evolution, but also a beneficial one in relation to the past. In relation to the future, however, it is an evil that will be destroyed.

CAPITALISM: THE THEORY APPLIED

The basic law of social development, according to the Marxists, has been stated above. But what are the proofs of its operation in capitalist society? First and foremost, not unlike the societies which preceded it, capitalism creates within itself an inner opposition. Just as feudalism created an inner opposition, bringing forth the *bourgeoisie* to destroy it, so the *bourgeoisie* bring forth the modern wage-earning class, the proletariat, which is to overthrow bourgeois society. Capitalism brings forth the proletariat because it needs it to operate the factories, etc. But it exploits the propertyless wage-earner, for he cannot buy back all that he has produced. He does not get paid for all that he does; some is held back.[3]

Secondly, the position of the worker gets worse as time goes on. The rich get richer and the poor get poorer. Economic power tends to centralize and wealth accumulates in large fortunes. This centralization of wealth robs the proletariat of purchasing power, which results

---

[2] While Engels did not disagree with this analysis, he did concede that there were brief periods when the warring classes were so nearly equally balanced that the power of the state for the moment assumed a certain independence in relation to both.

[3] This is the Marxian labor theory of value, that is, labor produces capital as well as the actual goods of consumption. This idea was not original with Marx.

in crises—overproduction, unemployment, economic depressions, and panics. These crises, Marx was convinced, would destroy the entire capitalist system, for not only does the lot of the workers become more and more unbearable, but in addition, the ranks of the proletariat are greatly enlarged by more and more of the *bourgeoisie* being pushed out and forced to make a living as wage-earners. Thus revolution becomes imminent as capitalism ripens.

Finally, bourgeois society is doomed, for it has not done away with class antagonisms, but has established new classes, new conditions of oppression, new forms of struggle in place of the old.[4] While the "history of all hitherto existing society is the history of class struggles,"[5] earlier societies had many classes. "In ancient Rome we have patricians, knights, plebeians, slaves; in the Middle Ages, feudal lords, vassals, guild-masters, journeymen, apprentices, serfs. . . ."[6] The epoch of the *bourgeoisie*, however, has simplified the struggle. Instead of many classes, there are only two, the *bourgeoisie* and the proletariat.

Moreover, as Plekhanov was to suggest, the evolution of bourgeois society would result in a more enlightened proletariat, and hence one ready to revolt.[7] There is an immense difference, he observed, between being conscious of the restrictiveness of laws and consciously striving to abolish this restrictiveness. Where man does not strive to abolish old institutions and to create new ones, there the way for the new system has not been properly prepared by the economics (the productive forces) of the society. But as science and technology reduce ignorance, man will better understand natural phenomena. As a consequence, he will better understand social and economic phenomena. When he does, he will revolt.

LENIN'S CONTRIBUTION TO MARXISM

V. I. Lenin, who was to become the leader of the Bolshevik Revolution, is the immediate doctrinal authority for the Russian Communists, as well as for many other Marxists. The Russian Communists almost always speak of Marxism-Leninism when referring to the ideological doctrine by which they profess to be guided. Although other Russian Marxists, notably George Plekhanov, preceded Lenin in laying the doctrinal foundations for Russian Marxism, Lenin has

---

[4] *Communist Manifesto* (New York: International Publishers edition, 1932), p. 9.

[5] *Ibid.*

[6] *Ibid.*

[7] *Essays in Historical Materialism* (New York: International Publishers edition, 1940), pp. 36–37.

come to be regarded by the Russian Communists as the true inter-preter of Marx.

Lenin made two principal contributions to Marxism. The first adds to the analysis of capitalism, while the second concerns the question of techniques for the overthrow of bourgeois society.

Lenin condemned capitalism for all the evils Marx had attributed to it, and he added others. In its later stages of development, capital-ism, because of its monopoly controls, fostered scarcity at home. The reduced domestic buying power sent capitalists in search of markets abroad, which led to imperialism. Consequently, capitalism pro-duced competing imperialistic ventures by the capitalist countries, thus leading to war.[8] At the same time, the "state machinery" was strengthened, with a notable growth of the bureaucracy and the mili-tary. Simultaneously, repressive measures against the proletariat were on the increase.[9]

Closely related to this idea was Lenin's argument that the pro-letarian revolution did not need to wait until society had gone through the evils of the capitalist phase, although this was contrary to his earlier thinking on the subject. The peasantry, he said, could be allied with the industrial workers to bring about the revolution. In this change in outlook, he may have been guided by his desire to con-summate the proletarian revolution in Russia, which was still a back-ward country and not yet developed as a bourgeois society. The Russian peasantry, because of the lingering evils of serfdom, was, in his "more mature opinion," ready to join with the workers in seeking power.

Lenin's other contribution was his development of the concept of the professional revolutionary. Marx had viewed the proletarian revo-lution as inevitable. Lenin accepted Marx's analysis but was more insistent upon the need for leadership to bring it about. Marx and Engels paid little attention to the idea of a communist political party. Lenin, on the other hand, talked constantly about the need of a party of professional revolutionaries, and devoted more than 20 years to building that kind of party. While Marx and Lenin agreed that cap-italism prepares the way for the revolution, Lenin was somewhat skeptical about the proletariat rising spontaneously. Consequently, he argued that a small, tightly organized party of dedicated and trained revolutionaries was needed. These people would lead the proletariat in its successful revolution.

---

[8] See his *Imperialism, the Highest Stage of Capitalism* (originally published in 1916).

[9] *State and Revolution* (New York: International Publishers edition, 1932), p. 29.

MARXISM AS A POSITIVE PROGRAM

Although Marxists are first of all preoccupied with an interpretation of capitalism, they utilize this interpretation as the foundation upon which their positive program rests. Unlike other philosophers who have sought to explain the world, the Marxists also seeks to change it. Once their analysis of the existing order is made, they see two tasks confronting the proletariat. First is the seizure of political power, or converting their potential superiority into an actual one. Secondly, once political power is secured, the proletariat must go about the task of building the new economic and social order.

POLITICAL POWER: DICTATORSHIP OF THE PROLETARIAT

Marx argued that while history produces a revolutionary situation, it would be necessary for the proletariat and history to work together. The proletariat must have a program whose function is to show the workers how they can achieve political power. In democratic countries they should organize politically so as to win the battle of democracy. In countries where the democratic process was forbidden to them they should use organized force. Thus Marx's program was at once both evolutionary and revolutionary.

Lenin, who was impatient to witness the revolution in Russia, placed a greater emphasis on action. Every step in the real movement is more important than a dozen programs, he declared. Moreover, he insisted that it was impossible to win by democratic means so long as the *bourgeoisie* commands the army and the police. He frequently emphasized that unless revolutionary theory is combined with revolutionary practice it is not Marxism but opportunism.[10] "The replacement of the bourgeois by the proletarian state is impossible without a violent revolution."[11]

Lenin, moreover, was much more preoccupied than Marx with the form of the new political authority once political power had been captured. While asserting that the bourgeois state must be destroyed root and branch, Lenin insisted that the Communists would for a time need the state. This new workers' state would function during the period of transition from capitalism to communism. Its functions would be to suppress the *bourgeoisie* and to build socialism. It would be

---

[10] See V. Adoratsky, *Dialectical Materialism* (New York: International Publishers, 1934), especially chapter 6.

[11] *State and Revolution*, p. 20.

a dictatorship of the proletariat. So as not to leave any of his followers in doubt, Lenin declared: "He who recognizes *only* the class struggle is not yet a Marxist. . . . A Marxist is one who *extends* the acceptance of class struggle to the acceptance of the dictatorship of the proletariat."[12]

BUILDING SOCIALISM

The dictatorship of the proletariat would do away with the *bourgeoisie* by nationalizing capital, that is, by seizing all income-producing property, including natural resources as well as capital industries. Those who sought to resist would be liquidated. Nothing must stand in the way of the new proletarian authority "to abolish all exploitation," to crush "the resistance of the exploiters," and to guide the masses "in the work of organizing socialist economy."[13]

The gains from the productive property, now in state hands, would accrue to the entire community and be distributed by public authority. Presumably there would be private property in income, although this could not be invested for the purpose of making a profit. Although there are contradictory statements among Marxists as to the relative equality of reward, Marx and Engels, in the *Communist Manifesto*, asserted that the ultimate objective was a society in which everyone would contribute according to his ability and in turn be rewarded according to his need. Lenin, although speaking of immediate aims, was more specific when he talked of paying workingmen's wages to managers, technicians, bookkeepers, and government officials.[14]

As conceived by Marx, however, the dictatorship of the proletariat would not be a dictatorship of one man or a few. As he envisioned it, the proletarian state would be a dictatorship of the majority (proletariat) over the minority (*bourgeoisie*), and hence in reality a democracy.

MARXISM AS THE CLASSLESS, STATELESS SOCIETY

The struggle between the capitalists and the proletarians, according to Marx and his followers, represents the last historic clash between classes. With the abolition of private ownership of the means of production, the basis for the existence of classes will disappear. Everyone will be in the same "class," or more correctly, classes will

[12] *State and Revolution*, p. 30. Italics his.
[13] *State and Revolution*, pp. 22–23.
[14] *State and Revolution*, p. 43.

disappear, for the concept of class has no meaning unless there are two or more of them.[15]

Since the state is the oppressive instrument of the dominant class, according to Marxian theory, there will be no need for it in a classless society. Therefore, the state will "wither away," but Marxists have not been too precise as to how soon this would take place. In 1918, Lenin thought of the transition period in terms of "ten years or perhaps more." A year or two later, he admitted that perhaps he had been overly optimistic, and for a time dwelt on the need of strengthening the state in the transition period. But he does not seem to have departed from his assertion in *State and Revolution* that what the proletariat needs is "only a state which is withering away, *i.e.*, a state which is so constituted that it begins to wither away imme- diately. . . ."[16] In any case, irrespective of the time it took, Lenin expected the withering away of the state to be progressive and continuous.

Assuming the disappearance of classes and the withering away of the state, it still remains to be asked how the classless society will be organized and how it is to function without state authority. Here the Marxists are even more vague than in the matter of the duration of the dictatorship of the proletariat. Somehow, all production would be concentrated in the hands of vast associations of the whole people. The administrative functions normally associated with the state would become part and parcel of the productive process. Presumably, the people would choose representatives who would determine the basic policies to be pursued. They would plan the utilization of the material resources for the good of all. In essence, everyone would be a member of a cooperative commonwealth of the world in which cooperation would take the place of compulsion. The profit motive would give way to the service motive and people would do the right thing because it was the right thing to do.

If the classless, stateless society may seem utopian and unrealistic, the Marxists would be the first to deny it, on paper at least. "We are not Utopians," said Lenin, "and we do not in the least deny the possibility and inevitability of excesses on the part of *individual* persons, nor the need to suppress *such* excesses. But . . . no special machinery . . . is needed for this; this will be done by the armed

---

[15] In 1957, the Chinese Communist leader, Mao Tse-tung, revised Marxian doctrine to the extent of admitting that "contradictions" existed in China, that there were differences between the Communist government and the people. The Russians, however, have denied that such contradictions exist in the Soviet Union.

[16] Page 22.

people itself, as simply and as readily as any crowd of civilized people, even in modern society, parts a pair of combatants or does not allow a woman to be outraged."[17] In practice, of course, the Russians have yet to produce any evidence of the withering away of the state, although they are now in the fifth decade of the dictatorship of the proletariat.

CRITIQUE OF MARXISM

The foregoing discussion of Marxian theory is far from being exhaustive.[18] Similarly, an extensive evaluation of that theory is beyond our scope here. Yet, some critical analysis seems in order.

THE MARXIAN ANALYSIS OF CAPITALISM

Unquestionably, Marxist writings have had an important impact on the world. There are elements of truth in these writings, else they could not have had such influence. However erroneous he may have been with respect to his predictions of future developments or however naive he may have been with respect to a future Communist system, Marx did contribute to man's knowledge about the past. By tracing social and especially political institutions to their materialistic or economic bases, he at least called our attention to the importance of materialistic factors, although most of us would not agree that they were always the decisive ones. Moreover, his exposition of the conflict between the proletariat and the *bourgeoisie* gave us an added insight into social relationships. And his demonstration of some of the instabilities of capitalism has contributed to more meaningful insights with respect to the workings of a free enterprise economy. Finally, because of his many assertions, other researchers have been challenged to probe deeper, in order that they might contribute to a better understanding of our social order.

First among the criticisms that might be made of Marx's theories concerns the basic assumption that materialistic forces are primary in the shaping of all human development, that all other forces are derivative and secondary. The findings of most modern social scientists, however, indicate that society is much more complex than the Marxian formula assumes. There is evidence that ideas and other

---

[17] *State and Revolution*, p. 75.

[18] Much of what Marx wrote deals with highly technical questions in the field of economics, as any perusal of *Capital* will confirm. Our main aim has been to concentrate on those aspects of his theory which would be most meaningful to a student of Soviet politics and government.

considerations do motivate people, quite independently of materialistic forces. Moreover, Marx did not say that technical changes
(inventions, etc.) were governed by materialistic forces alone. Why, it
might be asked, does creativity in human affairs have to be limited to
the technical sphere?

A second criticism that might be made of Marx's analysis is that the
consequences of the Industrial Revolution which he saw are not to be
associated with capitalism alone.[19] The Industrial Revolution, whether
engineered by private enterprise or by the state, as in Russia, creates
new social classes. State-initiated industrialization produces an industrial working class, while the bureaucracy, sometime euphemistically
refered to by the Russians as the "toiling intelligentsia," becomes the
ruling class.[20] The plight of the workers under state-engineered industrialization, in the sense that they are materially exploited and emo-
tionally disoriented, is not unlike that of the western European
workers during the early capitalist period. Exploitation of the workers, therefore, is not the result of capitalism or of socialism but of the
early stages of the Industrial Revolution.

Thirdly, Marx did not foresee that when the Industrial Revolution
had run its course, the lot of the worker would improve and a certain
social balance would be achieved. The position of the proletariat
improved for several reasons. Free speech and a free press, by making
possible a thorough discussion of workers' grievances, aroused the
social conscience of the educated people. In addition, workers were
able to organize in unions and thus push their demands. Moreover,
they gained the right to choose members of legislative bodies and were
influential in securing legislative enactments favorable to them. Without denying the great influence which capitalism wielded, it can be
seen that political liberty and representative institutions enabled
Western democracy to evolve a system characterized by a considerable balance among social classes.

Another defect in Marxian theory lies in its underestimation of the
strength and flexibility of capitalism. Instead of impoverishing the
middle class and driving more and more of its members into the ranks
of the proletariat, capitalism has enabled the middle class to become
more prosperous and to grow in numbers. In democratic countries,
capitalism has showed no driving need for imperialistic expansion.

---

[19] See the series of articles by Hugh Seton-Watson in the *Manchester Guardian
Weekly*, January 28, February 4, 11, and 18, 1954, under the general title, "Some Myths
of Marxism."

[20] See Milovan Djilas, *The New Class* (New York: Frederick A. Praeger, 1957).

Moreover, it has demonstrated a remarkable ability to adjust to public regulation of some of its important activities. By making concessions, it has provided untold opportunities for the middle class and for the workers, demonstrating a dynamic flexibility.

In their revolutionary appeal for unity among all of the workers of the world, Marx and his followers underestimated the strength of the appeals of nationalism. National loyalties have proved to be stronger than loyalties to class, something which is true of the capitalist class as well as of the proletariat.

Finally, the Marxists erred in their assumption that workers would act, and act rationally, in given circumstances. Studies in the political behavior of human beings indicate that people are often exceedingly irrational in their political choices. More important, perhaps, is the fact that people are seldom moved to action. Thus, Marx was wrong when he assumed the revolutionary character of the workers, as well as when he assumed that they would act rationally in support of their class interest.

MARXISM AND SOVIET PRACTICE: STALIN AND KHRUSHCHEV

Since the Bolshevik victory in 1917, Marxism, or Marxism-Leninism, has meant whatever the Soviet leaders have chosen to have it mean. In the first place, the men who set up the dictatorship, aside from a few educated Marxists such as Lenin, could not have known much about Marxism. Many peasant lads, like Nikita Khrushchev, who joined the movement in 1917, were barely literate. Secondly, Soviet Communist leaders, including Lenin, Stalin, Khrushchev, and their successors, have never hesitated to revise Marxist postulates when it was thought necessary to defend certain policies or programs. By and large, the Soviet leaders have been guided by their cardinal aim—the abolition of private property. To achieve this, they have found it necessary to strengthen the state and in the process to protect the interests of the dominant class—the party apparatus.

Stalin's main contribution to Marxism-Leninism is the idea of "socialism in one country." When the Bolshevik revolution was not followed by similar revolutions elsewhere, Stalin saw in the outside world a threat to the Soviet system (the so-called "capitalist encircle-ment"). To meet this threat, Stalin believed that the Soviet state had to be strengthened, and this could be done, in his opinion, only by a rapid transformation of the Soviet economic system. This required forced industrialization, which in turn called for collectivization of agriculture in order that the new proletariat be fed. Marx had stressed the importance of the proletariat. Lenin had put greater emphasis on the party. Stalin sought to merge the party and the state so as to make the Soviet Union the chief instrument of proletarian revolutions.

From the notion of "socialism in one country" flowed certain other ideas. The dictatorship of the proletariat had to be viewed as the dictatorship of the one-party state. This dictatorship had to be strengthened in the so-called transition period, and especially the army and the police as guardians of that dictatorship. Moreover, the period of this dictatorship was to be relatively long, during which the economic and cultural prerequisites for "socialist victory" were to be created. These ideas led to the destruction of all opposition and to the strengthening of the monolithic character of the regime. The withering away of the state was, for all practical purposes, forgotten.

Stalin's idea of "socialism in one country" had other interesting implications and consequences. For example, revolutionary movements in foreign countries would be staged or called off depending upon whether Soviet foreign policy was furthered thereby. Similarly, in order to increase labor productivity, Stalin introduced significant wage differentials and worker-discipline legislation. Moreover, he departed from Lenin's emphasis on internationalism, stressing the achievements of the Russian state, claiming Russian firsts in inventions, and elevating heroes of Tsarist Russia to positions of veneration. Although a member of a minority nationality (Georgian), Stalin became more Russian than the Russians.

Khrushchev, although not looked upon as much of a theorist even when he was in power, advanced three ideas to which reference should be made. Allegedly correcting Stalin's errors, he in effect revised Lenin when he asserted that a clash between the Communist and non-Communist camps was not inevitable. Similarly, he revised Lenin when he proclaimed that it was possible for proletarian revolutions to be achieved by nonviolent means. More interesting than either one of these notions were his observations on the withering away of the state, which revised Marx as well as Lenin. Instead of being the last stage in political development prior to the establishment of the classless and stateless society, the dictatorship of the proletariat gives way to the "state of all the people." Instead of ceasing to exist, the state apparently dissolves itself slowly into organized society. In this organized society, the Communist party will replace the government and therefore its role will become even more important than in the past.

MARXISM AND SOVIET PRACTICE: THE ROLE OF IDEOLOGY

Among the so-called experts there is some disagreement as to the role of ideology in the Soviet system. A few maintain that it is a body of "ceremonial political functions," a type of "Sunday creed" to which most Communists pay lip-service. A much larger group contends that ideology is a guide to action, a type of instruction manual of pragmatically extracted precepts from Marxist teachings, which permits the greatest flexibility in the practical implementation of fundamentally inflexible principles. This means that each Marxist-Leninist postulate expresses the position of the Communist party concerning some specific question at a particular time. When a goal is reached or circumstances change, the postulate loses validity, and the party's ideological position can be changed. Thus, adherence to traditional concepts can be interpreted as "faithfulness to the party line" or as "dogmatism." Readiness to modify such concepts can be interpreted as "revisionism" or as "creative Marxism." Similarly, peaceful coexistence can be "a form of the class struggle on a worldwide scale" or "downright capitulation." As a guide to action, therefore, ideology is viewed less as a collection of dogmas and more as an instrument of communication and leadership.

Other experts, while agreeing that ideology as a guide to action assists the leaders in coping with practical needs, whether economic or political, maintain (correctly in the opinion of this writer) that ideology has an influence on policy beyond these needs. As a guide to action, Marxist-Leninist teachings are utilized to enhance and extend the role and power of the Soviet Communist party, but these teachings also reflect the party's world outlook. In this ideology are found most of the basic teachings of Marx: the class struggle, the overthrow of capitalism, and the establishment of a system of social (collectivist) production. Ideology in the Soviet Union is thus "a continuous process resulting from the interplay of Communist theory and practice, affected at times—perhaps continually—by the interests of ruling groups, by Communist internecine struggles and by the personal characteristics of dictators, but with a logic of its own."[21]

Some writers have suggested that Soviet ideology be viewed in terms of its various components.[22] For example, one part constitutes dogma, a set of beliefs or axioms based on Lenin's interpretation of Marx. This set of beliefs is never subjected to logical analysis. Expansions of this dogma, however, would seem to be flexible and are altered from time to time as Soviet practice changes or as it is resisted

---

[21] C. Olgin, "What is Soviet Ideology?", *Bulletin* (Institute for the Study of the USSR), Vol. XI (November, 1964), p. 9.

[22] Joseph M. Bochenski, "The Three Components of Communist Ideology," *Studies in Soviet Thought*, Vol. II (March, 1962), pp. 7–11.

by reality. Moreover, in some areas of activity, such as the natural sciences, ideology does not seem to dictate, although even the scientists are obliged to help the ideologists fit new theories into the Marxist-Leninist framework.

The above brief summary of the role of ideology in the Soviet Union is merely suggestive. Undoubtedly much more study will be necessary before we can more adequately assess its role in the Soviet system.

BIBLIOGRAPHICAL NOTE

There are several editions of Marx's writings, among which one of the more convenient brief collections is *Capital, The Communist Manifesto, and Other Writings* (New York: Modern Library, 1932). A useful biography of Marx is Isaiah Berlin, *Karl Marx: His Life and Environment* (2d ed.; London: Oxford University Press, 1948). Some of the views of an influential nineteenth century Russian Marxist may be found in George Plekhanov, *Essays in Historical Materialism* (New York: International Publishers, 1940).

Among Lenin's numerous works, several deserve mention: *What Is To Be Done; Two Tactics of Social Democracy; Imperialism: The Highest Stage of Capitalism;* and *The State and Revolution.*

Recent analyses and critiques of Marxism include those of H. B. Acton, *The Illusion of the Epoch: Marxism-Leninism as a Philosophical Creed* (London: Cohen & West, 1955); Sidney Hook, *Marx and the Marxists* (Princeton: D. Van Nostrand, 1955); Robert N. Carew Hunt, *The Theory and Practice of Communism* (3d ed., London: Bles, 1957); Hans Kelsen, *The Political Theory of Bolshevism* (Berkeley: University of California Press, 1955); Alfred G. Meyer, *Leninism* (Cambridge, Mass.: Harvard University Press, 1957) and *Marxism: The Unity of Theory and Practice* (Cambridge, Mass.: Harvard University Press, 1954); John Plamenatz, *German Marxism and Russian Communism* (London: Longmans Green & Co., 1954); Ernest J. Simmons (ed.), *Continuity and Change in Russian and Soviet Thought* (Cambridge, Mass.: Harvard University Press, 1955); and Gustav A. Wetter, *Dialectical Materialism; A Historical and Systematic Survey of Philosophy in the Soviet Union* (New York: Praeger, 1958).

CHAPTER **26**

THE COMMUNIST
PARTY AND
ITS ROLE

THE COMMUNIST party is the driving force in the Soviet system. It is the dictatorship, not really *of* the proletariat, but *over* the proletariat and over all other groups in Soviet society. It has a complete monopoly of political power; no competing groups or influences are tolerated. The Soviet "Government" is not a government in the Western sense, for it is not an autonomous force. It cannot function independently of the party. As Stalin once said, "Not a single important political or organizational question is decided without direction from the party. . . ." The party makes the decisions, while the governmental apparatus serves as the party's agent to carry out these decisions.

In any study of the Soviet system, therefore, the key role of the Communist party must remain in the foreground, but, as a subsequent chapter will show, this role is not confined to the spheres of economics and politics. Every phase of human endeavor is within the scope of its all-embracing authority and concern.

BACKGROUND OF RUSSIAN COMMUNIST PARTY

The early Russian Marxists, as did those in Western Europe, thought of themselves as social democrats and initially called their party the Russian Social Democratic Labor party. As a consequence of internal quarrels, the faction that was to gain dominance called itself the Russian Social Democratic party (B).[1] In 1918, they changed the name to Russian Communist party (B), and in 1925 it became the All Union Communist party (B). Following the Nineteenth Party Congress in 1952, the official name became the Communist party of the U.S.S.R.

---

[1] The "B" stood for Bolsheviks; see pp. 339–40.

ORIGINS OF RUSSIAN MARXISM

Russian Marxism grew out of a split in the *Narodnik* (populist) organization, referred to in Chapter 24. The *Narodnik* movement was initiated by intellectuals who hoped and expected the peasantry to be responsive to their agitation, that is, to their explanations of the peasants' plight and their suggested remedies. When the peasantry proved unresponsive, and indeed hostile, many of the *Narodniki* turned more and more to direct action and violence. They acted through an organization called *Narodnaya Volya* (the people's will). Those who opposed violence established a rival organization, called the *Chernyi Peredel* (the black partition). Subsequently, leaders of the latter group, such as George Plekhanov, became convinced that the peasantry was a nonrevolutionary, conservative, and indifferent element. After searching for a new faith, they embraced Marxism, and founded the first Russian Marxist organization, called the Emancipation of Labor.

Declaring its disillusionment with the peasantry, this group, under the intellectual leadership of Plekhanov, declared that the revolutionary movement in Russia could triumph only if it were based on the working class. This constituted a break with the important *Narodnik* idea, which they had once shared, that Russia could skip the capitalist phase of development. Plekhanov and his cohorts were in effect saying that Russia was launched on the course of capitalist development, which would produce the working class, and which in turn would overthrow Russian bourgeois society.

Marxism, however, meant different things to many Russians who professed to be Marxists.[2] Some equated it with industrial development, others with traditional trade unionism, still others with idealistic reforms and opportunism. Plekhanov and his pupil, V. I. Lenin, viewing themselves as orthodox Marxists, sought in the 1890s to defend the orthodox Marxist analysis and particularly to reassert its revolutionary content. They agreed with the *Communist Manifesto* that the proletarian revolution would come in the wake of capitalist development. Because Russia was industrially backward, they believed that the initial task was to facilitate a bourgeois-democratic revolution in Russia. While Plekhanov remained loyal to his position to the end, Lenin was to find it increasingly inconvenient, for it got

---

[2] See Leopold H. Haimson, *The Russian Marxists and the Origins of Bolshevism* (Cambridge: Harvard University Press, 1955).

in the way of his activist bent. Other Russian Marxists were to find themselves similarly divided.

MENSHEVIKS AND BOLSHEVIKS

The Russian Social Democratic Labor party, founded in 1898, developed a split of major proportions at its second congress, held in London in 1903.[3] Out of it emerged two distinct groups of Russian Marxists, the result of a split which had been in the making for several years. The groups came to be known as Mensheviks and Bolsheviks. These words are derived from the Russian words *Menshe* and *Bolshe*, meaning less and more, respectively. The split between the Mensheviks (or minority men) and the Bolsheviks (or majority men) continued to widen in the years ahead, leading to their complete and formal separation in 1912.

The Mensheviks and Bolsheviks found themselves divided on two primary and several subsidiary questions. The first of the major questions concerned the political implications of Russia's industrial backwardness. The Mensheviks, led by Plekhanov, held to the orthodox view that socialism would come to Russia only after the bourgeois-democratic revolution, and this was to be a long-term affair. The opposite view, often identified with Leon Trotsky, originally a Menshevik, held that the capitalist class was not strong enough to bring forth the bourgeois revolution. Hence, the proletariat should bring on the revolution and keep it going (in "permanence") until the proletarian revolution should be completed. This would mean telescoping two revolutions into one. While continuing to pay lip service to the orthodox doctrine, Lenin and the Bolsheviks were in spirit close to the latter group. Subsequently, Lenin was to add his own contribution to Bolshevik theory by suggesting an alliance with the peasantry so as to give the proletariat a broader base. By tactically combining the proletariat with the peasantry to complete the democratic revolution, and subsequently with the village poor to bring on the proletarian revolution, industrial backwardness, in Lenin's view (and later Stalin's), could actually be turned to the advantage of socialism.

The second of the major questions in the split in the Russian Social Democrats involved the nature of the party. Lenin, as leader of what

---

[3] The first congress had met secretly at Minsk, but the principal participants were arrested before anything could be done beyond the appointment of the central committee and the decision to publish a party organ. The second congress had to be held abroad, originally convened in Brussels, but soon transferred to London for fear of police pressure.

was to become the Bolshevik faction, argued for a relatively small, closed party of carefully selected and dedicated revolutionaries. This would be a disciplined organization run from the center. While sympathizers would be encouraged, they would not be members of the party. The leaders of what was to become the Menshevik faction, on the other hand, argued for a broadly based party which would admit all who believed in its program. Such a party would of necessity have to accord some voice to the rank and file. Moreover, such a party would collaborate with other parliamentary parties when it was in its interest to do so, something that was anathema to Lenin. Although initially in a minority, Lenin, through tactical maneuvers, gained a majority of the delegates for his side. In the years ahead, he did all in his power to consolidate his position of leadership and to rebuff all challenges to his authority.

The definitive split in 1912 resulted in no small part from Lenin's precarious hold on the leading committees, which he was afraid he could not maintain, and therefore directed the formation of a separate Bolshevik organization with a separate central committee. The Bolsheviks, however, resisted his suggestion that they call themselves Communists, a name they adopted only after their seizure of power.

The collapse of tsarism and the establishment of the bourgeois-democratic provisional government seemed to favor the Menshevik position. The gains of the Bolsheviks, however, and particularly their seizure of power in November 1917, irrevocably settled the argument in favor of the Bolsheviks, at least insofar as Russia was concerned. The Menshevik arguments were answered by revolutionary action. The events of 1917, for all practical purposes, resolved the Bolshevik-Menshevik controversy in favor of the former. The Mensheviks, as well as others, continued an uneasy and harassed existence as opposition parties until the end of the civil war, when the Bolsheviks put an end to opposition groups.

ELASTICITY OF BOLSHEVIK TACTICS

The history of Russian Marxism in the early part of this century, and particularly the history of what transpired in 1917, has provided us with the major clue to Bolshevik success. In no small measure, their success may be attributed to the elasticity of their tactics. Their firm dedication to the goal of achieving political power was certainly important. Perhaps other political groups were equally dedicated to their respective goals, but they had none of the ingenuity or the willingness of the Bolsheviks to alter their methods, to change their positions, or to take seemingly contradictory positions when doing so would advance them toward their objective.

Lenin, for the most part, was the master tactician in all Bolshevik maneuvers. The elasticity of his tactics enabled him to bring the peasants into his theories because he believed that their discontent could be channeled to Bolshevik ends. Similarly, he was convinced that the discontent among the non-Russian nationalities could be harnessed in the interests of the proletarian revolution. His changes in attitude as to whether or not the Bolsheviks should participate in the soviets, whether they should take part in the Duma elections, etc., further confirmed his influence on Bolshevik tactical elasticity. Lenin's dedication to this principle has by and large been observed by his party successors.

BOLSHEVIK CONCEPT OF PARTY

Out of this factious and discordant background and out of the experience of governing in subsequent years, the Bolsheviks developed a concept of party which embraces certain definite characteristics. In the main, these characteristics are identified with questions concerning what the party is supposed to be and what it is supposed to do. The answers to these questions have not varied materially during the period of Soviet rule.

MONOLITHIC REVOLUTIONARY ELITE

The early formative years gave the party an indelible cast. That cast was in the nature of a monolithic revolutionary elite. Lenin was especially insistent upon the elitist principle: only the most qualified and dedicated persons should be permitted membership. They all must be of one mind, or at least capable of accepting iron discipline and obedience once the party line had been handed down. No deviations were to be permitted; in other words, no internal factions could exist. The party was to speak with one voice and to act as one unit. Sympathizers (fellow travelers) were encouraged to cooperate and to lend themselves to party ends, but they would not be permitted to become encumbrances on the party's disciplined and monolithic machine.

All of these ideas, predicated upon the assumption that the party would be the instrument for the seizure of political power in the name of the proletariat, were reinforced under the leadership of Lenin's successor, Joseph Stalin. By comparison with Stalin, Lenin's intolerance of disagreement and compromise were mild indeed. Rigidity in the interpretation of the party line increased constantly during Stalin's reign. Slightly varying points of view became known as major and treasonous deviations, which were punished with increasing severity.

Stalin's successors, although making certain modifications in the Soviet system, have not departed from basic Bolshevik tenets concerning the nature of the Communist party. It continues to be viewed as a monolithic, highly centralized, and disciplined organization. There has been no suggestion that factions be permitted within the party or that top leaders of the party be subject to criticism any more than they have been in the past.

VANGUARD OF THE WORKING PEOPLE

The Russians have described the Communist party as the most conscious segment of the working class, whose role it is to lead and to speak for the proletariat. As the all-wise and only true defender and expounder of socialism, the party is supposed to know what needs to be done during the period of transition from capitalism to communism. Since no one else can be trusted with this task, the party not only becomes the source of all initiative, but also the all-wise judge of human actions and motivations, and of good and evil. Moreover, the party not only assumes the role of guarding and protecting the interests of the proletariat against all other movements that would seek the favor of the proletariat, but in addition, prevents the formation or operation of any group whose aim is to appeal to any segment of society for support.

In other words, the party is the sole instrument for the totalitarian remaking of society. The party organization is charged with facilitating the execution and acceptance of the policies of the party's high command. Moreover, it must from time to time assimilate into its ranks various individuals, while at the same time making sure that their devotion to the party is unquestioned, so that the party may continue to be a trustworthy instrument of its leaders. The party, in short, operates as a machine of the party leadership for the total reconstruction of society.

INTRAPARTY DEMOCRACY

The Bolsheviks have often defended their totalitarian dictatorship by arguing that democracy prevails inside the party. They have said that until the party takes a position on a certain question, party members are free to discuss and debate the various aspects of that question. Moreover, they have asserted that even after the party line has been established, rank and file members, as well as those at the top, are encouraged to engage in criticism and self-criticism.

In practice, as a subsequent section of this chapter will show, dissent within party ranks was discouraged from the outset, and progressively repressed until it came to an end. The criticism which today remains is a controlled criticism, directed from the top. The lesser figures in the party and their work are the invariable objects of this criticism. On occasion a more prominent figure is accorded the "opportunity" of indulging in self-criticism, admitting his sins and bringing down wrath upon his own shoulders. But high party leaders, as well as party policies, are immune from criticism from below, unless for some reason these leaders decide that a change is needed and that it would be facilitated by controlled and directed criticism.

But even controlled criticism does not assert that the party erred in a given situation. As a general rule, the criticism centers on bureaucratic inefficiency, venality, and on outright refusal to carry out assigned tasks. Sometimes governmental officials are charged with being unimaginative, slow, and inept in adapting party policies to the circumstances at hand. Other times they are accused of misinterpreting party directives. Such criticism, the leaders hope, will have the effect of diverting attention from them as well as from the party when things go wrong.

Party leaders who die or are removed from office may be subject to criticism. This has been true even of top leaders such as Stalin and Khrushchev. But the contention is always made that their misdeeds are not the fault of the party. In the downgrading of Stalin, for example, it was even asserted that other party leaders had no choice but to carry out his evil directives. The system which permits or enables a personal dictator to arise is seemingly never at fault.

ORGANIZATIONAL STRUCTURE AND AUTHORITY WITHIN THE PARTY

THE PARTY: SIZE AND COMPOSITION

The Russian Communists have by and large adhered to Lenin's precept that the party should be kept relatively small. The party has grown numerically, but for the most part this has been a controlled growth. The years of World War II were somewhat of an exception. Because casualties among party comrades were particularly high, recruitment policies were liberalized, with the result that Russia came out of the war with the party membership nearly doubled. New members were often taken in more because of their contribution to the war effort than for their knowledge of and dedication to Marxism-Leninism. The present membership is approximately 11 million, with more than 500,000 candidates for membership. Most of the candidates are among the 18 to 20 million members of the *Komsomol* (Communist youth organization). In a total population of some 225 million, the Communist party is still a relatively small and select organization.

In the light of Marxian theory, one might expect to find the Communist party the party of the proletariat. Soviet industrial workers, however, while constituting an important core of the party membership, are by no means in a majority. In fact, they account for approximately one third of the total. The rural areas account for something less than a third of the total, although Soviet statistics in this area are exceedingly meager.[4] The remainder is made up from the "toiling intelligentsia," or the bureaucracy, which, together with the workers, enables the party to retain its predominantly urban character.

The really important development in party membership is to be found in the shift in emphasis from the workers to the technical and administrative intelligentsia. Party membership among the workers and among farmers has been in relative decline, while among the growing class of technicians, factory managers, engineers, and party and government bureaucrats, party membership has been on the increase. This has had the effect of raising the intellectual level of the party membership. It has also resulted in an increasing influence being wielded by the new Soviet administrative and intellectual elite, with a corresponding decline in the influence of the workers and the farmers. It is interesting in this connection that Khrushchev in 1961 observed that in time there would be no need to divide party members into workers, farmers, and white-collar workers.

For a long time rank and file representation in the party of various nationalities favored the Slavs, especially the Great Russians. This was especially true in Stalin's time. In recent years, however, there has been a considerable redressing of the balance, with the avowed aim of bringing the percentage of party membership among the non-Russian nationalities up to that of the RSFSR. While this goal has in a large measure been realized, the Great Russians still seem to enjoy a disproportionate representation in the party's top leadership groups.

---

[4] Soviet authorities have admitted that as late as 1958, some collective farms had no party units, while on others they were small and weak.

From time to time party ranks are purged of "undesirables."[5] The Russian Communists have looked upon the purge as a rational and desirable way of keeping the ranks pure by cleaning out the undesirable elements. This is in conformity with the Leninist notion that the party should be a monolithic organism. The need for the purge presupposes that the rigid process for admission to the party is not foolproof, that some persons will get in who should have been excluded. In the post–World War II period, many of those who had been hastily admitted to the party were expelled because they could not be educated to accept their roles as dedicated Leninists.

In the struggles for power within the party, however, the concept of the purge was broadened to include mass expulsions and a large-scale liquidation of party leaders at all levels.[6] Purges to this end could hardly be defended as merely a cleaning out of persons of doubtful dedication to Marxism-Leninism, for some of Lenin's most devoted followers perished in the purges.

Where the penalty is mere expulsion, on the other hand, many members become undesirable deliberately, for being thrown out is by and large the only way out of the party. Once a person becomes a party member he dares not give thought to leaving the party on his own volition. To leave, or to suggest leaving, is tantamount to treason. Yet some persons have found it difficult to continue living a lie, that is, to pretend to believe the party's propaganda. The way out for some of these people is expulsion, which can sometimes be induced by failure to pay dues, attend meetings, or perform assigned tasks. Excessive consumption of alcohol may also produce undesirables, and hence candidates for expulsion.

PRINCIPLE OF ORGANIZATION: DEMOCRATIC CENTRALISM

Ostensibly, the Communist party is organized on the basis of the principle of "democratic centralism." This means, as Soviet spokesmen have explained it, that the party is a pyramidal organization. At the bottom are some 300,000 primary units, once called cells. Above these are several layers of intermediate bodies, each layer having fewer units until the top is reached, where there is one supreme party organization. This setup is allegedly democratic because, in theory at least, members of the lower units in the pyramid elect persons to the

---

[5] For an excellent work on the purge as a technique of Soviet totalitarianism, see Zbigniew K. Brzezinski, *The Permanent Purge: Politics in Soviet Totalitarianism* (Cambridge, Mass.: Harvard University Press, 1956).

[6] The struggle for power within the party is discussed in a subsequent section of this chapter.

unit above, and these in turn are responsible to those who elected them. The centralist aspect is to be found in that it is incumbent upon the lower layers to obey the directives and to carry out the orders of the units above them.

In Soviet practice, however, the accent has been on centralism. First of all, the elective principle has been largely meaningless, for so often members have been co-opted, that is, named by someone above, a practice admitted by the Russians, although in the form of a criticism. Secondly, the leaders at the very top, so long as they stick together, are in no danger of being ousted, and they in turn can virtually dictate the selection of those immediately below. These, in turn, because they have the confidence of the top leaders, can dictate the selection of those below them, and so on down the line. The one possible exception involves local party secretaries, some of whom have been ousted, following the introduction of the practice of voting for each member of the local committee individually and by secret ballot. Secretaries of city and district committees must be approved by committees of higher units, which sometimes means that approval from top leaders is necessary. Finally, the practice of ruthlessly punishing dissenters has discouraged members from questioning the adequacy of individuals whom they have "elected."

Moreover, party rules protect members of the executive bodies at all levels from disciplinary action by the respective primary organization to which they belong. Punishment can be inflicted only if a two-thirds majority of the executive body concerned, meeting in plenary session, gives its consent. In this way the leaders run no risk, if indeed one ever existed, of being embarrassed by a "defeat in their own precinct."

Democratic centralism, as theoretically conceived, operated only at the beginning—while the Bolshevik party was in the process of organization. Even then the leaders were in large measure self-appointed, reaching the top through ability and the force of their personalities. Once the top group was fairly well established, the members of that group, and not those below, determined who should join them in positions of leadership. From that time on, democracy gave way to centralism and to authority.

NATIONAL PARTY GOVERNING BODIES

The party congress, according to party rules, is the "supreme organ" of the party. In practice it is anything but that. It is supposed to meet at least once every four years, but even this party rule has not always been observed. Between 1939 and 1952, for example, no congresses were held. Since 1952 there have been four congresses: 1956, 1959, 1961, and 1966. Aside from the infrequency of their meetings, which, in any event, last but a few days, congresses are handicapped by their sheer size, recent ones having several thousand delegates. Moreover, their proceedings give every outward indication of being carefully prepared in advance, with no dissenting debate and all decisions being taken unanimously. Party congresses are, in reality, huge manifestations or rallies of the party faithful who merely sit, perhaps also listen to, and applaud the party leaders. Conversely, the congresses provide a platform for the leaders to extol their alleged accomplishments, to call for renewed efforts on behalf of old or new goals, and to proclaim changes in the party line.

Far more important than the party congress is the Central Committee, ostensibly elected by the congress and meeting at least once every six months. Its membership has been characterized by large turnovers from one congress to another. The greatest turnovers occurred in the 1930s following the great purges, but more recent changes have been quite extensive. At the Twentieth Party Congress in 1956, for example, 133 members were elected, over a third of them for the first time, while of the 122 candidate members over half were chosen for the first time. At the Twenty Second Party Congress in 1961, the membership of the Central Committee was increased to 175 members and 155 candidate members. Among these, the holdovers constituted approximately thirty-seven per cent. These large turnovers have not resulted from actions freely taken by the respective congresses, for no one is elected to the Central Committee unless his name is proposed by the top leadership of the party.

The new party rules adopted in 1961 set forth the principle of "systematic renewal of the composition of party bodies." More specifically, they provide that not less than one-fourth of the composition of the Central Committee and of the Presidium shall be renewed at each regular election (i.e. once every four years). In the case of the central committees of the party in the republics, as well as in the case of territorial and provincial committees, one-third of the membership is to be renewed. In the case of local committees, one-half of the members should be changed at each election. Moreover, the rules provide that normally a person should not be re-elected for more than three successive terms (two in the case of local committees). This provision may be ignored in the case of individuals of recognized prestige and high political and organizational talents. In such circumstances a three-fourths vote is required, but this proviso should not endanger the positions of the top leaders or of those whom the top leaders want to retain in their posts.

The Central Committee is charged with directing the work of the party between congresses, and its powers, at least on paper, are extensive. Aside from its authority to manage party resources, appoint editors, and set up various party institutions, the Central Committee "directs the work of central government bodies and social organizations of working people through the party groups in them." While basic directives are issued in the name of the Central Committee, in actuality these functions are performed by and under the direction of the Presidium and the Secretariat (discussed below). While the Central Committee was relatively important in the 1920s, it rarely met during the latter years of Stalin's rule and, according to one-time party secretary Khrushchev, it was never called into session during World War II.[7] In more recent years, the Central Committee has met with fair regularity, but there is no evidence to suggest that it has seriously impeded the proposals or programs of the recognized leader or leaders. Because many of its members are prominent in the governmental bureaucracy, in science and technology, in the military, and in the cultural field, the Central Committee serves as a link between the party elite represented in the Presidium and the Secretariat and the important scientific-technical-administrative apparatus that supervises the operation of the Soviet system.

For most, if not all, of the Soviet period, the most powerful party body has been the Presidium, prior to 1952 known as the Politburo (or policy bureau), numbering about a dozen men. In 1952, it was merged with the Orgburo (organizational bureau), resulting in a body of 25 members and 11 candidates. After Stalin's death in 1953, the membership of the Presidium was cut to its former size. In recent years its size has fluctuated between 10 and 14 members and 6 to 9 candidates. As the group that is supposed to direct the work of the Central Committee between its plenary meetings, the Presidium is the supreme policy-making body in all spheres of Soviet life. Although elected by the Central Committee, Presidium members are chosen only upon recommendation by the Presidium, a recommendation that in the past originated with the recognized leader.

The Secretariat is a type of management board of the party apparatus. In recent years it has consisted of five to ten secretaries (several of whom are also members of the Presidium) who are chosen

[7] *New York Times*, June 5, 1956.

by the Central Committee in much the same way as the members of the Presidium. With a staff of approximately 100,000 full-time party professionals, the Secretariat is charged with directing the current work of the party. This means that it selects personnel for positions of responsibility in various parts of the Soviet system, and that it verifies fulfillment of party decisions in all fields—political, economic, social, propaganda, and so on. In this way, the Secretariat not only serves to implement policies, but is at the same time the eyes and ears of the Presidium.

In the Presidium and in the Secretariat there is a broad division of labor. These general areas of responsibility include foreign affairs, heavy industry, agriculture, party affairs, agitation and propaganda, political administration of the armed forces, and other spheres of activity with which the party is concerned.[8] Because of their intimate association with the party, state, military, and police apparatus, the members of the Secretariat are now thought to be in a position to exercise a decisive influence in the party Presidium on all matters of high policy. One writer refers to the Presidium as "merely a weekly gathering, a 'little party parliament,' a 'talking shop,' while the Secretariat is the permanently active, sole repository of supreme power, even though from the juridical standpoint it is subordinate to the Presidium."[9]

Although party rules have emphasized the principle of collective leadership, the general tendency in the Soviet system has been toward one-man rule. This was true in Lenin's day, but much more so after Stalin consolidated his power in the late 1920s. It was Stalin's position as general secretary of the party, and his determination to use that position to the utmost, that enabled him to rise to a position of unquestioned ascendancy. Nikita Khrushchev, although never using the title of general secretary (merely first secretary), was able to rise to one-man leadership in a brief span of time. His successor, Leonid Brezhnev, also assumed the title of first secretary, but it is not possible at this writing to predict whether he will achieve a position of unquestioned one-man leadership.[10]

One other organ of the Central Committee, the Control Committee,

---

[8] For an excellent discussion of the various reorganizations of the Secretariat, see Merle Fainsod, *How Russia is Ruled* (rev. ed., Cambridge, Mass.: Harvard University Press, 1963), pp. 190–208.

[9] Abdurakhman Avtorkhanov, "The General Implications," *Bulletin: Institute for the Study of the USSR*, Vol. XI (December, 1964), p. 15. Also see Leonard Schapiro, *The Communist Party of the Soviet Union* (New York: Random House, 1960), pp. 563, 580.

[10] For a discussion of one-man rule versus collective leadership, see the subsequent sections of this chapter.

deserves mention. Its task is to check on members to see that party discipline is observed, that its rules and its program are loyally adhered to, and, in case of violations, to punish the guilty. In addition, it passes on appeals from disciplinary actions of the central committees of the republics.

* * * * *

It is of importance to note that most of the men who have reached the top of the party hierarchy in recent years have spent most of their lives in administrative and organizational work. Most of the men in the Secretariat and in the Presidium have had long careers in the party apparatus, Aleksei Kosygin, an economic administrator who was named Chairman of the Council of Ministers in October 1964, being the only exception. Some of the men at the top have been consistently identified with a single area of competence, while others have had responsibilities in a number of fields. Most of them were graduated from institutions of higher learning, with a majority having only narrow, highly specialized technical training.

In the Central Committee the situation is not too different. About a third of its membership is made up of men whose primary background is work in the party apparatus. The next largest group represents men who have devoted most of their adult years to the state bureaucracy. The third largest group has primarily a military background. In view of these facts, it is perhaps not surprising to find that approximately sixty per cent of Central Committee members have had a technical-scientific education. Some fifteen per cent have had no higher education, while the remainder have had military or general educational training.

LOCAL PARTY ORGANS

The party governing bodies at the national level, as the above suggests, are by all odds the most important. Each republic, except the largest, the RSFSR, has governing bodies corresponding to those on the national level. In almost every instance the names of the institutions are the same: congress, central committee, etc. Below the national level, however, the executive of party committees is called a bureau instead of a presidium. Party organizations below the national level are subservient to the national organization of the party, where all the important decisions are made, as well as many of lesser significance.

The party organizations of the various subdivisions of the RSFSR report directly to the governing bodies of the national party. The desire of certain leaders in the RSFSR to establish a separate organization for their republic led to the celebrated "Leningrad case," following World War II. The result was the purge and liquidation of a number of party leaders, including one Politburo member. In 1956, however, the Twentieth Party Congress established a special Bureau of RSFSR Affairs in the Central Committee. Its chairman is the first secretary of the Central Committee.

The first duty of party organizations in the republics is to see to it that the decrees and instructions emanating from the Central Committee in Moscow are carried out. The latter seeks to insure that this will be done (1) by specifying in great detail the duties of party organizations at all levels, and (2) by providing extensive controls in the party apparatus from top to bottom.

THE PARTY BUREAUCRACY

The bureaucratic apparatus of the party is vast, although the exact number of individuals engaged in full-time paid party work remains a secret. Various estimates have run from 100,000 to 500,000, with the first figure probably being more accurate as of this writing.[11] Since 1956 there has been a conscious effort to reduce the number of full-time party functionaries. At the same time, however, the number of part-time unpaid party workers has increased considerably.

The initial core of *apparatchiki* (men of the apparatus) emerged from the Bolshevik pre-tsarist conspiratorial underground organization. Stalin's rise to supreme power can in large part be attributed to his close association with this group. In the early years of the Soviet regime, his chief party work was in the Orgburo, which constituted his first base of operations. From that position, he built, shaped, and controlled the party's bureaucratic apparatus. It was in connection with this work that in 1922 he was named to the post of general secretary, a position that has come to be regarded as that of unchallenged supreme authority in the party.[12]

The party's bureaucratic machine serves to make the authority of the dictatorship effective. As the long arm of the dictatorship, operating under the respective sections of the party Secretariat, it handles the detailed work of the party. It transmits directives and orders, supervises local party organizations, checks on fulfillment of tasks, assigns personnel, calls party secretaries to render an accounting of

---

[11] See Fainsod, *op. cit.*, pp. 205–07. Also, see Schapiro, *op. cit.*, pp. 572–73.

[12] For an excellent summary of the growth of the party apparatus, see Fainsod, *ibid.*, chap. 6.

their work, and reports its observations to the appropriate party leaders in Moscow. The following chart depicts the division of the Secretariat of the Central Committee into various departments:

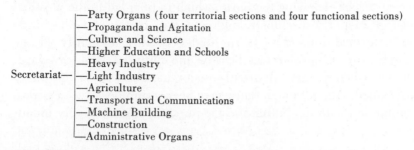

Secretariat—
—Party Organs (four territorial sections and four functional sections)
—Propaganda and Agitation
—Culture and Science
—Higher Education and Schools
—Heavy Industry
—Light Industry
—Agriculture
—Transport and Communications
—Machine Building
—Construction
—Administrative Organs

In addition, there are four other departments which are of particular importance. They are: Main Political Administration of the Soviet Army and Navy, Foreign Affairs, Liaison with Bloc Parties, and Liaison with Non-Bloc Parties. It must be noted, however, that changes in the organization of the Secretariat have been made periodically and these have not always been publicized. Because of this fact, the above scheme may not completely reflect the existing organization.

THE KHRUSHCHEV REORGANIZATION OF 1962

In November 1962, the Central Committee approved a proposal by the party's first secretary, Khrushchev, to reorganize the party structure into two hierarchies, one to be concerned with agriculture and the other with industry. The resulting hierarchies of party committees would be coordinated for the first time at the republic level, where only one central committee and only one presidium existed. The avowed reason for this reorganization was to make more effective the party's control function, i.e. in seeing to it that the policies and programs of the top leadership were carried out. This scheme apparently did not produce the desired results. In any case, Khrushchev's successors declared it a failure, and abandoned it, presumably going back to the territorial principle of organization.

THE STRUGGLE FOR POWER WITHIN THE PARTY

In the writings of Marx, Lenin and other Marxian theorists, there is the presumption that unity of purpose would characterize the dictatorship of the proletariat. The Russian experience has demonstrated, however, that irreconcilable differences arose. This should not have been too surprising in view of the ideological splintering that has prevailed during the past century in the whole socialist movement, including its Russian component. Uncompromising from the outset, the leaders of the Bolshevik faction, once in power, were determined not to tolerate factions inside the party. To this end, they embarked upon a course of cleansing the party, which in turn led to the physical liquidation of party dissidents, high and low. In the end, the purge was transformed into mass terror under Stalin; the unity of the dictatorship of the proletariat became the unity of the graveyard. Under Khrushchev, and apparently under his successors, the purge was continued. And although there have been a number of executions, by comparison with the Stalin era, the purge has been largely bloodless.

LENIN AND THE STRUGGLE FOR POWER

Lenin remained the unquestioned leader of the young Communist regime until his death in 1924, but he laid the psychological basis for purging party ranks, which was to become the decisive instrument in the struggle for power within the party.[13] His utter rejection of compromise and his equating of disobedience in party ranks with treason left no room in the party except for those who unquestioningly accepted the party's course as it was defined by the leader. During Lenin's lifetime, however, the purge of party ranks meant no more than expulsion from the party.[14] More frequently, discipline took the form of transferring the person to work in more remote regions of the country. But the groundwork for more severe measures was laid in his lifetime.

In the initial years of Lenin's rule there were some party members who believed that a certain amount of opposition within the party was possible. In 1920, a group calling itself Democratic Centralists appeared at the Ninth Congress of the party and, among other things, accused the Leninist Central Committee of being a "small handful of party oligarchs," who were exiling comrades because of their "deviant views." Simultaneously, party rank and file unrest developed into the so-called Workers' Opposition, which demanded that industry be controlled and managed by the trade unions.[15]

---

[13] For a discussion of the instruments of the purge as means of subduing non-Communist groups and individuals, see Chapter 28.

[14] The outbreak at Kronstadt in March 1921 among the Red Navy sailors, one-time supporters of the Bolshevik revolution who demanded, among other things, civil liberties and the end of the party dictatorship, was nevertheless crushed with armed force. This cannot, however, be viewed as a party purge.

[15] For an excellent summary of party opposition under Lenin, see Fainsod, *op. cit.*, pp. 141–48.

Lenin's answer to the Democratic Centralists and the Workers' Opposition, his one-time supporters who were turning against the regime, was to get the Tenth Party Congress (1921) to declare these and similar groups dissolved and to prohibit the formation of groups which were critical of the general line of the Central Committee. Moreover, he insisted on a proviso, kept secret for a time, which in effect forbade agitation against the party line even by leading members of the party. Although Lenin on occasion employed threats which clearly implied physical violence, he did not punish dissenters with anything more severe than expulsion from the party. But his suppression of all opposition within the party inevitably led to resolving struggles for power by force and violence.

STALIN AND THE STRUGGLE FOR POWER

In his position as general secretary of the party, Stalin had laid the basis for consolidation of power in his hands. This proceeded slowly. For a time, while Lenin lay dying and for two or three years thereafter, power seemed to be shared by a triumvirate in the Politburo, composed of Stalin, Leo Kamenev, and Gregory Zinoviev, who had banded together to keep Trotsky from succeeding Lenin. In response to Trotsky's open criticism of the state of things, Stalin's two cohorts demanded firm action (including arrest) against Trotsky, while Stalin appeared to be moderate and restrained. Gradually, Trotsky was removed from one position and then another until he had no power left.

In the meantime, differences between Stalin and his two cohorts had been developing. But Stalin had been preparing for a showdown. As general secretary, he was building a faithful machine of party workers who would increasingly control delegations to party congresses. Secondly, he was forging a coalition in the Politburo against Kamenev and Zinoviev, which included Nikolai Bukharin, Aleksei Rykov, and Mikhail Tomsky. Step by step, Stalin was able to isolate Kamenev and Zinoviev to such an extent that they abjectly confessed their errors and promised to abide by party discipline. But they were expelled from their positions and from the party, although they were later readmitted.

Once the so-called "leftist deviationists" (Kamenev, et al.) were subdued, Stalin borrowed their program (collectivization of agriculture and intensive industrialization) and introduced it as Soviet policy. The so-called "rightists" (Bukharin, et al.) became restive. Stalin alleged that he had discovered a plot of the right-wing group to consolidate forces with the remnants of the leftist faction. Under Stalin's attack, Bukharin, Tomsky, and Rykov capitulated; they confessed their sins and asked to be permitted to do battle against all deviations from the general line of the party. But they were soon removed from the important positions which they had held.

At the beginning of 1934, Stalin could boast of complete victory. "The anti-Leninist Trotskyite group has been defeated and scattered. . . . The anti-Leninist group of the right deviationists has been defeated and scattered . . . . the national deviationist groups have been defeated and scattered . . . . the party today is united as it has never been before."[16] Thus, in his struggle for absolute power, Stalin narrowed the margin of permissible dissent for the opposition until it disappeared.[17]

STALIN AND THE GREAT PURGE

Throughout the period when he was consolidating his power, Stalin and his henchmen repeatedly declared that the need of purging party ranks increased after the proletariat had gained power. Power, they said, tended to attract opportunists, many of whom were able to conceal their real motives. Moreover, the *bourgeoisie* had not accepted defeat and was instead resorting to all sorts of vicious means in an effort to undermine the Soviet system. The opportunists in the party became convenient and ready tools of the class enemy. Therefore, said the Stalinists, the party had to be vigilant against the wrecking activities of these elements.

The road of repression moved from expulsion to arrest and imprisonment in the late 1920s and early 1930s. By the mid-1930s it had led to the extermination of the old Bolsheviks and to mass terror. A most revealing document concerning the Great Purge of the 1930s is the speech of the one-time party secretary, Nikita S. Khrushchev, to a closed session of the Twentieth Party Congress in February 1956.[18] Although question marks remain, Khrushchev's speech provided many previously unknown details of a purge whose main features have long been known.

The Great Purge ostensibly had its origin in the assassination in

---

[16] Stalin, *Problems of Leninism*, pp. 515–16.

[17] For a more detailed discussion of Stalin's consolidation of power, see Fainsod, *op. cit.*, pp. 148–60. Also see Brzezinski, *op. cit.*, especially chaps. 3 and 4.

[18] For a purported text, see *New York Times*, June 5, 1956. Also see text published by the *New Leader* under the title, *The Crimes of the Stalin Era*, and annotated by Boris I. Nicolaevsky. Also see Bertram D. Wolfe, *Khrushchev and Stalin's Ghost* (New York, 1957).

December 1934 of the Leningrad party secretary, Sergei M. Kirov, by a fellow Communist. The circumstances surrounding his assassination remain vague, or, to use Khrushchev's words, "inexplicable and mysterious." Khrushchev clearly asserts that there are grounds for believing that the killer was aided by people inside the secret police, and asserts that the leaders of the secret police in Leningrad, after being given light sentences for their negligence, were shot in 1937 "in order to cover the traces of the organizers of Kirov's killing." This would seem clearly to implicate Stalin.

In any case, "the next four years claimed victims in the hundreds of thousands."[19] Trotsky had been exiled, but Kamenev, Zinoviev, Bukharin, Rykov, and countless of their alleged followers paid the supreme penalty. The blood bath also engulfed other important party figures and many more lesser ones. Tomsky committed suicide, as did a number of lesser figures. Many who escaped liquidation were sent to camps in Siberia, from which few returned. Expulsions from the party were on a mass scale. One fifth of the total membership was expelled; in the Ukraine one out of four was turned out.

The Great Purge also devoured many officers of the Red Army. Among those who perished was the chief of staff, Marshal Tukhachevsky. A number of generals and many lesser officers shared his fate.

Scarcely a segment of Soviet society remained unscathed. Many of those who perished, both inside and outside party ranks, were innocent, even by Stalin's admission. But since the infallible Stalin could not be responsible, the liquidation of innocent people was attributed to "enemies of the people," who had infiltrated party and police ranks. In any event, a momentary halt to the purge was called, while many of the purgers were purged. In the meantime, Stalin continued to liquidate those who became suspect, but at a somewhat slower pace and with less attendant publicity.

Originally, the purge was associated with the difficulty of coordinating Communists in the making of policy. Lenin's answer was the authoritarian formula, which under Stalin developed into an unbridled liquidation of all opposition or competition in matters of policy determination within the party. Simultaneously, the party purge provided an opportunity for the regime to sweep away all opposition, party and nonparty, real and imagined.

In the absence of institutional or other limitations on the dictator-

---

[19] Fainsod, *op cit.*, p. 158.

ship, the purge gained momentum. As it progressed, it created the impression of a huge and continuing conspiracy against the regime, suggesting the need of extending the purge. This intensified already existing tensions and uncertainties. Fear bred fear. Had not a temporary halt been called, the purge might very well have consumed the system.

After a brief lull, during which many of the purgers lost their lives, the purge was resumed. Perhaps what we have come to refer to as "the purges" should be characterized as the violent eruptions of a purging process that is in continuous operation. Professor Brzezinski, in his cogently written book, concludes that the purge has become a permanent institution.[20] In his opinion, it serves to release or absorb tensions, conflicts, and struggles for power within the system. It facilitates the circulation of elites in a monolithic system where competition and free choice do not prevail. Moreover, it provides a way of maintaining revolutionary fervor by periodically weeding out corrupt and careerist elements.

THE NEW STRUGGLE FOR POWER: KHRUSHCHEV AND AFTER

Nikita Khrushchev's ascendancy to supreme power in the years after Stalin's death (1953), as well as his ouster in 1964, may have opened a new chapter in the struggle for power within the Communist party. Khrushchev's rise to a position of unquestioned leadership was somewhat reminiscent of Stalin's.[21] Within a month of the former dictator's death, he was the senior secretary of the party and not long thereafter was made first secretary. Almost simultaneously came the execution of Lavrenti Beria, Stalin's head of the secret police, and a number of his associates. Using his position as first secretary, Khrushchev asserted his leadership by assuming the role of the party's spokesman in the Central Committee and by becoming head of the government. At the same time, he sought to disassociate himself from the evils of the Stalin regime, primarily through his denunciation of the former dictator's misdeeds in a speech (discussed below) to a closed session of the party congress in February 1956. Moreover, he moved to discredit his principal rivals, Stalin's and his onetime

---

[20] *Op. cit.*, see especially pp. 168–75. Other and different views of the purges are to be found in such works as Isaac Deutscher, *Russia in Transition and Other Essays* (New York: Coward-McCann, 1957) and George Fischer, *Soviet Opposition to Stalin: A Case Study in World War II* (Cambridge, Mass.: Harvard University Press, 1952).

[21] For a detailed discussion of Khrushchev's struggle for power, see Fainsod, *op. cit.*, pp. 161–75.

associates in the Presidium. He was challenged briefly in 1957, but succeeded in outmaneuvering his foes and removing them from the party Presidium and the Central Committee. The "collective leadership" was dissolved.

By the end of 1958, Khrushchev's leadership was beyond challenge. While condemning Stalin's "personality cult" and extolling "collective leadership," he had built a personality cult of his own. He had achieved primacy without much bloodshed, it is true, and to a degree persuasion replaced preventive terror. Following the Twenty-First Party Congress in January 1959, however, Khrushchev launched a widespread purge of the party and governmental apparatus. He set the stage for the new purge by telling the congress that changes in the party hierarchy were necessary in order to make better use of young party members, to free old members from excessive burdens, and to replace those officials "who have remained behind the times." In the new party program of 1961, he sought to legitimize these actions by introducing the principle of a periodic renewal (discussed earlier in this chapter) of the composition of party bodies.

In October 1964, Khrushchev was replaced by some of the same men whom he had placed in positions of responsibility. The change resembled a palace revolution. An established Communist dictator was toppled for the first time as a result of a high level plot. Perhaps one of the consequences of the Khrushchev era may be that struggles for power at the top levels can take place without the danger of participants losing their heads. And it may be that the ouster of Khrushchev signified the replacement of a personal autocracy by a bureaucratic oligarchy, even though such a development would be contrary to past Soviet history. If that should take place, however, the problem of extending "intraparty democracy" cannot long be avoided. It is possible that the system may be forced to democratize the entire party or else revert to a new one-man dictatorship.

The overthrow of Khrushchev does not seem to be based on fundamental disagreements concerning the party's domestic and foreign policies. The disagreements seem to involve the methods by which these policies are executed, as well as Khrushchev's general style of leadership. As managers and technicians, Khrushchev's successors seem to be more concerned with action and deeds rather than with threats and "phrase-mongering." They would appear to be more interested in results than in impressive oratory. At the same time, Khrushchev became a convenient scapegoat for the political and economic failures of the system.

THE DOWNGRADING OF STALIN AND ITS MEANING

Following the death of Stalin in March 1953, his successors set about downgrading their former hero. Their efforts were by and large imperceptible until December 1953, when they liquidated Lavrenti Beria, for many years head of the secret police under Stalin. The first direct and extended criticism of Stalin was presented by Khrushchev at a closed meeting of the Twentieth Party Congress in February 1956. Although the Soviets did not publish it, a purported text was released by the United States.[22] In this speech, Khrushchev paid Stalin a tribute for his role in the Bolshevik Revolution and civil war and for his fight to build a socialist society in the USSR. But most of the speech was devoted to a criticism of his shortcomings and the grave consequences which ensued from them.

THE CRITICISM OF STALIN

The principal criticism of Stalin, in the Khrushchev speech, centered on the so-called "cult of personality" charge. Stalin had become a personal dictator. Unlike Lenin, he did not tolerate collegiality in leadership or in the work of the party and government. He ignored his colleagues in the Central Committee and even those in the Politburo. Often he did not even bother to inform them of important decisions which he had made. The cult of one-man rule, said Khrushchev, was contrary to the Leninist principle of collective leadership.

Moreover, the development of the cult of personality, according to Khrushchev, was promoted by Stalin himself, for he took an active part in the campaign of praise. Unlike Lenin, he was not a modest man. By taking credit for the achievements of the collective, Stalin arrogated to himself the attributes of an infallible superman. Stalin's vanity resulted in the establishment of many "monuments to the living" in the form of huge statues, busts, portraits, Stalin prizes, etc. All of this, said Khrushchev, was foreign to Marxism-Leninism.

More serious than the un-Leninist nature of the cult of personality were its dire consequences. It was the "source of a whole series of exceedingly serious and grave perversions of party principles, of party democracy, of revolutionary legality." Whoever opposed Stalin's concept of leadership or attempted to argue against it met with moral and physical annihilation. The result of Stalin's arbitrariness was the killing of countless thousands of innocent party comrades.

---

[22] See *New York Times*, June 5, 1956.

In describing the fabrications against his party comrades who perished, Khrushchev dealt in the main with the principal personalities, those who had achieved high positions.[23] In addition to citing individual cases by name, he reported that "of the 139 members and candidates of the party's Central Committee who were elected at the Seventeenth Party Congress, 98, or 70 per cent, were arrested and shot." And more than a majority of the nearly 2,000 delegates to that Congress were arrested.

Stalin originated the concept "enemy of the people" which "made possible the usage of the most cruel repression . . . against anyone who in any way disagreed with Stalin, against those who were only suspect of hostile intent. . . ." Many of those who in 1937–38 were branded "as 'enemies' were actually never enemies, spies, wreckers, etc., but were always honest Communists." Many were shot without trial, but trials were not too significant anyway, for convictions were made on the basis of confessions, which "were gained with the help of cruel and inhuman tortures."

Arbitrary behavior by one person, said Khrushchev, encouraged and permitted arbitrariness in others.

Khrushchev, however, did not criticize Stalin's struggle against dissident factions within the party. On the contrary, he praised his fight against the left deviationists (Trotsky, Kamenev, Zinoviev) and against Bukharin and other representatives of the right. Even Lenin had criticized the actions of Kamenev and Zinoviev, but, said Khrushchev, there was no suggestion on Lenin's part that they should be arrested and certainly no thought of shooting them.

The second major criticism in Khrushchev's speech, although he did not dwell on it, was aimed at Stalin's theory of the class struggle during the period of the dictatorship of the proletariat. The terror of the middle and late 1930s was defended by Stalin as a necessary retaliation against the class enemy. The use of extreme measures against the class enemy is perfectly justifiable and right, said Khrushchev. But, he added, this repression came after socialism was fundamentally constructed and the exploiting classes generally liquidated. It came at a time when "there were no serious reasons for the use of extraordinary mass terror." And in any case, he added, this terror was not directed at the defeated exploiting classes, "but against the honest workers of the party and of the Soviet state."

The third major criticism was directed at Stalin's role in World

---

[23] At one point he made reference to over 7,000 persons who, upon investigation after Stalin's death, were posthumously rehabilitated.

War II. In the postwar years, he was pictured as a "military genius" who was singlehandedly responsible for the success of the Soviet armed forces. This, according to Khrushchev, was far from the truth. Initially, he said, Stalin was not alert to the many warnings, from foreign and Soviet sources, that Germany would attack the Soviet Union. The failure to heed these warnings and to prepare for the attack had disastrous military consequences for the Soviet armed forces. Moreover, the earlier liquidations of the cream of the army's officer corps had left the Soviet Union in a weakened position.

Secondly, the military reverses in the early part of the war immobilized Stalin. He ceased to lead. He was convinced that all was lost, that everything that Lenin had built was lost in a brief period of time. Only when other Soviet leaders told him what must be done did he resume leadership.

When he did resume command of the war effort, however, he often hampered it. He interfered with field commanders, to the detriment of the army. Even urgent pleas from the front by Khrushchev and others for orders that would save the situation were ignored. He even refused to come to the telephone to talk to Khrushchev, who was desperately calling from the front. The net result was huge losses to the Soviet army.

In addition, Khrushchev criticized Stalin's wartime policy of deporting and exiling minority populations (such as the Volga Germans) who were near the front. This resettling was indiscriminate. Even Communist party members and their leaders among these nationalities were deported and exiled with the rest.

IMPACT OF CRITICISM OF STALIN

The successors of Stalin, by their criticism of a man theretofore depicted as infallible, may have set in motion forces which cannot be controlled. Their criticism of Stalin reverberated around the world, and within a brief period of time produced crises at home and abroad.[24] The most immediate impact of the criticism of Stalin was the ideological crises in Communist parties in the non-Communist countries. French, Italian, American, and other Communists suddenly discovered that their hero had feet of clay, and worse. For years they had been engaged in perpetrating a hoax. And this on the authority of Moscow itself! This was not easy to take, for it was perhaps the rudest shock experienced by the foreign apologists of the Soviet Union. Some

---

[24] This analysis is in part based on A. Avtorkhanov, "Current Soviet Political Problems," *Bulletin: Institute for the Study of the USSR*, Vol. IV (January, 1957), pp. 3–14.

left their respective parties. Some asked where Khrushchev and his colleagues had been when all the evil deeds were being done. Others fell in with the new party line without outward questioning. Fellow travelers, although not all, fell by the wayside in great numbers. But the crisis was not to end there.

The way had been prepared for the ideological crisis in the world Communist movement by Khrushchev's revision of Lenin in his opening address to the party congress. By declaring that there were various roads to socialism (that is, by declaring that force and violence were not necessarily the only means, that war is not inevitable, etc.), he appeared to be revising Stalin, but in effect he was revising Lenin also. This was far too flexible an interpretation for many comrades in the various Communist parties, with some openly declaring that such flexibility would deprive them of the very thing that distinguished them from other workers' parties. The theoretical revision of Lenin and the personal condemnation of Stalin were bound to keep the world Communist movement in a certain amount of ideological turmoil.

The crisis in Communist ranks was not confined to party comrades in the non-Communist world. The beginning of a series of political crises in Eastern Europe followed quickly on the heels of Khrushchev's declaration about "different roads to socialism" and his revelations of the abuses under Stalin's rule. The restiveness of the satellite countries exploded in the autumn of 1956 into a full-blown revolt in Hungary, together with more peaceful changes in Poland. In both instances the revolt was against domestic "Stalinists" and, by implication at least, against Russia's Stalinist methods in dealing with the satellites. The Hungarian revolution soon assumed a general anti-Communist character. It was phenomenally successful until crushed by Soviet troops which were sent into Hungary for that purpose. But this aggressive act of the Soviet Union did not end the political crisis in the countries of Eastern Europe.

This political crisis, particularly the events in Hungary, served to make more acute the psychological crisis which had been developing inside the Soviet Union in the wake of Khrushchev's revelations about Stalin. The Soviet rulers took note of unrest among their own students and workers some time before the blowup in Poland and Hungary. After the latter had occurred, Soviet citizens were warned in the party press about their criticism of the party and the government, while "hiding behind the slogan of the struggle against the cult of the individual." University students were seemingly most vocal and

Khrushchev was moved to tell the dissatisfied: "If you do not like our methods, then go to work and others will come to study in your place."[25]

In assessing the Khrushchev denunciation of the cult of Stalin, Avtorkhanov notes three main contradictions in it. The first is practical: Stalin's methods were declared to have been illegal and not in the best interests of the party, and yet it would have been impossible to maintain the Communist system without them. The second is theoretical: Stalin's theory of the class struggle during the period of the dictatorship of the proletariat was denounced, yet these theories were indispensable in justifying Communist practice. The third contradiction is moral: Stalin's treachery, suspiciousness, and hypocrisy were depicted as personal traits, whereas these qualities are an essential feature of the Communist system.

The various crises which followed in the wake of the criticism of Stalin could not but put a strain on the collective leadership. Suggestions to this effect were met with evasive denials until July 1957, when it was revealed that such old Bolsheviks as Molotov, Kaganovich, and Malenkov, as well as other members of the top leadership, had been removed from their posts because of their deviationism, that is, their attempt to oppose party policies as conceived by Khrushchev and his collaborators. Attacks upon this "antiparty group" have been repeated several times. At the Twenty-First Party Congress, the names of several other former party leaders were added to the antiparty roster, along with a demand for an explanation of their parts in the plot. At the Twenty-Second Party Congress in October 1961, Khrushchev, as well as his collaborators, returned to the attack, with further revelations concerning the crimes of the Stalin era. This time he portrayed the members of the "antiparty group" as accomplices of Stalin. It remains to be seen if one day his name may also be associated with those crimes.

Certain actions of the new Soviet rulers would seem to indicate that Stalinism, including the Stalinist aspects of Khrushchev's leadership, has been discredited. This in turn cannot but raise questions about the relevance of Leninism to a modern industrialized society. Party members, much better educated than in the past, will be more inclined to ask for explanations and be less satisfied with commands. Their right to question and to criticize is very much on the agenda. In brief, the available evidence suggests that the forces which were set in

---

[25] *Pravda*, November 10, 1956.

motion at the Twentieth Party Congress have not yet run their course.

BIBLIOGRAPHICAL NOTE

The best work on the Communist party is Leonard Schapiro, *The Communist Party of the Soviet Union* (New York: Random House, 1960). Insight into the role of the Communist party in the Soviet system may also be gained from Merle Fainsod, *How Russia Is Ruled* (Rev. ed., Cambridge, Mass.: Harvard University Press, 1963) and *Smolensk Under Soviet Rule* (Cambridge, Mass.: Harvard University Press, 1958); Barrington Moore, *Soviet Politics: The Dilemma of Power: The Role of Ideas in Social Change* (Cambridge, Mass.: Harvard University Press, 1950) and *Terror and Progress—U.S.S.R., Some Sources of Change and Stability in the Soviet Dictatorship* (Cambridge, Mass.: Harvard University Press, 1954); Howard R. Swearer, *The Politics of Succession in the U.S.S.R.* (Boston: Little, Brown, 1964); Adam B. Ulam, *The New Face of Soviet Totalitarianism* (Cambridge: Harvard University Press, 1963). Additional recent analyses include those of Columbia University, The Russian Institute, *The Anti-Stalin Campaign and International Communism* (New York: Columbia University Press, 1956); Leo Gruliow (ed.), *Current Soviet Policies II: A Documentary Record, 1953–1956, From the Purge of Beria Through the 20th Communist Party Congress and the Re-Evaluation of Stalin* (New York: Praeger, 1956); Boris Meissner (ed.), *The Communist Party of the Soviet Union* (New York: Praeger, 1957); John S. Reshetar, Jr., *A Concise History of the Communist Party of the Soviet Union* (New York: Praeger, 1960); and Bertram D. Wolfe, *Khrushchev and Stalin's Ghost* (New York: Praeger, 1957). A detailed look at the party in the purge years and after is John A. Armstrong's *The Politics of Totalitarianism: The Communist Party of the Soviet Union from 1934 to the Present* (New York: Random House, 1961).

CHAPTER 27

THE GOVERNMENTAL
STRUCTURE

SINCE THE party is the decision-making body in the Soviet system, government is mostly a matter of administration. Governmental forms, as well as the whole fabric of organizational and institutional life in the Soviet Union, constitute the administrative apparatus for implementing party policies and party aims. An appreciation of this basic fact is indispensable to an understanding of the Soviet system. All else is secondary. Soviet governmental forms, as well as the theories that ostensibly govern their functions and powers, must ever be viewed as subordinate to the party hierarchy.

DUALISM OF PARTY AND GOVERNMENT

Formally, the party and government structures are separate and independent.[1] Organizationally, they are similar, except at the lowest level. They are in the nature of twin pyramids or dual hierarchies. The governmental hierarchy parallels that of the party (described in the previous chapter) in that the Supreme Soviet of the USSR corresponds to the party congress, the Presidium of the Supreme Soviet corresponds to the party Central Committee, and the Council of Ministers is similar to the party Presidium, etc. A governmental hierarchy corresponding to that of the central government exists in each one of the union republics. At the lowest level, governmental powers are vested in a soviet of working peoples' deputies, whose executive and administrative organ is the executive committee.

In theory, authority is wielded by the constitutionally established governmental bodies. In practice, however, party predominance is guaranteed by the existence of the party pyramid, which parallels the governmental structure at every level, and by the knowledge of all

---

[1] The governmental and party changes which were announced immediately following Stalin's death in March 1953 were, however, allegedly decided upon at a *joint* meeting of the party's Central Committee, the Council of Ministers of the USSR, and the Presidium of the Supreme Soviet of the USSR.

412

INTERSECTING PYRAMIDS OF PARTY AND GOVERNMENT ORGANIZATION

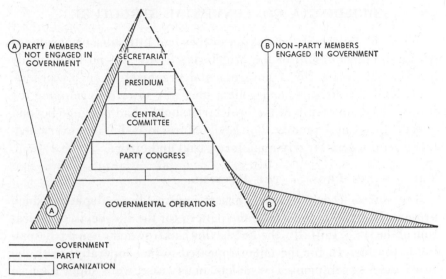

(A) PARTY MEMBERS NOT ENGAGED IN GOVERNMENT

SECRETARIAT

PRESIDIUM

CENTRAL COMMITTEE

PARTY CONGRESS

GOVERNMENTAL OPERATIONS

(B) NON-PARTY MEMBERS ENGAGED IN GOVERNMENT

——————— GOVERNMENT
— — — — PARTY
[ ] ORGANIZATION

Deviation in shape of Government pyramid due to the fact that non-party members are non-existent in the higher functions of government.

those in the governmental hierarchy that their basic task is to carry out party policy. Party and nonparty individuals in government offices are aware of and consult with party officials at their respective levels of authority. No governmental decision of any consequence is made except upon order or approval from competent party officials.

As implied above, party predominance is also guaranteed by an interlocking directorate of party members who simultaneously hold governmental and party posts. Party members who occupy governmental positions but who do not serve as party officials are nonetheless aware that they are primarily engaged in performing tasks pursuant to party decisions. Nonparty governmental employees are for the most part to be found in lesser jobs, but they, too, realize that the governmental structure is but an appendage of the party.

The Soviet constitution of 1936, to be discussed below, openly recognizes the predominant position of the party, a marked departure from previous Soviet constitutional documents. It is listed among the organizations which have the right to nominate candidates for public office and it is referred to as "the vanguard of the working people in their struggle to build Communist society and is *the leading core of all organizations of the working people, both public and state.*"[2]

---

[2] See articles 141 and 126. Italics added.

BUILDING A GOVERNMENTAL STRUCTURE

When the Bolsheviks seized power they had little idea of how to organize the dictatorship of the proletariat. There was no ready-made Marxian blueprint for a governmental organization in a workers' state. Lenin, to be sure, had gone a long way toward developing the idea of the dictatorship of the proletariat, but he had not gone beyond generalities. Consequently, Bolshevik efforts to fashion a governmental structure were largely a matter of trial and error.

THE SOVIETS PROVIDE THE PATTERN

The soviets (councils) of workers' and soldiers' deputies which arose in 1917[3] were to become the pattern for the Bolshevik organization of the state. Initially, the Bolsheviks had frowned upon participating in the soviets, for the latter appeared to be cooperating with the provisional government. The soviets, in any case, were under the firm control of the non-Bolshevik revolutionary parties, a fact not calculated to induce Bolshevik cooperation. Before long, as noted in Chapter 24 above, the Bolsheviks saw in the soviets the one potential instrument for the seizure of power. After having served this purpose, the soviets became the organizational pattern for the Bolshevik state, and governing bodies at national, local, and intermediate levels became known as soviets.

The soviets under the Communist regime differ markedly from their earlier prototypes. Initially they were loosely organized democratic bodies. Members of several different revolutionary parties engaged in free and vigorous debate. Decisions were reached by majority vote. There was no attempt to suppress minority opinion. Once the Bolsheviks had taken over, however, they were determined to make of the soviets monolithic organizations. The more moderate revolutionary groups soon withdrew, for they were not anxious merely to serve Bolshevik ends. By the spring of 1918, all non-Bolshevik representatives had withdrawn, leaving the Bolsheviks in complete control.

EARLY CONSTITUTION MAKING

The Bolshevik approach to a constitution is entirely different from that to which we have been accustomed. Constitutionalism in the West has been identified with limited government. Initially, it constituted a way of curbing and regulating the powers of kings and other monarchs.

---

[3] These were patterned on the short-lived Petrograd Soviet of 1905.

Once this was done, the next step was to deny certain powers to the new democratic governments, in accordance with the consent of the governed, and to provide procedural safeguards in the exercise of those limited powers which were granted to popular governmental authorities. This view of constitutionalism is foreign to the Soviet leaders, for their constitution neither imposes limitations upon government nor provides for meaningful procedural safeguards against the abuse of authority.

If the Soviet constitution does not serve the purposes normally associated with constitutions in the West, why, it may be asked, did the Russians bother with a constitution at all? There would seem to be at least two main reasons. First, a constitution makes the governmental-administrative structure explicit, providing for a smoother operation of the bureaucracy. Secondly, a fundamental law that stressed the rights of workers and peasants and proclaimed their participation in the government would serve Communist propaganda objectives at home and abroad. The latter, as will be noted below, was especially evident in connection with the 1936 constitution.

In the early months of the Bolshevik regime there was no constitution. When they had seized power, the Bolshevik leaders went to the Second All-Russian Congress of Soviets, which was then in session, with a resolution decreeing a temporary government, bearing the name "Council of Peoples' Commissars." The resolution was adopted, including the naming of Bolsheviks to all leading posts in the government. This government was to last until the convocation of the Constituent Assembly, which had been promised by the provisional government. The Bolsheviks set the election for November 25, 1917, but as noted earlier, the outcome was not favorable to the Bolsheviks. Nevertheless, they permitted the Constituent Assembly to convene in January 1918, but when they realized that it was not susceptible to manipulation by them, they disbanded it by force after it had been in session only one day.

A Bolshevik-framed declaration, setting forth the basic principles for the organization of the new state, which the Constituent Assembly refused to adopt, served as the basic law of the Russian state until the formal adoption of a constitution in July 1918.[4] The constitution, adopted by the Fifth All-Russian Congress of Soviets, provided a governmental structure for the Russian Socialist Federal Soviet Republic

---

[4] This declaration, in effect, became the preamble of the constitution. For texts of the declaration and the constitution, see James H. Meisel and Edward S. Kozera, *Materials for the Study of the Soviet System* (Ann Arbor, Michigan, 1950), pp. 57 and 79.

(RSFSR), by far the largest of the present 15 Soviet republics. For the most part, this constitution ratified the evolving structure of soviets, setting forth specific provisions concerning the composition and powers of soviets and their central executive committees, the organization of the Council of People's Commissars, the powers of the central and local governments, and electoral rights. The revolutionary functions of the constitution were said to embrace the establishment of a dictatorship of the urban and rural proletariat (including the poorest peasantry), the establishment of socialism, and the suppression of the *bourgeoisie* and exploitation.

By 1921, under Bolshevik guidance, socialist soviet republics had been set up in Belorussia, the Ukraine, and Transcaucasia, which had entered into a treaty relationship with RSFSR. In 1922, a Union of Soviet Socialist Republics was created, and in 1923 the constitution was revised to reflect this change.[5] The new constitution, formally ratified by the Congress of Soviets in January 1924, followed closely the RSFSR model of 1918. All powers of any significance were vested in the central government, leaving the union republics exceedingly little authority.

THE 1936 CONSTITUTION

By 1936 the number of soviet republics had grown to 11.[6] In addition, a drastic social and economic transformation had taken place in the years 1929–35. A new constitution was needed, said Stalin, in order to bring the fundamental law into conformity with those changes. Allegedly, classes had been abolished and society transformed. Therefore, it was possible to introduce universal suffrage, direct and secret elections, and to eliminate inequality between workers and peasants. But, said Stalin, the new constitution "preserves unchanged the present leading position of the Communist party," which provided "democracy for the working people, that is, democracy for all."[7]

The widespread discussion throughout the Soviet Union of the draft of the 1936 constitution, and particularly the publicity surrounding this discussion which the Soviet leaders purveyed abroad, suggests that foreign (as well as domestic) propaganda may have been the

---

[5] For text, see Meisel and Kozera, *op. cit.*, p. 152ff.

[6] The Uzbek, Turkmen, Kazak, Kirgiz, and Tadjik republics were added, while Transcaucasia was divided into three republics: Georgia, Armenia, and Azerbaijan.

[7] "On the New Constitution" in *Problems of Leninism*, pp. 578–79.

dominant motive behind the new constitution. Soviet leaders, anxious to find allies among the capitalist democracies against the Nazi, Fascist, and Japanese threat, were eager to demonstrate that the 1936 constitution was proof of an evolving democratic system which enjoyed the support of the Soviet peoples. Therefore, there existed a common bond between the capitalist democracies and the Soviet Union in the face of the Facist threat.

Although a new constitution has been promised for several years, the 1936 document was still in effect in 1966. Its broad divisions may be summarized briefly. The first 12 articles proclaim the basic principles underlying the organization of the socialist society. The next 17 articles (21, if the amendments are counted separately) describe the organization of the state and set forth the powers of the central government. Articles 30 through 56 describe the highest organs of state power of the central government, as well as some reference to their powers, while the next 6 articles set out the highest organs of state power in the republics. Articles 64 through 88 provide for the organs of administration of the central and republic governments. Articles 89 through 101 refer to organs of state power in governmental subdivisions below the republic level. The courts and the prosecutor's office are dealt with in articles 102 through 117, while fundamental rights and duties of citizens are taken care of in articles 118 through 133. The electoral system is depicted in articles 134 through 142. The final four articles deal with the coat of arms, the flag, the capital of the country, and the method of amending the constitution.

GOVERNMENTAL STRUCTURE: LEGISLATIVE AND EXECUTIVE

The governmental forms through which the party dictatorship is exercised resemble those to be found in a democracy, at least superficially. There is great emphasis on "popularly elected" legislative assemblies (soviets), which choose their respective executives and to which the latter are supposedly responsible. Moreover, the Soviet Union claims to be a federal state, with a distribution of governmental powers between the central government and the 15 republics. These governmental forms, upon closer examination, will stand revealed as a type of democratic façade behind which the party dictatorship functions. At the same time, something of the party's tactics in the operation of that dictatorship will be brought into sharper focus.

FEDERALISM AND THE NATIONALITY QUESTION

Ostensibly, the USSR is a federal state, formed on the basis of voluntary association of equal republics. Any impartial study of the Soviet system will reveal, however, that this is not the case. A governmental system cannot be called federal unless (1) the distribution of powers between the central government and its component subdivisions provides the latter with some real substance of power, and (2) the central government is prevented from altering this distribution of powers through its actions alone. The Soviet system meets neither of these two tests, either in theory or practice.

A reading of the Soviet constitution reveals that the grants of power to the central government are so all-embracing as to leave the republics with no real substance of power. Secondly, the power to amend the constitution is vested in the central government alone; the republics are not required to ratify amendments.

Yet, ironically enough, the constitution asserts that each of the union republics has "the right freely to secede from the USSR." Two 1944 amendments, moreover, provide that each union republic has the right to enter into direct diplomatic relations with other countries and to have its own military formations. These are not the attributes of a federal state, but of a confederation.

In practice, however, the Soviet Union is neither a federation nor a confederation. The republics have neither the powers usually associated with component units of a federation nor can they exercise the powers normally enjoyed by members of a confederation. None of the republics has been permitted to establish diplomatic relations with foreign countries. A British proposal in 1947 to exchange diplomatic representatives with the Ukraine was rejected. Additional Moscow disrespect for the "rights" of union republics was demonstrated when in 1956 the Karelo-Finnish Republic was abolished without any seeming effort to obtain its approval, although the constitution asserts that the boundaries of a union republic may not be altered without its consent. Again, it cannot too often be emphasized that the USSR is a highly centralized dictatorship where authority is wielded by the leaders of the Communist party, a unitary organization. Moreover, it is a sound generalization that a one-party dictatorship is a poor place to look for federalism, to say nothing of a confederate arrangement.

The Soviet nationality policy is the basis for Moscow's claim to federalism. This policy, ostensibly one of autonomy, was based on the need to weld together the diverse fragments of the Russian empire which had fallen apart with the Revolution and which the Red Army was bringing into the fold. Lenin had sought to harness minority discontent to the aims of the Revolution, hence a departure from tsarist policy was imperative. The departure was in the direction of autonomy and it was an improvisation.

From the outset, however, it was evident that there would be no national autonomy in the realm of political power or in the matter of social or economic organization of society, although for some years that followed many continued to hope. In May 1918, Stalin, who was made chairman for nationalities when the Bolshevik government was established, stated that Soviet authorities were "for autonomy, but only for an autonomy where all power rests in the hands of the workers and peasants." In 1925, he depicted Soviet nationality policy goals as being "proletarian in content and national in form." During World War II, however, even the basic right of autonomous existence was violated in the case of several nationalities, who were uprooted from the Caucasus because of alleged disloyalty.[8]

Similarly, it was made clear from the outset that the "right freely to secede" was meaningless. In 1920, Stalin reaffirmed the right, but at that stage of the revolution, he said, a demand for secession would be regarded as counterrevolutionary. Moreover, the history of Soviet nationality policy is replete with purges of party and nonparty "nationalists" in the Ukraine, Belorussia, Armenia, and in several of the other non-Russian republics. Under Stalin, deliberate systematic efforts were made to eradicate "local chauvinism." Many of those who were purged were charged with harboring a desire to detach their respective republics from the Soviet Union, although the constitution presumably gives them this "right."

What remained of the national autonomy, therefore, was largely linguistic and cultural. Soviet leaders, in their propaganda, made much of their policy of encouraging minority nationalities to advance themselves culturally, through the use of their native language and through the development of their native cultural heritage. But the basic aim of the party leadership in Moscow was not cultural advancement for its own sake. Rather, they saw in the native language, educational system, and culture the means through which the party could more effectively sovietize the minority peoples. This takes on added significance when one remembers that these means could not be utilized by any other group to pursue a different or contrary aim.

---

[8] In 1957, it was announced that five of the nationalities would be rehabilitated, and in 1965 it was announced that the Volga Germans had not really been disloyal.

It is also of interest to note that Stalin's principles of nationality did not recognize the Jews as a minority, although an autonomous region (Birobidjan) was set aside by Stalin for Jewish colonization. Ironically enough, however, they are a minority even in Birobidjan. In the early years of the Soviet regime many of the leading Communists were Jews, but Stalin purged most of them. In the last years of his life it was practically subversive to speak or write in Yiddish. Jewish schools, newspapers, and periodicals were closed down. Even Jewish prayer books were unobtainable. Articles in the official press were clearly derogatory.

During the Khrushchev era there seemed to be an increasing harassment of Jews. In 1963, for example, a blatantly anti-semitic book was published by the Ukrainian Academy of Science, although it was critically reviewed in the Soviet press. Moreover, articles in the press emphasized that Jews were involved in a large share of the economic crimes committed by Soviet citizens. In addition, Soviet newspapers reported that a number of Jews were arrested on espionage charges, allegedly having given state secrets to Israeli diplomats. At the same time, Soviet leaders took pains to point out that they were not anti-semitic, that many Jews held responsible positions, that so long as they were good citizens they had nothing to fear. Furthermore, they pointed to the reappearance of certain Jewish publications as a reversal of a trend, but as the Khrushchev era ended the evidence in this direction was meager indeed.

THE ELECTIVE PRINCIPLE

According to the constitution, all members of the various legislative bodies (the soviets) are elected "on the basis of universal, equal, and direct suffrage by secret ballot." If one goes beyond this formal proviso, however, any initial impressions of popular democracy are quickly dispelled. First of all, when the Russian voter goes to cast his ballot he finds only one list of candidates; there is only one candidate for each office to be filled. There are no alternative candidates to vote for, although by invalidating his ballot he can in effect cast a vote against the official list.[9] In practice, even this demonstration of opposition has become difficult simply because Soviet election officials do not require voters to enter the voting booth before casting their ballots, hence destroying the secrecy of the ballot. To vote for the list one need not mark his ballot, but one must do so if he is to invalidate it. Faced

---

[9] According to the Soviet electoral law, an election is not valid unless the list receives at least 50 per cent of all the votes cast.

with the spectacle of certain voters openly demonstrating their loyalty to the regime, other voters, who may or may not be inclined to invalidate their ballots, are discouraged from entering the voting booth before casting their ballots. Moreover, many voters believe, rightly or wrongly, that the voting booth itself does not insure secrecy, since the officials have ways of detecting those who invalidate their ballots. In view of these considerations, the reports that official lists receive more than 99% of the votes cast can better be understood.

Secondly, popular democracy is lacking in the nominating process. Soviet propagandists have defended the single list of candidates on the ground that these are chosen after long and thorough discussions, which allegedly characterize the nominating process. The right to nominate candidates is accorded to "Communist party organizations, trade unions, cooperatives, youth organizations, and cultural societies." Since the Communist party is the sole guiding force in all of these associations, there is no possibility of a person being nominated who is in any way repugnant to the party. Prior to an election, meetings of voters are held to discuss the various nominees. It is here that the party's view of who should be the candidate are made amply clear. No one will take a position against the party, although it does not follow that the nominee will be a party member. Often the party finds it expedient, particularly in local soviets, to have nonparty candidates. These are nonetheless persons whom the party can trust.[10]

Finally, if need be, the Communists can control the results of elections, for they count the ballots. Who is to question the accuracy of the count? There are no challengers, no demands for a recount, no critical press, or political opposition to reveal irregularities. Even if 99% of the voters did not cast their ballots for the official list, as reported, the election officials could make it so.

That the party should be in complete control of the nominating and electoral process is perfectly consistent with the Communist view that in their system only one program can exist. If no alternative to Communism is to be tolerated, why permit the nomination or election of persons who may oppose Communism? But then, the question may be asked: why have elections at all? Why are they necessary; what purposes do they serve? Why is there such a determined effort to get all eligible voters to the polls?

An analysis of the Soviet system suggests that, from the Communist

---

[10] In the Supreme Soviet of the USSR the percentage of Communist party members and candidates approaches 85 per cent, while in local urban soviets it falls near 50 per cent, and drops down to near 25 per cent in local rural soviets.

point of view, the elections serve several purposes. They provide a plausible façade by means of which the regime could claim popular support, especially in its propaganda abroad. Moreover, they constitute a technique by which the regime hopes to instill in the broad masses a sense of involvement in Communist undertakings. For those who do not cherish such an experience, their participation in Communist elections serves to create a climate of futility, moral despair, and hopelessness. No one who hates Communism can go through the symbolic approval of what he hates without a sense of personal degradation, of having destroyed his own personal integrity. In addition, Communist leaders find elections soul-satisfying, especially when they register such overwhelming majorities. The lesser Communists, on the other hand, are afforded an opportunity by the elections to show their importance and to experience a feeling of power. The efforts of thousands, if not millions, of party workers are required during a national election campaign. Finally, elections provide an excellent peg on which to hang domestic propaganda messages. Periodically, they furnish the regime with a convenient opportunity to praise itself, to explain away shortcomings, and to exhort the people to make new sacrifices.

Soviet leaders have admitted the propaganda function of their elections. One of them wrote openly: "The Soviet election system is a mighty instrument for further educating and organizing the masses politically, for further strengthening the bond between the state mechanism and the masses. . . ."[11] Similar statements are to be found in the Soviet press and in party pronouncements, especially in the days preceding an election.

THE LEGISLATURE: THE SUPREME SOVIET

The Supreme Soviet of the USSR is a bicameral[12] body, consisting of a Soviet of Union and a Soviet of Nationalities. The former is chosen directly by the people in electoral areas on the basis of one deputy per 300,000 inhabitants. The latter is designed to represent nationalities, with deputies distributed as follows: 25 to each union republic, 11 to each autonomous republic, 5 to each autonomous region, and 1 to each national area. They are also directly elected. Each chamber has between 600 and 700 members. Both chambers are elected for four-year terms and are said to have equal powers.

The Supreme Soviet, according to the constitution, is the highest organ of state authority; it is the exclusive wielder of the legislative

---

[11] Andrei Y. Vyshinsky, *The Law of the Soviet State* (New York, 1948), p. 722.

[12] Soviets of the republics and other subdivisions of the USSR are unicameral.

power of the central government. Despite these constitutional declarations, the Supreme Soviet cannot qualify as a parliamentary body, as that term is generally understood. This conclusion would be valid on the basis of any objective analysis of the Supreme Soviet's activities, even if one did not take into account the predominant role which the Communist party plays in the Soviet system.

First of all, the Supreme Soviet is supposed to meet twice yearly. An examination of the record in several post-World War II years reveals that it met only once yearly in the years 1947–52, inclusive. More important, however, is the fact that each annual session averaged no more than five days. Could anyone seriously suggest that the Supreme Soviet, with a membership exceeding 1,300, would be capable of legislating in the vast areas of authority which the constitution theoretically grants it by sitting five days a year?

Moreover, a cursory examination of its activities during these brief sessions indicates that the Supreme Soviet engages in little deliberation or debate, to say nothing of dissent. The rank and file members play a simple role. They sit quietly while government and party leaders deliver a series of speeches, applauding at the appropriate moments, and casting unanimous votes for all government proposals. Unrehearsed and free debates are out of the question. The members are well rewarded, however, receiving a monthly salary approaching that of a skilled worker (this is in addition to what they receive in their regular jobs), plus free annual passes on all railway and water transport facilities. During the sessions of the Supreme Soviet they receive a liberal per diem.

From the Communist point of view, this is perhaps as it should be. The Supreme Soviet, a large and unwieldy body, is the governmental counterpart of the party's congress. In both cases, these large gatherings serve essentially similar purposes. Their function is not to debate and discuss but to applaud and assent. In a twenty-year period (1937–1958), for example, the ministers enacted, through decrees and resolutions, some 390,000 pieces of "legislation," while the Supreme Soviet and its Presidium (discussed below) were passing some 7,000 laws, resolutions, and decrees. Moreover, many of the acts of the Supreme Soviet merely confirmed decisions already promulgated by its Presidium.

THE EXECUTIVE: PRESIDIUM AND COUNCIL OF MINISTERS

The Soviet Union may be said to have a dual executive, although a comparison with other countries in this respect would be misleading. There is the Presidium of the Supreme Soviet, a collegial executive body elected by the Supreme Soviet, which is a permanent nucleus of the Supreme Soviet. It consists of a president, a secretary, 15 vice-presidents (one for each of the union republics) and 16 members. It has become customary to elect the presidents of the presidia of the union republics to fill the vice-presidential posts. Several top party leaders are always members. The Presidium performs many of the functions of a formal executive in a parliamentary state. It receives credentials and letters of recall of diplomatic representatives, awards decorations, confers titles of honor, ratifies treaties, convenes sessions of the Supreme Soviet, exercises the right of pardon, and appoints and recalls diplomatic representatives.

At the same time, the Presidium is said to have powers which would make it correspond to a legislative body. In the interval between sessions of the Supreme Soviet, it performs many of the powers of the parent body. It has the power to issue decrees; to declare war; to order general or partial mobilization; to annul those decisions of the Council of Ministers of the USSR and of the union republics which do not conform to law; to appoint and remove the higher commands of the armed forces; to proclaim martial law; and to appoint and remove ministers. The last is subject to confirmation by the Supreme Soviet. The Presidium also has the power to interpret the laws of the USSR and to conduct nationwide polls (referenda) on its own initiative or on the demand of one of the union republics.

The Supreme Soviet also chooses the Council of Ministers, which is composed of the heads of the usual departments plus those ministries responsible for various parts of the economy.[13] The latter group was quite large at one time, but was considerably reduced in 1957, when the Communist leadership decided to decentralize the actual implementation of party economic goals. Formally, the Council of Ministers is selected by the Supreme Soviet, but the real ministerial assignments are made by the party leaders. As might be expected, the Council of Ministers is engaged not so much in policy discussions as in the means of implementing policies already arrived at. Even the constitution refers to it as an "executive and administrative organ."

The Council of Ministers also has a "presidium," or a type of cabinet, consisting of some half dozen ministers, although this is unknown to the constitution. Prior to 1953, there had been a "presidium" of the Council of Ministers and a "bureau of the presidium," although before that time neither had been publicly identified. They

---

[13] For a good account of the evolution of the Council of Ministers, see Julian Towster, *Political Power in the USSR, 1917–1947* (New York, 1948), pp. 272–76.

were no doubt made necessary by the unwieldiness of the Council of Ministers, which by 1952 had exceeded 50. In 1953, it was reduced to half its former size, while the reforms of 1957 reduced it to 15. By 1964, the number had jumped to 23, but even this seemed deceptive, because there were 43 "other ministers of the USSR" and 16 "heads of departments at ministerial level." Moreover, the fifteen chairmen of the councils of ministers of the union republics are *ex-officio* members of the Council of Ministers of the USSR.

The administrative powers of the ministers are vast and far reaching. One can appreciate how far reaching they are only if one bears in mind that in addition to the normal bureaucratic apparatus of a large industrial nation, there is added a bureaucracy to direct and administer the whole economy of the country. In such circumstances it is inevitable that the Council of Ministers be the source of much rule making as well as legislative proposals. Apparently, the decentralization projected in 1957 was at least in part based on the sheer inability of the ministries in Moscow to direct and supervise this huge bureaucracy in minute detail.[14]

There are two types of ministries represented in the Council of Ministers: all-union, and union-republic. All-union ministries are ministries of the central government which operate directly through their own bureaucracy down to the lowest level. Union-republic ministries, on the other hand, are said to function indirectly through corresponding ministries in the republics. Often in the past, however, they have exercised direct control over certain enterprises. Moreover, the union-republic ministries have occasionally controlled and directed the work of purely republic ministries, which are supposed to be the sole concern of the individual republics. By the end of the Khrushchev era, the classification of ministries into all-union and union-republic (discussed in more detail in Chapter 29) seemed to have lost much of whatever significance it may have had in the past.

Although ministers are technically responsible to the Supreme Soviet and, in between its sessions, to the Presidium of the Supreme Soviet, they are in reality responsible solely to the top party leaders. Most of these leaders are, of course, members of the party Presidium, and many of them are also members of the Council of Ministers. There is no such thing as "collective responsibility" of the cabinet, nor are there any resignations of ministries as a whole. There are no motions of censure, no political attacks on the ministry in the legislature, and

---

[14] For a discussion of the administration and the bureaucracy see Chapter 29.

no votes of confidence. As long as individual ministers can satisfy the top party leadership, they have no reason to fear incurring the wrath of anyone else.

GOVERNMENTAL STRUCTURE: JUDICIARY AND CIVIL RIGHTS

The judicial system in a dictatorship cannot be looked to as an instrument for limiting the arbitrary acts of the wielders of dictatorial power. More than that, Soviet courts have often been told publicly that it is their duty to act as faithful servants of the dictatorship. The provision in the constitution that the judges are independent and subject only to the law has been interpreted publicly to exclude any thought of political independence on the part of judges. On the contrary, it has been pointed out that the key phrase is "subject only to the law," and this means Communist law. Moreover, it should be noted that in the Stalinist period the secret police were not responsible to the courts nor subject to the law, even Communist law. Reforms instituted in the Khrushchev era were allegedly designed to establish "socialist legality," but Soviet leaders were quick to point out that this did not mean that they were concerned with the rights of individuals. To them "socialist legality" means strict observance of the law by government agencies and by individuals alike. This does not imply, however, that the regime is bound by the law as defined and enforced by the courts, for in the final analysis Soviet courts are the servants of the party dictatorship.

COMMUNIST CONCEPT OF LAW AND JUSTICE

As a general rule, laws and the means employed to enforce them are but a reflection of the ideas and principles which characterize any given political system. In this respect, Soviet laws and Soviet courts hold true to form. The Marxist-Leninist doctrine, upon which the Soviet system is founded, insists that law is not based on some abstract concept of justice. Rather, all law reflects the will of the dominant class. Accordingly, Soviet leaders have made it amply clear that their law and their courts are the instruments of the dictatorship of the proletariat, designed to strengthen and to defend the conquests of the Bolshevik Revolution, as these are interpreted by the top party leadership. Therefore, the primary objective of Soviet laws and Soviet courts is to preserve the Bolshevik regime and its achievements and to aid and protect those who faithfully seek to carry out its programs.

Conversely, the Soviet judicial system is to strike down all those who constitute a barrier to these ends.

In view of these basic concepts and in the light of the party's extensive program in all fields of human endeavor, the need for a centralized, uniform, and disciplined judicial system becomes strikingly evident. That system must be studied and judged in this context, for to condemn it solely on the basis of the results and thereby leave the impression that it conceivably could come near our own standards of justice, while remaining an integral part of the dictatorship, would be misleading and meaningless. Soviet law and the Soviet judiciary cannot be studied apart from the political system which they serve and whose instruments they are.

THE SOVIET BILL OF RIGHTS

The provisions in the Soviet constitution concerning the rights and duties of Soviet citizens are completely in harmony with basic Soviet ideas about law and justice. Contrary to the belief of many persons, who apparently have not bothered to read the constitution of the USSR, Soviet citizens *are not* guaranteed the basic rights of free speech, press, and association in the way that these are secured for the citizens of democratic countries. Article 125 of the constitution defines these "rights" so narrowly as to make them meaningless in any true sense. Their guarantee is prefaced by the following clause: "In conformity with the interests of the working people, and in order to strengthen the socialist system, . . ." Hence, these rights could not, even in theory, be said to guarantee a person the right to advocate anything except the socialist system. And the party is the all-wise judge as to what that system is and what will or will not strengthen it.

Similarly, Article 126 states: "In conformity with the interests of the working people, and in order to develop the organizational initiative and political activity of the masses of the people, citizens of the USSR are guaranteed the right to unite in public organizations. . . ." It cites examples, such as trade unions, cultural and scientific societies, youth organizations, and others, among which is included the Communist party, which is described as "the vanguard of the working people" and "the leading core of all organizations of the working people, both public and state." It would be difficult, therefore, to defend, even in theory, a right to any type of organizational life except that which accords with the party's wishes and desires.[15]

---

[15] For a discussion of how the Soviet regime utilizes its concept of civil rights to harness the masses to the dictatorship, see the following chapter.

Other articles speak of the right to rest and leisure, to education, and to maintenance in old age and in case of sickness or disability. They also refer to equality of women and the equality of the races. The freedom to worship or to engage in antireligious propaganda is recognized, but there is no recognition of a right to engage in propaganda in favor of religion. There is "the right to work," but there is no right to stop working, that is, the right to strike. Moreover, the inviolability of homes and of the person is guaranteed, but the actions of Soviet authorities have frequently made a hollow mockery of this alleged guarantee.

The declared duties of Soviet citizens form a part of the Soviet "Bill of Rights." Military service is an "honorable duty" and the defense of the USSR is a "sacred duty." It is the duty of every citizen to abide by the constitution, "to observe the laws, to maintain labor discipline . . . . to safeguard and fortify public, socialist property as the sacred and inviolable foundation of the Soviet system."

Taken as a whole, therefore, the so-called Bill of Rights not only specifies the purposes for which certain "rights" are to be utilized, but in addition, asserts that the defense and furtherance of these purposes and aims are among the fundamental duties of Soviet citizens. What gain is there, many Soviet citizens might ask, in being given the right to speak, to write, to organize in order to defend a system which they may not like? Or in being told that it is their duty to do so? Yet, in reality such is the Soviet Bill of Rights.

THE COURT SYSTEM

In the Soviet Union each republic has a court system, consisting of local and intermediate courts and a supreme court. In addition, there is the Supreme Court of the USSR, which is the highest court of the nation. Moreover, there are special tribunals, such as military courts. Some special tribunals have received little publicity, such as those in the concentration camps, and there may be others whose existence is known to only a limited number of people in the Soviet Union. On the other hand, the special transport courts, having jurisdiction over crimes affecting railroads and waterways, were abolished in 1957.[16]

The basis of the Soviet judicial system is the people's court, established in each district and consisting of a popularly elected judge and two people's assessors, chosen at a general meeting of persons at

---

[16] At the same time it was also announced that a "people's assessor," a representative of the public, would in the future sit on military courts.

their place of work, residence, or military unit. The judge, who is supposed to have legal training but often does not, is selected for a term of five years, while the assessors are chosen for two year terms.[17] There are no juries. These courts exercise original jurisdiction in various kinds of civil cases and in minor criminal cases.

A variety of courts are to be found between the people's courts and the supreme courts of the republics. These are based on territories, areas, regions, autonomous regions, and autonomous republics. The judges of these courts, five in number, are elected for terms of five years by the soviets of the respective geographic units. All of these courts have panels of people's assessors, but they are utilized only in cases of original jurisdiction, and not in appellate cases. All of these courts may review cases originating in the people's courts and they possess original jurisdiction in the more important civil and criminal cases.

The supreme court of each republic, consisting of five judges and a panel of assessors elected by the republic's supreme soviet for a term of five years, exercises both original and appellate jurisdiction. It has original jurisdiction in civil and criminal proceedings of major importance. It exercises a certain supervisory function over the courts below it and can set aside any of their verdicts. In 1957, the load of the supreme courts of the republics was increased when the Supreme Court of the Soviet Union was restricted largely to appellate functions.

The Supreme Court of the USSR is elected by the Supreme Soviet for a term of five years. Presumably because it has been restricted mainly to appellate jurisdiction, its size was reduced in 1957. It now consists of a chairman, 2 deputy chairmen, and 13 members, plus the 15 chairmen of the supreme courts of the union republics who serve ex-officio. In addition, there are 45 assessors, who serve when the court is exercising original jurisdiction in civil and criminal cases of exceptional significance. The court rarely sits as one body; in the performance of its actual work it is divided into several "colleges."

In addition to its other functions, the Supreme Court of the USSR is charged by the constitution "with the supervision of the judicial activities of all the judicial organs of the USSR and of the Union Republics" (Article 104). This power has been exercised to insure a centralized, uniform, and disciplined judiciary.

---

[17] Assessors at upper levels in the judiciary are selected by the respective soviet which appoints the professional judges.

EXTRA-JUDICIAL LAW ENFORCEMENT

In the late 1950s and in the 1960s, extra-judicial institutions of law enforcement were considerably augmented. These in the main consist of (1) comrades' courts, (2) anti-parasite tribunals, and (3) voluntary citizens' militia. The first have been in existence for a long time, but their jurisdiction and powers have been extended in recent years. The latter two are of relatively recent creation. All of them seem to be based on the assumption that direct public action is more effective in the case of certain offenders than the regular courts.

Comrades' courts may be created in places of residence (apartment building, collective farm, etc.) or in places of work (factory, office, etc.). The members are elected by the respective collective for a period of one year. The size of the court is not specified except that the members choose a chairman, vice-chairman, and a secretary from among their number. Comrades' courts concern themselves with violations of labor discipline, drunkenness and other improper social behavior, violations of apartment or dormitory regulations, petty theft, and similar offenses. Originally, they could impose reprimands and assess small fines. In 1965 they were empowered to impose fines up to approximately fifty-five dollars and to demand full repayment on damaged property. They may also decide to transfer a case to the regular courts. Decisions of comrades' courts may not ordinarily be reviewed by a court, although a trade-union committee or the executive committee of the local soviet may suggest that the case be heard over again.

The anti-parasite tribunals were established, ironically enough, at a time (1957 and after) when there was considerable emphasis on the need to establish "socialist legality." The anti-parasite laws provide for the exile to more remote regions of the country of persons who evade socially useful work or who live on unearned income. Sentences may be up to five years, with forced labor at the place of exile and possible confiscation of property not acquired by labor. The anti-parasite tribunals are not really courts, but mass meetings of the local population, conviction being by a majority of the quorum in attendance. The sentence is carried out when ratified by the executive committee of the local soviet. Certain types of parasitic offenses must come before the regular people's courts. These do not require confirmation by the executive committee of the local soviet, although the prosecutor (and not the defendant) may protest to the next higher court. The aim of the anti-parasite laws would seem to be two-fold: to combat "private-enterprise" activity and to further social conformity.

The voluntary citizens' militia, or public-order squads, came into being when the anti-parasite laws were being passed. Initially, these public-order squads were designed to combat drunkenness, rowdyism, and other breaches of the peace by patrolling the streets, usually during the evening hours. They work under the guidance of party organizations as well as the police. A significant portion of their membership comes from the ranks of the Komsomol. There have been reports of many abuses of authority (beatings, invasions of privacy, etc.) by the voluntary citizens' militia, but Soviet authorities insist that the streets have been made safer.

THE PROSECUTOR-GENERAL

The prosecutor-general is vested with "supreme advisory power to insure the strict observance of the law by all ministries and institutions subordinated to them, as well as by officials and citizens of the USSR generally" (Article 113). He is appointed by the Supreme Soviet for a period of seven years. He in turn appoints the prosecutors-general of the republics, territories, regions, autonomous regions, and autonomous republics, who serve for five years. Area, county, and city prosecutors are appointed for a like period by the prosecutors of the republics, but subject to the approval of the prosecutor-general of the USSR.

The powers of the prosecutor-general in the enforcement of laws are vast. According to the constitution, all officials of his office are in no way subordinate to any local organs of authority. In discussing the judicial reforms in 1957, however, Soviet officials revealed that a "special council" of the Ministry of the Interior, which included the secret police, had existed and had given instructions to the courts. Ostensibly, the full powers of the prosecutor have been restored and the court system has been divorced from the secret police.

SOVIET JUDICIAL PROCEDURES

Many Soviet judicial procedures have over the years come under considerable criticism in the democratic countries. Perhaps the most telling commentary on these procedures, however, have been the admissions by Stalin's successors that many innocent persons were imprisoned or executed during the Stalin era. It is now alleged that some of the notorious judicial practices have been or are being abolished. It still remains to be seen, however, to what extent this will be done. In any case, it does not seem likely that Soviet judicial procedures will be modified to such an extent that they will meet democratic standards of justice.

One of the most repugnant of Communist judicial practices stems from the absence of *habeas corpus*. The result is long pretrial incarceration and investigation. This period may last for months or even years, during which the imprisoned person may not be told why he is being held. Friends and close relatives may have no idea where the person may be or why. The 1961 RSFSR Code of Criminal Procedure empowers the prosecution to hold a suspect up to nine months without charges being filed. According to the announced judicial reforms of 1957, the right of counsel was to be accorded at some stage in the pretrial investigation, but the legal codes adopted in December 1958 limit this right to minors. Moreover, the persons conducting investigations are to be less subject to the orders of the prosecutor than heretofore. While these reforms, if actually put into practice, may result in an improved situation for some unfortunate persons, they do not go to the heart of the problem. The absence of *habeas corpus*, particularly in a society where the public cannot know who is being held or for what period of time, continues to constitute an abhorrent situation.

Another repulsive practice, perhaps made partially possible by the absence of *habeas corpus*, is the forced confession, the sole basis of countless convictions. Long pretrial imprisonment has given the police authorities ample time to torture and to wear down the victim to a point where he will sign anything. This has made possible the fabrication of a case against the accused which was false from beginning to end. Stalin's successors have admitted this, although the more specific references were to party comrades who were liquidated and not to the ordinary citizens who must have received even less consideration. Allegedly, proof of guilt will in the future require more than a confession. While this may be a modest gain, depending upon what weight courts continue to give to confessions, it does not do away with long pretrial imprisonment nor with the techniques for obtaining confessions. Nor does it forbid the use of such confessions in court.

The Soviet judicial system operates on the inquisitorial approach. In countries where democratic legislative bodies and a free press stand as guardians against the misuse of the judicial process, the inquisitorial approach has achieved high standards of justice. In the Soviet Union, however, it has made it possible for the judges to browbeat witnesses and to create an atmosphere of fear in the courtroom. The accused, who are obliged to take the stand and be grilled by the judge, often present a sorry spectacle. Even the so-called defense attorneys are often afraid to attempt a real defense, particularly in instances of the so-called crimes against the state. After the downgrading of Stalin, some Soviet jurists advocated the discarding of the presumption of guilt doctrine and the acceptance of the principle that a person is assumed to be innocent until proved guilty. While present statutes do not recognize this principle explicitly, they do state that the burden of proof rests on the prosecutor.[18]

In a somewhat similar situation are the ostensible guarantees to a public trial and to defense counsel. In the past, the right to a public trial has not been too meaningful, for the constitution permits legislation to deny it. Consequently, innumerable trials have been secret. It is possible, however, to overemphasize the value of public trials in the Soviet Union, for they have not been a barrier to miscarriages of justice. The right to defense counsel has in the past left much to be desired. By not being familiar with the case in the pretrial investigative period, defense attorneys have rarely had time to prepare a defense in the allotted time. Moreover, in certain types of cases, neither the defense attorney's nor the defendant's presence were required for conviction. It still remains to be seen whether significant reforms are instituted in this area.

Also of concern to many students of the Soviet judicial system is the absence of any protection against double jeopardy. Acquittal does not prevent additional trials for the same alleged offense. Similarly, moderate sentences may be appealed to higher courts and stiffer penalties imposed. It is altogether possible for a person to receive a moderate sentence in the court of original jurisdiction, thereby conveying a favourable impression of the Soviet judicial system, only to have a much more stringent sentence imposed by an appellate court without this fact becoming public knowledge. Now, however, appeals from acquittal or mild sentences must be made within a year.

Two procedures, said to be abolished in 1957, were not even a part of Soviet law, and therefore all the more repugnant. One was the practice of holding a person in violation of the criminal code in cases of minor negligence and other "administrative offenses" not foreseen by the law. Administrative officials, usually in the Ministry of Interior, imposed penalties, some of which banished the person for several

---

[18] Harold J. Berman, *Justice In The U.S.S.R.: An Interpretation of Soviet Law* (Rev. Ed., New York: Vintage Books, 1963), p. 71.

years. The second practice held that a person could be held in violation of the criminal code for crimes by analogy, that is, for acts that were analogous to illegal acts. These practices are allegedly no longer in existence. A similar procedure, also allegedly discarded, permitted punishment of relatives for crimes committed by their kin. The family of a soldier who deserted abroad, for example, was held collectively responsible for this act. A new type of offense has been added, however. Particularly dangerous state crimes committed against any other workers' state are now punishable under a new law.

Reports of improvements in Soviet judicial practices must, however, be tempered with the fact that the party has always reserved the right to go outside the law if considerations of policy demanded it. The setting up of the anti-parasite tribunals and the voluntary citizens' militia are but recent examples. The decree of the Presidium of the Supreme Soviet in 1961, authorizing a retroactive application of the death penalty for speculation in currency is another example.

It should also be remembered that new laws can be made any time that the regime's leaders desire them. At the time of the 1958 reforms, for example, the "counter-revolutionary" crime of "agitation or propaganda" against the Soviet system was retained, which is punishable by up to seven years imprisonment. And while the worst abuses of the Stalin era have apparently been eliminated, it may be significant that the death penalty has been extended in recent years to several new categories of crimes. Among these are: serious economic crimes, illegal transactions in foreign currencies, large-scale bribery, and resistance to a policeman which results in his death.

It is necessary also to note that Soviet courts are not impartial in dispensing justice. Party members usually receive more lenient sentences than nonparty citizens. Moreover, the Soviet press has from time to time printed stories indicating that prosecutors have been reluctant to bring party members to court at all. That some favoritism in favor of party members exists cannot be questioned, but its extent and prevalence are far from clear.

Finally, it needs to be noted that where there is no free press as a guardian of men's liberties, the existence of dubious judicial practices and procedures cannot be brought to light in a way that will have a serious impact upon the rulers. Moreover, where there is a corresponding emphasis upon secrecy, many odious practices can exist for years without becoming known to the most astute observers. Freedom would seem to be the first prerequisite for the type of judicial standards to which free men aspire.

THE ARMY IN THE SOVIET SYSTEM

In Marxist eyes, the army was the dreaded instrument of the bourgeois state, and, like it, had to be destroyed. But something had to be put in its place—an armed force of the new authority. But since the party was to become all-powerful in the Soviet system, it is quite understandable that the army (armed forces) could not become an autonomous force. New armed forces were established, but like their predecessors, they became the instrument of the prevailing political authority, only more so.

It needs to be re-emphasized that the Communist party is regarded as the source of all wisdom and authority. Any efforts to set up alternate or competing centers of political discussion, and any questioning of the party's program, have been viewed as treasonous and treated as such. The army, like other institutions in the Soviet system, is supposed to be subservient to the party. It can have influence only to the extent that what it wants to do is also what the party wants to do. If the army ever achieved an independent status the result would be a military dictatorship and not a dictatorship of the party.

The party's aim, of course, has been to produce the type of military man who will see no conflict between his role as a military man and his role as a party member. More than that, the party has sought to raise the political educational level of the military commanders, so that they will act as loyal party men. It should surprise no one that over 85% of the officer corps is made up of party members, and that the top command of the military forces is made up exclusively of party members. In other words, the military officer comes to his position imbued with the idea that the party is the most important part of the Soviet system, and that he, as a party member and as a military man, owes his highest allegiance to the party. And the party, for all practical purposes, means the top leadership. Military men, therefore, are party comrades, and it would be unthinkable for them to challenge the authority of the party leaders in the hierarchy above them. To do so would be to challenge the Soviet system itself.

Nevertheless, the party has also developed other means of insuring the loyalty of the armed forces. First of all, men in the armed forces live well, especially the officer class, and rarely do men cherish the loss of privileged positions which they happen to occupy. Secondly, there is the authority of the superior officers, who are also trusted party leaders, and upon whose good opinion promotion depends. In addition, the party's Central Committee has a special section whose responsibility is confined to political administration in the military forces. Its task is to convince all ranks that their first loyalty is to the party. Moreover, the party organizations in the armed forces have independent chains of command. They report to top party authorities and are not subject to the local party organization. Finally, the secret police operates within the military forces and, like the party organizations, is not subject to control by the local or regional party organization.

As a result, loyalty in the armed forces has been maintained, although not without purges, some of which have been of considerable proportions. We do not know to what extent there was any serious attempt on the part of military men to overthrow the system or to challenge the decisions of the political leaders. If they existed, they were not successful. Thus far, party leaders have been able to cope with troubles in the military forces, pretended or real.

There have been some indications, however, that military leaders have been made use of by political leaders in their struggle for power within the party. In 1957, for example, when an effort was made in the party Presidium to oust Khrushchev, the minister of defense, Marshal Zhukov, who owed his appointment to Khrushchev, employed military aircraft in order to get members of the Central Committee to Moscow quickly, enabling Khrushchev to frustrate the efforts of his opponents in the Presidium. Thereupon Khrushchev ousted his foes, and rewarded Zhukov, first as a candidate and then as a full member of the Presidium, the first time that a professional soldier achieved such a distinction. But Zhukov erred in thinking that he could curtail the work of party organizations in the military, and in a few months was ousted not only as minister of defense but also as a member of the Presidium and the Central Committee. Subsequently, the role of the party in the armed forces was strengthened, through explicit orders and through a re-affirmation of the principle that the leadership of the military cannot be outside the control of the party. As long as the authority of the party dictatorship is maintained, therefore, it seems safe to conclude that the armed forces will be loyal to whichever leaders remain at the top of the political ladder.

BIBLIOGRAPHICAL NOTE

A general view of the structure of the Soviet government may be found in Fainsod, *How Russia Is Ruled* (cited in chapter 25), and Herbert McClosky and John E. Turner, *The Soviet Dictatorship* (New York: McGraw-Hill; 1960). Particular studies of the Soviet legislature are few indeed, although useful discussions are included in Wladyslaw Wszebor Kulski, *The Soviet Regime, Communism in Practice* (4th ed. Syracuse: Syracuse University Press, 1964) and in Julian Towster, *Political Power in the U.S.S.R., 1917–1947: The Theory and Structure of Government in the Soviet State* (New York: Oxford University Press, 1948). George Barr Carson, *Electoral Practices in the U.S.S.R.* (New York: Praeger, 1955) is the first reliable study of that aspect of the Soviet system.

Information with regard to the political leadership in Russia is also meager. Nathan Leites, *The Operational Code of the Politburo, A Systematic Analysis of the Political Strategy of Communism and the Rules by Which It Operates* (New York: McGraw-Hill, 1951) and George K. Schueller, *The Politburo* (Stanford: Stanford University Press, 1951) are sources of information on the governmental organ now referred to as the party Presidium. Additional material may be found in Wolfgang Leonhard, *The Kremlin Since Stalin* (London: Oxford University Press, 1962); in Philip E. Mosely (ed.), *Russia Since Stalin* (Philadelphia: American Academy of Political and Social Science, 1956); in Victor Alexandrov, *Khrushchev of the Ukraine: A Biography* (New York: Philosophical Library, 1957); in Lazar P. Mikhailovich, edited by Konrad Kellen, *Khrushchev: A Political Biography* (New York: Praeger, 1959); and in the biographies of Lenin and Stalin cited under Chapter 25.

The basic reference work for the study of Soviet law is Andrei Y. Vyshinsky (ed.), *The Law of the Soviet State* (New York: Macmillan, 1948). Vladimir Gsovsky, *Soviet Civil Law: Private Rights and Their Background Under the Soviet Regime* (2 vols., Ann Arbor: University of Michigan Press, 1948 and 1949) is a comprehensive study, while Harold J. Berman, *Justice in the U.S.S.R.* (New York: Vintage Books, 1963) and John N. Hazard, *Law and Social Change in the U.S.S.R.* (London: Stevens, 1953) are excellent also. Additional information may be found in Vladimir Gsovski and Kazimierz Grzybowski (eds.), *Government, Law and Courts in the Soviet Union and Eastern Europe* (2 vols., New York: Praeger, 1959); Hans Kelsen, *The Communist Theory of Law* (New York: Praeger, 1955); Boris A. Konstantinovsky, *Soviet Law in Action,* edited by Harold J. Berman (Cambridge, Mass.: Harvard University Press, 1953); and G. G. Morgan, *Soviet Administrative Legality* (Stanford: Stanford University Press, 1962).

Among the outstanding general works on the Soviet system are Raymond A. Bauer, Alex Inkeles, and Clyde Kluckhohn, *How the Soviet System Works* (Cambridge, Mass.: Harvard University Press, 1956); George Bernard de Huszar, et al., *Soviet Power and Policy* (New York: Crowell, 1955); James H. Meisel and Edward S. Kozera (eds.), *Materials for the Study of the Soviet System: State and Party Constitutions, Laws, Decrees, Decisions and Official Statements of the Leaders in Translation* (2d.; Ann Arbor, Mich.: George Wahr Publishing Co., 1953); Jacob Miller, *Soviet Russia* (New York: Longmans, Green, 1954); W. W. Rostow, *The Dynamics of Soviet Society* (Mentor, 1955); and Bertram D. Wolfe, *Six Keys to the Soviet System* (Boston: Beacon Press, 1956).

Discussions of the Soviet military system include those of Harold J. Berman and Miroslav Kerner, *Soviet Military Law and Administration* (Cambridge, Mass.: Harvard University Press, 1955) ; Zbigniew Brzezinski (ed.), *Political Controls in the Soviet Army* (New York: Praeger, 1954) ; Augustin Guillaume, *Soviet Arms and Soviet Power* (Washington, D.C.: Infantry Journal Press, 1949) ; Basil Henry Liddell Hart, *The Red Army: The Red Army 1918 to 1945; The Soviet Army 1946 to the Present* (New York: Harcourt, Brace, 1956) ; and the translation of the Soviet military text: V. D. Sokolovskii, *Soviet Military Strategy* (Englewood Cliffs, N.J.: Prentice-Hall, 1963).

CHAPTER **28**

HARNESSING THE MASSES TO THE DICTATORSHIP

ONE OF THE most perplexing, and at the same time one of the least adequately answered, questions encountered by persons seeking to understand the workings of a Communist regime concerns the methods and techniques by which the masses are mobilized to do the regime's bidding. Since the number of persons belonging to the Soviet Communist party does not exceed 7 or 8 per cent of the adult population, how do they manipulate the other 90-odd per cent? Part of the answer is to be found in the fact that Soviet leaders have never operated on the assumption that it was sufficient not to have people against you. They must be for you. It is not enough to prevent undesirable acts. It is essential that people act positively. It is imperative that the people do the things that the party wants done, even if these are deeply repugnant to the people who are forced to do them. Explaining how the party gets the masses to do its bidding is the task of this chapter.

FORCE AND FEAR

From the outset, the new Soviet regime employed the instruments of force and fear to compel obedience, a practice that has been copied by every other Communist regime. Over the years, these instruments were developed and applied with increasing refinement. And although they were supplemented by various efforts at persuasion, behind each such effort there always lurked the possibility of a serious if not a frightful sanction.

LIQUIDATION AND IMPRISONMENT

Following Lenin's dictum that the Communists should not be squeamish about spilling blood, the wielders of the new authority lost no time in imprisoning and executing their opponents, real or imagined, even though they had violated no law. Those considered most dangerous to the new regime were put out of the way, often without benefit of any type of trial. In the initial years, it was the "class enemy" (former owners of productive property and persons who had been associated with the tsarist regime) that felt the brunt of the terror. In subsequent years, however, the terror was to seep into all segments of society—workers, peasants, and even the Communist party.

Those who were not considered dangerous enough to warrant physical liquidation were imprisoned for varying terms. People were banished to concentration camps for years on a no more serious charge than that they were found to be "socially dangerous," although there was no definition of social danger. Proceedings against a person did not have to be public, nor was it necessary for him to be present or to be represented by counsel. In some cases, sentences of people sent to camps contained the proviso, "without privilege of correspondence." The authority to pass such judgments was vested in special boards of the secret police, and they were in no way bound by provisions of the criminal code, nor were they responsible to the courts.

SECRET POLICE SURVEILLANCE AND INTIMIDATION

To take care of a vastly larger number of individuals whose loyalties were suspect, but who were not considered dangerous enough to liquidate or to imprison, the new Soviet regime created a secret police.[1] Initially it was known as the Cheka, extraordinary commission for combating espionage, counterrevolution, and dereliction of duty, but subsequently known under a variety of initials (OGPU, NKVD, MVD), reflecting changes in name and, to some extent, changes in function. In August 1954, its powers allegedly curbed, the secret police became the Committee for State Security (KGB), and was made responsible to the Council of Ministers. Its powers were further curbed in 1960 and 1962, when jurisdiction over the militia, or ordinary police, was transferred from a central ministry to ministries in the union republics.

Agents of the secret police are to be found in all segments of Soviet society, in the offices, in the army, in schools, in recreational clubs and in collective farms, but most people can only surmise as to the identity of the agents. They move about freely and are not subject to local control of any type.

People who are something less than enthusiastic about the regime are made aware of the existence of the secret police in a variety of

---

[1] See Simon Wolin and Robert M. Slusser, *The Soviet Secret Police* (New York: Praeger, 1957).

ways. Some are asked to report to the local office, where they may be questioned about remarks they or their associates have allegedly made. Or they may be asked to explain their absence from parades or other manifestations sponsored by the authorities. Or they may be held for a few hours or a day, with no hint as to the reason. Subsequent invitations to appear may follow, and one never knows when a more permanent stay may result.

In those cases where the authorities wish to go beyond intimidation, a person may be held for days or months, or even years, and without the person knowing the charge against him. Such imprisonment is usually accompanied by endless interrogation, particularly if a confession is desired. The methods used to extract confessions have been so adequately described in recent years that further comment would seem superfluous here. Suffice it to say that the methods of torture, mental as well as physical, have been systematically refined and developed. Once caught in the web, even high party dignitaries become helpless.[2]

The tactics of secret police agents are many and varied. Often the agents are provocateurs, posing as enemies of the regime and urging the creation of antiregime organizations. When the desired persons have been implicated, the net closes and the agents become star witnesses in court, admitting all. At other times, they are placed in prison, talking about their "crimes," and in the process learning as much as possible about the past activities of their cell mates, only to become more convincing witnesses at the trial.

Secret Police Auxiliary: The Informers

Secret police agents cannot be everywhere at all times. Hence, there is need for a sizable net of informers if surveillance is to be reasonably complete. Wherever a few people come together, for work or pleasure, there is certain to be one or more secret police informers. Everyone knows that they exist, although they are not known even to one another. Since people do not know who the informers are, they are led to suspect everyone, including close friends. The result is a general feeling of isolation and distrust.

Most informers are recruited, but there are those who volunteer, hoping thereby to build some good will with the authorities against the exigencies of more difficult times. Often enough the informers find that they are pitted against each other so as to insure a thorough

---

[2] See Khrushchev's speech to Twentieth Party Congress (February 24–25, 1956) for some notable examples.

reporting job. Failure of one informer to report even a minor matter results in his integrity being questioned. Once having begun to inform, the informer is at the mercy of the secret police. Even more onerous tasks are demanded of him. Should he hesitate, the question of changed loyalties immediately arises. Even past performances are examined for hidden and disloyal motives.

The end result of the techniques of force and fear is to eliminate or to cow and terrify all those who would be capable of offering an alternative to the Communists. The effect of the terror apparatus is made more frightful by virtue of the feeling that anyone could be next. It matters not whether the threat is real or not; it is sufficient that the people think so.

MOBILIZING PUBLIC OPINION

Supplementing force and fear, in harnessing the masses to do the bidding of the dictatorship, are a host of elaborately developed techniques for mobilizing and monopolizing public opinion. Unlike democratic governments, the Soviet regime is not interested in satisfying popular demands. But it knows that people will continue to do some thinking even if they cannot make their views known publicly. It is imperative, therefore, that the Soviet leaders learn something of the people's frame of mind so as to be able to channel their thinking more effectively along desired lines. In order to do this, the regime exercises complete and active control over the public opinion media and, in addition, seeks to exclude all competing influences.

OWNERSHIP AND CONTROL OF PUBLIC OPINION MEDIA

The extent of the government's monopoly in the public opinion field cannot be appreciated unless one bears in mind that there are no privately owned newspapers or press agencies in the Soviet Union. There are no privately owned stocks of newsprint or printing presses. There are no privately owned movie theaters, film producing, or film importing enterprises. There are no privately owned or operated television or radio stations, or privately produced programs. There are no privately owned theaters or privately produced plays. There are no privately published or privately imported books. It is illegal to publish anything privately, even with a mimeograph machine. In short, Soviet citizens may not attempt to spread their ideas except through channels which the government provides. And the official censor guards the access to these channels.

Such control over the instrumentalities of public opinion enables the leaders to control what the public is to know. Visitors to the Soviet Union never fail to be astounded at the extent of popular ignorance about world events that are well known to people in the democratic world. Even Lenin's testament was not published in the Soviet Union until some time after Stalin's death, 30 years after its publication in the outside world. Moreover, ignorance is compounded by a great deal of misinformation which the regime regularly purveys.

From time to time, the party leaders' ideas as to what the public should know changes, and history needs to be rewritten. For example, one-time Politburo member Lavrenti P. Beria was, like Orwell's Winston, "lifted clean out from the stream of history." After his execution in 1953, the official state publishing house supplied subscribers of the Soviet Encyclopedia with four pages on Friedrich Bergholtz and pictures of the Bering Sea, recommending that the four-page article on Beria and his picture in volume V be cut out and replaced with this new material. Beria will never have existed! Similar examples are legion.

The control over what the public can read or hear extends also to the outside world. The number of publications from non-Communist countries is pitifully small and these are permitted to come in only after the most careful screening by the censorship. Foreign radio broadcasts, especially those from the United States, were jammed prior to 1963 by an array of Soviet transmitters. In addition, Soviet citizens have not been free to travel outside their country except on official missions, a practice which was seemingly modified in a limited manner after 1956. Likewise, foreign visitors to the USSR were pretty well excluded during the heyday of the Stalin era and their contact with Soviet citizens was extremely dangerous to the latter. Since 1956, it has been much easier for foreigners to visit the Soviet Union and to talk with Soviet citizens, although the length of their stay and the areas they can visit have been rigidly limited.

The protective curtain against outside ideas has also been used to keep undesirable information about Soviet society from reaching the outside world. The few foreign news correspondents who have been permitted in the Soviet Union have not been permitted to gather news freely. They have had to rely, for the most part, on official handouts. Moreover, until 1961 their dispatches had to be submitted to the censor, with no knowledge at the time of what was passed and what was deleted. More recently, the Soviets have permitted correspondents of foreign radio networks to broadcast from Moscow. In all cases, however, the government has felt free to expel correspondents if what they reported met with official displeasure. The representatives of one American network were even expelled because that network produced a television show in the United States which was regarded in Moscow as being "anti-Soviet propaganda." Although news-gathering in the Soviet Union is still not free, the outside world gets considerably more news from there than it did ten years ago.

CREATING PROPAGANDA INSTRUMENTS

The Soviet authorities are not satisfied with owning and controlling the existing instrumentalities of public opinion. They are determined that all segments of society should be involved in the regime's propaganda effort to create an atmosphere of assent for the party's aims and policies, and especially for its current programs. To this end, the Soviet leaders have created a welter of new and different propaganda instruments.

These propaganda instruments are designed to reach groups and individuals who could normally avoid political polemics. Scientists, teachers, musicians, writers—all are given a propaganda outlet, which they are expected to utilize by way of praising the Communist way of life and the opportunities it affords them. Writers who might have pleaded that it was inappropriate for them to contribute to clearly political papers, such as *Pravda*, the official organ of the Communist party, discovered that the regime had created a newspaper for writers alone, *The Literary Gazette*. Writers could be reminded that in tsarist days they were unable to find an outlet for their views. Now, the government has set up a special newspaper for them wherein they can write about the great opportunities for writers and artists in a Communist society. Here was a means of expressing their gratitude. Here was an outlet for their views. Here were printing presses and stocks of newsprint—and here were party-furnished texts of what they should like to say. How much easier could it be!

Similarly, other groups in Soviet society are provided an outlet of their own. A biology professor, for example, cannot claim that it would be inappropriate for him to write in political journals. He does not have to. The government provides him a special and dignified platform, a specially created newspaper for professors. And the party is generous in providing themes to write about. If the professor can demonstrate that his official duties do not leave him enough time, some one will be found to write a piece for him. The greater the professor's reputation the more important it is, from the regime's point of view, to have his name associated with the party's goals and programs. The same can be said of the scientists, musicians, actors, engineers, and others.

Members of some groups are more effectively involved by various public meetings. Engineers and other respected personnel in a plant or other economic enterprise are asked to take part in party-sponsored political meetings or other propaganda manifestations. If they cannot always be prevailed upon to give a speech, or to take some other leading role, they are asked "just to sit on the platform," etc. In this way the rank and file can observe a visual connection between party leaders and the respected men in their enterprise. In other words, the regime does not want to leave uncommitted any men in whom the rank and file could see a leadership alternative to the Communists.

Since everyone cannot be counted upon to read the party's program or even to listen to it over the radio and television, the Soviet leaders have developed face-to-face agitation to a fine art, a technique always regarded as paramount. It has been estimated that the Communist party enlists the part-time services of some 2 million persons in face-to-face agitation.[3] They speak to groups in factories or on collective farms. They visit homes and small gatherings of apartment dwellers. In this way no one can escape getting the party's propaganda message, perhaps in several different forms.

GUIDANCE FROM AGITPROP

The primary responsibility for directing the Communist party's propaganda is vested in the Central Committee's agitation and propaganda section, commonly referred to as *Agitprop*. It must see to it that all propaganda outlets do their job. It issues directives and suggestions. And it furnishes various materials. Moreover, it sees to it that those who fail or falter are criticized for their shortcomings.

Once or twice a year (on the anniversary of the Bolshevik Revolution or on May Day, or both) *Agitprop* develops and the party issues officially a large number of slogans which constitute the keynote of the party's policies for the coming months. They are the principal guideposts for the various propaganda outlets. These are modified by subsequent party declarations on various subjects. In the absence of official party declarations, the party's different official organs offer ample clues as to the current party line on any subject. And, of course, there are the confidential instructions from *Agitprop*.

One or two examples of the more detailed work of *Agitprop* may be instructive. The face-to-face agitation, for example, is systematically

---

[3] See Alex Inkeles, *Public Opinion in Soviet Russia: A Study in Mass Persuasion* (Cambridge, Mass., Harvard University Press, 1950).

organized. At regular intervals, *Agitprop* publishes the *Agitator's Notebook*, which contains materials for speeches and themes to be stressed. Generally speaking, there are several brief articles, some dealing with domestic problems and some with foreign affairs. Thus the agitator is furnished a steady and current stream of propaganda materials. Moreover, the so-called "letters to the editor," which are often depicted by Soviet leaders or their sympathizers as examples of freedom of expression in the Soviet Union, are for the most part organized and controlled by *Agitprop* or its agents. Closely related to the letter writers are the so-called worker, peasant, youth, and soldier correspondents, who are trained and paid for their contributions. The various newspaper staffs are instructed in how these correspondents are to be trained and how they are to go about their work. In editorial conferences with these correspondents, there is often a party representative to give advice and guidance. Sometimes the party calls conferences of correspondents to discuss the important themes to be dwelt upon. Hence, it is obvious that these correspondents and letter writers deal only with those topics deemed appropriate by the party. Their function is to help the regime mold public opinion and not to express it as it actually exists.

THE MASS ORGANIZATIONS

In addition to the instruments of force and fear and the techniques of persuasion, the Soviet leaders have developed numerous organizations through which everyone is involved, in one way or another, in helping to carry out the party's program. Whereas force and fear are employed to destroy opposition and to instill fear, and whereas the public opinion media have been developed and organized to make sure that the party's propaganda message gets to everyone in a variety of contexts, the numerous party-sponsored organizations are designed to harness the masses to the dictatorship by having them help the party to realize specific and concrete aims. All mass organizations have been referred to by Soviet leaders as "transmission belts," linking the party with the masses. Not only are people not allowed to oppose or to stand aside; they must actively assist in carrying out Communist party programs.

THE SOVIETS

The most far flung of the mass organizations are the soviets. Although they constitute the administrative apparatus for carrying out governmental policies, they are also the principal means by which mass participation in community activities is secured. The majority of the members of local soviets, unlike those at the top, are not members of the Communist party, hence conveying the idea of popular control in administration. But, as noted in an earlier chapter, the soviets are organized on a pyramidal basis, with effective party control at all levels. Moreover, even the selection of nonparty members for local soviets is decided upon by the party.

Because they are a part of the governmental structure, and therefore have the authority of the state behind them, the soviets reach out to include everyone. They have officially been depicted as "the mass organization of all toilers." Because they are so described, no citizen can refuse to help the soviets in carrying out their tasks.

THE TRADE UNIONS

Unlike trade unions in democratic countries, Soviet trade unions are not expected to hold views that are essentially different from those of the employer. They were described by Stalin as "the mass organization of the proletariat, linking the party with the class primarily in the sphere of production." But in the Soviet Union the interests of the proletariat are not judged to be in conflict with the interests of any other group. Initially, the trade unions did conceive workers' interests more narrowly and sought to represent them as against the narrower interests of management. But within a brief period of time they were brought into line. The worker was depicted as being also the owner. If he should strike, therefore, he would be striking against himself.

Like other organizations in a Communist state, trade unions are organized in a pyramidal fashion, with authority being wielded by the All-Union Central Council of Trade Unions, which is at the apex of the pyramid. At the base of the pyramid is the factory committee, elected by the union in each factory. Between the base and the top are a number of intermediary committees at the district and republic level. Throughout the trade union organization, however, the real wielder of authority is the Communist party. In various enterprises, party control is achieved through the appointed director, the primary unit of the party, and the shop committee. The latter is nominally an agency of the trade union, but, in the past at least, it has been more of an adjunct of management than a representative of the workers.

Therefore, the trade unions have in the main functioned as instruments of the party in seeking to attain higher production quotas, labor discipline, efficiency, and other regime goals. Beyond this, in actual practice, their principal area of action has been in the social welfare field. They have been charged with the administration of social insurance and labor benefits. Interviews with Soviet workers who have left the USSR show that they regard Soviet trade unions solely as instruments of the party and of factory management.

In 1957, the Soviet leaders took steps that indicated that they wanted the trade union representation on the disputes commissions to at least uphold the legal rights of the workers. At the same time, they revealed that in the past a worker's complaint did not get much of a hearing, often not at all. His rights of appeal were narrowly limited. Often the union members of the disputes commissions had sided with the actions of management, even when they ran contrary to the law. While not suggesting that the trade unions defend traditional workers' rights, they were told that they should at least defend those legal rights which the workers in the Soviet Union do possess.

ACCENT ON YOUTH

It has been evident for a long time that the Soviet leaders, although jealously guarding top leadership positions, have staked everything on youth. The future of Communism is in their hands. Not only must the new leaders come from the youth, but in addition, new generations of supporters for the regime must be won there. The Communist way of life cannot be perpetuated unless a steady stream of new adherents can be recruited who are enthusiastic enough to want to perpetuate it.

Consequently, the Soviet leaders have left no stone unturned to develop the most elaborate organizational network of youth organizations.[4] These include the *Octobrists* for small children, the *Pioneers* for adolescents and the *Komsomol* (union of Communist youth) for the young adults. All children are *Octobrists*, but there is progressive elimination as one goes up the ladder. The cream of the youth, from the party's point of view, is to be found in the *Komsomol*, which in turn is the principal recruiting ground for new party members. Similarly, leadership is from the top down. Party members lead the *Komsomols*, which in turn are responsible for work among *Pioneers*, while *Pioneers* are supposed to help the *Octobrists*. The party, of course, is the final judge in all matters of youth organization and action. The activities of these youth organizations are carefully planned and supervised. In the case of the *Octobrists* and *Pioneers*, it is mostly a matter of implanting attitudes, but in the case of the

---

[4] The Soviet schools, as devices for harnessing the masses to the dictatorship, are treated separately in a subsequent section of this chapter.

Komsomols there is more serious work to be done. Broadly speaking, the work of the *Komsomols* can be said to comprise four basic functions: (1) assist in the ideological training of youth, (2) set an example, by hard work, which will help the regime realize its economic aims, (3) help the regime to spot trouble or disloyalty, by maintaining a sharp lookout at all times, (4) assist the regime in realizing its objectives in the armed forces. Moreover, *Komsomol* members are required to play an active role in the quasi-military civil defense agency (DOSAAF), which is directed by top-flight reserve officers of the Soviet armed forces. Here they are taught first aid, given shooting practice, trained to operate and manipulate parachutes, taught about guided missiles, and subjected to further political indoctrination.

To achieve their varied goals, the *Komsomols*, some 18 to 20 million strong, have the unstinting support of the party, which spares no effort in their behalf. In order to realize the ideological tasks of the *Komsomols*, for example, special courses, schools, and study groups are organized. Here the youth study the history of the party, the biographies of Soviet leaders, the works of Marx, Lenin, and others. In addition, over 200 youth newspapers and magazines are published with a total circulation of over 20 million copies.

Moreover, there are a number of other techniques which are designed to capture the youth for the regime. Among these are youth theaters, youth physical culture centers, and youth homes and recreation centers. To the end that new generations must be won for Communism, leisure as well as work time of young people is carefully planned, supervised, and directed by the Communist party.

But there are indications that all is not well in the *Komsomols*. Soviet newspapers continue to carry accounts of poor and unsatisfactory work in the youth organizations. The *Komsomolists* are negligent of their leadership duties among the *Pioneers*. Many of them are calculating careerists, using the *Komsomol* organization to advance personal ambitions and goals, being indifferent to everything that does not affect their careers. Many have fallen for bourgeois tastes in music, literature, art, dress, and manners. Many have not responded to special appeals to engage in various volunteer projects. Many who have completed their university or technical studies find ways of remaining in the larger urban centers, and thus avoiding service in the more remote provinces. Many have raised embarrassing questions about the regime's promises and declared goals. Soviet leaders have spoken of "unhealthy moods among the youth," and official *Komsomol* newspapers have written of "ultrarevolutionary demagogues," "apolitical persons devoid of ideals," and "nihilists, carrying out a reappraisal of values."

While it would be difficult to speak of opposition to the regime among youth, because it is impossible for opposition to organize or be manifested openly, it is possible, at least, to speak of a passive dislike for the regime.[5] There is a revulsion against the constant interference in the personal lives of young people. There is dissatisfaction with the material state of things. There is a feeling of isolation and a yearning for contact with the outside world. Even among the privileged youth, the system of completely limiting the individual tends to produce moods of depression.

Bits of evidence stemming from informal gatherings in private homes, apparently not so hazardous as in Stalin times, reveal a general desire for political and spiritual freedom. Although political topics are for the most part studiously avoided, unorthodox views on other matters are frequently expressed. Further testimony of the yearning for freedom is provided by the fact that the names of several underground student magazines have found their way into the Soviet press. Far from creating new generations of unconditionally obedient robots, devoid of feelings and ideas, the Communist party may, in the long run, produce the exact opposite.

More recently, young *Komsomol* members have been asking some difficult questions openly. They have been asking what the society which they are supposedly building will look like in the future. Having come face to face with the contradictions and injustices in the Soviet system, they are seeking an answer from their leaders as to the nature of the future society. Aware of the inequalities of the Soviet class structure, they want to know if Communism will mean the end of these inequalities. The regime's answer was the new party program (1961), which reiterates many old promises and whose avowed goal is to catch up with the United States in twenty years. By 1980, according to the program, Soviet citizens can look forward to certain free services, including most utilities, municipal transport, midday meals, education, medicine, and rent-free housing.

WRITERS AND ARTISTS

Writers and artists in the Soviet Union, unlike those in democratic countries, are expected to develop and to utilize their talents in order

---

[5] See the two articles by David Burg (a former Soviet student) in *The Bulletin of the Institute for the Study of the USSR*, entitled, "Soviet Youth's Opposition to the Communist Regime," Vol. IV (April and May, 1957), pp. 41–47; 44–50.

that they may more effectively support the Communist political system. There is no freedom to create except insofar as the creation assists the party in mobilizing support for the regime. The Soviet Bill of Rights gives writers and artists the "right" to create, but only for the purpose of defending and strengthening the socialist system. And the party leaders are the sole judges of what that system is and what strengthens it and what does not.

From time to time, the party conducts a literary purge, during which certain works and their authors are severely criticized and the magazines which published their pieces are censured. Sometimes the authors are expelled from the Union of Soviet Writers, an organization which serves to keep would-be mavericks in line. During Stalin's reign, many writers also went to prison camps. The usual criticism is that literary and artistic works are ideologically harmful, apolitical, imitative of bourgeois Western concepts, or based on the notion of art for art's sake. In the Communist party's view, Soviet art, literature, music—in short, all forms of artistic expression—must serve to glorify the Soviet system, the Soviet leaders, and the domestic and foreign policies of the Soviet Union.

But the party does not simply wait to judge artistic and literary works in a sort of postaudit. Through its official organ, *Pravda*, the *Literary Gazette* and other media, the party frequently sets forth tasks for writers and artists. They are told to stress the efforts of workers and peasants in the realization of the current economic plan, or some other objective with which the party is currently concerned. Occasionally, it bemoans the absence of a great poem, novel, opera, or other work depicting some Soviet scene, and calls for the production of such a work. In other words, great art or great literature is what contributes to the realization of whatever goals the Communist party is pursuing at any one time.

For those who live up to the party's expectations there are generous rewards. Artists of all types, but especially writers, actors, and singers, are held in high esteem by the regime, and consequently receive considerable note in the press and other publicity media. Moreover, they are the highest paid people in Soviet society, which makes the material rewards perhaps more important than the recognition. Soviet writers and composers receive royalties, which means that some of them are millionaires. Actors and singers, if considered good, are given special engagements for extra pay, even though their regular salaries are high. Finally, the better artists have an opportunity to travel, they have better clothes, and they have good housing, which is scarce everywhere. If an artist is willing to have his talents exploited for political purposes, therefore, he gets recognition from the regime and usually can be assured of excellent material rewards.

Following Khrushchev's revelations in 1956 of the crimes and abuses of the Stalin era, party publications called for an end to the narrow political approach to art. The Stalinist cult was held responsible for a debased cultural life. Certain writers who were sent to prison during the Stalin period were released, and some who had met a worse fate were posthumously "rehabilitated." Within a year, a tremendous change had occurred in the Soviet literary and artistic output. No longer was there an effort to hide or to avoid the facts of Soviet life, including illegal arrests, the prison system, and the fate of former colleagues. In print, on canvas and on the stage, Soviet artists and writers were presenting ambitious and greedy party officials and government bureaucrats as the villains of their pieces. Their heroes were simple people, often not even party members. Some writers, cautiously hopeful, were stressing the need for freedom of creative endeavor.

The victory of the anti-Stalinists in Poland, and more particularly the Hungarian Revolution, forced the Soviet leaders into a reappraisal of their new attitude toward art. Reportedly, stormy sessions of writers' and artists' associations followed, where the political leaders sought to reassert the party line in the artistic and literary fields. The meeting of artists fell in line, adopting a resolution in which they promised to reflect in their works "the beauty and grandeur of Communist ideals," and pledged to combat the infiltration of alien influences. Reports of the meeting of writers, however, indicated that the party leadership was not too pleased with the results. The author of the most controversial work of fiction at that time (Vladimir Dudintsev, author of *Not by Bread Alone*), far from confessing his errors, defended his work, despite the fact that the party leadership was displeased with it.

In 1957, before he knew that his novel, *Doctor Zhivago*, could not be published in the Soviet Union, Boris Pasternak arranged for its publication outside Russia by an Italian publisher. The latter, an alleged Communist, refused to suspend publication when, as a consequence of the decision that it would not be published in the Soviet Union, he was asked to do so. The book was awarded the 1958 Nobel prize for literature and translated into several languages. Before Soviet authorities could act, Pasternak signified acceptance of the award, but subsequently declined when he was bitterly attacked in the

Soviet press, expelled from the Union of Soviet Writers, and threatened with exile.

In the early 1960s there seemed to be room for optimism. The refreshing nature of Yevtushenko's poems, as well as those of other poets, and the forthright prose of Nekrasov and some of his colleagues gave rise to hopes for increasing relaxation. The publication of Alexander Solzhenitsyn's *One Day in the Life of Ivan Denisovich,* depicting life in one of Stalin's concentration camps, seemed to improve opportunities for critical realism. In 1963, however, Khrushchev made it clear that the party was on the side of those who insisted on maintaining ideological purity in the arts. His successors have said that creativeness requires experimentation, but that such experimentation must be within the bounds of dialectical materialism and socialist realism.

In the light of these developments, the future of literary and artistic expression in the Soviet Union seems unclear. For a brief moment, at least, Soviet writers felt a release from the deadening conformity into which they had for years been forced by the Stalinist dictatorship. They were able to experience a modicum of creativity which they had not known in the years before. Perhaps the tide cannot be completely reversed. It may be that the Soviet leaders will never again be able to resort to the type of ruthlessness which could silence all expressions of discontent. Only time will tell.

OTHER ASSOCIATIONS

The mass organizations discussed in the preceding pages are the ones which seem to get the greatest attention from the Communist party, and are, therefore, perhaps the most important in helping realize specific and concrete tasks. But there are also other organizations which have important roles to play. There are sports groups, an association of railway workers, an organization for war veterans, an association of collective farmers, reserve military organizations, and so on. All of these have their periodic meetings, at which they examine their problems, their past work, and, in the end, inevitably pledge to do their utmost to come up to the expectations which the party holds out for them.

The net result of the whole scheme of mass organizations is that nearly every person, at least in the cities, is caught up in the vortex of Communist organizational life, so that he finds himself belonging to several organizations, each of which strives to bend him to fit the Communist mold. The composition of each group may vary with changing occupational or avocational groupings, and the techniques may be altered by party edict, but the end is always and forever the same. The Soviet citizen, despite everything he can do, becomes entangled in the Communist web. In addition to his regular job, he finds himself going to meetings and conferences, taking part in parades or other manifestations, and involved in one or more so-called voluntary projects. Physically he finds himself in a state of perpetual exhaustion. Psychologically, if he does not like the Communist system, he sees himself compromised, involved as in a huge conspiracy, contributing to a perpetuation of the system, yet seeing no way out of the web in which he has become enmeshed.

SCHOOLS IN A STRAIT JACKET

Along with the youth organizations, the Soviet Communist party looks upon the schools as the main instruments for shaping the new generations. Since the launching of the first Soviet earth satellite in 1957, the Soviet educational system has received a good deal of attention in the West from educators and political leaders alike. It is beyond the scope of this book, however, to examine the Soviet educational system in all its ramifications. We are primarily interested in it as an instrument in the hands of the party for the molding of new generations to fit the requirements of its political leaders.

As all other institutions in the Soviet Union, the schools have a definite role to play. In addition to providing the type of training desired by the party, mostly professional and technical, the schools are supposed to turn out young citizens who will be enthusiastic supporters of the Communist system. The attempt to re-educate older generations has not borne much fruit. Hence there is an urgent need, from the point of view of the party, to redouble the effort to guide young people along the desired path. Therefore, little is left to chance. All educational programs are carefully planned with definite political objectives at all levels.

As might be expected, there is a desire to get to children at an early age. The much-advertised nurseries, or day care centers, where working mothers may leave their young ones, offer the first such opportunity. Here, in picture, song, and story, the young ones learn to glorify Soviet leaders and their achievements. In most instances the young one returns to the mother at the end of the day, although there are a growing number of centers which return the child to the parents only for the week end.

Understandably, the party sets the educational goals of the Soviet schools and assigns important personnel to check on their realization. Basic directives are usually in the form of resolutions of the party's Central Committee, which may be spelled out in greater detail by the Council of Ministers. Key articles from the party press or in educational journals offer further guidance. In addition, there are the ministries of education in the republics. Moreover, important school officials (administrators and teachers) are party members, and presumably familiar with the party line on education. Through all of these channels, Soviet teachers are told, time and again, that all education must be based on the one and only true science, the science of Marxism-Leninism.

To this end, textbooks and other teaching materials are expected to conform, with increased emphasis on ideology as one moves up the educational ladder. Moreover, the general tone is set by the most important general reference work for all citizens, the Large Soviet Encyclopedia, which is regarded as the final authority and the undisputed source of information on all subjects. It was produced on the basis of a political directive which in 1949 declared that the second edition "should widely elucidate the world-historical victories of socialism . . . in the USSR in the province of economics, science, culture, art." And "it must show the superiority of socialist culture over the culture of the capitalist world." All articles are thus written from the point of view of the Marxist-Leninist world outlook. This concept of an encyclopedia is foreign to the Western world, and foreign to the traditional concept of what an encyclopedia should be.

In their propaganda aimed at the outside world, Soviet leaders have expressed considerable pride in their educational system. Among other things, they have on innumerable occasions pointed to the banishment of illiteracy as one of their great achievements. While not denying this, an objective observer must also ask: What achievement is it if the purpose is to enslave the mind? What gain is it for an Armenian or a Ukrainian to have the party organ, *Pravda*, translated from the Russian into one of his own tongue? This is not to suggest that banishing illiteracy is not a desirable goal, but to point out that in the Soviet system it is not an unmixed blessing.

In their domestic output, in contrast to what is said about the educational system in propaganda destined for abroad, the Soviet leaders are frequently critical of the shortcomings of their schools. On the one hand, there are the material deficiencies, poor or inadequate physical facilities (necessitating double and even triple shifts), inadequate housing and work space for teachers, and the like. On the other hand, and seemingly more important, are the undesirable results. Too many students are receptive only to the type of learning which will get them into institutions of higher learning, while the latter can admit and accommodate only a portion of them. Moreover, many of the university graduates are often pictured as ideologically unprepared, enamored of cosmopolitan views and tastes and, in general, not possessing the ideological outlook which the party leaders expect and desire.

In late 1958 and early 1959, the regime launched an organizational overhaul of the Soviet school system, which came to be known as the "Khrushchev School Reform." Its avowed goal was to channel only a relatively small proportion of young people toward higher education. The remainder were to be trained for a specific niche in the labor force, while giving them a modicum of general knowledge. In support of his plan, Khrushchev observed that it was unwise and unrealistic for so many young people to aspire to a higher education, particularly when many of them did so because they found the idea of manual labor repugnant.

The objectives of the Khrushchev School Reform were to be achieved through an eight-year compulsory school, followed by on-the-job training for two or three years. While for some on-the-job training consisted mainly of going to school, 80 per cent of the university admissions quota was reserved for persons with at least two years of work experience. While on the job, these youngsters would prepare themselves for institutions of higher learning through special classes, night schools, or correspondence courses. Under this plan, Soviet authorities would be able to determine, at an earlier age than before, who would go to the university, to the technical institutes, or to the mines and factories.

This aspect of the Khrushchev School Reform was not enthusiastically received by a number of educators who doubted the wisdom of interrupting the educational careers of promising students. It came under fire in the Soviet press soon after Khrushchev's ouster in 1964, and in 1965 it was altered so that quotas would be in proportion to the number of applications received from high school graduates and from young workers. Moreover, new entrance examination requirements will make more difficult the admission of young people from industry who are not properly prepared for advanced studies.

Another aspect of the Khrushchev School Reform are the so-called boarding schools, which were described, at the time of their introduction in 1956, as "the basic form of common secondary and technical education for the rising generation." In 1959, they were referred to as the type of school which "creates the most favorable conditions for the education and Communist upbringing" of the new generation, mainly perhaps because they will in large measure isolate students from parents. These model schools may be set up with a curriculum of either 8 or 11 years. By 1965, according to Soviet estimates, these schools were to have 2.5 million students, compared to 180,000 in 1958. Available evidence suggests, however, that progress has been much slower than anticipated by Khrushchev, and with his fall from power their future may be in question.

ATTACK ON COMPETING INFLUENCES

In seeking to create the new "socialist man," the Communist party found it necessary to combat those influences which ran counter to its ideological position. As noted earlier in this chapter, foreign influences were in large measure excluded by policies which came to be referred to collectively as the Iron Curtain. Domestically, at the time when the Communists seized power, the family and the church were the most powerful influences in shaping new generations. Consequently, Soviet leaders lost no time in devising ways of eliminating or minimizing this influence.

THE ATTACK ON RELIGION

Marxian theory had explained society and the nature of its development in a "scientific" way and without the need of a deity. Previous political systems, according to Marx, had made use of religion to enslave the people more effectively. Religion was an opiate which served to divert the worker from his earthly woes. It was, in essence, one tool in the hands of the *bourgeoisie* for keeping the proletariat in its place. In view of the close association of the then-prevailing faith (the Russian Orthodox Church) with tsarist autocracy, this analysis must have seemed plausible to many Russians. In the new society, said Marx and his followers, religion will be relegated to the museum.

Soviet leaders were unwilling, however, to wait for the day when the people would discard religion as no longer useful. Consequently, they embarked upon the task of destroying churches. Countless thousands of them were physically demolished, although a few of the more impressive ones were left standing. Most of the churches were stripped of their religious appurtenances, including gold-covered Bibles, silver and gold crosses, the more impressive icons, robes, and other things of value. Many of these were placed in museums. In most instances, regime partisans prevented the use for religious purposes of the churches which were left standing. These gradually deteriorated over the years, although some have been refurbished since World War II. In most instances, however, they are not used for religious purposes, but are labeled as "architectural monuments." Their preservation at state expense is justified on the ground that they are examples of architecture of a certain period and therefore historically important to the nation. Some of the churches which were left standing were converted into atheistic museums.

The physical destruction of churches was accompanied by a corresponding attack upon the clergy. The more important ones were quickly liquidated, unless they succeeded in escaping. Others were imprisoned or herded into labor camps. Those who were neither liquidated nor imprisoned were mocked and persecuted. All sorts of indignities were heaped upon them. Moreover, they were left without any means of support, for they were forbidden to plead for any type of aid for themselves or their churches. They were forced to rely on voluntary and usually surreptitious gifts.

By 1935, Stalin seemed so firmly in power that the new Soviet constitution could proclaim freedom of religious worship, but the right to propagandize about religion was limited to those who were against it. Moreover, within a brief period of time new church leaders were permitted to evolve, but these swore allegiance to the new regime. During World War II, Russian church leaders prayed for Stalin and for the victory of the Red Army. Since that time, the Russian Orthodox Church, as well as a few Protestant churches, has been able to function in a limited way. In many areas there are no churches or clergymen, and even in cities like Moscow and Leningrad, they are few and far between. A few synagogues have also been permitted, although during the latter years of Stalin's reign a calculated antisemitic policy—never identified as such—was in effect. By 1965, there were only four seminaries for the training of Orthodox clergymen, and the number of new students who may enter each year is severely limited.

Religion is not regarded as a private affair in the Soviet Union. For members of the party and the *Komsomol* it cannot be, for both are dedicated to oppose actively all non-Communist ideological influences, especially on the young. Numerous visits to Russian churches by American tourists in recent years revealed an almost total absence of representatives of what we would call the high school and college generation. Woman and older people tend to stand out in any church congregation, although there is a fair sprinkling of persons in their 30s and 40s, with some in their late 20s.

In the case of the youth, the party and *Komsomol* organizations have an active campaign of providing them with other things to do on Sundays and other religious holidays. There are special parades and manifestations, youth work projects, visits to libraries, museums, and historical places, as well as circuses and carnivals. Religious instruction for the young is not permitted, while youth publications attack religion in all of its manifestations. In brief, the party will endeavor to make sure that the church cannot compete successfully for the allegiance of the young. As a totalitarian and materialistic philosophy, Communism cannot tolerate effective competition for men's minds by a spiritual force.

Moreover, by the time most youngsters reach adulthood they are made all too clearly aware that advancement in their society depends upon the party. The most desirable jobs, as well as promotions, are controlled by the party. A young person soon learns that his attitude toward the party and its policies can be decisive. Consequently, he is not likely to jeopardize his future knowingly. And he knows that if he goes to church or if he becomes known as a religious person, these matters will be noted in his *dossier*, or personal file. In such circumstances, some jobs will certainly be closed to him and his promotion in others impeded. Consequently, these are compelling reasons for avoiding even the appearance of being religious.

Finally, the party keeps a close watch on whatever religious activities are permitted. Official governmental councils for church affairs have been established to regulate the spiritual safety valve. There is something cruelly ironical in an avowed Communist being the supervisor of the Orthodox hierarchy. Like other organizations in the Soviet system, churches are expected to serve Communist propaganda purposes and to endorse the party's political decisions. From the regime's point of view, the basic battle has been won; only mopping-up operations remain, and the remaining vestigial remnants of worship will eventually dwindle to nothing.

On the other hand, regime actions in recent years suggest a growing concern about religion. During the Khrushchev era, for example, anti-religious activities were stepped up considerably. Additional churches, monasteries, and seminaries were closed or turned into museums. Many clergymen were arrested under pretexts of fraudu-

lent manipulations, insanity, or the exploitation of believers. A retroactive income tax was imposed on all priests. Anti-religious publications, anti-religious lectures, and other anti-religious activities were
markedly multiplied. A special institute of atheism was established
and a course in atheism was introduced in the schools. Prizes were
announced for literary and artistic works that most effectively conveyed anti-religious messages. It is perhaps significant that while the
struggle against religion in the early decades of the regime was
carried on by semiliterate party agitators, in the Khrushchev years it
was performed by scholars, scientists, writers, and poets who were
mobilized in the anti-religious crusade.

In spite of this systematic attack, there are indications of rumblings
beneath the surface. While it is not possible to speak of a religious
revival, there is some evidence of hostility toward a system that does
not regard religious attitudes as matters of personal and private
concern.

THE ATTACK ON THE HOME

In the early years of the new regime, youngsters were encouraged to
inform on their parents as a means of discovering anti-Communist
sentiment. Many parents stood in fear of their children, and many
went to prison because of them. As the years wore on, and particularly
as young citizens came to realize the hollowness of the regime's claims
and promises, and as they began to experience the same material fate,
informing by children dropped off sharply. But by that time the
regime had consolidated its position, won many new recruits, and
refined its techniques for controlling the masses.

At the same time, however, the number of the disaffected grew.
Young fathers and mothers came to realize that a great deal of the
"old-fashioned nonsense" which they had learned from their parents
now seemed to make sense. Consequently, parental disillusionment
with the regime has continued to be of constant concern to the Soviet
leaders. Inevitably, children are hearing things in the family during
their formative years which, in the opinion of the leaders, must be
unlearned.

It is in the light of this situation that one must look at the party's
intensive campaign among the young, in and out of school. It is in this
light that one must, at least partially, view the new boarding schools.
Aside from all the other things discussed in this chapter, as ways of
influencing and controlling the people's minds, there are two primary
means of countering family influence. One is to get hold of the child as

early as possible in his life, and the other is to monopolize his waking hours or, negatively, to leave as few days and waking hours as possible in which children can be with their parents.

* * * * *

In contemplating the future, it should be noted that in recent years naked force and violence have been less in evidence than in the past. Some observers feel that former inmates of Soviet prisons, many of whom now occupy important governmental posts, give the society an inner toughness and constitute a substantial barrier against the rise of a new police terror system. Some even suggest that the day of the informer may be past, and that Soviet society is no longer controlled by fear. This does not mean, however, that the Soviet leaders have rejected force and violence as instruments of political control or that they will not resort to them if less violent means fail to keep the people in line and thereby threaten the security of the regime and its leaders.

BIBLIOGRAPHICAL NOTE

An understanding of the extent to which force and fear are utilized under the Soviet system may be gained from F. Beck and W. Godin, *Russian Purge and the Extraction of Confession* (New York: Viking Press, 1951) ; Zbigniew Brzezinski, *The Permanent Purge, Politics in Soviet Totalitarianism* (Cambridge, Mass.: Harvard University Press, 1956) ; *Genocide in the U.S.S.R., Studies in Group Destruction,* done under the auspices of the Institute for the Study of the U.S.S.R., (New York: Scarecrow Press, 1958) ; Otto Heilbrunn, *The Soviet Secret Service* (New York: Praeger, 1956) ; Arthur Koestler, *Darkness at Noon* (New York: Macmillan, 1941) ; Nathan Leites and Elsa Bernaut, *Ritual of Liquidation, The Case of the Moscow Trials* (Glencoe, Ill.: Free Press, 1954) ; Vladimir and Evdokia Petrov, *Empire of Fear* (New York: Praeger, 1956) ; and Simon Wolin and Robert M. Slusser (eds.), *The Soviet Secret Police* (New York: Praeger, 1957).

Alex Inkeles, *Public Opinion in Soviet Russia: A Study in Mass Persuasion* (Cambridge, Mass.: Harvard University Press, 1950) is a pioneering study of the Russian use of the mass media and of their role in public opinion formation. Studies of the impact of the Soviet system upon education, literature, and the arts and sciences include those of Anthony Adamovich, *Opposition to Sovietization in Belorussian Literature* (New York: Scarecrow Press, 1958) ; Alexander G. Korol, *Soviet Education for Science and Technology* (New York: John Wiley & Sons, 1957) ; Walter Z. Laqueur and George Lichtheim, *The Soviet Cultural Scene, 1956–1957* (New York: Praeger, 1958) ; and Alexander Vucinich, *The Soviet Academy of Sciences* (Stanford, Cal.: Stanford University Press, 1956). Insight into *Komsomol* activities may be gained from Ralph Talcott Fisher, Jr., *Pattern for Soviet Youth: A Study of the Congresses of the Komsomol, 1918–1954* (New York: Columbia University Press, 1959).

CHAPTER **29**

PUBLIC
ADMINISTRATION

THE SOVIET state, more than any other political system known to man, is an administrative state. Soviet society is bureaucratized to the highest degree. Even the lives and daily decisions of individual Russians are guided by the decisions of the Communist party, as expressed in the all-embracing administrative system. A detailed treatment of this system is beyond the scope of this book. But it is important that its main features be examined, its formal organization depicted, and some of its major problems set forth.

NATURE OF SOVIET ADMINISTRATION

Prior to their seizure of power, the Bolsheviks—and especially Lenin—envisioned a new type of society, without bureaucracy, police, or army. Anyone knowing the four rules of arithmetic, in Lenin's view, possessed the qualifications of an administrator. After the initial establishment of the new society, administration would need to be only a part-time affair. It was not long, however, before the Bolshevik leaders learned how indispensable was a highly organized bureaucracy to the orderly functioning of a modern state, especially a state which was bent on speeding industrialization and embarking upon large-scale social engineering. This became particularly evident when they started the USSR down the path of successive five-year plans.

Vast Scope of Administration

The scope and extent of public administration in the Soviet Union would be sizable under any political system. There is a huge territory to oversee, with varied climates, peoples, and problems to cope with. An authoritarian system, of whatever type, would need an extensive bureaucracy to make sure that its edicts were obeyed and the empire held together. This is all the more true of a dictatorship which sets out to remake society and does not hesitate to run roughshod over everyone who might stand in the way.

Moreover, one can appreciate the size and scope of the Soviet bureaucracy if he keeps in mind the fact that virtually nothing in the USSR occurs as a result of private enterprise. The government runs or controls every form of economic activity—stores, factories, mines, farms, trains, ships, and all of the other things that we normally associate with private endeavor. In a broad sense, everyone works for the government.

The size and scope of the administrative machine becomes even more meaningful if one remembers that it is not merely a matter of a bureaucracy running the machinery of government which it has inherited. Under its control, nothing is supposed to happen by accident. Everything is planned and controlled. The bureaucracy not only runs things, but in addition, it plans them and runs them according to the plans. Under such a system and in such a large country, the size and scope of the administrative apparatus must be large indeed.

ADMINISTRATION AS INSTRUMENT OF ONE-PARTY STATE

In the Soviet Union, therefore, the administration works within the framework of the policy guidance which the party establishes. From the beginning it was the party which had to determine what the factories should produce, how raw materials, manpower and machinery were to be combined so as to realize the planned output, and how that output was to be distributed. As an arm of the party dictatorship, the Soviet bureaucracy has the task of building a Communist society, in accordance with the party blueprint. As such, the Soviet bureaucracy cannot be viewed as a nonpolitical and detached civil service. It is clearly partisan.

But the party does more than merely furnish policy guidance. It is constantly engaged in checking on the execution of its policies. The top political leaders must keep an eye on the bureaucrats, who have not been above falsifying records and engaging in a whole host of other "unsocialist" acts in order to receive material or political rewards from their superiors. The administrators all along the line have learned to expect the party's watchful eye, and to fear the attribution of political motives to some of their acts, with possible dire consequences, even when such motives may never have existed.

Simultaneously with checking on the fulfillment of its policies, the party is engaged in mobilizing popular support behind planned targets. This may range all the way from exhorting the workers to surpass planned output to urging a mass movement of people to an area where there is a manpower shortage; such exhortations very often are made without taking other circumstances into account, which may result in making matters worse. In short, the bureaucracy can expect to hear the party's voice at all stages of its operation.

CENTRALIZED CONTROL AND DIRECTION

As the above suggests, public administration in the Soviet Union is highly centralized, with control and direction from the center. The most important control agency is the party, which decides on the nature of all other controls. The latter have been altered so often that any description of them would soon be out of date. For example, the Ministry of State Control gave way in 1957 to the Commission of Soviet Control, which in turn gave way to the State Control Commission in 1961. In 1962, Khrushchev reorganized the party into two hierarchies, one to check performance in agriculture and the other in industry. As a part of this reorganization, the State Control Commission was replaced by the Committee for Party and State Control. Now that Khrushchev's successors have indicated that the dual hierarchy arrangement was a failure, further changes in the control apparatus can be expected.

Other controls are exercised by the office of the state prosecutor and by the secret police. In addition, various ministries, the Supreme National Economic Council, and the State Planning Commission perform control functions. Moreover, the Committee for Party and State Control was to be aided by advisory workers' committees and by a corps of volunteer inspectors.

This multiplicity of controls must be viewed against the party's shifting standard of what meets or does not meet the requirements of theoretical dogma. What is perfectly acceptable today may turn out to be un-Marxian tomorrow. What supports the strategy of party leaders becomes an impediment when that strategy changes, and it has changed often during the life of the Soviet regime. When something does not produce the desired result, there are changes which are often based on little more than the principle of trial and error, although the party leaders never admit this. In their words, each change is but another step toward the desired goal, a step which more appropriately corresponds to "the present stage of socialist development."

In their search for workable administrative arrangements, the party leaders have emphasized the desired objectives, usually to the exclusion of other considerations. To them, loyalty and adherence to party directives have been of the utmost importance. Efficiency is important, but secondary. The rights of individuals, on the other hand, are given little weight. The administrative machine, understandably, operates to achieve state-determined objectives and not to preserve abstract personal rights.

FORMAL ADMINISTRATIVE ORGANIZATION

Superficially, at least, the Soviet administrative organization bears a certain resemblance to that found in most other countries. There are ministries—until 1946 the Soviet leaders avoided this bourgeois term—and bureaus, offices, missions, etc. There is a civil service to staff these various offices. Moreover, from time to time there have been changes and reorganizations in the administrative structure. In other ways, however, the Soviet administrative organization is unique, which will become evident from what follows.

TYPES OF MINISTRIES

As noted in an earlier chapter, there are three types of ministries in the Soviet Union, all-union ministries, union-republic ministries, and republic ministries. All-union ministries are national ministries which operate from Moscow through their own employees down to the local level. The line of responsibility is vertical. Union-republic ministries are those ministries which exist on the national level and on the republic level. In other words, the ministries in Moscow which operate through corresponding ministries in each of the republics are known as union-republic ministries. The line of responsibility, therefore, is both vertical and horizontal, although the former is more important. In both all-union and union-republic ministries the final control rests in Moscow. Republic ministries, on the other hand, are ministries which exist on the republic level, with no corresponding ministries at the national level. These are responsible to their respective republics, although they may be engaged in carrying out programs which are determined in Moscow.

The number of ministries in the various categories has changed a number of times. The number of all-union ministries was increased and decreased several times. At the time of Stalin's death, for example, there were 60, but two days later these were reduced to 25. Within a year the number had increased to 46, and by 1956, it was up to 52. This number dropped sharply following the 1957 reorganization, discussed below, but by 1965 the number of ministers at the national level increased to about 70, although the majority of them were designated as chairmen of committees rather than heads of ministries, but they hold the rank of minister nonetheless. The other types of ministries have also experienced changes, as the Bolshevik leaders sought to square Marxist-Leninist theory with the political and economic facts of life.

THE 1957 REORGANIZATION

In 1957, the Soviet Union underwent a sweeping reorganization of its industrial-administrative structure. Most of the all-union ministries in the economic sphere, as well as many union-republic industrial ministries, were abolished. In their place, more than 100 regional economic councils were set up, corresponding to the number of economic regions into which the Soviet Union was divided. In most instances, these regions coincided with the existing administrative and territorial divisions of the USSR. The regional councils, which were given authority to run the vast industrial empire, were, in theory, to be chosen by the governments of the respective republics, but Moscow retained a veto power over members of the councils as well as over council decisions.

In some circles this reorganization was referred to as a decentralization of the Soviet economy. Soviet leaders, notably Khrushchev, insisted that it was, in effect, a more effective centralization. It was only the operative control which was being decentralized. Decisions concerning basic policy as well as planned targets were still to be made in Moscow. The regional councils and local authorities were merely to have more discretion in finding ways and means of carrying out basic economic directives. This meant that power once exercised by a departmental bureaucracy in Moscow had been transferred to the bureaucracy which was actually at the center of production. In addition, some of the powers previously exercised by ministries in Moscow had been transferred to local ministries and local party committees.

To insure basic control from the center, the functions (and to some degree the administrative apparatus) of the all-union ministries that were abolished were transferred to the reorganized State Planning Committee and to a whole host of other committees which in a way resembled skeletal ministries. Most of the heads of the abolished ministries were made chairmen or deputy chairmen of these new committees, with the rank of minister of the USSR.

Within less than a year after the 1957 reorganization went into effect, evidence began accumulating that all was not running smoothly. Complaints began appearing in the Soviet press that certain regional councils were putting local interests ahead of the national interest. After seeking to remedy the situation by providing bonuses for deliveries of goods to outside economic areas, the Soviet leaders found it necessary to resort to sterner measures. A decree was promulgated which made it a criminal offense to fail to deliver goods to other areas or to the government, a method of control that had been used in the past. Unless there was a valid excuse, the guilty would be subject to strict disciplinary measures or fines of up to three months of salary. Second offenders would be treated more harshly.

Further difficulties were evidenced by the fact that in 1960 a new agency, called the Russian Council for the National Economy, was established. It was charged with coordinating the work of the 70 regional economic councils in the Russian republic (RSFSR). In 1962, a new reorganization divided the country into 17 major economic regions, each with a council to be concerned with the development of resources and with the coordination of planning and production among the management bodies under its jurisdiction. In 1963, the Supreme National Economic Council was established to coordinate the planning and management of industry on a nationwide basis. The authority of the regional councils was further reduced when in 1965 several state committees, notably in the defense field, were converted into full-fledged ministries and thus removed from the jurisdiction of the councils. By late 1965, the Soviet leaders had abolished the regional councils altogether, thus continuing the search for more efficient ways of organizing and operating a vast planned economy.

COUNCIL OF MINISTERS AS DIRECTING AGENCY

At the top of the formal administrative structure is the Council of Ministers of the USSR. During most of Stalin's reign this was a large and unwieldy body, which really never decided anything important as a body. Really effective power was exercised by a small group, sometimes referred to as the Presidium of the Council, consisting of the chairman and the deputy chairmen of the Council. With the abolition of many national ministries, the Council initially decreased in size, but in more recent years the number of national ministries has again risen appreciably.

The Council of Ministers is the directing agency of the administrative machine. It is supposed to have the main responsibility in supervising the carrying out of the industrial plans. As such, it can overrule the councils of ministers of individual republics. It exercises wide decree powers in finance, taxation, pricing, and foreign trade. It is also empowered to issue decrees in the realm of military affairs, and it can promulgate measures to protect socialist property. Important decrees are often issued jointly with the Central Committee of the party. Sometimes there is a joint promulgation of decrees by the Council of Ministers and by the All-Union Council of Trade Unions. The latter has been empowered to issue binding decrees, especially in the labor legislation field, subject to approval by the Council of Ministers.

THE STATE PLANNING COMMITTEE

Centralized economic planning became an essential feature of the Soviet economy by 1921, although it is usually associated with the beginning of the era of the five-year plans. Established in 1921, *Gosplan* (State Planning Committee) did not come into prominence until the launching of the first five-year plan in 1929. That year also marked the consolidation of the Stalin dictatorship and the final abolition of private economic enterprise.

The principal aims of the five-year plans during Stalin's reign centered on the building of a heavy industry and the collectivization of agriculture. The former involved a series of successive drives to build new capital goods factories and plants at an ambitious rate. The latter was ostensibly aimed at increasing agricultural production by seeking to convert small and often scattered peasant holdings into large-scale mechanized units. These were monumental tasks, and in the case of the industrialized sector, there were some substantial gains, but the human and material costs in both were huge.

Centralized planning and direction are still the responsibility of *Gosplan*, although since the 1957 reorganization it is not supposed to interfere in the administrative management of the economic regions. How it will avoid this is a bit difficult to perceive, since it is not only to determine the direction and rate of economic development, but also to be concerned with long-range plans. It will no doubt coordinate its efforts with those of the planning committees in the respective republics, as well as with those of the economic ministries and the Supreme National Economic Council.

The planning operation is an involved and complicated affair. It begins with the aims and goals of the party, transmitted via party and governmental channels from top to bottom. Gosplan and the subsidiary planning bodies at the republic, regional, and local levels must work out the detailed plans, in collaboration with other governmental authorities as well as with economic ministries, regional officials, and individual enterprises. These plans involve not only planning for a set number of years, but in addition, planning for each year and each quarter of a year. The more detailed planning involves targets and timetables for each month.

THE CIVIL SERVICE

The precise number of people in the Soviet bureaucracy is difficult to determine, mainly because there is some question as to who should be included. Should one include, for example, the people who work full time in the trade unions, the party apparatus, the youth organizations, etc.? Depending upon how one conceives the bureaucracy, its estimated size runs from 10 to 15 million.

This vast army of civil servants is recruited under the watchful eye of the Communist party, which is the final judge in all personnel matters. The party's concern with personnel is understandable, for the highest duty of the bureaucracy is to carry out party policies. For years, the party's concern with personnel was exercised through the Cadres Administration of its Central Committee and through similar party organizations at all levels of government. Now, however, individual ministries recruit people at the lower levels, usually from the universities, where they can prescribe certain courses, or from schools that are attached to certain ministries. But as one moves up the bureaucratic ladder, the transfer and movement of personnel is subject to increasing party control.

The government (party) can shift personnel at will. Although the 1940 decree on the compulsory transfer of personnel was repealed in 1956, the government can employ other coercive means to achieve the same end. For example, it can appeal to the trade unions, the party, or the youth organization to *send* its members to new industrial sites, the virgin lands, or elsewhere. Uncooperative persons can be expelled from these organizations, a circumstance fraught with serious practical consequences for the persons concerned, such as the loss of job, position of responsibility, or privileges attendant to membership. Moreover, the government can, and does, promulgate new decrees at will. And it can, and often does, act without the benefit of any legal sanction.

As the above paragraphs suggest, the bureaucracy is first of all responsible to the party. In actual practice the control of the bureaucracy is complicated. The Committee for party and State Control has vast powers to investigate and to institute measures of correction, to reprimand, and to dismiss. The Council of Ministers exercises powers in the same realm. The Presidium of the Supreme Soviet can modify and interpret decrees and decisions of administrative bodies. The police, the courts, and the prosecutor's office, to say nothing of the "volunteer" inspectors (who are publicly encouraged), exercise a type of cross control. Finally, there is the criticism and self-criticism which is voiced through the press, in editorials, or letters to the editor. Despite the fact that the party ostensibly provides the necessary guidance, the nature of the control apparatus lends itself to confusion and abuse. And the Soviet press continues to assert that the work of the control organs is far from what it should be!

SETTLEMENT OF ADMINISTRATIVE DISPUTES

So as to deal more effectively with the large number of lawsuits between state economic enterprises, the Soviet leaders have established a system of so-called state arbitration tribunals. They have the power to summon witnesses, to request the submission of documents, to appoint expert examiners, and to issue decrees which must be obeyed. They are appointed by, are subordinate to, and their decisions may be reversed or altered by the supreme executive bodies of the areas in which they function. The chief arbitrator is attached to the Council of Ministers of the USSR. He supervises the arbitration work of state arbitrators at all levels, and issues general instructions to them. He is also empowered to review their decisions.

In the settlement of disputes, the state arbitration tribunals are supposed to protect the "property rights and lawful interests of enterprises." At the same time, they are to protect the basic concerns of the state, by declaring invalid all contracts between enterprises which do not conform to Soviet law or which run counter to the plans of the State Planning Committee. Most of the disputes between economic enterprises concern alleged breaches of contract, which may involve late or non-delivery of goods, poor quality of goods, or their delivery in poor or damaged condition. Some disputes concern prices and terms of payment. Other disputes involve damage claims resulting from the delivery of allegedly defective materials or machines. Arbitration tribunals are also called upon to resolve pre-contract disputes, where enterprises are legally required to enter into contracts and yet cannot agree on the terms.

MANAGEMENT OF GOVERNMENT ENTERPRISES

Lenin believed that capitalism had simplified and routinized industrial methods to such an extent that socialized industry could be operated by anyone who could read and write. "The ability to observe and record and to make out receipts—this, with knowledge of the four rules of arithmetic, is all that is required." Soviet leaders were to learn the hard way, however, that the role of management was much more important than that.

EVOLUTION OF MANAGERIAL CONCEPT

For years, the great problem in Soviet management was the lack of freedom to manage. The first phase in Soviet industrial management was characterized by the power of factory committees and the trade unions. They had to be consulted on virtually everything. But neither the factory committees nor the trade unions were trained to deal with problems of supply, manufacturing, and distribution. Consequently, Soviet industrial production dropped sharply. For a time, in the era of the New Economic Policy, many of the capitalist managers were called back. By the time the Soviet leaders were ready to launch the five-year plans (1928), they were convinced that the managerial concept must be accepted.

The philosophy behind the five-year plans was production at any cost. In order that nothing should interfere with the pursuit of the announced goals, the factory committees had to go. The five-day week and other labor gains also had to go, while the trade unions were made a part of the governmental machinery, with assigned roles to play. Their chief task now was to ride herd on their members in order that management might reach its assigned production quotas. To achieve the goals of the five-year plans, the managers needed to have the power to manage, and with minimum interference even from party organizations.

The purges of the 1930s, however, dealt the managerial concept a hard blow. Many old Bolsheviks who held high administrative or party posts were liquidated or displaced. Managers of various ranks were removed by the thousands, with many of them being shot or sent to slave labor camps. The net result was a widespread fear of making decisions. The safe way was to refer everything, even ridiculously minor matters, to Moscow. Soviet management was to suffer from this malady as long as Stalin lived. Since his passing, however, there have been indications that the new Soviet leaders have been engaged in restoring the power of management to the managers.

DRIFT TOWARD CAPITALIST PATTERN OF REWARD

The acceptance of the importance of the managerial role was accompanied by a trend toward capitalist type incentives. In the early years of the regime, when the trade unions sought to protect the workers, the five-day week was the rule, and there was a trend toward equality of wages. With the launching of the five-year plans, however, the previous trade union attitude was viewed as defensive and negative. Increasingly, the practice of rewarding people in proportion to their output became the rule of the Soviet society, receiving constitutional recognition in the fundamental law of 1936.

To the end that people would be rewarded "according to their work," the salaries of managers jumped phenomenally, for their work was regarded as much more important than that of the ordinary workers. In addition, managers were given bonuses for overfulfillment of planned goals, as well as compensation in kind, such as good apartments, special food, a radio, and even a private automobile. The work of engineers, technicians, and skilled laborers received similar recognition, with corresponding gradations in salary and rank.

Differentiation was also made even among the unskilled workers. Piece rates and production quotas were established for them, with increasing rewards for those who surpassed the so-called "norm" of production, which was raised steadily as more and more workers surpassed it. Those who consistently produced above the norm were designated as *stakhanovites* (shock workers), after a coal miner named Stakhanov whose work output was allegedly phenomenal. In setting wage scales in the Soviet Union, familiar capitalist principles, such as education, experience, and the arduousness, complexity, and exactness of work, are given weight. The net result is wider differentials and inequalities of reward than in the United States, where legal enactments and union activity have served to narrow the gap.

Those workers who are judged to be particularly deserving are awarded medals, trips to Moscow, special vacations and other honors. Negatively, the capitalist type of reward was accompanied by rigid controls, applicable particularly in the case of the less cooperative worker. Movement from job to job became almost impossible. Absenteeism without an acceptable excuse was punished progressively, in wages, ration coupons (during rationing), and, ultimately, in the loss of job and dwelling quarters. Drunkenness was also punishable.

Cautious Approach to Market Mechanisms

The drift toward capitalist patterns of reward was not, however, accompanied by any visible trend toward a free market as a regulator of the economy. Production and distribution were determined by the plans, as were the costs and profits. The plans were enforced, for the most part, by changing the rate of the turnover tax, a type of sales tax, which is also the principal source of government revenue. By increasing or decreasing the rate, the government can effectively encourage or discourage certain types of economic activity. It could, for example make shoes expensive and television sets inexpensive. In brief, this is the way in which the party's arbitrary decisions concerning the allocation of resources were carried out.

Under this system the preferences of the consumer were ignored. Moreover, the producing enterprise had no particular incentive to turn out quality goods. The result, all too often, was an accumulation of poor quality goods that went unsold. In order to remedy this situation, the government has made some cautious approaches to the use of certain market mechanisms, such as interest charges, profits, and consumer demands. The central planners will continue to set the basic targets, but many factories are now given greater authority in carrying out the plans. By requiring enterprises to pay interest on the money that they borrow and by permitting them to share in the profits, the government will in effect be rewarding those enterprises that make desirable goods at a reasonable price and punishing those that turn out goods that no one wants. In this way, enterprises are encouraged to make an effort to discover what the consumer likes and desires. Similarly, they are encouraged to improve the efficiency of their operations. As of this writing (1965), the results of the effort to employ certain market mechanisms in a planned economy are far from clear.

EVOLUTION OF TECHNICAL-ADMINISTRATIVE CLASS

As the Soviet industrial empire grew, the importance of the technical-administrative intelligentsia became more and more evident to the Soviet leaders. Increasingly, members of this group rose to higher and higher posts in the administrative hierarchy. During Stalin's dictatorship, however, they were sufficiently terrorized that they could not openly challenge party dictates, even when these were obviously faulty. By 1957, on the other hand, a number of them felt sufficiently secure to argue publicly against some of the theses put forward by party leaders. This became particularly evident in the discussion of Khrushchev's theses concerning industrial reorganization. Atomic energy specialist Kapitsa, metallurgist I. P. Bardin, and others pointed out that in the case of their particular specialties, the Khrushchev proposals would not work or needed modification.

It is, of course, impossible to tell if the discussion of Khrushchev's reorganization scheme by technical specialists is to be repeated in other contexts. A number of observers have for several years been noting the growing importance of the technical-administrative intelligentsia in the party membership itself. Most indications point to the growing importance of this group in Soviet society, although some observers have asserted that one of the aims of Khrushchev's economic reorganization plan was to reduce the power of the technical-administrative-intelligentsia and to increase the party's control over the economic apparatus.

MANAGEMENT IN AGRICULTURE

Despite the revolutionary cry of "all land to the peasants," the Bolshevik leaders did not intend to promote private ownership of land. In the early years they attempted, in effect, to confiscate agricultural produce through compulsory deliveries, a practice highly resented by the peasants. During the NEP period, however, the peasants were free to produce and to sell. The more enterprising ones leased land and even hired labor, leading to the growth of a moderately well-to-do group of peasants, subsequently called kulaks. In 1929, the party leaders called a halt, and embarked on a program to collectivize agriculture. Through heavy taxation, refusal of credit, making it illegal to own or lease farm machinery and, in the final analysis, through physical liquidation of the recalcitrants, the regime conducted its farm revolution, which was virtually complete by 1932. The original plans had called for the collectivization of 15 to 20 per cent of the land during the first five-year plan. At least in part because of peasant opposition, this figure was boosted to 75 and subsequently to 90 per cent.

Some form of collective ownership and operation of agriculture was required by the Marxian doctrine, although the details were far from clear. Seemingly of more importance to the Soviet leaders was the promotion of greatly increased agricultural production, which was necessary to feed the growing industrial-urban population. This could be achieved by mechanization, but there was some question of how effectively machinery could be used on the small and often scattered pieces of land. Hence the conclusion that mechanization would only be effective on large-scale agricultural units. Parenthetically, however, it might be noted that during the entire period of Stalin's dictatorship, productivity per acre was not raised. Increased yields were only achieved by adding acreage.

NATURE OF COLLECTIVE FARMS

Most of the land in the Soviet Union is in the form of collective farms (kolkhoz), although a small percentage of the agricultural acreage is in the form of state farms (sovkhoz). The latter are government owned and operated, the workers on them being ordinary wage earners. The former are also really government owned, but they resulted, in the main, from the merging of neighboring farms, under rules set forth by the government. Hence, the people who live on them have a right, at least in theory, to their exclusive use. Under rules handed down by the government, the members of the kolkhoz divide the profits of their labor. Moreover, in most instances, the individual family dwelling was retained by the family, together with an adjoining household or garden plot of from one half to three acres. The latter, theoretically, could be used as the family saw fit, but in practice the government could and does change the rules.

Over the years, it became increasingly evident to the Soviet leaders that these private plots were occupying a large part of the time of the collective farm members. Instead of planting a few vegetables and berries for the family table, the peasants were using these plots to grow major produce, as well as to support the maximum livestock permitted (a cow and two calves, a pig, a few goats or sheep and an unlimited number of poultry). Prior to World War II, the average member of a kolkhoz was earning approximately one half of his total income from these plots, a fairly good indication that "collective" farmers were not giving the collective effort a very high priority.

Soon after legalizing the private plot, the government began to hedge it in with restrictions, designed to make it so costly that the peasant would ultimately abandon it. High taxes were imposed on produce from these plots. After World War II, the government inaugurated compulsory deliveries on a portion of the produce, even requiring the delivery of milk, eggs, wool, etc., whether the farmer owned the livestock or not. Moreover, there was an attempt to reduce the size of the plots in 1950, during an amalgamation of small collective farms into larger ones. After a temporary relaxation in 1953–54, the regime returned to the attack. In 1956, it inaugurated a program designed to eliminate the private plots. In 1961 decrees urged consumer cooperatives to step up the purchase of surplus produce from the farmer, pointing to the elimination of the last remnants of a free market. By 1965, however, shortages in agricultural produce forced the government to encourage peasants to grow food on the private plots, and to sell the surplus at local markets, where supply and demand determine the price.

In the 1950s there were several developments indicating that the collective farm itself may be on the way out. A number of the smaller collective farms were amalgamated, with the result that the total number was reduced by more than one-half. Almost simultaneously there was a move to promote the construction of *agrogorods* (agricultural cities), where the collective farmers would live, commuting to work. While this idea fell by the wayside after Khrushchev's rise to power, he nevertheless promoted the further merger of collectives as well as the creation of additional state farms at the expense of the collective farm idea. The 6 million acres of virgin land which were opened up in 1955, for example, were all organized on the state farm principle.

In 1965, Khrushchev's successors declared that the farm-merger policy had resulted in agricultural units of unmanageable size. At the same time, they criticized the policy of encouraging the conversion of collectives into state farms. They indicated that the two systems would be continued in the future.

More important than these declarations, however, was their decision to provide greater investments in agriculture. These are to be accompanied by policies which would bring higher prices for farm produce, lower rural taxes, and lower prices for consumer goods that the farmer needs. The general aim is to raise the peasants' purchasing power, and hence to reduce the differences in living standards between urban and rural areas.

MANAGEMENT OF COLLECTIVE FARMS

Ostensibly, the members of each collective farm meet in an annual assembly and elect a management committee to run the affairs of the farm for the year. In actual practice, the Communist party, by and large, controls all such elections. In any case, the management committee must operate under the general laws dealing with collective farms and it must fit its operations into the over-all agricultural plan.

In accordance with the general rules, applicable to all collective farms, the land, farm buildings, draft animals, and major tools are owned in common. Each able-bodied adult is required to put in a minimum number of labor days in the collective effort, which means about one half of his annual work time. But in view of the fact that a large part of agricultural work is seasonal, this normally means much more than half time. A labor day is supposed to represent the average daily output of an average worker. If, for example, the average worker will hoe 10 rows of corn in a day, that becomes the norm, and a worker who hoes 20 rows in one day has two labor days to his credit. This is the agricultural counterpart of piece rates in industry, and it is on this basis that the profits from the collective enterprise are distributed. Credit and other things furnished by the government must, of course, be paid for by the collective.

Prior to 1958, the collective farms were not allowed to own the major agricultural machines. These were leased by the government through the Machine Tractor Stations (MTS), which were important instruments of political control. They also acted as effective collecting centers of agricultural produce, for each collective was obliged to sell a certain proportion of its produce at a low government-established price. In 1958, however, all of this was changed. Collective farms now own their own machinery. In place of the MTS there is now the Farm Machinery Association, whose job it is to sell and repair machines, and to sell fertilizer and other farm needs. The practice of obligatory deliveries of farm produce at low prices has given way to a more realistic price system.

The day-to-day operation of a collective farm is under the direction of the manager or farm chairman. Assisting him is an administrative staff—bookkeepers, brigade leaders, watchmen, storekeepers, day and night guards, an agronomist, and the manager of the livestock unit. Obviously, by American standards, Soviet collective farms are top-heavy with administrative personnel.

PROBLEMS OF AGRICULTURAL MANAGEMENT

The two outstanding facts about Soviet agriculture are: (1) the goals have not been met, and (2) the party insists on attempting to meet those goals within the confines of collectivized agriculture (state and collective farms). Consequently, there has been a great deal of experimentation, which has involved the power and roles played by the ministry of agriculture, local soviets, local party organizations, regional economic councils, farm procurement agencies, and the collective and state farm managers.

In the early 1960s the powers of the ministry of agriculture were drastically reduced, being limited largely to scientific research and the training of personnel. The overall responsibility of coordinating agricultural production and checking on the fulfillment of quotas was vested in the All-Union Committee on Agriculture. Similar committees were created to function at the republic level. Regional producing and marketing associations were established. At the time of his overthrow in 1964, Khrushchev was planning other innovations in agricultural management.

In 1965, the ministry of agriculture seemed to have regained most, if not all, of its administrative and management functions which it had lost three years earlier. A decree of the Presidium of the Supreme Soviet placed the ministries of the republics, which were charged with the procurement of farm products and with the management of agriculture, under the jurisdiction of the central ministry of agriculture. At the same time, the Soviet leaders announced plans for greater investments in the agricultural sector of the economy, together with promises of greater authority for the farm managements, as well as prospects of greater material rewards for the farmers.

SOME CONCLUSIONS ABOUT SOVIET ADMINISTRATION

It is difficult to evaluate the effectiveness of the Soviet administrative apparatus. First of all, the operations of the Soviet government are treated with such great secrecy that we are not sure just how much of the picture we do not see. Secondly, there is the matter of what yardstick should be used in passing judgment. And finally, we have no way of balancing the costs against what the Soviet citizen would be willing to pay for the services he receives. In spite of these difficulties, however, it is possible to make some reasonably sound observations about the administrative machine, based in large part on revelations in the Soviet press.

BUREAUCRACY HAS GROWN

Contrary to Lenin's expressed hope that the organized state bureaucracy would dwindle and ultimately disappear, it has actually grown. There would seem to be several explanations for this trend. First of all, Stalin found in the bureaucracy the only firm foundation of his power. Under this rule, the Soviet regime operated on the premise that no one could be trusted, including the more seasoned party members. Consequently, a system of checking and crosschecking required the services of countless people. Secondly, the sheer size of the country and the assumption that the party should direct or at least have its eye on all developments required a huge bureaucratic machine, often resulting in duplication and endless paper work. Finally, there has been a tendency toward overstaffing in government agencies, accounted for, in part at least, by an inefficient distribution of manpower and by the growing tendency of people to prefer office employment to work on farms or in factories. Moreover, the shortage of qualified personnel in the earlier years of the regime encouraged establishments to recruit and to hang on to more people than they actually needed.

While there may be other reasons which would explain the growth of the bureaucratic apparatus, the essential fact remains that it has grown to considerable proportions. And equally important is the fact that this development is at variance with the promises of the regime when it came to power, a consideration which would seem of no small consequence to the citizen who pays the bill.

CONFUSION CONCERNING RESPONSIBILITY

There is no clear-cut line of responsibility in the Soviet bureaucracy. Technically, responsibility is vertical to the Council of Ministers, which, in turn, is supposed to be responsible to the Supreme Soviet. In practice, the picture is far from clear. The bureaucracy is, in the end, certainly responsible to the party, but the party has set up various channels of control, with no clear lines of authority. The trade unions and local soviets are told, for example, not to interfere in the management of government enterprises. At the same time, they are told to assist enterprises and to oversee their work, creating a situation which often leads to a conflict in jurisdiction. Simultaneously, the *Komsomol* organizations are urged to be vigilant, and the secret police is expected to be ever watchful.

For the most part, it seems that the party wants it this way. By avoiding firm and set channels, the party leadership is able to skip intermediate control centers and to go directly to the lowest level if intervention seems necessary. Knowing this, and believing that party officials will ultimately hear about it, managers tend to take their problems to party committees rather than to the appropriate governmental agencies. One consequence of this is that there is an absence of a close working relationship up and down the bureaucratic ladder. Such a close relationship exists only with immediate superiors and immediate subordinates.

On the whole, however, the party is probably in a position of firmer control than it was a decade ago. This is especially true in agricultural management, where party organizations and party members have come to play a more decisive role. In industry, too, as state enterprises have expanded, so has the party. Moreover, by institutionalizing the practice of frequent promotion, demotion, or transfer of local officials, the party seeks to minimize the opportunities for local arrangements that might be detrimental to its basic objectives.

NETWORK OF PROTECTIVE ALLIANCES

The demands upon the administrative apparatus are such, and the bureaucratic restrictions so confining and often contradictory, that responsible administrators have found it necessary to go outside the law if they are to achieve what is expected of them. This means finding informal ways of by-passing technical bureaucratic requirements. More specifically, it involves asking for favors, which beget requests for favors in return. Sometimes, it is necessary to falsify reports or to employ other means of concealing the real situation. Often, the net result is a whole network of protective evasions, which the Soviet press has sometimes labeled "the building of family relationships."

Such extralegal arrangements are officially condemned, but despite its secret police and its other means of control, the regime has often seemed helpless to cope with them. Paradoxical as it may seem, the administrative apparatus, as it has grown, has to a certain extent been able to resist manipulation, while at the same time it was becoming more and more indispensable to the Soviet dictatorship.

LACK OF POPULAR TRUST

Since the people do not have any control over the administration, the absence of popular trust in it is not strange. This is particularly true when we remember that the Soviet regime has made countless promises which it has subsequently failed to fulfill. Even such solemn obligations as the repayment of loans made to the government have been broken. Soon after World War II, the government, without warning, proclaimed a currency reform, as a result of which the citizens received one ruble for every ten. A similar reform was promulgated in early 1961. Similarly, in 1957 it was announced that the government would postpone payment of state loans for 20 to 25 years. Moreover, no interest is to be paid on this money. This is all the more repugnant to the holders of government securities, for although their purchase was theoretically voluntary, almost no one could avoid "investing" less than one month's salary annually in these loans.

These are but some of the more obvious ways in which the Soviet administration has broken faith with its people. Reference has already been made elsewhere concerning arbitrary administrative acts, such as arrests and imprisonment. Various citizens of the USSR could no doubt provide an endless catalog of administrative acts which have caused them to lose confidence in the regime. But the Soviet regime is not dependent upon popular support, and most of the available evidence suggests that popular support is not very high on the regime's list of desired goals or priorities.

SOME OBSERVATIONS ON THE SOVIET ECONOMIC REVOLUTION

Irrespective of what has been said in the foregoing about the Soviet system, one cannot deny that it has been able to produce some desired results. There has been an economic revolution in the Soviet Union. Through a series of successive five-year plans, the economy has in large measure been industrialized. The regime was ruthless in its takeover of the economy and in its direction. It appropriated the means of production and distribution. Nothing was permitted to stand in the way of the government's aims. As a result of the regime's determined and impatient approach, there has been considerable progress, particularly in those areas where the best talent and the best materials were allocated. Generally speaking, however, the trial and error method resulted in huge costs, both material and human. But the country was moved ahead, and this is what the leaders wanted.

The motivation behind the industrialization drive was largely political. There was a firm conviction that the economy should be exploited for political purposes, for example, to build a strong industrial and military state. The prolonged emphasis on the development of heavy industry and a large military establishment, together with the extremely low priority accorded to consumer's goods, was ample proof. Consequently, the building of socialism became a distinctly secondary consideration.

At the same time, the Soviet leaders had to provide incentives to those who were made responsible for the achievement of the regime's goals. To some extent, these persons, as loyal party functionaries, could be relied upon to carry out the party policies in any case. But social and economic inducements were seemingly more important. The managerial class was provided with better wages, better living quarters, bonuses, and increased opportunities for promotion and recognition. The method of positive and negative incentives was applied with considerable success.

BIBLIOGRAPHICAL NOTE

Among the more useful of the numerous studies of Soviet administration and economic policy are Alexander Baykov, *The Development of the Soviet*

Economic System (New York: Macmillan, 1947); Abram Bergson (ed.), *Economic Trends in the Soviet Union* (Cambridge: Harvard University Press, 1963; ——, *Soviet Economic Growth* (Evanston, Ill. and White Plains, N.Y.: Row, Peterson and Co., 1953); John N. Hazard, *Soviet Housing Law* (New Haven: Yale University Press, 1939); Naum Jasny, *The Soviet 1956 Statistical Handbook: A Commentary* (East Lansing: Michigan State University Press, 1957); Alex Nove, *The Soviet Economy* (New York: Praeger, 1961) Harry Schwartz, *Russia's Soviet Economy* (2d ed.; New York: Prentice-Hall, 1954); and Alexander Vucinich, *Soviet Economic Institutions: The Social Structure of Production Units* (Stanford: Stanford University Press, 1952).

Specialized studies of agricultural administration include those of Fedor Belov, *The History of a Soviet Collective Farm* (New York: Praeger, 1955); Naum Jasny, *The Socialized Agriculture of the U.S.S.R.* (Stanford: Stanford University Press, 1949); and Roy D. Laird, *Collective Farming in Russia* (Lawrence, Kans.: University of Kansas Press, 1958).

Useful discussions of Soviet labor, trade unions, and industrial management are A. Arakelian, *Industrial Management in the U.S.S.R.* (Washington, D.C.: Public Affairs Press, 1950); Joseph S. Berliner, *Factory and Manager in the U.S.S.R.* (Cambridge, Mass.: Harvard University Press, 1957); David Dallin and Boris I. Nicholaevsky, *Forced Labor in Soviet Russia* (New Haven: Yale University Press, 1947); Isaac Deutscher, *Soviet Trade Unions* (London: Royal Institute of International Affairs, 1950); Margaret Dewar, *Industrial Management in the U.S.S.R.: An Outline Study* (London: Royal Institute of International Affairs, 1945); and David Granick, *Management of the Industrial Firm in the U.S.S.R.: A Study in Soviet Economic Planning* (New York: Columbia University Press, 1954) and *The Red Executive: A Study of the Organization Man in Russian Industry* (Garden City, N.Y.: Doubleday, 1960).

Information on local administration is included in Merle Fainsod, *How Russia Is Ruled* (rev. ed., Cambridge, Mass.: Harvard University Press, 1963); in W. W. Kulski, *The Soviet Regime, Communism in Practice* (4th ed., Syracuse: Syracuse University Press, 1964); and in Maurice F. Parkins, *City Planning in Soviet Russia* (Chicago: University of Chicago Press, 1953). Also of interest is John A. Armstrong, *The Soviet Bureaucratic Elite: A Case Study of the Ukrainian Apparatus* (New York: Praeger, 1959).

Also of interest are some of the early surveys of Soviet economic policy. Thomas Campbell, *Russia, Market or Menace* (London: Longmans, Green, 1932) and Louis Fischer, *Machines and Men in Russia* (New York: H. Smith, 1932) are products of a period when Americans viewed the Soviet experiment with greater amazement than fear or hostility. Both of these works display a certain admiration for the thoroughness of Soviet planning and for the system of Soviet controls.

CHAPTER 30

THE SOVIET
CHALLENGE

BECAUSE our political system rests on popular approval, many of us are apt to think of other political systems as having the consent of the majority of their respective peoples, at least at the time of their initial establishment. This is not true, however, of the Soviet or any other Communist system. In no country has a majority voted freely in favor of Communism, either before or after its inauguration. And yet, the Soviet leaders (and their ideology) assert that all other countries must sooner or later go their way. This is the Soviet challenge, in its most elemental form, to the non-Soviet world. Although this chapter deals with the Soviet challenge, the reader should bear in mind the evolving challenge of other Communist systems, notably that of China.

UNIVERSALITY OF THE CHALLENGE

All societies around the world are told, in effect, that the laws of historical development are pushing them inevitably toward revolution and the proletarian dictatorship. The all-embracing Marxian ideology not only professes to explain the basic laws of social development, and thereby to predict the shape of the future society, but in addition, it seeks to provide the instruments with which the transformation is to be brought about. In the hands of Soviet and other Communist leaders, this ideology and the systems which they have built constitute a type of declaration of war on the non-Communist world. Hence, this world finds itself, whether it wishes it or not, in the midst of a life and death struggle.

There are three aspects to this struggle. The first is essentially domestic, that is, the challenge (or threat) that the Soviets will provide a viable political, economic, and social system which best meets the needs of the members of society and which provides the greatest measure of social justice. Or, to put it in question form: Will they succeed in building a social order which by its sheer success in meeting human and social problems will constitute a powerful attraction and a persuasive argument for conscious imitation?

The second aspect of the struggle—really a part of the first—is the challenge to the non-Soviet world to establish and maintain a social system (or systems) that will continue to be superior to anything that the Soviets may devise. By and large, this is a dual problem. On the one hand, there are the highly developed industrial nations which have, in the main, established viable social systems, but which must be able to adjust to the changing needs of evolving industrial societies. On the other hand, there are the nonindustrialized nations, sometimes referred to as underdeveloped countries, which find themselves in varying degrees of economic and political development. The challenge to these two broad groups of non-Soviet nations (industrialized and nonindustrialized), although related, is of considerably different magnitude for each.

The third aspect of the struggle concerns the militant effort of the Soviet leaders to utilize the power of the Soviet Union and her allies to alter the international status quo in their favor. To this end, they are employing a variety of means. Because of the nature of modern weapons of war, this aspect assumes major proportions, for it is here that the life and death of nations and peoples may hang in the balance.

HOW VIABLE A SOCIAL ORDER?

An evaluation of a changing social order must remain tentative. While Stalin was alive, an appraisal of Soviet society was less difficult. But gone are many of the rigidities of that era. Although many things remain as before, some changes are taking place, and any current estimate must take this into account. This is not to suggest that extraordinary departures are expected, but merely to call attention to the fact that Stalin's successors are less resistant to experimentation.

UNEVEN ECONOMIC GROWTH

Without doubt, great strides have been made in the Soviet Union toward industrializing a backward nation. The rate of economic growth in the past decade has been particularly impressive. The world has witnessed dramatic proof of the achievements of Soviet science and technology. But progress has been uneven, with some aspects of the economy receiving much more attention than others. And the human and material costs have been high. The judgment of a onetime Soviet citizen is still valid: there has been considerable progress for those who survived. Also, there is a marked contrast beween new buildings and equipment and the neglect with which they are often treated.

Moreover, there is a marked contrast between the growth in industrial production and the slow pace in agriculture. In most food items, production per inhabitant is below that of 1913. In December 1958, Khrushchev admitted that "the agricultural situation was grave," and that some earlier Soviet agricultural statistics had been a "fraud" and a "deception," an interesting description of official data by a Soviet leader. In the same year, he admitted that to produce a unit of milk the Soviet farmer put in three times as many man-hours as the American farmer. And in the case of wheat it was seven times the man-hours. In the ensuing years he continued to express dissatisfaction with the results of Soviet agriculture, frequently accompanying his declarations with changes in farm management. In 1963–1964, the Soviet Union was forced to buy large quantities of wheat, mainly from the United States and Canada.

It should also be noted that general backwardness prevails in a large segment of the rural areas. Roads are often poor or virtually nonexistent. Transportation and housing are inadequate. Perhaps a majority of peasant houses, for example, have neither electricity nor running water. These conditions are in sharp contrast with the large urban centers, where considerable modernization has taken place.

Low Standard of Living

On the whole, the Soviet Union has a low standard of living. Most, if not all, European countries have a higher one. This means that the Soviet rate of national economic growth has not been reflected in such consumer items as food, clothing, or housing. Rather, it is to be found in the build-up of capital goods industries and in the Soviet military establishment. It needs to be noted, however, that in the Khrushchev years there was a far greater emphasis on consumer goods and services than in the preceding years, resulting in an increased standard of living, particularly in the urban areas.

The boasts about surpassing the United States standard of living are not apt to materialize in the near future. Substantial increases in consumer items cannot be brought about without encouraging individual initiative, providing better living conditions, and increasing agricultural production. At present, the low agricultural output still ties up nearly half of the Soviet labor force, which is in sharp contrast to the small percentage of the United States labor force which produces large agricultural surpluses.

The low standard of living is coupled with an uneven distribution of consumer goods. The "new class," the privileged in Communist society, gets the most of what there is to get. But within other groups in Soviet society (for example, the workers) there is also a large disparity in rewards. The gap between the low and high paid in virtually every group is greater than gaps within similar economic groups in the United States. In any event, and however else the Soviet Union may be described, it certainly is not an egalitarian society.

Moreover, the Soviet standard of living, such as it is, is in part dependent upon the work of many women. Although there are laws on the "protection of female labor," a substantial percentage of steam furnace stokers, metal welders, blacksmiths, and stevedores are women. Moreover, they handle hot asphalt, lay bricks and stone, handle ties and rails in railway construction and repair, and unload coal, cement and grain—to say nothing of their work as janitors, street cleaners, and farm workers. What may be even more important is the fact that the percentage of women in the Soviet labor force has increased over the years. This would seem to be a strange way of "emancipating" women.

No Political Democracy

While there are some uncertainties as to the ability of Soviet society to achieve a large measure of balanced economic growth and to provide its citizens with an improving standard of living, no such uncertainties are to be found in the political realm. Barring a cataclysmic upheaval, the Soviet Union seems condemned indefinitely to dictatorial rule. The Communist party remains an all-powerful elite, and its leaders are determined to keep it that way. For the foreseeable future, therefore, there is no indication that the Soviet Union will be anything except a one-party dictatorship.

This means that whatever aspirations for political freedom the peoples of the Soviet Union may have, and there are various indications that such aspirations exist to a considerable degree, will go unrealized. It means also that the secret police and other instruments of totalitarian control will continue to function. It seems ironic that an ideology whose avowed and declared purpose was to liberate people should produce the opposite. Over the past century and a half, man's personal liberty has increased in most countries, but in the Soviet

Union, as in other Communist states, it has become more restricted.

Nevertheless, certain contradictions beset the leaders of the USSR. On the one hand, they may be able to make concessions in a number of areas, but they will not be able to make them in the one significant area of giving people a voice in deciding who should govern. To do so would be to invite the people to replace them with someone else. This they can never do. Moreover, it is doubtful if they can even permit open and free criticism, for to do so would be to pave the way for the next step in the democratic process, that is, to throw out of power those leaders whose policies and programs are the bases of the criticism.

On the other hand, the leaders are beset with demands, particularly from young people, that there be a more realistic discussion as to the nature of the future society. To the young people the single most intriguing aspect of Communism is the promise that goods are to be distributed in conformity with the principle of "to each according to his needs." The young people, even the Communists among them, have come face to face with the contradictions and injustices of the Soviet system. The less fortunate, particularly, are anxious to know if there is going to be an end to the inequalities with which they are so familiar.

That the young people are asking questions, and arriving at independent answers, suggests that they are unwilling to accept what they are told by their leaders. The latter would rather not discuss such questions at all. But they know that whether they wish it or not, these discussions will "go on without us, without our intellectual influence." Consequently, they have attempted to provide answers. From the reactions which their answers have provoked, however, they must know that the young people are far from satisfied.

STATUS OF INTELLECTUAL AND CULTURAL FREEDOM

The absence of the most significant freedom—political liberty—has its crucial implications for all other freedoms. As was pointed out in chapter 6, a dictatorship of the modern totalitarian variety seems to need control over all aspects of human endeavor, and cannot, therefore, permit unbridled freedom in any area. From time to time, it may be able to make some concessions. But without political freedom, man cannot feel secure in any of his other liberties.

The period of liberalization (1955–57) in literature and other forms of cultural expression is instructive in this regard, although far from conclusive. In 1958 and 1959, the all-powerful government was able to reimpose more rigid controls and to get pledges of reform and rededication from artist and literary associations. But it does not seem likely that the educated younger generation, which responded so favorably to the liberalization, will be easily reconciled to the Kremlin's reimposition of orthodoxy. The Soviet public, as one Soviet writer pointed out to an audience of critics, is tired of "the same steam shovel, the same dam, the same road." Moreover, there is reason to believe that the post-Khrushchev leadership will be forced to seek an accommodation with the increasing desire of writers and artists to be free of the fetters of socialist realism.

VIABILITY OF THE NON-SOVIET WORLD

What the above suggests is that Soviet society is far from being a viable social order. But viability is a relative matter. The crucial question, particularly in the long run, may be: Does the non-Soviet world present examples of a more viable social order or orders? In this respect it is difficult, if not impossible, to speak of the non-Soviet world, or even of the Western world, as if it were one. Many of the nations of the non-Soviet world vary a great deal from each other in their historical and cultural heritage, as well as in their political, economic, and social experience.

For the purposes of this discussion the countries of the non-Soviet world may be divided, although somewhat arbitrarily, into the industrialized or developed nations and the underdeveloped countries. It must be kept in mind, however, that there are some nations which will not fit into either category, or rather, they will fit both categories partially. They are the countries which are either in transition or experiencing serious social crises.

For the most part, the countries in the first category (United States, Great Britain, France, Canada, Germany, Italy, Japan, Switzerland, Scandinavia, and the Low Countries) are sometimes referred to as the free nations. Most of them have experienced political freedom long enough to appreciate keenly what is at stake, what there is to lose. Most of them, too, have evolved in the direction of an improving standard of living for their peoples. They want to remain free.

There is some question, however, if even these nations are fully aware of the nature and extent of the Communist challenge and what they must do to remain free. Certainly, there is some division among the peoples of these countries on this question. When the domestic Communist party is weak or non-existent, it is difficult for many inhabitants of the country to perceive the danger. Similarly, when the Communist movement is gaining ground in another country, people who are somewhat removed from the scene do not become excited easily, especially if what is taking place is in little known areas and in countries which have only recently achieved their independence.

Most Western leaders, however, have come to realize that Communist victories anywhere constitute a threat to the free world. Such victories enhance the power of the Soviet Union and its allies, and reduce the actual or potential area of the free world. This view is not shared by certain nations, sometimes labeled neutralist, whose leaders deliberately seek to avoid involvement in great power controversies. Even in some democratic countries there is a sizable neutralist opinion.

To meet the Communist threat in various parts of the world, the major nations in the free world have embarked upon programs of economic and other aid, particularly to underdeveloped countries and especially to those which are seeking to establish or perpetuate democratic political systems. The hope is that such aid will help these countries to make the transition from backwardness to industrialization without sharp and violent political and social upheavals.

In many of these countries the situation is favorable to the Soviet Union. Among large segments of the people there is mass ignorance, backwardness, resentment of the wealth which the West holds, and little or no experience with political freedom. There is great impatience to get things done; slow growth has few supporters. Moreover, their political leaders, often naive and almost always ambitious, are attracted by the Soviet experiment in radical social and industrial engineering. They are impressed by the rapid transformation of peasant Russia into an industrial and military power.

Moreover, the Soviet Union has embarked upon its own aid program to certain underdeveloped countries. Having no electorate to whom an accounting must be made, the Soviet leaders can dispense aid irrespective of cost. Even if they cannot win people over to their side, the Soviets can foment unrest or augment already existing trouble. Sometimes, however, Communist actions have helped the West by betraying Soviet bloc intentions. The ruthless suppression of the Hungarian revolution and the takeover in Tibet are but two examples.

MILITANT SOVIET EFFORTS TO CHANGE THE STATUS QUO

The Soviet challenge to the non-Soviet world is made particularly acute by the militant campaign waged by the Soviet leaders and their allies to change the international status quo. Their violations of World

War II agreements, which were designed to guarantee free and unfettered elections to the countries of Eastern Europe, are well known. And Korea is a matter of record. In short, the Kremlin and its allies are engaged in a determined campaign to hoist the red flag of tyranny on every continent and on every ocean of the globe. In this campaign all sorts of weapons are employed, and many others, including the most destructive of modern armament, are held in reserve. For some time to come, therefore, mankind must live under a threat of nuclear conflict.

Soviet Policy Conditioned by Tsarist Inheritance

While the objectives of Soviet foreign policy and the means for its implementation are in large measure dictated by the Marxist-Leninist world outlook, it would be a mistake to ignore the influence of historical and other factors that antedate the Soviet era. The Soviet leaders inherited tsarist Russia's geography, population, natural resources, and her drive to gain access to warm-water outlets to the sea. Although the Bolsheviks consented to great losses in territory in the German-imposed treaty of Brest-Litovsk, they waged a concerted and largely successful military campaign to regain the tsarist patrimony after Germany was defeated in the West. Among the first foreign policy ventures of the new regime, therefore, was the one to reclaim the fruits of tsarist expansionist policies. Soviet leaders may deny the influence of the tsarist inheritance on their foreign policies, but in this case actions speak louder than words.

Influence of Marxian World Outlook

Marxian theory tells the Soviet leaders that the world is in a process of conflict and change. This process, the same theory tells them, will lead to proletarian revolutions in all nation states, and the overthrow of their capitalist social orders. Most Soviet leaders have been convinced, however, that this process needs assistance. Consequently, they have believed that one of the missions of the Soviet regime is to promote revolutions. In other words, world revolution is the maximum goal of Soviet foreign policy, the minimum goal being the survival of the USSR.

In the pursuit of this goal (or goals) the Soviet leaders have utilized a variety of means. At varying times, they have employed espionage networks, infiltration, foreign trade, propaganda, domestic Communist parties, the secret police, and such organizations as the Comintern and Cominform. And finally, they have utilized their military establishment. For them, war and diplomacy are two sides of the same coin, but they distinguish between *just* and *unjust* wars. Among the just wars are wars of liberation from colonialism and capitalism. In the words of the 1961 party program, it is the duty of Communists "to support the sacred struggle of the oppressed peoples and their just anti-imperialist wars of liberation." By definition, any war engaged in by the Soviet Union would to them be a just war. By the same token, wars waged by capitalist countries, particularly the leading ones, would be unjust wars.

Soviet leaders have on many occasions insisted that Marxism teaches the inevitability of violence as the final arbiter in international affairs. They have no faith in the idea that Communist and non-Communist states could exist side by side, with common legal principles or moral precepts regulating their relations. This, combined with the Marxian notion of the inevitability of proletarian revolutions, the Soviet doctrine of just and unjust wars and the Kremlin's possession of nuclear and other capabilities, presents the remainder of the world with some unpleasant prospects.

In more recent years, however, the Soviet leaders have said that "peaceful coexistence is an objective necessity," a point of view not shared by their Chinese comrades.[1] Meanwhile, they have not hesitated to exploit the universal fear of war to gain some of their objectives without war.

It has been argued that once the Soviet regime achieves the basic objectives of Communism at home the need to foment revolutions will fade or disappear. A more persuasive argument, it seems, is that the preservation of the totalitarian system at home will be more difficult to justify as the objectives of Communism at home are met. In order to continue exacting sacrifices and denying basic freedoms, the Soviet leaders will need to show that this is required in the interests of aiding the Soviet brand of Marxism to advance in the world at large.

COEXISTENCE: A REALITY?

From time to time, Soviet leaders have said that they believed in the coexistence of differing social systems. In Stalin's time, such expressions were meant for foreigners and not for the Soviet public. Moreover, such declarations did not speak of permanent coexistence, nor of the conditions for its establishment and maintenance. On the contrary, a careful examination of those statements revealed that the basic condition would be the willingness of the non-Soviet world to yield to

---

[1] These and other differences in the Communist camp are discussed below.

the Kremlin's world revolutionary objectives. Coexistence, from Stalin's point of view, was the time the Communists needed to achieve superiority—the period during which the Soviet Union would seek to destroy or weaken the military and political solidarity of the free world.

There is reason to believe that Stalin's successors have been forced to alter his concept of coexistence. Available evidence suggests that they do not accept nuclear war as a realistic means of achieving their objectives. Moreover, they have asserted that peaceful coexistence is the "highest form of class struggle." Yet, there are contradictions. On the one hand, they asserted in the 1961 party program that "Marxist-Leninist parties prefer to achieve the transference of power from the hands of the bourgeoisie to those of the proletariat, without a civil war." But at another point, they say: "Leninism teaches and historical experience confirms that the ruling classes do not yield their power voluntarily." And in their instructions to writers, Stalin's successors have made it quite clear that political and military coexistence does not mean that there should be ideological coexistence.

In this, as in other areas, the Soviet leaders have demonstrated that while they may be inflexible where goals are concerned, they are exceedingly flexible in strategy and tactics. They do not believe that their system can be safe so long as free nations exist as beacons of hope for those who live in tyranny. Yet, if they reject nuclear conflict as a means to an end, they can be counted on to work harder in the exploitation of other instruments to reach the same goal. Therefore, it ill behooves a world that is tired of conflict to accept, at face value, the disarmingly attractive doctrine of peaceful coexistence. If it is to have any real meaning for the non-Communist world, peaceful coexistence, as a concept, will require further modification by the Communists, so that it constitutes a genuine effort on both sides to reach a workable accomodation.

DISCORD IN COMMUNIST CAMP

The seemingly monolithic nature of the Communist camp in the early post-World War II years proved to be deceptive. The first open break came in 1948, with the public airing of differences between Yugoslavia and the Soviet Union. For a time a form of unity was re-established, with the "isolation" of Yugoslavia. Following Stalin's death in 1953, and particularly after Khrushchev's denunciation in 1956 of many of the actions of his predecessor, the bonds between Moscow and her Eastern European satellites began to loosen. While varying degrees of attachment to Moscow are to be found in these nations, signs of independence have been notably on the increase. In the main, however, most of the Communist regimes in these countries, including Yugoslavia, support the Soviet Union in its approaches to foreign policy.

The most acrimonious discord in the Communist camp has involved the Soviet Union and China. Apparently, there are four major issues in dispute. The first concerns the question of leadership of the international Communist movement. The Chinese have stressed the equality of Communist states and they have accused the USSR of "great power chauvinism." The Soviets have at least paid lip-service to the principle of equality, but at the same time they have pointed out that power and responsibility cannot be separated. At a time when the Communist camp must ultimately rely upon the power of the Soviet Union, the Kremlin leaders believe that the decisive voice should be theirs.

The second question at issue concerns the matter of revolutionary tactics and strategy. The Chinese leaders want the Communist camp to pursue global revolution, stressing the point that Communists should not be deterred by nuclear blackmail. They have attacked the peaceful coexistence policy of Moscow as being un-Marxist and un-Leninist, and therefore devoid of theory. They criticized Khrushchev bitterly for his withdrawal of Soviet missiles from Cuba in 1962, and for his signing of the nuclear test-ban agreement in 1963. The Soviet leaders view the position of the Chinese leaders as devoid of an appreciation of practical realities. They have asserted that the prevention of nuclear war is feasible, and have pointedly asked the Chinese if they really thought that all bourgeois governments lacked all reason in everything that they did. The Moscow leaders are convinced that their knowledge of what is possible in foreign affairs is superior to that of the comrades in Peking. They are convinced that the Chinese strategy for global revolution could easily result in global suicide.

The third problem dividing Moscow and Peking involves the nature and form of intra-bloc assistance. The Chinese leaders have complained that the newer Communist states, notably China, have not received sufficient aid or even the right type of aid from Moscow. They have criticized the Soviet leaders for their reluctance to provide massive aid for the Chinese industrialization program. And they have been critical of Soviet aid to such non-Communist states as Egypt. Moreover, they have charged that Moscow has used its aid to exert political pressure. To all of these charges, the Soviet leaders have replied by citing statistics as to the extent of their assistance (military and economic), made at great sacrifices to the people of the Soviet Union. In addition, the Kremlin has on occasion pointed out the uneconomic nature of certain plans of the newer Communist regimes. Finally, the Soviet leaders have made it quite clear that in the current stage of development of their society, it is necessary to provide greater and greater material incentives to their people. In addition, they have maintained that it was their international duty to so build Communism at home as to provide their foreign comrades with an appealing example.

Finally, the Chinese leaders have been critical of some of the consequences of de-Stalinization. They insist that they see the re-emergence of capitalist forms in several of the smaller Communist nations and in the USSR itself. Liberalization, they believe, will lead to the liquidation of Communism. Their own experience in China leads them to conclude that they cannot build the new society without the employment of Stalinist tactics which, they assert, had been necessary in the Soviet Union also. And those tactics, they argue, must be justified by reference to doctrine. De-Stalinization tends to rob them of the necessary doctrinal support.

While the above would seem to be the major elements in the disagreement between China and the Soviet Union, there may be others. There have been hints of disagreements as to territorial boundaries. And Peking has publicly suggested that the Kremlin rulers regard the colored peoples as something less than equal to the whites. Whatever else may be at issue, it should be noted that nationalism is still the great force of our age, and Communist national states, not too much unlike non-Communist nations, are beset with different internal problems, and their views of their respective national interests are far from identical. Consequently, they have different ideological needs. In this atmosphere of diversity, the discord in the international Communist camp is not likely to be resolved in the near future.

BIBLIOGRAPHICAL NOTE

The attempt to evaluate the Soviet challenge on the international front may be facilitated by the following works: Robert Loring Allen, *Soviet Economic Warfare* (Washington, D.C.: Public Affairs Press, 1960); Gabriel A. Almond, *The Appeals of Communism* (Princeton, N.J.: Princeton University Press, 1954); Frederick C. Barghoorn, *The Soviet Cultural Offensive: The Role of Cultural Diplomacy in Soviet Foreign Policy* (Princeton, N.J.: Princeton University Press, 1960); Howard L. Boorman, et al., *Moscow-Peking Axis* (Council on Foreign Relations: Harper, 1957); Chiang Chung-cheng, *Soviet Russia in China* (New York: Farrar, Straus and Cudahy, 1957); David J. Dallin, *Soviet Foreign Policy After Stalin* (Philadelphia: Lippincott, 1961); Herbert S. Dinerstein, *War and the Soviet Union: Nuclear Weapons and the Revolution in Soviet Military and Political Thinking* (New York: Praeger, 1959); Ruth Fischer, *Stalin and German Communism: A Study in the Origins of the State Party* (Cambridge, Mass.: Harvard University Press, 1948); Raymond L. Garthoff, *Soviet Strategy in the Nuclear Age* (New York: Praeger, 1958); Elliot R. Goodman, *The Soviet Design for a World State* (New York: Columbia University Press, 1960); George C. Guins, *Communism on the Decline* (New York: Philosophical Library, 1956); Robert N. Carew Hunt, *A Guide to Communist Jargon* (London: Bles, 1957); John Kautsky, *Moscow and the Communist Party of India* (New York: John Wiley & Sons, 1956); Malcolm D. Kennedy, *A History of Communism in East Asia* (New York: Praeger, 1957); Evron M. Kirkpatrick (ed.), *Target: The World, Communist Propaganda Activities in 1955* (New York: Macmillan, 1956), and *Year of Crisis: Communist Propaganda Activities in 1956* (New York: Macmillan, 1957); J. M. Mackintosh, *Strategy and Tactics of Soviet Foreign Policy* (New York: Oxford University Press, 1963); and Marshall Shulman, *Stalin's Foreign Policy Reappraised* (Cambridge: Harvard University Press, 1963).

Also useful are David Floyd, *Mao Against Khrushchev* (New York: Praeger, 1964), Philip E. Mosely, *The Kremlin and World Politics: Studies in Soviet Policy and Action* (New York: Vintage Books, 1960), and Harry Schwartz, *Tsars, Mandarins, and Commissars: A History of Chinese-Russian Relations* (Philadelphia: Lippincott, 1964).

Communist activities in Eastern Europe are discussed specifically in Stephen Borsody, *The Triumph of Tyranny: The Nazi and Soviet Conquest of Central Europe* (New York: Macmillan, 1960); Zbigniew Brzezinski, *The Soviet Bloc: Unity and Conflict* (Cambridge, Mass.: Harvard University Press, 1960); Hawthorne Daniel, *The Ordeal of the Captive Nations* (New York: Doubleday and Co., 1958); Melvin J. Lasky (ed.), *The Hungarian Revolution—A White Book* (New York: Praeger, 1957); and Paul E. Zinner (ed.), *National Communism and Popular Revolt in Eastern Europe* (New York: Columbia University Press, 1956). More recent developments are discussed in Stephen D. Kertesz (ed.), *East Central Europe and the World: Developments in the Post-Stalin Era* (Notre Dame, Ind.: University of Notre Dame Press, 1962).

THE STUDY OF
COMPARATIVE GOVERNMENT

BROADER vistas are opened to the student once he gains a basic understanding of the government and politics of several countries. He begins to make some preliminary comparisons. He sees similarities and differences. He asks questions, views political phenomena from a different perspective, and seeks to utilize new concepts. This chapter is not designed to compare the political systems treated in this book. Rather, it is an effort to suggest some ways in which comparison can be undertaken, to outline some categories and topics that will make comparison more meaningful. The approach outlined here is by no means the only one available, and not necessarily the one which will produce the most fruitful results. It happens to be one which the author believes will be useful to the student who has studied the political systems discussed in the preceding pages.

COMPARISON: NATURE AND PURPOSE

Comparison of political systems is not new. Aristotle made a good beginning when he attempted to classify the constitutions of several city states. But how well have we done since his day? Not too well, in the opinion of some observers.[1] These critics say that political scientists, in their more recent attempts at comparison, have been "merely descriptive." They do not condemn description, because description, if based on systematic investigation and evidence, is the objective of scientific inquiry. What these critics are suggesting is that the descriptions are based on superficial observations, on a mere look at laws, constitutions, and formal structures, without an effort to investigate political practice and the significant forces that move a particular political system. In other words, they want us to be as systematic and as precise as our research tools will permit.[2]

---

[1] For example see Roy C. Macridis, *The Study of Comparative Government* (New York: Random House, 1955).

[2] For two recent discussions of problems in political science research see Robert A. Dahl, *Modern Political Analysis* (Englewood Cliffs, N.J.: Prentice-Hall, 1963), and Eugene J. Meehan, *The Theory and Method of Political Analysis* (Homewood, Ill.: The Dorsey Press, 1965). Also see Gunnar Heckscher, *The Study of Comparative Government*

The purpose in making comparisons of political systems is to enhance our knowledge of the ways in which they function, and to attempt to discover the factors that account for the differences and similarities among them. In this respect we may want to know what in a particular system is interesting or worthwhile studying. What is significant? How is political power institutionalized? Who plays what roles? What checks are there on the exercise of political power? What is the relationship between the political leadership and the citizens? Our purpose in seeking answers to these and similar questions is not unlike that of those engaged in other fields of learning—to extend the frontiers of knowledge in our chosen discipline. If we do that, our studies should have predictive value, both in terms of broad policy decisions and in terms of the impact of changes in the variables in political systems.

POLITICAL CULTURE: SETTING FOR GOVERNMENT

Anyone who has lived for a time in a nation other than his own becomes aware that there are differences in outlook toward politics and government. These are often difficult to be precise about, yet they are there.[3] They involve such things as citizens' expectations and perceptions about acceptable or unacceptable behavior of political leaders (e.g. observance of procedural niceties, graft, nepotism, unfair electoral or propaganda tactics, etc.). They also involve the citizens' notions about their own place in the political process. Citizen attitudes on these and similar matters are generally the result of long historical and cultural conditioning. The traditional family relationships and the nature of a people's religious experience help to condition attitudes toward political authority. Often cataclysmic historical events (e.g. civil war or foreign occupation) also play their part in shaping political attitudes.

Similarly, the assumptions of those who exercise political power are influenced by their nation's political culture, which may be defined as the sum total of the attitudes and expectations of the vast majority of the society toward politics and government. Dictators, of course, are in a better position than democratic rulers to slight the

---

and Politics (New York: The Macmillan Co., 1957); Charles S. Hyneman, *The Study of Politics: The Present State of American Political Science* (Urbana, Ill.: University of Illinois, 1959).

[3] See the pioneering work by Gabriel A. Almond and Sidney Verba, *The Civic Culture: Political Attitudes and Democracy in Five Nations* (Princeton: Princeton University Press, 1963). Also see Lucian W. Pye, *Politics, Personality, and Nation-Building* (New Haven: Yale University Press, 1962).

dictates of the political culture, although they cannot ignore them. In fact, clever dictators seek to exploit those attributes of the political culture which can facilitate their aims.

The political culture is therefore the setting in which politics and government operate. In making comparisons of political systems, the student must take this factor or variable into account. Yet he must try to prevent it from becoming a stumbling block to meaningful comparisons. Dahl's characteristics, referred to above, can be applied to different political systems even though some of the findings may be attributable to elements in the political culture. In some countries, for example, the important place accorded to fate may account for a relatively limited quest for political influence, but the extent of this quest can be measured or at least approximated.

THE MACHINERY OF GOVERNMENT: INSTITUTIONALIZING POLITICAL POWER

All political systems set up what we might call the machinery of government. Political power is institutionalized, i.e. instruments of government are created and functions assigned to them. The relations among these instruments are defined and ways are provided for resolving possible conflicts among them. Moreover, the relations between citizens and their government are specified or stipulated. In this arrangement, therefore, it is stated who makes policies, who carries them out, who adjudicates conflicts, and who obeys and under what conditions or possible sanctions.

Political power is institutionalized through what we normally call a constitution. But a constitution must be broadly defined; usually it is more than just a document that bears the name "constitution." In Britain, as we have seen, there is no one document. The British constitution includes the law of the constitution (certain basic charters, laws of a constitutional nature, and certain judicial decisions), as well as the conventions or usages of the constitution. The United States constitution includes the document ratified in 1789, as well as certain usages that have grown up with it (e.g. political parties and presidential nominating conventions), certain enactments of Congress, and the judicial decisions that interpret the written constitution and govern political practice under it. In the Soviet Union, on the other hand, the rules and practices of the Communist party are more nearly the real constitution of the Soviet Union than the document which they call the constitution.

Comparisons of the ways in which political power is institutionalized can be interesting and useful. But looking at documents is not enough, although necessary. An effort must be made to ascertain the nature of political reality and to assess the ways in which the "real" constitution may be altered or amended. This leads to the study of political dynamics, which for most students is the most interesting aspect of politics.

POLITICAL DYNAMICS

A constitution is the body of rules (written and unwritten) which establishes institutions of government for a particular nation and specifies the ways in which the political processes are to function. But political institutions and political processes are manned by people, because in politics only individuals can take conscious actions. Of course, the ways in which political institutions have been operated in the past cannot but have some influence on their functioning in the future. Traditional ways of performing certain governmental tasks are not easily changed. This interaction of institutions, the people who man them, and the citizens on whose behalf they are operated is what the author calls political dynamics.

Political dynamics as thus conceived can be studied in its several aspects. The author is aware that some other arrangement than the one set forth below is possible, and may even be preferable. But whatever the division, the student who seeks to make comparisons of the things that give life to the political process cannot exclude consideration of the electorate and all that goes into the electoral process. Nor can he avoid the problem of political leadership, or the role that legislative bodies play. Similarly, he must take into account the administrative and the judicial processes. And some attention must be accorded to the question of "levels" of government, particularly in the case of nations organized on the federal principle. In a broad sense, whatever the breakdown, the questions that need to be answered come down to these: How are the governors selected? How is leadership organized and how does it function? What role or roles does the legislature play? What are the significant features of administration? What is the role of the judicial process? Is there a federal or a unitary form of organization and what is its significance?

THE ELECTORAL PROCESS

The process by which the citizens choose their rulers has several aspects. There are the formal election laws which stipulate who may vote, who may be a candidate, how the ballots are to be cast and counted, and what practices may be forbidden. There may be informal rules, too, such as a residence requirement for candidates even if one is not stipulated by law. Other laws or constitutional guarantees (e.g. freedom of speech and press, the right to organize and assemble, etc.) may be closely related to a meaningful electoral right. The reader will readily appreciate that laws pertaining to elections have considerably different meanings in a democracy and a dictatorship. Moreover, the study of voting behavior, electoral trends, etc. can be meaningful in a democracy but not in a dictatorship.

Another aspect of the electoral process is the political party system. Generally speaking, there are one-party, two-party, and multi-party systems. These can be studied not only in terms of the factors that contribute to a particular party system, but also in terms of its impact on the nation's political system as a whole. In addition, party systems can be studied from the point of view of types of organizational structure and the exercise of power therein. Moreover, there are the factors of party loyalty, party discipline, party finances, and the patterns of recruitment of members. And there is the question of the relationship of the elected officials and the party officials who do not hold elective office.

Political parties may also be studied in terms of their basic function. In democratic countries, for example, do they not today concern themselves more with the claims of different segments of the electorate and how these might be compromised, rather than being the custodians of ideological positions? Good examples are the Labor party in Britain and the Social Democratic party in Germany. And what about the acceptance of a certain amount of welfare state activity by the Conservative party in Britain and the Republican party in the United States?

Another element in the electoral process is the part played by group interests. What groups are attracted to what parties? How are interest groups organized, formally and informally, and what techniques do they utilize to achieve their aims? In some nations interest groups may exert their greatest activity in the electoral process, while in others they may choose to devote more of their energies to the legislative process. Similarly, certain interest groups may be very active in the pursuit of their aims, while others may appear relatively inactive. Interest group activity in democratic nations certainly offers a rich field for comparison. Although considerably more limited in dictatorial countries, interests apparently do exist, at least within the governing party, and their study would be interesting if reliable information were available.

LEADERSHIP: THE POLITICAL EXECUTIVE

Democracy in the modern world is government by and through elected representatives. Except for a few town-meeting type institutions at the local level, which are exceedingly rare, popular government everywhere is representative government. Therefore the argument of democracy *vs.* republic is a sterile one. It is true that some democratically governed nations have a monarch as head of state (Britain), but he has little or no real political power. Whether we call a representative form of government a democracy or a republic is perhaps not too significant, although democracy is preferable in that it is much older and has historically conveyed the notion of popular government.

But traditional democratic theory does not tell us from where leadership is to stem. Democratic practice, however, has demonstrated that leadership does not readily and easily evolve from a large representative assembly. Consequently, a political institution, called the executive, emerged. In Great Britain, as we have seen, the need for executive leadership was recognized relatively early. In the United States, on the other hand, this recognition came only in this century. One evidence of this is to be found in the fact that late in the last century Woodrow Wilson wrote a book called *Congressional Government,* signifying that Congress was at the center of our system and not the president.

The United States experience, however, is in a way unique. The U.S. Constitution was drafted at a time when the separation powers scheme was widely hailed as the way of avoiding tyranny. Provision was made for the election of the president quite independently of the election of Congress. And the drafters were careful not to lodge all (or even most) governmental powers in one person or body of persons. In Britain, as we have noted, the prime minister is selected only after he has become a member of the legislature. He was never independently elected as is the American president. And the British legislature, of which the prime minister is a member, is legally omnipotent.

A study of political executives, therefore, can be the subject of fruitful comparison. The methods of selecting the executive, his tenure, his relationship to the legislature, his powers, and his accountability generally—to the public and to other branches of government—are the principal points of comparison. The types of persons chosen and their styles of leadership are also worthy of consideration, although a meaningful comparison of these attributes is admittedly more difficult.

THE LEGISLATIVE PROCESS

The legislative process in democratic countries offers a variety of opportunities for comparison. In the broadest sense there is the question of what role the legislature is supposed to play. Is it a partner in policy making or does it primarily perform the function of criticism and control? On the more specific level, several factors or attributes suggest themselves. There is the question of legislative organization—the formal and informal rules of procedure. In all legislative bodies there are subgroups, the power movers and the followers. There are the committees, and the written and unwritten rules concerning their operation. In some legislative bodies the committees and their chairmen are powerful, while in others they are largely servants of the parent body. How political parties organize in the legislature, and the extent to which the leaders can maintain discipline over the rank and file members, are significant aspects for comparison. Other features, such as the ways and means by which legislative leaders are selected, and the roles which they play, are also of interest.

Another aspect of the legislative process that is significant concerns the relationship of the legislature to other branches of government. We normally think of the legislature's relationship to the executive, but there is also the legislature's concern with administration and the work of the bureaucracy. And there is the question of the judiciary, particularly in countries like the United States, where the judiciary is empowered to declare legislative acts null and void if they are in conflict with the constitution. Finally, the relationship of the legislative body to the public at large cannot be neglected. The public image of the legislature in one country, for example, may be quite different from what it is in another one.

A study of specific policy decisions, in domestic as well as in foreign affairs, can reveal a great deal about how a particular political system works.[4] Such studies illustrate what steps were necessary, particularly by executive and legislative leaders, in order for a specific proposal to become law or for a definite foreign policy to become an accomplished fact. They may also indicate interest group

---

[4] See James B. Christoph (ed.), *Cases in Comparative Politics* (Boston, 1965).

activity, different notions of "fair play," and the interaction of political institutions. Policy decisions, as they are ironed out, cannot but have some impact on the political environment and on the political processes themselves.

THE ADMINISTRATIVE PROCESS

Public administration, although perhaps less glamorous for study than other areas of politics, is in large part what day-to-day government is all about. Because of the vast expansion of governmental activities over the past several decades, the administrative process has become more and more important. Not only are more people touched by the administrative arm of government, but in addition, the administrators have been given expanded rule-making authority. Legislation is often drafted in general language, leaving the more detailed provisions for the administrators to fill in. This type of delegated legislative authority in the hands of non-elected officials has been the subject for considerable discussion and debate. The question of how to over-see the operation of nationalized industries is far from being solved. In general, the whole question of future trends in the role of public administration is very much a matter of legitimate concern for all citizens.

More specifically, students of public administration are concerned with the question of efficiency of the bureaucracy. This in turn involves questions of sound organization and good staffing. The latter takes into account recruitment policies, salaries, working conditions, and promotion systems. Good policies can be made ineffective and unpopular by poor organization and incompetent personnel. On the other hand, sometimes bad policies can be made to look tolerable by an effective and efficient bureaucracy. Not all nations tackle the problems of organization and staffing in the same way. In France, as we have seen, the administrative system is highly centralized, while in Great Britain it is much less so, although there are also some similarities, particularly in staffing.

A second major problem that concerns the students of public administration is that of responsibility. Since civil servants are not elected, and for the most part have security of tenure, how are they to be made accountable for the ways in which they govern? How effectively does the executive perform the control function, what authority does he have, and what procedures are employed to this end? What techniques or institutions are utilized to provide the necessary coordination between and among agencies of government where their activities affect each other? What of the bureaucracy's attitude toward the public? What opportunities are there for citizens to be heard? These are but a few questions that are significant in any consideration of the accountability of the administrators.

THE JUDICIAL PROCESS

Normally, we think of the courts as adjudicating conflicts. In so doing, however, they are interpreting as well as applying the law. They do this in all countries, although the degree of judicial independence is severely circumscribed in dictatorships. In democratic nations, one important aspect of the rule of law is its application by an independent and impartial judiciary. But even in democratic countries there may be significant differences in the ways that the courts function. Moreover, in some countries, the power to interpret the law is augmented by the power to nullify it, if judged to be in conflict with the constitution.

The way that the judicial process operates may be influenced by a number of factors. First of all, there is the system of law under which a particular judiciary operates. But even within the same system of law, judicial practice may vary. Great Britain and the United States, for example, both operate under the common law system, yet there are significant differences in practice. Moreover, the role of precedent is important in common law systems, but rarely so in Roman law countries. Secondly, judicial tradition is important in all legal systems. Thirdly, the men who staff the judiciary cannot be overlooked. After all, judges are human beings, and their backgrounds cannot but condition their outlook on social, economic, and political questions. Moreover, courts are not free from political influence. This has been particularly noticeable in the United States, where the powers of Congress to legislate in certain areas have been expanded considerably by judicial interpretation.

Another phase of the judicial process concerns the work of administrative tribunals. In certain countries (e.g. France) there is a separate system of courts for the adjudication of conflicts arising from challenges to administrative authority. Other countries have administrative tribunals, but more often than not they are a part of the administrative apparatus. As such, the question could be treated as an administrative one. It is mentioned here because of the contention by some observers that often the citizen must accept governmental decisions of a judicial nature, without right of appeal to the judiciary. A man does not always have his day in court. Questions arising from this situation offer opportunities for considerable additional research. Much the same could be said about comparative judicial institutions and processes generally, because there are exceedingly few studies in this area of political science.

LEVELS OF GOVERNMENT: FEDERALISM

One of the interesting problems in the study of politics is that of the distribution of powers geographically, i.e. between the central government and the component subdivisions of the nation. To most students, the United States is the best known example of federal organization. But Germany, Canada, Australia, and a few other countries are federations. Some, such as the Soviet Union, call themselves federations, but in fact they are not. As might be expected, there are differences among federal systems, and these offer ample opportunities for comparative study.

Similarly, significant changes have taken place within the same federal system. In the United States, where the individual states are less inclined to go it alone than they once were, some writers now describe the system as "cooperative federalism." More and more problems extend beyond state lines, and these are often dealt with through some cooperative arrangement, with the national government providing the bulk of the necessary funds. In other federal systems, notably those of Canada and Germany, changes are also taking place.

* * * * *

The foregoing discussion was not meant to be exhaustive. In a sense it is but a type of outline, designed to call the student's attention to certain problems in the study of comparative government, and to sort out some of the significant aspects that lend themselves to comparative study. Some of the topics are merely suggestive, although they embody important and interesting questions. If this chapter has opened some new vistas to the student, and made the study of comparative government more meaningful for him, the author will consider himself sufficiently compensated.

BIBLIOGRAPHICAL NOTE

Because I have decided to limit the number of titles included below, the selection may appear somewhat arbitrary, as indeed it is. The books were selected mainly because they seemed to constitute a good beginning. In this connection, the titles listed following the Introduction might also be consulted, as well as the footnote references in this chapter.

On constitutions: C. F. Strong, *Modern Political Constitutions: An Introduction To The Comparative Study of Their History and Existing Form* (London: Sidgwick & Jackson, 1963); K. C. Wheare, *Modern Constitutions* (New York: Oxford University Press, 1951); Arnold J. Zurcher (ed.), *Constitutions and Constitutional Trends Since World War II* (2nd ed., New York: New York University Press, 1955).

On parties and interest groups: Maurice Duverger, *Political Parties: Their Organization and Activity in the Modern State* (New York: Wiley, 1954); Avery Leiserson, *Parties and Politics: An Institutional and Behavioral Approach* (New York: Knopf, 1958); David B. Truman, *The Governmental Process: Political Interests and Public Opinion* (New York: Knopf, 1951); Henry W. Ehrmann (ed.), *Interest Groups on Four Continents* (Pittsburgh: Pittsburgh University Press, 1958).

On executives: There is no really significant book limiting itself to a comparative analysis of executives. Douglas V. Verney, *The Analysis of Political Systems* (London: Routledge and Kegan Paul, 1959) does deal with parliamentary and presidential executives. And, of course, there are a number of excellent books dealing with the American presidency, as well as a number of similar works on the British cabinet system.

On legislatures: John C. Wahlke and Heinz Eulau (eds.), *Legislative Behavior: A Reader in Theory and Research* (Glencoe, Ill.: The Free Press, 1959); K. C. Wheare, *Legislatures* (London: Oxford University Press, 1963).

On administration: Poul Meyer, *Administrative Organization: A Comparative Study of the Organization of Public Administration* (London: Stevens, 1957); Joseph La Palombara (ed.), *Bureaucracy and Political Development* (Princeton: Princeton University Press, 1963); William J. Siffin (ed.), *Toward the Comparative Study of Public Administration* (Bloomington: Indiana University Department of Government, 1957).

On the judiciary: Henry J. Abraham, *Judicial Process: An Introductory Analysis of the Courts of the United States, England, and France* (New York: Oxford University Press, 1962); Freda Castberg, *Freedom of Speech in the West: A Comparative Study of Public Law in France, the United States and Germany* (London: Allen and Unwin, 1961); Glendon Schubert (ed.), *Judicial Decision-Making* (New York: Free Press of Glencoe, 1963).

On federalism: William S. Livingston, *Federalism and Constitutional Change* (Oxford: Clarendon Press, 1956); Edward McWhinney, *Comparative Federalism: States' Rights and National Power* (Toronto: University of Toronto Press, 1962); K. C. Wheare, *Federal Government* (4th ed., New York: Oxford University Press, 1964).

INDEX

INDEX

513

This book has been set on the Linotype in 12 point Bodoni Book, leaded 2 points, and 10 point Bodoni Book, leaded 1 point. Chapter numbers are in 10 point Bodoni Modern caps with 30 point Bodoni Bold Condensed figures. Chapter titles are in 18 point Bodoni No. 375 caps. The size of the type page is 27 by 46½ picas.